The American Flag

The American Flag

An Encyclopedia of the Stars and Stripes in U.S. History, Culture, and Law

JOHN R. VILE

An Imprint of ABC-CLIO, LLC
Santa Barbara, California • Denver, Colorado

Library of Congress Cataloging-in-Publication Data

Names: Vile, John R., author.
Title: The American flag : an encyclopedia of the Stars and Stripes in U.S. history, culture, and law / John R. Vile.
Description: Santa Barbara, California : ABC-CLIO, 2018. | Includes bibliographical references and index.
Identifiers: LCCN 2018010859 (print) | LCCN 2018011774 (ebook) | ISBN 9781440857898 (eBook) | ISBN 9781440857881 (alk. paper)
Subjects: LCSH: Flags—United States—History—Encyclopedias.
Classification: LCC CR113 (ebook) | LCC CR113 .V55 2018 (print) | DDC 929.9/20973—dc23
LC record available at https://lccn.loc.gov/2018010859

ISBN: 978-1-4408-5788-1 (print)
978-1-4408-5789-8 (ebook)

22 21 20 19 18 1 2 3 4 5

This book is also available as an eBook.

ABC-CLIO
An Imprint of ABC-CLIO, LLC

ABC-CLIO, LLC
130 Cremona Drive, P.O. Box 1911
Santa Barbara, California 93116-1911
www.abc-clio.com

This book is printed on acid-free paper ∞

Manufactured in the United States of America

"To the Republic, for which it stands."
May it always seek "liberty and justice for all."

Contents

Topical List of Entries

Artists, Paintings, and Exhibits

Cases

Causes, Events, and Organizations

Civil Rights Movement
Flag Manufacturers Association of America
Hard Hat Riot (1970)
Immigrants and Flag-Waving
Jehovah's Witnesses
Olympic Protocol
Suffragists and the U.S. Flag
Xenophobia, Nativism, and the U.S. Flag

Desecration of the Flag

Advertising
Cowgill v. California (1970)
Ex Parte Starr (1920)
Flag Desecration Amendment
Halter v. Nebraska (1907)
Smith v. Goguen (1974)
Spence v. Washington (1974)
Street v. New York (1969)
Texas v. Johnson (1989)

Design Elements

Colors of the Flag
Constellation
Eagle
Flag Apparel
Flag Houses
Flag Patches
Lapel Pins
Proportions of the American Flag
Stars, Arrangement of on U.S. Flags
Stars and Stripes
Stripes on the Flag

Designers and Makers of Flags

Heft, Robert G.
Hopkinson, Francis
Pickersgill, Mary Young
Ross, Betsy

Famous Flags

Bennington Flag
Betsy Ross Flag
Brandywine Flag
Campaign Flags
Christian Flag
Confederate Flags
Cowpens Flag
East India Company Flag
Easton Flag
Exclusionary Flags
Forster Flag
Fort Niagara Flag
Fort Sumter Flag
Great American Flag
Guilford Flag
Human Flag
Liberty Trees, Liberty Poles, and Liberty Caps
Lincoln Flag
Old Glory Flag
Pine Tree Flag
Rattlesnake Flags
Revolutionary War Battle Flags
Schuyler Flag
Star-Spangled Banner (Flag)
Stafford Flag
Thirteen-Star Flags
Union Flag
Union Jack

Flag Collectors and Collections

Folk Art and Popular Culture

Holidays and Commemorations

Laws and Executive Orders

Flag Act of 1794
Flag Act of 1818
Freedom to Display the American Flag Act (2005)
All-American Flag Act
Respect for America's Fallen Heroes Act
Sedition Act of 1918

Miscellaneous

American's Creed
Capitol Flag Program
Guthrie, William N.
Identifying the Age of Flags
Immigrants and Flag-Waving
"Long May It (She) Wave"
Nicknames for the U.S. Flag
See You at the Pole (SYATP) Events
Top of the Flagpole
Washington's Coat of Arms

Organizations

American Flag Foundation, Inc.
American Legion
Citizens Flag Alliance (CFA)
Daughters of the American Revolution (DAR)
Grand Army of the Republic (GAR)
National Flag Foundation (NFF)
United States Flag Association

Photographs and Photographers

American Flag (Photograph)
American Gothic, Washington, D.C. (Photograph)
Frank, Robert
Iwo Jima Flag Raising
Mapplethorpe, Robert
New York City Firemen Photograph
The Soiling of Old Glory (Photograph)

Places, Including Statues and Memorials

Flag Day Monument
House of Flags Museum
Iwo Jima Flag Raising
Lafayette Gravesite
Landscape
Space Program, American Flag and the
Star-Spangled Banner Flag House
Twenty-Four-Hour Flag Displays
Vietnam Memorial
Washington Monument Flag Display

Pledge of Allegiance

Balch, George Thacher
Bellamy, Francis J.
Mennonites and Amish
Minersville School District v. Gobitis (1940)
Pledge of Allegiance
Tremain, Russell
Under God
West Virginia State Board of Education v. Barnette (1943)
Youth's Companion

Poets, Poems, and Other Literary Works

Campbell, Thomas
Child, Lydia Maria
Fritchie, Barbara
"Man without a Country"
"Old Ironsides"

Protocol Surrounding Flag

Baxter, Percival P.
Flag Code
Flying the Flag

Songs and Anthems

Speeches

Wars and War-Related

Preface

Throughout most of my academic life, I have focused on issues related to American Founding Fathers (and Mothers), the Constitutional Convention of 1787, the constitutional amending process, the U.S. Constitution and its interpretation, and other related issues. A number of my works, including titles devoted to the First and Fourth Amendments, civil liberties, and proposed constitutional amendments, have been encyclopedic in nature. But I had not, prior to this volume, given much academic thought to the American flag. I probably never would have done so if Kevin Hillstrom from ABC-CLIO had not contacted me about taking on the project.

As I pondered the proposal, I learned that there were some great books about both the general history of the flag and about subtopics as well as numerous articles and Internet sources. I quickly became excited about the possibility of focusing on a new area of scholarship that I thought might strike a popular chord with general audiences. Throughout my career, I have enjoyed speaking to local civic groups, and the American flag was a topic that would be an especially appropriate topic around such holidays as Flag Day, Independence Day, and Memorial Day. As I write this, I am only now beginning to get such invitations, but I may never be able to top my first, which was a talk to the local Rotary group. It was having a breakfast not in its usual upstairs spot at a local country club but in the basement. When the time arrived for the pledge to the flag, the Rotary president realized that the flag was upstairs. After someone pointed out that I was wearing a tie with images of the American flag, the audience began directing its attention in my direction and saluting the flag on my tie!

When I was about six years old, I spent a year with my parents in Costa Rica, where they were learning Spanish in preparation for missionary work. One of the highlights that I remember was a day (probably Independence Day) for Americans at the American ambassador's house. The building was decked out for the day in American flags and featured an appearance by an Uncle Sam dressed in red, white, and blue and walking on stilts.

I grew up during the Cold War. I well remember pictures and films about exploding nuclear bombs, the Cuban Missile Crisis, and the assassination and funeral of President John F. Kennedy, whose flag-draped coffin was carried on a caisson to Arlington National Cemetery, which he had visited just weeks earlier. A picture of George Washington adorned the classrooms in the elementary school that I attended in the Shenandoah Valley of Virginia, where we began each day with a salute to the American flag. During this time, I was fortunate enough to have a Mennonite friend who joined me (a Baptist) in refusing to sing any worldly "dancing songs" in class. But he also stood silently as the rest of us saluted the flag, an action which he thought was a form of idolatry. Although my family and I did not share this view, I admired his display of conviction and have thus recognized from a fairly early age that people interpret symbols and ceremonies differently. I continue to believe that one of the beauties of the American system, and the flag that symbolizes it, is that it remains open to individuals of various religious and political persuasions.

In upper elementary school, I was one of a small number of students who helped make announcements over the school's loudspeaker system as buses arrived and who participated in the lowering of the flag every afternoon. Although I don't recall receiving a specific lesson in flag protocol, I knew that the flag was not supposed to touch the ground and that it was to be respectfully folded into a triangle at the end of each day, and I took pride in my role and the badge that accompanied it.

I first became interested in politics during the Kennedy/Nixon election of 1960 and the Johnson/Goldwater election of 1964. I recall proudly waving a small flag on a wooden stick in my bedroom, especially enjoying the sound of air rustling through the folds of the flag. Just as wind makes flags appear to be alive, the flag has almost always been a living symbol to me, not only representing what the United States has been but also pointing to the high ideals to which it has aspired.

Despite this personal link to the flag and to the constitutional system that it represents, prior to writing this book I did not have more than a passing intellectual interest in the flag per se. I was unfamiliar with the term "vexillology," which refers to the study of flags, or even of the fact that there were organizations and journals devoted to the subject. Indeed, I might well have associated the study of flags with individuals (and there probably aren't that many) who are even geekier than I am. The writers of the television comedy *The Big Bang Theory*, with its periodic episodes about "Fun with Flags," clearly associate the study of flags with intellectual trivia; in a recent episode, the only person who called in to the "Fun with Flags" vodcast was a friend who wanted to give an update on his love life.

Although I don't think the writers of *The Big Bang Theory* are far from the mark in guessing that there are probably not many Americans who have much interest in flags in general, I have found that many *are* quite interested in the flag of the United States and its history. Although veterans are particularly likely to associate the flag with their service and devotion to their country, almost all the groups to which I speak begin with a salute to the flag, and from my experience, those who participate take the ceremony quite seriously.

Because I so value history and the context that it provides, I do not believe that the flag is whatever contemporaries choose to make it, but I do believe that respect for the flag rises and falls with respect for the nation and its congruence with its highest ideals. I know that there are many men and women, including my father, all three of his brothers, and his father (my dad's sister remembers displaying a flag in the window with five stars during World War II), who were willing to serve under its colors in times of national peril from foreign foes. I further recognize that our national defense continues to rest on the willingness of our people to cherish and protect it, if necessary, at the cost of their lives. I think that both civilians and military personnel show their devotion to the flag and to the republic for which it stands not only by their service on the battlefield but by faithfully carrying out their family responsibilities and their daily jobs with appreciation for their heritage and with aspirations to make the nation even better.

Although many myths surround the history of the American flag, I have tried to treat them respectfully. I know that just as contemporary scholars have pointed out past errors, so too future scholars will further refine our understanding of both the substance and symbols of American representative government. I have done my best to see that this book represents the best contemporary scholarship available at the time of its publication.

This encyclopedia is not designed to provide a comparative study of flags in general, but many of the articles I have read suggest that America's enthusiasm for its flag is fairly unique among nations. The flag is waved from schools, displayed in many churches and classrooms, flown over post offices and other government buildings, carried in parades, incorporated into clothing designs and objects of art, and is especially associated with major patriotic holidays. Indeed, it was not until I began this formal study that I realized how ubiquitous the American flag and its colors truly are.

John R. Vile
Middle Tennessee State University

Acknowledgments

One of the most enticing aspects of this book is that I have often gotten ideas for entries after simply asking people if they knew any stories about the American flag or if they had visited any historic sites where the flag was displayed in a particularly impressive way. Almost every member of the Honors College staff has offered suggestions. Librarians at the reference desk and in the interlibrary loan office at the MTSU Walker Library have rendered considerable assistance in locating sources. I have relied particularly heavily on two of our student workers, Miranda Dodson and Abby Armour, to help me locate articles and websites.

I am, of course, deeply indebted to the editors at ABC-CLIO, especially Kevin Hillstrom, who first suggested this project. I owe a particular debt of gratitude to the scholars, some of whom are MTSU colleagues, who have written the introductory essays and to Susan Lyons, who has helped with my correspondence with them.

Introduction

The Flag in American History

It has been said that history is a trail of symbols. Michael Waltzer's observation that the image of the body politic "does not so much reinforce existing political ideas (though it may later be used for that purpose) as underlie them" (1967, 194) could just as easily be applied to the flag. As a political scientist who was trained as a political theorist, I have been most interested in the symbols of written language expressed in documents like the Declaration of Independence, the Articles of Confederation, the U.S. Constitution and its amendments, and in speeches that articulated values.

Many of these documents, however, take a fair degree of sophistication to understand, and they may not evoke the same emotions as the picture of a beloved president, a carving of a bald eagle, or the display of an American flag. In monarchical nations—even those like Great Britain, where the king or queen is largely a figurehead—pictures of the monarch are everywhere, especially on currency and postage stamps. It is possible that the absence of such a figure in the United States has over time elevated the flag (and arguably the Constitution) to a similar status; Jenna Joselit (2017) has recently argued that the Ten Commandments have played a similar role. In a notable speech entitled "The Old Flag," James S. Ostrander, a first lieutenant from Indiana, used religious language to describe this phenomenon. He observed, "Men seal their devotion to an idea, a principle, with their lives; but the mind is so constituted that the abstract thought must have material existence, and this the flag supplies, for by some occult process of transubstantiation it becomes in the eyes of the patriot the visible State, the embodiment of all that is grand and good and true in the structure of the nation" (Ostrander 1887, 63).

Flags, banners, and totems go back to Biblical times, and their use has continued through the course of empires and republics. The first flags to appear in the New World were originally the coats of arms of those monarchs who sent explorers. Indeed, the British flag, which combined the red cross of St. George on a white field with the white cross of St. Andrew on a blue field, is often called the King's Colours. By contrast, despite futile attempts to associate the American flag with George Washington's coat of arms, it appears to have had a more organic growth.

The cross, the likeness of which the British flag bears, emerged far earlier than the flag itself. Carried in the crusades, it became the symbol of one of the world's largest relief agencies and was incorporated into numerous other flag designs. The cross is itself an ambiguous symbol. Viewed by orthodox Christians as a symbol of God's loving willingness to sacrifice his own son for the sins of the world, Muslims may associate the symbol with the militarism of the Crusades, while some Protestant Christians view it, and other attempts to represent Jesus, Mary, and the saints, as temptations to idolatry. Iconoclast forbears of America's Pilgrim Fathers ransacked British churches destroying such images, and long before flag burning became a symbol of opposition to governmental policies, New England Puritans themselves sometimes cut out the cross from the British flag because they considered it to be a papist symbol.

Colonial History

Although the Swedish, Dutch, Spanish, and French governments all staked claims to parts of North America, in time the 13 colonies that hugged the Atlantic below French Canada all became subject to the British monarch, on whom they also relied for protection. Most residents of this New World considered themselves to be British citizens, with the rights that they associated with Englishmen. Initially, the king granted the colonies considerable autonomy, a salutary neglect that was furthered by the physical distance between the colonies and the motherland. The colonists in Virginia prided themselves on having established their own House of Burgesses in 1619, and other colonies exercised similar forms of self-government. The Virginians traded almost exclusively with the British and their colonies, but they might have largely done so even if commercial regulations had not required it.

After the French and Indian War, which lasted from 1754 to 1763, the British began to exert increased influence in the colonies that they had defended. In particular, Parliament, which English legal theorists considered to be legally sovereign, began to assert its authority to tax the colonies. By contrast, colonists took the position that the Magna Carta (1215) and other documents prohibited their taxation without parliamentary representation. They reasoned that since representatives from the colonies were not seated in Parliament, that body had no right to tax them.

They initially sought the support of George III to oppose what they considered to be parliamentary pretension. Over the course of the ensuing decade, however, the king's actions convinced the colonists that he would offer no help and that the time for independence had arrived. When the colonists formally declared their independence in July 1776, their troops had already been in the field for more than a year. At the time, it was common for troops to march under the colors of their regiments, which often were firmly tied to individual colonial identity. New Englanders marched under flags with pine trees, South Carolinians under trees with palmettos, and others with rattlesnakes (Don't Tread on Me) and other local symbols.

The Founding Period

It was not until 1777 that Congress officially authorized a distinctive U.S. flag. The move appears to have been largely dictated by the need for American ships on the high seas to have a banner that would distinguish them from pirate ships. The resolution was concise:

> Resolved, that the flag of the United States be made of thirteen stripes, alternate red and white; that the union be thirteen stars, white in a blue field, representing a new constellation.

Prior to this time, Washington's troops on Prospect Hill, outside Boston, appear to have raised a flag. It consisted of the British Union Jack (itself formed by combining the flags of England and Scotland) in the upper-left-hand canton and 13 alternating red and white stripes in the field.

It seems appropriate that Congress would take the imagery of the flag from the sky (Shalev 2011). Just as the word "revolution" derived from the terminology of astronomy, so too the new nation was asserting its independence from the gravitational pull of the British empire. Although numerous individuals have subsequently gone to considerable lengths to describe the origin of the colors of the flag, the first congressional resolution is surprisingly silent on the matter. The most obvious explanation, however, is that the colors red and white were borrowed from the nation from which the colonies were now declaring their political independence.

Because the 1777 resolution did not specify the arrangement of the stars, there was considerable variation in early usage. This ranged from the typical flag design attributed to Betsy Ross (13 five-pointed stars arranged in a circle within the canton) to flags with rows of stars or 12 stars surrounding a 13th. Despite a number of paintings that anachronistically portray scenes of battle in which such flags were flying, most troops in the field continued to use battle flags that often reflected greater regional than national influences. Moreover, works of folk art from the period following the war indicate that the U.S. flag had not yet achieved its later status. Pictures of George Washington, carvings of the bald eagle, and pictures and carvings of female figures (Native American maidens, Lady Liberty, and Columbia) embodying liberty appear to have been far more prominent than flags or depictions thereof.

As the Second Continental Congress was preparing for independence, it was also drafting plans for a new government. The resulting Articles of Confederation, headed by a single unicameral Congress in which states were equally represented, highlighted individual state sovereignty. American diplomats were among those who pressed for a stronger national union, which delegates formulated in Philadelphia at the Constitutional Convention of 1787. It created a more powerful national government representing "We the People" while preserving the states. It divided this strengthened national government into three coequal branches, split Congress into two Houses (one of which was apportioned by population), and soon was modified by amendments that put certain rights beyond the reach of this new government.

The Early Republic

In advocating ratification of the United States Constitution in *Federalist No. 10*, James Madison had argued for the merits of a large republic. In such a republic, representatives would refine and enlarge public opinion and would better be able to control the "mischiefs of faction" and thus better preserve justice than smaller nations. Madison also thought that a single faction, or combination of factions, was less likely to prevail in such a large republic (Hamilton, Madison, and Jay 1961, 77–84). Americans thus undoubtedly took pride in the addition, in 1795, of two additional stars and stripes on the flag representing Kentucky and Vermont. Stars continued to be added to the flag throughout the next century as the nation realized what it increasingly believed was its manifest destiny to push all the way to the Pacific Ocean.

As America's first president, George Washington did much to establish historic protocols for his successors (Bruff 2015), but he could not tamp down the rising partisanship that he had hoped to avoid. Although this certainly distracted from the national unity that the flag might otherwise represent—even Independence Day celebrations became partisan events (Warren 1945, 254)—the nation passed an important milestone in 1801. At that time, it survived a malfunctioning in the Electoral College, which had created a tie between the two Democratic-Republican candidates that the House of Representatives had to resolve, and power peacefully passed from the Federalist administration of John Adams to the Democratic-Republican control of Thomas Jefferson. After the demise of the Federalists in the wake of the War of 1812, the Whig party rose to take its place, and the United States has continued to have a strong two-party system (often with third-party alternatives) ever since.

Although Washington had used his *Farewell Address* to warn Americans of excessive entanglement in European affairs, America barely avoided war with France during the administration of John Adams, and the Jefferson administration imposed an embargo on Great Britain. War with Britain followed during the administration of James Madison. It was largely precipitated by British impressment of U.S. sailors and not a little by American hopes to bring Canada, which Britain had gained during the French and Indian War, into its growing sphere.

The war, like earlier embargoes, brought about sharp internal divisions within the United States, with representatives from the New England states even considering disunion. Soldiers continued to march under regimental colors, but the U.S. flag became immortalized by Francis Scott Key, who wrote "The Star-Spangled Banner" to express his relief and pride at seeing the flag flying over Fort McHenry after the unsuccessful nighttime British bombardment of Baltimore. Andrew Jackson's great military victory over the British in New Orleans at the end of the war further heightened national pride. Indeed, combatants fought after the formal peace treaty had already been signed but prior to the time that this news had reached America.

Between the end of the War of 1812 and the beginning of the Civil War, the number of stars on the flag grew from 15 to 33. In 1818, Congress wisely decided that while it would continue to symbolize the addition of new states to the constitutional constellation with new stars, it would reduce the number of stripes back to 13, lest the addition of new stripes reduce them to mere pinstripes.

Despite the composition of "The Star-Spangled Banner," prior to the Civil War, the U.S. flag did not yet occupy the pervasive place in the American geographical or psychological landscape that it later would. The Jacksonian Era did, however, expand suffrage among white males, and beginning with the presidential election of 1840, campaigning took a popular turn that would lend itself to rallies, parades, and other events that treated flag-waving as a symbol of patriotism.

From the Mid-19th Century to World War I

The Mexican-American War, which lasted from 1846–1848, marked the first occasion that American troops regularly carried the U.S. flag, rather than just their regimental colors, into the battlefield. Although American victory further augmented both American territory and national pride, it also aggravated sectional tensions. By expanding southward and westward, the nation was opening up new territory for the spread of slavery, which would therefore become even more difficult to eradicate. The so-called Wilmot Proviso attempted to forestall this, and in 1854, individuals created the Republican Party specifically to prevent further expansion.

The Civil War marks the period in which the U.S. flag came into its own as a popular icon. Lincoln attended a flag raising at Independence Hall in Philadelphia on his way to his inauguration. The war began with the Confederate defeat of federal forces, who were forced to lower their flag at Fort Sumter, and ground through the continent's four bloodiest years. During this time, Lincoln's initial aim to preserve the Union was over shadowed by a rededication, which Lincoln announced in his Gettysburg Address, to the founding principle that all men are created equal. Days after the war officially ended, the American flag was raised back over Fort Sumter. That same day, Lincoln was shot. There are reports that as Lincoln lay dying at Ford's Theatre, a flag cradled his head and that when his body was transported to the White House, another flag was used to cover his remains.

Officers who had served together under the Stars and Stripes during the Mexican-American War fought under different banners during the Civil War. The Confederate battle flag eventually replaced the Stars and Bars (which was difficult to distinguish from the U.S. flag on the battlefield) as the official symbol of the confederacy. Gen. Benjamin Butler executed a Confederate sympathizer who had desecrated a U.S. flag in Union-occupied New Orleans, and Edward Everett Hale pulled at the national heartstrings with his fictional tale (often taken as nonfiction) "The Man without a Country." The war also popularized the term "Old Glory" as a reference to the American flag. The term owes its origins to a flag that one-time sea captain William Driver had hidden in his Nashville house. When Union forces recaptured the city, Driver offered it to Union troops to fly over the state capitol building.

Many African Americans had actively participated in the Civil War, and the Thirteenth Amendment eliminated the institution of slavery at the end of the war in 1865. Promises of equal protection of the laws, which the Fourteenth Amendment (1868) guaranteed, like similar protections for voting rights in the Fifteenth Amendment (1870), received little judicial protection for the next 80 years, as former Confederate leaders reasserted renewed white control throughout most of the South during the same time.

The Civil War marked the first creation of national cemeteries. The following decades saw the creation of Decoration Day (later Memorial Day), the issuance of the first stamp with the image of an American flag (1869), and the creation of the myth of Betsy Ross as a Founding Mother, after her grandson William J. Canby gave a speech bringing her alleged role as creator of the first American flag to the public's attention in 1870. This time also witnessed the designation of Independence Day as a national holiday (1870) and the celebration of the centennial of the Declaration of Independence in Philadelphia. Although this celebration included the display of some notable paintings of the U.S. flag, the nation chiefly used the event to celebrate scientific progress. The next year, however, was the first in which Flag Day was celebrated.

Just as the Liberty Bell had emerged as a national symbol among abolitionists during the years leading up to the Civil War, so too the dedication of the Statue of Liberty in 1886 provided another potent symbol of American ideals. While this statue welcomed immigrants, some Americans (like Know-Nothing forbears) viewed increasing immigration—particularly from southern European Roman Catholic nations—as a threat to national identity and promoted instruction about and reverence for the flag as a way to bring about national assimilation and unity.

This and the successive decade thus saw the birth of increased attention to "the cult of the flag"—that is, to attempts to make the flag into an even more sacred object. Efforts to honor the flag were led by a variety of veterans and hereditary groups such as the Daughters of the American Revolution and the Grand Army of the Republic. Once used primarily as a form of identification at sea, the flag began increasingly appearing at public buildings and at schoolhouses. This time also marked the formulation of the pledge to the flag, which gradually became a standard feature of the public school day. The Pledge of Allegiance became much more prominent, for example, after a successful nationwide effort to mobilize students for this purpose in 1892, the 400th anniversary of Columbus's discovery of America.

As the flag became an increasingly popular symbol, businesses often exploited it for commercial purposes. Despite an occasional conviction, state laws against such commercial exploitation proved to be largely ineffective and remain so to this day. Red, white, and blue colors are so pervasive that it takes effort to realize how ubiquitous they are.

The period of congressional reconstruction of southern states ended in 1877. Afterward, there was an increasing disjunction between American ideals as expressed in such documents as the Declaration of Independence and the Gettysburg Address and the reality that faced many Americans, especially African Americans. While Americans won the Spanish-American War in relatively short order, it also complicated American identity. Patriotism, which was increasingly symbolized by reverence for the U.S. flag, became associated with the acquisition of foreign colonies, whose people did not always welcome such rule. Americans subsequently engaged in the tactics that they had used to suppress Native Americans when putting down a guerrilla insurgency in the Philippines (O'Leary 1999, 141).

World Wars I and II

In 1912, President William Howard Taft finally issued a proclamation intended to standardize the dimensions of the U.S. flag and its arrangement of stars. Four years later, President Woodrow Wilson issued an order making "The Star-Spangled Banner" the official anthem of the U.S. Armed Forces. Although the United States initially kept out of World War I, when it entered the conflict in 1917, it entered full bore and brooked little domestic opposition. Flags shouted from recruiting posters, and Congress adopted a Sedition Act that made it a crime to criticize the flag or to fly the flag of an enemy nation. Streets were splashed in the colors of the United States flag and those of the flags of American allies, and such tableaus (as well as flags themselves) became an increasingly common subject of paintings. Suffragists who ultimately succeeded in pushing for the adoption of a constitutional amendment granting women the vote added to the effectiveness of their campaign by parading with American flags.

Many Americans became isolationist at the end of World War I, and the U.S. Senate rejected any American participation in the League of Nations, for which President Wilson had advocated. As a new group of veterans joined American civilian ranks at the end of the war, conferences sponsored by the American Legion in 1923 and 1924 articulated an elaborate flag code that treated the flag as an increasingly sacred symbol. In 1931, Congress officially designated "The Star-Spangled Banner" as the national anthem and established November 11 as Armistice Day to honor those who had served in World War I.

By the time that Kate Smith began singing Irving Berlin's "God Bless America" in 1938, many were watching "As the storm clouds gather, far across the sea." However disillusioning it must have been to realize that the "war to end all wars" had not succeeded in accomplishing this objective, the Japanese attack on Pearl Harbor on December 7, 1941, mobilized Americans in a war that generated little internal dissent. A year prior to U.S. entry into the war, the Supreme Court upheld a repressive Pennsylvania law that suspended students and punished the parents of students who refused on religious grounds to salute the American flag in public schools. The court reversed this decision during the course of the war (Flag Day of 1942), in part because the Axis nations seemed to offer a chilling example of what happened when nations refused to tolerate dissent. That same year, Congress officially recognized the pledge and the flag code, although it did not provide legal penalties for violating them.

The flag can be an especially unifying symbol during times of war. In July 1942, over 400 American magazines joined in printing pictures of American flags on the covers of their issues. Many private citizens also followed the practice, first established during World War I, of hanging service flags from their windows denoting the number of family members serving in the armed forces. Gold stars represented members who had died. The flag was considered to be so valuable to the war effort that the Star-Spangled Banner, which had waved over Fort McHenry during the War of 1812, was removed from display at the Smithsonian Institution and taken to a storage facility outside Luray, in the Shenandoah Valley of Virginia, to preserve it from possible enemy attack. Meanwhile, millions of men and women continued to march, toil, and fight under the banner of the Stars and Stripes.

One of the most iconic images that emerged from World War II was the photograph, later memorialized in sculpture, of American marines raising an American flag at the top of Mount Suribachi on Iwo Jima. The war finally ended when U.S.-led Allied forces defeated Hitler in Berlin and American planes dropped two atomic bombs on Japan. This latter action ushered in a new fear of thermonuclear war that would dominate American consciousness for the next 50 years. When the Japanese surrendered to the United States on the battleship *Missouri*, the ship waved the American flag that Commodore Perry had flown on the ship that traveled to Japan in 1853 to open trade with that country.

From the Cold War to the Present

American allies in the war quickly became rivals as it ended. Although former combatants agreed to form the United Nations (UN), this international forum was unable to bring about world peace, as the Soviet Union retained a veto in the UN's all-important Security Council. Soviet forces installed puppet communist regimes in the nations that they had liberated in Eastern Europe as communists gained control of mainland China. For its part, the United States reconstructed Japan and used the Marshall Plan to help prop up those tottering Western nations that it had liberated but that were still staggering from war losses and displaced refugees. Germany remained long divided between East and West, and in 1948 and 1949, the United States had to launch a major airlift to Berlin, which was also divided when the Soviets cut off Western access to the city.

America largely followed a policy of containment to halt the further spread of communism. It sent military forces to Korea, Vietnam, and other theatres to halt the expansionist ambitions of the Soviets. Congress sought to highlight the ideological divisions between democracy and communism by adding the words "under God" to the nation's pledge in 1954 and by declaring in 1956 that "In God We Trust" would be the nation's official motto. In 1962, the United States and the Soviet Union approached the brink of nuclear war over the placement of Soviet missiles in Cuba.

The Korean War began on June 25, 1950, when communist forces from the North invaded South Korea. It expanded when Chinese forces entered on behalf of their communist allies after an offensive led by American forces pushed back through North Korea close to the Chinese border. Designated by President Harry S. Truman as a "police action" that did not need congressional sanction, American participation in Korea, although ending in stalemate at the boundaries where it had begun, prepared the basis for further interventions. America continues to post troops in South Korea, and the American flag is still revered there.

No Cold War intervention was more controversial than America's extended participation in the conflict between North and South Vietnam, which was less an invasion than a guerilla conflict in which it was difficult to distinguish combatants from civilians. The increasing numbers of American troops involved in the Vietnam War between 1964 (when the first U.S. ground troops arrived) and 1975 (when the last American personnel left the war-torn country) led to rising casualties and to antiwar protests, especially on American campuses, that roiled American society. The act of burning both U.S. flags and draft cards in protest of the war led to the enactment of a flag desecration bill in 1968, although it did little to quell the protests. Artists increasingly began to play on the ambiguous role of the flag as a symbol not only of what was good about America but also of its flaws.

When African American soldiers returned home at the end of World War II, where they had served in racially segregated units, many became leaders in the movement for equal rights at home. It was not until its decision in *Brown v. Board of Education* (1954) that the Supreme Court finally reversed the decision of *Plessy v. Ferguson* (1896) and ended the segregationist policies of "separate but equal." At least initially, mainstream civil rights demonstrators marched with U.S. flags waving, sometimes as they confronted rival crowds who were waving the Confederate Flag. One of the era's most iconic photographs, *The Soiling of Old Glory*, emerged from anti-busing demonstrations that sprouted in Boston and other cities in response to court-ordered busing to desegregate schools. In the famous 1976 photograph taken by journalist Stanley Forman, a young white protestor is poised to use the staff of an American flag to spear an African American bystander.

As some civil rights leaders, Martin Luther King Jr. among them, began to question the Vietnam War, their criticism was sometimes mistakenly taken as disregard for the flag. When a memorial was constructed to those who had died in Vietnam, it was far less militaristic and heroic than most previous war monuments. A solid black wall with the names of thousands of casualties, although initially highly criticized, has subsequently been recognized as a place of healing. In time, a more traditional statue of three soldiers was added to the entrance of the memorial along with an American flag.

As America was extracting its forces from Vietnam, the nation faced a major constitutional crisis with revelations that President Richard M. Nixon's reelection campaign had bugged the Democratic National Headquarters in the Watergate complex in Washington, D.C., and then sought to cover it up. As the House of Representatives inched closer to impeaching President Nixon for high crimes and misdemeanors, he resigned—not long after his vice president had done the same, after pleading no contest to charges that he had accepted bribes while acting as the governor of Maryland. Gerald Ford took Nixon's place and sought to heal the nation, even though his pardon of Nixon led many to think that he had created a double standard.

In 1976, the nation celebrated the bicentennial of the Declaration of Independence. Far more dispersed that the celebrations held 100 years earlier, the celebrations glorified American history and led to renewed respect for the Red, White, and Blue. As embarrassing as the events surrounding the Watergate break-in had been, Nixon's resignation appeared to show that the system of checks and balances that the Founders had set in place still worked.

After several years of a national energy crisis and a sort of societal malaise, in the words of President Jimmy Carter, the 1980 election of Ronald Reagan appeared to bring a more confident nationalism, which was often reflected in increased use of the flag. As a former Hollywood actor, Reagan was particularly effective at using the American flag and other symbolic props and sites as effective backdrops, a technique that has not been lost on subsequent candidates.

His successor, President George H. W. Bush, repulsed an Iraq invasion of Kuwait only to see his political popularity sink under economic problems. He was replaced by a charismatic Bill Clinton, who over two terms exercised great political skill, which he needed to salvage his presidency in the aftermath of an impeachment brought about by his sexual infidelity and attempts to cover it up. The presidency of his successor, George W. Bush, became defined largely by the terrorist attacks of September 11, 2001, which not only highlighted the threat of radical Islam but also led to renewed flag-waving, increased domestic surveillance, another invasion of Iraq, and the use of harsh interrogation tactics to extort information from America's enemies. An iconic photograph from the aftermath of the 9/11 attacks showed New York City firefighters raising an American flag amid mounds of gray debris in a pose reminiscent of the soldiers who earlier raised the flag at Iwo Jima.

During this time, the flag that flew over Fort McHenry was being painstakingly restored and repositioned at the Smithsonian Institution. This project was completed in 2005, just two years before the 50-star flag became the longest serving in U.S. history. That Star-Spangled Banner remains perhaps the most hallowed object at the Smithsonian.

In 2008, the nation elected its first African American president, which would have seemed almost inconceivable a century earlier. Barack Obama served out two full terms and managed to push through a national health care program that had eluded many prior presidents. In 2016, Hillary Clinton became the first female presidential nominee of a major political party and actually captured the popular vote but lost the electoral vote to businessman Donald Trump, who had expressed concern over flag desecration and represented the resurgence of populist nationalism. In 2017, NFL quarterback Colin Kaepernick initiated a movement in which players kneeled during the national anthem to protest police brutality against African Americans. On September 22, 2017, President Trump responded to this by asking a crowd, "Wouldn't you love to see one of these NFL owners when somebody disrespects our flag, to say, 'Get that son of a b**** off the field right now. Out! He's fired!'" At least initially, these remarks appeared to unite owners and players (who locked arms on the field) more than it divided them.

Schoolchildren and members of many civic groups continue to salute the flag. Individuals continue to wave flags from their houses, particularly on national holidays. Some Americans undoubtedly associate the flag with support of all American endeavors, military or otherwise, while others distinguish the ideals of liberty and justice for which the flag stands from those who currently occupy political offices or the nation's current policies. Most presidential candidates appear to seek to outdo one another in expressions of loyalty to that banner, and many ordinary citizens remain willing to sacrifice their lives on behalf of the flag and the nation for which it stands.

The Organization of This Book

This book is organized into two main divisions. The first is a series of comprehensive essays about the American flag and its place in U.S. history and culture, written by knowledgeable scholars. The second is a series of alphabetical entries on just over 200 different topics that span U.S. history.

As the topical table of contents reveals, these entries are fairly wide ranging. They include artistic depictions of the flag, famous photographs and monuments to the flag, musical selections focusing on the flag, poems and speeches about the flag, and accounts of how the flag has been incorporated into sporting events and other institutions of American life and culture.

Yet another set of entries focuses on some of the designers and designs of the flag. These include entries on the colors of the flag, the stars, the stripes, and flag proportions. Other entries discuss how the flag relates to other American symbols and how these symbols are displayed in a variety of ways. The encyclopedia is also generously stocked with entries covering legal decisions related to the display, treatment, and meaning of the flag. Some court decisions deal with flag salutes, and other entries in the book also focus on the pledge to the flag and how it developed and has been applied.

Although the flag is designed to represent all Americans, this encyclopedia devotes special attention to certain groups that have been particularly prominent in promoting the flag and ceremonies related to it, such as the Grand Army of the Republic, the Daughters of the American Revolution, the American Legion, and the Veterans of Foreign Wars. Similarly, the encyclopedia highlights individuals known for their connection with, or contributions to, our understandings of the flag or to flag-related holidays.

Although the current 50-star flag is the longest-serving official flag in U.S. history, it was preceded by many other designs. Indeed, because law did not specify the arrangement of stars on the flag until 1912, early iterations of the flag showed great variety, and many flags have special names denoting where and by whom they were displayed. Individual entries on some of the most prominent flag designs, like the Rattlesnake Flag, the Pine Tree Flag, and the flag that flew over Fort Sumter at the beginning of the Civil War, are also included in this work.

The entries in this encyclopedia also include cross-references to other entries and scholarly references for those who want to engage in further research. Other informational aids include a table of contents, a topical list of entries, an extensive bibliography, a detailed timeline, and a comprehensive subject index.

Timeline

1492 Christopher Columbus comes ashore in San Salvador with the Spanish flag bearing the arms of Castile and Leon.

1497 John Cabot, a Venetian, flies the English flag for the first time in North America (Newfoundland). The flag would probably have been a white flag with a rectangular red cross.

1603 As James I (formerly James VI of Scotland) becomes King of England, the two nations are merged and St. George's Cross is joined with the cross of St. Andrew to form the new flag. From the beheading of Charles I in 1649 to 1660, the partnership was dissolved, but it was afterward renewed.

1634 Pilgrims slash out the St. George's Cross from the English flag because they think it is a relic of Roman Catholicism.

1707 Parliament adopts the King's Colours as the official flag of the kingdom.

1754–1763 Conflict between the French (and their Indian allies) and British (and their 13 North American colonies) results in British acquisition of Canada, and the British desire to tax colonies to help pay for their defense.

1775 Fighting breaks out between the colonists and Great Britain.

1776 The Second Continental Congress issues Declaration of Independence proclaiming the separation of 13 North American colonies from Great Britain.

On November 16, the Dutch become first to salute U.S. flag (Continental Union) off the Dutch West Indies.

1777 Congress authorizes a flag with stars and stripes and proposes a new form of government known as the Articles of Confederation.

1779 The first known painting of the stars and stripes on a naval vessel is completed, a painting by Francis Holman of an engagement between the British ship *Bridgewater* and the American privateering ship *Hampden*. The white stars in the flag's blue canton are arranged in a circle.

1781 The Articles of Confederation, drawn up by the Second Continental Congress, are ratified by the final state.

British forces surrender to Americans and French at Yorktown, Virginia.

1782	George III acknowledges American independence.
	John Singleton Copley finishes a portrait of Elkanah Watson by adding an American flag to a ship in the background.
1783	British troops withdraw from New York City (Evacuation Day) on November 25, 1783.
	George Washington resigns his commission as head of U.S. military forces.
1787	The convention in Philadelphia draws up the U.S. Constitution.
1788	Conventions in nine states ratify the U.S. Constitution.
1789	The U.S. Constitution goes into effect; Washington is inaugurated as the first president.
1801	Power is peacefully transferred from a presidency headed by Federalist President John Adams to Democratic-Republic President Thomas Jefferson.
1795	Congress adds 2 stars and 2 stripes to the original 13 to mark the admission of Vermont and Kentucky.
1799	George Washington decides not to run for a third presidential term.
1800	John and Abigail Adams become the first family to live in the White House.
1812	The United States declares war on Great Britain.
	Residents who live outside of Colrain, Massachusetts, gather around a flag that they raised near a log-cabin schoolhouse
1814	The British burn the White House.
	Francis Scott Key composes "The Star-Spangled Banner" after Americans rebuff a British attempt to invade Baltimore.
1815	The War of 1812 comes to an end.
1818	Congress reduces the number of stripes on the flag back to 13, but stipulates that new states would be symbolized by the addition of new stars, thus raising the number to 20.
1819	Congress adds a 21st star on the flag to acknowledge the admission of Illinois.
1820	The number of stars on the flag increases to 23 to acknowledge admission of Alabama and Maine.
1822	The number of stars on the flag increases to 24 to mark the admission of Missouri.
1824	William Driver coins the term "Old Glory" for a flag that he had flown on his ship.
1828	Disputes over the national tariff lead to the development of the doctrine that states have the power to nullify federal laws.
1830	Oliver Wendell Holmes Sr. writes "Old Ironsides."

1836 The number of stars on the flag increases to 25 to mark the admission of Arkansas.

1836 The number of stars on the flag increases to 26 to mark the admission of Michigan.

Texas declares its independence from Mexico.

1840 In a campaign with the slogan "Tippecanoe and Tyler Too," ribbons portray Whig candidate William Henry Harrison with a log cabin with a flag flying outside.

1841 A flag is displayed at half-mast over the White House for the first time on the death of President William Henry Harrison.

1843 To mark the death of Francis Scott Key, the U.S. Supreme Court adjourns for January 11, and flags in Washington and Baltimore are lowered to half-staff.

1845 The number of stars on the flag increases to 27 to mark the admission of Florida.

1846 The number of stars on the flag increases to 28 to mark the admission of Texas.

The U.S. engages in a war with Mexico. This is the first war in which troops regularly marched under national colors rather than those of their regiments.

1847 The number of stars on the flag increases to 29 to mark the admission of Iowa.

1848 The number of stars on the flag increases to 30 to mark the admission of Wisconsin.

The Seneca Falls Convention in New York proposes woman's suffrage.

1851 The number of stars on the flag increases to 31 to mark the admission of California.

1853 Commodore M. C. Perry becomes the first to sail a ship flying an American flag into a Japanese port.

1854 The Republican Party is formed in Ripon, Wisconsin, dedicated to opposing the further expansion of slavery.

1858 The number of stars on the flag increases to 32 to mark the admission of Minnesota.

1859 The number of stars on the flag increases to 33 to mark the admission of Oregon.

1860 Abraham Lincoln is elected as the first Republican to hold the office of the presidency.

1861 Southern attack on federal garrison at Fort Sumter initiates the U.S. Civil War; during the war, the flag becomes known as Old Glory.

The number of stars on the flag increases to 34 to mark the admission of Kansas.

Confederate Congress issues a proclamation on March 4 creating its own flag consisting of stars in a blue canton and two red stripes and one white stripe (of equal dimensions). This was later replaced in part because it was hard to distinguish it from the U.S. flag on the battlefield.

1862 The U.S. military executes William B. Mumford for tearing down an American flag flying over New Orleans and dragging it through the mud.

In December, before the Battle of Stones River, the floor at a wedding ceremony in Murfreesboro, Tennessee, is covered with American flags, on which people dance.

1863 The number of stars on the flag increases to 35 to mark the admission of West Virginia, which had joined the union side in the Civil War after separating from Virginia.

Edward Everett Hale publishes "The Man without a Country."

1864 The words "In God We Trust" first appear on a U.S. coin (the two-cent piece).

1865 The Civil War ends, and John Wilkes Booth assassinates President Abraham Lincoln. A flag is used to cushion Lincoln's head.

Congress increases the number of stars on the flag to 36 to mark the admission of Nevada.

1866 A group of Union veterans founds the Grand Army of the Republic (GAR).

The Capitol Dome is completed.

1867 The number of stars on the flag increases to 37 to mark the admission of Nebraska.

1868 Gilbert H. Bates takes a four-month trip through the South carrying an American flag.

Decoration Day is established to honor Civil War dead.

The Fourteenth Amendment declares all persons born or naturalized in the United States to be citizens.

1869 The first stamp with a picture of the U.S. flag is issued.

1870 Congress designates July 4 as a national holiday.

William J. Canby gives speech claiming that Betsy Ross made the first U.S. Flag.

The Fifteenth Amendment prohibits discrimination in voting on the basis of race or previous condition of servitude.

1876 The nation celebrates the centennial of the Declaration of Independence in Philadelphia. One of the displays includes the painting *The Spirit of '76*.

1877 The number of stars on the flag increases to 38 with the admission of Colorado.

Flag Day is first celebrated.

A special commission awards disputed electoral votes to Republican presidential candidate Rutherford B. Hayes, giving him the election over Democrat Samuel B. Tilden.

Federal troops cease to occupy the U.S. South as the period of congressional Reconstruction comes to an end.

1879 C. T. Russell founds the Watchtower Society (later known as Jehovah's Witnesses), whose members would later object to saluting the U.S. flag.

1886 The Statue of Liberty is dedicated.

1887 George Balch composes what is believed to be the first pledge to the U.S. flag.

President Grover Cleveland revokes an order that he had given to return captured Confederate flags to the southern states.

1888 *The Youth's Companion* begins efforts to install a flag at every school and to adopt the pledge of allegiance.

The first memorial to Francis Scott Key is dedicated in Golden Gate Park in San Francisco on July 4.

The Washington Monument is completed and opened to the public.

1890 George Balch publishes his *Methods for Teaching Patriotism in the Public Schools*, which includes instructions on flag rituals.

Congress increases the number of stars on the flag to 43 to mark the admission of North Dakota, South Dakota, Montana, Washington, and Idaho.

The Daughters of the American Revolution (DAR) is founded.

1891 The number of stars on the flag increases to 44 to mark the admission of Wyoming.

1892 Schools celebrate Columbus Day with children repeating pledge developed by Francis Bellamy.

1893 Katharine Lee Bates of Wellesley College pens "America the Beautiful."

1896 The Olympic Games are reestablished in Athens, Greece.

Congress increases the number of stars on the flag to 45 to mark the admission of Utah.

1897 John Philip Sousa's "The Stars and Stripes Forever" is publically performed for the first time.

1898 Spanish-American War is sparked by the sinking of the *Maine*, an American battleship, in Cuba. Through the war, the United States acquires its first foreign colonies.

	The New York state legislature passes the first flag-salute statute.
	A memorial is dedicated to Francis Scott Key in Frederick, Maryland.
1906	"You're a Grand Old Flag" is first performed.
1907	Kansas becomes the first state to mandate that all public school students salute the flag.
	In *Halter v. Nebraska*, the Supreme Court upholds the conviction of an individual who used the flag on a beer bottle for advertising purposes.
	A Republican Congress and president (Theodore Roosevelt) authorize the return of Confederate flags captured during the Civil War.
1908	The number of stars on the flag increases to 46 to mark the admission of Oklahoma.
1909	Robert E. Peary reaches what he believed to be the North Pole and leaves a fragment of an American flag there.
1912	President William Howard Taft signs an executive order (No. 1556) prescribing the proportions and dimensions of the flag.
	The Smithsonian gains possession of the flag that flew over Fort McHenry and inspired "The Star-Spangled Banner."
	The number of stars on the flag increases to 48 to mark the admission of New Mexico and Arizona.
1914	President Woodrow Wilson establishes June 14 as Flag Day.
1915	A German U-boat sinks the *Lusitania*, which results in 128 American deaths and leads to calls for American intervention in World War I.
1916	President Wilson signs an order making "The Star-Spangled Banner" the anthem for America's armed forces.
	Bouck White leads a group of New York Socialists who cast their respective flags, including the American flag, into a burning "melting pot," for which they are successfully prosecuted.
1917	The United States enters World War I on the side of the Allies.
	The Federal Trade Commission (FTC) asks Congress to protect the people from price gouging, including the rising prices of flags.
	The fall of Russia to communist forces leads to increased fear of communism in the U.S., including periodic "Red Scares."
1918	Ora Troyer, a Mennonite from West Liberty, Ohio, is successfully prosecuted because his daughter refused to salute the flag.
	William Tyler Page's "The American's Creed" is selected from more than 3,000 entries in a nationwide contest as the best distillation of American ideals.
	Congress adopts a Sedition Act that makes it a crime to criticize the U.S. flag or fly the flag of a foreign enemy.

A Montana man is sentenced to 10–20 years in jail after refusing a mob's demand that he kiss the American flag.

President Wilson proclaims November 11 as Armistice Day to commemorate the end of World War I.

1919 The American Legion is founded.

William Guthrie publishes *The Religion of Old Glory*.

1920 The Nineteenth Amendment prohibits discrimination in voting on the basis of sex.

1922 In the first national presidential radio address, President Warren G. Harding dedicates a sculpture at Fort McHenry.

The Lincoln Memorial in Washington, D.C., is completed.

1923 Governor Percival P. Baxter of Maine orders the flag over the Augusta statehouse to be flown at half-mast to honor his dog, Garry, who had just died.

1923 The first flag conference meets and changes the words in the Pledge of Allegiance from "my flag" to "the flag of the United States." It also agrees on a flag code.

1924 The second flag conference adds the words "of America" to the pledge after "United States."

Taxicab drivers forcefully raise a U.S. flag over the German embassy in Washington, D.C., after it fails to lower its flag in honor of the death of Woodrow Wilson.

1925 Over 40,000 members of the Ku Klux Klan march down Pennsylvania Avenue in Washington, D.C., carrying U.S. flags.

Congress used Defenders Day to designate Fort McHenry as a national park.

1926 Congress calls on the president to call for a display of the flag on all governmental buildings for Armistice Day.

The Rockefellers begin making plans to restore Colonial Williamsburg, which had served as Virginia's colonial capital.

1931 Congress makes "The Star-Spangled Banner" the official anthem of the nation.

In *Stromberg v. California*, the U.S. Supreme Court overturns a conviction for waving a red flag.

1935 Having previously decided that it was wrong to salute Adolf Hitler, Jehovah's Witnesses decide that it is also wrong to salute the U.S. flag.

1936 American athletes refuse to dip the flag to Adolf Hitler at the international Olympic Games.

1938 Congress designates each November 11, the date of the official end to World War I, as Armistice Day, to honor those who died in the war.

1940	U.S. Supreme Court rules in *Minersville Board of Education v. Gobitis* that schoolchildren may be compelled to salute the flag. Jehovah's Witnesses who refuse to comply are subsequently subjected to widespread violence.
1941	On July 4, Chief Justice Harlan Fiske Stone leads the Pledge of Allegiance over the radio after a speech by President Franklin D. Roosevelt.
	On December 7, a Japanese surprise attack on the U.S. military base at Pearl Harbor leads the United States to declare war against Japan, marking America's formal entrance into World War II.
1942	Congress officially recognizes the Pledge of Allegiance.
	Congress establishes an official flag code.
	The United States drops the so-called Bellamy salute (right hand extended toward the flag with an upward palm) and replaces it with placing one's hand over one's heart.
	Four hundred magazines coordinate efforts to put U.S. flags on their covers to mark the first Fourth of July since the Japanese attack on Pearl Harbor.
	The Supreme Court rules in *West Virginia State Board of Education v. Barnette* that schoolchildren may not be compelled to salute the U.S. flag. The court announces its opinion on Flag Day.
	The original sheet music for "The Star-Spangled Banner" is temporarily moved from the Smithsonian Institution in Washington, D.C., to a warehouse in Shenandoah National Park in Virginia, for safekeeping.
	Gordon Parks takes the iconic photograph *American Gothic, Washington, D.C.*
1943	The Jefferson Memorial in Washington, D.C., is completed.
1944	Composer Igor Stravinsky's performance of a symphonic arrangement of "The Star-Spangled Banner" is criticized for some discordant chords.
1945	American marines raise a U.S. flag on Mount Suribachi, on Iwo Jima, and become the subjects of an iconic photograph that later became the basis for a famous sculpture.
	The United States drops two atomic bombs on Japan. A short time later, Japan surrenders, bringing World War II to a close.
	The White House flies an American flag that flew over Pearl Harbor during the Japanese attack.
	The UN is founded.
1949	Congress passes an act asking to observe Flag Day each year on June 14.

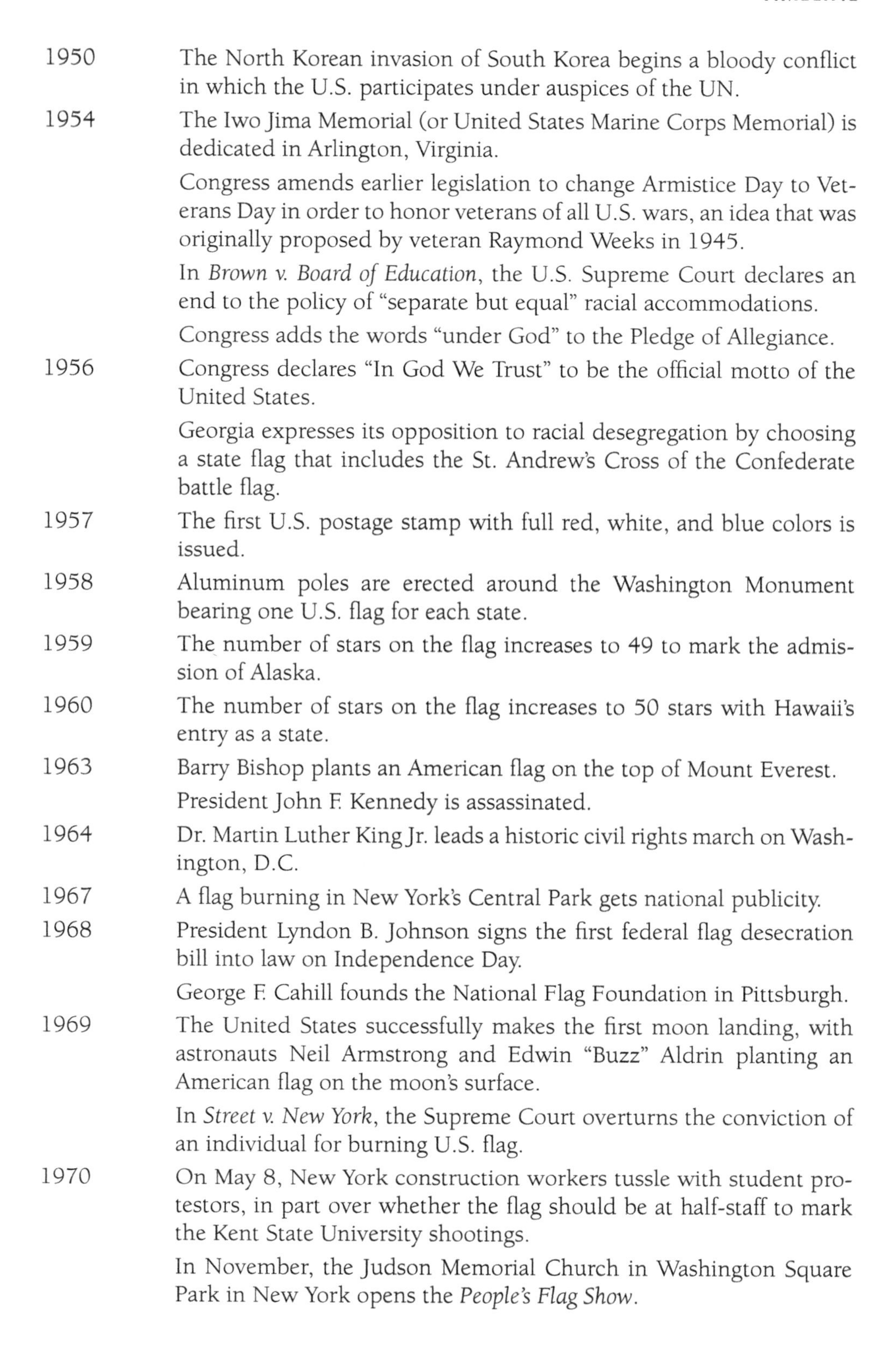

1950	The North Korean invasion of South Korea begins a bloody conflict in which the U.S. participates under auspices of the UN.
1954	The Iwo Jima Memorial (or United States Marine Corps Memorial) is dedicated in Arlington, Virginia.
	Congress amends earlier legislation to change Armistice Day to Veterans Day in order to honor veterans of all U.S. wars, an idea that was originally proposed by veteran Raymond Weeks in 1945.
	In *Brown v. Board of Education*, the U.S. Supreme Court declares an end to the policy of "separate but equal" racial accommodations.
	Congress adds the words "under God" to the Pledge of Allegiance.
1956	Congress declares "In God We Trust" to be the official motto of the United States.
	Georgia expresses its opposition to racial desegregation by choosing a state flag that includes the St. Andrew's Cross of the Confederate battle flag.
1957	The first U.S. postage stamp with full red, white, and blue colors is issued.
1958	Aluminum poles are erected around the Washington Monument bearing one U.S. flag for each state.
1959	The number of stars on the flag increases to 49 to mark the admission of Alaska.
1960	The number of stars on the flag increases to 50 stars with Hawaii's entry as a state.
1963	Barry Bishop plants an American flag on the top of Mount Everest.
	President John F. Kennedy is assassinated.
1964	Dr. Martin Luther King Jr. leads a historic civil rights march on Washington, D.C.
1967	A flag burning in New York's Central Park gets national publicity.
1968	President Lyndon B. Johnson signs the first federal flag desecration bill into law on Independence Day.
	George F. Cahill founds the National Flag Foundation in Pittsburgh.
1969	The United States successfully makes the first moon landing, with astronauts Neil Armstrong and Edwin "Buzz" Aldrin planting an American flag on the moon's surface.
	In *Street v. New York*, the Supreme Court overturns the conviction of an individual for burning U.S. flag.
1970	On May 8, New York construction workers tussle with student protestors, in part over whether the flag should be at half-staff to mark the Kent State University shootings.
	In November, the Judson Memorial Church in Washington Square Park in New York opens the *People's Flag Show*.

	The Merv Griffin Show blocks out radical activist Abbie Hoffman's flag shirt, which some states considered to be a form of flag desecration, when he appears on the television program.
1971	Congress specifies that Memorial Day will be celebrated on the last Monday in May.
1974	The U.S. Supreme Court rules that President Nixon does not have adequate executive privilege to withhold information that might be related to criminal wrongdoing.
	President Richard M. Nixon resigns from office rather than face the possibility of congressional impeachment and conviction.
1976	White anti-busing protestor Joseph Rakes uses the staff of an American flag to attack African American lawyer Ted Landsmark in Boston, an incident that photographer Stanley Forman captured in a photo he called *The Soiling of Old Glory*.
	The United States celebrates the bicentennial of the Declaration of Independence.
1978	Gilbert Baker invents the rainbow flag to symbolize gay pride.
1982	The American Flag Foundation, Inc., is chartered as a 501(c)(3) organization in Maryland.
1983	A flag is added to the entrance of the Vietnam Veterans Memorial in Washington, D.C.
1987	John Philip Sousa's "The Stars and Stripes Forever" is named the national march.
	The nation celebrates the bicentennial of the writing of the U.S. Constitution.
1989	*Texas v. Johnson* invalidates a Texas flag desecration statute.
	Congress adopts the Flag Protection Act of 1989.
1990	*U.S. v. Eichman* invalidates a congressional flag desecration statute.
1996	The world's largest flag is hung from the Hoover Dam in the run-up to the Olympic Games.
2000	In *Bush v. Gore*, the U.S. Supreme Court closes the recount in Florida for the presidential election, effectively giving the election to George W. Bush.
2001	Terrorist attacks on the World Trade Center in New York and other targets stimulate intense patriotism.
	Firefighters raising a flag at Ground Zero of the World Trade Center become the subject of an iconic photograph.
	Charlie Daniels and his band produce "This Ain't No Rag, It's a Flag."
2002	The Ninth Circuit Court of Appeals decides that the words "under God" in the pledge violate the establishment clause of the First

Amendment. More than 100 members of the House recite the pledge on the Capitol steps in protest.

U.S. ships are instructed to fly the Don't Tread on Me flag from their low bows until the war on terrorism is ended.

Toby Keith releases "Courtesy of the Red, White, and Blue."

2004 In *Elk Grove Unified School District v. Newdow*, the Supreme Court decides that the individual who challenged a school flag salute over the words "under God" did not have appropriate standing.

2005 The restoration of the Star-Spangled Banner that flew over Fort McHenry is completed at a cost of $18.6 million.

2007 The current 50-star flag became the longest-serving flag in U.S. history.

2011 NBC News upsets viewers by omitting the words "under God" from the Pledge of Allegiance during video aired during the U.S. Open Golf Tournament. The network subsequently apologizes.

2014 Some U.S. embassies begin displaying rainbow flags during LGBT pride week.

2015 As a sign of renewed diplomatic relations, the U.S. flag is raised over the U.S. embassy in Cuba, having been lowered in 1961.

2016 President-elect Donald Trump reacts to a flag-burning incident by suggesting possible loss of citizenship and jail time for individuals who burn the U.S. flag.

2017 Donald Trump is inaugurated as the 45th president of the United States.

President Trump fires FBI Director James Comey amid investigations that the Russians interfered in the U.S. presidential election of 2016.

Part I
Flag Overview Essays

The Creation, Design, and Symbolism of the Stars and Stripes

Eran Shalev

A fateful resolution of the Naval Committee of the Continental Congress declared on June 14, 1777, that "the Flag of the thirteen United States, be Thirteen Stripes, alternate red and white; That the Union be Thirteen Stars, white in a Blue Field, representing a new Constellation." This laconic decree did not elaborate or explain the meaning of the flag's use of stripes or the colors red, white, and blue. It did not stipulate the shape or size of the stars, their order, or their layout. In fact, not until 1912, during the presidency of William Howard Taft, would the exact shape, arrangement, and proportions of the flag be established. The authorization of the flag and its design in 1777 were, according to one authority, "a highly practical affair, without fanfare"; hence we know nothing about the forces and motivations contained in the creation of the Stars and Stripes (*New York Gazette and Weekly Mercury*, April 28, 1783).

Since the United States was the first modern nation, the adoption of a new national flag was by definition an unprecedented move. Unprecedented, it may have been, but as we have seen, its official order was also concise to the extreme. To understand the sparse language of the Flag Resolution, we must remind ourselves that early modern flags were not the effective vehicles for rallying national and patriotic passions that they are nowadays and that their symbolic meaning tended to be local and obscure. Flags served mostly as military standards for identification and communication devices, and it was at sea that their use as large, colorful, and distinguishable objects of identification had become established practice (hence Congress's naval committee's ordering of the Flag Resolution). In the colonies, Americans could glance at the English Union Jack waving over Crown property such as official buildings and military installations. They could—but rarely would. As the North American colonies were overwhelmingly rural, most Americans spent their whole lives in the vicinity of their farms, and local centers of English power were few and far dispersed. Thus, a majority of colonial Americans rarely encountered flags, while many never even observed a billowing English flag. Consequently, in the English imperial world, flags did not spontaneously capture the average citizen's adoration. Even the American flag would become a universally revered and beloved icon of freedom and liberty only late in the 19th century, as a direct consequence of the Civil War. In paintings and drawings of the Early Republic, the flag often appears as a decorative element framing more-favored national icons, such as the goddess of liberty and George Washington. For a long while, the Stars and Stripes would stay on the margins of the cultural and symbolic world of the new nation.

At the moment of imperial disintegration and the creation of the United States, the language of nationalism, including its visual lexicon, had yet to be born. That may explain the tardiness at which the new United States moved toward adopting a national flag, a concept that would mature only decades later. At a time when the use of a national flag was still limited to a small number of buildings, installations, and ships, a great seal seemed to be a more pressing issue (indeed, a special committee was asked to formulate such a device immediately following independence). It took almost a full year for the Second Continental Congress to pass the Flag Resolution, which was, at least in retrospect, minimalist to a fault. The congressional resolution on the flag left many variables, and their meanings, including the choice of colors, shapes, and proportions, were arcane. We may only attempt to come to terms with those fateful choices, deconstruct the motivations behind them, and reveal the ideas that drove them. It is a worthy endeavor, however, as those variables were important in creating the pervasive and revered visual language that still saturates our lives centuries later.

"That the flag of the thirteen United States be thirteen stripes"

With the surge of colonial resistance to strong-handed imperial measures in the 1760s, local and symbolic representations began to show up on colonial standards and flags. Among those were the snake (likely Benjamin Franklin's creation), more specifically an indigenous rattlesnake, which symbolized vigilance and opposition; the liberty pole and the pine tree, which were local New England symbols of self-reliance and moral rectitude; and liberty caps and the Goddess of Liberty. These emerged as useful emblems for rallying support to the American cause, gaining traction in certain locales and times during the tumultuous revolutionary years. Among those local flags was the Rebellious Stripes, a banner first raised by the Sons of Liberty in 1767 and consisting of nine vertical red and white stripes in alternating order (Guenter 1990, 27).

The Rebellious Stripes may have posed a precedent for the American Patriots, but it was not the direct predecessor of the American flag. That role was preserved for the Continental Colors, the first generally accepted continental flag, used between 1775 and 1777. Also known as the Great Union and the Grand Union Flag, the Continental Colors had 13 horizontal stripes of alternating red and white (as opposed to the Rebellious Stripes' vertical columns), meant to represent the unity of the 13 mainland colonies, with the crosses of St. George and St. Andrew adorning its canton (the upper inner quarter of the flag's field). The stripes manifested a degree of variation, as various flags displayed red and blue stripes, or red white and blue, and while 13 stripes was the norm, some had 9 (Teachout 2009, 30). Some of the choices for the design of the Continental Colors are somewhat perplexing. Was the retention of the British cross (which customarily represented the king of England or Scotland) an intentional gesture, hinting at the possibility of reconciliation, or was it a "signal of submission," as George Washington asserted (quoted in Guenter 1990, 28)? Whatever the reason may have been, that temporary flag never won the hearts and minds of the American rebels. Even as a banner for naval identification, for which it was predominantly used, it proved a poor choice, as its design made it difficult to distinguish from the British flag. It did bequeath, however, the concept of a single national flag, and its 13 horizontal alternating red and white stripes became established as a symbol of Confederate unity.

"Alternate red and white . . . in a blue field"

The anonymous designer(s) of the flag and the author of the decree that gave birth to it may have felt that the use of red, white, and blue as well as of a canton and field did not necessitate explanation because those elements were already in widespread use in late 18th-century flags and standards. Nevertheless, five years *after* the Flag Act was decreed, and in the context of elaborating on the design of the Great Seal, which bore similar colors, Congress bestowed meaning on that particular choice of colors: the white signified purity and innocence; the red signified vigor and valor; and the blue stood for vigilance, perseverance, and justice. However, as historian Arnaldo Testi points out, these may have been ex post facto rationalizations, as the colors may have well been adopted for prosaic, not affectionate, reasons. They were familiar from other designs, fabrics, and dyes that were in common use; in other words, the colors of the British flag were adopted because they were available for the struggling wartime and preindustrial economy of the young American nation (Testi 2010, 17). White purity, red valor, and blue vigilance were all surely noble, but it was their immediate accessibility that helped drive Americans to dye their flags with those recognizably English pigments.

"Thirteen stars, white in a blue field . . . representing a new constellation"

Accompanying the red and white horizontal stripes were 13 white stars, which appeared in a blue canton in the flag's upper-left corner. While each star obviously represented a state in the new confederacy, the vague and sparse specifications of the Flag Resolution meant that any possible arrangement of the stars would be theoretically legitimate. Consequently, there were numerous variations of the 13-star flag. A circular arrangement of stars was a favorite of painters, designers, and flag makers, since the ring suggested unity and perpetuity. Called the medallion pattern, that circular arrangement of fame is better known as the Betsy Ross flag, named after the Philadelphia seamstress whom myth credits with making the first American flag. That pattern was, however, only one of many variants that emerged during the evolutionary stage of the American flag, a time in which a spectacular variety of arrangements appeared and disappeared. The stars could be arranged in a full circle, sometimes in a circle of 12 with a central star (such as on the Cowpens Flag, further discussed below); in horizontal rows, sometimes forming a square frame around the blue center; in an arch over the number 76; and even forming the shape of a larger star. With the expansion of the republic, as additional stars were added to the original 13, they could appear in configurations in horizontal rows, in vertical columns, or in a square border. Star shapes varied too, as stars came with six or seven points, as in the heraldic tradition. Only occasionally did they have the now-familiar five points.

Beyond the possible arrangement and exact shape and alignment of the stars, historians have struggled to determine their exact origin—or even why a given star shape was used in the first place. While studies have been dedicated to the history of most of the elements contained in the American flag, the origins of the stars, the most distinct shapes imprinted on the flag, have remained more obscure and typically less explored (Fawcett 1937; Moeller 1976). Regardless of the prominent place of the symbol of the state as star and the consequent "American constellation" in the American political vocabulary (Keim and Keim 2007, 40–42), vexillologists and historians of the American flag seem to have accepted somewhat unsubstantiated conjectures regarding the origins of this idiom. While many have simply disregarded the question of the stars' source or meaning, the leading assumptions of those who have explored the origins of the stars seem to be that they pedigree from the star-laden Masonic visual tradition or, alternatively, from the coat of arms of George Washington's family (Teachout 2009, 30).

While remaining silent on all elements of the flag other than the stars, that the Resolution elaborated only the 13 states as forming "a new Constellation" points to the remarkable originality of the new American flag: the flag implied that United States was written in the skies, a novel and unprecedented political constellation. It is thus worth dwelling upon the symbol of the state as star and the consequent image of the United States as a new constellation, as it involved a remarkable intellectual reconfiguration tightly linked to the emergence of American republicanism and nationhood. Bearing in mind how little we know beyond the actual wording of the Flag Resolution, it may be futile to investigate the exact moment of origin, or identity of the originator, of the representation of the star as state. It would be more fruitful to uncover the meaning and significance of that epoch-making language.

The republicanism and anti-monarchism of the American Revolution shattered a traditional conception of political order based on the imagery of a single solar power center. In the European world of monarchic absolutism, kings were viewed as suns, an outlook epitomized in the image of Louis XIV but prevalent across the continent, England included. In that view, kings were suns placed in the middle of a solar "system," the nation, which reigned over harmoniously revolving "planets" (traditionally understood as standing for either social orders, state apparatuses, or magistrates). A crucial revolutionary move took place in America: from a monarchic sun, the political universe was transformed into an egalitarian starry constellation—from a celestial kingly hierarchy to an astro-republican (nonmonarchical) firmament. The revolution (initially, we should remind ourselves, an astronomic term denoting the rotation of the heavens) gave rise to a wholly new mode of communicating the political-national order. Now, with the American states viewed as stars, no single sun or kingly star overshadowed and dominated others; together the American state-stars constituted a novel political system in which a plurality of individual stars held together, comprising a republican "constellation" that was more perfect than its discrete parts.

Instead of a realm in which all politics revolved around the sunlike king, in the 1770s an alternative and revolutionary political cosmology emerged and was enshrined in the new nation's symbols: a diffuse constellation of uniform floating stars devoid of a solar center, a constellation that embodied egalitarian and republican values. Throughout the republic's founding and expansion and the consequent addition of stars to the "new American constellation," and even when it temporarily collapsed during the Civil War, that constellational image has provided a distinct vocabulary to articulate and express Americans' shifting attitudes toward, and understanding of, their unique nation.

This idea that a republican solar system was benevolent and benign, not monarchically coercive, was expressed graphically during the years following its adoption, first and foremost on the flag but also on the likes of paper money and other insignia. As we have already seen, that image had several variations in its initial evolution. Within the process of the formation of the Star-Spangled Banner, the Cowpens Flag signifies a link in the evolution from a solar to a constellational model of the American flag. On that celebrated flag, which was famously carried during its namesake battle (1781) by the 3rd Maryland Regiment, 12 states were represented by stars revolving around a 13th similar, central star. Tellingly, the central star (presumably standing for Maryland, but potentially representing any of the states) was a five-point-star design indistinguishable from the rest of the stars in the constellation. In the Cowpens design, the central body was still distinguishable through its pivotal position, but it was not a domineering sun anymore. The American flag would abandon a hierarchal representation and eventually convey the fully egalitarian constellational model, boasting indistinguishable state-stars, of the American republican federacy.

While the ideas behind the Flag Resolution, adopted with little ceremony by the obscure marine committee of the Congress, do not echo with modern audiences, politically conscious Americans seem to have understood perfectly well the motivations behind the design of the new flag and its novel starry symbolism in particular. In a letter that paraphrased the wording of the Resolution, Benjamin Franklin, who had—not surprisingly for such a Renaissance man—a lifelong interest in astronomy, was proud to acquaint the ambassador of Naples with "the Flag of the United States of America [that] consists of thirteen Stripes, alternately red, white and blue; a small Square in the upper angle, next the flag staff, is a blue field, with thirteen white Stars, denoting a new Constellation" (Sparks 1829, 1:470.). Notably, Franklin took the Flag Resolution's example in elaborating only on the novel celestial element of the flag. Benjamin Rush, another revolutionary scientific and political savant, proposed on October 21, 1777, to introduce "a constellation to be worn on the breast containing 13 stars as a reward for military exploits" (Taylor 2006, 5:319). And on April 16, 1778, the Bostonian Patriot James Lovell revealingly remarked in a letter to Abigail Adams that "the rising Constellation which is now in place of the British Union [Jack] is a Device greatly admired in our Colours" (Smith 1976, 9:423). Ezra Stiles, president of Yale University, commented that "The Congress have substituted a new Constella of Stars (instead of the Union) in the Continental Colours" (quoted in Furlong and McCandless 1981, 101–2). The United States was viewed from the outset as a new constellation that replaced a corrupt older European solar-monarchical system. A republican assemblage of stars formed that constellation, an idea still manifested on numerous flag poles across the land, even if its original meaning has been since lost and obscured.

Influence

On April 4, 1818, President James Monroe signed an act that "Provided for 13 stripes and one star for each state, to be added to the flag on the 4th of July following the admission of each new state." This official decree stipulated what contemporaries hoped: additional stars would not ruin the federal harmony and balance but rather strengthen the American republican constellation. By then, Americans of the early republic had formulated and perpetuated a powerful political cosmology that analogized celestial bodies to the American political world. State flags indicate the pervasiveness of that language: 17 out of the 37 (46 percent of) American states that joined the Union after 1776 explicitly included stars on their flags. Most notable, perhaps, was Texas, "the Lone Star Republic," which was founded as an independent state under the sphere of American political culture and eventually attached its star-spangled state-banner to the incrementally growing constellation. The "new American constellation," the image of the American federation as a fraternity of stars, which originated deus ex machina in the Flag Resolution of 1777, is consequently manifested on countless flagpoles, currency notes, and numerous other cultural mannerisms.

No less striking is the fact that the United States provided starry inspiration not only to the states that joined the Union but also to numerous nations and states that established their independence during the 19th century and beyond. Scores of new countries, from the Philippines and Australia to Brazil, took their cue from the American starry idiom and adorned their national flags with shining stars. A remarkable array of polities as diverse as the European Union and the Cook Islands incorporated rings of stars into their flag designs. If many nations are chosen, as the revealing title of a study of national chosenness indicates (Smith 2004), many likewise seem to perceive themselves as written in the skies. In this light, the connection between the Stars and Stripes and those complex ideas associated with exceptionalism seems somewhat ironic: While Americans came to understand themselves in celestial-exceptional terms, they also paved the way for other nations to understand themselves in similar terms. The United States' heavenly image has thus not only shaped Americans' understanding of their nation but has also had a powerful global effect on the ways in which numerous communities around the world imagine themselves. The state as star and consequent image of the American constellation, born uneventfully in a mundane wartime pronouncement of the Continental Congress, has become remarkable evidence of America's wielding of soft power.

The American flag was the first modern national flag. Unlike its predecessors, it did not represent a sovereign or a monarchic dynasty, nor was it centered on a coat of arms. Moreover, it was used liberally and was not confined to military installations and ships. It was a new breed, a cloth that represented a people, a nation state. The Stars and Stripes was the creation of a republican revolution: egalitarian, without a symbolic monarchical center to which to pay homage. It would take years (and a civil war) before the flag could truly become a democratic symbol of popular identity that would enter, literally, into people's homes and backyards. By then, however, its rich symbolic meaning would be mostly dimmed and forgotten.

Further Reading

Fawcett, Charles. 1937. "The Striped Flag of the East India Company, and Its Connexion with the American 'Stars and Stripes.'" *The Mariner's Mirror* 23 (4): 449–476.

Furlong, William Rea, and Byron McCandless. 1981. *So Proudly We Hail: The History of the United States Flag*. Washington, D.C.: Smithsonian Institution Press.

Guenter, Scot M. 1990. *The American Flag, 1777–1924: Cultural Shifts from Creation to Codification*. Rutherford, NJ: Fairleigh Dickinson University Press.

Keim, Kevin P., and Peter Keim. 2007. *A Grand Old Flag: A History of the United States through Its Flags*. New York: DK.

Leepson, Marc. 2006. *Flag: An American Biography*. New York: St. Martin's Press.

Moeller, Henry W. 1976. *Shattering an American Myth: Unfurling the History of the Stars and Stripes*. Mattituck, NY: Amereon House.

New York Gazette and Weekly Mercury. 1783. "Philadelphia, April 17, In Congress." April 28.

Smith, Paul M., ed. 1976. *Letters of Delegates to Congress*. Vol 9. Washington, D.C.: Library of Congress.

Sparks, Jared, ed. 1829. *The Diplomatic Correspondence of the American Revolution*. Vol. 1. Boston: N. Hale and Gray & Bowen.

Taylor, Robert J., ed. 2006. *The Adams Papers*. Vol. 5. Cambridge, MA: Harvard University Press.

Teachout, Woden. 2009. *Capture the Flag: A Political History of American Patriotism*. New York: Basic Books.

Testi, Arnaldo. 2010. *Capture the Flag: The Stars and Stripes in American History*. New York: NYU Press.

Flag Etiquette

Marc Leepson

For about a century after the 1777 adoption of the Stars and Stripes as the flag of the United States, very few, if any, Americans paid attention to flag etiquette. That's because during that time, Americans felt very differently about their flag. For example, it was almost unheard of for individuals, businesses, or schools to fly the flag. Until 1861, the flag was used primarily by the federal government, mainly by the U.S. military—most particularly the navy—as a signaling and communications device.

That situation changed markedly in the northern states when the Civil War started in 1861. Almost as soon as the fighting began in March 1861, Americans from every strata of society in the North for the first time embraced the flag as a symbol of American patriotism. In short order, the Stars and Stripes became a beloved, cherished icon in the North, a widely held symbol of the Union and the fight to keep it whole.

The Civil War, said the noted flag expert Whitney Smith, "became a fight for the flag, and it was expressed in those terms. The flag was everywhere. Every school flew a flag and prior to that there is only one known instance—in 1817—of a school flying an American flag. Union soldiers even carried miniature flags called Bible flags, small enough to fit in the Bible they would take with them to the battlefield. The start of the Civil War was the beginning of the sense we have today of the American flag as an everyday object and of something that belongs to everyone."

That sense of the flag spread nationwide in the last two decades of the 19th century as what has become known as the "cult of the flag"—the near-religious feelings Americans have for the flag—took hold throughout the country. This enormous change in the cultural meaning of the flag wound lead directly to the movement to codify flag etiquette.

A large part of that had to do with the explosive growth in the 1880s and early 1890s of scores of patriotic, hereditary, fraternal, and veteran-focused organizations, many of which took a strong interest in promoting the American flag (and later in defining proper flag etiquette) during what has been called the Golden Age of Fraternalism. Most of the groups established national organizations, augmented with affiliated groups in the states.

In 1897, some 5.4 million Americans belonged to secret fraternal orders—about 1 in 8 adult males. That did not include the 400,000-plus members of the first large veterans' service organization, the Grand Army of the Republic (the GAR) or other veterans' and military groups.

The largest fraternal organizations included the Masons, the Odd Fellows, the Knights of Pythias, the Ancient Order of United Workmen, the United Order of Odd Fellows (African American), the United American Mechanics, the Junior Order, the Masons (African American), and the Independent Order of Good Templars.

The newly formed organizations included patriotic groups that worked to foster an appreciation of the nation's history by supporting historic preservation, love of country, and respect for and adoration of the American flag. This would lead directly to the nation's first flag protection laws, and, later, the U.S. Flag Code. The most active groups concerned with flag protection and etiquette were the hereditary societies that looked to the American Revolution for inspiration: the Sons of the Revolution (SR), the Colonial Dames of America, the Society of Colonial Wars, the Sons of the American Revolution (SAR), and the Daughters of the American Revolution (DAR).

The Veterans of Foreign Wars of the United States (VFW), which was formed when several Spanish-American War veterans' organizations merged in 1913, and the American Legion, which received its congressional charter in 1919, also heavily promoted flag etiquette. The VFW did so through its flag-oriented Americanism Program, which grew out of its Committee on Americanization's drive to "Americanize America" in the early 1920s. The idea was to promote the use of the English language among immigrants and encourage them to become American citizens, institute a nationwide Buy American campaign, and work to take "un-American" textbooks out of the nation's schools.

The First Flag Protection Laws

In the late 1880s, veterans' and patriotic organizations—led by the Grand Army of the Republic and the Sons and Daughters of the American Revolution—played the leading role in the first concerted effort to formalize flag etiquette. This became known as the flag protection movement. The movement grew out of what many saw as the out-of-control commercialization of the use of the flag.

In the absence of laws governing the use of the flag's image or any accepted rules of flag etiquette, marketers and advertisers routinely printed American flags directly on their products and on advertisements for them. And they had no qualms whatsoever about printing their messages directly on American flags. An 1878 advertisement for McFerran's Magnolia Hams, for example, had Uncle Sam pointing to a ham sitting in front of a flag with the words "The Magnolia Ham is an American Institution" printed across the stripes.

Politicians also took liberties with the American flag both before and after the Civil War, including inserting candidates' names and messages across the stripes and among the stars. The stripes of a flag produced for the Republican ticket in the 1884 presidential campaign, for example, contained the words "For President James G. Blaine—For Vice President John A. Logan 1884." The canton had the requisite 38 stars, as well as likenesses of Blaine and Logan, who had been the GAR commander in chief from 1868 to 1871.

Another factor that led directly to the first flag protection laws was the large-scale development of color printing as the nation rapidly industrialized in the last third of the 19th century. Low-cost color postcards proliferated in the 1880s and 1890s; many featured red-white-and-blue American flags. Flag business cards also were common, and the flag was a common letterhead theme embossed on private and commercial stationery.

Advertising in newspapers and magazines and on billboards and signs also flourished in this period. Images of the flag found their way into an astonishing number of advertisements for scores of different types of products: from baking powder, bicycles, and beer to cigarettes, corned beef, toilet paper, tobacco products, window shades, and whiskey barrels.

The rampant use of the flag for commercial purposes did not sit well with the veterans' and patriotic organizations and with some members of Congress. The first attempt to legislate against misuse of the flag in advertising and political campaigns was a bill introduced in the House of Representatives in 1878 by Rep. Samuel Sullivan Cox of Ohio. Cox's measure called for criminal penalties for anyone who "shall disfigure the national flag, either by printing on said flag, or attaching to the same, or otherwise, any advertisement for public display." That bill died in committee.

Beginning in the mid-1890s, the patriotic and veterans' groups launched a strong nationwide campaign to lobby the state and federal governments to enact flag protection laws. U.S. Army captain Philip H. Reade, a Civil War veteran, amateur historian, and the head of the Illinois Society of Colonial Wars, was instrumental in the campaign. In 1895, Reade helped shape a society resolution that called on Congress to enact legislation reigning in the commercial use of the flag.

Reade formed a society committee that compiled a list of the names and addresses of companies and organizations that used the flag for commercial purposes. The committee published *Misuse of the Flag*, a pamphlet describing the advertising excesses of the flag, and distributed it widely to politicians, colleges, clergy, and newspaper editors as well as to the patriotic and veterans' groups.

Reade heavily lobbied other patriotic and veterans' organizations to join the movement to protect the flag with legal sanctions. He achieved great success, winning support from many state branches and the national organizations of the leading groups, including the SAR, SR, DAR, GAR, and the Loyal Legion. From 1897–1899, those groups established committees to work for flag protection legislation.

In February 1898, representatives of the flag committees of the patriotic and veterans' organizations met in New York City. That meeting resulted in the founding of the United States Flag Association, made up of representatives of 30 state and national flag committees. That included national and state SAR and DAR flag committees along with representatives of the Loyal Legion, the Order of Founders and Patriots, the Society of the War of 1812, the National Society of Naval Veterans, and the Society of the Army of the Potomac.

The association soon attracted many more groups. Its objective was to foster "public sentiment in favor of honoring the flag of our country and preserving it from desecration, and of initiating and forwarding legal efforts to prevent such desecration."

In 1897, Pennsylvania, Illinois, and South Dakota enacted flag protection laws; by 1905, 29 states and the Arizona and New Mexico territories had followed suit. By 1932, flag protection laws were on the books in all 48 states.

There were other successes as well. In 1899, U.S. Army inspector general Joseph C. Breckinridge, a member of the United States Flag Association executive committee, ended the long-standing military practice of inscribing flags with unit names and the battles in which they had participated. Four years later, the U.S. Commissioner of Patents ruled that his office would no longer register any trademarks on commercial products that made use of the flag. Congress in 1905 codified that ruling into law.

The association and the various national flag committees also worked hard to convince Congress to enact legislation. Despite years of lobbying, however, no legislation on the issue passed on Capitol Hill until 1968. That first federal flag protection act was aimed primarily at acts of flag desecration rather than at the commercial use of the flag's image. That law and all the state flag protection laws, however, were declared unconstitutional on First Amendment grounds in 1989 by the U.S. Supreme Court.

That action (and a 1990 Supreme Court decision reaffirming that ruling) led to the movement to adopt a flag protection constitutional amendment. Legislation has come to the floors of the House and Senate regularly since 1990, but has failed to get the required two-thirds vote needed for the first step of adopting what would be the Twenty-Eighth Amendment to the Constitution.

Flag Etiquette and Protection during World War I

The United States entered World War I on April 6, 1917. Shortly thereafter, the U.S. Department of Justice let it be known that Germans and other foreigners living in the United States who were discovered "abusing or desecrating" the American flag "in any way" would be subject to "summary arrest and confinement" as a "danger to the public peace or safety" for the duration of the war. In 1918, Congress passed and President Woodrow Wilson signed into law an addition to the June 1917 Espionage Act, known as the Sedition Act. Among other things, this measure made it illegal to "willfully utter, print, write or publish any disloyal, profane, scurrilous, or abusive language" about the Constitution, the government, or the "flag of the United States." The Sedition Act also banned the willful display of the flag "of any foreign enemy." Those acts were punishable by a fine of not more than $10,000 or 20 years in jail. The law also mandated that any U.S. government employee or official who "in an abusive and violent manner criticizes the Army or Navy or the flag of the United States shall be at once dismissed."

During the World War I era, several states strengthened the language and increased the penalties in their flag protection laws, which originally had been designed primarily to cut down on the commercial use of the flag. Kansas, for example, passed a law in 1915 making it a misdemeanor to "publicly mutilate, deface, defile, or defy, trample upon, or cast contempt, either by words or act upon any" American flag.

Three years later, Frederick Shumaker Jr. of Wetmore, Kansas, was convicted under the statute for making "a very vulgar and indecent use of the flag." He was accused of using language in a blacksmith's shop so foul that the court would not spell it out because it would become part of the official record. Shumaker apparently had referred to the flag as "a rag." He appealed his case to the Kansas Supreme Court and lost.

Texas's Disloyalty Act, enacted on March 11, 1918, made flag desecration punishable by up to 25 years in jail. The law imposed that strict penalty on those convicted of using "any language" in public or private that "cast contempt" on the American flag.

Montana enacted a similarly worded law in February 1918. Six months later, a man named E. V. Starr was arrested, tried, and convicted in Montana for the words he said after a mob tried to force him to kiss an American flag. "What is this thing anyway, nothing but a piece of cotton with a little paint on it and some other marks in the corner there," Starr said. "I will not kiss that thing. It might be covered with microbes."

It is unclear from court records and newspaper accounts if the mob turned on Starr for political reasons. What is clear is that the federal and state flag protection laws were enforced during World War I primarily against those who spoke out against the war effort—typically labor activists, pacifists, socialists, anarchists, and communists—as well as German immigrants, German Americans, and those who expressed sympathy for the German cause.

A New York City woman, for example, was arrested and sent to jail for six months in March 1918 for displaying a German flag and taking down an American flag put in her window and then saying the words, "To hell with the American flag. I want my own flag."

Outside of the law, citizens took measures against German Americans and others who spoke out against the war effort. Typically, vigilante actions of this sort involved forcing the allegedly unpatriotic person to salute the flag, recite the Pledge of Allegiance, or kiss the flag.

The self-appointed flag defenders may have taken their cue from the stern words of President Wilson in his April 2, 1917, war message to a special session of Congress. Speaking about Americans "of German birth and native sympathy who live among us," Wilson warned what would happen if they were not loyal during the upcoming war. "If there should be disloyalty," he said, "it will be dealt with with a firm hand of stern repression."

The 1923 National Flag Conference

In 1917, the National Conference of Commissioners on Uniform State Laws—an organization that since the early 1890s had been drawing up suggested model laws for state legislatures—approved a uniform flag law. It was almost identical in wording to New York's 1905 flag protection law. That measure provided that "no person shall publicly mutilate, deface, defile, defy, trample upon, or by word or act cast contempt upon any such flag, standard, color, ensign or shield." It was adopted by only a handful of states, however.

In 1919, Garland W. Powell, a World War I veteran and former Maryland state senator who had a strong interest in the American flag, became the national director of Americanism for the recently formed American Legion. In *Service for God and Country*, Powell presented a treatise on Americanism, including advice about flag etiquette.

Powell contacted other groups interested in the flag, proposing that they meet in a national conference to put together a uniform national code of flag etiquette. An executive order signed in 1912 by President William H. Taft gave specifications for the proportions and design of the flag and had thus cut down drastically on freelance American-flag design. Despite this, flags with many different arrangements of the stars were used well into the early 1920s. Powell and others wanted that situation rectified. What's more, the U.S. Army and Navy had developed their own flag etiquette regulations, as had the veterans' service organizations. The conference's goal would be to come up with one codified etiquette standard.

Powell's organizing efforts came to fruition on June 14, 1923, when the Legion's Americanism Commission convened the first National Flag Conference. It took place at Memorial Continental Hall in the DAR's national headquarters in Washington, D.C. In addition to the Legion and the DAR, 66 other groups took part in the gathering. The U.S. Army and Navy sent representatives. Samuel Gompers, the president of the American Federation of Labor, attended, as did representatives from groups such as the SAR, the Boy Scouts of America, the National Congress of Mothers, the United Daughters of the Confederacy, and the Ku Klux Klan.

"I hope you will succeed in forming a code that will be welcomed by all Americans," President Warren G. Harding said during his 40-minute speech at the opening ceremonies, "and that every patriotic and educational society in the republic will commit itself for the endorsement and observance and purposes of that code."

The conferees did, indeed, agree on the nation's first flag code. It was based heavily on a War Department *Flag Circular* that had been published earlier in the year. Much of what the code contained was apolitical and had to do with practical matters, such as the proper ways, times, positions, and occasions to display the flag. The code also included the Pledge of Allegiance and the proper ways to recite it as well as a section on the proper ways to respect the flag.

There was a political dimension to the conference, however. Harding Administration secretary of labor James J. Davis warned the conference that "disrespect for the flag" was one of the "first steps" toward communist revolution. The conference also agreed to replace the words "my Flag" in the Pledge of Allegiance with "to the Flag of the United States." The second National Flag Conference on May 15, 1924, amended that language slightly to read, "to the Flag of the United States of America."

The U.S. Flag Code

The Flag Code that the conference agreed upon was big news. In the weeks after the 1923 conference, virtually all of the nation's large newspapers published the new code in its entirety. Others followed suit on the Fourth of July. The American Legion and the other organizations that took part in the conference published booklets explaining the new code and distributed them by the millions.

Fifty-one additional patriotic, hereditary, and veterans' organizations took part in the second National Flag Conference in Washington in 1924. That gathering made only minor revisions to the work done the year earlier.

The flag code, however, did not become the law of the land until 1942, during World War II. On June 22 of that year, Congress passed a resolution, which was signed into law by President Franklin D. Roosevelt, adopting the code with several small changes as part of Title 36 of the United States Code. The code was slightly amended in December 1942 and several other times in subsequent years.

It remains in effect today. Although the U.S. Flag Code is a national public law, it is not enforced—nor is it enforceable. The code is a set of guidelines that carries no penalties for noncompliance; it doesn't even have enforcement provisions. It tells American civilians (the military branches have their own flag codes) what to do and what not to do with their national emblem.

Today the 10-part code is part of title 4, chapter 1 of the U.S. Code. It includes guidelines for

- the design of the flag, including the position of the stars and the flag's dimensions;
- respect for the flag;
- the use of the flag advertising purposes;
- the mutilation of the flag;
- the manner of delivery of the Pledge of Allegiance;
- the display and use of the flag, including times and occasions and the positions and manner of display; and
- conduct during hoisting, lowering, or passing the flag.

Several parts of the code contain detailed guidelines. What follows, for example, is the complete text of the "Time and Occasions for Display" and "Respect for the Flag" sections.

Section 6: Time and Occasions for Display.

(a) It is the universal custom to display the flag only from sunrise to sunset on buildings and on stationary flagstaffs in the open. However, when a patriotic effect is desired, the flag may be displayed 24 hours a day if properly illuminated during the hours of darkness.

(b) The flag should be hoisted briskly and lowered ceremoniously.

(c) The flag should not be displayed on days when the weather is inclement, except when an all-weather flag is displayed.

(d) The flag should be displayed on all days, especially on New Year's Day, January 1; Inauguration Day, January 20; Martin Luther King Jr.'s birthday, the third Monday in January; 15 Lincoln's Birthday, February 12; Washington's Birthday, third Monday in February; Easter Sunday (variable); Mother's Day, second Sunday in May; Armed Forces Day, third Saturday in May; Memorial Day (half-staff until noon), the last Monday in May; Flag Day, June 14; Independence Day, July 4; Labor Day, first Monday in September; Constitution Day, September 17; Columbus Day, second Monday in October; Navy Day, October 27; Veterans Day, November 11; Thanksgiving Day, fourth Thursday in November; Christmas Day, December 25; and such other days as may be proclaimed by the President of the United States; the birthdays of States (date of admission); and on State holidays.

(e) The flag should be displayed daily on or near the main administration building of every public institution.
(f) The flag should be displayed in or near every polling place on election days.
(g) The flag should be displayed during school days in or near every schoolhouse.

Section 8: Respect for the Flag

No disrespect should be shown to the flag of the United States of America; the flag should not be dipped to any person or thing. Regimental colors, state flags, and organization or institutional flags are to be dipped as a mark of honor.

(a) The flag should never be displayed with union down, except as a signal of dire distress in instances of extreme danger to life or property.
(b) The flag should never touch anything beneath it, such as the ground, the floor, water, or merchandise.
(c) The flag should never be carried flat or horizontally, but always aloft and free.
(d) The flag should never be used as wearing apparel, bedding, or drapery. It should never be festooned, drawn back, nor up, in folds, but always allowed to fall free. Bunting of blue, white, and red, always arranged with the blue above, the white in the middle, and the red below, should be used for covering a speaker's desk, draping in front of the platform, and for a decoration in general.
(e) The flag should never be fastened, displayed, used, or stored in such a manner as to permit it to be easily torn, soiled, or damaged in any way.
(f) The flag should never be used as a covering for a ceiling.
(g) The flag should never have placed upon it, nor on any part of it, nor attached to it any mark, insignia, letter, word, figure, design, picture, or drawing of any nature.
(h) The flag should never be used as a receptacle for receiving, holding, carrying, or delivering anything.
(i) The flag should never be used for advertising purposes in any manner whatsoever. It should not be embroidered on such articles as cushions or handkerchiefs and the like, printed or otherwise impressed on paper napkins or boxes or anything that is designed for temporary use and discard. Advertising signs should not be fastened to a staff or halyard from which the flag is flown.
(j) No part of the flag should ever be used as a costume or athletic uniform. However, a flag patch may be affixed to the uniform of military personnel, firemen, policemen, and members of patriotic organizations. The flag represents a living country and is itself considered a living thing. Therefore, the lapel flag pin being a replica, should be worn on the left lapel near the heart.
(k) The flag, when it is in such condition that it is no longer a fitting emblem for display, should be destroyed in a dignified way, preferably by burning.

Some of the U.S. Flag Code guidelines are often misquoted or misunderstood. That includes section 8, paragraph K (above), on the proper disposal of the flag. The code gives no details on how a dignified ceremony should be performed. However, ceremonies are regularly performed that contain what are purported to be "official" step-by-step details. Many include snipping out the stars or detaching the stripes before burning. Others call for reciting the Pledge of Allegiance or contain words describing the "meaning" of the red, white, and blue colors—although no official document exists with that information.

Many local veterans' service-organization posts and chapters (such as Vietnam Veterans of America, the Veterans of Foreign Wars, and the American Legion) conduct flag-retirement burning ceremonies, often on June 14, Flag Day. The American Legion provides a script and details for its ceremony in its *Manual of Ceremonies*. It calls for local posts to hold the ceremony on Flag Day, outdoors, at night, with a flag-disposal detail, a color guard, a bugler, a chaplain and for a preburning inspection of the flags by a post's first and second vice commanders.

The most recent additions to the code deal with conduct during the hoisting, lowering, or passing of the flag and while reciting the Pledge of Allegiance. In 2002, wording was added giving American veterans and members of the armed forces not in uniform the option of saluting the flag during hoisting and lowering ceremonies and when the flag is passing in a parade, instead of placing one's right hand over one's heart. The same language was added with respect to recitation of the Pledge of Allegiance in 2013.

The U.S. Flag in America's Historic-House Museums*

Marla R. Miller

Among the nation's roughly 15,000 historic-house museums are three sites devoted to the interpretation of moments in the history of the U.S. flag: the Betsy Ross House in Philadelphia, Pennsylvania; the Star-Spangled Banner Flag House in Baltimore, Maryland; and the Barbara Fritchie House and Museum in Frederick, Maryland. The sites—created between 1896 and 1927—both separately and together reflect the evolution of the flag's place in American culture. In *Domesticating History: The Political Origins of America's House Museums*, historian Patricia West reminds us that all historic-house museums are inherently political, in that their founding inevitably reflects the contemporary agendas of their founders; meanwhile, Seth Bruggeman's *Born in the USA: Birth, Commemoration and American Public Memory* underscores the entangled ways that boosterism, civic pride, and commercial interests inform the creation of many such sites, including those surrounding the "birth" of the U.S. flag. And so, unsurprisingly, each of the places considered here emerged from postwar reverence for the national colors and corresponding spikes in gestures of patriotism (a period that also saw flourishing nationalism and nativism), impulses that easily sat alongside municipal interests in both community identity and tourism.

Each site has also confronted challenges to its historical veracity as skeptics challenged its very foundational narrative. Interestingly, all three house museums here are devoted to women; as we shall see, the homes of two men who would seem to have been likely candidates for this kind of memorialization—Francis Scott Key and William Driver—were not preserved. These origin stories are also deeply enmeshed, then, in larger tensions around women's place in society, and particularly the more-than-70-year struggle to secure suffrage, as well as broader issues surrounding house museums, domesticity, and the history of women's history. Taken together, these three historic-house museums document the evolving place of the flag in American collective memory.

* For their assistance with this essay, the author wishes to thank Kimberly Staub (collections and exhibitions manager at the Betsy Ross House) and Lisa Moulder (director, Betsy Ross House); Amanda Shores Davis (executive director, the Star-Spangled Banner Flag House); Carrie Blough (formerly of the Historical Society of Frederick County, Maryland, and today with the DAR Museum); Chris Haugh (History Shark Productions); and Sarah Leavitt (National Building Museum).

The Betsy Ross House

Opened to the public in 1898, the Betsy Ross House (239 Arch Street) interprets the life and times of Philadelphia upholsterer and flag maker Elizabeth Griscom Ross Ashburn Claypoole (1752–1836). The ca. 1740 house's origins as a historic place can be traced to the 1870 speech made by William J. Canby (1826–1890) to the Historical Society of Pennsylvania, in which he shared what he remembered of his grandmother's account of her role in the making of the first "stars and stripes." Canby had, from his childhood, heard the story of how, at the onset of the American Revolution, George Washington had come to Ross's shop with a request that she fabricate a new national emblem. In the family narrative, Washington had in hand an initial sketch involving a blue canton with 13 six-pointed stars; Ross, an experienced craftswoman in the upholstery trades, showed Washington how she could more quickly and easily produce five-pointed stars, and the star's appearance was so altered. A "specimen" flag was produced and approved by Congress, and so the flag of the new United States of America was born.

Long simply a Claypoole family story—and one that, in the flag maker's telling, emphasized the encounter with Washington and not the "firstness" of any flag—that narrative entered national collective memory in the middle decades of the 19th century. In the late 1850s, Clarissa Claypoole Wilson (Ross's daughter and Canby's aunt), mindful of the various histories of the Revolution and the flag then taking shape, asked Canby to record the family story before she left Philadelphia for retirement in Iowa. The exigencies of the American Civil War prevented Canby from pursuing the matter further, but after the war, and amid surging interest in the flag that represented the now-preserved union, Canby resumed his research. In 1870, on the eve of the centennial of Independence, he delivered an address before the Historical Society of Pennsylvania in which he shared the "report" (as he preferred to call it) of the making of the first "Stars and Stripes." In the wake of Canby's address, the house on Arch Street where Ross was remembered to have once lived became a site of public interest, even though questions concerning the story's veracity were raised quickly. (There is some debate about whether this address is the same as that which Ross once occupied. Her descendants identified it as the correct house in the late 19th century, but by that time, many residences along this block of Arch Street had been demolished, making the isolated remaining dwelling stand out as her likely home. More-recent research suggests that Ross may have occupied either this house or the house next door. Whether or not this house is the one in question, it is certainly true that in her lifetime, Ross and her family members inhabited a number of houses along Arch Street.) The family of Charles P. Mund, in residence there for some 35 years, posted a sign declaring "First Flag of the US Made in this House." An 1876 advertisement for the Mund family tavern read: "Original Flag House, Lager, Wine and Liquors. This is the house where the first United States flag was made by Mrs. John Ross."

Canby's claim about his family's history gained public traction in part because it came at just the right moment. The 1876 centennial as well as the post–Civil War reverence for the flag as the symbol of union and the ongoing debate over woman suffrage all served to heighten interest in the Ross site. As attention turned to the birth of the nation, and consequently the national emblem, the Ross story struck chords with both pro- and antisuffrage activists, as it put a woman in the center of the war for independence—not in any military or political role but rather through an activity (sewing) that had been framed (by that time) as domestic (rather than artisanal) work. The story's popularity persisted. In 1892, in response to a competition for artwork depicting an historical event and inspired by the Mund family's activities at the Ross site, Charles Weisgerber painted the monumental (9 x 12') *Birth of Our Nation's Flag*. The work was exhibited at the World's Columbian Exposition the following year. In 1898, in an effort to stop the demolition of the house where the scene may have unfolded, the American Flag House and Betsy Ross Memorial Association was formally organized, with Weisgerber as a founding member. The association sold memberships for 10 cents; members received certificates bearing an image of Weisgerber's painting as well as views of the Betsy Ross House and her grave at Mount Moriah Cemetery. Individuals were encouraged to form "clubs" of 30 members; each member would receive the certificate, while the club's founder would receive a 10-color chromolithograph of Weisgerber's painting. Meanwhile, the Weisgerber family, in residence, opened two rooms to the public.

Only three years later, Weisgerber began seeking another source of support for the venture, first looking to the federal government. In 1906, bills were introduced into both the House of Representatives and the U.S. Senate "providing for the acceptance by the United States Government of the Old Flag House, tendered by the American Flag House and Betsy Ross Association." Resolution 17949 was introduced by Rep. Reuben Moon of Pennsylvania on April 9, 1906, and referred to the House Committee on Public Buildings and Grounds; Senate bill 5739 was introduced by (Philadelphia native) Sen. Boies Penrose of Pennsylvania on April 17, 1906, and first referred to the Senate Committee on Buildings and Grounds before being referred to the Committee on Library. The House bill noted that the American Flag House and Betsy Ross Memorial Association represented "a uniform membership from every State and Territory of the United States and many foreign counties of one million forty-six thousand two hundred and seventy persons, irrespective of creed, color, condition, sect, or age." But neither bill moved out of committee, and no reports were published, suggesting that the prospect held little appeal for the nation's legislators. In 1907, the Memorial Association recycled the language in the proposed federal legislation to offer possession of the house to the City of Philadelphia, where it was likewise declined. After Weisgerber's death in 1932, the association became defunct, and the house gradually fell into disrepair. The building's deterioration eventually came to the attention of inventor, manufacturer, and philanthropist Atwater Kent (1873–1949), and in 1937 the house underwent a thorough restoration, funded by Kent and led by architect Richardson Brognard Okie (1875–1945). All eight rooms of the house opened to the public on Flag Day, June 14, 1937.

In 1941, the American Flag House and Betsy Ross Memorial Association—by that date some 35 years behind on real estate taxes—gifted the house to the city of Philadelphia in exchange for the waiver of back taxes (*Gazette and Daily*, May

2, 1941; *Inquirer*, May 2, 1941; *Inquirer*, May 16, 1941; *Inquirer*, May 21, 1941). A board of 10 men—all previously directors of the American Flag House and Betsy Ross Memorial—were appointed to oversee the site in its new municipal role (*Inquirer*, May 28, 1941). Charles's son Vexil Domus Weisgerber (1902–1959; born in the house in 1902 and named for the Latin word *vexillum*, for "flag," and *domus*, for "house") served as secretary of the Association until he passed away in 1959. His sister Augusta Marguerite Weisgerber Spruance (1895–1945) was also heavily involved with the organization, acting as secretary during World War II, when Vexil Weisgerber was in the armed services.

The bicentennial year, unsurprisingly, saw heightened attention to the Ross house. As part of the celebration, remains deemed to be those of Ross and her third husband, John Claypoole, were reinterred in graves in the courtyard adjacent to the site. That year saw an astounding 1,105,677 people visit the house. Around that same time, the Betsy Ross House began to cultivate ties with the academic community in ways that would support more-scholarly interpretation. In the 1970s, University of Pennsylvania graduate student Debra Force first presented academic research about the house to the board of directors. And in the 1990s, historians like Avi Decter, Sandra Lloyd, and Stephanie Grauman Wolf contributed research that informed fresh interpretive work at the site.

In 1995, Historic Philadelphia, Inc. (a private nonprofit organization founded in 1994), began leasing the property from the municipality; HPI continues to manage the site today. In the early 21st century, site staff—drawing on the flourishing scholarship in women's history, the American Revolution, and early American labor history that had emerged in recent years—began widening the site's interpretive emphasis to address the lives of women in Revolutionary Philadelphia. In 2010, in order to draw firmer connections to Ross's well-documented work in the upholstery trades, they opened a new installation interpreting an 18th-century upholstery shop. In 2015, the Betsy Ross House was recognized with an American Association for State and Local History Leadership in History award for the exhibition *Dressing the Bed: A Living Demonstration of 18th-Century Needlework*. In 2016, the museum won a Willing Hands award from the New Century Trust for its work in women's history. Today, close to 200,000 visitors tour the house each year (Hilario 2017).

The Star-Spangled Banner Flag House

The 1914 centennial of the writing of "The Star-Spangled Banner" doesn't appear to have attracted any special attention at the Betsy Ross House, but that milestone would produce two additional historic-house museums associated with the American flag, both in Maryland. One hundred years earlier, on September 14, 1814, Francis Scott Key drafted a poem, "Defence of Fort M'Henry," to capture his emotions as he witnessed the bombarding of the Baltimore fort during the War of 1812. An attorney charged with negotiating a prisoner exchange, Key was detained aboard a British ship in the city's harbor when the shelling began. His poem described his great relief, the following morning, to see the U.S. flag—called the "star-spangled banner" in Key's concluding verse—still flying. The work was quickly published in William Pechin's *American and Commercial Daily Advertiser,* and it was set to music not long thereafter. During the Mexican-American War and American Civil War, the song caught on. In 1889, Secretary of the Navy Benjamin Tracy's General Order #374 declared that "The Star-Spangled Banner" be played at the raising of the national flag, and in the 1890s, the song began to be played at army posts. By the turn of the 20th century, it was widely considered (if not yet formally designated) the U.S. national anthem.

The song's centennial in 1914 was marked with lavish events in Baltimore. A National Star-Spangled Banner Centennial Commission was formed (Baltimore mayor James H. Preston presiding), and festivities were planned for September 1914. The commemorative program articulates the civic motivations that drove the event: "We want you to know," said Mayor Preston, "our city—big, enterprising, progressive, successful; we want you to know our people—hospitable, courteous, patriotic, chivalrous; we want you to know our history—important, creditable, nation-wide in its influence" (O'Connell 1914, 6). Honorary presidents of the Centennial Commission included President Woodrow Wilson and former presidents William H. Taft and Theodore Roosevelt, while honorary vice presidents included U.S. vice president Thomas R. Marshall, the speaker of the House of Representatives, and the governor of Maryland, together with the governors of all 18 states that were members of the union in 1814 and other leading figures.

The centennial included both ordinary and extraordinary parades and pageantry. A floral automobile parade progressed through Baltimore. The U.S. Congress funded the repair of USS *Constellation* and ordered that the frigate be stationed at Baltimore. The Star-Spangled Banner itself, by that time under the stewardship of the Smithsonian Institution, was likewise restored. During the ceremonies at Fort McHenry, more than 6,000 Baltimore schoolchildren, arranged in a "human flag" formation, sang the anthem to an audience of thousands (O'Connell 1914, 50). The event also gave the city occasion to mark other important histories: Tablets were unveiled to mark the site of the first Baltimore and Ohio Railroad station; Mount Clare, the site of the oldest house in the city; Carroll Mansion, where the last surviving signer of the Declaration of Independence died; and others. Larger memorials included the Memorial to the American Privateersmen of the War of 1812 and another to Lt. Col. George Armistead, commander of Fort McHenry during the bombardment (the Francis Scott Key Monument, by French sculptor Jean Marius Antonin Mercie, having been raised three years earlier, in 1911). Most importantly, the Centennial Monument, in Baltimore's Patterson Park, was erected; the sculpture, by J. Maxwell Miller, depicts two children unfurling a scroll that reads: "To commemorate the centennial of the writing of the Star-Spangled Banner, the pupils of the public schools of Baltimore have erected this memorial upon Hampstead Hill where in September, 1814, the citizen soldiers of Maryland stood ready to sacrifice their lives in defense of their homes and their country."

Amid this frenzy of memorial activity, Baltimoreans did not overlook the contributions of Mary Young Pickersgill (1776–1857), the known maker of the large garrison flag that Key had been so glad to see that September morning. Pickersgill was the daughter of Philadelphia flag maker Rebecca Flower Young; she and her widowed mother had moved into the house in 1806 (Leepson 2005, 70–72). A 37-year-old widow at the time she was commissioned to make both a large (30-by-42-foot) garrison flag and a smaller storm flag for the installation at Fort McHenry, Pickersgill's role in the making of the Star-Spangled Banner had survived in Baltimore's collective memory through the agency of both Caroline Pickersgill Purdy (1800–1884; Mary's daughter) and Georgiana Armistead Appleton (1817–1878; daughter of Commander Armistead). The centennial's official program notes Mary Pickersgill's role in making the flag and observes that her home at the corner of Pratt and Albemarle Streets still stood. One of the tablets unveiled during the weeklong series of festivities marked the site of the "flag house," extant at 844 E. Pratt Street (O'Connell 1914, 23–25).

Key to the house's evolution at this stage were Baltimore physician James Iglehart and his wife Monterey Watson Iglehart (1846–1924; daughter of William H. Watson, born on the day her father was killed in the Battle of Monterey), charter members, in 1915, of the Star-Spangled Banner Association (SSBA). According to the Ritual of the Star-Spangled Banner Association of the United States of America, together with the charter, constitution, by-laws, and list of charter members, the SSBA sought "to help make the American flag and our American life synonymous with the loftiest of ideals and with the noblest of actions. To that end, the Association plans to focus public attention persistently on the flag, in all of its bearings, hoping thereby to stimulate a worth and patriotic Americanism."

Influential among Baltimore's past keepers, the Iglehart were deeply involved in an array of patriotic societies, which they tapped to promote the association's aims. James D. Iglehart (1850–1934) was active in the Sons of the American Revolution and a force behind the successful 1903 effort to raise a monument (erected by the Maryland Association of Veterans of the Mexican War to honor men killed during the U.S.-Mexican War) to William H. Watson. Monterey Iglehart was regent of Baltimore's Francis Scott Key chapter of the Daughters of the American Revolution, and a member of the Colonial Dames, the Daughters of the Confederacy, the Daughters of the Cincinnati as well as founding president in Maryland of the United States Daughters of 1812 and the corresponding secretary of the SSBA. In 1916, she addressed the Congress of the DAR on the work of the association, while James carried word to the National Society of the Sons of the American Revolution (Harnit 1917, 394; Orton 1917, 73; Clark 1913, 14).

From the 1914 centennial celebration and ensuing SSBA would in time emerge the Star-Spangled Banner Flag House Association. In the decade to follow, Fort McHenry itself would evolve from active military installation to a site of national memory; retired from their role in the nation's coastal defense, the fortifications were recreated as Fort McHenry National Park in 1925. (In 1933 the National Park Service succeeded the War Department as the site's administrative home, and the fort was renamed Fort McHenry National Monument and Historic Shrine.) Meanwhile, interest in the Pickersgill home as a historic site grew; that baton would be taken up by Ruthella and Arthur Bibbins, another power couple in the memory circles of Baltimore. Johns Hopkins University alumnus Arthur Barneveld Bibbins

(1860–1936) had served as chairman of the 1914 Star-Spangled Banner centennial celebration as well as chairman of the Washington Bicentennial Commission, an officer in the Maryland Society of the Sons of the American Revolution, and president of the Society for the Preservation of Maryland Antiquities. Arthur and Ruthella had been charter members of the SSBA, and in February 1927, Ruthella Mory Bibbins (1865–1942) proposed the effort to "Save the Flag House" at a meeting of the Maryland Historical Society. Bibbins graduated from Goucher College and went on to study history and political science at Oxford University before completing her PhD at the University of Chicago in 1900. She chaired the WCTU department of legislation and enforcement and served as secretary of the Maryland Federation of Republican Women, but it was her work as a historian that drew her into the preservation of the Pickersgill House. Bibbins chaired the history and political science programs at the Maryland Academy of Sciences and was deeply involved as historian for the Star-Spangled Banner Centennial Commission. A native of Frederick County, Maryland, her remains would be interred in Mount Olivet cemetery, not far from those of Barbara Fritchie.

But the Bibbinses' attempt to raise the money necessary to purchase the house was ultimately unsuccessful. When those private fund-raising efforts failed, the City of Baltimore prepared to purchase the house, then owned by the Samuel Ready estate. The Star-Spangled Banner Flag House Association formally incorporated in Spring 1927 and assumed responsibility for the stewardship of the house on June 14, 1927, the 150th anniversary of the adoption of the first official United States flag.

The house began welcoming visitors and became a symbol of the city of Baltimore; for instance, in the 1930s, when steel beams were installed to strengthen the structure, timbers removed from the house were carved into "keys to the city" that were offered luminaries and honored guests. The site's first curator, Arthur P. Sewell (1900–1946), oversaw the restoration of the house to its 1813 appearance, removing some late-19th and early-20th-century alterations. In the mid-1940s, a proposal emerged to move the building to Fort McHenry, but the building remained at its original location and in fact expanded its footprint. That work made the veracity of the flag narrative a matter of court attention in 1949, when the Maryland Court of Appeals heard the complaint of Annie Flaccomio, owner of the three-story red brick rooming house adjacent to the Flag House. The City of Baltimore had condemned Flaccomio's building, which they sought to convert into office space for the historic-house museum next door. The arguments hinged in part on whether Pickersgill's massive flag was completed in a nearby brewery, which—Flaccomio's attorney's suggested—would diminish the historical significance of Pickersgill's house and thus the city's need to expand the Flag House's footprint at this site. The court ruled unanimously that the city did possess the right to seize the property in order to create a "symbolic memorial." By summer 1950, "Flag House Square" had been dedicated, and the block surrounding the square was cleared of garbage and derelict buildings.

In 1953, the city built a one-and-a-half-story building behind the historic house to create a museum with an exhibition area and space for offices. In 1969, the site received National Historic Landmark status. Like the Betsy Ross House, management of the museum became increasingly professional in the 20th century. Most recently, the permanent exhibition *A Family of Flagmakers* interprets Mary Pickersgill and her household in the context of Baltimore's women's, labor, and military history.

An Opportunity Lost? The Home of William Driver

Interestingly, the 1920s—a key decade in the preservation of Baltimore's Flag House—had seen additional attention to the history of "Old Glory" and the source of that nickname for our national standard, but no effort was made to preserve the Nashville, Tennessee, home of William Driver (1803–1886) that was associated with that history. Driver's mother and others had made a U.S. flag that Driver flew during his years as a ship captain, which he came to call Old Glory; he took the flag with him when he later moved to Nashville, Tennessee, where he was compelled to conceal it during the Civil War. After Union troops expelled Confederate forces from the city, Old Glory was raised over the city.

The phrase entered the national consciousness (the effort to rescue the Betsy Ross House referred to it as the birthplace of Old Glory), though the house associated with it apparently never garnered memorial attention. Auctioned in September 1886 in the wake of Driver's death on March 3, 1886, the home had "long since" been demolished by 1917, when an article in the *Tennessean* on July 9 narrated the history of Old Glory. In the 1940s, the American Legion would place a marker at its site. Two surviving flags were claimed to be Old Glory, and in 1922, both were sent to the Smithsonian Institution (Jenkins 2013). But it seems that Driver's house was lost before any notion of converting it to a museum could take shape, and no subsequent effort emerged to recreate it.

The Barbara Fritchie House

The enterprising residents of Frederick would pursue a different course. The year 1927, which had witnessed the purchase of Baltimore's Star-Spangled Banner House, was an important one for the larger memory of the United States flag. In that year, the Technicolor short *The Flag: A Story Inspired by the Tradition of Betsy Ross*—starring Enid Bennet as Ross and Francis X. Bushman as George Washington—traveled to American theaters (Leepson 2005, 40). Meanwhile a musical, *My Maryland*, interpreting the legend of Barbara Hauer Fritchie (1766–1862) opened on Broadway to a warm reception. And in the same year that the Star-Spangled Banner House was purchased by the City of Baltimore, the Barbara Fritchie House and Museum opened at 15 West Patrick Street in Frederick, Maryland.

Barbara Fritchie had gained fame as the subject of John Greenleaf Whittier's 1863 poem "Barbara Frietchie" [sic]. Fritchie, like Ross, was a young woman from the American Revolution who lived to see the outbreak (and resolution) of another war with England. And both women were members of artisanal families: Fritchie's husband, John Casper Fritchie, was a glove maker. Widowed in 1849, Fritchie remained in her home on West Patrick Street, on the banks of Carroll Creek, through the American Civil War. During the conflict, as the story was first told, Confederate troops under the command of Stonewall Jackson marched through Frederick en route to Antietam; as the men moved past the home of the 96-year-old widow Fritchie, she was remembered to have flown in defiance a U.S. flag, prompting a soldier to fire at the banner. In July 1863, the Washington, D.C., novelist E. D. E. N Southworth (1819–1899) told Whittier (1807–1892) this story of Fritchie's defense of the Union flag, and he was moved to commemorate this "hater of the Slavery Rebellion" in verse. The poem, published in the *Atlantic Monthly* in October 1863, recounts the events as Whittier understood them at the time (he later acknowledged that the poem might have been based on a flawed or incomplete understanding of events); the couplet describing her reply—"Shoot if you must this old gray head, but spare your country's flag, she said"—became the poem's most memorable line.

It is difficult to overestimate the cultural influence of John Greenleaf Whittier—a journalist and editor, poet, and antislavery activist—on 19th- and 20th-century American thought and culture. The poem was enthusiastically embraced. But, like the narrative about Betsy Ross in Philadelphia, once shared, the Fritchie story was quickly contested (Marling 2004, 33). Competing claims emerged that it was neighbor Mary Quantrill, or perhaps Nannie Crouse, who in fact bravely waved the union banner, and the general whose troops were on the march may have been A. P. Hill rather than Stonewall Jackson. But Fritchie, once introduced to the public, never lost her charm. Like the story of Betsy Ross and the making of the first flag, the story appealed to post–Civil War Americans caught up in the new symbolic force of the flag. And, also like Ross, Fritchie had descendants as well as nieces and other relatives to champion the tale as it was initially reported.

But unlike Ross or Pickersgill, the Fritchie story at first had no physical site around which to organize. In 1869, Fritchie's house—damaged when Carroll Creek flooded the previous year—was demolished. For more than 40 years, only Fritchie's simple marble marker in Frederick's German Reformed cemetery could serve as the site of remembrance. But her popularity flourished in the arts. Generations of schoolchildren memorized Whittier's poem, and in 1899, Jules Jordan composed "Barbara Frietchie: Patriotic Ballad," which set the verse to music. An 1899 play by Clyde Fitch (*Barbara Frietchie, the Frederick Girl: A Play in Four Acts*) proved a success and was followed by silent films in 1908 and 1911.

As interest in Fritchie flourished, her original gravesite proved insufficient to public demand. In the early 20th century, the events of the Civil War were still in living memory, and the coming centenary of "The Star-Spangled Banner" activated those recollections: "In the long line of heroic American women," the Washington, D.C., *Evening Star* would claim on June 9, 1912, "none appeals so vividly to the imagination of the children as she who defied the marching Confederate hosts for the sake of that flag for which Francis Scott Key watched with such straining eyes in the dawn of that morning in 1812 after the night-long bombardment of Fort McHenry by the British." In 1912, a Barbara Fritchie Memorial Association was formed to fund a memorial that could stand alongside that already raised for

Francis Scott Key. Launched at a meeting held in the rooms of the local Young Men's Christian Association, organizers planned to "enlist the children" across the nation's elementary school classrooms. Noting that "the Barbara Fritchie poem is taught where reading is studied," planners aimed to ask "each school child in the country" to "contribute a penny to the fund." One thousand buttons were produced and sold for 10 cents each. The local papers reported steadily on the project's progress, and in time, the penny campaign—likely influenced by the penny campaign to preserve the Betsy Ross House—succeeded. In Spring 1913, Fritchie's remains were relocated to Mount Olivet Cemetery, near the gravesite of Francis Scott Key. Unveiled in September 1914, a large granite obelisk—designed by Alexander Doyle (1857–1922), who also designed the Francis Scott Key memorial—bears a bronze tablet containing Whittier's poem beneath a medallion, created by sculptor James Edward Kelly (1855–1933), depicting Fritchie, in profile, before a waving U.S. flag. Theatrical productions in 1915 and in 1924 continued to drive interest in her life. As mentioned above, a Broadway musical, *My Maryland*, based on Fitch's play, opened in September 1927 and ran into June 1928 (Everett 1993, 2–8).

The play and the house would open in the same year. Frederick native Henry Dorsey Etchison (1867–1939), an attorney, became head of the Barbara Fritchie Society; in that role, he would open and dedicate the Barbara Fritchie Museum, a replica of the original Barbara Fritchie house, built in 1926 and opened to the public the following year. Preparations had begun in earnest in summer 1926 when a company formed to purchase the site and supply financing for the reconstruction. Eleanor Dorff Abbott (1870–1955; Fritchie's great grand niece and an ardent promoter of the Whittier narrative) served as president, and H. Lee Hanshew (Fritchie's great-grandnephew) as secretary. The architect for the reconstruction was Joseph Walker Urner (1898–1987), another Frederick native. The dwelling was reconstructed from photos and documents of the original home. Some historicity was conferred by the mantel in the exhibit room as well as hardware from the house's doors, repurposed from Fritchie's home, and the banisters and stairway in the 1920s project were recycled from a stone tavern believed to be among the oldest in the community. Various relatives and others furnished the house with items believed to have belonged to Fritchie: Abbott donated ceramics and silverware, a Mrs. D. C. Brish provided a mahogany table and chairs as well as Fritchie's bed coverings, and Hanshew brought other furniture. Some 3,000 people attended the July 1927 dedication, a turnout that convinced some in the community that the house was destined to become an top tourism destination.

The Barbara Fritchie Memorial Association initially engaged Eleanor Abbott as hostess (1927–1933). Reminiscent of the small replica American flags made by Rachel Albright (Betsy Ross's granddaughter) and Sarah M. Wilson (Betsy Ross's great-granddaughter), and sold in the East Wing of Independence Hall from about 1898 to 1913, were mementos produced by Abbott, who

> cut pieces from linen sheets that Fritchie supposedly wove herself, turned them into bookmarks with 'Barbara Fritchie' and the American flag embroidered on them.

> Abbott hand-wrote cards to go with each book mark authenticating it. In this same manner, crocheted doilies were also produced with the same authenticating cards written and signed by Abbott. (Blough 2012)

In the mid-1930s, the Fritchie house was popular enough that when Henry and Edsel Ford planned an expansion of the Dearborn Inn (the "country's first 'airport hotel'") near Ford's celebrated Greenfield Village, a replica of the replica joined an imagined "colonial village" of such replicas: the Fritchie house still stands there in the company of the Governor Oliver Wolcott House in Litchfield, Connecticut; the Patrick Henry House in Red Hill, Virginia; the Edgar Allan Poe House in the Bronx, New York; and the Walt Whitman Birthplace in Huntington, New York (Haugh 2008; Swigger 2014). Ford, born the same year in which Whittier's poem appeared, had an affinity for poets and poetry, and he likely knew the verse that launched Fritchie's fame, leading to this Michigan echo of the Maryland replica.

Situated along the National Road, the Fritchie house enjoyed robust tourism in its first decade. More than 21,000 visitors reportedly crossed its threshold in its 1927, and some 40,000 by its first anniversary. But the Fritchie home, like both the Ross and Pickersgill houses, struggled in the 1940s. Skepticism about the poem's veracity and the effects of wartime rationing suppressed visitation, and by November 1944, the house went into foreclosure; the Barbara Fritchie Home, Inc., assumed responsibility for the house's management (Blough 2012). In the 1950s, attendance continued to decline, from over 13,000 in 1953 to 7,873 in 1957, in part apparently due to changes in traffic patterns, though larger cultural forces were surely afoot as well.

After passing through the hands of a series of private owners, in 1967, the property was purchased by the family of Richard and Margaret Mitchell Kline, who owned the Fritchie House for several more decades. In July 2015, the Ausherman Family Foundation purchased the Barbara Fritchie House, then at risk for public auction. The house remained open to the public as a site along the Civil War Trail, but in January 2018, the foundation sold the property to new owners, who planned to open it as an Airbnb.

The Francis Scott Key House

Perhaps ironically, the author of the national anthem has no historic-house museum dedicated to his memory, though he nearly did. The 1795 Georgetown home in which Francis Scott Key lived for 30 years, and from which he traveled to Baltimore in September 1814, became the subject of attention from prospective museum builders in the early 20th century. Key and his family had left the house in 1830, and over the course of the following century, this section of Georgetown became increasingly industrial. In 1907, Admiral George Dewey led an attempt—inspired by the successful effort to preserve the Betsy Ross House a decade earlier—to open a museum here, and the following year, the building opened on Flag Day. Organizers reached out to Charles Weisgerber, who was hired to raise funds toward the preservation of the Key house; Weisgerber's painting *The Inspiration*, depicting Key on a ship's deck looking out toward Fort McHenry, was used on the Francis Scott Key Memorial Association certificate, just as *Birth of Our Nation's Flag* had been used in the Betsy Ross House initiative. But the effort failed. The neighborhood had lost its association with Key. Its commercial setting made it difficult to imagine the building as it was when the Key family resided there, and none of their possessions survived to help furnish the home.

The Key house stood until 1947, when it was dismantled to make way for the Whitehurst Freeway; the structure was to be assembled at a new location (Kelly 2013). But although the building materials were moved to the new site, the reconstruction never occurred, in part because the project exceeded the funds available and in part because, by the 1940s, interest for replicas and reconstructions had waned. In 1948, President Harry S. Truman scuttled the project, and over time the building fabric was lost.

What the Houses Collectively Tell Us

The histories of these sites taken together illuminate the ways in which collective memory around the history of the United States flag has intersected with the evolution of American historic-house museums. The half century (more or less) flanking the turn of the 20th century comprised decades in which Americans expressed their reverence for the national standard through the medium of the house museum, creating spaces in which to revere important moments in that history. These museums sit at the intersection of two cultural impulses of late-19th-century America: the increasing veneration for the flag as a symbol of patriotism, and rising interest in the preservation of historic houses as documents of U.S. history. In the wake of the Civil War, the need to achieve some sort of national reconciliation, followed by the easing of sectional tension, helped propel the flag to prominence, as did the rise of veterans' groups (particularly the Grand Army of the Republic) and patriotic societies (e.g., the Sons of the American Revolution and the Daughters of the American Revolution). The rise of Decoration (later Memorial) Day and the 1876 centennial of Independence provided occasions for the mass celebration of the flag. The growth of Flag Day observations in the 1880s and 1890s and the emergence of the Pledge of Allegiance in the 1890s through the 1910s also primed Americans to want to know the flag's history and visit sites associated with the national emblem (Leepson 2005).

In those same decades, the commemorative genre of the historic-house museum was established, drawing thousands to visit domestic spaces associated with public figures and events. The 1850s preservation of Hasbrouck House in Newburgh, New York, and George Washington's home at Mount Vernon launched this phenomenon, along the way "inexorably" linking "love of home and love of country"—a development buoyed further, as the century progressed, by an expanding interest in museums as sites able "to promulgate national loyalty in an increasingly polyglot citizenry" and with the emergence of automobile travel, facilitating tourism (West 1999, 43). About 20 historic-house museums had opened by the time the Betsy Ross House welcomed its first visitors. By 1910, that number had expanded to almost 100, and by 1933, the Pickersgill and Fritchie sites joined some 400 house museums that offered Americans an opportunity to learn and celebrate U.S. history in domestic settings (Coleman 1933, 18).

The small subset of house museums devoted to the history of the flag looked to one another for inspiration and support. The penny campaigns and membership certificates and the small flags sold by Abbott, Albright, and Wilson suggest ways that these sites learned from one another. The sites also connected more directly, as the same individuals swirled through these circles; for instance, pathbreaking Ohio attorney Harriet Jean Willis in 1904 was recognized for her contribution to the preservation of the Betsy Ross House, and she received recognition in 1910 from the Francis Scott Key Memorial Association for her assistance in the effort to preserve Key's home. Creators of the Fritchie and Key sites looked directly at the work done to preserve the Ross site as models and in some cases tapped that expertise directly.

Today, the Ross and Pickersgill Houses have become vehicles to interpret not only the history of the flag and its evolving place in collective memory and popular culture but also intertwined themes in women's and labor history. The Ross house explores histories of artisanal skill and women's work more generally in Revolutionary Philadelphia, while the Pickersgill residence educates visitors about not only women, work, and family in 19th-century Baltimore but also employment and indentured service and women in reform movements. Together these places serve as vehicles through which to interpret the history of the flag and as documents of how the American understanding of the flag has evolved over time.

Further Reading

Blough, Carrie. 2012. *The Fritchie Phenomenon: Barbara Fritchie in Popular Culture*. Museum exhibition. Historical Society of Frederick County. June–December.

Bruggeman, Seth. *Born in the U.S.A.: Birth, Commemoration, and American Public Memory*. Amherst: University of Massachusetts Press, 2012.

Clark, A. Howard. 1913. "Abstract of Proceedings of Chicago Congress." *Official Bulletin of the National Society of the Sons of the American Revolution* 8: 9–17. Washington, D.C.: National Society of the Sons of the American Revolution.

Coleman, Laurence Vail. 1933. *Historic House Museums*. Washington, D.C.: American Association of Museums.

Dearinger, Kevin Lane. *Clyde Fitch and the American Theatre: An Olive in the Cocktail*. Madison, NJ: Farleigh Dickinson University Press, 2016.

Everett, William A. 1993. "Barbara Frietchie and *My Maryland:* The Civil War Comes to Operetta." *Passing Show* 16 (2): 2–8.

Harnit, Fanny. 1917. "The Twenty-Fifth Continental Congress." *Daughters of the American Revolution Magazine* 48.

Haugh, Chris. 2008. "Spare Your Country's Flag: Women Flag Wavers in Civil War Frederick County." *Historical Society of Frederick County Journal* (Fall): 4–47.

Hilario, Kenneth. 2017. "New Project to Make Old City Landmark More 'Authentic,' Aims to Boost Visitation." *Philadelphia Business Journal*. January 26.

Jenkins, Sally. 2013. "How the Flag Came to Be Called 'Old Glory.' " *Smithsonian Magazine*. October.

Kelly, John. 2013. "O Say Can You See the Missing Key House?" *Washington Post*. June 22.

Leepson, Marc. 2005. *Flag: An American Biography*. New York: Thomas Dunne.

Leepson, Marc. 2014. *What So Proudly We Hailed: Francis Scott Key, A Life*. New York: Palgrave Macmillan.

Marling, Karal Ann. 2004. *Old Glory: Unfurling History*. Piermont, NH: Bunker Hill Publishing.

Miller, Marla R. 2010. *Betsy Ross and the Making of America*. New York: Henry R. Holt.

O'Connell, Frank A., ed. 1914. *Official Programme, National Star-Spangled Banner Centennial, Baltimore, Maryland, September 6 to 13, 1914*. Baltimore: Munder-Thomsen Press.

Orton, Mary Anderson, ed. 1917. "Speakers During the Congress." *Report of the National Society of the Daughters of the American Revolution* 19. Washington, D.C.: Government Printing Office.

Swigger, Jessie. 2014. *History is Bunk: Assembling the Past at Henry Ford's Greenfield Village*. Amherst: University of Massachusetts Press.

Ulrich, Laurel Thatcher. 2007. "How Betsy Ross Became Famous." *Common-Place* 8 (1). www.common-place-archives.org/vol-08/no-01/ulrich/.

West, Patricia. 1999. *Domesticating History: The Political Origins of America's House Museums*. Washington, D.C.: Smithsonian Institution Press.

The Confederate Flags

Derek W. Frisby

Contentious debates over the design and meaning of the Confederate flag have raged since the Confederacy's inception in 1861. The Confederacy itself created confusion and controversy regarding the flags and banners it employed to represent the nascent and ultimately doomed nation throughout the American Civil War. Yet even in the Confederacy's defeat, the unofficial Confederate flag, often referred to as the Confederate battle flag, transcended the war and became infused with a myriad of meanings dependent upon context, being displayed for a variety of political causes and movements around the world. To some, this symbol is one of pride, patriotism, independence, democracy, and respect for heritage; to others, it is an emblem of shame, treason, prejudice, repression, and hate. Regardless of the controversies swirling around it, this "embattled emblem" remains ingrained in American history and culture to the extent that vexillologists have referenced it as "America's second national flag" (Coski 2005, viii; Moss 1998, 36).

The Stars and Bars

The Provisional Confederate Congress in February 1861 created a Committee of the Flag and Seal with South Carolinian representative William Porcher Miles as chair. The unenviable task of Miles's committee was to choose an emblem for the Confederacy that acknowledged the old flag (the Stars and Stripes) that many still revered but would still be distinctive enough to establish a new national identity. Citizens submitted scores of suggestions to the committee, including the popular but unofficial Bonnie Blue Flag, a five-pointed white star on a blue field. The committee's choice for the first Confederate flag (later approved by the Provisional Congress) would be known as the Stars and Bars, designed by Prussian immigrant Nicola Marschall, a prominent painter and art professor at the nearby Marion Female Academy. Marschall's submission closely resembled the Stars and Stripes. It featured "true republican colors"—a white horizontal stripe representing purity between two red horizontal stripes symbolizing valor and, on the canton, a blue field for truth containing a circle of white five-pointed stars, each star denoting a Confederate state (Coski 2005, 4).

Initially raised over the Confederate capitol in Montgomery, Alabama, on March 4, 1861, with great élan, the Stars and Bars quickly fell out of favor. The similarity of the

Stars and Bars to the Stars and Stripes added to the fog of war at the first major clash of the American Civil War, at Manassas, Virginia (First Bull Run). Confederate commander brigadier general P. G. T. Beauregard noted that the resemblance of the Stars and Bars to the U.S. flag contributed to battlefield confusion, including a number of friendly-fire incidents. Beauregard subsequently resolved to adopt a "battle flag . . . different from any State or Federal flag" and reached out to his former aide, William Porcher Miles, for advice. Miles reported Beauregard's complaints to his committee, but the committee overwhelmingly rejected the call for a change. Thus, the senior commanders of the Confederate forces in Virginia met at Fairfax Court House in September 1861 to discuss adopting a "war flag," issued by the War Department, to be used instead of the "peace or parade flag" (i.e., the Stars and Bars) (Coski 2005, 8).

Miles's Design and Battle Flags

Miles adamantly believed that the Stars and Stripes symbolized tyranny and was greatly disappointed in the adoption of Marschall's Stars and Bars over his own design (Coski 2005, 3). Miles's submission had included a variation of the flag used at the 1860 South Carolina secession convention, a red field with the palmetto tree and crescent of South Carolina's flag alongside an upright blue (or St. George's) cross sporting 15 white five-pointed stars, one for each slaveholding state. Surprisingly, Miles's design met with significant opposition on religious grounds. Protestants objected to the use of the cross, and Jews took issue with the crescent, for both sides hoped to avoid associating the new nation with any particular religion. Miles altered his design by removing the palmetto tree and crescent and changing the upright cross to a diagonal saltire, or X-shaped cross, sometimes referred to as a St. Andrew's cross, with stars for each Confederate state. (Occasionally, the number of stars on a Confederate flag may vary from 11 to 13 because people sometimes considered Missouri and Kentucky to be Confederate states, although they never officially seceded.) Seemingly vindicated by the military dissatisfaction of the Stars and Bars, Miles later showed his design to Beauregard, who championed it at the September 1861 command conference. By November 1861, Confederate units in Virginia had been issued new "Beauregard flags"—battle flags based on Miles's design, although the Army had dictated that the flags be square rather than oblong and of different sizes based upon branch.

Beauregard and several other subordinate officers subsequently transferred to different theaters and attempted to use their flags with their new commands. The western Confederate armies, however, had already adopted emblems and flags of their own, as well as state flags for use in battle. Although Beauregard and others issued orders for these units to conform to Beauregard's standard, many western units preferred their original flag patterns and continued to use them throughout the war. Nevertheless, by 1863, pressure to change the national flag and the pervasive dissemination of the battle flag throughout the Confederate ranks resulted in a search for a second Confederate flag.

The first official Confederate Congress convened in February 1862 at Richmond, Virginia, and again addressed the issue of the national flag. This time, public sentiment favored something that was completely different from the Stars and Stripes. By April, the Confederate Congress had rejected several designs and adjourned without a decision. The Second Confederate Congress of 1863 revived the issue and considered numerous requests for alterations or new flag designs. Beauregard lobbied the Congress to include the battle flag design as part of the canton, with a blue or white field behind it. Once more, Miles intervened and pushed through a design that featured his battle flag as the union on a field of white, ostensibly to mimic the French flag of the Bourbon Restoration. At least one Southern newspaper, in Savannah, Georgia, equated the white field with white supremacy, with the paper's editors referring to it as "the white man's flag," but few if any similar references are extant (Coski 2005, 18). The second national flag, popularly referred to as the Stainless Banner, flew over Richmond by mid-May 1863 and draped Lt. Gen. Thomas "Stonewall" Jackson's coffin as it lay in state in the Capitol.

The Stainless Banner

The second Confederate national flag, or Stainless Banner, satisfied proponents of the battle flag, but the white field still created confusion and consternation. Critics asserted that the white field might be mistaken for a flag of truce or surrender, particularly at sea. In addition, few units unfurled the banner in battle as it became easily soiled (often soldiers simply cut the white field off and used just the battle flag canton), and much of the flag's use was limited to displays at military headquarters and during ceremonial activities. As Confederate military fortunes collapsed and discontent with the Stainless Banner grew, the Confederate Congress adopted a third national flag in March 1865. This new flag simply added a vertical red stripe to the Stainless Banner's far edge. As its chief proponent, Confederate major Arthur L. Rogers, argued, the colors and heraldic devices were reminders of the British and French heritage of the Confederacy. The so-called Blood-Stained Banner saw little use before the surrender of the Army of Northern Virginia in April 1865 or the capitulation of other Confederate units in the ensuing months.

By 1865, the battle flag had become synonymous with the Confederate cause during the war—the use of states' rights to defend slavery. Confederate citizens preferred the design as it was distinctive from the Stars and Stripes. Beyond its symbolic use to represent their nation's defense of slavery, they had imbued the battle flag, according to historian John Coski, with "additional layers of meaning related to duty, soldierly valor, ancestry, heritage, and tradition" (2005, 27). Indeed, the military's use of the battle flag created a flag culture that Confederate citizens enshrined in song and literature to extol the South's martial virtues. The Confederate Army became the epitome of Confederate national identity—for as long as the Army survived, the idea of the Confederacy endured—and the Army's identity was the battle flag. Therefore, although it had been incorporated into the various national flags designated by the Confederate Congress, the battle flag had evolved in the pantheon of Confederate nationalism as *the* Confederate flag.

Postbellum Flags

Despite the Federal authorities' mildly enforced "implied prohibition" on Confederate flag displays during Reconstruction, some white southerners, particularly veterans, continued to display the emblem as a testament to "honor, courage, patriotism, and camaraderie" (Coski 2005, 29). Many southerners venerated original flags used by military units as holy relics or preferred to keep these relics furled in honor of those who perished. Even the original Ku Klux Klan refused to use the flag in its Reconstruction-era terror campaigns.

Reconstruction's demise brought about the Confederate flag's resurgence. Federal veterans had established the Grand Army of the Republic (GAR) as a veterans' advocacy group in 1866, but Confederate memorial groups were mostly informal extensions of wartime assistance groups. On occasions, most notably Decoration Day events, remembrance of the wartime dead involved the placing of flowers and small Confederate flags upon the soldiers' graves. Monument dedications and funerals for veterans frequently used the Confederate flag image, too. By the 1890s, the Confederate veterans' groups eventually coalesced into the United Confederate Veterans (UCV), the United Daughters of the Confederacy (UDC), and the Sons of Confederate Veterans (SCV). These organizations embedded the use of original and replica Confederate flags in their ceremonies, rituals, and publications and made the Confederate flag "part of the rhythm of public life in the South well into the twentieth century" (Coski 2005, 56). Adding to the growing acceptance of the Confederate flag was the spirit of reunion and reconciliation that peaked from the formation of the first national military parks. The establishment in the 1890s of Chattanooga and Chickamauga as the nation's first Civil War military parks not coincidentally came as the UCV was being organized in Chattanooga, and by 1913, the creation of Gettysburg National Military Park brought about a marked increase in the Confederate flag's display and dissemination in both Southern and national culture. Although there were still complaints about the use of the battle flag in certain instances at reunions or memorial functions, Reconstruction-weary white Americans sought reconciliation and developed a greater tolerance for the battle flag as a symbol of the South.

Unlike the diverse and conflicting flags displayed by various Confederate units during the war, the UCV preferred the battle flag pattern, and it futilely attempted to set regulations for reproductions of Confederate flags, going so far as to create the Committee to Arrange for Manufacture and Distribution of the Correctly Designed Battle Flag of the Confederacy. Well into the 20th century, Confederate veterans' organizations employed the battle flag to promote "the Lost Cause" and as a memorial to Confederate veterans. Less successful was these organizations' desire to restrict the commercial and political use of their venerated symbol.

The Confederate Flag in the 20th Century

Renewed interest in the Confederate flag during the early 20th century initiated a wave of commercialism that threatened the reverence for the flag often demanded by the memorial organizations. The patriotic nationalism of the Spanish-American War and the Great War eclipsed the segment of the American populace that still harbored resentment and suspicion of those proclaiming "dual loyalty" to both the Confederate and American flags (Coski 2005, 77). The premiere of D. W. Griffith's *The Birth of a Nation*, an unapologetic ode to the "redeemed" Jim Crow South, where whites who had fought for the Confederacy regained power, initiated a rebirth of the Ku Klux Klan not only in the South but the Midwest as well. The Klan's use of Confederate iconography still included marginal use of the Confederate flags by the more-national Klan membership, who preferred to use American rather than Confederate flags in parades (such as their infamous 1925–1926 Washington, D.C., marches). Throughout the 1930s, the Klan's resurgence and the commercial success of *Gone With the Wind*, in both print and cinema, created a desire for "Southern culture" and paved the way for an upsurge of the battle flag's acceptance in a variety of contexts. This broader acceptance of the battle flag allowed it to escape from the regional confines of the American South into national and global politics and popular culture. Soldiers in World War II, especially Southern servicemen, used the battle flag as unit symbols, aircraft nose art, and even adorned the yardarms of naval vessels to proclaim their martial heritage and regional pride. The military frowned upon its use, however, and directed commanders to strike the battle flag when it appeared, despite a lack of official regulations against its use.

The wave of Southern martial traditions carried over into the growing collegiate culture, especially in athletics. The 1926 Rose Bowl, often referred to as "the game that changed the South," pitted the University of Alabama in its first bowl appearance against the Washington Huskies. Alabama's victory inaugurated an era of Southern sports prowess, and college football became an arena to showcase the South's alleged athletic and cultural superiority over the traditional northern powerhouse teams. Campuses across the South used the battle flag, the "Dixie" fight song, and "Rebel" monikers to turn victories in athletic contests into a substitute for the battlefield successes that had eluded them in the Civil War. Students formed fraternities steeped in the Southern martial traditions, none more so that of the Kappa Alpha Order, supposedly ordained by Gen. Robert E. Lee himself when he was the postwar president of Washington College. The fraternity centered its rituals and events around Confederate themes and flags as an homage to the values of the "Southern gentleman" and culture of Southern honor.

Further Changes in the Flag's Meaning

In the late 1940s and 1950s, popular culture across the South steadily transformed the Confederate battle flag from a symbol of commemoration to one of defiance, pride, and prejudice. The defection of the Dixiecrats (conservative southern Democrats) from the Democratic Party in 1948 reminded the nation of Reconstruction's failures regarding race relations. The southern-based Dixiecrats defiantly opposed federal civil rights mandates and adopted the Confederate battle flag to link their cause with that of the South's earlier rebelliousness against similar laws. The Confederate battle flag soon became omnipresent at any event opposing the civil rights movement throughout the 1950s and 1960s. Alabama governor George Wallace had the flag flown over the state capitol building to protest the integration of the University of Alabama in the 1960s. The close of the Civil War Centennial and Martin Luther King Jr.'s assassination forced many to reconsider the history of racial intolerance inherent in Confederate iconography. Beginning in 1968, many universities phased out use of the Confederate flag, the "Dixie" fight song, Confederate-themed mascots, and other images associated with the Old South. Fans and alumni chafed at losing these reminders of their colleges' identity, but as more African American and minority students arrived on campus, few institutions weathered the purge of campus Confederate iconography. Still, the battle flag persisted in popular culture.

The Civil War Centennial (1961–1965) provided a new influx of the battle flag's use in Confederate kitsch, appearing on T-shirts, bikinis, and other merchandise. With the centennial wave of kitsch and its prominent use among college students, the battle flag during the 1970s and 1980s became a symbol of cultural nonconformity and Southern regional pride. Even several leftist student and political activist groups have used the flag in futile attempts to reappropriate the battle flag for their causes and capitalize on its iconic status. The pinnacle of Confederate battle flag commercialism came from the popular TV series *The Dukes of Hazzard*, which appeared on CBS from 1979–1985. The action-comedy series featured rebellious but honorable youth driving an orange 1969 Dodge Charger stock car nicknamed "the General Lee." The stars of the show often used the car, which was emblazoned with a Confederate battle flag on its roof, to elude or best blundering and corrupt authorities. The show's popularity among all demographics, but particularly younger viewers, transformed the seven-season series into a merchandising juggernaut and spawned feature films, reboots, and profitable syndication deals. The flag fad, however, soon gave way to flag flaps as the national demographic became increasingly multicultural and several high-profile incidents erupted that revolved around the meaning of the battle flag and its relationship with white supremacy (Coski 2005, 111, 130, 183).

State Appropriations of the Confederate Flag

At the end of the 19th century, many Southern states had approved state flags that incorporated elements of the previous Confederate national flags, a trend that many believe to be inspired by the rise of the Jim Crow South and segregation. In 1885, North Carolina adopted a modified version of its secession-era flag in a bill sponsored by a Confederate veteran, and although a slight symbolic modification occurred in 1991, its similarity to the first Confederate national flag is evident. In 1900, Florida voters approved a flag with a red saltire resembling the same blue feature of the battle flag, and the 1895 Alabama legislature included a red saltire very similar to that of a Confederate infantry regiment as the state flag. Tennessee's current state flag, approved in 1905, is also believed to be influenced by the Confederate flag designs. Arkansas's 1912 flag appeared suggestive of the Confederacy as well. It originally featured a red field with a diamond pattern containing five-pointed white stars, with three blue stars inside the diamond. In 1923, the Arkansas legislature mandated a fourth blue star above the word "Arkansas," in the diamond's interior, to represent the Confederacy. The Texas flag also closely resembles the first Confederate national flag, but its 1839 adoption predates the Confederacy.

Two southern states, Georgia and Mississippi, overtly included the battle flag pattern in their state flags. From 1879 to 1956, Georgia used a flag, designed by a Confederate veteran, that was based upon the first Confederate national flag. From 1956 to 2001, two-thirds of the Georgia flag featured a large battle flag, in opposition to federal integration efforts. Calls to remove the battle flag element from the state flag intensified during the 1990s and resulted in a short-lived flag that featured a Georgia state seal with each of the previous historical Georgia state flags beneath it. In 2003, Georgia voters ratified by a 3-to-1 margin a new flag closely approximating the first Confederate national flag. Mississippi, the only current state flag still bearing the battle flag design, adopted the emblem in 1894. After decades of legal wrangling over the official status of the flag (stemming from a 1906 revision in the state legal code that omitted mention of the flag), Mississippians reaffirmed in a referendum the 1894 state flag with the battle flag design, achieving nearly a two-to-one margin among voters over a revised design that again was reminiscent of the first Confederate national flag.

Free Speech Issues

Displays of the battle flag have also tested the tenets of free speech. Since *Tinker v. Des Moines Independent Community School District* (1969), elementary and secondary schools have enjoyed broad discretion when creating student dress codes. In response to the racial tension and unrest across the country, schools specifically prohibited student attire with the battle flag, citing *Tinker* for their authority to ban Confederate symbols because they possessed offensive messages that in a racially charged atmosphere would "materially and substantially" disrupt the educational environment. This exclusive focus on banning Confederate symbols brought immediate challenges in Federal courts, beginning with *Melton v. Young* (1972). In this case, the student (Melton) wore a battle flag patch on his jacket to his high school in Chattanooga, Tennessee, after a ban on Confederate symbols, and was suspended. The court invoked the *Tinker* test in upholding the ban and suspension, finding that the flag's display amid the school's racial tensions would create a substantial disruption and thus that the ban was reasonable to preserve order and discipline. The courts noted that such cases threatened the delicate balance of "the exercise of the fundamental constitutional right to freedom of speech, and . . . the oft conflicting, but equally important, need to maintain decorum in our public schools." *Melton* ushered in a temporary pause in battle flag ban challenges, until 1997, when courts began to see a new influx of Confederate flag–related cases. The courts have upheld the ban in the vast majority of those cases, based upon *Tinker*; however, the few rulings that overturned bans and punishments regarding Confederate symbols, particularly the battle flag, involved situations that lacked racial tensions like those present in *Melton* that satisfied the *Tinker* test. Furthermore, courts mindful of viewpoint discrimination have directed that schools may not single out the Confederate flag or symbols "for special treatment while allowing other controversial racial and political symbols to be displayed." Yet courts have stressed that decisions favorable to flag proponents should not be interpreted as providing "a safe haven for those bent on using the flag in school as a tool for disruption, intimidation, or trampling upon the rights of others." Subsequent cases, such as *B. W. A. v. Farmington R-7 School District* (2009) and *Hardwick v. Heyward* (2013) indicated court receptivity to school administrators who employ bans on Confederate symbols without the precedent of tension or violence because of fear of potential problems if such symbols are displayed in the school.

Similar challenges to state-sponsored battle flag displays have escalated in the early 21st century. In 2000, South Carolina ended a four-decade-long tradition of flying the battle flag atop the state capitol after the National Collegiate Athletic Association (NCAA) imposed a ban on locating postseason events in the state due to the capitol flag's prominence. The tradition had begun in 1961 both as a way to recognize the Civil War Centennial and to reject the civil rights movement. Officials subsequently moved the battle flag display to an area on the capitol grounds near a Confederate memorial and prohibited any removal of the flag at that site without further legislative action. This relocation failed to appease the NCAA, which imposed a noncompulsory moratorium on members from holding postseason activities in the state, and the National Association for the Advancement of Colored People (NAACP), which continued a tourism boycott against South Carolina. Ostensibly as the result of a remodeling effort at the Florida state capitol in 2001, Republican governor Jeb Bush removed to a museum a flag display that was erected in 1978 and featured the Stainless Banner alongside the British, French, and Spanish flags that had flown in homage of the nations that once governed the state.

In 2012, the Equal Employment Opportunity Commission (EEOC) found in *Dawson v. Donahoe* (2012) that an African American post office employee in Dothan, Alabama, had suffered from discriminatory harassment when his coworkers and supervisors failed to take "immediate and appropriate corrective action" to stop employees at the post office from wearing attire depicting the Confederate battle flag. California prohibited the state government from the display or sale of merchandise featuring the battle flag in 2014. The legislation came in response to state senator Isadore Hall's mother's complaints about replica currency featuring the Confederate flag sold at the statehouse gift shop. Opponents labeled the California prohibition as too broad, forcing supporters to provide assurances that the law allowed for historic and educational uses as well as the use by private individuals.

Specialty license plates are another area for prominent opposition to state-sanctioned battle flag displays. In 1961, the NAACP protested the use of the battle flag on license plates in Spotsylvania County, Virginia. The county agreed to allow registrants to place a sticker over the battle flag image and issued plates without the battle flag the following year. States, however, eventually began offering specialty license plates to convey messages with graphics or slogans to raise funds for select organizations and causes. Maryland and nine states (Alabama, Arkansas, Georgia, Louisiana, Mississippi, North Carolina, South Carolina, Tennessee, and Virginia) from the former Confederacy offered registrants the opportunity to purchase car license plates with a portion of the proceeds going to the Sons of Confederate Veterans, as of 2017. Prior to 2010, all but Arkansas's plates featured the SCV seal, featuring the battle flag as part of the organization's crest. Mississippi redesigned the SCV plate in 2010, substituting the SCV crest with a Civil War sesquicentennial logo, but it kept in the upper-left corner the state flag that features the battle flag.

The Texas Sons of Confederate Veterans applied to the state Department of Motor Vehicles for its own specialty license plate featuring the SCV crest in 2009 and 2010. Texas denied the application on the grounds "that a significant portion of the public associate the Confederate flag with organizations advocating expressions of hate directed toward people or groups that is demeaning to those people or groups." In 2012, the Texas SCV filed suit against Texas for denying its application, claiming that the denial was a violation of free speech and amounted to viewpoint discrimination. The case eventually reached the U.S. Supreme Court. It ruled with a five-to-four decision in *Walker v. Texas Div., Sons of Confederate Veterans, Inc.* (2015) that a state's specialty license plate–program constitutes government speech and may be regulated to a greater extent than private speech. Significantly, Clarence Thomas, the court's only African American justice and typically a staunch conservative, joined the largely liberal majority opinion.

On June 17, 2015, the evening prior to the *Walker* decision, a 21-year-old white man named Dylann Roof murdered nine African Americans, including one South Carolina state senator, as they attended a Bible study at the historic Emanuel African Methodist Episcopal Church (or the Mother Emanuel Church) in Charleston, South Carolina. The arrest and investigation of Roof uncovered evidence of his disturbed nature and fascination with white supremacist ideology. On his social media accounts and registered web pages, Roof outlined his racist perspectives and posed in pictures with flags from the former white-minority-ruled African nation of Rhodesia (now Zimbabwe), the former apartheid-era flag of South Africa, and the Confederate battle flag. Roof's car additionally bore a bumper sticker that displayed the three versions of Confederacy's national flags. Roof's murderous rampage and blatantly racist motivations shocked the world, and calls for the removal of the battle flag and other Confederate monuments from public spaces intensified. Statements from political candidates in the upcoming U.S. presidential primaries, protesters surrounding the state capitol, and public petitions supporting the flag's removal spurred quick action from the state. Republican governor of South Carolina Nikki Haley and other past and present prominent South Carolina Republicans implored the state legislature to remove the battle flag from the statehouse grounds. Following Senate passage and a two-thirds vote in the South Carolina House, officials removed the capitol's battle flag display on July 10, 2015.

Other states and businesses addressed the Confederate flag issue after the Charleston murders. Alabama's governor also had the Confederate flags removed from a memorial park near the state capitol in Montgomery on June 24, 2015.

In Mississippi, many state universities and the city of Biloxi refused to fly the state flag due to its continued inclusion of the battle flag. Retailers and corporations divested themselves from the Confederate battle flag after the murders as well. Amazon, Apple, eBay, Walmart, Target, and others ordered a halt to sales of merchandise displaying or featuring the battle flag. Warner Brothers, which holds merchandising rights to the General Lee car from *The Dukes of Hazzard*, prohibited replicas and related products with the battle flag on its roof. Even prominent flag manufacturers ceased production and sales of Confederate flags. Virginia ordered the SCV crest removed from the SCV specialty license plate, and several other states threatened to remove the SCV crests from their specialty plates too, but those efforts were later abandoned. NASCAR, a sport long associated with Southern culture, requested that fans no longer fly or display the Confederate flags at their events. This type of request is comparable with those of other public and private entities that have requested a voluntary ban on Confederate flags and related products featuring the flags, such as voluntary vendor ban at the New York State Fair. All of these voluntary policies have met with limited success and in some cases outright defiance. Many companies still profit from the sale of Confederate battle flag items despite the voluntary ban. Dixie Outfitters, for example, still sells attire emphasizing the rustic, natural aspects of the South and featuring a logo of the battle flag with the motto "Preserving Southern Heritage since 1861." Following recent controversies and bans on merchandise with the battle flag, the company, like many other heritage organizations, has shifted to using the Gadsden Flag. Nonetheless, much of their product line still features the battle flag and is available through web retailers who had earlier proclaimed bans on such items.

After the Charleston murders, the U.S. National Park Service (USNPS) issued guidance to parks, particularly those associated with the American Civil War, to halt voluntarily all sales of items in the park bookstores and gift shops that feature a stand-alone image of the battle flag. Park units may still fly Confederate flags to provide historical context, on certain recognized holidays (for example, in a state celebrating Confederate Memorial Day) and, on occasion, by groups wishing to undertake the placement and removal of small Confederate flags at the graves of Confederate veterans. At no time may the Confederate flag be flown from a fixed USNPS cemetery flagpole (the Department of Veterans Affairs has a similar policy, mandated by Congress in 2016). The USNPS site at Fort Sumter in Charleston ended its display of Confederate flags shortly after the Charleston murders. The Washington National Cathedral's stained-glass windows and the New York statehouse's War Room murals are conspicuous examples of Confederate flag imagery incorporated into design elements, detailing historical events surrounding the Civil War, which, despite protests and debate, remain in place as of 2017.

Many statues, portraits, and busts related to the Confederacy came under increased scrutiny after Charleston. In August 2017, a number of white supremacist groups who used the Confederate flag prominently in their marches, literature, and materials gathered in Charlottesville, Virginia, to protest the proposed removal of a statue of Gen. Robert E. Lee. A white supremacist plowed his car into a group of counterprotesters, killing one woman and injuring dozens of others. This incident, like Roof's Charleston attack, once again sparked debate on Confederate iconography and memorials. Officials began removing Confederate memorials across the South, in addition to those in the Midwest, the Pacific Northwest, and additional northern states. Between the events in Charleston and Charlottesville, many states passed legal protections for Confederate memorials on public property to block further efforts at removal, so many such memorials remain in place. But in the wake of Charlottesville, the Six Flags Over Texas, the flagship of the Six Flags Entertainment Corporation, replaced all six flags that had flown over Texas, including the Confederate flag, with six American flags.

Ironically, the Confederate battle flag has become more popular internationally, although the confusing cultural baggage the flag carries has accompanied it overseas, too. Naples, in southern Italy, declaring a historical linkage with the Confederacy due to its defeat at the hands of Rome in 1861, has used the battle flag as the emblem of the city's soccer team for years. So have some fans of soccer clubs in Scotland, Spain, Portugal, and France, who often recite chants and songs with racist or anti-Semitic themes while flying Confederate flags. Swedish and United Arab Emirates muscle-car enthusiasts, fascinated by American culture, display the flags from their vehicles, while British country music fans wave Confederate flags at festivals. Descendants of Confederate expatriates and fans of Southern culture in Brazil hold celebrations of their "heritage" featuring Confederate iconography and battle flags. The battle flag has been associated with Northern Ireland's paramilitary groups, who use the flag to honor immigrants who fought for the Confederacy, and it has been used by self-proclaimed "Jewish rednecks" in Israel. Neo-Nazis use the battle flag as a substitute for Nazi flags, often banned by law there; other extremist groups in Europe, especially given the recent rise in anti-immigration and right-wing activism, employ the battle flag for their cause as well. Europeans' fascination with reenacting the American Civil War has further popularized the battle flag. The battle flag and similar variations have also appeared in Bosnia and the Ukraine to symbolize independence and resistance.

Although the Confederate flag had been diminished in the American public landscape after Charleston, the battle flag continues as a potent and nebulous symbol that generates mixed messages. Proponents stress the flag's heritage, while opponents emphasize its hate. An East Tennessee state legislator in the wake of the 2017 Charlottesville incident echoed the proflag heritage arguments, proclaiming the Confederate battle flag "a symbol of freedom" representing the history, courage, and honor of Confederate ancestors and heroes (Whetstone 2017). But others see the same symbol very differently, perceiving it as a symbol of exploitation, cruelty, and bigotry from one of the darkest chapters in the nation's history.

Further Reading

Bonner, Robert E. 2002. "Flag Culture and the Consolidation of Confederate Nationalism." *Journal of Southern History* 68 (2): 293–332.

Cannon, Devereaux D., Jr. 1988. *The Flags of the Confederacy: An Illustrated History*. Wilmington, NC: Broadfoot Publishers.

Coski, John N. 2005. *The Confederate Battle Flag: America's Most Embattled Emblem.* Cambridge, MA: Harvard University Press.

Martinez, J. Michael, William D. Richardson, and Ron McNinch-Su, eds. 2000. *Confederate Symbols in the Contemporary South.* Gainesville: University Press of Florida.

Moss, Rosalind Urbach. 1998. "'Yes, There's a Reason I Salute the Flag': Flag Use and the Civil Rights Movement." *Raven: A Journal of Vexillology* 5:16–37.

Teachout, Woden. 2009. *Capture the Flag: A Political History of American Patriotism.* New York: Basic Books.

Whetstone, Tyler. 2017. "Confederate Battle Flag 'Is a Symbol of Freedom,' Says Tennessee Lawmaker." *USA Today*. August 16.

The Flag in American Art

Kenneth Hartvigsen

In René Magritte's 1929 painting *The Treachery of Images*, viewers encounter a realistic-looking pipe above the slogan "*Ceci n'est pas une pipe*" (This is not a pipe). This may seem like a bit of surrealist fun, that the artist negated the image he created. The title, however, points toward more serious concerns. All images are treacherous because they are not what they appear to be. Magritte is right; this is not a pipe—it is a picture of a pipe. But is this always the case?

In 1964, Alan R. Solomon asked a question about Jasper Johns's artwork *Flag* (1954)—which has 13 red and white stripes and a blue field of stars—that would have made Magritte smile: "Is it a flag, or is it a painting?" he queried (Solomon 1964). This question is not as easy to answer as whether one could smoke some aged Cavendish using Magritte's painting. The easiest answer to Solomon's question would probably be yes. While Johns invited this confusion in various ways, the very nature of flags seems to confuse the relationship between a real thing and a representation. A flag is flexible, both literally and symbolically. When it flies, it shows the direction of the wind. Symbolically, it reveals prevalent attitudes and beliefs about the world in which it flies, and simultaneously that world reveals the flag's true shape.

This essay analyzes six examples of flag art—two from the 19th century, three from the 20th, and one from the 21st—that behave almost like real flags by revealing prevalent "winds of change" from their historical moment. These artworks are iconic; they are not, however, monolithic in meaning. Like real flags, they can mean different things to different people. By analyzing these artworks and their historical contexts, this essay will explain some of the ways that flags insert themselves into cultural discourse and how the art world has participated in creating the flag and the America that we know today.

John Trumbull, *Surrender of Lord Cornwallis*

In 2016, 22 million people visited Washington, D.C., and the United States National Park Service recorded 33.8 million individual visitors to the National Mall (Destination DC 2017). A highlight for many visitors was the United States Capitol, where John Trumbull's cycle of monumental history paintings is permanently installed in the rotunda. The *Surrender of Lord Cornwallis* (1820) is thus seen by millions of people every single year. In the center, Maj. Gen. Benjamin Lincoln, astride a white charger, receives the sword of surrender from a British officer while lines of soldiers on both sides provide a visual balance that suggests tensions are now at rest. Subtle asymmetries in the background, however, hint at the turmoil that led to this. Smoke rises diagonally from behind the French forces on the viewer's left, and beneath the smoke, a seemingly endless column of British soldiers curves into view.

Lincoln's horse bends to its left, its head pointing at Gen. George Washington, who presides from under the billowing folds and the authority of the Stars and Stripes. Washington and flag together manifest an iconographic center of gravity around which the rest of Turnbull's composition spins. The white flag flying on the painting's opposite side—a French flag flying above French soldiers—flies higher than the American flag, perhaps as a gesture on Trumbull's part that acknowledges the role Rochambeau's troops played in securing victory. Despite the flag's height, it arches downward, leading the eye toward Washington's rampant colors. The American flag, in contrast, billows upward, pointing out of the canvas toward a future dominated by an American story. Its fly, curling in the breeze, almost resembles a face in profile caught in a victorious shout.

Though it may look unremarkable, this flag is an early design seen in other Trumbull paintings, with eight-pointed stars arranged in a square with one in the center. Based largely on its appearance in Trumbull's paintings, Grace Rogers Cooper supposed that this was an authentic early design (Cooper 1973, 9), but not all historians are convinced that Trumbull can be trusted when it comes to the details of his paintings (Guenter 1990, 35). Still, as a veteran of the war, Trumbull would have been familiar with the flags that were used. In his painting *General George Washington at Trenton*, the more familiar Betsy Ross design (five-pointed stars in a circle) flies over an artillery crew in the distance. Placed in the composition below General Washington's horse, this flag does not enjoy the same victorious position as its sibling at Yorktown but may be the earliest depiction of this more-familiar design in a painting (Cooper 1973, 9).

Trumbull's use of multiple flag designs indicates that this young nation was still finding its way in the world. This is not to say that he intentionally used different flags for this reason, but if Cooper was correct that both of these designs were used during the war, Trumbull's awareness and use of these designs documents a time when America was still deciding what symbols it would use—a decision that would have wide-ranging effects.

Trumbull was a first-hand witness to the flag's emergence as a symbol of international significance. The son of the only colonial governor to support the Revolution, Trumbull served for a time as George Washington's aide-de-camp and rose to the rank of colonel by the age of 21. A gifted artist from his youth who had encountered American masters, including the great Bostonian portraitist John Singleton Copley while studying at Harvard, Trumbull left his promising military career—after a disagreement with Congress about the date of a promotion—and pursued art studies in England, of all places.

In England, Trumbull absorbed a European academic style infused with Benjamin West's and John Singleton Copley's flare for contemporary subjects. He also managed to get himself thrown in prison on suspicion of treason after he travelled to Paris to rendezvous with Benjamin Franklin and Thomas Jefferson. Though threatened with execution, he was released after seven months and returned to America. By 1783, he was back in London, where Benjamin West suggested the massive project for which Trumbull would forever be known—the history paintings commemorating the American Revolution that hang in the Capitol Rotunda (Staiti 2011, 181).

As West had taught him, Trumbull never let the literal truth get in the way of a good painting or a grand story. Nonetheless, Trumbull enjoyed a social position that allowed him to work with many of the individuals pictured in his paintings (Paulson 1982, 349). The resulting paintings became visual texts around which an evolving mythos of Revolutionary America could develop and were part of a program to rebuild the U.S. Capitol, which the British had burned in the War of 1812.

As Staiti explained, during and after the Revolution, the nation was "in urgent need of images, rituals, and mythologies not only that could replace the old British ones, but that might also bring a disparate population together in functional union" (Staiti 2011, 7). While Staiti is writing of artwork, the flag itself was one of those tools used to construct these new mythologies. Its design represents the unification of the states, as its stars suggest the independent states rising together as a new constellation. It is no surprise that this need for images, a need for American icons, would merge with the arrival of the new American flag.

Emanuel Leutze, *Washington Crossing the Delaware*

The European style that inspired Trumbull continued to be the dominant model for American history painters, as evidenced in the career of German American artist Emanuel Leutze. Born in Germany, raised in Virginia and Philadelphia, Leutze studied in Germany, where his best-known painting was influenced not only by European style but by political unrest.

Washington Crossing the Delaware (1851) is one of America's most iconic paintings. Even more than Trumbull's Yorktown, this is a monument to George Washington, who stands majestically in the prow of a boat cutting through the icy waters of the Delaware River. Additional boats extend from the right of the canvas in a receding diagonal line, suggesting not only the troops under Washington's command but future citizens who would symbolically follow Washington in defending freedom through challenging conditions.

The flag itself has been wrapped for the journey but not stowed. Though the small boat is rowed, the flag seems like a sail hurrying the craft along. Managed by two men, the flag billows within their grasp as though it could unfurl any moment. While the cold wind of a winter night is evident, something more stirring than this energizes the flag as if from within. This flag is no prop but is a participant in the scene, a figure as animate as any other in this story.

Despite the painting's popularity, many observers would be surprised to learn of the political context that inspired Leutze. As multiple scholars have shown, Leutze's initial stimulus was revolutionary activity in Germany, where he was studying (Groseclose 1975; Howat 1960; Wierich 2001). Sympathetic to the revolutionaries of 1848, Leutze wanted to paint a series of canvases that would, in Groseclose's words, "[illustrate] the struggle of the religiously and politically oppressed citing landmarks on the road to new world freedoms" (1975, 75). George Washington leading the colonial forces thus symbolizes the potential of all people to rise in defense of freedom.

For a picture that is so ubiquitous in American culture to arise from a failed German revolution is strange enough. It is stranger still that scholars are divided as to whether Leutze intended this picture for an American audience at all. Groseclose points out that Leutze's request to Congress for financial support in painting a second canvas was inspired by and did not precede the painting's reception in the U.S. Karsten Fitz, however, insists that the painting's European connections do not detract from the fact that Leutze had expressed a desire to find "an American national art" (Fitz 2007, 34). Jochen Wierich makes the additional observation that this painting, among others, "spoke to the political aspirations of German immigrants who came to America in the aftermath of failed European revolutions" (2001, 54). Despite these differing perspectives, the record shows that the picture was exhibited to enthusiastic crowds in the United States. It continues to enjoy a powerful place in public memory—as well as in the permanent collection of the Metropolitan Museum of Art in New York City.

Childe Hassam, *The Avenue in the Rain*

Trumbull's and Leutze's paintings enjoy pride of placement in two of the most powerful buildings in the United States—Trumbull's in the United States Capitol and Leutze's in the Metropolitan Museum of Art. Childe Hassam's *The Avenue in the Rain* (1917) also resides in a proud location: since 1963, it has been in the permanent collection of the White House, where it serves as a backdrop to the public performance of the American presidency. While Hassam's impressionistic canvas may not seem as historically rich as Trumbull's or Leutze's, understanding its true subject reveals a symbolic punch that justifies the painting's presence in the nation's most powerful residence.

With its focus on atmospheric conditions, its loose brushstroke, and its vibrant color, *The Avenue in the Rain* is textbook Impressionism, one of a series of at least 30 different flag pieces inspired by patriotic displays in New York City in which flags by the thousands filled Fifth Avenue. Ilene Susan Fort has identified the initial inspiration as a May 13, 1916, parade that was "the first large-scale public demonstration in support of the creation of a large, well-trained army and represented the beginning of the United States' involvement in [WWI]" (1988, 8). America's entry into the war required a massive change in public opinion. President Wilson had run for reelection with the campaign slogan "He Kept Us Out of the War," and the escalation of hostilities continually challenged his stance. Acts of aggression against

American interests, including the sinking of the *Lusitania* in May 1915 and the interception of communications attempting to establish an alliance between Germany and Mexico, eventually changed Wilson's mind, resulting in a declaration of war against Germany in April 1917. Hassam's flag paintings, which many consider to be his best work, capture this period of change through an explosion of color.

The vertical orientation of this canvas recalls the hanging forms of the flags that fill the avenue, and the hues of the rainy day allow for a palette of red, white, and blue. The effect is striking, and as William Kloss has noted, the painting becomes "not a street scene, not a painting of flags, but in essence a vibrant flag itself" (Kloss 1992, 238). This analysis is consistent with the patriotic fervor of the time. As Fort explained, "It became the duty of all citizens to participate in a heroic manner, if not in battle, then in a war-related activity at home" (1988, 8). Hassam was politically active from the start, and his flag series is a grand example of personal flag-waving.

America's entry into the war was a moment of international acceptance: the adolescent nation took its seat at the table of global affairs. At the same time, America was setting itself apart financially and technologically, reflected in the rise of the modern city in which Hassam witnessed these displays. In fact, scholars have read Hassam's narrow canvases, such as this one, as evocative of the city's skyscrapers. As H. Barbara Weinberg explained of a similar canvas, "Hassam's narrow vertical canvas—twice as high as it is wide—is a perfect format for this 'urban landscape,' whose compression of upward thrust contrasts so markedly with [Hassam's] open, sprawling pastoral panoramas" (2004, 208). Fort likewise wrote that "New York at this period had come to stand for America and its technological prowess, which had surpassed that of Europe . . . and the skyscraper, draped with flags of freedom and liberty, symbolized the power to be victorious" (1988, 98).

In an act of patriotism, Hassam exhibited nearly his complete flag series only four days after the armistice was signed. While not all enjoy the skyscraper dimensions, or the famous provenance of *Avenue in the Rain*, all celebrate the emergence of modern America as a technological and political superpower.

Jasper Johns, *Flag*

While Hassam's paintings were explicitly patriotic, other artists that followed would create more politically complicated flag art—including Jasper Johns, whose *Flag* (1954) still avoids easy categorization more than 60 years after its creation. This owes much to the work's medium, as Johns created his flag by dipping strips of newspaper in pigmented wax and smoothing them out on a fabric background. In other words, rather than painting the famous design, he assembled a flag out of nontraditional materials.

The newsprint can still be read within the layers of wax, and some scholars have puzzled over whether the stories contained therein provide additional meaning. Of these texts, Anne Middleton Wagner explained, "the familiar press repertoire [was] sampled with each utterly ordinary fragment . . . speaking to and of the texture of everyday life" (2012, 13). This prosaic smattering of news texts seems appropriate for Johns, for whom meaning is slippery. He insisted that he created *Flag* not out of patriotism or in protest but in reaction to a dream in which he was painting a large American flag. He believed the work could be acknowledged as a flag but should be recognized as other things as well. In one interview, he said, "The painting of a flag is always about a flag, but it's no more about a flag than it is about a brushstroke or about a color or about the physicality of paint, I think." Further, he suggested that—apart from the dream—he found inspiration in objects that were perfectly ordinary: "The most conventional thing, the most ordinary thing—it seems to me that these things can be dealt with without having to judge them" ("Interview with David Sylvester—Jasper Johns" 1992, 721, 723).

Johns attempted to sidestep politics and focus attention on the thing itself rather than on its contestable meaning, but as Fred Orton has observed, 1954 was a year full of significant flag events. It is difficult to believe that Johns had none of them in mind when he created *Flag*. Among the most prominent events were President Eisenhower's Flag Day Proclamation, in which he encouraged all citizens to display their flags; the incorporation of the phrase "under God," into the Pledge of Allegiance by act of Congress; and the dedication of the Marine Corps War Memorial, or Iwo Jima Memorial, in Arlington, Virginia (Orton 1994, 100–103).

The last of these was an exceptionally powerful event to have occurred concurrently with the creation of *Flag*. The memorial, which incorporates an actual flagpole, together with the Pulitzer Prize–winning photograph on which it was based, are supreme examples of American myths being created through pictures of flags. The memorial and the photograph have much in common with Trumbull's and Leutze's paintings, which have been accused of being light on historical accuracy. While Joe Rosenthal never hid the fact that his photograph captured the second raising of the American flag over Iwo Jima, many viewers assumed that this was the first flag to fly that day. Others believed the raising of the flag signaled American victory over the island—which was also not true. Parades, speeches, tours, and a Hollywood film took Rosenthal's photograph as raw material to be molded into a powerful American myth. By the time the memorial was dedicated, this image had become much more than a press picture, more than a celebration of the soldiers pictured within it, whose names were left off the memorial. The raising of the flag over Iwo Jima, perpetually reenacted in the monument, signifies American success now and forever and the triumph of the American flag as a symbol of national and individual pride. What then to make of Jasper Johns, who chose that historical moment, bathed as it was in political excitement and flag ritual, to create his masterpiece?

Flag's reception was complicated from the start. Johns destroyed most of his earlier works, marking this as the genesis of all that was to come. He exhibited it frequently, and in 1958, Alfred H. Barr, director of the Museum of Modern Art (MOMA), proposed acquiring *Flag* and a handful of other works by Johns. While *Flag* is now a destination work at MOMA, Barr's recommendation was initially denied by members of the Museum Committee of Collections and the Trustees, who feared that *Flag* would be read as a protest piece (Messer 1978, 292). The fact that the trustees of such a powerful organization would be afraid to display a flag—or a painting of a flag—testifies to the power of flag art in American society and indicates the political turmoil of the 1950s.

Dread Scott, *What Is the Proper Way to Display a U.S. Flag?*

Flag is a turning point; it is the first work on this list to be overtly American in subject *and* style, and it is also a signpost of things to come, a flying flag revealing the changing direction of the wind. While *Flag's* politics may be harder to discern than the newsprint trapped within its wax, most American flag art that followed has been unafraid to broadcast its point of view.

In 1989, while a student at the Art Institute of Chicago, Dread Scott exhibited an instantly infamous installation piece: *What Is the Proper Way to Display a U.S. Flag?* Consisting of a photo collage of flag-draped coffins and South Korean protesters burning American flags, a blank ledger with pens available for audience commentary, and a three-by-five-foot American flag positioned on the floor, the installation invited visitors to write down reactions while standing on the flag. It was possible to stand to either side of the flag to access the pens and ledger, but the artist's intention was clear.

Scott's website displays some of the book's entries (Scott 2017). It is not surprising that a large number of visitors were deeply offended. A number of comments contain racial slurs and demand that Scott be jailed or murdered. The most surprising comments are those that offer a positive view, including several whose authors saw the installation as an affirmation of free speech. One visitor wrote:

> There are many questions you have raised. For that I thank you. It does hurt me to see the flag on the ground being stepped on. Yet now after days have passed, I have realized tat [*sic*] this is the ultimate form of patriotism. Our country is so strong in believing what it stands for that we would allow you to do this. You have made me really think about my own patriotism, which has grown stronger. (Scott 2017)

Most reactions were far less affirmative, and the installation became a national controversy (Goldstein 1996, 78). President George Bush and Senator Bob Dole publically denounced the work, and Congress enacted legislation to prevent similar exhibitions from taking place in the future. This reaction, however, was not a reaction to this work alone. As provocative as it was, *What Is the Proper Way to Display a U.S. Flag?* was exhibited at a time when the public was already enraged by flag desecration. In the same month, the United States Supreme Court heard *Texas v. Johnson* (1989), a historic flag-burning case. The court ruled five to four that burning the flag was protected as free speech, which overturned statutes banning flag desecration in 48 states.

Justice Kennedy's concurrence to Justice Brennan's majority opinion contained sentiments similar to those expressed by the positive comments at Scott's installation: "It is poignant but fundamental that the flag protects those who hold it in contempt." Dissenting opinions offered by Justices Stevens and Rehnquist eloquently laid out a case for protecting the flag's unique position. Justice Stevens argued that it was not Mr. Johnson's opinion that was under assault by flag desecration laws but merely his means of expression. Justice Rehnquist was more emotive in his dissent:

> The flag is not simply another "idea" or "point of view" competing for recognition in the marketplace of ideas. Millions and millions of Americans regard it with an almost mystical reverence regardless of what sort of social, political, or philosophical beliefs they may have. I cannot agree that the First Amendment invalidates the Act of Congress, and the laws of 48 of the 50 States, which make criminal the public burning of the flag.

While *What Is the Proper Way to Display a U.S. Flag?* is iconic in its own right, its fame was part of a charged historical moment. By engaging with the American flag, the installation revealed the prevalent ideologies at play in its contentious present. And, like the examples discussed above, it revealed and was revealed by the strength of those cultural winds.

Conclusion—Robert Longo, *Untitled (The Pequod)*

These examples show that the flag has always been a common yet uncommonly powerful subject in American art. There is no reason to doubt this will continue to be the case. Still, I cannot predict which flag artworks of today will become iconic tomorrow, no more than I can define for later historians what way the wind is blowing in the early 21st century. Is this the post-9/11 era? Post-Obama? The age of Trump? In a day when Americans are deeply divided about whether black, blue, or all lives matter, what will be the cultural touch points that taken together define this somehow-still-sailing ship of state? Without answers to these questions, I nonetheless conclude with one final artwork. I don't know if it will become iconic to future generations, but it resonates with this author, who has long contemplated the relevance of flag art in 21st-century America.

Robert Longo's *Untitled (The Pequod)* (2014) is a monumental black flag made of steel, wood, and wax. Reaching 17 feet above the ground, the imposing form jabs into the floor at a precarious, gravity-defying angle. It is a broken flag, yet still undeniably powerful. It is a gigantic razor blade slicing into the gallery floor. It is, as the name suggests, a doomed ship being dragged by its own weight into an eerily calm foam.

The subtitle *The Pequod*, in referencing the ship from *Moby Dick*, doubles down on the sculpture's Americanness—if that's possible for a gigantic Stars and Stripes—as Melville's tome is often on the shortlist of "Great American Novels." A book about power and obsession, Melville's masterpiece is famously complicated and inscrutable. The book slides between ecstasy and boredom as it strains to reveal mysteries of the universe and obsesses over quotidian details. If the *Pequod* is a microcosm of America (which I would not be the first person to suggest), the reader should be horrified when the *Pequod*, and nearly her entire crew, are lost to the raging sea, not victims of the whale alone but of Captain Ahab's maniacal will.

Is this the message Longo intends? Is this massive sinking ship of a flag a prophetic warning that the nation will succumb to unchecked will and outpaced ambition? If so, it is worth remembering that someone survived the whale's attack and Ahab's mania: Ishmael lived and floated away to safety on a coffin. This undignified salvation was salvation just the same, and so perhaps Longo's sculpture is not as fatalistic as it may seem. If this flag represents the sinking ship of state, it also hints that survival is possible—but that this survival may not take the form one expected.

The same must surely be said not just of the future but also of the future of flags in American art. They will continue to fly, to reveal us, and to be revealed by us. But they will probably not take the form we expect.

Further Reading

Cooper, Grace Rogers. 1973. *Thirteen-Star Flags: Keys to Identification*. Washington, D.C.: Smithsonian Institution Press.

Destination DC. "Washington, DC Visitor Research." DC Press. Accessed September 2017. https://washington.org/press/DC-information/washington-dc-visitor-research.

Fitz, Karsten. 2007. "The Düsseldorf Academy of Art, Emanuel Leutze, and German-American Transatlantic Exchange in the Mid-Nineteenth Century." *Amerikastudien / American Studies* 52 (1): 14–34.

Fort, Ilene Susan. 1988. *The Flag Paintings of Childe Hassam*. New York: Henry N. Abrams.

Goldstein, Robert Justin. 1996. *Burning the Flag: The Great 1989–1990 American Flag Desecration Controversy*. Kent, OH: Kent State University Press.

Groseclose, Barbara S. 1975. "Washington Crossing the Delaware: The Political Context." *The American Art Journal* 7 (2): 70–78.

Guenter, Scot. 1990. *The American Flag, 1777–1924: Cultural Shifts from Creation to Codification*. Rutherford, NJ: Farleigh Dickinson University Press.

Howat, John K. 1960. "Washington Crossing the Delaware." *The Metropolitan Museum of Art Bulletin* 26 (7): 289–299.

"Interview with David Sylvester—Jasper Johns." 1992. In *Art in Theory, 1900–1990: An Anthology of Changing Ideas*, pp. 721–726, edited by Charles Harrison and Paul Wood. Malden, MA: Blackwell Publishers.

Kloss, William. 1992. *Art in the White House: A Nation's Pride*. Washington, D.C.: White House Historical Association in cooperation with the National Geographic Society.

Messer, Ruth. 1978. *Moma: Museum in Search of an Image*. Diss., Columbia University.

Orton, Fred. 1994. *Figuring Jasper Johns*. Cambridge, MA: Harvard University Press.

Paulson, Ronald. 1982. "John Trumbull and the Representation of the American Revolution." In "Romantic Texts, Romantic Times: Homage to David E. Edman," special issue, *Studies in Romanticism* 21 (3): 341–356.

Scott, Dread. 2017. "What Is the Proper Way to Display a U.S. Flag?" Dreadscott.net. Accessed September. http://www.dreadscott.net/works/what-is-the-proper-way-to-display-a-us-flag

Solomon, Alan R. 1964. *Jasper Johns*. New York: Jewish Museum.

Staiti, Paul. 2011. *Of Arms and Artists: The Revolution through Painters' Eyes*. New York: Bloomsbury Press.

Wagner, Anne Middleton. 2012. *A House Divided: American Art Since 1955*. Berkeley: University of California Press.

Weinberg, H. Barbara. 2004. *Childe Hassam: American Impressionist*. New York: Metropolitan Museum of Art.

Wierich, Jochen. 2001. "Struggling through History: Emanuel Leutze, Hegel, and Empire." *American Art* 15 (2): 52–71.

The Flag in American Music

Gregory N. Reish

When George M. Cohan's three-act musical comedy *George Washington, Jr.* opened at New York's Herald Square Theatre on February 6, 1906, it became an immediate commercial success. Cohan had already established himself as the all-around man of popular musical theater—playwright, composer, actor, singer, dancer, director, and impresario—and he had begun to taste the fruits of rising American patriotism masterfully transformed into popular entertainment. The rather straightforward plot of *George Washington, Jr.* focuses on the patriotic son of a U.S. senator who foils his father's scheme, an arranged marriage into an aristocratic British family. The show's theatrical centerpiece was what came to be one of Cohan's most enduring songs: "You're a Grand Old Flag." Starring in the title role, as he usually did, Cohan sang it while marching up and down the stage with an American flag, at certain points even wrapping himself in it. It was resplendent patriotic spectacle, and Cohan used it to full effect.

Critics blasted the inherent shallowness of Cohan's brand of chauvinistic theater, even as they acknowledged its commercial power. *Life Magazine*'s James Metcalfe characterized parts of the show as "original musical trash" and concluded that "if [Cohan] can bring himself to coin the American flag and national heroes into box office receipts, it is not his blame, but our shame" (1906). Writing for *The Evening World* little more than a week after the show's debut, theater critic Charles Darnton wrote that "it pays to be patriotic. . . . Mr. George M. Cohan found this out with *Little Johnny Jones*, and now, with a keen eye to business, he has gone in for being the son of his country" (Darnton 1906). Cohan's earlier show *Little Johnny Jones* premiered in 1904 and is now widely recognized as a milestone, the first dramatically integrated American musical. In it Cohan had staged a bombastic, flag-waving march to accompany the show's biggest hit, "Yankee Doodle Dandy." Surely it was not lost on Cohan, ever sensitive to his audiences' reactions, that such displays of patriotism, taking full advantage of the flag and other symbols, had almost unlimited power to excite and engage.

George Washington, Jr. was thus conceived, composed, and staged as an extended presentation of this strongly patriotic ethos, with the American flag at its core. However superficial those critics like Metcalfe and Darnton found this tactic ("*George Washington Jr.* won't make history," Darnton gibed, "but it will make money"), Cohan, the consummate showman, understood the potential appeal of an entire show that trafficked in staged patriotism, and he had already witnessed the power of the flag as the ultimate nationalistic symbol. Indeed, Cohan went out of his way to position "You're a Grand Old Flag" not only as the show's big number but as its genesis, part of the Cohan mythology. In a story that may well be apocryphal, as beautifully and sentimentally conceived as one of Cohan's stage plots, he later reported that the idea for the song, and eventually the entire show, came from a chance encounter with a Civil War veteran and member of the Grand Army of the Republic (GAR) during a memorial event at Gettysburg. Holding a carefully folded but tattered flag in his lap, the veteran explained to Cohan that what he and his comrades had suffered was all for this "grand old rag." Indeed, Cohan's original title for the song was "You're a Grand Old Rag," used in the first sheet music printings and in early performances of *George Washington, Jr.* Cohan even recreated the story of the old soldier in the script. In the scene, veterans of the Civil War are visiting Mount Vernon when a GAR veteran emerges from that onstage chorus with a tattered flag as a prelude to the song. Critics like Darnton found the effect "slangy," while various patriotic organizations objected to Cohan's calling the treasured national symbol a "rag." He obviously meant no disrespect, but he quickly bowed to external pressure and changed "rag" to "flag" in both stage performances and subsequently published sheet music.

Use of the American flag in popular music and other types of entertainment was certainly nothing new to Cohan and his early 20th-century audiences. The power of the flag as patriotic image had grown steadily through the 19th century, and popular song had helped to fuel that growth. Throughout this period, the popular-song and musical-entertainment industries were blossoming into one of the nation's most vibrant economic sectors. Coincident with this development were waves of political populism, vast improvements in the nation's commercial infrastructure, an increasing sense of America's importance in the world as a political force for democracy, and numerous wars that sparked repeated waves of American nationalist sentiment.

The Flag in Early American Music

The flag was not always been widely employed as a symbol of American patriotism. References to the flag in music of the Revolutionary and Federalist eras were extremely rare, even after the passing of the Flag Resolution in June 1777. Popular and patriotic songs of this period were largely composed, often by crafting new words to existing melodies, in response to specific events. Their lyrics emphasize themes of freedom, bravery, and resistance to tyranny; their imagery draws chiefly on the armaments of war, the bodies of the fallen, and a range of Biblical references. A noteworthy composer of 18th-century American patriotic songs was Francis Hopkinson, judge, congressman, artist, essayist, harpsichordist, signer of the Declaration of Independence, and designer of the first U.S. flag with stars and stripes. Hopkinson's "The Battle of the Kegs" (1778) typifies songs of the Revolutionary War, commemorating an attempted American attack on British ships by floating kegs of gunpowder down the Delaware River to the Philadelphia Harbor.

Although Hopkinson never used flag-related imagery in his songs, he did, around 1790, write the first American lyrics to "The Anacreontic Song," the melody of which later became "The Star-Spangled Banner."

The earliest published reference to an American flag in popular music seems to be "Song for the 5th of March." Published almost simultaneously in March 1774 in *The Massachusetts Spy* and *The Newport Mercury* to commemorate the fourth anniversary of the Boston Massacre, this anonymous poem is set to the tune of "Once the Gods of the Greeks," a popular song once a favorite of John Quincy Adams. The patriotic adaptation makes two references to the flag. Its fourth verse evokes the flag as a symbol of fallen Americans' just cause:

But the Banner of Freedom determin'd we'll stand
Waving high o'er our Countrymen's Graves;
From the deep vault of Death they give forth the Command,
"Revenge us, or live to be Slaves."

The song's seventh, penultimate verse cites "the American Ensign," the maritime flag flown to identify a vessel's nationality, and evokes the star as both a design feature of the flag and a symbol of American resilience and triumph.

A ray of bright Glory now Beams from afar,
Blest dawn of an Empire to rise;
The American Ensign now sparkles a Star,
Which shall shortly flame wide thro' the Skies.

In the early 19th century, interest in the flag as a patriotic symbol in popular culture began to increase, and the number of songs associated with it rose accordingly. Sheet music examples from America's fledgling popular-song publishing industry include William Taylor's "Our Flag: A National Song" (New York, 1829), W. Nash's "The American Flag" (Baltimore, 1835), and George F. Cole's "Our Country's Flag: A New National Song" (Baltimore, 1836). In the latter, allegiance to the flag is necessary and absolute:

Honor to those who its fame would save,
To its foeman's ranks the felon's grave

The music of these patriotic songs, in settings for piano and solo voice, is generally marchlike and sometimes even martial in character. Melodic lines tend to be uncomplicated but follow chordal arpeggios to generate excitement and to suggest the valveless bugle of military music. Piano accompaniments are simple and chordal beneath the melody but take on more aggressive and repetitive figures in introductions and interludes. These songs share lyrical content and imagery too. Several include cheers such as "Huzzah!" and refer to the flag's "stars and stripes." Also of note are their published dedications, almost invariably to specific military men or, in the case of Nash's song, "To the Officers of the United States Navy."

Even more abundant in the early 19th century are flag-centered song lyrics published without music in modest collections called songsters or their single-sheet equivalents, broadsides. Songsters and broadsides were small-format and cheaply printed song lyrics, a common means of commercially disseminating new and already popular songs. The tunes that accompanied the printed lyrics were usually familiar airs, often identified by name at the top of each page, but the structural consistency and straightforwardness of the verses also allowed consumers to adapt whatever melodies they knew to the printed words. That the text of William Taylor's "Our Flag" appears in the famous *Forget-Me-Not Songster* (New York, 1847) reveals the enduring popularity of this "national song" that had been printed as sheet music 18 years earlier. Other flag songs displayed comparable staying power. "The Banner of Freedom High Floated and Unfurl'd," sung to the tune of "Ye Tars of Columbia," first appeared in a songster entitled *The Columbian Naval Melody* (Boston, 1813) and was published again two decades later in *The American Naval and Patriotic Songster* (Baltimore, 1834). Still others were more fleeting, tied to specific people and events that did not remain long in the popular imagination. "The American Flag and Harrison" is found in *The Harrison Medal Minstrel, Comprising a Collection of the Most Popular and Patriotic Songs* (Philadelphia, 1840). The entire songster is dedicated to the military service of William Henry Harrison and to his victorious presidential campaign of that year. Harrison died of pneumonia in 1841, just 31 days into his presidency; "The American Flag and Harrison" was never reissued.

The Star-Spangled Banner

By far the most popular song of the American flag in the early 19th century was "The Star-Spangled Banner," a song copiously printed and widely circulated more than a century before it became the nation's official anthem. Francis Scott Key, a lawyer and poet from Frederick County, Maryland, wrote the now-familiar words as a poem entitled "The Defence of Fort M'Henry" in 1814. Detained aboard a British ship he had boarded in the Patapsco River while attempting to negotiate the release of his friend, Dr. William Beanes, Key helplessly witnessed the British bombardment of Fort McHenry during the Battle of Baltimore. His poem was printed with its original title one week later, on September 21, 1814, by the *Baltimore American and Commercial Daily*. Shortly thereafter, Key approached Thomas Carr, who ran a successful music-publishing and retail business in Baltimore with his brother. Carr adapted Key's text to a popular tune called "The Anacreontic Song," composed a simple piano accompaniment in two-voice counterpoint and a flute part that doubled the melody, and published the first sheet music edition of "The Star-Spangled Banner" in late 1814.

Composed by British organist John Stafford Smith, the Anacreontic melody was originally paired with words by Ralph Tomlinson and associated with the Anacreontic Society, a musicians' club in London. The famously awkward tune made its way across the Atlantic in the 18th century and had become popular in the colonies, particularly as a vehicle for new, parodic words. In his careful study of the song's complicated history, Marc Ferris tallies an astonishing 84 settings of the Anacreontic melody in America before 1820 (2014, 19). In fact, Francis Scott Key had already used the tune once before, for his 1805 poem "When the Warrior Returns." In this earlier work, written to honor U.S. naval heroes of the First Barbary War in North Africa, Key had employed the descriptor "star spangled" to describe the flag, its metaphorical light overpowering the crescent of the Tripolitanian banner:

In the conflict resistless, each toil they endured,
'Til their foes fled dismayed from the war's desolation:
And pale beamed the Crescent, its splendor obscured
By the light of the Star Spangled flag of our nation.
Where each radiant star gleamed a meteor of war,
And the turbaned heads bowed to its terrible glare.

Key's "The Defence of Fort M'Henry," transformed into "The Star-Spangled Banner" by Thomas Carr, uses some of the same poetic devices he had employed in "When the Warrior Returns." In both poems the flag's radiance, with special emphasis on its stars, symbolizes power, and in both poems military power is equated with higher moral ideals. But whereas Key's earlier poem refers to the flag only in the third of its five verses, his 1814 text employs flag symbolism throughout its prominent opening verse (the one sung today) and carries it over into the second. Here the flag's resilience, representing that of the nation, is evoked through images of light. Just as the sun rises on a new day, so does the flag endure:

What is that which the breeze, o'er the towering steep,
As it fitfully blows, half conceals, half discloses?
Now it catches the gleam of the morning's first beam,
In full glory reflected now shines in the stream:
'Tis the star-spangled banner, O long may it wave
O'er the land of the free and the home of the brave

Although the third and fourth verses veer away from evocations of the flag and its symbolic power, Key returns to the flag at the end of each remaining verse with a version of the following refrain (which is, in fact, a chorus):

And the star-spangled banner in triumph shall wave
O'er the land of the free and the home of the brave.

The song's immediate success after its 1814 publication, its startlingly rapid spread throughout the young nation, and its unusually durable popularity over many decades seem to have contributed significantly to the rise of the flag as a national emblem and to the proliferation of other flag songs during the rest of the 19th century and into the 20th. The phrase "star-spangled banner" became widely accepted as a nickname for the flag through the ubiquity of Key's song. New patriotic songsters featuring or even named for "The Star-Spangled Banner" began to appear within just a few years of the song's first printing. The first was *The Diamond Songster* (Baltimore, 1817), the subtitle of which identifies it, somewhat curiously, as a collection of "Scottish, Irish, and National Songs." Another collection featuring the song was *The Star Spangled Banner, Being a Collection of the Best Naval, Martial, Patriotic Songs, Chiefly Written During and in Relation to the Late War*. Published in Wilmington, Delaware, this collection was already in its second edition before the end of 1817.

"The Star-Spangled Banner" prompted scores of imitations and parodies and was treated to many instrumental arrangements. Variation sets for piano were especially common, with noted composer-artists using the beloved melody as the basis for bravura showpieces. Perhaps the earliest instance is W. A. King's "The Star Spangled Banner, Arranged with Introduction and Variations for the Pianoforte with a Grand Finale a la Valce" (New York, 1835). In a sign of the song's growing cultlike status, King performed his showpiece during a concert of music by Haydn, Handel, and Mozart sponsored by the New York Sacred Music Society. Charles Grobe's "The Star-Spangled Banner with Brilliant Variations," Op. 490 (Baltimore, 1854) offers another virtuosic example. A thunderous, fortissimo introduction using nearly the full range of the keyboard but restricted to the diatonic consonance of the key of C major leads to a simple but spirited presentation of the theme, mostly voiced in octaves. There follow three variations that treat the tune and its harmonic underpinning to a variety of textures, and a grand finale brings back the melody in octaves leading to a decisive, if somewhat melodramatic, conclusion. America's most esteemed composers of art music took up the tune, as well. John Knowles Paine, one of America's best composers of orchestral music and the nation's first professor of music (at Harvard), composed a set of "Concert Variations on 'The Star Spangled Banner'" for organ in 1861. Paine's contemporary Dudley Buck, also a highly respected classical composer, is today best remembered for his similar set of organ variations on the patriotic melody, published in 1868.

Civil War Tunes and the Flag

As the country built up to and exploded in civil war just after midcentury, patriotic sentiment intensified on both sides of the conflict. The increasing complexity of the situation is reflected in the diversity of the era's popular music. New songs and new treatments of old ones arose to fill people's need for emotional reinforcement, and the symbolism of the opposing flags took on greater import. In the north, the Stars and Stripes became an emblem of loyalty to the Union. "Stand by the Flag of the Nation" (Cincinnati, 1863), with words by C. C. Butler and music by R. M. Hastings, includes on its cover page the shockingly stark admonition, "If any man attempt to pull down the American flag, shoot him down as a Traitor." The song's second verse reinforces the notion that the flag itself must be preserved, for if it survives, so will the nation.

And tho' the vile traitors have rended
This glorious Union so fair,
Those stars and those stripes still are blended,
Unfurl'd in their majesty there.

Similar adulation for the flag itself as the thing worth fighting for appears in "God Save the Flag of Our Native Land" (Louisville, 1861), which is dedicated to "the Lovers of the Union." Several songs of the war focus on the flag's 34 stars as a powerful symbol of the nation's threatened unity. "The Flag with 34 Stars" (Cincinnati, 1862) makes explicit that "every patriot volunteer" is "battling for our flag, with every stripe and star." The same publisher, A. C. Peters of Cincinnati, produced a set of instrumental variations on this melody under the title "The Bonnie Blue Flag with 34 Stars," credited to composer "U. Nion."

Confederate musicians and publishers, for their part, produced a fascinating assortment of material that expressed the difficulty in letting go of the nation's treasured emblem—and a powerful desire to establish a worthy Southern replacement. J. R. Boullcott's and Ella Clark's "Adieu to the Star Spangled Banner Forever" (New Orleans, 1861) conveys a sincere sadness about leaving the Union and its symbols: "How dear to each heart was the Star Spangled Banner." A more defiant goodbye to the flag of the Union appears in "Farewell to the Star Spangled Banner" (Richmond, VA, ca. 1862), "Respectfully Dedicated to the Army and Navy of the C.S.A." The violently resistant temper of the first verse is chilling in its brutality:

Let tyrants and slaves submissively tremble,
And bow down their necks 'neath the juggernaut car;
But brave men will rise in the strength of a nation,
And cry give me freedom or else give me war.

"Up With the Flag" (Richmond, 1863) takes a less violent tack, exalting the Confederate flag as a "symbol of freedom" and "banner of hope," while "The Star Spangled Cross in the Pure Field of White" (Richmond, VA, 1864) attempts to replace the nation's cherished symbol with a new, modified version.

One of the best-known songs of the Civil War was "The Battle Cry of Freedom" (Chicago, 1862), a recruiting march composed by George F. Root. A native of Massachusetts and prodigious musical talent, Root studied under the renowned hymn composer and music educator Lowell Mason in Boston before spending time in New York. Just before the war, he resettled in Chicago, where his brother owned a thriving publishing company. Root called "The Battle Cry of Freedom" a "rallying song," meant to bolster support for the Union's cause among both abolitionists and anti-secessionists. Its opening line, "Yes, we'll rally 'round the flag, boys," gave rise to an alternate, flag-centered title. In the original sheet music, Root provided another set of lyrics, slightly different from the "rallying song"; he calls this alternate version a "battle song." Here, too, the flag takes center stage in the opening verse, now as a proud emblem of soldiers marching into battle. "We are marching to the field, boys, we're going to the fight," Root proclaims. "And we bear the glorious stars for the Union and the right" equates the American flag—placing special emphasis on the stars as symbols of the states—with both the Union itself and the moral high ground. Both versions of the lyrics, the rallying song and the battle song, reinforce this imagery in their choruses: "Down with the traitor, up with the star." The immense popularity of "The Battle Cry of Freedom" during the war produced a Confederate version under the same title. With new lyrics by William Barnes and published in Macon, Georgia, in 1864, the Confederate adaptation of the song turns Root's rallying cry upside down, replacing the Union flag's imagery with that of the Confederate banner:

> Down with the eagle and up with the cross,
> We'll rally 'round the bonny flag, we'll rally once again.

Postbellum Patriotic Music

George Root's popularity and output continued into the decades following the war. After the destruction of the family's publishing firm in the great Chicago fire of 1871, he concentrated on the composition of church hymns and educational materials but still responded to political and other developments. In the last year of his life (1895), Root composed a large-scale work for soloists and choir, *Our Flag with the Stars and Stripes*. He called it a "patriotic cantata for school and choir," and conceived its dramatic arc as a historical sketch of U.S. history, from the Revolutionary period to the Civil War. This remarkable work, which incorporates Root's earlier Civil War songs "The Battle Cry of Freedom" and "Tramp, Tramp, Tramp," tells the story of the nation through the symbolism of the flag with narration by both Father Time and Uncle Sam. Its opening choral exhortation ("Come! Come! Come! Let us honor our flag today") establishes the mood and the predominant imagery, while a children's choir connects the narrative arc with the life of the personified flag ("Tale of the flag that we love. . . . Freedom has written her story, Into its red, white and blue"). After "Making the Flag" explains its colors and symbolism in a soprano-alto duet, 13 children sing "We Are the Thirteen Stars" and 48 young women proclaim "Oh, We Are Sisters Forty-Eight." A marching chorus ("Salute we our beautiful flag") gives way to a portrait of George Washington leading his men across the Delaware ("While o'er them the bright banner waved"). An extended section on the Civil War, which was still fresh in the nation's collective memory, introduces Lincoln and then moves through a variety of martial, mournful, and prayerful songs. The cantata's finale is a rousing conflation of religion, patriotism, and flag worship entitled "Praise Be to God and Hail to the Flag."

George Root's *Our Flag with the Stars and Stripes* is a truly remarkable work, but its message and mood were not unusual at the time. Still recovering from its greatest crisis, the nation sought to heal the metaphorical wounds of the Civil War with unabashed patriotism, much of it manifesting in the publication of patriotic songbooks for schools and churches. Collections such as *Patriotic Songs for School and Home* (Boston, 1899) and *Songs of Flag and Nation* (New York, 1904) circulated widely. Charles Johnson, editor and compiler of *Songs of the Nation* (New York, 1896), opened his preface by stating plainly that his book "has been prepared in response to a demand for a collection of songs inculcating patriotism, love of country, and devotion to the flag." Francis Scott Key's "The Star-Spangled Banner" appears third in the collection, following "America" and "Hail, Columbia!" *Uncle Sam's School Songs: For Schools, Colleges, Institutes, and the Home Circle* (Chicago, 1897) includes not only "The Star-Spangled Banner" but other flag-focused numbers such as "Flag of Freedom," "Oh! We Love the Flag," "Proud Flag of the Free," "Flag of Our Union Forever," "We'll Stand By the Flag," "A Song for Our Banner," and "Wave On, Thou Banner of the Free."

The Flag in Band Music and Tin Pan Alley

The Civil War had also given rise to brass and concert band music, much of it martial and patriotic in tone, as a primary medium of American popular entertainment. Nearly every unit of both the Union and Confederate forces included some kind of modest brass band, used to recruit and rally troops. After the war's end, these bands continued to play in their home towns, maintaining some of the most popular marches and sentimental ballads of the war in their repertory and thus helping the wounded communities to heal. In time, bands began to professionalize and to grow in size and instrumental diversity, leading to nationally known concert bands led by Patrick Gilmore and John Philip Sousa. After he stepped down from the Marine Corps Band in 1892, Sousa quickly built his band into one of the most sophisticated and beloved entertainment acts of the next 30 years. The Sousa Band, which by 1925 had swelled to include 76 musicians, toured widely and tirelessly. Sousa scholar Paul Bierley has documented more than 15,000 public concerts by the Sousa Band between 1892 and 1931. As a composer, arranger, and concert programmer, Sousa's range was impressively eclectic. A typical performance included operetta overtures, programmatic suites, arrangements of popular ragtime and sentimental songs, operatic arias, symphonic excerpts, and, of course, a strong dose of military marches and other rousingly patriotic material. It was this last category, more than any other, that accounts for Sousa's fame and success and that made him, in Bierley's phrase, "the symbol of an era" (2006, 6).

The piece that launched Sousa's popular success was his most famous composition, "The Stars and Stripes Forever." Composed on Christmas Day, 1896, aboard an ocean liner as Sousa returned home from a European vacation, "The Stars and Stripes Forever" premiered the following May and was an immediate sensation. Its form is that of the standard American military march: a brief introduction followed by four distinctive melodic strains, each repeated. The third strain, designated as the "Trio" for its contrasting key and reduced instrumentation, became the work's most recognizable section. Lesser known today are the lyrics that Sousa wrote for the piece, a paean to the flag and, by extension, the cause of freedom America represented in the national, and increasingly the international, imagination. In the opening strain, Sousa identifies the flag as "The banner of the Western land," positioning the U.S. on the global stage. "The red and white and starry blue, Is freedom's shield and hope." The lyrics of the famous Trio reinforce this notion, recalling language and imagery used in patriotic flag songs since the beginning of the 19th century:

Hurrah for the flag of the free!
May it wave as our standard forever,
The gem of the land and the sea,
The banner of the right.
Let despots remember the day,
When our fathers with mighty endeavor,
Proclaimed as they marched to the fray
That by their might and by their right
It waves forever.

"The Stars and Stripes Forever" has been performed, recorded, adapted, and parodied countless times. A tune that practically every American knows, and recognizes as intrinsically patriotic, it is now an essential thread in the fabric of American culture. In 1987, 90 years after its debut, "The Stars and Stripes Forever" became the official march of the United States by an act of Congress.

The wave of patriotic nationalism that made John Philip Sousa the biggest name in American popular entertainment around the turn of the 20th century also manifested in other arenas. George M. Cohan reshaped popular musical theater and laid the foundation for the "Golden Age of Broadway" with his jingoistic, flag-centered spectacles. Commercial recordings featuring patriotic material sold well, such as popular vocalist Billy Murray's 1906 recording of Cohan's "You're a Grand Old Flag" (released the same year as the song's publication and theatrical debut) and Murray's 1908 recording of Cohan's "Under Any Old Flag at All" (from the show *The Talk of New York*). Around the same time, America's popular songwriting and publishing industry coalesced in a concentrated area of New York City (West 28th Street, between 5th and 6th Avenues) that became known by its nickname, Tin Pan Alley. With this consolidation of the popular-song industry, the songwriters and publishers of Tin Pan Alley were able to respond to, and in some cases establish, cultural trends for the bulk of the nation. Popular songs reflected changing demographics, technological developments, political affairs, fashion and dance trends, and the aggressive patriotism fueled in part by the Spanish-American War of 1898, the United States' subsequent emergence as a world power, and its involvement in World War I.

Among the hundreds of patriotic songs churned out by Tin Pan Alley hit makers during this period, a significant percentage continued to seize upon the flag as the ultimate symbol of American pride, unity, and power. Even those songs that made no reference to the flag in their content often featured flag imagery on the cover of the sheet music. Charles K. Harris, the composer often credited with helping to establish Tin Pan Alley, wrote "There Is No Flag Like the Red, White and Blue" (Milwaukee, 1898) and republished its lyrics in *Chas. K. Harris' Complete Songster* (New York, 1903). In 1913, Andrew Dinegan and Hugo Hamlin published "Decoration Day," its cover featuring an old Union veteran embracing a young army cadet, who stands in salute, the draped American flag in the background. One of the most elaborate celebrations of the flag in Tin Pan Alley song was E. T. Paull's "The Triumphant Banner," its cover rendered in the vivid color and detailed design for which Paull's publishing company was known.

Flag Songs from the World Wars

America's entry into World War I in 1917 produced a fresh wave of patriotic songs, many of which employed the flag as a symbol of American military determination and justice. The development had even been anticipated in popular song one year earlier with Edwin Skedden's and Katherine Pike's "Old Glory (A Song of Preparedness)." Its lyrics profess the need for American military might, but with an eye toward a pacifist solution. With the commitment of American troops to the European conflict, the tenor of published popular song shifted to enthusiastic support of the troops and the families they left behind. The cover of Laura O'Neal's "The Stars and Stripes" (Chicago, 1919) shows an American infantryman, arm extended and rifle by his side, bidding farewell to his wife and idyllic rural home. The artwork of "Our Banner" (Chicago, 1918) portrays a soldier in combative stance, rifle and bayonet protruding, against a stylized arrangement of stars and stripes that reinforce the flag's metaphorical radiance. "We'll Carry the Star Spangled Banner thru the Trenches" by Daisy Erd—identified on the cover as a chief yeoman of the U.S. Naval Reserve Force—depicts in its graphic design a flag-waving Uncle Sam with a platoon of American infantrymen marching in step behind him.

The economic boom of the Roaring Twenties followed immediately by the sharp downturn of the Great Depression produced a decline in American patriotic entertainment and, with it, musical representations of the flag. "The Star-Spangled Banner" retained its popularity, particularly after becoming the nation's official anthem in 1931. Sousa's "The Stars and Stripes Forever" also continued to be heard in concert halls, parades, and other celebrations, but such turn-of-the-century patriotism seemed nostalgic, trite, even naïve to an American generation that had endured the "war to end all wars" and the Great Depression.

With the outbreak of World War II, Americans once again had reason to rally around the flag and other patriotic symbols as young men and women marched off to military service around the globe. In this era, however, references to the flag in patriotic popular song are less numerous, less powerful, and less idealistic. Fred Coots's "Goodbye Momma (I'm Off to Yokohama)" (New York, 1941), a jaunty, somewhat comical number popular near the beginning of the war, seems almost sarcastic when its protagonist claims he's off to fight "for my country, my flag and you." The combination of lively music and lines such as "soon have those Japs right down on their Japa-knees" make patriotic allusions to the flag difficult to take seriously. Other songs were more resolute and sincere in their calls to arms, such as "Let's Put New Glory in Old Glory." Created as a propaganda machine in 1942, the U.S. Office of War Information produced radio shows and films to promote the American war cause. It established guidelines for the composition of "freedom songs" to "wave the flag and shout Hallelujah for all conquered and oppressed peoples" (Smith 2003, 69) The powerful and lasting image of American soldiers planting the flag atop Iwo Jima's Mount Suribachi in February 1945, one of the most immediately recognizable images from the war and a symbol of American determination and victory in the Pacific, reignited interest in the symbolism of the flag. Two popular songs commemorated the event and helped to enshrine the image: "Stars and Stripes on Iwo Jima" by Bob Wills and Cliff Johnsen—the Sons of the Pioneers' recording of which recording reached no. 4 on the *Juke Box* folk chart—and "There's a New Flag on Iwo Jima" by Jimmy McHugh, popularized in a recording by Eddie Cantor.

Flag Music in the Vietnam Era

With the rise of rhythm and blues, country and western, the "big singers" like Frank Sinatra and Ella Fitzgerald, and eventually rock and roll in the immediate postwar era, patriotic songs once again receded out of mainstream popular entertainment. In the civil rights and Vietnam War era, the flag reappeared in American popular music, now often wielded to express dissent with American political and military action. Jimi Hendrix's now legendary rendition of "The Star-Spangled Banner" at Woodstock in 1969 (and in other venues before and after) turned the notion of the flag as a rallying symbol of American loyalty inside out. In Hendrix's wordless performance, played as a virtuoso on his highly amplified and distorted Fender Stratocaster guitar, the violence of the song's original imagery is brought to life, its "bombs bursting in air" mutating into the sounds of air raid alarms and machine guns. But more than the performance's musical surface features, the Hendrix version of "The Star-Spangled Banner" was a milestone for its attitude, its willingness to take a nearly-200-year-old symbol of American unity and use it to evoke the horrors of the Vietnam War and social injustices here at home (Clague 2014).

Allusions to the flag in popular-song content during the protest era supported both sides of the national debates and culture wars of the time. On his eponymous debut album released in 1971, folk singer–songwriter John Prine lambasted the self-righteous, empty symbolism of the flag with characteristically sardonic humor in his antiwar song "Your Flag Decal Won't Get You into Heaven Anymore." Much soberer in tone is the remarkable "Day for Decision" by Johnny Sea, the opening track on a concept album of the same name released in 1966. Sea's recited text outlines a cynical picture of American shame and self-loathing, in which "old glory has never fallen so close to earth." Against a backdrop of bleak string pizzicato, Sea locates the sources of America's real problems at home, not in Asia. The mood of the track changes to one of determination and resilience as the background music evolves into a choral rendition of "America the Beautiful." Likewise, the entire album moves through wide-ranging and heavy-handed moods, culminating in a jingoistic recitation of "The Star-Spangled Banner" in the album's final track.

Country songs of the Vietnam era appealed to the genre's largely patriotic fan base, using images and associations comparable to those wielded by popular-song composers during World War II, including the flag. "Keep the Flag Flying," composed by hit songwriter Cecil Null, was recorded and released by country star Johnny Wright in late 1965 as a follow-up to his highly successful "Hello Vietnam" (written by Tom T. Hall). "Keep the Flag Flying" tells the tragic story of a fallen U.S. soldier from the perspective of his comrade and brother; the song's chorus employs flag symbolism to express steadfast American optimism and purpose: "Keep the flag flying, Keep freedom from dying." By the end of the decade, the antiwar and counterculture movements reached their peaks, and country music resorted to traditional patriotic images to represent old-fashioned American values under attack. One notoriously complex example is Merle Haggard's "Okie from Muskogee," released in September 1969. Although the sincerity of the song's sentiment has been questioned (and Haggard himself later insisted that he wrote it as a joke), on its surface the song proudly distinguishes those who "still wave Old Glory down at the courthouse" from the "hippies out in San Francisco" who burn draft cards and indulge in drug use and free sex.

Such explicit lyrical references to the flag were relatively rare in American popular music of the time, but its image became commonplace on album covers, in stage designs, and on artists' clothing. Jefferson Airplane's *Volunteers* (1969) and Sly and the Family Stone's *There's a Riot Going On* (1971) both feature prominent American flags on their album covers, clearly meant to invoke a different, more questioning, brand of symbolic patriotism. In the wake of the Watergate scandal, Johnny Cash released his album *Ragged Old Flag* in 1974. A politically conscious album, its title track offers a stunning, mostly spoken-word history of the flag that includes references to Washington crossing the Delaware, Francis Scott Key, the Battle of New Orleans, Civil War generals, and World War I's Flanders Field, before taking aim directly at Nixon and his conspirators.

Even in the post–Vietnam era, the symbolism of the flag remained powerful in evoking the nationwide angst of that conflict. Released in 1984, Bruce Springsteen's *Born in the U.S.A.* was among the most commercially and critically successful pop records of the decade. The album reflects on the devastating effects of the Vietnam War on Americans generally and veterans in particular. The image on its cover, shot by the famous photographer Annie Leibovitz, offers a rear-end view of Springsteen as working-class hero in faded jeans and white T-shirt, against a large backdrop of the flag's red and white stripes. In a *Rolling Stone* interview shortly after the album's release, Springsteen denied that the shot's composition was intended to suggest anything disrespectful but emphasized that "the flag is a powerful image" (Loder 1984).

The Flag in Contemporary Popular Music

In contemporary popular music, the flag reappears routinely in song and image, its meaning varying widely and articulated entirely by context. Its use in hip-hop imagery is widespread, where it often suggests an abstract military-economic power base against which American minorities continually struggle. Early hip-hop rapper from Harlem 2 Black 2 Strong and his group, MMG, featured a burning flag on the cover of the provocative 1990 album, *Burn Baby Burn*. The title track and its associated music video reject the relevance of the flag's symbolism for African Americans in the strongest terms. Rage Against the Machine, a politically active rock band from Los Angeles whose style mixes elements of punk, heavy metal, and hip-hop, drew sharp criticism for burning an American flag on stage during their 1999 performance at Woodstock. This flag burning was cited as one of many factors that induced widespread crowd violence at the notorious event (McIver 2014, 129–30). The cover of *Stankonia*, a 2000 release by influential Atlanta hip-hop duo Outkast, features a black-and-white version of the American flag, suggesting a different America, economically and socially oppressed, out of the mainstream. The group continued to use the symbol as part of its stage design in live performances as late as 2014.

In 2013, rapper Lil Wayne was shooting a music video in New Orleans for his song "God Bless Amerika" when an onlooker captured him stepping on the American flag. The cell phone video went viral. In the context of the song's lyrics, Lil Wayne's physical debasement of the flag was assumed by many to be deliberate. The artist quickly took to social media to vindicate himself, saying that his walking on the flag was an unfortunate accident. "I didn't step on the flag on purpose," he proclaimed on Twitter. Later, on Facebook, he offered a more detailed explanation and reassured his audience that "it was never my intention to desecrate the flag of the United States of America" (Holpuch 2013). Other contemporary artists, however, are more deliberate in their use or rejection of the flag. Pop singer–songwriter Lana Del Ray makes abundant use of nostalgic American imagery in her songs, videos, and stage shows. In a July 2017 interview for *Pitchfork*, however, she explained that she would no longer use the American flag as a backdrop to her stage performances, at least not in the era of President Donald Trump. "I definitely changed my visuals on my tour videos," she said. "I'm not going to have the American flag waving while I'm singing 'Born to Die.' It's not going to happen" (Frank 2017). While Del Ray had taken advantage of the flag's rich symbolism and nostalgia in her previous work, she did not want to run the risk of it being misconstrued as a show of support for the Trump administration.

Other artists, particularly in mainstream country music, have reclaimed the flag as a symbol of American patriotic pride. One of the most outspoken examples came from country rock singer Charlie Daniels, whose career has engaged openly with politics occasionally over its 50-year span. In direct response to the terrorist attacks of September 11, 2001, Daniels wrote "This Ain't No Rag, It's a Flag" and released it as a bonus track on his *Live!* album to much attention. He was scheduled to perform the song at a country music festival in Nashville in October of that year but pulled out when the executives at Country Music Television asked him to soften the lyrics' militantly anti-terrorist rhetoric.

Having established himself as a hip-hop artist in the 1990s, Detroit's Kid Rock has moved increasingly toward the kind of Southern rock ethos pioneered by Daniels and others in the 1970s. Kid Rock's ongoing controversies have revolved around his complex relationship with African American and Southern white culture, his outspoken right-wing political views, and his repeated use of both the U.S. and Confederate flags as symbols. In 2004, he performed during the Super Bowl halftime show wearing a Stars and Stripes poncho. A mild dustup ensued—largely overshadowed by Janet Jackson's now-infamous "wardrobe malfunction" during the same show—when U.S. senator and former Georgia governor Zell Miller called Kid Rock an "ignoramus with his pointed head stuck up through the hole he had cut in the flag of the United States of America." Miller decried Kid Rock's disrespectful use of the flag to which Americans pledge allegiance and use to drape over the coffins of men and women who sacrifice their lives in military service. Miller declared that the musician should be "tarred and feathered and ridden out of this country on a rail" (de Sola 2004). More recently it was Kid Rock on the offensive, speaking harshly of Colin Kaepernick and other NFL players who kneeled during pregame performances of the national anthem to protest institutional racism. During a concert in Grand Rapids, Michigan, in September 2017, Kid Rock interrupted the music to speak against the Ku Klux Klan and other racist groups, while also lashing out at Kaepernick and the Black Lives Matter movement. Wearing a U.S. flag–inspired scarf and with a real flag mounted beside his podium (designed to look like a presidential podium), Kid Rock shouted, "If you want to take a knee or sit during our 'Star-Spangled Banner,' call me a racist 'cause I'm not PC and think you have to remind me that black lives matter" (Champion 2017). He ended the concert with a performance of his 2010 hit "Born Free" against the backdrop of a massive U.S. flag unfurled behind the stage.

What these episodes, along with those surrounding Lil Wayne, Lana Del Ray, Charlie Daniels, and others reveal is that the ability of the flag to elicit a wide range of powerful emotional responses has not diminished since Francis Scott Key wrote his "The Defence of Fort M'Henry" in 1814. On the contrary, this power seems only to have intensified, its use by popular entertainers both a cause and a symptom of the flag's symbolic strength. In our era of increased political and social divisiveness, the flag is a touch point, an evocation of American pride and shame, of the country's glorious but problematic history. Since the social and political upheavals of the Vietnam era, the flag has relinquished its unified, shared meaning but lost none of its power. Indeed, as perhaps the most potent symbol of America's complicated past and equally complicated future, musicians will certainly continue to wield the flag's power in ways we can scarcely predict.

Further Reading

Bierley, Paul Edmund. 2006. *The Incredible Band of John Philip Sousa*. Urbana, IL: University of Illinois Press.

Champion, Brandon. 2017. "Kid Rock Gets Political During Electric Show at Van Andel Arena." MLive. Last modified September 7. http://www.mlive.com/news/grand-rapids/index.ssf/2017/09/kid_rock_gets_political_during.html

Clague, Mark. 2014. "'This is America': Jimi Hendrix's Star Spangled Banner Journey as Psychedelic Citizenship." *Journal of the Society for American Music* 8:435–478.

Darnton, Charles. 1906. " 'George Washington, Jr.,' a Red-White-and-Blue Success." *The Evening World's Home Magazine*, February 15.

De Sola, David. 2004. "The Politics of Music." CNN.com, August 30. http://www.cnn.com/2004/ALLPOLITICS/08/29/gop.music/index.html

Ferris, Marc. 2014. *Star-Spangled Banner: The Unlikely Story of America's National Anthem.* Baltimore: Johns Hopkins University Press.

Frank, Alex. 2017. "Life, Liberty, and the Pursuit of Happiness: A Conversation with Lana Del Rey." *Pitchfork*, July 19.

Holpuch, Amanda. 2013. "Lil Wayne Defends Trampling on American Flag during Music Video Shoot." *The Guardian*, June 18.

Loder, Kurt. 1984. "The *Rolling Stone* Interview: Bruce Springsteen on 'Born in the U.S.A.' " *Rolling Stone*, December 6.

McCabe, John. 1973. *George M. Cohan: The Man Who Owned Broadway*. New York: Doubleday.

McIver, Joel. 2014. *Know Your Enemy: The Story of Rage Against the Machine*. London: Omnibus Press.

Metcalfe, James. 1906. "George Washington, Jr." *Life Magazine*, March 1.

Smith, Kathleen E. R. 2003. *God Bless America: Tin Pan Alley Goes to War*. Lexington: University Press of Kentucky.

Watkins, Glenn. 2003. *Proof Through the Night: Music and the Great War*. Berkeley: University of California Press.

The Flag in American Journalism

Larry L. Burriss

The history, lore, and mythology of the American flag easily can be traced back to the earliest days of the republic. But like the nation itself, the history, lore, and mythology of the flag continue to change and evolve, often through the agency of the news media. This chapter looks at four stories that, in their own way, refuse to die—or perhaps, on a more positive note, continue in their own way to live in the collective memory and life of the citizens whom the flag represents.

A discussion of the flag on Iwo Jima reviews the iconic story (and image) from one of World War II's deadliest battles, fought over one of the smallest Pacific islands. But just which flag and picture are we actually talking about?

The story of Robert Heft has, in some ways, had more of an impact on the American flag than any other person in United States history. How did a 17-year-old create the nation's longest-serving flag design?

Texas v. Johnson (1989), the original flag-burning case (although not the original flag desecration case), offers an example of how a Vietnam-era Supreme Court decision still reverberates through society. But the issue is not as clear cut as proponents and opponents would have us believe. What exactly is "desecration"?

The final discussion in this essay examines the story of the flags on astronaut uniforms and flags on the moon in light of numerous conspiracy theories about the "supposed" moon landings. Are there really flags on the moon, or are they actually on a soundstage somewhere?

The Flag on Iwo Jima

On February 23, 1945, Associated Press photographer Joe Rosenthal took one of the most iconic images of World War II: five U.S. marines and a U.S. Navy corpsman raising a large American flag atop Mount Suribachi (sometimes misspelled Surabachi), a 528-foot-high volcanic mountain at the southwestern tip of Iwo Jima, an eight-square-mile island in the northwest Pacific Ocean. The image won a Pulitzer Prize, was the inspiration for a memorial in Arlington National Cemetery and for a postage stamp . . . and more than 70 years later, is still the center of controversy and confusion.

Because Mount Suribachi gave the Japanese a commanding view of American landing positions during the invasion of Iwo Jima, it was essential to capture it. On

February 23, 1945, 1st. Lt. Harold G. Schrier, the executive officer for Easy Company, 2nd Battalion, 28th Marine Regiment, 5th Marine Division, was told by his battalion commander, Lt. Col. Chandler W. Johnson, to assault the mountain. He was also given a 28-by-54-inch American flag that had been brought to Iwo Jima by the battalion adjutant, 1st. Lt. George G. Wells, to place at the top of the crater.

The 40-man Marine patrol reached the top at about 10:00 a.m. and spent 15–20 minutes clearing Japanese defenders from their hidden positions. With the group was a photographer for *Leatherneck* magazine, S.Sgt. Louis R. "Lou" Lowery.

Members of the patrol found a water pipe, attached the flag to it, and raised it at 10:20 a.m. A few minutes later, a Japanese officer emerged from hiding and tried to cut the flag down with his sword. He was shot and killed a few yards from the flag.

Coincidently, navy secretary James Forrestal and marine Lt. Gen. Holland Smith, overall invasion commander, were at that moment on their way ashore.

Shortly afterward, more marines began to climb the mountain, one of whom was carrying a four-by-eight-foot flag that had been on one of the landing ships assigned to the invasion, *LST-779*. Three photographers were with the marines: Rosenthal, motion picture photographer Sgt. Bill Genaust, and another still photographer, PFC. Bob Campbell.

Part of the confusion stems from which of three photographs that Rosenthal took of the flag raising on that day is the "real" picture:

> Associated Press photographer, Joe Rosenthal, made three photographs atop Suribachi, a Japanese observation post on the island of Iwo Jima during World War II. His first picture became the most reproduced photograph in history and won for him a Pulitzer Prize. His third photograph became the source of accusations that the first picture had been set-up.
>
> The first picture is the image most remembered. It shows six soldiers [marines] erecting a large, American flag on a long, diagonally slanted flagpole. Rosenthal's third shot shows 18 soldiers smiling and waving for the camera under that same flag. (Lester 2017)

The second photograph Rosenthal took shows the first flag being lowered while the second flag is anchored in the ground. The third photograph shows a group of Marines posing in front of the second flag.

Back with the invasion ships, Forrestal asked that the first flag be returned to him as a keepsake. Smith, however, thought the flag should stay with his unit, although he apparently intended to give the second flag to the secretary. Both flags were later given to the National Museum of the Marine Corps in Quantico, Virginia, thus thwarting both Forrestal and Smith.

In fact, Rosenthal barely got the photograph. Using a Speed Graphic set to a shutter speed of 1/400 of a second and an f-stop between f/8 and f/11, he was trying to find a good vantage point when he saw the flag being raised:

> Out of the corner of my eye, I had seen the men start the flag up. I swung my camera and shot the scene. That is how the picture was taken, and when you take a picture like that, you don't come away saying you got a great shot. You don't know. (Rosenthal [1955] 2017)

After the flag raising, Rosenthal asked the marines to pose for a group photograph, which has been described as a "gung ho" shot. This photograph led to controversy and unfairly tarnished both Rosenthal's reputation and the iconic photograph itself.

Rosenthal, who was unsure of the image he had captured, sent the film to Guam for processing, and from there, the most famous photograph in the war was transmitted to New York City for distribution to Associated Press newspapers across the country. *The New York Times* ran a cropped version of the photograph on the front page of the Sunday, February 25, 1945, edition, below the headline, across columns five through seven.

Rosenthal soon returned to Guam. Before he had seen either of the photographs, he talked with another correspondent who remarked on how great the photograph (flag raising) was and asked if it had been staged. Apparently thinking his interrogator was referring to the "gung ho" photograph, Rosenthal replied "Sure." A third person present overheard the conversation and assumed Rosenthal's comment referred to the flag photograph. Word subsequently circulated in both print and broadcast media that Rosenthal had staged the flag-raising photograph, and he was repeatedly criticized to the point that some people called for his Pulitzer Prize to be revoked (Hariman 2002).

Fortunately, Rosenthal was not the only photographer on the scene. Sgt. William Genaust, standing almost shoulder-to-shoulder with Rosenthal, shot a motion picture film of the flag raising, which contains three sequences: preparations for raising the flag, the flag raising itself, and the "gung ho" scene. Genaust's film clearly shows the flag raising was not staged.

Despite the controversies, the image has taken on a life of its own: It was reproduced on 3.5 million posters printed for the seventh war bond drive. It was the subject of two United States postage stamps (in 1945 and 1995). It was featured in a 1949 film, *Sands of Iwo Jima*, in which three of the surviving marines (Ira Hayes, Rene Gagnon, and Harold Schultz) made cameo appearances. It has been emulated in Lego blocks and Etch A Sketch. Additionally, it has been the subject of numerous parodies, including the 2015 Syfy television movie *Sharknado3: Oh Hell No!*

Robert Heft

Any detailed story of the American flag will, of course, include references to the very first American flag, the origins of which have become shrouded in myth and speculation.

But there is no doubt or controversy about who designed the 27th version of the Stars and Stripes, which has flown across America since 1960, when Hawaii became the 50th state. That person is Robert Heft.

Heft was a junior at Lancaster High School in Ohio in 1958 when it became obvious two new states would be added to the union, thus necessitating a replacement for the 48-star flag that had been in use since New Mexico and Arizona were admitted in 1912. Redesigning the flag became a project for teacher Stanley Pratt's history class.

Over the course of 12 hours in his grandparent's living room over a weekend, Heft first cut up a 48-star flag, for which his mother said he was being disrespectful. He then used $2.87 of supplies (blue cloth and white adhesive material) to make 100 hand-cut stars (50 on each side), placed in nine alternating rows of 6 stars and 5 stars. Finally, using his mother's Singer sewing machine and an iron, he attached the stars to the field and the field to the remnants of the stripes.

Heft took the flag to school, but the response from his teacher was less than enthusiastic:

> I had my flag on the teacher's desk.
>
> The teacher said, "What's this thing on my desk?"
>
> And so I got up and I approached the desk and my knees were knocking.
>
> He said, "Why you got too many stars? You don't even know how many states we have."
>
> And he gave me a grade of a B-minus. Now a B-minus ain't that bad of a grade. However, a friend of mine, Jim, he'd picked up five leaves off the ground—he's taping these leaves down to the notebook and labeling them elm, hickory, maple—and the teacher gave him the grade of an A.
>
> I was really—I was upset.
>
> The teacher said "if you don't like the grade, get it accepted in Washington. Then come back and see me. I might consider changing the grade." (StoryCorps 2009)

Accepting his teacher's challenge, Heft wrote 21 letters and made 18 telephone calls to the White House. He eventually sent the actual flag to Rep. Walter Moeller, asking him to keep it until a 50-star flag was needed. Moeller later presented the flag to the four-member congressional committee appointed to screen designs for the new flag, and President Eisenhower then made the final selection.

Later, while at work as a draftsman, Heft received a personal call from President Eisenhower. He went to Washington, D.C., on July 4 for the official adoption of the flag.

It should be noted of the 1,500 designs sent to President Eisenhower, at least 3 were identical to Heft's. In addition, Secretary of the Army Wilbur M. Brucker sent several designs to Secretary of Defense Neil H. McElroy, which also included designs identical to Heft's.

As for the grade, Heft stated the following:

> And so I have the grade book. It's encased in plastic; it's kept in a bank.
>
> My teacher, he said "I guess if it's good enough for Washington, it's good enough for me. I hereby change the grade to an A." (StoryCorps 2009)

More than 1,500 designs had been submitted for review, but with Executive Order No. 10834, on August 21, 1959, Eisenhower made Heft's flag design the official flag of the United States.

In 2010, Frederick N. Rasmussen, a reporter for *The Baltimore Sun*, described the introduction of the new flag 50 years earlier:

> By presidential order, [Secretary of the Interior Fred A.] Seaton was selected to . . . rais[e] the new 50-star flag in a ceremony scheduled for 12:01 a.m. July 4, 1960.

> An estimated 40,000 spectators jammed the grounds of the historic fort where 146 years earlier, Mary Pickersgill's original star-spangled banner had flown over Fort McHenry during the British attack in 1814, to witness the raising of the 50-star flag on an 87-foot flagpole.
>
> A red rocket soared high over the fort to announce the first appearance in the world of the new flag. At one minute past midnight, it rose to the top of the flagstaff and unfurled itself in a stiff breeze that blew up the Patapsco River.
>
> The crowd broke into singing "The Star-Spangled Banner" under the direction of Camille Elias, a secretary in the National Park Service's Washington headquarters. As soon as the last note of the song had ended, four Army 105-mm howitzers placed along the Patapsco shoreline roared out a 50-gun salute. (Rasmussen 2010)

Heft's flag has flown over every state capital and over 88 American embassies.

A few weeks after the class project, Heft designed a 51-star flag, with six alternating rows of 9 and 8 stars. If the flag is later adopted in the event of the awarding of statehood to a 51st state, Heft will be the only person in U.S. history to have designed two American flags.

> "I never thought when I designed the flag that it would outlast the 48-star flag," said Heft, who later became a teacher and the mayor of Napoleon, Ohio, for seven terms. "I think of all the things it stood for in the past, the things we've done as a nation that we're proud of. It's not a perfect country, but where else would I like to live?" (Rasmussen 2010)

Heft, who was born January 19, 1942, died on December 12, 2009, at age 67, in Saginaw, Michigan. He is buried in Saginaw's Holy Cross Lutheran Cemetery

Flag Desecration

Perhaps no issue in society or politics is as divisive and controversial as burning the American flag, an action that individuals alternatively regard as either unmitigated desecration or symbolic expression of constitutionally protected speech. This dichotomy of desecration or expression has informed much of the debate about flag burning.

Throughout history, symbols including flags have been imbued with mystical meanings. Early cave paintings suggest a belief that if the picture of an animal was "killed," the hunt for the real animal would be successful. Some cultures believe that injuring an effigy will also injure the subject of the effigy. Similarly, some people believe defacing a flag is somehow injurious to the country the flag represents.

Even those who do not believe that the flag embodies the country may still think that defacing the flag is showing disrespect to both the flag and the country that it represents. Then there are those who believe that the flag does represent the country but that desecration is in itself a symbolic act that does no actual damage. Finally, there are those who see flag desecration as an act actually represented by the flag: the flag represents a commitment to free speech, no matter how offensive. Thousands of people have died to protect the right to speech and self-expression, and desecration is in itself an act protected by the ideals the flag represents.

As might be expected, this continuum from harm to no harm has numerous variations and adherents. This naturally leads to the question, Should flag burning as an act of desecration be allowed? And if not, what should be the penalty for such acts? Then comes the follow-up question: Who has the authority to answer these questions and apply the answer on a national level?

In the United States, the Supreme Court is tasked with providing ultimate answers to questions and controversies. Because the court only deals with "live" controversies, abstract legal theory and philosophy have little impact on court decisions, which often can be reduced to simple yes-or-no questions and answers and are called "court opinions" and become the law of the land.

Court decisions generally follow precedents based on past decisions. Precedent tells us that speech on public policy issues are the most protected form of speech. So the question is, Since burning the flag is a symbolic act, is symbolic speech protected? And if it is, is desecrating a flag a form of symbolic speech protected by the First Amendment?

In some respects, the First Amendment is very clear: "Congress shall make no law . . . abridging the freedom of speech, or of the press." These words apply to spoken and printed words. Obviously, these "strict constructionist" or "original meaning" theories have been expanded to include radio and television, commercial speech, and the Internet. These forms of media are, nevertheless, forms of printed and spoken words.

But what about forms of communication such as protests and demonstrations, arm bands, and actions that have no clear spoken or printed form? Are these also forms of "speech" protected by the First Amendment? If not, then obviously flag burning would not be protected speech. But if these actions are protected, do they rise to the level of discourse involving discussion of public policy issues? Again, a simple yes-or-no answer would decide the fate of flag desecration.

For years, the court skirted the issue of "symbolic speech," releasing opinions that touched on nonspeech and nonpress issues but ruling on nonspeech grounds. In *Tinker v. Des Moines Independent School District* (1969), the court overturned the school suspension of students who had worn black armbands to school to protest the war in Vietnam. However, in issuing its decision, the court was more concerned with the *result* of the symbolic speech than with symbolic speech itself:

> They neither interrupted school activities nor sought to intrude in the school affairs or the lives of others. They caused discussion outside of the classrooms, but no interference with work and no disorder. In the circumstances, our Constitution does not permit officials of the State to deny their form of expression.

In *United States v. O'Brien* (1968), David Paul O'Brien was arrested and convicted for burning his draft card. In upholding the conviction, the court ruled that destruction of the card was a significant interference with government operations, thus negating any free speech interest O'Brien asserted:

> Both the governmental interest and the operation of the 1965 Amendment are limited to the noncommunicative aspect of O'Brien's conduct. The governmental interest and

> the scope of the 1965 Amendment [to the Universal Military Training and Service Act of 1948] are limited to preventing harm to the smooth and efficient functioning of the Selective Service System. When O'Brien deliberately rendered unavailable his registration certificate, he willfully frustrated this governmental interest. For this noncommunicative impact of his conduct, and for nothing else, he was convicted.

Not until the flag-burning case *Texas v. Johnson* (1989) did the court finally rule on the constitutionality of symbolic speech as speech. This case stemmed from an incident at the 1984 Republican National Convention in Dallas, during which Gregory Lee Johnson, a member of the Revolutionary Communist Youth Brigade, set an American flag on fire. A witness, Daniel E. Walker, retrieved the remnants of the flag and buried them in his backyard, following military protocols for properly disposing of an American flag.

Johnson was arrested and convicted under a 1989 Texas law prohibiting the desecration of a venerated object. He was sentenced to one year in prison and fined $2,000. The Texas Court of Criminal Appeals, however, overturned the conviction, ruling that Johnson's actions were symbolic speech and protected by the First Amendment. The court also said Johnson's actions did not cause a breach of the peace. Texas then appealed to the United States Supreme Court, which in 1989 issued a controversial five-to-four decision overturning Johnson's conviction.

The court said that the First Amendment protects "symbolic speech." Interestingly, the Court relied on a 1931 flag decision, *Stromberg v. California*, which said that display of a red flag was a form of protected speech. Texas had already conceded Johnson's actions were expressive conduct. The state's argument, however, that there was a compelling state interest in preserving the flag, that O'Brien's conduct was unrelated to the speech, and that the First Amendment was not therefore implicated.

As to the claim that the flag needed special protection, the court said there were neither previous decisions nor historical justifications for carving out a special exemption for the flag:

> There is, moreover, no indication—either in the text of the Constitution or in our cases interpreting it—that a separate juridical category exists for the American flag alone. Indeed, we would not be surprised to learn that the persons who framed our Constitution and wrote the Amendment that we now construe were not known for their reverence for the Union Jack. The First Amendment does not guarantee that other concepts virtually sacred to our Nation as a whole—such as the principle that discrimination on the basis of race is odious and destructive—will go unquestioned in the marketplace of ideas. See *Brandenburg v. Ohio*, 395 U.S. 444 (1969). We decline, therefore, to create for the flag an exception to the joust of principles protected by the First Amendment.

The Court further said that, as in *Brandenburg v. Ohio,* no actual breach of the peace had occurred, nor were there any threat of "imminent lawless action."

In response to the Supreme Court decision, Congress has attempted numerous times to enact legislation to protect the flag and to propose constitutional amendments that would prohibit flag desecration. All of these measures have failed, either because of subsequent Court decisions (see 1990's *United States v. Eichman*) or a lack of congressional approval.

In order to be effective, laws have to detail what is or is not prohibited and what *exactly* are the physical aspects of the tangible item being discussed. As proponents of such law soon discovered, defining "desecration" was fairly easy; describing an "American flag" is quite another matter.

The "official" American flag has 50 stars and some very specific dimensions specified by the U.S. Flag Code, using the hoist (height) of the flag as one unit. For example, the diameter of a star is defined as four-fifths of one-thirteenth (the width of a stripe). The space between the edge of the blue canton and the first horizontal column of stars is one-twelfth of two-fifths of the flag width (which itself is 1.9 times the height).

Enter the "paradox of the heap" (Williamson 2016), which asks, If one starts with one grain of sand and adds one grain at a time, how many grains does one add before having a "heap" of sand? In terms of the flag, how different does a "flag" have to be before it is no longer an "American flag" and thus no longer subject to proposed desecration laws?

Is a 48-star flag an "American flag"? Is a flag with different dimensions than the official flag still an American flag? What if the red and white stripes are reversed, or the canton moved to the right side, or the blue canton colored green, or the stars replaced with spirals, or the spirals arranged in a triangle shape? Is wearing a flag as an article of clothing "desecration"?

None of these questions has come before the Supreme Court, which, whether intentionally or not, has chosen to avoid all of these questions and opt for a First Amendment solution.

Flags on the Moon

Historically, nations claimed new lands by planting a flag. But in September 1959, at the height of the Cold War, the Soviet Union crash-landed a probe containing a Soviet flag on the moon. An immediate concern was whether or not the Soviet Union could or would claim the moon. Certainly the official position of the U.S. government was that such a claim would not be recognized. In sending a subdued congratulatory message to the Soviet government, for example, Vice President Richard Nixon reminded the Communists that "planting" the flag conveyed no territorial claim.

In June 1965, Gemini IV astronauts James A. McDivitt and Edward H. White II (the first American to complete a space walk) bought their own small flags and had them placed on the left shoulder of their spacesuits. It's interesting to note that many times the iconic photograph of White floating in space is reversed, so the flag appears to be on his right shoulder. The NASA website (2017), however, clearly shows the flag on the left shoulder.

Curiously, the Gemini IV astronauts were the first to wear the flag on the left shoulder, a pattern followed by all other astronauts, with the exception of the Apollo I crew, who wore the flag on the right shoulder. Sadly, the Apollo I crew was killed in a launchpad fire in 1967. That crew consisted of Virgil I. "Gus" Grissom, Roger B. Chaffee, and Edward H. White (the flag-on-the-left-shoulder space-walking astronaut from Gemini IV).

Over the years, several other nations have landed or crashed probes on the moon and other celestial bodies, but only the United States has actually gone through the motions, in the manned moon landings, of actually "planting" a flag on the moon.

But nothing involving the NASA space program was simple, even the planting a flag on the moon. First, there were international political considerations. International treaties specified no one could stake a claim to the moon. And during his presidential inaugural address in January 1969, President Nixon emphasized the international nature of lunar exploration: "As we explore the reaches of space, let us go to the new worlds together—not as new worlds to be conquered, but as a new adventure to be shared."

In February 1969, when preparations were all but completed for the first moon landing, acting NASA administrator Thomas O. Paine created the Committee on Symbolic Activities for the First Lunar Landing. The committee studied several options, including leaving a flag of the United Nations, a United States flag, and a set of small flags from every nation. The committee ultimately recommended leaving an American flag and attaching a plaque to the lunar lander to be left on the moon.

Congress, apparently trying to catch up with lunar reality, passed a bill in November 1969 (four months after the landing):

> The flag of the United States, and no other flag, shall be implanted or otherwise placed on the surface of the moon, or on the surface of any planet, by members of the crew of any spacecraft . . . of the United States. . . . [T]his act [of planting the flag] is intended as a symbolic gesture of national pride in achievement and is not to be construed as a declaration of national appropriation by claim of sovereignty. (Jasentuliyana 1992, 81)

On to the development and deployment of the Lunar Flag Assembly (LFA): How would the flag and pole be carried in the cramped confines of the Apollo command module and the lunar lander? Picture safely fitting a 66-inch-tall pole with a three-foot horizontal extension into cramped small car! How would the astronauts, in their bulky spacesuits, which limited their reach, actually deploy the flag on the lunar surface? What about weight considerations?

To make the pole easy to handle, engineers, led by Jack Kinzler, devised a telescoping pole made of one-inch gold-anodized aluminum tubing. The horizontal portion of the assembly would be swung out from the vertical portion once the flag was pushed into the lunar surface.

The assembly would be carried behind the ladder on the lunar module and was not attached until about 4:00 a.m. on the morning of the launch.

But early on it was discovered that carrying the flag outside the lunar lander would introduce a new set of engineering challenges: how to protect the flag assembly from the hot exhaust of the descent engine, which was estimated to range from 250 degrees to 2,000 degrees during the final phase of landing.

The solution was a stainless steel outer jacket with several layers of aluminum, Thermoflex, and Kapton insulation, limiting the internal temperature to 180 degrees. This shroud assembly was used for Apollo 11 to Apollo 14. For the final three missions (Apollo 15 to Apollo 17), the flag assembly was carried in a storage drawer that opened from the side of the lander.

And what of the flag itself? Throughout the space program, NASA was known for its attention to detail and the apparent necessity to custom design and build each of the millions of parts from *Explorer I* through the Apollo landings. But some NASA sources say the American flag carried by Apollo XI, the first manned landing, was an off-the-shelf flag purchased at Sears by a group of secretaries on their lunch break. Other NASA sources claim the flag was purchased from a government supply catalog (Platoff 1993).

Regardless of where the flag came from, it was a simple matter to sew a seam into the flag and slip it over the horizontal bar for the flag assembly. The horizontal and vertical pieces were attached by a locking hinge mechanism, which on Apollo 11 jammed, leaving the flag not fully extended.

So in what condition are the six flags placed on the moon during the Apollo program? Evidence suggests that the Apollo XI flag was knocked over by the blast of the lunar module as it left the moon because, according to Edwin "Buzz" Aldrin, the flag was only about 27 feet from the lander. Later crews placed their flags further away from the landers.

Photographs taken by the *Lunar Reconnaissance Orbiter* seem to show the flags of Apollo 12, 16, and 17 are still standing. Engineers suspect that the flags have been faded to white by the intense lunar sunlight and that in some cases the fabric may have disintegrated.

But, of course, all of this presupposes we actually landed on the moon. And at the heart of moon-landing conspiracies is the idea that the American flag is waving in a nonexistent lunar breeze and fluttering against a field of nonexistent stars.

In fact, the flag is fluttering—but due to inertia, not the wind.

As Aldrin tried to push the pole holding the flag into the lunar surface, he had to twist the pole into the dirt. This twisting motion was transferred to the horizontal brace. In addition, the horizontal rod designed to extend the flag to its full width jammed, giving the flag the appearance of rippling. This "ripple" in the airless atmosphere of the moon sparked "evidence" of a fake landing.

The process of unrolling the flag also caused some motion, which quickly subsided. And as can be seen in video that Armstrong shot of Aldrin, as Aldrin's hand moves during his salute, the flag remains motionless, with no actual ripple visible.

A Symbol of Continuing Debate

For more than 250 years, the American flag has stirred patriotic feelings, controversy, and argument. Is it a symbol of freedom or a symbol of oppression? Is the flag merely a piece of decorated cloth, or is it, somehow, a reality beyond the symbolism? Even asking the seemingly simple question "What is an American flag?" can spark sometimes violent passions and debate.

But, in fact, these debates and issues represent a tautology, a circular argument. If the flag represents freedom, then it represents all sides of the debate and all actions that flow from the notion of freedom. Does desecration dishonor the flag and the memory of the hundreds of thousands who have died to defend its ideals? But didn't those hundreds of thousands die to preserve one of ideals the flag represents: free speech and free expression?

As a symbol, the flag can mean many things to many different people. Or, to put it another way, it can mean anything to anyone. But the beauty—and hope—of our democracy is that no individual, group of individuals, or the government has the right to stop that debate.

Further Reading

Hariman, R., and J. L. Lucaites. 2002. "Performing Civic Identity: The Iconic Photograph of the Flag Raising on Iwo Jima." *Quarterly Journal of Speech* 88:363–392.

Jasentuliyana, N. 1992. *Space Law: Development and Scope*. Westport, CT: Praeger.

Lester, P. M. 2017. "Faking Images in Photojournalism." Accessed June 1. http://paulmartinlester.info/writings/faking.html

Lillian Goldman Law Library. (1969) 2008. "First Inaugural Address of Richard Milhous Nixon." The Avalon Project, Yale Law School. Accessed August 3, 2017. http://avalon.law.yale.edu/20th_century/nixon1.asp

NASA. 2017. Photograph of Edward White. Accessed June 1. https://www.nasa.gov/sites/default/files/ed_white.jpg

Platoff, A. M. 1993. "Where No Flag Has Gone Before: Political and Technical Aspects of Placing a Flag on the Moon." Johnson Space Center, NASA. https://www.jsc.nasa.gov/history/flag/flag.htm

Rasmussen, F. N. 2010. "A Half-Century Ago, New 50-star American Flag Debuted in Baltimore." *Baltimore Sun*, July 2. http://articles.baltimoresun.com/2010-07-02/news/bs-md-backstory-1960-flag-20100702_1_48-star-flag-blue-canton-fort-mchenry

Rosenthal, J. and W. C. Heinz. (1955) 2017. "The Picture That Will Live Forever." Internet Archive Wayback Machine. Accessed June 1, 2017. https://web.archive.org/web/20130323213838/http://oldmagazinearticles.com/1955_Joe_Rosenthal_Io_Jima_Article_pdf. Originally published in *Colliers Magazine*, February 18, 1955.

Story Corps. 2009. "Bob Heft." NPR Morning Edition interview. Originally aired July 3. Accessed June 1, 2017. https://storycorps.org/listen/bob-heft

Williamson, T. 2016. "On Vagueness, or, When Is a Heap of Sand not a Heap of Sand?" Last modified November 15. https://aeon.co/ideas/on-vagueness-when-is-a-heap-of-sand-not-a-heap-of-sand

The Flag in American Politics

Woden Teachout

The American flag has been a powerful tool in American politics. It has represented multiple themes throughout its history in the American political arena: democracy, expansion of the electorate, opposition to immigration, the abolition of slavery, capitalism, segregation, integration, and hawkish war policy. A vast range of political and social groups, both idealistic and shrewd, have claimed the flag to legitimize their versions of the American dream. Each of these iterations has been a site of conflict and conversation over what it means to be an American.

Throughout this complex history, the flag has moved back and forth between two basic political frameworks. The first is humanitarian patriotism, an ideological commitment to democracy as a political and social system. Humanitarian patriots see the political state not as a good unto itself but rather as a means to an end: the individual potential of each of its citizens. Their patriotism celebrates the Declaration of Independence, civil liberties, and individual rights. They view dissent as a key patriotic activity, a necessary check against the power of the state.

Nationalist patriotism, by contrast, takes its legitimacy from the idea of a nation, an imagined community, in Benedict's framing, defined by a shared culture, language, geography, and ethnic heritage. Nationalist patriots emphasize the collective over the individual, the transcendence of shared values over the rights of any individual citizen. They stress allegiance to the state as the best way to sustain the collective power of the nation, emphasizing personal sacrifice for the greater good. They look askance at skepticism and dissent, seeking instead to create a culture of reverence.

These two frameworks—humanitarian and nationalist patriotism—have been constants through the flag's varied political history. As theory, they are ideal types; in practice, they are often less tidy. But they allow us to conceptualize two very different sets of convictions about the relationships among the individual, the nation, and the state, along with the political implications that follow. They reveal that each iteration of the flag's political meanings has drawn on one of these traditions more strongly than the other. And they allow us to see a historical shift from a predominantly humanitarian patriotic tradition in the 19th century to a predominantly nationalist one in the 20th and 21st, in which the flag takes center stage.

The history of the flag in American politics has been not a history of slow and careful evolution but rather flashpoints of change that show the historically expanding power of the flag in American politics. The flag was first imbued with political meaning by a disenfranchised section of the population during the Revolution, came into its own as a powerful and widely recognized symbol of the Union during the Civil War era, and was imbued with reverence around the turn of the 20th century, gaining it the status that it has in contemporary American politics. Tracing this history from the Revolution to the present allows us to see the defining cultural moments that have shaped the flag into the politically potent symbol it is today.

Revolutionary Meanings

In order to understand the origins of the political meanings of the flag during the American Revolution, it is important to recognize that the flag was not yet a central symbol of the nation. Its influence was highly circumscribed, belonging to a specific tradition of rebellion on the waterfront of port cities. Flags were a feature of sailing ships: emblems that indicated the nationality of a ship across the distances of the water, not fully developed symbols with emotional power. During the Revolution, they began to be used on land as a symbol of defiance against Great Britain, but that use was still defined primarily by sailors and dockworkers. Thus, their political meaning was deeply influenced by the values of the waterfront.

Revolutionary maritime culture was radical. In the years leading up to American independence, popular resistance to Great Britain focalized in the ports up and down the coast. The resistance to the Stamp Act in Boston in 1765, dominated by sailors and other dockworkers, exemplified this spirit. Their demonstration—which featured flags, objects dangling from the liberty tree, a mock "stamping," and a burning effigy of stamp director Andrew Oliver—forced Oliver's resignation; it also articulated a distinctly colonial tradition of humanitarian patriotism based on political liberty, the rejection of hierarchy, and egalitarianism. In the following decade, other instances of port-city defiance invoked similar themes. And they increasingly featured liberty poles (which were tall ship masts erected in public spaces) and flags: the red and white stripes of the Sons of Liberty, the coiled rattlesnake with its motto "Don't Tread on Me," Pine Tree flags symbolizing New England, and the solid-red flags that were traditional British symbols of protest. The Stars and Stripes did not yet exist.

The American flag, when it did come into being, served as a statement of defiance from the start. The Continental Colors was flown from the Continental Navy ship Alfred in 1775; the design was an amalgam of the Sons of Liberty stripes and the Union Jack, reflecting the ambivalent political status of the colonies at the time. When the Continental Congress passed the Flag Resolution in 1777, it authorized not so much a design as a set of constituent elements. The flags that flew over the official Continental Navy and American privateers boasted red and white stripes and white stars in a blue field, with endless variations as to the number and arrangement of those elements. But in all of them, the flag marked political separation from Great Britain: the Union Jack that had occupied the canton of the Continental Colors was gone.

Of those who fought in the Revolutionary War, these sailors were most attached to the flag. The delegates at the Continental Congress did not talk about the flag other than to authorize it; for them, the symbol of the nation was the female figure of

Columbia. But the sailors lived and worked under the flag, and for them, it became both an emblem of the state and a powerfully personal symbol that drew on the flag culture of maritime resistance. The first people to develop their own ceremonies and rituals around the flag were American sailors—often privateers—imprisoned in British prisons. The most extensive historical account describes a Fourth of July ceremony held in Old Mill prison on the English coast, in which 200 American prisoners hoisted Stars and Stripes into paper hats as a sign of defiance. The author of the account described his fellow prisoners' readiness to "return to a free country, to enjoy our just rights and privileges"—a radically egalitarian statement for a sailor, in a moment when the privileges of full citizenship were confined to landholding men. This was a humanitarian expression of patriotism. But despite the sailors' adoption of the flag and the political meaning with which they infused it, the flag appeared in mainstream American culture mostly as a minor symbol in paintings and drawings. It had not yet become a political force.

The 19th Century: The Flag's Growing Political Power

The War of 1812 was a defining moment for the flag. As the first war since the Revolution, the war—and its victory—became a key part of American identity. The war served to establish the young nation as a political and military force. Georgetown lawyer Francis Scott Key wrote "The Star-Spangled Banner" after witnessing the British attack on Fort McHenry, and the text was published in the newspapers, publicly performed as a song, and then published and sold as sheet music. The song served to elevate the flag from a naval emblem into a powerful source of American identity; it was a symbol of a young country that was able to defeat the power of Great Britain for a second time.

This changed with the nativist movement that began in the 1830s and surged in the 1840s as a response to large-scale immigration from Ireland and other countries. Nativists were alarmed by the political machines that were springing up in immigrant communities in cities and feared the influence of Catholicism. In Philadelphia, a nativist preacher named Lewis Levin helped found the American Republican party (later the Know-Nothings), which held secret meetings that opened with the raising of the American flag. When nativists went into Irish neighborhoods to hold their meetings in defiance, they brought the flag. During one scuffle, Irish immigrants shot a young man named George Shiffler while he was carrying the flag. Shiffler quickly became a martyr for the nativist cause, igniting the Philadelphia Riots of 1844, in which nativists burned entire Irish neighborhoods. The flag became a nativist banner. Merchants sold lithographs of a dying Shiffler clutching the flag, and nativist women sewed red, white, and blue silk into flags for a massive Independence Day parade that doubled as a nativist display of power.

The Philadelphia riots quickly established the American flag as a nativist symbol in Eastern cities where most of the immigrants lived. Nativist groups sprung up, notably the Order of United Americans in New York (1844) and the Order of the Star Spangled Banner in New York City (1849). Nativism became a political force as Lewis Levin was elected to Congress from the American Republican Party, and similar-thinking nativist (known as Native American) parties sprung up in other locales. These were not the only people laying claim to the flag—both Whigs and Democrats incorporated it in their party banners for the 1844 elections—but they were the most important. At the height of its power, the American Party (or "Know-Nothings) carried six states in the 1854 elections and came close to carrying seven more, replacing the Whigs as the dominant party opposing the Democrats. The flag meant a commitment to a white, Protestant America in which immigrants had all but disappeared: a nationalist vision of patriotism.

At the same time, the Mexican War was reviving the flag's military implications in a way that dovetailed with this vision of a triumphant white and Christian nation. As the United States annexed Texas in 1845 and American troops marched into Mexico in 1846, the flag became a symbol of American imperialism. When American troops rode into the main square of Mexico City, they pulled down the Mexican flag and replaced it with the Star-Spangled Banner. This was the first war in which soldiers carried the national flag into battle, and many of them developed an almost mystical relationship with the flag. One captain called it "an emblem of American possession to the Sierra Madre." This imperialist vision resonated with the American people, who bought flags at such an unprecedented rate that the nation's first flag company was founded. The war ended with the Treaty of Guadalupe Hidalgo granting Texas to the United States, but it continued to reverberate in politics as war hero Zachary Taylor was nominated by both Whig and Know-Nothing parties and elected as president in the 1848 election.

In the years leading up to the Civil War, the flag was a canvas for political statements. In 1856, a Charleston captain flew a flag of 15 stars—a star for each state that he believed loyal to the South. Abolitionist flags bore stars only for those states that had banned slavery; other northern flags carried stars for each state that was pledged securely to the Union. The Peace Flag used a diagonal to divide the American flag into two—the top for the upper half and the bottom for the lower half—with the hope of reuniting the two halves when South and North were able to reconcile. When Mississippi seceded from the Union in 1861, Jefferson Davis made a speech describing his desire to tear the state's star from the flag; as a result, Bonnie Blue flags proliferated throughout the South, each featuring a single star on a blue background.

With the attack on Fort Sumter, the American flag catapulted to the center of the political discussion about the war. When Major Robert Anderson lowered the flag as a sign of surrender, South Carolina Governor Pickens was giddy: "We have made the proud flag of the Stars and Stripes, that never was lowered before to any nation on this earth—we have lowered it in humiliation before the Palmetto and the Confederate flags." The Sumter flag, battered and torn, was taken to New York City, where it was flown from the equestrian statue of George Washington as the centerpiece of an enormous patriotic rally. Contemporaries estimated 100,000 flags in the city—decorating hats, lapels, hands, windows, housetops, railroad cars, hotels, barrooms—and *The New York World* coined a new term: "flag mania." The political meanings were clear: support for the Union. And crowds enforced this, using a litmus test of the flag. The Democratic publisher of *The New York Herald* was chased by a crowd who threatened him until he hung two flags out the window; a similar incident happened with the publishers of the southern-leaning *Journal of Commerce*.

At the same time, ceremonial flag raisings in major cities were attended by tens of thousands of people. As a witness in Boston wrote, "Never before had the national flag symbolized anything to me. But as I saw it now, kissing the skies, all that is symbolized as representative of government and emblematic of national majesty became clear to my mental vision. . . . It was this holy flag that had been insulted." For northerners, the flag became an icon marrying the political and religious dimensions of the war: the Union troops and a transcendent sense of nation. This feeling was especially pronounced among the troops who fought under the flag and marched from encampment to encampment to the rhythm of "The Stars and Stripes" and other popular flag songs. For Union prisoners, the flag provided a way to stay true to their convictions, and prisoners at Libby Prison in Virginia created a flag from red, white, and blue shirts.

Over the course of the war, the flag came to signify not only the Union but opposition to slavery. Few northerners were abolitionists at the beginning of the war: the Northern cause and the flag were a commitment to the Union. But Lincoln's Emancipation Proclamation in 1863 placed slavery directly at the center of the conflict. And as Union fortunes improved during the spring and summer of 1863, soldiers increasingly supported the proclamation. The inclusion of African American troops into the Union army made a huge difference. At the battle of Milliken's Bend, Louisiana, newly freed slaves in the United States Colored Troops repulsed a Southern assault and defended the Union supply point. Experiences like this changed the minds of many white northerners who had scoffed at the idea of black troops. Lincoln won 78 percent of the soldier vote in the 1864 Presidential election, cementing support for his antislavery policies. And as the war drew to an end, celebrations of freedmen and freedwomen featured the American flag: the freedmen and freedwomen's parade in Charleston, for example, featured an American flag, which was met with uproarious applause, and a coffin declaring the death of slavery. The flag of the Union had become the flag of emancipation.

During Reconstruction, the flag was occasionally used in this same vein: as a political tool by Republican politicians who used the memory of the Civil War as a way to embarrass Democrats as disloyal. But mostly it was seen as too volatile a symbol for a nation that continued to be fiercely divided, at a time when many Northerners hoped for a real reunification. In the 1870s, this tension lessened somewhat—first with the centennial celebration and a shared emphasis on Revolutionary history and then with the Compromise of 1877, which gave Rutherford Hayes the election and ended Reconstruction. But for a while, the red-white-and-blue banner still spoke to the divisions of the Civil War.

The Long 20th Century: The Flag as a Force in American Politics

The flag began to creep back into popular culture in the late 1880s. In large part, this was an expression of nationalism that took shape in many countries during this era: an emphasis on a shared culture, ethnic background, and language and marked by a celebration of traditions, both real and manufactured. Certain factors defined the shape that this nationalism took in the United States. One was the memory of the Civil War. As the veterans aged, holding "Blue-Gray" reunions in which Confederate and Union veterans gathered together, they began to reshape their understanding of the war. Amidst the excesses of the Gilded Age, they came to think of the war as a crucible of manhood and the flag as the banner under which they had learned responsibility, sacrifice, and allegiance to something greater than themselves. At the same time, groups like the Daughters of the American Revolution, alarmed at the number of immigrants in American cities, began to use the flag as a way to teach patriotism in schools. These groups had varied political agendas. George Balch's flag salute, developed in New York City schools, was a militaristic expression of national patriotism, while Francis Bellamy's Pledge of Allegiance, first performed at the Chicago Exposition in 1893, was an expression of Christian socialism. Merchants took advantage of this newfound celebration of the flag, waving flags from their establishments and printing advertisements on small handheld flags.

The election of 1896 took this flag culture and politicized it. In the wake of the Depression of 1894, the defining issue was the economy: Republican William McKinley supported the gold standard to insure investments, while Democrat William Jennings Bryan promoted putting more currency into circulation with free silver. The election pitted "the money power" of Eastern bankers against a vision of anarchy and mobs run wild. Into this charged atmosphere stepped Mark Hanna, McKinley's campaign manager. He printed flag buttons for McKinley during the Convention, organized a Patriotic Heroes Brigade that stumped for McKinley on a train car swathed in bunting, and counseled McKinley to use the flag as a central trope in his speeches. Most important, he organized a special Flag Day on the last Saturday before the election, in which large crowds waving flags paraded for McKinley through all the major cities. The Democrats protested, but the strategy was effective: McKinley won. Contemporary newspapers wrote that the election had given the Republicans "the monopoly of patriotism" and "a sort of divine right to the flag." The icon that had been a symbol of the North and the Union was now reincarnated as a symbol of the Republican Party, sound money, and the status quo. And it had arrived as a central feature of American politics.

The Spanish-American War of 1898 marked deep divisions as Americans argued about their role in the world. The conflict was promoted as a means to assist Cubans in throwing off Spanish colonial power and achieving self-rule. But it opened up serious questions about imperialism, a discussion in which the flag had a central place. The anti-imperialists, like Mark Twain, argued that the flag was a symbol of democracy and self-rule; American senator Carl Schutz invoked "the old, the true flag, the flag of George Washington and Abraham Lincoln, the flag of the government of, for and by the people." But when Teddy Roosevelt's Rough Riders carried the flag up San Juan Hill in Cuba and placed it on the top in conquest, it became an emphatic symbol of imperial power. As a result of the war, the United States acquired Cuba as an American protectorate and took ownership of Hawaii, Guam, and Puerto Rico. The conquest of the Philippines followed in 1902. The flag, for many, had come to mean empire.

World War I, too, was marked by deep divisions between those who supported the war and the pacifists and labor activists who criticized it. Starting in

1916, Americans held "preparedness parades" with marching bands and rows of flag-waving citizens—parades designed to show support for the war. President Woodrow Wilson declared Flag Day an official holiday. When Wilson requested a declaration of War from Congress in 1917, hawkish Congressmen wore flag pins in their lapels. A raft of legislation, including the Espionage and Sedition Acts, drastically curtailed individual rights; immigrants were held in internment camps for "enemy aliens." Images of the flag decorated war-recruitment posters and anti-German propaganda, "The Star-Spangled Banner" was declared the official anthem of the army and navy, and demand for flags doubled. The Sedition Act outlawed disloyal talk about the flag, and a Texas state law raised the penalty for flag desecration from 30 days to 25 years in jail. Lynch mobs forced German Americans to kiss the flag or sing "The Star-Spangled Banner." The flag had become a litmus test for loyalty, the marker of a nationalist vision of patriotism in which individual rights were subsumed by the rights of the state.

The Ku Klux Klan, emerging at the same time, drew on these meanings of the flag and added a new one that hearkened back to the nativists: white nationalism. From their founding moment in 1915 at the top of Stone Mountain, Klan members had adopted both the flag and the cross as defining symbols. The flag waved at the front of their parades and featured heavily in their ceremonies; fully cloaked members would appear in churches during the service and lay folded flags on the altar. The flag's adoption by the Klan drew on the superpatriotism of the war: their manual stated "The military form of government must and will be preserved for the sake of true, patriotic Americanism, because it is the only form of government that gives any form of success." During the war, Klansmen saw themselves as a civic adjunct to the government forces, harassing striking workers and Wobblies (members of the International Workers of the World). After the war, their focus shifted to Jews, Catholics, African Americans, and immigrants, and they increasingly articulated a vision of a white Protestant country. Their claim to this vision was cemented by their 1925 march in Washington, in which 30,000 Klansmen strode right under the Capitol Dome waving American flags. Shortly after, corruption and moral turpitude weakened the Klan, but the association between the flag and their white nationalist vision continued.

World War II brought forth both nationalist and humanitarian strains of patriotism. On the first Independence Day after Pearl Harbor in 1942, 400 magazines coordinated to feature the flag on their covers. An artist's rendering of the Iwo Jima flag raising was printed as a liberty bond poster, and the marines photographed in the famous image were pulled home to go on tour and sell war bonds. Moviegoers and baseball fans sang "The Star-Spangled Banner" before shows and games. But the nature of the wartime enemy defined the flag's meaning in a very different way than World War I. Hitler's massive flag rallies and his anti-Semitism were uncomfortably reminiscent of World War I and segregation. Comedian Will Rogers compared the Nazis and the Klan, saying "[Hitler] don't want to be emperor; he wants to be kleagle." In 1942, President Roosevelt eliminated the straight-armed flag salute in favor of hand over heart. His Four Freedoms speech—and to an even greater extent, Norman Rockwell's paintings by the same name—emphasized a humanitarian and incipiently multicultural version of patriotism.

One of the flag's swiftest and most interesting shifts in political meaning happened in the 1950s. While Joseph McCarthy and Hollywood blacklisting set clear markers of acceptable patriotism, the flag itself was not a particularly potent presence early in the decade. If anything, it meant a defense of the status quo, and White Citizens Councils, middle-class cousins to the Klan, placed the American flag alongside the Confederate one on their insignia. But over the course of the 1950s, federal actions—such as Supreme Court decisions like *Brown v. Board of Education* (1954) and Eisenhower's troops forcing the integration of Central High School—alienated the segregationists, and they turned increasingly to the Confederate flag. By 1959, American flags had all but disappeared from segregationist gatherings. Civil rights workers, some of whom were black veterans, saw an opening. They drew on the legacy of World War II, comparing segregation to Nazism and making a claim that the values of democracy and civil rights should be extended to all Americans. The movement adopted the symbol, using it at the Greensboro lunch counter and Raleigh sit-ins and more fully at the Jackson student protests. Most powerful of all was a stirring photo essay of the march from Selma to Montgomery, which featured the flag prominently. The flag allowed black Americans to make a claim to full citizenship and facilitated the willingness of white Americans to extend the rights of citizenship to that larger circle.

The Vietnam era saw a radical politicization of the flag, as disillusioned war protesters began to see it as a symbol of an irredeemable government. During the Central Park protest in April 1967, when a number of war resisters burned their draft cards, several young men set fire to an American flag nearby. The event catalyzed a series of flag burnings intended as public speech, which outraged many citizens and led to the first federal flag desecration bill, signed by President Lyndon Johnson on July 4, 1968. The American population was split between those for whom the flag symbolized sacrifice and honor and those for whom it represented a government that had betrayed its people and American ideals. The Hard Hat Riot of 1970, in the wake of Kent State, marked the flag as a prowar, pro-Nixon symbol. Construction workers beat up protestors and marched to City Hall, where they raised the flag and sang "The Star-Spangled Banner." The flag-waving marches that followed this event tied the flag explicitly to Nixon with signs and speeches. And they marked a turning point in support for Nixon. In response, he and his cabinet began to wear flag pins on their lapels, followed by other Republican politicians. "American flag lapel pins," wrote one political commentator, "became a sort of GOP costume."

This legacy defined cultural politics through the next four decades as the Republican party claimed the flag and the left abandoned it. Ronald Reagan used a rich panoply of flag imagery in his Morning in America campaign series, and at campaign stops, he and his wife Nancy waved smaller flags against the backdrop of an enormous one. In the 1988 campaign, Republican George H. W. Bush pointedly noted Democrat Michael Dukakis's veto of a bill that would have required Massachusetts students to recite the Pledge of Allegiance. "What is it about the American flag which upsets this man so much?" Bush asked. From 1989 to 2006, flag-burning legislation came before Congress seven times. It was a largely partisan issue, with

Republicans wanting to outlaw flag burning and Democrats thinking it should be legal. The flag had become a relatively static symbol of American conservatism.

Contemporary Politics

For a moment after the events of September 11, 2001, the flag was apolitical: a symbol of grief, resilience, and most of all unity. Americans of all political stripes hung it out, especially in Manhattan, and so did citizens of other countries in an expression of solidarity. But when President George W. Bush and his staff appeared on television wearing flag pins and American forces began bombing Afghanistan in search of Osama bin Laden, the flag took on the hawkish, proadministration meanings that it often has in times of war. Protests against the war featured thousands of signs and banners but only a handful of American flags, and those who carried them were viewed with suspicion. Not everyone ceded the flag to the right. Television host Bill Moyers's statement on the flag flew round the Internet when he said "The flag belongs to the country, not the government." Nonetheless, the flag's prowar, Republican connotations were unmistakable.

During the immigration reform protests of the spring of 2006, a different facet of the flag emerged. The protests were a response to legislation proposing a crackdown on undocumented workers. Starting in Chicago and continuing to a number of major cities, large numbers of Latino workers came into the streets. In the early protests, many of them carried the Mexican flag as a symbol of unity and pride in their roots. Conservative talk show hosts responded harshly, asking why the marchers did not go back to Mexico. The Border Guardians, a new anti-immigration group, burned Mexican flags in Tucson. As protests spread, marchers responded to criticism by bringing American flags. On April 10, marked as the "national day of action for immigration justice," and May 1, the "Day without an Immigrant" boycott, hundreds of thousands of demonstrators marched in more than 140 cities, waving American flags and banners reading "We are America" and "We Have a Dream Too." These events marked the emergence of Hispanic voters as a force in American politics. They also showed the flag in two of its faces: as a symbol of anti-immigration sentiment and as a symbol adopted by an immigrant community making a bid for inclusion in the humanitarian tradition, much as the civil rights movement had done.

The era of Barack Obama also revealed the flag to be a site of contest between nationalist and humanitarian strands of patriotism. Obama's race and personal history challenged the white normative definition of what it meant to be an American. Internet rumors circulated that he refused to wear a flag pin and that he had removed the American flag insignia from his campaign and presidential planes. At the same time, Obama made a deliberate attempt to redefine patriotism as a bipartisan tradition, describing the flag as belonging to both political parties. In his stump speech, he described how Democrats and Republicans and independents "fought together and bled together and some died together under the same proud flag." On the night of his election as the first Black president, many African Americans described feeling a connection to the flag that they had never felt before. Throughout his presidency, Obama continued to invoke the flag, as during the

2012 State of the Union address when he described one of his proudest possessions: the flag that the Navy SEALs took on their mission to get Osama bin Laden. During these years, the flag became a symbol with ambivalent political meaning, not belonging fully either to left or right.

With the election of President Trump, the flag's conservative associations became ascendant once again. In the wake of the election, students burned flags at three American colleges and removed and lowered them at several more. In response, Trump tweeted that anyone burning the flag should be punished with loss of citizenship or jail time. After debates on campus, Hampshire College announced that it would not fly any flags, a decision that was met by protest from veterans' groups; it has since reversed the decision. Trump's supporters wave the flag at rallies and fly it from their homes more frequently than do his critics. Liberal singer Lana Del Rey, who previously used American flag imagery in her concerts, has decided to drop the iconography because it feels too politicized in the Trump era.

The flag remains a contested symbol, invoked and waved by both political parties during elections. It is both defined by, and defines, American politics. It draws on both humanitarian and nationalist traditions of patriotism, often by turn and sometimes together. Its associations with the political right continue to be particularly strong in the modern era. But as the flag's expansive history illustrates, this association is not immutable. The flag's political power comes from its elasticity as a symbol. It draws on a rich and complex history of American political thinking, and it is always ripe for the next reinvention.

Further Reading

Bonner, Robert E. 2002. *Colors and Blood: Flag Passions of the Confederate South*. Princeton, NJ: Princeton University Press.

Budiansky, Stephen. 2008. *The Bloody Shirt: Terror after Appomattox*. New York: Viking.

Chalmers, David Mark. 1987. *Hooded Americanism: The History of the Ku Klux Klan*. Durham, NC: Duke University Press.

Feldberg, Michael. 1975. *The Philadelphia Riots of 1844: A Study of Ethnic Conflict*. Westport, CT: Greenwood Press.

Gilje, Paul A. 2004. *Liberty on the Waterfront: American Maritime Culture in the Age of Revolution*. Philadelphia: University of Pennsylvania Press.

Goldstein, Robert. 1995. *Saving "Old Glory": The History of the American Flag Desecration Controversy*. Boulder, CO: Westview Press.

Guenter, Scot M. 1990. *The American Flag, 1777–1924: Cultural Shifts from Creation to Codification*. Rutherford, NJ: Fairleigh Dickinson University Press.

Kinzer, Stephen. 2017. *The True Flag: Theodore Roosevelt, Mark Twin, and the Birth of American Empire*. New York: Henry Holt.

Mastai, Boleslaw, and Marie-Louise D'Otrange. 1973. *The Stars and the Stripes: The American Flag as Art and as History from the Birth of the Republic to the Present*. New York: Alfred A. Knopf.

O'Leary, Cecelia. 1999. *To Die For: The Paradox of America Patriotism*. Princeton, NJ: Princeton University Press.

Teachout, Woden. 2009. *Capture the Flag: A Political History of American Patriotism*. New York: Basic Books.

Wells, Tom. 1994. *The War Within: America's Battle over Vietnam*. Berkeley: University of California Press.

Part II
A–Z Entries

A

ADVERTISING

Although most modern controversies over flag desecration center on flag burning, this was not always so. Especially near the end of the 19th century, there was great concern over the use of the U.S. flag in advertising, which critics thought cheapened the image. A majority of states adopted legislation designed to limit the practice.

Although some courts struck down such laws as being discriminatory, the U.S. Supreme Court upheld a Nebraska anti–flag desecration statute in *Halter v. Nebraska* (1907), arguing that it promoted patriotism.

Notably, the decision was issued prior to decisions that applied First Amendment protections to the states (they had originally applied only against the national government) via the due process clause of the Fourteenth Amendment (1868) and before the court began to view advertising as a form of speech covered by those amendments. The case also preceded decisions in *Texas v. Johnson* (1989) and *United States v. Eichman* (1990), which ruled that laws against flag burning were unconstitutional.

Today it is quite common to see huge flags flying from automobile dealerships or incorporated into logos on packaging. Given the way that the flag can be represented through red, white, and blue designs and through symbols (such as Uncle Sam) that embody them, it would appear very difficult to administer any such laws in a nondiscriminatory fashion.

Section 8 of the Flag Code, provides that "The flag should never be used for advertising purposes in any manner whatsoever" nor "be embroidered on such articles as cushions or handkerchiefs and the like" (Luckey 2008, 7). This admonition, which carries no penalties, appears to be largely ignored.

Kalle Lasn, the author of *Culture Jam*, founded *Adbusters* magazine, which launched a campaign known as the Corporate American Flag, based on a flag that substitutes corporate logos for the stars in the canton of the U.S. flag. The campaign, which itself uses the flag as a kind of logo for corporate America, is designed to encourage customers to end corporate rule (Goddard 2008).

See also Flag Code; *Halter v. Nebraska* (1907); *Texas v. Johnson* (1989); *United States v. Eichman* (1990)

Further Reading

Gey, Steven G. 1990. "This is Not a Flag: The Aesthetics of Desecration." *Wisconsin Law Review* 1990 (November/December): 1549–1595.

Goddard, Kristian. 2008. "The Resilience of the Stars and Stripes." December 4. http://www.kristiangoddard.net/Blog/americanflag.htm

Goldstein, Robert Justin. 1990. "The Great 1989–1990 Flag Flap: An Historical, Political, and Legal Analysis." *University of Miami Law Review* 45 (September): 19–106.

Luckey, John R. 2008. *The United States Flag: Federal Law Relating to Display and Associated Questions*. CRS Report for Congress. Washington, D.C.: Congressional Research Service.

ALL-AMERICAN FLAG ACT

Governments, like individuals, sometimes have a choice in deciding between making purchases domestically, which might sometimes cost more, or from foreign sources that might be cheaper. Prior to the Civil War, most bunting, which was the chief material used to make flags, was imported from England (Corcoran 2002, 50).

On March 3, 1865, President Lincoln signed a bill providing that it should be "lawful for the Secretary of War, [and] the Secretary of the Treasury, to enter into contract for Bunting of American manufacture as their respective services require for a period not exceeding one year, and at a price not exceeding that at which an article of equal quality can be imported" (quoted in Cooper 1973, 17). This law appears to have been advocated in part by Gen. Benjamin F. Butler, who had personally invested in an American company that produced bunting.

The All-American Flag Act was proposed in the 114th Congress (January 2015–January 2017). It provided that "only such flags of the United States of America, regardless of size, that are 100 percent manufactured in the United States, from articles, materials, or supplies 100 percent of which are grown, produced, or manufactured in the United States, may be acquired for use by the Federal Government." The 114th Congress did not adopt this law.

The act, which would complement an earlier provision added to the omnibus appropriations act of 2014, which required the U.S. military to purchase only American-made flags. That law was sponsored by California congressman Mike Thompson, a Vietnam War veteran who did not think the U.S. should be spending money on flags produced abroad. Thompson found out that this was happening when he visited North Bay Industries in his district and discovered that the military had been buying some American flags in China, where they were cheaper (CBS News, February 19, 2014).

The Buy American Act generally requires governmental agencies to purchase items that have 50 percent or more American components, but it, like the Berry Amendment, provides for waivers in certain cases (*All-American Flag Act* 2).

See also Flag Manufacturers Association of America

Further Reading

All-American Flag Act: Report of the Committee on Homeland Security and Governmental Affairs United States Senate to Accompany S. 1214 to Require the Purchase of Domestically Made Flags of the United States of America for Use by the Federal Government. 2014. Washington, D.C.: U.S. Government Printing Office.

CBS News. 2014. "American Flags Made in China Now Banned in U.S. Military." February 19. https://www.cbsnews.com/news/american-flags-made-in-china-now-banned-in-us-military/

Cooper, Grace Rogers. 1973. *Thirteen-Star Flags: Keys to Identification*. Washington, D.C.: Smithsonian Institution Press.

Corcoran, Michael. 2002. *For Which It Stands: An Anecdotal Biography of the American Flag*. New York: Simon and Schuster.

AMERICAN FLAG (PHOTOGRAPH)

Photographer Robert Mapplethorpe (1946–1989), who is chiefly known for his homoerotic photographs and the controversies that their exhibit provoked, is also known for a black-and-white photograph entitled *American Flag* (1977). In the photograph, which is owned by the Getty Museum, a low sun appears to be practically burning through the canton, and the stripes are torn and threadbare.

Jon Rendell (2014) observes that the flag was flying above "Fire Island's infamously gay district of the Pines; four years before anyone had even heard of AIDS," from which Mapplethorpe would die. Kristian Goddard (2008) acknowledges that there "is something fragile and defeated about the image," but he also sees it as "one of the greatest examples of the resilience of the American Flag," noting that "it is testimony to the endurance of the flag that, despite its appearance, still flies in the wind." By contrast, Rendell interprets the image as a symbol of "an empire in decline, barely hanging on."

Further Reading

Goddard, Kristian. 2008. "The Resilience of the Stars and Stripes." December 4. Accessed May 7. www.kristiangoddard.net/Blog/americanflag.htm

Rendell, Jon. 2014. "Shoot." Last modified August 22. Accessed May 7, 2017. https://jonrendell/gumblr.com/post/95463030568/american-flag-robert-mapplethorpe-1977-i

AMERICAN FLAG FOUNDATION, INC.

The American Flag Foundation is headquartered in Riderwood, Maryland. Formerly known as the National Flag Day Foundation, the American Flag Foundation was chartered as a 501(c)(3) organization in December 1982. It describes its vision as that of being "the source for inspiring patriotism and encouraging honor for the American flag." Its specific mission is "to create and distribute educational materials, and facilitate or conduct events in communities across the United States that inspire patriotism and encourage honors for the American flag."

The organization works with Fort McHenry to create the Living American Flag, the original (the Human Flag of 1914) of which consisted of an arrangement of 6,500 Baltimore schoolchildren. The organization is chiefly educational in nature and sells educational resources for third-, fourth-, and fifth-grade students. Its website contains a variety of FAQs pertaining to the display of the U.S. flag as well as numerous educational resources, speeches about the flag, and biographies of individuals related to the flag.

The foundation sponsors the Annual National Pause for the Pledge of Allegiance, which has taken place every Flag Day at 7:00 a.m. local time since 1982.

See also Human Flag

Further Reading

American Flag Foundation. 2017. "About Us." Accessed January 27. http://americanflag foundation.org/about/

AMERICAN GOTHIC, WASHINGTON, D.C. (PHOTOGRAPH)

One of the most iconic photographs to utilize the symbolism of the American flag was taken by Gordon Parks (1912–2006). Entitled *American Gothic, Washington, D.C.*, the photo features a posed black-and-white photograph of an African American charwoman (essentially a janitor) standing before the flag, holding a mop in one hand and a broom in the other. The title reflects back on a famous painting by Grant Wood of a father and daughter (Grant's sister and his dentist, often thought by viewers to be husband and wife) posing in front of a house in Wood's Iowa hometown that features a second-story Gothic-shaped window. The man, dressed as a farmer, is holding a pitchfork in his hand.

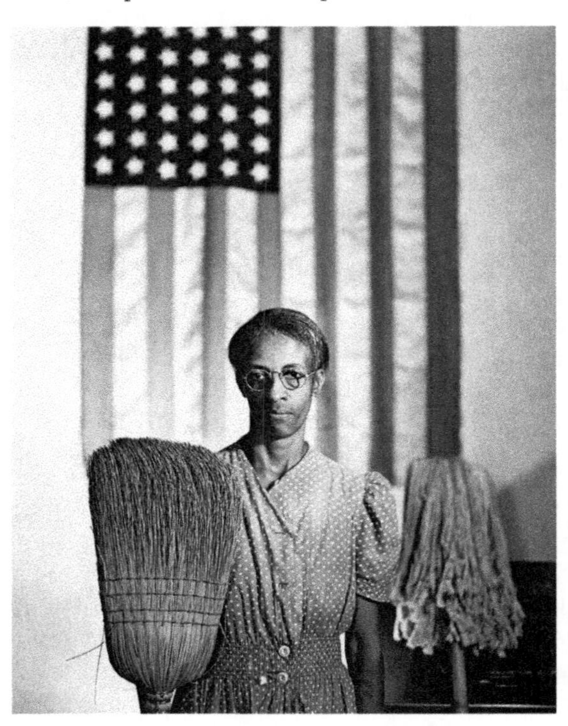

Mrs. Ella Watson, a charwoman employed in a federal office building in Washington, D.C., stands in front of an American flag with her mop and broom in a pose reminiscent of Grant Wood's *American Gothic*. Gordon Parks documented Mrs. Watson's daily life for the Farm Security Administration in 1942, as part of a nationwide photography project on America's poor. His photo essay on Mrs. Watson brought special focus to the lives of poor African Americans in an era of war, depression, recovery, and social segregation. (Corbis via Getty Images)

At the time he took the photograph in 1942, Parks was in Washington, D.C., on a fellowship from the Julius Rosenwald Fund, under the tutelage of photographer Roy Stryker. Parks, who had experienced discrimination growing up in rural Kansas, was frustrated to find similar racial discrimination being practiced in the nation's capital, where places of public accommodations often denied him equal service. Encouraged by Stryker to talk with others, Parks took time to talk with Ella

Watson, who was working in his building, and discovered the story of a woman whose home life had been beset with discrimination and tragedy. The picture highlighted the manner in which the nation depended on African Americans to do much of its physical and often unseen labor. In so doing, Parks also highlighted the gap between the dreams and aspirations that the flag symbolized and the actual lives of many individuals who lived and worked under it.

Parks took a whole series of photographs of Watson, especially of her involvement in church. In addition to taking photographs that highlighted the grit of modern life and promoted social change and justice, Parks also established himself as a fashion photographer. Although he did not graduate from high school, he received numerous honorary degrees and wrote a number of books, including a number of autobiographical accounts.

See also Civil Rights Movement

Further Reading

Burrows, Barbara Baker. 2006. "Remembering Gordon Parks (1912–2006)." *American Art* 20 (Fall): 118–121.

Estrin, James. 2011. "Empathetic Portraits of a Segregated Nation." Lens, *New York Times*. July 18.

Library of Congress. 2017. "Farm Security Administration, Lot 156." Accessed April 18. https://www.loc.gov/pictures/collection/fsa/docchap7.html

AMERICAN LEGION

The American Legion is one of a number of patriotic veterans' groups like the Grand Army of the Republic and the Veterans of Foreign Wars that has been especially active in promoting respect for the flag.

Founded in 1919, just after World War I, the group was largely the brainchild Lt. Col. Theodore Roosevelt III, the son of the 26th U.S. president (Ebel 2010, 171). Organized into state posts, the Legion was open to all veterans and was influential in both the development and later congressional recognition of the flag code. The legion sponsored events to increase awareness of the flag in schools, and it distributed millions of copies of a booklet on flag etiquette entitled *Respect the Flag* (Guenter 1990, 178–179). Metro-Goldwyn-Mayer Studios collaborated with the organization to produce a film entitled *The Flag Speaks*.

The group has sponsored both the Boys Nation and the Boys State programs and pushed for the establishment of the U.S. Veterans Bureau (and its successor, the Department of Veterans Affairs), the GI Bill of Rights, and for other governmental programs for veterans (Boulton 2014, 30–31). The legion has supported traditional renderings of the national anthem and in 2012 sponsored a resolution to designate March 3, the day President Hoover signed the bill making "The Star-Spangled Banner" the national anthem, as Star-Spangled Banner Day (Leepson).

The legion has been a strong supporter of Armistice and Memorial Day commemorations as well as Flag Day celebrations. In elementary schools, it developed a speech focusing on the letters of the flag, which it associated respectively with

"Faith, Loyalty, Amo (Love), and Glory" (Pencak 1989, 290). Manuel Madriaga (2007, 57–58) observes that legion meetings include a flag salute and recitation of the preamble to the American Legion Constitution and appear to affect their members' respect for the flag.

The American Legion has been particularly active in attempts (so far unsuccessful) to adopt a constitutional amendment that would protect against flag desecration.

See also Flag Code; Flag Desecration Amendment; Grand Army of the Republic (GAR); Veterans of Foreign Wars (VFW)

Further Reading

The American Legion. https://www.legion.org/history

Boulton, Mark. 2014. *Failing Our Veterans: The G.I. Bill and the Vietnam Generation*. New York: NYU Press.

Ebel, Jonathan H. 2010. *Faith in the Fight: Religion and the American Soldier in the Great War*. Princeton, NJ: Princeton University Press.

Guenter, Scot M. 1990. *The American Flag, 1777–1924: Cultural Shifts from Creation to Codification*. Cranbury, NJ: Associated University Presses.

Leepson, Marc. 2017. "'Long May It Wave.'" The American Legion. Accessed April 24. https://www.legion.org/magazine/224572/long-may-it-wave

Madriaga, Manuel. 2007. "The Star-Spangled Banner and 'Whiteness' in American National Identity." In *Flag, Nation and Symbolism in Europe and America*, edited by Thomas Hylland Eriksen and Richard Jenkins, 53–67. New York: Routledge.

Pencak, William. 1989. *For God and Country: The American Legion, 1919–1941*. Boston: Northeastern University Press.

AMERICAN'S CREED

The American's Creed is a statement, patterned on Christian affirmations of faith, that was written by William Tyler Page (1868–1942). Page, a descendant of President John Tyler and Carter Braxton, who signed the Declaration of Independence, was a long-serving public servant who became Clerk of the U.S. House of Representatives after winning a contest sponsored by James H. Preston, the mayor of Baltimore. The creed was selected in 1918 from among more than 3,000 entries as an articulation of American values and is regularly recited by the Daughters of the American Revolution (DAR) at their meetings.

Unlike the Pledge of Allegiance, the American Creed is drawn directly from documents and speeches and specifically acknowledges the U.S. Constitution. The creed is as follows:

> I believe in the United States of America
> as a Government of the people, by the people, for the people;
> whose just powers are derived from the consent of the governed;
> a democracy in a republic, a sovereign Nation of many sovereign
> States; a perfect union, one and inseparable;
> Established upon those principles

Of freedom, equality, justice,
And humanity for which American patriots
Sacrificed their lives and fortunes.
I therefore believe it is my duty to my country to love it;
To support its Constitution; to obey its Laws; to respect its Flag;
And to defend it against all enemies.

In a 1937 article, Page wrote, "We have pledged allegiance to the Flag of our Country and to the Republic for which it stands. But without the Constitution there could be no Republic, there could be no flag." Perhaps with a view of incorporating some of his creed within the pledge, he proposed that we should say, "I pledge allegiance to the Constitution of the United States of America, protector of the liberties of a free people, and to the Republic which it created" (Page 1937, 40).

The William Tyler Page Elementary School in Silver Spring, Maryland, is named for Page. Page gave a speech the night before he died to the members of the DAR, who were commemorating the 50th anniversary of the writing of the pledge. He was last photographed as he was pledging allegiance to the flag that he so loved (Quaife, Weig, and Appleman 1961, 156). While not widely known by the American public, Page's American Creed became "gospel" within the DAR (Anderson 1974, 75), and it continued to be highly valued by that organization in the 21st century.

See also Daughters of the American Revolution (DAR); Pledge of Allegiance

Further Reading

Anderson, Peggy, 1974. *The Daughters: An Unconventional Look at America's Fan Club—The DAR*. New York: St. Martin's Press.

Editorials. 1918. *The Journal of Education* 87 (June 6): 630–632.

Page, William Tyler. 1937. "The Romance of the Constitution." *Records of the Columbia Historical Society* 37/38:31–40.

Quaife, Milo M., Milvin J. Weig, and Roy E. Appleman. 1961. *The History of the United States Flag from the Revolution to the Present, Including a Guide to Its Use and Display*. New York: Harper and Brothers.

"AN APPEAL TO HEAVEN"

See Pine Tree Flag

ARMISTICE DAY

See Veterans Day

B

BALCH, GEORGE THACHER

George Thacher Balch (1828–1894) was born in Maine and graduated from West Point in 1852. He served in the Civil War, where he was increasingly recognized for his administrative abilities. He taught a year at West Point before resigning. After some unsuccessful business ventures, he became an auditor of the Erie Railway Company and later of the New York Health Department, after which he got a job with the New York City Board of Education, where he became increasingly interested in teaching citizenship.

After observing patriotic ceremonies in the classroom that had been introduced by Col. DeWitt C. Ward (Guenter 1990, 115), Balch identified what he thought was "the germ of a patriotic movement, which, in the hands of wise and judicious teachers, could be made to produce results, the far-reaching consequences of which it would be impossible to prognosticate at this time" (Balch 1890, vii). Seeking to further greater patriotism, he developed what is believed to be the first pledge to the U.S. flag: "We give our Heads!—and our Hearts!—to God! And our Country! One Country! One Language! One Flag."

Balch further promoted flag rituals in his *Methods for Teaching Patriotism in the Public Schools*, which was published in 1890. Balch's emphasis on "one language" shows that he thought learning English was an important aspect of immigrant assimilation, which has been arguably reflected in subsequent movements to make English the official national language. Balch developed a program that awarded flags to the best-behaved students in each class and developed a catechism that stressed good conduct and obedience (Guenter 1990, 116).

Balch's pledge was superseded by a pledge developed by Francis Bellamy and subsequently modified at least twice, most notably by the addition of the words "under God," which brought Bellamy's salute closer to Balch's original.

See also Bellamy, Francis J.; Pledge of Allegiance; Under God

Further Reading

Balch, George T. 1890. *Methods of Teaching Patriotism in the Public Schools*. New York: D. Van Nostrand.

"George Thacher Balch." http://balchipedi.wikidot.com/georgethatcher.balch

Guenter, Scot M. 1990. *The American Flag, 1777–1924: Cultural Shifts from Creation to Codification*. Cranbury, NJ: Associated University Presses.

O'Leary, Cecilia, and Tony Platt. 2002. "Pledging Allegiance: The Revival of Prescriptive Patriotism." In *Beyond September 11: An Anthology of Dissent*, edited by Phil Scraton, 173–176. Chicago: Pluto Press.

Teachout, Woden. 2009. *Capture the Flag: A Political History of American Patriotism*. New York: Basic Books.

BATES'S FLAG MARCH THROUGH THE FORMER CONFEDERATE STATES

Perhaps influenced by the pedestrianism movement advocated by Edward Payson Weston, Sgt. Gilbert Bates (1836–1917), a former Union soldier, took two long trips carrying an American flag to show that animosities had healed after the Civil War. The first and most heralded of these journeys, which he took from January through April 1868, was triggered by a bet from a Wisconsin neighbor. It consisted of a 1,300-mile trek through the states of the Confederacy, designed to show that southerners would treat him and the flag hospitably. The journey started in Vicksburg, Mississippi, and proceeded through Alabama, South Carolina, North Carolina, and Virginia before ending at the nation's capital.

Bates's neighbor was not his only skeptic. Writing in the *Territorial Enterprise*, Mark Twain observed:

> This fellow will get more black eyes, down there among those unconstructed rebels, than he can ever carry along with him without breaking his back. I expect to see him coming into Washington some day on one leg and with one eye out and an arm gone. He won't amount to more than an interesting relic by the time he gets here and then he will have to hire out for a sign for the Anatomical Museum. Those fellows down there have no sentiment in them. They won't buy his picture. They will be more likely to take his scalp. (Quoted in Keim and Keim 2007, 129)

Bates's critics were wrong, though. In fact, Bates had a highly successful trip. Ladies in Vicksburg made a five-by-three-foot silk flag for him to carry, and crowds greeted and feted him enthusiastically through most of his trip. He did face numerous storms, however, which sometimes forced him to walk on railroad tracks rather than on muddy roads. On one occasion, he encountered a pack of dogs, which he warded off with the staff of his flag after observing that he could only account for their hostility "on the ground that they are 'rebels yet,' and have not yet been reconstructed, nor taken the test oath" (Bates 1868, 13). On another occasion, he faced a threat from African Americans in a theatre, which he attributed to "unscrupulous white men, who infest the country, [and] are constantly putting them up to all sorts of mischief" (15).

Bates was among those who thought that Reconstruction was too harsh. In the journal that he kept of his trip, he frequently accused African Americans of being shiftless and lazy. He also opposed African American suffrage, declaring that "such a loathsome mass of ignorance never before exercised political power in a civilized community" and that he had "certainly never fought for any such object" (Bates 1868, 10–11). Bates recorded many testaments of southern allegiance to the U.S. flag, including one from a Confederate veteran who told him: "We are willing to-day to fight for the stars and stripes and the Constitution against any nation in the world. Just tell your friends that, Sergeant, and they won't think so badly of us. We are all Americans, and love the old flag, every one of us" (17).

However, it seems unlikely that elite white southerners would have extended as warm a welcome had his own politics not been amenable to theirs. Bates tellingly observed that in Charlotte, North Carolina, a former Confederate soldier "proposed three cheers for Sergeant Bates, the United States flag, and the white man's government" (19).

When he arrived at the nation's capital, Radical Republicans opposed to his hasty reconciliation with the South tied up in red tape his request to wave the flag above the Capitol Building. Undeterred, Bates went to the still-unfinished Washington Monument. There, after a speech by E. O. Perrin, the newly appointed chief justice of the Supreme Court of Utah, Bates climbed to the summit of the monument, where he raised the flag to the cheers of the crowd that had gathered below (Lomask 1965).

In 1872, Bates conducted a shorter journey of just over 300 miles from the Scottish border to London, where the citizens, who had been thought to have sympathized with the Confederacy, received him with similar acclaim.

See also Civil War; Washington Monument Flag Display

Further Reading

Bates, Gilbert H. 1868. *Sergeant Bates' March Carrying the Stars and Stripes Unfurled from Vicksburg to Washington: Being a Truthful Narrative of the Incidents Which Transpired During His Journey on Foot, Without a Cent, through the Late Rebellious States, and Showing How the Good Old Flag Was Received as the Harbinger of Peace and New Hope to the Distressed People of the South*. New York: B. W. Hitchcock.

Keim, Kevin, and Peter Keim. 2007. *A Grand Old Flag: A History of the United States through Its Flags*. New York: DK.

Lomask, Milton. 1965. "Sergt. Bates March." *American Heritage* 16 (6). http://www.americanheritage.com/content/sergt-bates-march?page=show

BAXTER, PERCIVAL P.

One of the most unusual controversies surrounding a U.S. flag occurred in 1923 when Percival Proctor Baxter (1876–1969), the governor of Maine from 1921 to 1925, ordered the flag over the State House in Augusta to be lowered to half-mast to mark the death of his dog Garry, an Irish setter.

Baxter, an unmarried graduate of Bowdoin College and the Harvard Law School, initially received criticism from the Grand Army of the Republic and the American Legion, both of which thought that Baxter's actions dishonored the flag. Most critics apparently changed their minds after Baxter explained that "I did it, not because Garry was my dog and a member of my family, but to teach a lesson, to draw people's attention to the qualities of the dog, qualities which so often are forgotten in human relationships" (*New York Times*, July 8, 1928).

Baxter further explained his action in a small pamphlet:

> My faithful dog, unlike many of my human friends, never betrayed or believed ill of me. It may be that comments made upon my action will arouse our people to a new realization of their responsibility to dumb animals. I firmly believe that when the

> men and women of this State and nation think through what I have done, they will see that a lesson in the appreciation of dumb animals has been taught, and that my act heightens the significance of our flag as an emblem of human achievement that has been made possible largely through the faithful services and sacrifices of dumb animals. I should esteem it an honor when my times comes to have the same Capitol flag that was lowered for my dog, lowered for me. (Quoted in *New York Times*, July 8, 1928).

Baxter was an outdoorsman who is probably best known for leaving 200,000 acres of forest land to the state. In 1933, Maine converted it into a state park named in his honor.

See also American Legion; Grand Army of the Republic (GAR); Half-Staff

Further Reading

New York Times. 1928. "Governor Who Honored Dog Makes Reply to His Critics." July 8.

BEECHER, HENRY WARD

Henry Ward Beecher (1813–1887) was one of the most influential Protestant (Congregational) preachers of the 19th century. He was also a social reformer and brother of Harriet Beecher Stowe, who composed *Uncle Tom's Cabin*.

In 1861, Beecher delivered a speech to the Brooklyn 14th Regiment in which he sought to identify the flag with the abolitionist calls for liberty. With some exceptions, most notably Francis Scott Key's writing of "The Star-Spangled Banner" in 1814, the American flag did not figure that prominently in the early nation's history. After the southern attack on the federal garrison at Fort Sumter in April 1861 that initiated the U.S. Civil War, however, there was renewed emphasis in the northern states on the flag as a symbol of national unity, which began to replace earlier associations ("scars and stripes") between the flag and slavery.

Beecher reflected this sentiment with a rousing speech, likening the stars to "the bright morning stars of God" and its stripes to "beams of morning light." Unlike the flag of monarchies, it had "no ramping lions and no fierce eagle; no embattled castles, or insignia of imperial authority" but "symbols of light." Beecher proclaimed: "It is the banner of Dawn. It means Liberty; and the galley-slave, the poor, oppressed conscript, the trodden-down creatures of foreign despotism, sees in the American flag that very promise and prediction of God: 'The people which sat in darkness say a great light; and to them which sat in the region and shadow of death light is spring up.' " Significantly, Christians generally interpret the scripture passage from Isaiah to which Beecher referred as a reference to the Christ, the Messiah.

Beecher's closing words are the most significant. He urged the men, "Accept it, then, in all its fullness of meaning." He continued:

> It is not a painted rag. It is a whole national history. It is the Constitution. It is the government. It is the free people that stand in the government on the Constitution. Forget not what it means; and for the sake of its ideas, be true to your country's flag.

Beecher thus sought to tie the flag to the America's noblest principles and especially to liberty, which he hoped the Civil War would bring to the slaves.

At the end of the war, Beecher was invited to Fort Sumter to give a speech when the U.S. flag was raised there. In this speech, he observed:

> We raise our fathers' banner that it may bring back better blessings than those of old; that it may restore lawful government, and a prosperity purer and more enduring than that which it protected before; that it may win parted friends from their alienation; that it may inspire hope, and inaugurate universal liberty . . . giving to us the glorious prerogative of leading all nations to juster laws, to more humane policies, to sincerer friendship, to rational, instituted civil liberty, and to universal Christian brotherhood. (Quoted in Whipple 1910, 88)

Henry Ward Beecher was a nationally prominent minister, against slavery and for women's rights. Beecher gave a number of speeches, including one at the end of the Civil War, in which he associated the American flag with liberty. (Library of Congress)

He further expressed the hope that like the rainbow, the flag would serve as "the memorial of an everlasting covenant and decree that never again on this fair land shall a deluge of blood prevail" (quoted in Whipple, 88). Beecher gave this speech on Good Friday when, unknown to him or the crowd, John Wilkes Booth assassinated President Lincoln (Applegate 2007, 1–17).

In yet another speech entitled "The Meaning of Our Flag," Beecher chiefly associated the flag with liberty. He noted thus:

> This American Flag was the safeguard of liberty. Not an atom of crown was allowed to go into its insignia. Not a symbol of authority in the ruler was permitted to go into it. It was an ordinance of liberty by the people, for the people. That it meant, that it means, and, by the blessing of God, that it shall mean to the end of time! (Quoted in Whipple 1910, 131)

See also Campbell, Thomas; Civil War; Fort Sumter Flag; Key, Francis Scott: Star-Spangled Banner

Further Reading

Applegate, Debby. 2007. *The Most Famous Man in America: The Biography of Henry Ward Beecher*. New York: Three Leaves.

Kass, Amy A., and Leon R. Kass. 2013. *Flag Day: The American Calendar*. Washington, D.C.: What So Proudly We Hail.

Whipple, Wayne. [1910]. *The Story of the American Flag*. Bedford, MA: Applewood Books. [Philadelphia: Henry Altemus Company].

BELLAMY, FRANCIS J.

Francis Julius Bellamy (1855–1931) authored the pledge to the U.S. flag in preparation for nationwide celebrations that *The Youth's Companion*, a popular children's magazine, had organized to commemorate the 400th anniversary of Christopher Columbus's discovery of America. Bellamy worked so closely on this project with James B. Upham, another employee at *Youth's Companion*, that for a time, authorship of the pledge was disputed.

The son of a Baptist minister, Bellamy was born in Mount Morris, New York, and educated at the University of Rochester, where he also studied theology. Although he began his career preaching, he left the pastorate of Boston's Bethany Baptist Church to join *The Youth's Companion* because of conflicts stemming from his advocacy of Christian socialism. As the celebration of Columbus's discovery approached, Bellamy and Upham expressed dissatisfaction with an existing pledge that had been penned by George Thacher Balch. After Upham had difficulty penning words to the pledge, Bellamy authored the following: "I pledge allegiance to my Flag and to the Republic for which it stands—one Nation indivisible—with Liberty and Justice for all." In time, "my flag" was changed to "the flag of the United States" and later "of America," and the words "under God" were added in 1954.

Bellamy was very concerned about the need to integrate immigrants into the United States, and despite advancing Columbus Day celebrations, he emphasized America's Anglo-Saxon heritage. He was a first cousin of Edward Bellamy, who wrote the popular utopian novel *Looking Backward*.

See also Balch, George Thacher; Pledge of Allegiance; *Youth's Companion*

Further Reading

Ellis, Richard J. 2005. *To the Flag: The Unlikely History of the Pledge of Allegiance*. Lawrence: University Press of Kansas.

Harris, Louise. 1971. *The Flag Over the Schoolhouse*. Providence, RI: C. A. Stephens Collection, Brown University.

Jones, Jeffrey Owen. 2003. "The Man Who Wrote the Pledge of Allegiance." *Smithsonian Magazine*, November. https://www.smithsonianmag.com/history/the-man-who-wrote-the-pledge-of-allegiance-93907224/

New York Times. 1957. "Pledge Author Named: Library of Congress Decides Bellamy Wrote of Flag." September 13.

BENNINGTON FLAG

One of the most popular patterns of flags that people enjoy purchasing is the so-called Bennington Flag, so named because it was incorrectly believed to have been flown as Americans, led by Gen. John Stark, battled the British in Bennington, Vermont, on August 16, 1777. In addition to the alternating red and white stripes, the flag has the numeral 76 inscribed in the canton with an arc of 11 stars over it and 1 star in each of the canton's two upper corners.

The Bennington Flag (sometimes called the Filmore Flag after the individual who donated it), which is part of the collection of the Bennington Museum, is now known to have been made in the 19th century. It is similar to some flags that were made during centennial celebrations of the Declaration of Independence in 1876. By contrast, a green flag with 13 stars in the canton, which is also believed to have been carried by Stark's men, is still thought to be authentic (Corcoran 2002, 52–53).

See also Centennials, Bicentennials, and Other Commemorations; Thirteen-Star Flags

Further Reading

Cooper, Grace Rogers. 1973. *Thirteen-Star Flags: Keys to Identification*. Washington, D.C.: Smithsonian Institution Press.

Corcoran, Michael. 2002. *For Which It Stands: An Anecdotal Biography of the American Flag*. New York: Simon and Schuster.

BETSY ROSS FLAG

The flag most generally attributed to Betsy Ross contains the traditional 13 red and white stripes with 13 five-pointed stars arranged in a circle in the canton.

Although most scholars now doubt the story advanced by Ross's grandson William Canby that Ross designed the first American flag, she and her descendants certainly made flags, and it is common to refer to a flag with 13 alternating red and white stripes and a canton with 13 stars arranged in a circle as a Betsy Ross flag.

The earliest flag legislation did not specify how stars were to be arranged, and this Betsy Ross pattern remains one of the most popular flag designs. It was widely reproduced during the nation's centennial and bicentennial celebrations.

See also *Birth of Our Nation's Flag*; Ross, Betsy; Thirteen-Star Flags

Further Reading

Miller, Marla R. 2010. *Betsy Ross and the Making of America*. New York: Henry Holt and Company.

BIRTH OF OUR NATION'S FLAG

One of the paintings that has done the most to shape American understandings of the U.S. state flag is a large 9-by-12-foot painting by an amateur painter, Charles

This painting by Charles H. Weisgerber, which was first displayed at the World's Columbian Exposition in Chicago in 1893, gave rise to the myth that Betsy Ross designed the first American flag. George Washington, George Ross, and Robert Morris represent a congressional committee. (Library of Congress)

H. Weisgerber (who died in 1932). Weisgerber's *Birth of Our Nation's Flag* was first displayed at the World's Columbian Exposition in Chicago in 1893.

The painting depicts Betsy Ross seated to the right, in her home, with a flag on her lap, and George Washington, Gen. George Ross, and Robert Morris, who are supposed to represent a congressional committee, on the left. Washington and Betsy Ross are looking at one another, while General Ross (a relative of Betsy's) and Robert Morris (the financier of the American Revolution) look toward the viewers.

Light streams from a window to Betsy Ross's right, and the 13 five-pointed stars on the flag that she is holding are arranged in a circular pattern. Some of the stars and stripes are portrayed as being on the floor, which was apparently not considered to be disrespectful at the time of the painting (as it is now). To Betsy Ross's right is a paper with a design of the flag, presumably from George Washington.

Although Betsy Ross did make flags, the myth that she made the first flag is anachronistic, in part because Congress did not authorize a flag design until June 14, 1777, and in part because there is no contemporary evidence that Washington met with Ross. The story of Ross's role originated from a paper that her grandson William J. Canby read before the Pennsylvania Historical Society in 1860 entitled "The Origin of the American Flag." He claimed to have heard the story from his grandmother before she died in 1836, and he subsequently gathered some affidavits from other family members to confirm the story. It was so well received that the Betsy Ross House at 239 Arch Street in Philadelphia, which was partially owned by Weisgerber (who named a son Vexil Domus, meaning "flag house" in Latin [Worden 2002]), has long been a cherished national landmark even after questions arose about the authenticity of Canby's story.

In analyzing Weisgerber's painting, Joann Menezes finds that it "is reminiscent of both an Annunciation and a Nativity scene" (Menezes 1997, 80), effectively identifying Betsy Ross as the mother of the nation.

The painting was widely distributed as a chromolithograph and later exhibited at the World's Fair of 1934. It also was the subject of a three-cent stamp that commemorated the 200th anniversary of Betsy Ross's birth. Vandalized by an attack in the 1950s while being displayed at the old State Museum in Harrisburg, the painting was rolled up for a time and subsequently restored. It was put on permanent display at the Pennsylvania State Museum in Harrisburg, shortly after the 9/11 terrorist attacks (Worden 2002).

Other paintings connecting Ross to the flag include a painting by Elloie Sully Wheeler of Philadelphia from 1851 and a glass plate negative that depicts a proposed fresco for the Capitol building (Harker 2005, 96–97). Edward Percy Moran (1862–1935), who specialized in historic themes, painted another picture of Betsy Ross and two girls showing the flag to George Washington and three other men in a work that he painted about 1917, titled *The Birth of Old Glory*.

See also Ross, Betsy

Further Reading

Harker, John B. 2005. "Betsy Ross: An American Legend and Patriot Revisited." *Raven: A Journal of Vexillology* 12:87–99.

Lidman, David. 1971. "Betsy Ross Stamp Perpetuates a Myth." *New York Times*, April 25.

Menezes, Joann. 1997. "The Birthing of the American Flag and the Invention of an American Founding Mother in the Image of Betsy Ross." In *Narratives of Nostalgia, Gender, and Nationalism*, edited by Jean Pickering and Suzanne Kehde, 74–87. Washington Square: New York University Press.

Worden, Amy. 2002. "Betsy Ross Painting Finds a New Home." *Baltimore Sun*, January 13. http://articles.baltimoresun.com/2002-01-13/news/0201130008_1_ross-sewed-betsy-ross-weisgerber

BRANDYWINE FLAG

A flag believed to have been flown at the Battle of Brandywine—sometimes called Brandywine Creek—on September 11, 1777, is on display at the Independence National Historical Park in Philadelphia. Flown at a time when units marched under regimental rather than national colors, the so-called Brandywine Flag is unique because it consists of a red-and-white-striped canton with its own white canton bearing 13 red six-pointed stars (Leepson 2005, 26–27) set against a field of red. The stars are arranged in three horizontal rows of four stars, five stars, and four stars. According to historian Grace Rogers Cooper, the earliest use of this pattern was in 1779 (1973, 10).

Possibly the first flag of stars and stripes carried into battle, it belonged to the 7th Pennsylvania Regiment's Company, commanded by Capt. Robert Wilson. During the course of the battle, Gen. George Washington's Patriot forces were forced to retreat from British forces under the command of Gen. Sir William Howe. This exposed the city of Philadelphia to subsequent capture and occupation by the British.

A 33-cent postage stamp commemorating this flag was released in 2000.

See also Revolutionary War; Thirteen-Star Flags

Further Reading

Cooper, Grace Rogers. 1972. *Thirteen-Star Flags: Keys to Identification.* Washington, D.C.: Smithsonian Institution Press.

Leepson, Marc. 2005. *Flag: An American Biography*. New York: St. Martin's Press.

BRUNER, FRANK C.

The U.S. flag has been a frequent subject for orations and declamations, so it is perhaps unsurprising that it has sometimes also been the object of prayer. It's probable no prayer has done more to highlight the flag than the one delivered by the Rev. Frank C. Bruner, the chaplain in chief of the Grand Army of the Republic, at its encampment in Cincinnati, Ohio, on September 8–9, 1898. At the time of the meeting, a month had not yet passed since the end of the Spanish-American War, which lasted from April 21 to August 13 and through which the United States acquired a number of foreign colonies.

Bruner was pastor of the First Methodist Church of Harvey, Illinois. His father and grandfather were veterans. Bruner himself had enlisted in the 9th Illinois Calvary at the age of 15. As quoted in the *Journal of the Thirty-Second National Encampment of the Grand Army of the Republic* (1898, 7), Bruner's prayer began by invoking "the Almighty God, Everlasting Father, [and] Prince of Peace." Bruner also referred to God as "the Father of Nationalism," which he associated with Mount Sinai, the site where God delivered the Ten Commandments to Moses and entered into a covenant with his people.

The second paragraph of his prayer uttered thanks for George and Martha Washington, for the Declaration of Independence and Constitution, and for Abraham Lincoln and the Emancipation Proclamation.

The third paragraph proceeded to thank God "for Liberty in Education," for the Grand Army of the Republic, and for "these men who have gone forth in 1898"—presumably those who had served in the Spanish-American War. The paragraph ends with "Give us greater love for the old flag which has seemed to come from the hand of God itself" (8).

The next and most extensive paragraph further offers thanks for "this emblem that we are to carry forth for civilization and to make the nations who have been blackened by superstition and darkness, brighter and more beautiful." Bruner opined that "the evolution of our flag gives a wider truth to humanity. It has become a patriotic schoolhouse, a symbolism of those elements which make good government: justice born of God." Likening the peace that had followed the recent conflict to "a snowy cataract . . . spilling its snow white waters upon the islands of the sea," he noted how "its silver billows are marching in white battalions across the continents resulting from the international liberty of the old flag" (8). He continued in perhaps his most expansive language:

> A flag for the national capital; a flag for every temple of justice; a flag for every church steeple; for every mountain top; a flag for every ship mast; a flag for every schoolhouse; a flag for all the world. All hail the banner of the free! May it continue to kiss the breeze until distant unborn generations rise up and look on its dancing folds. (8)

Bruner ended with the hope that men of the GAR will "take hold of the golden key of the Son of God that will unlock the gates and take us into the Grand Encampment above the stars" (8).

Stuart McConnell observes that this and similar statements from members of the Grand Army of the Republic framed the flag "as a quasi religious symbol with meaning that transcended national borders" (McConnell 1996, 110).

President William McKinley subsequently defended the U.S. decision to keep the Philippines as a colony by saying that he had prayed to God about the matter. Afterward, he said that he had concluded that "there was nothing left for us to do but to take them all, and to educate the Filipinos, and uplift and civilize and Christianize them, and by God's grace do the very best we could by them, as our fellow-men from whom Christ also died" (Rusling 1903, 17). Skeptics of McKinley's motivations, however, observed that most Filipinos were already Catholic Christians.

See also Cult of the Flag; Grand Army of the Republic (GAR); Spanish-American War

Further Reading

Chicago Tribune. 1896. "Bruner Is in the Race." September 2. http://archives.chicagotribune.com/1896/09/02/page/4/article/bruner-is-in-the-race

Journal of the Thirty-Second National Encampment of the Grand Army of the Republic. 1898. Cincinnati, September 8–9. Philadelphia: Town Printing Company.

McConnell, Stuart. 1996. "Reading the Flag: A Reconsideration of the Patriotic Cults of the 1890s." In *Bonds of Affection: Americans Define Their Patriotism*, edited by John Bodnar, 102–119. Princeton, NJ: Princeton University Press.

Rusling, James. 1903. "Interview with President William McKinley," *The Christian Advocate* January 22, p. 17. Accessible in "Decision on the Philippines, Digital History. www.digitalhistory.uh.edu/disp_textbook.cfm?smtID=3&psid=1257

C

CAMPAIGN FLAGS

Although the practice is now frowned upon as a violation of flag etiquette, in the 19th century it was common to print the names of presidential candidates on the stripes of the flag or place their pictures in the canton. This practice appears to have originated largely in the raucous campaign of 1840 in which the Whig Party competed with Democratic-Republicans (who had long prided themselves on their identification with the people) by portraying their candidate, William Henry Harrison, as having been born in a log cabin over which a flag commonly flew. Further emphasizing Harrison's military service in a campaign against the Native Americans, the Whigs ran with the slogan "Tippecanoe and Tyler too," referring to the Battle of Tippecanoe and John Tyler, the candidate for vice president. Flags also contained slogans such as "Harrison and Reform" and "The Hero of Tippecanoe" (Collins 1979, 102–103).

The practice of intermingling campaign messages on flags was so widespread that in 1880, the Cheney Brothers' American Silk Flags, of South Manchester, Connecticut, advertised attachments for the bottoms of U.S. flags with the names of party candidates (Guenter 1990, 136). Individuals could thus switch the names from one campaign to another.

Although slogans varied from one campaign to the next, this practice continued well into the late 19th century. During that same time, candidates' pictures often

Woodcut for the Whigs' "log cabin" campaign of 1840 for William Henry Harrison and John Tyler. The untitled woodcut was created to illustrate broadsides, banners, and ribbons during the campaign. (Library of Congress)

were also included on bandanas and campaign posters, often in conjunction with American flags, eagles, or other prominent American symbols. Politicians had an interest in portraying themselves as patriotic and their opponents as traitors. This was reinforced by the Republican tendency to "wave the bloody shirt"—that is, to continue to associate their Democrat opponents with the rebellion that led to the Civil War. Their opponents pushed back, however, against partisan attempts (such as that of Republicans in the election of 1896) to claim the flag or flag-related holidays for themselves (Guenter 1990, 134).

As the 19th century came to a close, organizations like the United States Flag Association began pushing back against the use of the flag in commercial advertising. This campaign, which eventually resulted in anti–flag desecration laws, probably help bring an end to the practice of writing candidates' names or including their pictures on flags, but it has not stopped politicians from attempting to link their campaigns to the flag and to other traditional symbols of patriotism.

See also Advertising; Lapel Pins

Further Reading

Collins, Herbert Ridgeway. 1979. *Threads of History: Americana Recorded on Cloth 1775 to the Present*. Washington, D.C.: Smithsonian Institution Press.

Guenter, Scot M. 1990. *The American Flag, 1777–1924: Cultural Shifts from Creation to Codification*. Cranbury, NJ: Associated University Presses.

Troy, Gil. 1992. "Stars, Stripes, and Spots." *Design Quarterly*, no. 157 (Autumn): 2–10.

CAMPBELL, THOMAS

Typically idealized by citizens and patriots, the U.S. flag can be a symbol of American shortcomings as well as of it successes. Although African Americans participated on the Patriot side during the American Revolution, it was not until the middle of the Civil War that Union forces finally allowed them to fight for their own freedom.

Prior to this time, most African Americans had little cause to celebrate the U.S. flag. During the American Revolution, the English literary figure Samuel Johnson had rhetorically asked, "How is it that we hear the loudest yelps for liberty among the drivers of negroes?" (Midgley 2016). No foreign author brought this point home more clearly than Thomas Campbell (1777–1844) of Scotland. Campbell's father had been a merchant in Virginia who lost much of his fortune at the time of the American Revolution.

In 1838, Thomas Campbell wrote a poem entitled "To the United States of North America," in which he likened the 13 stripes on the U.S. flags to scars; the term "stripes" can also refer to scars left by a beating. His words were as follows:

United States, your banner wears
Two emblems—one of fame.
Alas! The other that it bears
Reminds us of your shame

Your banner's constellation types
White freedom with its stars,
But what's the meaning of the stripes?
They mean your negroes' scars.

Campbell was writing at a time when *Sommersett's Case* (1773) had set a precedent that slaves became free once they reached England simply by reason of breathing English air.

Campbell's analogy of stripes was sometimes incorporated into U.S. abolitionist literature. In his famous Fourth of July address of 1852, the former slave Frederick Douglass observed, "The sunlight that brought light and healing to you, has brought stripes and death to me" (quoted in Vile 2016, 172). Earlier pointing to the evils of the fugitive slave clause, Douglass had observed: "Wherever waves the star-spangled banner there the bondman may be arrested and hurried back to the jaws of slavery. This is your 'land of the free,' your 'home of the brave' " (Kosek 2017, 38). In her "melo-drama" about the Underground Railroad entitled *The Stars and Stripes*, Lydia Maria Child has slaves carry the U.S. flag on stage. In a letter that former slave Harriet Jacobs wrote in 1853, she observed that the stripes and stars "should be stripes and scars" (quoted in Perry 2008, 597).

One "New Version of the National Song" that parodied "The Star-Spangled Banner" and was featured in William Lloyd Garrison's *The Liberator* featured the following verse:

Oh, say do you hear, at the dawn's early light
The shrieks of those bondmen, whose blood is now streaming
From the merciless lash, while our banner in sight
With its stars mocking freedom, is fitfully gleaming?
Do you see the backs bare? Do you mark every score
Of the whip of the driver trace channels of gore?
And say, doth our star-spangled banner yet wave
O'er the land of the free and the home of the brave? (Quoted in Ferris 2014, 30–31)

Harriet Jacobs gave a much more positive speech lauding the flag at a flag-presentation ceremony to the 9th Army's Colored, or L'Ouverture, Division in Alexandria, Virginia, in 1864, on the occasion of celebrating British West India Emancipation (Perry 2008). The Civil War is associated with increased appreciation of the flag—not only among African Americans, who would soon share in its freedoms, but also among white Americans, especially in the North, who regarded it as a symbol of national unity.

In a speech he delivered in Charleston, South Carolina, on March 19, 1867, Rev. E. J. Adams observed: "The flag that once floated over four millions of slaves, today waves in triumph over more than thirty millions of freemen. The bloody crimson stripes of that banner, once emblematic of the bloody furrows ploughed upon the quivering flesh of four million of slaves, today is emblematic of the bloody sacrifice offered upon the altars of American liberty."

See also Child, Lydia Maria; Civil Rights Movement; Civil War; "Star-Spangled Banner" (Anthem)

Further Reading

Adams, E. J. 1867. "These Are Revolutionary Times." BlackPast.org. http://www.blackpast.org/1867-rev-e-j-adams-these-are-revolutionary-times

Child, Lydia Maria. 1997. *The Stars and Stripes. A Melo-Drama.* Edited by Glynis Carr. The Online Archive of Nineteenth-Century U.S. Women's Writings. http://www.facstaff.bucknell.edu/gcarr/19cUSWW/LB/S&S.html

Ferris, Marc. 2014. *Star-Spangled Banner: The Unlikely Story of American's National Anthem.* Baltimore: Johns Hopkins University Press.

Kosek, Joseph Kip, ed. 2017. *American Religion, American Politics: An Anthology*. New Haven, CT: Yale University Press.

Midgley, Anne. 2016. "How Is It That We Hear the Loudest Yelps for Liberty Among the Drivers of Negroes?" *Saber and Scroll* 5 (3). http://digitalcommons.apus.edu/saberandscroll/vol5/iss3/10

Perry, Lewis. 2008. "Harriet Jacobs and the 'Dear Old Flag.'" *African American Review* 43 (Fall/Winter): 595–605.

Vile, John R. 2016. *The Jacksonian and Antebellum Eras: Documents Decoded.* Santa Barbara, CA: ABC-CLIO.

CANBY, WILLIAM J.

See Ross, Betsy

CAPITOL FLAG PROGRAM

The Capitol Building, which houses the U.S. Congress, is a unique symbol of the nation. Originally designed by Dr. William Thorton, it was burned by the British during the War of 1812 but repaired and significantly expanded by Thomas U. Walter. It is capped by a dome that is topped by a 19-foot statue of freedom. At one time, the building was also occupied by the Library of Congress and by the U.S. Supreme Court, which now have their own buildings.

Early engravings show that flags flew on either side of the low dome above the corridors connecting today's Statuary Hall and the Old Senate Chamber, just as they now fly over both wings of the building. Flags have flown continuously over both the east and west fronts since World War I. The flags are actually flown from a deck that is not visible from the street. After some employees were found to be skipping the flag raising, cameras now verify that they have done so (Corcoran 2001, 145).

Ever since it received a request in 1937 from a member of Congress for a flag that had flown over the nation's capital, Congress has overseen a Capitol Flag Program by which members of Congress may request flags that have flown over the capital and subsequently been retired from use. According to the official website of this organization, this group now fulfills more than 100,000 requests from private citizens or organizations each year. Each comes with a certificate indicating when it was flown (they are flown every day except Thanksgiving, Christmas, and New Year's Day). Flags may not exceed 8 feet by 12 feet.

See also Twenty-Four-Hour Flag Displays; War of 1812

Further Reading

Architect of the Capitol. 2017. "Capitol Flag Program." Accessed January 18. https://www.aoc.gov/flags

Corcoran, Michael. 2001. *For Which It Stands: An Anecdotal Biography of the American Flag.* New York: Simon and Schuster.

Federal Citizen Information Center. 2017. "Flags at the United States Capitol." Our Flag. Accessed March 27. https://publications.usa.gov/epublications/ourflag/capitolflag.htm

Luckey, John R. 2008. *The United States Flag: Federal Law Relating to Display and Associated Questions.* CRS Report for Congress. Washington, D.C.: Congressional Research Service.

Stern, Philip Van. 1969/1970. "The Capitol." *Records of the Columbia Historical Society, Washington, D.C.* 69/70:178–189.

CAPTAIN AMERICA

The comic book character Captain America, like Uncle Sam, wears clothes that distinctly tie him to the American flag. His cap and pants are blue, he has red and white stripes on his shirt, and he wears red boots. Most distinctively, since the second issue of the comic book, he carries a round shield (thus somewhat distinguishing himself from other allegorical figures in U.S. history with more traditionally shaped shields) with red and white stripes and a star in the blue center.

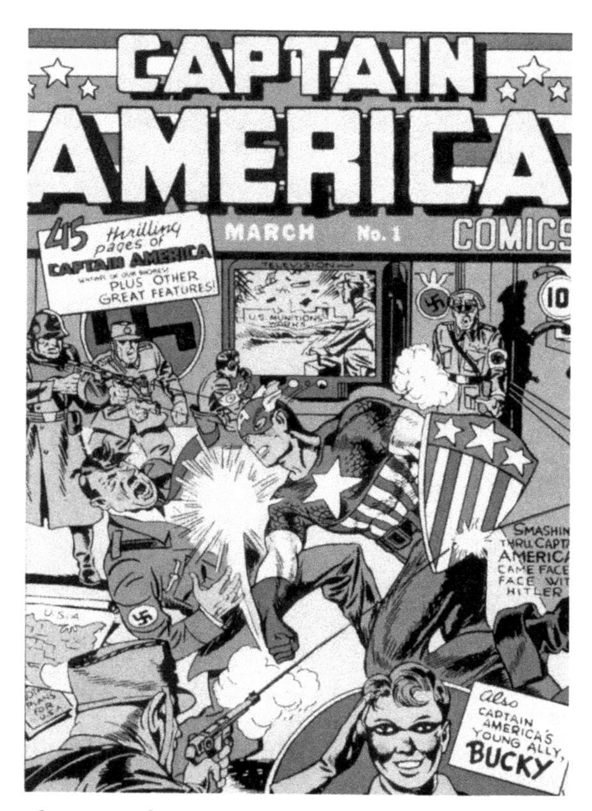

The cover of the very first issue of a *Captain America* comic book, published by Marvel Comics, 1941. This comic took the superhero genre into a whole new arena by pitting Captain America against a real-life wartime enemy, Hitler, and proved fantastically successful as a result. (Marvel Comics/Photofest)

In the first Marvel Comics issue in the Captain America series, released in March, 1941, he is introduced as a frail young man named Steve Rogers who is determined to join the U.S. Army. To his great disappointment, he cannot pass the physical exam, but he is given a serum by a Dr. Reinstein (a stand in for Albert Einstein) and becomes a super-soldier. Captain America does not, however, have the super-powers (the ability to fly or x-ray vision) of Superman and other superheroes. Significantly, he is characterized by a defensive shield rather than by an offensive weapon, and most early issues of the comic pair him with Bucky Barnes, a younger sidekick who ends up doing most of the actual killing of evildoers, when it proves necessary.

Later descriptions of Captain America tie his development less to wonder drugs than to his courage, hard work, and persistence (Dittmer 2013, 69–70). Three Captain America movies have been released from 2011 to 2016, each of them starring actor Chris Evans in the title role. In addition, the Captain America character has appeared in several other popular movies about Marvel superheroes during these same years.

In the same year that Captain America was introduced by Marvel Comics, a competing comic book company named DC Comics introduced a character known as the Star-Spangled Kid, whom Marc Ferris describes as "the alter ego of fifteen-year-old Sylvester Pemberton" (Ferris 2014, 175). This character was phased out within a matter of months, however.

See also Uncle Sam; World War II

Further Reading

Boime, Albert. 1990. "Waving the Red Flag and Reconstituting Old Glory." *Smithsonian Studies in American Art* 4 (Spring): 2–25.

Dittmer, Jason. 2013. *Captain America and the Nationalist Superhero*. Philadelphia: Temple University Press.

Ferris, Marc. 2014. *Star-Spangled Banner: The Unlikely Story of America's National Anthem*. Baltimore: Johns Hopkins University Press.

Scott, Cord. 2007. "Written in Red, White, and Blue: A Comparison of Comic Book Propaganda from World War II and September 11." *The Journal of Popular Culture* 40:325–343.

CENTENNIALS, BICENTENNIALS, AND OTHER COMMEMORATIONS

Some historic sites, including presidents' houses, national monuments, Pennsylvania Hall in Philadelphia, and Colonial Williamsburg in Virginia, to name but a few, serve as permanent reminders of America's past. Similarly, holidays like Independence Day, Flag Day, and Labor Day are almost always associated with patriotic displays that almost invariably place the American flag in positions of prominence. Likewise, anniversaries of historic events, especially centennials and bicentennials, place heavy emphasis on the American flag and other patriotic symbols.

The 1876 centennial celebration of the Declaration of Independence and the Revolutionary War was a particularly noteworthy event. Coming not long after the nation had fought a bloody Civil War and just before the end of Congressional Reconstruction, there is general agreement that the celebration, which was held in Philadelphia, was a chance for the nation both to celebrate its progress and to bridge sectional tensions.

The exposition was opened with a speech by then president Ulysses S. Grant and the raising of the American flag. Among the many exhibits were Archibald

Willard's painting *The Spirit of '76*. An exhibit of relics from George Washington included an American flag as a backdrop; although the Star-Spangled Banner that had flown over Fort McHenry was sent, it does not appear to have been exhibited, apparently for fears that it would be damaged (Taylor, Kendrick, and Brodie 2008, 97). The most popular flag offered for purchase during the celebration was probably the 13-star flag, many of which have subsequently been mistaken for originals from the Revolutionary War era. The celebration included sales of a wide range of commemorative souvenirs depicting representations of the flag, the bald eagle, the Liberty Bell, and other patriotic symbols. Boosted by huge crowds on opening day and July 4, the exposition was widely regarded as a success.

The World's Columbian Exposition of 1893 was held in Chicago. The celebration corresponded with generally successful nationwide efforts to fly flags at U.S. schools and to begin each day with salutes to the flag. Unlike on the centennial, the bicentennial celebrations of 1976 did not center in a single city but were diffused throughout the country. Like the celebrations that preceded them, the celebrations that year resulted in numerous commemorative items, many featuring red, white, and blue, including caskets (Klein 1977, 260). The Allentown Museum hosted an exhibit from June 14 through November 14, 1976, entitled *The American Flag in the Art of Our Country*, which was illustrated in a book that same year. The bicentennial also featured numerous reenactments of historic events, many of which were not particularly noted for their accuracy (Lowenthal 1977, 259–261).

See also Independence Day; Flag Day; *Spirit of '76*; Thirteen-Star Flags

Further Reading

Allentown Art Museum. 1976. *The American Flag in the Art of Our Country*. Allentown, PA: Allentown Art Museum.

Burstein, Andrew. 2001. *America's Jubilee: How in 1826 a Generation Remembered Fifty Years of Independence*. New York: Knopf.

Carson, Hampton L., ed. 1889. *History of the Celebration of the One Hundredth Anniversary of the Promulgation of the Constitution of the United States*. 2 vols. Philadelphia: J. J. Lippincott.

Gores, Stan. 1974. *1876 Centennial Collectibles and Price Guide*. Fond Du Lac, WI: Haber Printing Co.

Kammen, Michael. 2003. "Commemoration and Contestation in American Culture: Historical Perspectives." *Amerikastudien / American Studies* 48 (2): 185–202.

Klein, Milton M. 1977. "Commemorating the American Revolution: The Bicentennial and Its Predecessors." *New York History* 58:257–276.

Little, David B. 1974. *America's First Centennial Celebration: The Nineteenth of April 1875 at Lexington and Concord, Massachusetts*. 2nd ed. Boston: Houghton Mifflin.

Lowenthal, David. 1977. "The Bicentennial Landscape: A Mirror Held Up to the Past." *The Geographical Review* (July): 253–267.

Taylor, Lonn, Kathleen M. Kendrick, and Jeffrey L. Brodie. 2008. *The Star-Spangled Banner: The Making of an American Icon*. Washington, D.C.: Smithsonian Books.

CHILD, LYDIA MARIA

Lydia Maria Child (1802–1880) was a Massachusetts-born writer and social reformer who is probably best known for writing the Thanksgiving poem "Over the River and Through the Woods." She also published *The Stars and Stripes. A Melo-Drama*. This 1857 work tells the tale of a married mixed-race couple who use the Underground Railroad to flee from Mr. Masters, a southern slave owner and the father of the fleeing wife. During the course of the story, the couple make their way across the Ohio River, then through Detroit to Canada.

The drama begins at a Fourth of July celebration in the South, where the men sing lines from "The Star-Spangled Banner," but other than the opening scene, the play does not put much emphasis on the flag.

The play also contains "The Filibusters' Song"—at the time, a filibuster was an illegal military action typically undertaken against Caribbean nations by slave owners. In the song, slave owners laud the capture of Mexican territory and look forward to the capture of Cuba and Haiti as they defy John Bull (the symbol for Great Britain) to stop their advances. One stanza from Scene I proclaims thus:

> And if it suits our sov'reign will
> T'annex the planet Mars,
> What business need it be to you,
> How we increase our stars?

Similarly, the next stanza proclaims:

> 'Tis plain that Fate marks us to be
> The masters of the world!
> O'er Sandwich Isles, and far Niphon,
> Our flag shall be unfurled.

"Niphon" probably refers to Nippon, a name for Japan. The play is notable for playing off the theme of the Fourth of July and contrasting the liberty of the slave owner with the servitude of the slaves in the American South.

See also Campbell, Thomas; "Star-Spangled Banner" (Anthem)

Further Reading

Child, Lydia Maria. 1997. *The Stars and Stripes. A Melo-Drama*. Edited by Glynis Carr. The Online Archive of Nineteenth-Century U.S. Women's Writings. http://www.facstaff.bucknell.edu/gcarr/19cUSWW/LB/S&S.html

Lewis, Jone Johnson. 2017. "Lydia Maria Child: Reformer, Speaker and Writer." ThoughtCo. Last modified April 13. http://womenshistory.about.com/od/childlydiamaria/a/lydiamariachild.htm

CHRISTIAN FLAG

The use of a flag with a cross dates at least as far back as the Crusades and possibly to the Roman emperor Constantine (Wescher 1977). Indeed, Wescher believes that the desire to distinguish crusaders from France, England, and the Flemings led to the design of distinctive crosses of red, white, and green.

Whatever the antecedents, the modern idea for formulating a distinctively Christian flag apparently dates back to an impromptu speech that Charles C. Overton, a New York Sunday school superintendent at Brighton Chapel, Staten Island, delivered on a Rally Day (associated with a new Bible school year, typically soon after the end of summer) on September 26, 1897. He subsequently joined Ralph Diffendorfter, who was secretary to the Methodist Young People's Missionary Movement, to produce a flag consisting of a blue canton with a red cross against a field of white. Some churches recognized the flag, but critics such as the editor of *Christian Century* were dismissive, describing it as a particularly poor substitute for the cross (Sidwell 1998, 1).

Ironically, Puritan settlers in Massachusetts were offended that the flag that the king asked them to fly included a cross in the canton, which they sometimes removed because they thought the cross was an idolatrous remnant of Roman Catholicism (Martucci 2006).

The Civil War appears to mark the period in which churches began displaying U.S. flags. By April 1861, for example, flags were reportedly raised over Episcopal, Baptist, Dutch Reformed, and Roman Catholic churches across New York City, often to the accompaniment of ceremonial music such as "Yankee Doodle" or "Red, White, and Blue" (Guenter 1990, 85). Somewhat later, the Grand Army of the Republic (GAR), a Civil War veterans' organization, urged churches to display flags to emphasize the connection between God's Providence and the nation. In 1889, a GAR member named George W. Gue, who was also pastor of the First Methodist Church of Rock Island, Illinois, convinced the Central Illinois Conference of the Methodist Episcopal Church to adopt a resolution to place the flag in churches and Sunday schools "as an emblem of our Christian civilization" (quoted in Guenter 1990, 106).

The Flag Code, a set of recommendations adopted by patriotic organizations on Flag Day of 1923, has specified that when both the Christian flag and the U.S. flag are flown on a pole, the U.S. Flag should be in the higher position. Similarly, in a procession, it should have the lead place. The Federal Council of Churches questioned this in a resolution adopted on January 23, 1942, and in at least one case in Milford, New Jersey, a local chief of police attempted to change flag placement within the First Presbyterian Church.

In an account of the history of the flag of the American Episcopal Church, an author has observed:

> It may be questioned whether a secular code or military precedent should govern the display of the Church's own flag within the chancel of a church, but it seems reasonable that even inside the church, precedence should be given to the American flag. This does not contravene the declaration of the House of Bishops that "the cross is above the flag"; the cross, as the symbol of Christianity, of course, takes precedence over any national emblem. But the flag of the Episcopal Church, which represents a particular division of Christendom, is not entitled to the same precedence. (Luce 1958, 330)

The presence of two flags may always suggest the possibility of conflicting loyalties, but Americans are already accustomed to living in states that have their own emblems in addition to the national flag.

Lynn Harold Hough, a Methodist minister, wrote a pledge in 1908 that declared, "I pledge allegiance to my flag and the Savior for whose kingdom it stands; one brotherhood uniting all mankind in service and love" (quoted in Morgan 2014, 115). Another version, more common in conservative congregations, says: "I PLEDGE ALLEGIANCE TO THE Christian Flag and to the Savior for whose Kingdom it stands. One Savior, crucified, risen, and coming again with life and liberty to all who believe" (Coffman 2008).

One of these pledges is often used in Vacation Bible Schools, often in conjunction with a pledge to the Bible. That pledge is as follows: "I pledge allegiance to the Bible, God's Holy Word, I will make it a lamp unto my feet and a light unto my path and will hide its words in my heart that I might not sin against God."

During World War I, students were often encouraged to participate in flag pageants, which often featured both the U.S. and Christian flags. "The underlying message throughout seems to be that the United States will prosper as long as she remembers she is a Christian nation" (Guenter 1990, 165).

Writing in 1931, Robert Phillips observed that U.S. Navy ships carry a Christian flag and that "every Sunday morning, at eight o'clock, it is hoisted to a position above the Stars and Stripes, and is kept there for one hour. During that time religious services are held, the band participating by playing 'Onward Christian Soldiers' and the 'Star Spangled Banner'" (176). He further said, "No object except the Bible [or other such holy book] should be placed upon our national standard" (175).

Today churches often display Christian flags in conjunction with the U.S. flag. Ordinances in Dallas, Texas, and in Raleigh, North Carolina, have been challenged for forbidding the display of flags (including the Christian flag) other than the U.S. flag and were in both cases eventually changed to exempt the Christian flag (Sidwell 1998, 2).

See also Civil War; Cult of the Flag; Flag Code; Flag Etiquette (thematic essay); Pledge of Allegiance; World War I

Further Reading

Coffman, Elesha. 2008. "Do You Know the History of the Christian Flag?" *Christianity Today*, August 8. https://www.christianitytoday.com/history/2008/august/do-you-know-history-of-christian-flag.html

Guenter, Scot M. 1990. *The American Flag, 1776–1924: Cultural Shifts from Creation to Codification*. Cranbury, NJ: Associated University Presses.

Juster, Susan. 2017. "Planting the 'Great Cross': The Life, and Death, of Crosses in English America." *The William and Mary Quarterly* 74 (April): 241–270.

Luce, Jane Houghtaling. 1958. "The History and Symbolism of the Flag of the American Episcopal Church." *Historical Magazine of the Protestant Episcopal Church* 27 (December): 324–331.

Martucci, David B. 2006. "Flag and Symbol Usage in Early New England." *Raven: A Journal of Vexillology* 13:1–40.

Morgan, David. 2014. "The Image of the Protestant Bible in America." In *The Bible in the Public Square: Its Enduring Influence in American Life* (pp. 93–114), edited by Mark A. Chancey, Carol Meyers, and Eric M. Meyers. Atlanta: Society of Biblical Literature.
Phillips, Robert. 1931. *The American Flag: Its Uses and Abuses*. Boston: Stratford Company.
Sidwell, Mark. 1998. "The Christian Flag: A Fundamentalism File Research Report." December 18. http://libguides.bju.edu/ld.php?content_id=919093
Wescher, H. 1977. *Flags*. Winchester, MA: North American Vexillological Association.

CITIZENS FLAG ALLIANCE (CFA)

The Citizens Flag Alliance (CFA) describes itself on its website as a "broad-based, nonpartisan, nonprofit, national organization, which was formed to persuade Congress to pass a constitutional amendment that would return to the American people the right to protect their flag." In decisions in *Texas v. Johnson* (1989) and *United States v. Eichman* (1990), the U.S. Supreme Court respectively struck down state and federal laws prohibiting flag desecration on the grounds that they violated the First Amendment free speech clause of the U.S. Constitution.

The organization claims that it was incorporated in June 2004 and that it now includes more than 140 different organizations. Under "Frequently Asked Questions," the CFA notes that it has a board of directors drawn from member organizations and that this organizational structure serves "as a big, red, white and blue tent where all of our supporters can gather as equals to achieve our purpose."

In answering a number of commonly raised questions, the organization says that the amendment that it favors provides simply that "Congress shall have power to prohibit the physical desecration of the flag of the United States." It further says that the amendment that it favors would only apply to actual flags and not pictorial representations thereof and that the proposed amendment would apply only to American flags and not other revered objects like the Constitution, the Bible, or other symbols.

See also Flag Desecration Amendment; *Texas v. Johnson* (1989); *United States v. Eichman* (1990)

Further Reading

Citizens Flag Alliance. Accessed April 29, 2018. http://www.citizensflagalliance.org/

CIVIL RIGHTS MOVEMENT

Although the movement opposing the war in Vietnam often involved flag burning, early participants in the civil rights struggle of the 1960s more typically sought to evoke the flag on the side of their cause. This identification might symbolically reach back to the Civil War, where Union forces carried flags (that included the stars of the seceding states) as a sign of national unity.

African Americans had not, of course, always identified with the flag. In 1852, Frederick Douglass had delivered a speech in which he asked "What to the Slave Is the Fourth of July?" (Vile 2017, 171–176). Speaking around the turn of the 20th century, Henry McNeal Turner, the bishop of the African Methodist Episcopal Church who headed the Back to Africa movement, observed that "to the Negro the American flag is a dirty and contemptible rag" (quoted in Masur 2008, 107). Psychologist Kenneth Clark encountered an African American man in the 1960s who stated:

> The flag here in America is for the white man. The blue is for justice; the fifty white stars you see in the blue are for the fifty white states; and the white you see in it is the White House. It represents white folks. The red in it is the white man's blood—he doesn't even respect your blood, that's why he will lynch you, hang you, barbecue you, and fry you. (Quoted in Masur 2008, 109)

In 1959, segregationists carried both U.S. and Arkansas state flags when they came to the state capital to support Governor Orval Faubus's prosegregationist stand against public school integration (Moss 1998, 16), but in the early 1960s, segregationists more typically carried Confederate banners. The first American flag to be presented as a civil rights banner was displayed by students at North Carolina's A&T State University (Teachout 2009, 161) who protested segregation at local lunch counters. This tradition of carrying flags was extended to demonstrations led by Medgar Evers in Jackson, Mississippi, where opponents often took the flags out of the students' hands and threw them to the ground. Not surprisingly, many local whites who opposed the protest waved Confederate flags, which were considered to be a sign of resistance to the U.S. Supreme Court decision in *Brown v. Board of Education* (1954) that overturned racial segregation.

Flag-bearing demonstrators march from Selma to Montgomery, Alabama, in the historic voting rights protest of March 1965. The march led directly to the 1965 Voting Rights Act, which outlawed Southern states' attempts to prevent African Americans from voting. (Library of Congress)

When Dr. Martin Luther King Jr. gave his historic "I Have a Dream" speech in Washington D.C. in 1963, there were American flags in the background. By using this backdrop, he and other civil rights demonstrators attempted to appeal to common values that had been articulated in the Declaration of Independence and other American documents, including the Fourteenth Amendment, which had extended citizenship to all persons born or naturalized in the United States. During the historic civil rights march from Selma to Montgomery in 1965, James Karales took an iconic photograph of a marcher draped in the flag as though it were "his comfort and his hope" (Masur 2008, 109). This photograph is similar to one that Eric Gay took in 2005 of an African American woman, a victim of Hurricane Katrina, with a flag draped over her shoulders as if it were a "mourning shawl" (Masur 2008, 180).

The tradition of carrying American flags in favor of desegregation began to erode in the late 1960s, when the flag was often viewed as a symbol for support of the War in Vietnam. Sidney Street was arrested in New York for burning an American flag when he learned of the assassination of Medgar Evers. Moreover, police departments across the nation "begun adding American flag patches and pins to their uniforms and stickers to their patrol cars" in the late 1960s and early 1970s (Moss 1998, 16). The flag thus became a symbol of law and order, the forces of which were sometimes arrayed against demonstrators. Jackie Robinson, who desegregated Major League Baseball, thus observed: "I wouldn't fly the flag on the Fourth of July or any other day. . . . When I see a car with a flag pasted on it, I figure the guy behind the wheel isn't my friend" (quoted in Moss 1998, 16).

By the late 1960s, some civil rights groups began using Black Liberation flags (red, green, and black vertical tricolors) either in conjunction with or instead of U.S. flags. Followers of Marcus Garvey, founder of the United Negro Improvement Association (UNIA), had previously used a tricolor flag of three horizontal stripes of red, black, and green to symbolize African Americans. In the early 1970s, some black troops in Vietnam displayed a red Black Power flag with a black fist in the center and "Black Unity" emblazoned in black letters across the top (Moss 1998, 35).

Albert Boime observes that "the American flag was a recurring theme in the canvases of African American artists active in the Civil Rights movement," many of whom used the flag to point out discrepancies in the implementation of national ideals. He cites Faith Ringgold's *Flag for the Moon* and *The Flag Is Bleeding*, Dana Chandler's *Land of the Free # 3—Golden Prison* and her *Ted Landsmark Incident*, David Hammons's *Injustice Case*, and Dread Scott's *What Is the Proper Way to Display a U.S. Flag?* (Boime 1990, 18–23).

In 2016, San Francisco quarterback Colin Kaepernick refused to stand for the playing of the national anthem as a way of protesting racial injustices that had been highlighted by the Black Lives Matter movement. Even though Kaepernick did not find immediate employment in 2017, other NFL players that year followed Kaepernick's example and kneeled during the national anthem to protest alleged police brutality against minorities and other forms of racial injustice. President Trump and other critics vocally disparaged such behavior as unpatriotic. Others, however, defended the players' choice to peacefully exercise their free speech rights. Several team owners and players subsequently locked arms in a show of solidarity and support of such peaceful expressions of dissent during the playing of the national anthem at several NFL games.

A number of writers have pointed out that the third stanza of Francis Scott Key's "The Star-Spangled Banner," which serves as the national anthem, refers disparagingly to African Americans who had joined the British to gain their freedom. In January 2017, a group of protestors set fire to American flags in an Iowa City pedestrian mall in apparent protest of racial and other social injustices.

The Black Lives Matter movement has also been met with a Blue Lives Matter response. The latter asserts that police officers are not sufficiently valued or supported in communities and that they are subject to too much unfair criticism. This movement sometimes uses a black-and-white American flag with a blue strip just below the canton, emphasizing the role of police as a "thin blue line" between order and disorder.

See also Civil War; Confederate Flags; Hard Hat Riot (1970); *The Soiling of Old Glory* (Photograph); "Star-Spangled Banner" (Anthem); *Street v. New York* (1969)

Further Reading

Boime, Albert. 1990. "Waving the Red Flag and Reconstituting Old Glory." *Smithsonian Studies in American Art* 4 (Spring): 2–25.

Cummings, Melbourne S. 1982. "The Rhetoric of Bishop Henry McNeal Turner." *Journal of Black Studies* 12 (June): 457–467.

Ferris, Marc. 2015. " 'The Star Spangled Banner': A Slave-Owner's Anthem?" *Baltimore Sun*, September 10. http://www.baltimoresun.com/news/opinion/oped/bs-ed-anthem-change-20150910-story.html

Goddard, Kristian. 2008. "The Resilience of the Stars and Stripes." December 4. http://www.kristiangoddard.net/Blog/americanflag.htm.

Johnson, Jason. 2016. "Star-Spangled Bigotry: The Hidden Racist History of the National Anthem." TheRoot.com. Last modified August 4. https://www.theroot.com/star-spangled-bigotry-the-hidden-racist-history-of-the-1790855893

Masur, Louis P. 2008. *The Soiling of Old Glory: The Story of a Photograph That Shocked America*. New York: Bloomsbury Press.

Moss, Rosalind Urbach. 1998. "'Yes, There's a Reason I Salute the Flag': Flag Use and the Civil Rights Movement." *Raven: A Journal of Vexillology* 5:12–33.

Teachout, Woden. 2009. *Capture the Flag: A Political History of American Patriotism*. New York: Basic Books.

USA Today. 2017. "Flag Burning Sets Off Clash at Pedestrian Mall." Supplement to *The Tennessean*. January 28.

Vile, John R. 2017. *The Jacksonian and Antebellum Eras: Documents Decoded*. Santa Barbara, CA: ABC-CLIO.

CIVIL WAR

Few events in American history have done more to solidify reverence for the U.S. flag than the Civil War (1861–1865). Suddenly, the nation, which had been consistently adding new stars to the flag since its inception, faced the prospect of 11 such states seceding, largely out of their determination to preserve slavery within their borders. Even before southern states had agreed on the first of a number of flags under which its troops would fight (the U.S. flag had largely replaced regimental flags during the Mexican-American War), some abolitionists had proposed exclusionary flags that would be reworked to eliminate the stars and stripes of slave-holding states.

At the outset of the war, it was not clear which side had the advantage. As he reflected on citizens' ties to their state and to the nation, Nathaniel Hawthorne (1862) observed thus of "the anomaly of two allegiances":

> The State comes nearest home to a man's feeling, and includes the altar and the hearth, while the General Government claims his devotion only to an airy mode of law and has no symbol but a flag.

Never underestimating the power of the U.S. flag, Abraham Lincoln insisted that it would continue to retain stars for all of the states, even those fighting in rebellion. This was consistent with his view of the war as a "rebellion" rather than as a "war between the [nation] states," which was the preferred southern designation for the conflict. On his way to his inauguration, Lincoln participated in a flag-raising ceremony at Independence Hall in Philadelphia. During the service, he observed, "I have never had a feeling politically that did not spring from the sentiments embodied in the Declaration of Independence" (Lincoln 1953, 4:240).

At the beginning of the war, southern troops fired on Fort Sumter, forcing it to surrender and lower its flag. This flag became something of an icon in the North and was cited in a notable speech by Robert C. Winthrop to the 22nd Regiment Massachusetts Volunteer Infantry. This flag was raised again over the fort at the end of the war on the same day that Lincoln was assassinated.

Those who had previously fought under the U.S. flag must have been extremely conflicted when the South adopted a rival standard. It is reported that there was weeping, as well as celebration, when the U.S. flag was lowered and the Confederate flag was raised over the Confederate Capitol in Montgomery, Alabama, in 1861 (Keim and Keim 2007, 116). A story similar to the poem of "The Old Violin" tells how an auctioneer in Charleston, South Carolina, contemptuously referred to an American flag as something not worth bidding for, only to receive what was then considered a very substantial bid of $10 (Schauffler 1917, 67).

At the beginning of the war, James Jackson raised a large Confederate flag from his house in Alexandria, Virginia, where it could be clearly seen from the White House. Col. Elmer Ellsworth subsequently marched into Virginia to lower the flag, and both he and Jackson were killed and became martyrs for their respective sides. During the war, numerous songs and anthems were composed to pay tribute to the flags of both the North and the South (McWhirter 2012).

Often states were themselves divided in their loyalties. Samuel Bell Palmer, a Confederate soldier in a northern prison camp, composed a drawing of a scene of

Gay Street in Knoxville in which people were lined up in the foreground under a U.S. flag to join the Union side and under a Confederate flag on the far side of the street to join the Confederacy. Prisoners of war often fashioned flags representing their respective sides to boost morale of fellow prisoners.

The first Confederate flag borrowed its color and design from the U.S. flag, so much so that the initial flag was sometimes confused for the Union banner during battle. The design of the regimental colors of Gen. Robert E. Lee's Army of Northern Virginia was eventually incorporated into the design of the next two Confederate flags.

Proponents of both sides cast contempt on rival flags. Just prior to the Battle of Stones River in Murfreesboro, Tennessee, in December 1862, confederates danced on floors that were carpeted with American flags (Preble 1872, 373). Gen. William Butler executed William Mumford for desecrating a U.S. flag that he had taken down from a public building after federal troops captured New Orleans. William Driver hid the flag, which he had flown from his ship and dubbed "Old Glory," in a coverlet at his house in Nashville and then offered it to Union troops to fly over the state capitol when they recaptured that city.

Another story recounts how a southern lady offered to present a Union colonel with a flag on the Fourth of July and presented him with Confederate colors, which she identified in her presentation speech with liberty. The colonel turned the tables by noting how he and his men had already captured a number of similar flags and saying that he would keep her offering in a similar spirit. He also framed the woman's speech as a eulogy for a flag that would soon be no more (Schauffler 1917, 75–77).

Women often presented flags to soldiers on both sides as they marched off to war. A book by Mary Livermore entitled *My Story of the War* has an illustration of a woman wearing a skirt, serving as a flag-bearer in a battle under the title of "Michigan Bridget" (Bonner 2003). She appears to have been an Irish immigrant (whose maiden name may have been Biddy Diver) who participated in a number of battles in Virginia (Hannum, n.d., 6). Other women living in the South appear to have hidden flags during the war (Bonner 2003).

John Greenleaf Whittier penned the emotional poem "Barbara Frietchie" in 1863 to describe the loyalty of an aged woman to the American flag as Confederate troops marched through Frederick, Maryland. That same year, Edward Everett Hale pulled even stronger on heart strings with his fictional tale "The Man without a Country," the story of a man punished by never being able to set foot in the United States nor see the U.S. flag.

Another tale that originated in East Tennessee tells of a Confederate leader (identified simply as Lieutenant White) who was tasked with capturing weapons from local Unionists but who was warned by a local judge about disrespecting a U.S. flag flying in Chilhowee Gap. When the lieutenant and his men approached and surrounded the flag, he reputedly gave a speech in which he said:

> Men, that was the flag under which we were born. It was under that flag our fathers fought and many of them died. While we are fighting under a new flag, still, that was

> the flag of our fathers. Let us honor it for its history and for the memory of the blood poured out so freely by our brave ancestors in its defense. Instead of doing it injury, I propose that we salute it. (Ewing 1986, 52)

The story further says that had the lieutenant done otherwise, he and his men would have been the recipient of hostile fire from Union loyalists wielding the guns they were unsuccessfully seeking.

In 1861, the number of stars on the U.S. flag increased to 34 with the admission of Kansas. In 1863, the number increased to 35 as West Virginia split from Virginia so that it could remain loyal to the Union. For many in the South, the final sign of the end of the war was the lowering of the Confederate Flag and the raising of the U.S. flag. As a woman from Richmond, Virginia, wrote in her diary:

> Exactly at eight o'clock the confederate flag that fluttered above the Capitol came down and the Stars and Stripes were run up. We knew what that meant! . . . We covered our faces and cried aloud. All through the house was the sound of sobbing. (Quoted in Chang 1994, 84)

The Civil War resulted not only in the defeat of the idea of secession but also in increased power to the national government. One visible sign of this increased presence was the construction of battlefield cemeteries, like that in Gettysburg, which, especially on holidays, are draped with flags.

President Lincoln was assassinated shortly after the end of the war when attending a play at Ford's Theatre in Washington, D.C. As he lay dying, people tending to him reportedly cradled his head in an American flag. After the war, Sgt. Gilbert Bates took an American flag on a 1,300-mile march through several southern states before ending his journey at the nation's capital. Groups of army veterans, most notably the Grand Army of the Republic, and hereditary societies like the Daughters of the American Revolution were influential in promoting respect for the flag in the postwar era.

See also Bates's Flag March through the Former Confederate States; Beecher, Henry Ward; Confederate Flags; Daughters of the American Revolution (DAR); Davis, Jefferson; Ellsworth, Elmer E.; Exclusionary Flags; Fort Sumter Flag; Fritchie, Barbara; Grand Army of the Republic (GAR); Lincoln, Abraham; Lambkin, Prince; Old Glory Flag; "Man without a Country"; Prisoners of War; Winthrop, Robert C.

Further Reading

Bonner, Robert E. 2003. "Star-spangled Sentiment." *Common-Place* 3 (2). http://www.common-place-archives.org/vol-03/no-02/bonner/bonner-5.shtml

Chang, Ina. 1994. *A Separate Battle: Women and the Civil War*. New York: Scholastic, Inc.

Ewing, James. 1986. *It Happened in Tennessee*. Nashville: Rutledge Hill Press.

Hannum, James S. n.d. "Michigan Bridgett: Discovering The Truth Behind the Legend." http://spartanhistory.kora.matrix.msu.edu/files/7/29/7-1D-530-36-MichiganBridget.pdf. Accessed April 30, 2018.

Hawthorne, Nathaniel. 1862. "Chiefly About War Matters, by a Peaceable Man." *The Atlantic*. https://www.theatlantic.com/magazine/archive/2012/02/chiefly-about-war-matters-by-a-peaceable-man/308816/

Keim, Kevin, and Peter Keim. 2007. *A Grand Old Flag: A History of the United States through Its Flags*. New York: DK.

Leib, Jonathan I., Gerald R. Webster, and Roberta H. Webster. 2002. "Rebel with a Cause? Iconography and Public Memory in the Southern United States." *GeoJournal* 52:303–310.

Lincoln, Abraham. 1953. *The Collected Works of Abraham Lincoln*. Edited by Roy P. Basler. New Brunswick, NJ: Rutgers University Press.

McWhirter, Christian. 2012. *Battle Hymns: The Power and Popularity of Music in the Civil War*. Chapel Hill: University of North Carolina Press.

O'Leary, Cecilia Elizabeth. 1999. *To Die For: The Paradox of American Patriotism*. Princeton, NJ: Princeton University Press.

Preble, Henry. 1872. *Our Flag. Origin and Progress of the Flag of the United States of America, with an Introductory Account of the Symbols, Standards, Banners and Flags of Ancient and Modern Nations*. Albany, NY: Joel Munsell.

Schauffler, Robert Haven, ed. 1917. *Our Flag in Verse and Prose*. New York: Moffat, Yard and Company.

Zelinsky, Wilbur. 1988. *Nation into State: The Shifting Symbolic Foundations of American Nationalism*. Chapel Hill: University of North Carolina Press.

COHAN, GEORGE M.

See "You're a Grand Old Flag"

COLORS OF THE FLAG

Many individuals have speculated about the significance of the red, white, and blue colors of the American flag. It is important to note that these colors are far from unique and are shared by such nations as Australia, France, Costa Rica, and Russia.

Historically, the flag appears to have derived largely from the contemporary flag of Great Britain (the Union Jack), which had the same three colors. Quite apart from any symbolic meaning, it is further logical that the stars in the canton would be white and be set against either a blue or black sky. In presenting the Great Seal with the same colors to Congress, Charles Thomson, the secretary of the Continental Congress, said: "The colors are those used in the flag of the United States of America. White signifies purity and innocence. Red, hardiness & valor, and Blue . . . signifies vigilance, perseverance & justice" (quoted in Greenstein 2013).

In pondering the colors of the flag, scholar Robert Phillips discussed a number of possible inspirations. He quotes George Washington, for example, as saying, "We take the stars from Heaven, the red from our Mother Country, separating it by white stripes, thus showing we have separated from her, and the white stripes shall go down to posterity representing liberty" (Phillips 1931, 53). Later scholars, however, deny that Washington made such remarks (Marling 2004). Phillips further cited A. S. Gumbart, a Boston pastor, as saying that "the red connotes sacrificial love; the white, purity; the blue, heavenly protection." Phillips, however, expressed his personal belief that "one of the strongest interpretations of the flag symbolism is that which takes the red as the sign of the nation's wars; the white, of its years of peace; the blue, of its faith in God" (1931, 55). After reviewing such characterizations, Michael Corcoran (2002, 37) has observed that almost all are ex post facto rationalizations rather than arguments grounded in actual evidence.

See also Constellation; Union Jack

Further Reading

Bernard, Jim. 2011. "Three Cheers for Red, White and Blue." *Phi Kappa Phi FORUM* 92 (Summer): 16–18.

Corcoran, Michael. 2002. *For Which It Stands: An Anecdotal Biography of the American Flag*. New York: Simon and Schuster.

Greenstein, Nicole. 2013. "Why the U.S. Flag is Red, White and Blue." *Time*, July 4. http:swampland.time.com/2013/07/04/why-the-u-s-flag-is-red-white-and-blue/

Marling, Karal Ann. 2004. *Old Glory: Unfurling History*. Washington, D.C.: Library of Congress.

Phillips, Robert. 1931. *The American Flag: Its Uses and Abuses*. Boston: Stratford Company.

CONFEDERATE FLAGS

Just as the colors of the U.S. Flag are those of Great Britain (now the United Kingdom), so too the colors of the flag of the Confederate States of America were the same as those of the Union.

Although the Confederate flag is often called the Stars and Bars, this designation best applies to the first official flag, which was adopted in March 1861. It consisted of a blue canton of seven white stars (the number of states who initially seceded) and three horizontal parallel bars, of which the top and bottom were red and the middle was white.

This flag so resembled the flag of the United States that the two could be confused in the smoke of battle. Generals therefore preferred to use their own battle flags, which were often presented to them when they went off to war (Durrill 2006). In time, the most popular Confederate flag, which was especially associated with Gen. Robert E. Lee's Army of Northern Virginia, consisted of a square flag with a diagonal St. Andrew's cross of blue and 13 white stars highlighted in white, set against a red background. The 13 stars represented the 11 states that had officially joined the Confederacy as well as Kentucky and Missouri, where loyalties were divided.

On May 1, 1863, this design was incorporated into the canton of a larger rectangular white field and called the Stainless Banner (Coski 2006, 228). Just as the first flag could be confused with that of the Union, so too this one could be confused with a flag of surrender, thus making it largely inappropriate for battlefield usage. Perhaps for this reason, just before the fall of the Confederacy, a vertical red bar was added to the end of the flag.

As the war ended, Father Abram J. Ryan, who had served as a chaplain in the Confederate Army, penned a mournful poem entitled "The Conquered Banner," in which he ended with the lines:

> Furl that Banner, softly, slowly;
> Treat it gently—it is holy,
> For it droops above the dead;
> Touch it not—unfold it never;
> Let it droop there, furled forever,—
> For its people's hopes are fled. (Scott 1915, 161)

Consciously or not, Ryan's poem advocated that the Confederate flag be treated in the same way that Jefferson Davis had once proposed for the U.S. flag.

The flag which is today most frequently associated with the Confederacy is actually the Confederate Navy Jack, which is a diagonal version of the Confederate battle flag. Often used to express southern pride, this flag was also used by southern whites who opposed civil rights protests in the 1950s and 1960s and to express opposition to the Supreme Court's desegregation decision in *Brown v. Board of Education* (1954). A number of southern states either incorporated this design into their state flag during this period or defiantly flew the flag over the state capitol. One of the most recent to be removed was the flag waving over the South Carolina Capitol. However, as of 2017, five southern states still have state flags that are based in part on the Confederate flag.

While this flag has sometimes been used by those opposing racial desegregation, the flag is sometimes simply used as a symbol for the South. Tim Marshall, an expert on foreign affairs who writes on flags, thus observes that when two cousins rode around in the *Dukes of Hazzard* television series in a Dodge Charger with a Confederate flag painted on the roof, "this was not intended to suggest that the Dukes supported segregation, simply that they were 'good ol' boys' from the South" (Marshall 2017, 27–28).

See also Civil Rights Movement; Civil War; Colors of the Flag; Davis, Jefferson; Exclusionary Flags; Lincoln, Abraham

Further Reading

Bonner, Robert E. 2002a. "Flag Culture and the Consolidation of Confederate Nationalism." *Journal of Southern History* 68 (May): 293–332.

Bonner, Robert E. 2002b. *Colors and Blood: Flag Passions of the Confederate South.* Princeton: Princeton University Press.

Coski, John M. 2006. "Flag, Confederate." In Vol. 4, Myth, Manners, and Memory *of The New Encyclopedia of Southern Culture* (pp. 228–229), edited by Charles Reagan Wilson. Chapel Hill: University of North Carolina Press.

Coulter, E. Merton. 1953. "The Flags of the Confederacy." *The Georgia Historical Quarterly* 37 (September): 188–199.

Durrill, Wayne K. 2006. "Ritual, Community and War: Local Flag Presentation Ceremonies and Disunity in the Early Confederacy." *Journal of Social History* 39 (Summer): 1105–1122.

Leib, Jonathan I., Gerald R. Webster, and Roberta H. Webster. 2002. "Rebel with a cause? Iconography and public memory in the Southern United States." *GeoJournal* 52:303–310.

Marshall, Tim. 2017. *Worth Dying For: The Power and Politics of Flags*. London: Elliott and Thompson.

Scott, Emma Look. 1915. *How the Flag Became Old Glory*. New York: Macmillan Company.

CONSTELLATION

The origins of the stars on the American flag remains uncertain, but the symbolism was quickly appropriated in early America to distinguish American Republicanism from European monarchism (Shalev 2011).

In Europe, it was common to describe monarchs as planets or stars, with King Louis XIV (1638–1715) of France widely designated as the Sun King but with similar titles sometimes used for other monarchs, including Britain's Elizabeth I and George III. Such imagery suggested that the government revolved around the monarch as planets revolved around the sun. Prior to the American Revolution, America was sometimes likened to a planet that revolved around Britain. The term "revolution" itself derives from astronomy. David Rittenhouse, a friend of Francis Hopkinson and Benjamin Franklin, the latter of whom he succeeded as president of the American Philosophic Society, had created an orrery (a mechanical model of the solar system) in Philadelphia (as well as one for the College of New Jersey) designed to illustrate the movement of stars and planets, and had tied nature and its laws to the colonial struggle for liberty (Keim and Keim 2007, 41).

In colonial and early U.S. history, flags were used most frequently as a means of identifying ships at sea (Teachout 2009, 9–10). Sailors, who often set their courses by the stars, might be particularly attracted to a flag that had links to the starry night.

With independence, Americans transferred imagery so that individual states were likened to stars, which together constituted a new orderly "constellation" (Shalev 2011, 50) or system, held together both by their own constitutions, and, in time, by the Articles of Confederation and the U.S. Constitution. This imagery fit well with the nation's motto "E Pluribus Unum," meaning "Out of many, one." Just as new planets and stars were discovered (Sir William Herschel discovered Uranus in 1781), so too new states could be added to this constellation as the nation grew. Shalev further believes that imagery, which would be incorporated into the flag, was consistent with later images of the U.S. as "the redeemer nation" or "God's new Israel." He observes that 17 of the 37 states that joined the Union after 1776 would include one or more stars on their own flags (Shalev 2011, 62, 66). In early American flags, stars were sometimes organized into a circle, sometimes into row, and sometimes in other configurations.

Joseph Rodman Drake (1795–1820) wrote a widely published poem titled "The American Flag," which touted the flag's heavenly origins and tied them to freedom. The opening stanza read:

When Freedom from her mountain height
Unfurled her standard to the air,
She tore the azure robe of night
And set the starts of glory there.
She mingled with its gorgeous dyes
The milky baldrick of the skies,
And striped its pure celestial white
With streakings of the morning light. (Bonner 2003)

As the Civil War approached, northerners tended to stress the need for preserving the constellation intact, while southerners stressed that the attraction among the state "stars" was purely voluntary. Notably, the creators of the Confederate flag incorporated stars into its design.

One scholar of Native American history has observed that the Pawnee Indians were particularly enamored with the stars of the flag:

> These Pawnees know the stars, and they understand the heavens, and they understand their importance . . . when they [first saw the American flag in 1819] they saw the blue, representing the blue skies of the heavens, and they saw the stars upon the blue, which they knew were from the heavens, they thought God must have put it into the hearts of the people to make such a flag, and they have honored it from that day to this. (Kavanagh 1996, 94)

In speaking of the flag in 1918, Representative Frederick C. Hicks of Long Island, New York, sought to tie the constellation to those serving in World War I:

> Our forefathers took from the skies the eternal stars, emblazoned them upon our banner, forming a new constellation emblematic of the aspirations of our people. As the stars in the firmament of God are countless, so without number are the hosts of our patriots, marching to victory in vindication of the lofty principles of our Republic. (Hicks 1918, Appendix, 2)

See also Confederate Flags; *Our Banner in the Sky*; World War I

Further Reading

Bonner, Robert E. 2003 "Star-Spangled Sentiment." *Common-Place* 3 (2). http://www.common-place-archives.org/vol-03/no-02/bonner/bonner-5.shtml

Hicks, Frederick C. 1918. *The Flag of the United States: Address Delivered by Hon. Frederick C. Hicks of Long Island in the House of Representatives, June 14, 1917*. Washington, D.C.: Government Printing Office.

Kavanagh, Thomas W. 1996. *North American Indian Portraits: Photographs from the Wanamaker Expedition*. New York: Konecky and Konecky.

Keim, Kevin, and Peter Keim. 2007. *A Grand Old Flag: A History of the United States through Its Flags*. New York: DK.

Schmittou, Douglas A., and Michael H. Hogan. 2002. "Fluidity of Meaning: Flag Imagery in Plains Indian Art." *American Indian Quarterly* 26 (Autumn): 559–604.

Shalev, Eran. 2011. "'A Republic Amidst the Stars' Political Astronomy and the Intellectual Origins of the Stars and Stripes." *Journal of the Early Republic* 31 (Spring): 39–73.

Teachout, Woden. 2009. *Capture the Flag: A Political History of American Patriotism*. New York: Basic Books.
"Our Federal Sun: Planetary Politics before the Civil War." 2018. *American Political Thought: A Journal of Ideas, Institutions, and Culture* 7 (Spring): 189–215.

"COURTESY OF THE RED, WHITE AND BLUE"

Just as "The Star-Spangled Banner" emerged from conflict, later military conflicts in U.S. history have spawned other musical tributes to the American flag, which often serve as a rallying symbol against America's enemies.

In 2002, Oklahoma-born country music star Toby Keith (b. 1961) released a song on his *Unleashed* album entitled "Courtesy of the Red, White and Blue (The Angry American)." It expressed full-throated support for American military actions in Iraq and Afghanistan in the aftermath of the 9/11 terrorist attacks on New York and elsewhere.

Initially written as a tribute to his father who died in a car accident, the first verse ties the sight of "Old Glory Flying" to men who died to protect the nation. The second verse ties his father's service in the military and the loss of his right eye during his service to his practice of flying a flag in his yard.

Verse 3 mentions the "mighty sucker punch" that the nation took on 9/11, giving it a "big black eye," but ties the response to lighting up the enemy's worlds "Like the 4th of July."

Verses 4 and 5 cite Uncle Sam, the Statue of Liberty, the bald eagle, and the Liberty Bell and assert that when the enemy suffers the consequences of its actions, it should know those consequences were "brought . . . Courtesy of the Red White and Blue." The next verse anticipates giving a boot to American enemies.

Natalie Maines of the Dixie Chicks, a group that was known for its outspoken opposition to President George Bush's military actions, was a strong critic of the song: "I hate it. It's ignorant and it makes country music sound ignorant. It targets an entire culture—and not just the bad people who did bad things. You've got to have some tact. Anybody can write, 'We'll put a boot in your ass'" (quoted in Rudder 2005, 215). Similarly, ABC news anchor Peter Jennings objected to having the song performed on his station's Fourth of July special. In response, hundreds of Toby Keith fans sent boots to ABC (Yahr 2017).

See also Independence Day; Uncle Sam; Terrorist Attacks of September 11, 2001

Further Reading

Rodnitsky, Jerry. 2010. "Iraq is Arabic for Vietnam: The Evolution of Protest Songs in Popular Music from Vietnam to Iraq." In *Homer Simpson Marches on Washington: Dissent through American Popular Culture* (pp. 203–217), edited by Timothy M. Dale and Joseph J. Foy. Lexington: University Press of Kentucky.
Rudder, Randy. "In Whose Name? Country Artists Speak Out on Gulf War II." In *Country Music Goes to War*, edited by Charles K. Wolfe and James E. Akenson. Lexington: University Press of Kentucky.
Yahr, Emily. 2017. "Toby Keith Was a Loud Political Voice in the Bush Years. What about the Trump Era?" *Washington Post,* March 23. https://www.washingtonpost

.com/lifestyle/style/toby-keith-was-a-loud-political-voice-in-the-bush-years-what-about-the-trump-era/2017/03/22/135fd312-0a73-11e7-93dc-00f9bdd74ed1_story.html?utm_term=.125c56463551

COWGILL V. CALIFORNIA (1970)

In *Cowgill v. California*, 396 U.S. 371 (1970), the U.S. Supreme Court dismissed an appeal from the appellate department of the Supreme Court of the County of Los Angeles, California, in a per curiam opinion consisting of a single sentence. As sometimes happens in such cases, Justice John Marshall Harlan II authored a brief explanation, which was joined by Justice William Brennan, as to why he had not voted to give full review to the case.

Harlan explained the case had originated out of a prosecution of an individual who had worn a vest fashioned from a cut-up American flag. In *Street v. New York* (1969), the court had overturned the conviction of an individual who had burned a U.S. flag upon hearing of the death of civil rights leader James Meredith. In so doing it had expressed the fear that Street had been convicted for what he said rather than what he did. Citing this decision, Harlan said that he did not think the issue of whether the Fourteenth Amendment prohibited punishment for wearing a "mutilated" flag was insubstantial, but he did not think the record in this case provided an adequate means for addressing this issue.

Harlan cited a variety of cases to show that the court had, "as yet, not established a test for determining at what point conduct becomes so intertwined with expression that it becomes necessary to weigh the State's interest in proscribing conduct against the constitutionally protected interest in freedom of expression." Although the plaintiff claimed that his conduct conveyed a symbolic message, the trial court did not determine whether this was so, thus presenting an inadequate record for review.

Justice William O. Douglas noted that he thought "that probable jurisdiction should be noted."

In *Texas v. Johnson* (1989) and *United States v. Eichman* (1990), the court would later invalidate flag-burning laws, and presumably other laws designed to protect the symbolic integrity of the flag, as contrary to First and Fourteenth Amendment protections.

See also Flag Desecration Amendment; *Street v. New York* (1969); *Texas v. Johnson* (1989); *United States v. Eichman* (1990)

Further Reading

Waldman, Joshua. "Note: Symbolic Speech and Social Meaning." *Columbia Law Review* 97 (October): 1844–1894.

COWPENS FLAG

The 13-star flag with 12 five-point stars surrounding a 13th star in the middle of the canton is often called a Cowpens Flag because it was originally believed to have been flown at the Battle of Cowpens, South Carolina, on January 17, 1781, by C.Sgt. William Batchelor, a member of the Maryland Light Infantry. According to the legend, the Revolutionary War flag was also flown during the War of 1812, after which it was given to the Old Defender's association in 1843, which reputedly later turned it over to the state of Maryland in 1907.

This flag is quite similar to the flag generally attributed to Betsy Ross, except that the Ross flag has a circle of 13 stars with none in the middle. However, based on its materials, the Cowpens Flag appears to have been made in the mid-19th century, perhaps for the Mexican-American War. If there was such a Revolutionary War flag with the 13-star design, it is not the one now owned by Maryland (Cooper 1973, 28).

The Cowpens Flag is depicted in Archibald MacNeal Willard's painting *The Spirit of '76*.

See also Ross, Betsy; Revolutionary War Battle Flags; *Spirit of '76*; Thirteen-Star Flags

Further Reading

Cooper, Grace Rogers. 1973. *Thirteen-Star Flags: Keys to Identification*. Washington, D.C.: Smithsonian Institution Press.

Revolutionary War and Beyond. 2017. "The Cowpens Flag." Accessed February 27. http://www.revolutionary-war-and-beyond.com/cowpens-flag.html

CULPEPER FLAG

See Rattlesnake Flags

CULT OF THE FLAG

The "cult of the flag" is a term that historians have coined to explain the emphasis that various veterans' and hereditary organizations placed on promoting rituals surrounding the flag during the last two decades of the 19th century (Davies 1955, 218). The organizations most prominent in this movement were the Daughters of the American Revolution (DAR), the Sons of the American Revolution (SAR), the Grand Army of the Republic (GAR), and the Woman's Relief Corps. Reverence for the flag led to state laws seeking to regulate the use of the flag in advertising and in adopting laws against flag desecration.

Such organizations also sought to bring veterans into schools to talk with students, to introduce pictures of George Washington and flags into classrooms, to promote the Pledge of Allegiance to the U.S. flag, and to punish students or teachers who did not choose to participate. Many of these organizations also worked to create Flag Day and to see that other patriotic holidays were observed respectfully and not simply as days of leisure.

Much of this effort appeared designed to promote unity in a nation that was increasingly populated by immigrants, amid fears that those immigrants were not properly acquiring American values. The veterans' and hereditary groups make efforts to identify, restore, and preserve historical monuments and battle sites; to establish professorships at major colleges; to oversee textbooks; and to sponsor patriotic exercises in the schools. Some also worked unsuccessfully on the idea of establishing a national university in Washington, D.C.

As the members of the Grand Army of the Republic died out, the American Legion was formed. It has put special emphasis on educating schoolchildren on flag etiquette (Pencak 1989, 290–291). William Guthrie probably pushed the cult of the flag to its most extreme in a book that he published in 1919 entitled *The Religion of Old Glory*.

The developing cult of the flag, and the corresponding creation of military training, may have been one of the catalysts of the Spanish-American War in 1898. It was the first American war that resulted in the acquisition of noncontiguous foreign colonies.

See also American Legion; Daughters of the American Revolution (DAR); Grand Army of the Republic (GAR); Guthrie, William N.; Pledge of Allegiance; Spanish-American War

Further Reading

Davies, Wallace Evan. 1955. *Patriotism on Parade: The Story of Veterans' and Hereditary Organizations in America 1783–1900*. Cambridge, MA: Harvard University Press.

Guenter, Scot M. 1990. *The American Flag, 1777–1924: Cultural Shifts from Creation to Codification*. Cranbury, NJ: Associated University Presses.

Guthrie, William Norman. 1919. *The Religion of Old Glory*. New York: George H. Doran Company.

McConnell, Stuart. "Reading the Flag: A Reconsideration of the Patriotic Cults of the 1890s." In *Bonds of Affection: Americans Define Their Patriotism*, edited by John Bodnar, 102–119. Princeton, NJ: Princeton University Press.

Pencak, William. 1989. *For God and Country: The American Legion, 1919–1941*. Boston: Northeastern University Press.

D

DAUGHTERS OF THE AMERICAN REVOLUTION (DAR)

One of the organizations that has been at the forefront of efforts to instill respect for the American flag, especially in school classrooms, is the Daughters of the American Revolution (DAR). Open to individuals who can trace their ancestry to a veteran of the Revolutionary War, the society resembles the Society of the Cincinnati, which was founded in 1783 by former Revolutionary War veterans and raised some initial fears about the role of hereditary organizations with a republic (Davies 1948).

The DAR was founded in 1890 at a time of rising nationalism and increasing concern about an alleged erosion of patriotism due to rising immigration. The organization joined the Grand Army of the Republic, the American Legion, and other groups in advocating for the pledge to the flag in American classrooms and in sponsoring speech contests focusing on American history. At the beginning of the 20th century, its members were often involved in pageants that recreated important moments in American history (Glassberg 1990).

The organization is organized into local chapters, which send delegates to yearly Continental Congresses at the national headquarters in Washington, D.C., Constitution Hall, which covers a full city block and includes a huge auditorium, museum exhibits, and genealogical records. One of the highlights of each DAR Continental Congress is the unveiling of one of the world's largest American flags.

The society, which once drew political elites who advocated progressive causes, has in more recent years been associated largely with conservative stances. After the DAR expressed opposition to a stained glass window that the artist Grant Wood (most notable for his *American Gothic*) had made for the Veterans Memorial Building in Cedar Rapids, Iowa, because he had used glass from Germany, Wood took his revenge with a painting entitled *Daughters of Revolution*. It depicted three elderly matrons sipping tea in front of a picture of *Washington Crossing the Delaware*, in which James Monroe is hoisting an American flag. Not coincidentally, this work had been painted by German American artist Emanuel Leutze, who portrayed a river that looked far more like the Rhine than the Delaware. Wood's painting is on display at the Cincinnati Museum of Art.

The DAR encountered additional disapprobation when it denied Marian Anderson, a noted African American contralto, the right to sing at Constitution Hall in 1939. First Lady Eleanor Roosevelt was among those who arranged for her to sing on the steps of the Lincoln Memorial instead. Stung by the torrent of public criticism it received in the wake of its treatment of Anderson, the DAR later allowed her to sing at Constitution Hall as well.

The DAR motto is "God, Home, and Country," which thus ties together its concern with the religious, domestic, and political spheres of American life. The DAR's website identifies its chief efforts as historical preservation, education, and patriotism. It further boasts 185,000 members in more than 3,000 chapters. It publishes a leaflet about the U.S. Flag Code designed to educate students and citizens on the flag and encourage its proper use. The organization encourages the celebration of Constitution Week. Its own rituals include not only a salute to the American flag but a recitation of the American's Creed, which was authored by William Tyler Page.

The DAR often works in association with chapters of the Sons of the American Revolution (SAR), which was founded in 1889 (but excluded women) and was especially influential in establishing Constitution Day and Flag Day, and the Children of the American Revolution (CAR), which was founded in 1895.

See also American's Creed; American Legion; Flag Day; Grand Army of the Republic (GAR); Revolutionary War; *Washington Crossing the Delaware*

Further Reading

Anderson, Peggy. 1974. *The Daughters: An Unconventional Look at America's Fan Club—The DAR*. New York: St. Martin's Press.

Davies, Wallace Evan. 1948. "The Society of the Cincinnati in New England 1783–1800." *William and Mary Quarterly* 3 (5): 3–25.

Glassberg, David. *American Historical Pageantry: The Uses of Tradition in the Early Twentieth Century*. Chapel Hill: University of North Carolina Press.

Teachout, Woden Sorrow. 2003. *Forging Memory: Hereditary Societies, Patriotism and the American Past, 1876–1898*. PhD thesis, Harvard University.

Truesdell, Barbara. 1996. "Exalting 'U.S.Ness': Patriotic Rituals of the Daughters of the American Revolution." In *Bonds of Affection: Americans Define Their Patriotism*, edited by John Bodnar, 278–289. Princeton, NJ: Princeton University Press.

The Vintage Traveler. 2015. "Daughters of Revolution, Grant Wood." November 29. https://thevintagetraveler.wordpress.com/2015/11/29/daughters-of-revolution-grant-wood/

DAVIS, JEFFERSON

Jefferson Davis (1808–1889) served as president of the Confederate States of America during the Civil War. Prior to the outbreak of war, he was a U.S. senator representing Mississippi. On January 10, 1861, just 11 days before he would announce that he was leaving the body, Davis gave a speech in which he evoked the United States flag and his affection for it. Notably, Davis had graduated from West Point and served with distinction in the Mexican-American War, which was the first war in which troops routinely fought under the U.S. flag rather than various battle flags. The last book that Davis had checked out of the Library of Congress prior to this speech was Schuyler Hamilton's *History of the American Flag* (Leepson 2005, 92), and his speech suggests that he had read it.

Davis largely devoted his speech to arguing that U.S. forces should withdraw from Fort Sumter and that the national government should let states depart from the Union in peace. He recognized, however, the bonds of affection that President Lincoln would soon cite in his inaugural address. Davis thus asked, "Is there a Senator who does not daily receive letters appealing to him to use even the small power which one man here possesses to save the rich inheritance out fathers gave us?" He further observed the "tears now trickling down the stern face of man; and those who have bled for the flag of their country, and are willing now to die for it."

Jefferson Davis was a distinguished U.S. senator from Mississippi and secretary of war before becoming president of the Confederate States of America. Before leaving the Senate, Davis gave a speech suggesting that the U.S. flag should be folded and kept as a "sacred memento" to the past. Instead, it became a symbol of union. (Library of Congress)

Denying that President Washington would have authorized troops or forts to move against states, he pointed out that federal troops were now garrisoning themselves at Fort Washington and Fort McHenry, "memorable in our history as the place where, under bombardment, the star-spangled banner floated through the darkness of night, the point which was consecrated by our national song." Davis also addressed arguments that it would be shameful for the Union to lower the flag at Fort Sumter, asking, "Does any man's courage impel him to stand boldly forth to take the life of his brethren?"

In a passage that appears to contradict Schuyler Hamilton's *History of the American Flag,* who attributed the first Union flag to Washington's forces at Prospect Hill in Boston, Davis continued:

> These are your brethren; and they have shed as much glory upon that flag as any equal number of men in the Union. There are the men, and that is the locality, where the first Union flag was unfurled, and where was fought a gallant battle before our independence was declared—not the flag with thirteen stripes and thirty-three stars, but a flag with a cross of St. George, and the long stripes running through it. When the gallant Moultrie took the British Fort Johnson, and carried it, for the first time, I believe, did the Union flag fly in the air: and that was in October, 1775.

He further described how after repeated enemy attacks "the flag still floated there, and, though many bled, the garrison conquered." Asking again, "Can there be a point of pride against laying upon that sacred soil to-day the flag for which our fathers died?" Davis said his pride was different. He explained:

> My pride is that that flag shall not act between contending brothers; and that, when it shall no longer be the common flag of the country, it shall be folded up and laid away like a vesture [piece of clothing] no longer used; that it shall be kept as a sacred memento of the past, to which each of us can make a pilgrimage, and remember the glorious days in which we were born.

But even as Davis justified the right of states to secede from the Union, he remained gripped by the nostalgia of the old flag:

> All will feel the deprivation of that high pride and power which belong to the flag now representing the greatest Republic, if not the greatest Government, upon the face of the globe. . . . I here express the deep sorrow which always overwhelms me when I think of taking a last leave of that object of early affection and proud association, feeling that henceforth it is not to be the banner which, by day and by night, I am ready to follow, to hail with the rising and bless with the setting sun.

He further showed his understanding of the origins of the stars of the flag. Describing how America arose amid despotism, Davis waxed eloquent as he described the "confederation" that he thought it represented:

> The earth, the air, and the sea, became brilliant; and from the foam of ages rose the constellation which was set in the political firmament as a sign of unity and confederation and community independence, coexistent with confederate strength. That constellation has served to bless our people. Nay, more, its light has been thrown on foreign lands, and its regenerative power will outlive, perhaps, the Government as a sign for which it was set.

Davis insisted, however, that northerners had disrupted the flag constellation:

> If our Government shall fail, it will not be the defect of the system, though its mechanism was wonderful, surpassing that which the solar system furnishes for our contemplation; for it had had no center of gravitation; each planet was set to revolve in an orbit of its own, each moving by its own impulse, and all attracted by the affections which countervailed each other. It has been the perversion of the Constitution; it has been the substitution of theories of morals for principles of government; it has been forcing crude opinions about things not understood upon the domestic institution of other men, which has disturbed these planets in their orbit; it is this which threatens to destroy the constellation which, in its power and its glory, has been gathering one after another, until, from thirteen, it had risen to thirty-three stars.

Although the Confederate states adopted its own banner, Davis kept the U.S. flag under which he had fought during the Mexican-American War. It is now in the Mississippi Department of Archives. The stars have, however, been removed;

apparently Davis's wife Varina distributed stars from the flag to those who had remained loyal to her husband during the war (Bonner 2002, 18).

See also Civil War; Constellation; Fort Sumter Flag; Lincoln, Abraham; Mexican-American War

Further Reading

Bonner, Robert E. 2002. *Colors and Blood: Flag Passions of the Confederate South*. Princeton, NJ: Princeton University Press.

Davis, Jefferson. 1861. Speech of January 10. *Congressional Globe*. 36th Congress, 2nd Session, 306–312.

Hamilton, Schuyler. 1852. *History of the National Flag of the United States of America*. Philadelphia: Lippincott, Grambo, and Co.

Leepson, Marc. 2005. *Flag: An American Biography*. New York: St. Martin's Press.

DECORATION DAY (MEMORIAL DAY)

Nations have long honored their war dead. Pericles of Athens gave one of his greatest speeches to commemorate warriors lost in the Peloponnesian War, and the Gettysburg Address, which commemorated the war dead at Gettysburg, Pennsylvania, during the Civil War, remains one of Abraham Lincoln's greatest speeches. The Civil War lasted from 1861 to 1865 and resulted in the death of more than 750,000 soldiers as well as widespread devastation. The war began when newly elected President Abraham Lincoln sought to preserve the Union by resisting efforts by 11 southern states to secede for fear that the national government would interfere with slavery. After southern troops attacked Fort Sumter, off the coast of South Carolina, American forces were forced to withdraw. But they took the fort's flag with them when they left, and it quickly became a rallying symbol for the Union.

In 1868, three years after the war had ended in a Union victory, a group of Union veterans known as the Grand Army of the Republic (GAR), led by John A. Logan, established May 30 as Decoration Day, on which the graves of Union dead would be decorated with flowers and flags. Although southern states sometimes designated different days to honor Confederate war dead, the holiday, which is now known as Memorial Day, in time expanded to honor all war dead. Over time, certain traditions have become strongly associated with this day of remembrance. For example, the president of the United States typically lays a wreath at the Tomb of the Unknown Soldier in Arlington National Cemetery on Memorial Day. Once known chiefly for its solemnity, the day is now often also marked by picnics and sports events, a trend which the GAR opposed but which the American Legion, largely composed of World War I veterans, did not (Sacco 2015).

One modern scholar points out that while some critics bemoan the apparent "indifference" to the holiday, others are more concerned about the "levity" that now often surrounds the event. The scholar further suggests that the conflicting images of "parade and picnic together achieve a reconciliation of the conflicting claims of life and death. Each makes the other more meaningful" (Albanese 1974, 396).

Decoration (Memorial) Day festivities at the Soldiers' and Sailors' Monument in Riverside Park, New York City, May 30, 1917. The day, now known as Memorial Day, grew out of the Civil War, and often involves decorating graves with flags and flowers. (Library of Congress)

In 1971, Congress designated Memorial Day as a national holiday to be celebrated on the last Monday in May. In 2000, Congress further adopted "The National Moment of Remembrance Act," which encourages individuals to pause at 3:00 p.m. local time for a minute of silence to honor those who have died in the service of the nation.

A diverse number of cities have claimed to be the first to hold a formal Decoration or Memorial Day, but in 1966, President Lyndon B. Johnson and Congress bestowed this honor on Waterloo, New York. It is the site of the Memorial Day Museum, also known as the William H. Burton House. It is open on weekdays and Saturdays from Memorial Day through Labor Day.

See also Civil War; Grand Army of the Republic (GAR)

Further Reading

Albanese, Catherine. 1974. "Requiem for Memorial Day: Dissent in the Redeemer Nation." *American Quarterly* 26 (October): 386–398.

Blair, William A. 2004. *Cities of the Dead: Contesting the Memory of the Civil War in the South, 1865–1914*. Chapel Hill: University of North Carolina Press.

D'Imperio, Chuck. 2013. *Unknown Museums of Upstate New York*. Syracuse, NY: Syracuse University Press.

O'Leary, Cecilia Elizabeth. 1999. *To Die For: The Paradox of American Patriotism*. Princeton, NJ: Princeton University Press.

Sacco, Nicholas W. 2015. "The Grand Army of the Republic, the Indianapolis 500, and the Struggle for Memorial Day in Indiana, 1868–1923." *Indiana Magazine of History* 222 (December): 349–380.

U.S. Department of Veterans Affairs. 2015. "How Decoration Day Became Memorial Day." May 23. Special to the Whig. http://www.cecildaily.com/bonus-articles/memorial_day/how-decoration-day-became-memorial-day/article_216ad0f6-013d-11e5-91d9-6774a541cac3.html

DIMENSIONS OF THE AMERICAN FLAG

See Proportions of the American Flag

DIPPING THE FLAG

See Olympic Protocol

DON'T TREAD ON ME FLAG

See Rattlesnake Flags

DRIVER, WILLIAM

See Old Glory Flag

E

EAGLE

Like the American flag, the bald eagle serves as a symbol of the United States. It should not be surprising to find that in addition to being incorporated into the Great Seal of the United States, many early flags, including the Schuyler Flag and the Kingsboro Flag, included an eagle, most often in the canton. The bride of American explorer (and eventual California governor, U.S. senator, and Republican presidential nominee) John C. Fremont designed such a flag for him when he embarked on his first expedition into the western territories in 1842 (Mastai and D'Otrange 1973, 96).

Grace Rogers Cooper has observed that the eagle and star design "may well have been one of the more common early designs for national flags. It continued in use in the nineteenth century as late as the 1840s" (1973, 6). The symbol was particularly popular among Native Americans. Moreover, in quilts and early American folk art, the eagle was often a more prominent symbol of the nation than the flag.

Today, the eagle is at the center of the Seal of the President of the United States, which is also incorporated into the presidential flag. It carries a banner in its mouth saying "E Pluribus Unum" (From many, one) and has 13 stars and 13 cloud puffs over its head. It has a shield with red and white stripes below a blue top and holds an olive branch in its left talon and arrows in its right. This is a fitting symbol of the president's role as commander in chief of the armed forces, which is sometimes called "the power of the sword." The imagery appears on a blue background decorated with 50 stars, which is in turn surrounded with the words, in blue print on a gold background saying "SEAL of the PRESIDENT of the UNITED STATES."

A brass eagle often sits at the top of poles for the U.S. flag.

See also Quilts; Schuyler Flag; Top of the Flagpole

Further Reading

Cooper, Grace Rogers. 1973. *Thirteen-Star Flags: Keys to Identification*. Washington, D.C.: Smithsonian Institution Press.

Mastai, Boleslaw, and Marie-Louise D'Otrange. 1973. *The Stars and the Stripes: The American Flag as Art and as History from the Birth of the Republic to the Present*. New York: Alfred A. Knopf.

EAST INDIA COMPANY FLAG

There has been long-standing controversy over whether the flag of the East India Company (EIC) influenced the design of the Grand Union Flag and hence subsequent versions of the U.S. flag.

The East India Company (EIC) was chartered in 1600 and was largely responsible for British trading in contemporary India. Its ships typically flew flags that featured the red cross of St. George (or later the crosses of both St. George and St. Andrews) in the upper canton and a series of red and white stripes in the main field.

America's Grand Union Flag contains the British Union Jack in the canton and nine alternating red and white stripes in its field. Moreover, there is a 1754 engraving of two ships anchored off Philadelphia, one of which portrays an ensign with a Union Jack in the canton and what appear to be eight alternating red and white stripes.

Evidence suggests, however that few, if any, Americans other perhaps than sailors would have known of the EIC flag; the company did not trade with the American colonies, nor was it permitted to fly the flag in that part of the world (Ansoff 2008, 1–2). Moreover, extensive investigation of the engraving suggests that it had been taken from an earlier image of 1732, which had portrayed a harbor scene in Bombay, India, where the company would have been active (6–8).

There is also evidence that stripes were a fairly popular flag design during that era. One historian, for example, observed that "the merchant vessels of at least eleven nations and cities sailed under striped ensigns, and of these, six featured red and white stripes in their designs" (Rankin 1954, 341).

See also Stripes on the Flag; Union Flag

Further Reading

Ansoff, Peter. 2008. "A Striped Ensign in Philadelphia in 1754?" *Raven: A Journal of Vexillology* 15:1–22.

Fawcett, Charles. 1937. "The Stripes Flag of the East India Company, and Its Connexion with the American 'Stars and Stripes.'" *Journal of the Society for Nautical Research* 23. https://flagspot.net/flags/gb-eic2.html

Rankin, Hugh F. 1954. "The Naval Flags of the American Revolution." *The William and Mary Quarterly* 11 (July): 339–353.

EASTON FLAG

Part of the allure of early flags in the United States is their variety. One of the most interesting flags is a silk standard that looks as though it could have been produced by a modern artist because it reverses the typical pattern. It features a canton of 13 alternating red and white stripes and a large field of blue with 12 eight-pointed white stars arranged in a circle and surrounding a 13th. The flag, which is displayed at the Easton Area Public Library, Pennsylvania, was long reputed to have been flown at one of three readings of the Declaration of Independence that took place on July 8, 1776 (the others were in Trenton, New Jersey, and Philadelphia,

Pennsylvania). This would have predated the time that Betsy Ross was alleged to have made her flag for General Washington.

Apart from this legend, however, the flag, which adorns the city streets and has been adopted by Easton as its official flag, is not recorded again until 1814. At that time, a 14-year-old resident, Rosanna Beidleman, presented it to a company headed to avenge the burning of Washington, D.C., during the War of 1812, with the instructions, "Under this flag, march to glory" (Jones 2013). Although most historians now believe the flag to have been produced near the time that Miss Beidleman presented it, the standard U.S. flags of that day, like the Star-Spangled Banner that flew over Fort McHenry, had 15 stars and stripes.

See also Revolutionary War Battle Flags; Ross, Betsy; Star-Spangled Banner (Flag); Thirteen-Star Flags

Further Reading

Jones, Kyle M. 2013. "A Short History of Easton's Flag (Retyped)." *Easton Patch*, June 28. https://patch.com/pennsylvania/easton/retyped-a-short-history-of-eastons-flag

Landauer, Bill. June 13, 2015. "Did Betsy Ross Rip Off Easton?" *The Morning Call*. http://www.mcall.com/news/local/easton/mc-easton-flag-20150613-story.html

Leepson, Marc. 2005. *Flag: An American Biography*. New York: St. Martin's Press.

ELK GROVE UNIFIED SCHOOL DISTRICT V. NEWDOW (2004)

Elk Grove Unified School District v. Newdow, 542 U.S. 1 (2004), was a major U.S. Supreme Court decision on the First Amendment. It overturned a decision by the U.S. Ninth Circuit that had given Michael A. Newdow standing to intervene on behalf of his daughter, a California kindergarten student who had been joining her classmates at the beginning of each school day in reciting the Pledge of Allegiance, which since 1954 has included the words "under God." Newdow's contention was that forcing his daughter to recite the pledge violated the Establishment Clause and Free Exercise Clause of the First Amendment.

The Supreme Court's majority opinion, written by Justice John Paul Stevens, was joined by Justices Kennedy, Souter, Ginsburg, and Breyer. It focused almost exclusively on issues of standing. After reviewing the history of the pledge and of its inclusion of the words "under God," Stevens focused on the fact that Newdow shared custody of his daughter with his wife, who had final legal authority on issues related to her education. The mother indicated that neither she nor her daughter had any objection to the practice of reciting the pledge or to the words "under God."

Although Stevens appeared to believe that the case presented a genuine controversy, he pointed out that the doctrine of prudential standing also cautioned the court against intervening in domestic issues, which were typically resolved in state courts. Moreover, California not only permitted students to excuse themselves from the pledge but also did nothing to impair Newdow from instructing his daughter in religious matters as he chose.

Chief Justice William Rehnquist wrote a concurring opinion, which was joined by Justices O'Connor and Thomas. Justice Scalia, who had publicly questioned the Ninth Circuit decision, did not participate in the case. Rehnquist believed that Newdow had established standing and that the court had attempted to fashion an exemption for his case rather than deal with it directly. Rehnquist cited not only the pledge but also a number of presidential oaths, speeches, and declarations to establish that it was common to invoke God in national discourse. He further cited the words "In God We Trust" on American currency, the words of "The Star-Spangled Banner," and the words spoken at the beginning of each session of the Court. He believed that such usage was sufficient to establish that the words "under God" did not convert the salute to the flag into a religious exercise.

Justice Sandra Day O'Connor wrote a separate concurring opinion. Her opinion was designed to show that the inclusion of the words "under God" did not violate the endorsement test that she had devised to ascertain whether actions violated the Establishment Clause. In this case, she believed that the words served a secular purpose of helping to solemnize public occasions. After noting the history and ubiquity of the practice, she concluded that the words were not "a serious invocation of God" or "an expression of individual submission to divine authority" but an acceptable example of ceremonial deism.

Justice Clarence Thomas authored a separate concurring opinion in which he too argued that Newdow had standing but rejected the idea that the pledge was unconstitutional. Thomas believed that the pledge would be considered unconstitutional if the court applied the opinion in *Lee v. Weisman*, 505 U.S. 577 (1992), which had emphasized the coercion inherent in listening to a graduation prayer, but Thomas did not agree with that precedent. Thomas further articulated his view that the Establishment Clause was designed to protect existing state religious establishments and not to protect individual rights.

See also Pledge of Allegiance; Under God

Further Reading

Collins, Dan. 2003. "Scalia: One Nation Under God, Please." CBS News, February 18. http://www.cbsnews.com/news/scalia-one-nation-under-god-please/

Wheeler, Brian. 2008. "The Pledge of Allegiance in the Classroom and the Court: An Epic Struggle over the Meaning of the Establishment Clause of the First Amendment." *Brigham Young University Education and Law Journal*, 281–324.

ELLSWORTH, ELMER E.

Flags have tremendous evocative powers. Flags with differing symbols may evidence radically different loyalties. The beginning of the Civil War was marked by the fall of Fort Sumter in South Carolina. The federal troops who withdrew from Fort Sumter took the fort's flag with them, and this flag became a symbol of northern resolution to vindicate their cause.

On May 24, 1861, the day after Virginians ratified their state's decision to secede, Col. Elmer Ellsworth (1837–1861) marched into Alexandria, Virginia.

Born in New York, the highly ambitious Ellsworth, a Unionist determined to do his part to tamp down secession, had already mustered several regiments of Zoaves (named after acrobatic soldiers of the Crimean War), who became known for their precision drills and for adhering to the high moral standards that Ellsworth set for them.

Perhaps because Ellsworth recognized the provocative effect that the display of the Confederate flag had on his men, Ellsworth had entered the Marshall House to remove an 8-by-14-foot Confederate flag, which its owner, James Jackson, had been waving from a 25-foot staff from his house to make it visible across the Potomac River in Washington, D.C. Jackson, who was a strong advocate of slavery, mortally wounded Ellsworth with a shotgun, making him the first officer to be killed in the war. Jackson was in turn killed on the scene by Francis E. Browell, who later received the Medal of Honor for his actions. Ellsworth's slaying caused Lincoln deep sorrow (Ellsworth's body was laid out in the White House), and Ellsworth and Jackson were lionized by northerners and southerners respectively (Bonner 2002, 307–309). Lincoln wrote a particularly compassionate letter to Ellsworth's parents in which he referred to himself as "your friend in common affliction" (quoted in Ingraham 1918, 373).

See also Civil War; Confederate Flag; Lincoln, Abraham

Further Reading

Bonner, Robert E. 2002. "Flag Culture and the Consolidation of Confederate Nationalism." *The Journal of Southern History* 68 (May): 293–332

Edwards, Owen. 2011. "The Death of Colonel Ellsworth." *Smithsonian Magazine*, April. http://www.smithsonianmag.com/history/the-death-of-colonel-ellsworth-878695/?page=1

Goode, James M. 2003. "Civil War Washington: Rare Images from the Albert H. Small Collection." *Washington History* 15 (Spring/Summer): 62–79.

Ingraham, Charles A. 1918. "Colonel Elmer E. Ellsworth: First Hero of the Civil War." *The Wisconsin Magazine of History* 1 (June): 349–374.

ETIQUETTE

See Flag Code

EVACUATION DAY

November 25, 1783, is known as Evacuation Day because it marks the exit of British troops from the City of New York, where they had remained in control of the city long after Americans and their French Allies had won the battle of Yorktown on October 19, 1781.

On the morning of the departure of the British, a Mrs. Day reportedly raised the Stars and Stripes (probably the Betsy Ross flag) over her Murray Street tavern and used a broom to bloody the nose of a British captain, William Cunningham, when he attempted to take it down on the argument that the British retained possession of the city until noon (Bryk 2004).

Prior to that, British forces had nailed their flag defiantly over the Battery, removing the halyards and greasing the pole to make it more difficult to take down. In a scene depicted in a number of paintings and illustrations, John Van Arsdale, a Continental soldier, is credited with nailing cleats into the poll, ripping down the British flag and throwing it into the crowd, stringing the halyards, and raising the Stars and Stripes to a 13-gun salute. That night, Sons of the Revolution went to Fraunces Tavern and raised their glasses in 13 toasts, which included "May America be an Asylum for the persecuted of the Earth" and "May the remembrance of this day be a lesson to Princes" (Kaplan 2014).

Celebrations of Evacuation Day continued intermittently for almost a century but were gradually overshadowed by other holidays and then discontinued during World War I when the United States was allied with Britain.

See also Betsy Ross Flag; Revolutionary War

Further Reading

Byrk, William. 2004. "The British Are Going!" *New York Sun*, November 24. http://www.nysun.com/on-the-town/british-are-going/5343/

Kaplan, James S. 2004. "A Short History of 'Evacuation Day Day' in NYC." *New York History Blog*, December 31. http://newyorkhistoryblog.org/2014/12/31/a-short-history-of-evacutaion-day-in-nyc/

EX PARTE STARR (1920)

The case of *Ex Parte Starr*, 263 F.145 (1920), which was decided by a U.S. District Judge, is among a number of cases that demonstrate the degree to which war can generate intolerance against those who fail to hold the American flag in high regard.

In a decision affirmed by the state supreme court, an individual named Starr had been convicted by a Montana court of violating the state's sedition act. This state law was similar to the Federal Espionage Law of May 1918, which had prohibited language bringing the U.S. flag into contempt. Apparently, when told by a mob that he must kiss the flag, Starr had responded:

> What is this thing anyway? Nothing but a piece of cotton with a little paint on it and some other marks in the corner there. I will not kiss that thing. It might be covered with microbes.

After being fined and sentenced to 10–20 years at hard labor, Starr argued that the law was unconstitutional because it dealt with a matter for the national government and violated the Thirteenth and Fourteenth Amendments.

Unfortunately for Starr, his conviction and sentencing occurred before the U.S. Supreme Court delivered its decision in *Gitlow v. New York* (1925), applying the free speech clause of the First Amendment to the states via the due process clause of the Fourteenth Amendment. Moreover, in *Halter v. Nebraska* (1907), the court had upheld a state law prohibiting what it considered to be desecration of the flag in advertising, and no federal law had sought to preempt this field.

Judge George M. Bourquin was the magistrate who denied Starr's appeal of his conviction. Bourquin had faced other cases involving such intolerance, including one where he had exonerated a rancher accused of opposing the war (Gutfeld 1968). From Bourquin's perspective, Starr "was more sinned against than sinning." He called the sentence "horrifying" and stated that "a nominal fine would serve every end of justice." In addition, he likened mob members to slackers, profiteers, and enemy sympathizers. Despite all of this, however, he did not think that the law afforded the habeas corpus relief that Starr was seeking. His only recourse was thus to seek an executive pardon. In the course of his decision, Bourquin ruefully observed:

> Patriotism is the cement that binds the foundation and the superstructure of the state. The safety of the latter depends upon the integrity of the former. Like religion, patriotism is a virtue so indispensable and exalted, its excesses pass with little censure.

Subsequent Supreme Court decisions in *Texas v. Johnson* (1989) and *United States v. Eichman* (1990) demonstrated that the Supreme Court became increasingly disposed to curb such excesses under authority of the First and Fourteenth Amendments.

See also Advertising; *Halter v. Nebraska* (1907); *Texas v. Johnson* (1989); *United States v. Eichman* (1990)

Further Reading

Gutfeld, Arnon. 1968. "The Ves Hall Case, Judge Bourquin, and the Sedition Act of 1918." *Pacific Historical Review* 37 (May): 163–178.

EXCLUSIONARY FLAGS

Although the flag is generally a symbol of national unity, there have been a number of flags that have highlighted national discord. The most obvious is the flag of the Confederate States of America, but it is not the only one.

At the beginning of the Civil War, the official U.S. flag had 33 stars and 13 stripes. Some abolitionists, however, crafted flags with 7 stripes (for each of the original free states) and 19 or 20 stars (for the existing free states). In a somewhat related development, some members of the underground railroad apparently hung out flags with 5 stars—4 to represent the bowl of the big Dipper (the edge stars pointed toward the North Star) and the other to represent the North Star, by which slaves guided themselves to free territory.

An early southern secessionist flag includes 11 stripes (for each member of the Confederacy) and 15 stars (for each of the slave states that the Confederacy hoped to attract).

After hearing about secession, Samuel F. B. Morse, who invented the telegraph, proposed, perhaps not in complete seriousness, that the flag should be split into two parts, with the North to fly the top half, the South the bottom half, and with the stars and stripes to be proportionally divided between them (Ness 2008, 29).

Lincoln insisted that Northern troops fight under a U.S. flag representing all the states, including those in Confederacy, because he did not recognize the legitimacy of southern states seceding from the Union. Similarly, he consistently referred to the conflict as a civil war or rebellion, rather than as the War between the States, which would imply that the conflict involved two separate nation states.

See also Civil War; Confederate Flag; Lincoln, Abraham

Further Reading

Iasso, Anthony. 2014a. "American National Flag 5 Stars Obverse, 19 Stars Reverse, 7 Stripes, A Rare Exclusionary Flag with Abolitionist and Underground Railroad Symbolism, 1861." Rare Flags. http://www.rareflags.com/RareFlags_Showcase_IAS_00400.htm.

Iasso, Anthony. 2014b. "A Tale of Two Flags—The Abolitionist Flag and the Secessionist Flag," Rare Flags. Last modified 2014. http://www.rareflags.com/RareFlags_Collecting_TaleOfTwoFlags.htm.

Ness, William Boyd. 2008. *"Burning with Star-Fires": The National Flag in Civil War Poetry*. PhD thesis, University of Iowa.

Parry-Jones, Cai. 2014. "Flying the Flag for Freedom: The Star Spangled Banner and the American Abolitionist Movement." October 16. http://www.amdigital.co.uk/m-editorial-blog/flying-the-flag-for-freedom

EXECUTIVE ORDER NO. 1556 OF 1912 AND ITS SUCCESSORS

Although the Flag Acts of 1777, 1794, and 1818 provided guidelines for the numbers of stars and stripes on the U.S. flag, there was tremendous variety in the early years as to the proportions of the flag and how the stars were arranged.

On June 24, 1912, President William Howard Taft issued Executive Order No. 1556, which provided that the proportions of the fly (length) of the flag would be 1.9 times the hoist (width). He also specified that the width of the Union (or canton) would be seven-thirteenths, that the length would be 0.76, and that each of the stripes would be one-thirteenth of the length. The order further provided that Union Jacks flown at sea would be the "Union of the National Flag with which it is flown." It further specified that stars should be arranged according to a blueprint, which provided for six horizontal rows of eight stars each.

President Woodrow Wilson issued a similar order (2389) on May 29, 1916, which also provided for the president's flag.

President Eisenhower subsequently issued executive orders on June 3, 1959, and August 21, 1959, that provided for the addition on the flag of a 49th and then 50th star to acknowledge the statehood of Alaska and Hawaii.

See also Flag Act of 1777; Flag Act of 1794; Flag Act of 1818; Proportions of the American Flag; Stars, Arrangement of on U.S. Flags

Further Reading

Smithsonian. 2017. "Facts about the United States Flag." Accessed May 14. https://www.si.edu/spotlight/flag-day/flag-facts

F

FEDERAL FLAG PROTECTION ACTS OF 1968 AND 1989

The war in Vietnam was one of the longest and most bitter conflicts in U.S. history. The U.S. intervened on the side of South Vietnam to oppose what it believed to be aggression by the communist North Vietnam. As an increasing number of Americans, most of whom had been drafted, were killed or wounded, and the toll on Vietnam's land and people intensified, public protests over American participation in the war escalated, especially on college campuses. A number of these demonstrations included antiwar protestors who burned either flags or draft cards.

In response to these very emotional displays, Congress enacted Public Law 90-38, which was approved on July 5, 1968, and which was designed to prevent desecration of the United States flag. The law expanded on an earlier statute that had applied only within the District of Columbia. Section a of the law, embodied as section 700 of the U.S. Code, provided that "whoever knowingly casts contempt upon any flag of the United States by publicly mutilating, defacing, defiling, burning, or trampling upon it shall be fined not more than $1,000 or imprisoned for not more than one year, or both."

Section b of the law complicated the issue by broadly defining a flag as:

> any flag, standard, colors, ensign, or any picture or representation of either, or of any part or parts of either, made of any substance or represented on any substance, of any size evidently purporting to be either of said flag, standard, colors, or ensign of the United States of America, or a picture or a representation of either, upon which shall be shown the colors, the stars and the stripes, in any number of either thereof, or of any part or parts of either, by which the average person seeing the same without deliberation may believe the same to represent the flag, standards, colors, or ensign of the United States of America.

Section c further indicated that the law was not designed to withdraw jurisdiction over such matters from states and territories.

After the U.S. Supreme Court invalidated a similar Texas law in its decision in *Texas v. Johnson* (1989), Congress adopted Public Law 101-131 to tighten the law, limiting penalties to anyone who "knowingly mutilates, defaces, physically defiles, burns, maintains on the floor or ground, or tramples upon any flag of the United States." It further limited the definition of the flag to "any flag of the United States, or any part thereof, made of any substance, of any size, in a form that is commonly displayed" and permitting "the disposal of a flag when it has become worn or soiled" in Section 2(a)(2).

The court subsequently invalidated this law as a violation of the First Amendment in *United States v. Eichman* (1990). Both Supreme Court decisions have led to calls, unsuccessful as of early 2018, for an anti–flag desecration amendment to the U.S. Constitution.

See also Flag Desecration Amendment; *Texas v. Johnson* (1989); *United States v. Eichman* (1990)

Further Reading

Dorsen, Norman. 2000. "Flag Desecration in Courts, Congress, and Country." *Thomas M. Cooley Law Review* 17 (Michaelman Term): 417–442.

Goldstein, Robert J. 1995. *Saving "Old Glory": The History of the American Flag Desecration Controversy*. Bolder, CO: Westview Press.

Goldstein, Robert J. 2000. *Flag Burning and Free Speech*. Lawrence: University Press of Kansas.

Luckey, John. 2003. *Flag Protection: A Brief History and Summary of Recent Supreme Court Decisions and Proposed Constitutional Amendments*. Washington, D.C.: Congressional Research Service of the Library of Congress.

FLAG ACT OF 1777

On June 14, 1777, the Second Continental Congress adopted the following resolution:

> Resolved, that the flag of the United States be made of thirteen stripes, alternate red and white; that the union be thirteen stars, white in a blue field, representing a new constellation.

By this time, Americans had been fighting (albeit somewhat intermittently) with the British for more than two years, and America had formally proclaimed its independence the previous July 2 (with its explanation in the Declaration of Independence following two days later). Although the design differed, the colors of the flag were the same as those of the flag of the United Kingdom.

The congressional resolution, although fairly succinct, specifies the colors of the flag, the number of stars and stripes (albeit not that seven are red and six are white), and the symbolism of a "new constellation" (prior to independence, the colonies were commonly compared to stars revolving around King George III and Great Britain). The resolution does not specify the arrangement of the stars in the canton, or union, and that appears to have varied significantly in early flag designs.

Significantly, Congress adopted this resolution after Betsy Ross was alleged to have made the first flag. Most troops would have fought under regimental colors even after the resolution. It is logical to suggest that designing a flag was not initially considered to be as important as pursuing the war effort, drawing up a plan of government, and seeking foreign allies. Even after Congress adopted its resolution, there were a number of variants of the U.S. flag, including some with alternating red, white, and blue stripes (Young 1977, 830).

On May 1, 1795, after the admission of Kentucky and Vermont to statehood, Congress increased the number of stars and stripes on the flag to 15. In 1818, Congress subsequently reduced the number of stripes back to the original 13, with the number of stars continuing to reflect the total number of states and the 13 stripes now representing the original 13 states. Francis Hopkinson, who worked on designing the seal of the United States, appears to have been the chief designer of the flag. The day on which the resolution was adopted is now designated as Flag Day.

See also Colors of the Flag; Constellation; Flag Day; Hopkinson, Francis; Ross, Betsy; Stripes on the Flag; Thirteen-Star Flags

Further Reading

Young, Rowland L. 1977. "'Liberty and Justice for All.'" *American Bar Association Journal* 63 (June): 828–831.

FLAG ACT OF 1794

On January 13, 1794, Congress adopted a law to redesign the American flag. It read as follows:

> Be it enacted, etc., That from and after the first day of May, one thousand seven hundred and ninety-five, the flag of the United States be fifteen stripes alternate red and white, that the union be fifteen stars, white in a blue field. (Preble 1872, 223)

This law modified the congressional resolution of June 14, 1777, which had originally established the flag as having 13 stars and 13 alternating red and white stripes. Like that law, however, this one did not specify how the stars were to be arranged on the canton. This led to considerable variety in flag designs throughout America's first decades of existence.

The congressional action of 1794 was the result of the admission of the states of Vermont on March 4, 1791, and Kentucky on June 1, 1792.

Massachusetts representative Benjamin Goodhue was among those who thought the existing flag of 13 stars and 13 stripes "ought to be permanent." Fellow Massachusetts representative George Thatcher thought the whole matter was "a consummate piece of frivolity." By contrast, Elias Boudinot of New Jersey thought that it was "of consequence to keep the citizens of Vermont and Kentucky in good humor" (all quoted in Preble 1872, 222). James Madison, who was a friend of the West, was among those who agreed.

The law, which remained in effect until April 4, 1818, is the only such law that authorized a U.S. flag of 15 stripes. The practice of increasing the number of stripes with the addition of new states proved less practical than reverting to the original number of stripes and simply adding a new star.

The flag that flew over Fort McHenry and inspired Francis Scott Key to write "The Star-Spangled Banner" contained 15 stars and stripes, as specified in the 1794 legislation.

See also Flag Act of 1777; Flag Act of 1818; Star-Spangled Banner (Flag)

Further Reading

Preble, George Henry. 1872. *Our Flag. Origin and Progress of the Flag of the United States of America, with an Introductory Account of the Symbols, Standards, Banners and Flags of Ancient and Modern Nations*. Albany, NY: Joel Munsell. Reprinted by Forgotten Books.

FLAG ACT OF 1818

Congress had acted to alter the design of the flag in 1794, after the admission of Vermont in 1791 and Kentucky in 1792; however, it was slower to alter the flag after the admission of Tennessee in 1796, Ohio in 1803, Louisiana in 1812, and Indiana in 1816. Thus, these states were not officially recognized on the flag that flew during the War of 1812.

After the admission of Indiana, Rep. Peter Wendover of New York (1768–1834) proposed establishing a committee to review the matter. Wendover had also sought suggestions from Capt. Samuel Chester Reid (1783–1861), who had commanded the *General Armstrong* at the Battle of Fayal during the War of 1812. Reid suggested reducing the number of stripes back to 13, symbolizing each state with a star, and configuring the stars into a five-sided star design for public buildings and in parallel lines for ships.

Reid intended for the five-pointed star design to represent national unity as embodied in the national motto "E Pluribus Unum" (Eggenberger 1959, 104). Proposals to configure the stars themselves into a giant star were abandoned because "It was plainly evident that as the number of States increased, it would be necessary to make the individual stars so small as to be almost indistinguishable as stars" (Smith 1908, 86).

During congressional debate on the subject, Rep. George Poindexter of Mississippi proposed balancing the 13 stripes for old states with 7 stars for new states, and Rep. Walter Folger Jr. of Massachusetts proposed restoring the original flag. Congress apparently also considered a flag with 20 stars against a blue background in the upper-left quadrant; 13 alternating red and white stripes on the bottom-right quadrant; an eagle in the upper-right quadrant, against a white field; and a depiction of the Goddess of Liberty on the bottom-left quadrant, against another field of white (Preble 1872, 255–56).

On April 4, 1818, Congress adopted the following legislation:

> AN ACT TO ESTABLISH THE FLAG OF THE UNITED STATES
> SEC. 1. *Be it enacted, &c.*, that from and after the fourth day of July next, the Flag of the United States be thirteen horizontal stripes alternate red, and white; that the union have twenty stars, white, in a blue field.
> SEC. 2. And be it further enacted, that on the admission of very new state into the union, one star be added to the union of the flag, and that such addition shall take effect on the fourth of July next succeeding such admission. (Preeble 1872, 257–258)

The law thus reduced the number of stripes from 15 to 13 and provided not only for adding stars when new states were admitted but also for specifying when new flag designs would go into effect. It tied the latter date to the nation's Independence Day. Notably, this law did not specify how the stars would be arranged in the canton, resulting in further considerable variation over the following years.

See also Flag Act of 1794; Independence Day

Further Reading

Eggenberger, David. 1959. *Flags of the U.S.A.* New York: Thomas Y. Crowell Company.

Preble, George Henry. 1872. *Our Flag. Origin and Progress of the Flag of the United States of America, with an Introductory Account of the Symbols, Standards, Banners and Flags of Ancient and Modern Nations.* Albany, NY: Joel Munsell. Reprinted by Forgotten Books.

Smith, Nicholas. 1908. *Our Nation's Flag in History and Incident.* 2nd ed. Milwaukee: Young Churchman Co.

FLAG APPAREL

Although modern flag etiquette now frowns on wearing an actual flag as an item of clothing, as communications professor Jennifer Marmo (2010, 53) has observed:

> Wearing the flag on the body has become a phenomenon in American society. Many Americans show their support for the country by wearing the flag. Flag trends began emerging in fashion early on. Signature designers and corporations such as Tommy Hilfiger, Polo Ralph Lauren, the Gap, and Old Navy began incorporating patriotic symbols in their fashion.

Another scholar cites a program on National Public Radio about the challenge of composing a flag protection amendment since flag representations are so ubiquitous. The program noted that "there had been flag hats, flag pantyhose, and flag bathing suits during five hours of debate but no Bill of Rights bathing suits" (Marvin 1991, 119).

There is an early kerchief dated between 1775 and 1778 that features George Washington on a horse, surrounded by a number of flags (Monsky 2002). One scholar has observed that "as the nation started to celebrate her history, commemorative bandannas, kerchiefs and handkerchiefs were a standard souvenir issued for celebrations and events, including the U.S. centennial, the Chicago World's Fair, 'Presidential Victims of Assassinations,' the Louisiana Purchase and Exposition in St. Louis, and the 'Jamestown Ter-Centennial Exposition" as well as later celebrations of the Spanish-American War, and the two world wars (Kidd 2007, 41). Flags with candidates' names were also commonly used in the late 19th century.

During the late 1960s, pro- and antiwar forces used flag clothing and accoutrements to indicate both support and opposition to American policies. From the end of the 20th century to the present day, designers have increasingly incorporated flag designs into clothes. "It is common to see the American flag on shirts, shorts, capes, vests, and even socks; surprisingly (or not), the American flag is also donned on

In addition to lapel pins, there are a variety of articles of clothing, including neckties with flag designs, that allow wearers to show their patriotism or interest in American history. (John Vile)

American beauties wearing flag bikinis. American flags are now seen on scarves, hats, bandanas, and ties" as well as on "tube tops, slippers, sheets, and even evening gowns" (Marmo 2010, 53). The number of individuals choosing flag tattoos apparently also increased after the 9/11 terrorist attacks, and flag lapel pins and flag patches have become common decorative items.

Although many such displays are undoubtedly meant to display the wearer's patriotism, a combination of profit and poor taste would appear to be the only motives that would lead companies to distribute condoms with stars and stripes, star-shaped pasties, or "Little Patriot" disposable diapers (Marmo 2010, 54).

It is common for U.S. Olympic athletes to wear uniforms that feature red, white, and blue colors. Saba Ahmed, the president of the Republican Muslim Coalition, however, was criticized in 2015 when she appeared on *The Kelly File* wearing the flag as a hijab. She explained, "People are concerned that I'm disrespecting the flag, but that was never my intent" (Pesce 2015). In 2009, Sarah Palin, the vice presidential running mate of Republican John McCain in 2008, was photographed wrapped in a flag "as if it were a beach towel" (Guenter 2010, 16).

See also Campaign Flags; Flag Patches; *Hoffman v. United States* (1971); Lapel Pins; Olympic Protocol; Terrorist Attacks of September 11, 2001; Washington Kerchief Flags

Further Reading

Guenter, Scot M. 2009. "Flag Tattoos: Markers of Class and Sexuality." In *Proceedings The XIX International Congress of Vexillology, York, 23–27 York July 2001*. U.K.: Flag Institute. https://www.flaginstitute.org/pdfs/Scot%20Guenter.pdf

Guenter, Scot M. 2010. "Juxtaposing Symbols in Civil Religion: The Lady and the Flag." *Raven: A Journal of Vexillology* 17:1–2.

Kidd, Laura K. 2007. "Wave It or Wear It? The United States Flag as a Fashion Icon." *Raven: A Journal of Vexillology* 17:35–60.

Marmo, Jennifer. 2010. "The American Flag and the Body: How the Flag and the Body Create an American Meaning." *Kaleidoscope: A Graduate Journal of Qualitative Communication Research* 9:45–63.

Marvin, Carolyn. 1991. "Theorizing the Flagbody: Symbolic Dimensions of the Flag Desecration Debate, or, Why the Bill of Rights Does Not Fly in the Ballpark." *Critical Studies in Mass Communication* 8:119–138.

Monsky, John R. 2002. "From the Collection Finding America in Its First Political Textile." *Winterthur Portfolio* 37 (Winter): 239–264.

Pesce, Nicole. Updated November 19, 2015. "Muslim Woman Defends Her Wearing of American Flag as Hijab on Fox News to Debate Donald Trump Mosque Stance." *New York Daily News*. http://www.nydailynews.com/news/politics/muslim-woman-defends-wearing-american-flag-hijab-article-1.2439132

FLAG BEARERS, STANDARD-BEARERS

Both regimental and national flags have served not only to identify sides in a battle but also as rallying points. A flag flying from a battle position generally indicates that the side whose flag is flying has possession of that place.

Carrying the banner has traditionally been considered to be a great honor, and it was particularly important for the flag or standard-bearer to prevent the flag from touching the ground or falling into enemy hands. During the Civil War, for example, "if the flag bearer fell, any soldier at hand was bound by his honor and his allegiance to regiment, state, and nation to take his place" (Hartvigsen 2011, 415). One of the goals of Civil War battles was to capture the enemy's flag.

These sentiments were put to music in a song published by H. Lovegrove in 1864 entitled "Let Me Hold It Till I Die." The lyrics were as follows:

> See, the one who bears the banner
> Where the guns are crashing loud,
> Staggers now, for he is wounded,
> And his comrades round him crowd;
> Hands are raised to grasp the standard;
> But on it he turns his eye.
> Murmuring, "Comrades, do not take it,
> Let me hold it till I die! Let me hold it till I die!
> I have borne it into battle,
> When we forced our foes to fly.
> Do not take it from me comrades,
> Let me hold it till I die! Let me hold it till I die! (Hartvigsen 2011, 415)

Similarly, *Harper's Weekly*, a magazine known for its flag imagery, especially during the Civil War era, published a cover on September 20, 1862, of "A Gallant Color-Bearer," which featured a picture of a member of the 19th New York Regiment holding a flag even though he is mortally wounded (Hartvigsen, 2011, 415).

In his novel of the Civil War, *The Red Badge of Courage*, Stephen Crane recounted how a youth under fire headed for a flag in the woods with great enthusiasm:

> Within him . . . was born a love, a despairing fondness for this flag which was near him. It was a creation of beauty and invulnerability. It was a goddess, radiant, that bended its form with an imperious gesture to him. It was a woman, red and white, hating and loving, that called him with the voice of his hopes. Because no harm could come to it he endowed it with power. He kept near, as if it could be a saver of lives. (Crane 1957, 348)

As the color sergeant holding the flag is mortally wounded, the youth and a companion both spring forward to grab the flag. Crane explains:

> The youth and his friend had a small scuffle over the flag. "Give it t' me!" "No, let me keep it!" Each felt satisfied with the other's possession of it, but each felt bound to declare, by an offer to carry the emblem, his willingness to further risk himself. The youth roughly pushed his friend away. (Crane 1957, 349)

Historian Robert Bonner observes that southerners adopted a similar stance:

> The figure of the noble standard-bearer, bravely defending the troops' colors, became a favorite theme of Confederate sentimentalists. The risks that came with this position often transformed common soldiers into heroes. Their patriotism was affirmed in songs that praised their willingness to be vulnerable and that celebrated their happy deaths under the colors that all true soldiers should learn to love. (Bonner 2002, 317)

He cites southern lyrics from "The Banner of the Starry Cross," which was published in New Orleans in 1863:

> A ray of light was in his eye,
> A smile upon his mouth.
> While to his death-chilled breast he clasped,
> The banner of the South.

The Iwo Jima Memorial is an indication that flags continue to rally troops, but modern soldiers often use flag patches to identify themselves in battle rather than battle flags.

See also Civil War; Confederate Flags; Iwo Jima Flag Raising

Further Reading

Bonner, Robert E. 2002. "Flag Culture and the Consolidation of Confederate Nationalism." *The Journal of Southern History* 68 (May): 293–332.

Crane, Stephen. 1957. *The Red Badge of Courage and Other Stories*. New York: Dodd, Mead and Company.

Hartvigsen, Kenneth. 2011. "Picturing Flag Violence in Civil War Sheet Music: The Case of 'Down with the Traitors' Serpent Flag.'" In *Proceedings of the 24th International Congress of Vexillology*, 407–424. Washington, D.C.

FLAG CODE

The rules of flag etiquette are laid out in provisions of the U.S. Code, most of which follow guidelines suggested by the first National Flag Conference that took place at the Memorial Continental Hall of the Daughters of the American Revolution in 1923. Garland W. Powell, the American Legion's National Director of Americanism and author of *Service for God and Country*, played a major role in organizing this conference (Leepson 2005, 197). Another conference made amendments in the following year. Although the rules are generally designed to promote respect for the flag, some may appear quaint by modern standards (Cheung 2015).

Section 4 of the code recommends that civilians saluting the flag should place the right hand over the heart and face the flag. Those in military uniform give a military salute.

Further sections focus chiefly on civilians. Section 6 says that the typical times for displaying a flag are from sunrise to sunset. Those seeking to display it during darkness should illuminate the flag. Only all-weather flags should be flown in inclement weather. Special days for displaying the flag include presidential inaugurations, Easter and Christmas, and state and federal holidays. This section also says that flags should be displayed "daily on or near the main administration building of every public institution" (CRS-3), at polling places, and at schoolhouses during schooldays.

Section 7, which deals with the "Position and Manner of Display" of the flag, is the longest. It says that flags should not hang from floats during parades or be draped over vehicles. The U.S. flag should be raised higher than other national flags, except at the United Nations, where the U.N. flag is higher and the U.S. flag is in the same position as other national flags. When displayed with others, the U.S. flag should always "be hoisted first and lowered last." The code further outlines special rules for displaying flags on a speaker's platform. Contrary to popular myth, the code had no provision allowing the Texas state flag (which once represented an independent republic) to be flown on a level equal to the United States flag.

Section 7, Subsection M, specifies the procedures and occasions for displaying the flag at half-staff, on the deaths of important officials. It says that on such occasions, the flag "should be first hoisted to the peak for an instant and then lowered to the half-staff position." It further lists a number of occasions and lengths of time that the flag should be lowered, generally depending on the rank of the individual being honored. When covering a casket, the code further requires that the union should be "at the head and over the left shoulder." Similarly, when displayed across a corridor or lobby in the main entrance of a building "it should be suspended vertically with the union of the flag to the observer's left upon entering" (Luckey, 5–6).

Section 8 deals with "Respect for the Flag." It prevents dipping the flag and specifies that the flag is only displayed with the union down during times of "dire distress." It also warns against allowing the flag to touch the ground or floor and against its use "as wearing apparel, bedding, or drapery." In a rule that seems largely to be ignored, it also proves that "the flag should never be used for advertising purposes in any manner whatsoever" nor "be embroidered on such articles as cushions or handkerchiefs and the like." While it specifies that the flag should never "be used as a costume or athletic uniform," it permits flag patches on certain uniforms. It suggests disposing of the flag "in a dignified way, preferably by burning" (Luckey 2008, 6–7).

Section 9 deals with conduct during flag raisings, while section 10 permits the president to alter rules by official proclamations.

Although Congress has subsequently adopted a flag desecration law, which the Supreme Court declared in *United States v. Eichman* (1990) to violate the First Amendment, "the Flag Code does not prescribe any penalties for noncompliance nor does it include enforcement provisions; rather the Code functions simply as a guide to be voluntarily followed by civilians and civilian groups" (Luckey 2008, 1).

See also Advertising; American Legion; Flag Apparel; *United States v. Eichman* (1990)

Further Reading

Cheung, Kylie. 2015. "11 American Flag Rules That Are Bizarrely Patriotic, Picky, and Outdated." Bustle, July 10. https://www.bustle.com/articles/96257-11-american-flag-rules-that-are-bizarrely-patriotic-picky-and-outdated

Leepson, Marc. 2005. *Flag: An American Biography*. New York: St. Martin's Press.

Luckey, John R. 2008. *The United States Flag: Federal Law Relating to Display and Associated Questions*. CRS Report for Congress. Washington, D.C.: Congressional Research Service.

FLAG DAY

The origin of Flag Day generally has been attributed to Bernard Cigrand, a schoolteacher who started a celebration to honor the flag in the town of Wuabeka, Wisconsin, in 1885. He later moved to Batavia, Illinois, and that city is now contemplating establishing a Flag Day monument. Others believe that the commemorations began in 1861 after Dudley Warner, who edited the *Evening Press* of Hartford, Connecticut, suggested that individuals throughout Connecticut should display the nation's flag (Corcoran 2002, 147).

Whoever started the tradition, Woodrow Wilson issued the first presidential proclamation of a Flag Day in 1916, prior to U.S. entry into World War I. In his proclamation of May 30 of that year, Wilson suggested setting aside June 14, the day on which Congress adopted its first Flag Act, as "a day of renewal and reminder." He further suggested that this "FLAG DAY" be commemorated

> with special patriotic exercises, at which means shall be taken to give significant expression to our thoughtful love of America, our comprehension of the great mission of liberty and justice to which we have devoted ourselves as a people, our pride in the history and our enthusiasm for the political programme of the nation, our determination to make it greater and purer with each generation, and our resolution to demonstrate to all the world its vital union in sentiment and purpose, accepting

only those as true compatriots who feel as we do the compulsion of this supreme allegiance.

The following year, after the nation had entered the war, Wilson endorsed the flag on the grounds of the Washington Monument as "the emblem of our unity, our power, our thought and purpose as a nation." He further recognized that this was the first war in which the United States had sent armies "across the seas." In an essay entitled "The President's Appeal," which accompanied a pamphlet entitled *Our Flag and Its Message* (1917), Wilson focused not on the flag but on the need for farmers to plant crops to feed the troops.

President Woodrow Wilson at an event honoring the American flag, Washington, D.C., May 1915. On June 14, 1916, Wilson issued his Flag Day Proclamation, officially establishing June 14 as Flag Day. (Library of Congress)

Encouraged by the Sons of the American Revolution (SAR) and other organizations, in 1949, Congress adopted a joint resolution officially recognizing each June 14 as Flag Day and "authoriz[ing] and request[ing] the president to issue an official declaration of this holiday each year," and President Harry S. Truman did so the next year. The day was especially significant to Truman because it marked the day in 1904 when he had enrolled in the Missouri National Guard.

Flag Day is often marked by celebrations and parades. Philadelphia now holds a Stars and Stripes Festival to commemorate the occasion and the birth of the U.S. Army (Jenkins 2015). In 1914, Franklin K. Lane, the secretary of the interior, delivered a famous address on the flag. In 1943, the Supreme Court used the occasion for its decision in *West Virginia State Board of Education v. Barnette*, which reversed an earlier decision requiring the compulsory salute to the flag in public schools.

See also Flag Day Monument; Lane, Franklin K.; Washington Monument Flag Display; *West Virginia State Board of Education v. Barnette* (1943); World War I

Further Reading

Corcoran, Michael. 2002. *For Which It Stands: An Anecdotal Biography of the American Flag*. New York: Simon and Schuster.

Harry S. Truman Presidential Library and Museum. 2017. "This Day in Truman History, June 14, 1950. President Truman Proclaims Official National Flag Day." Accessed February 22. https://www.trumanlibrary.org/anniversaries/flagday.htm

Jenkins, Kristina. 2015. "The Stripes and Stars Festival Celebrates Flag Day in Philadelphia with a Patriotic Parade, Ceremonies and More, Sunday, June 14." Last modified June 10. https://www.uwishunu.com/2015/06/the-stripes-and-stars-festival-celebrates-flag-day-in-philadelphia-with-a-patriotic-parade-ceremonies-and-more-sunday-june-14/

Moss, James A., and M. B. Stewart. 1917. *Our Flag and Its Message Including the President's Appeal for Unity*. Philadelphia: J. B. Lippincott Company.

Schauffler, Robert Haven. 1912. *Flag Day: Its History, Origin, and Celebration as Related in Song and Story*. New York: Moffat, Yard and Company.

FLAG DAY MONUMENT

The town of Batavia, Illinois, has at least two connections to the American flag. One is that it became the home of Dr. Bernard Cigrand, who is most frequently identified as the father of Flag Day in recognition of his untiring efforts to establish official governmental recognition for the day. The other is that the town is the home of FlagSource, a flag manufacturer.

In addition to its annual Flag Day celebrations, the town has a plan to construct a Flag Day memorial on its river walk. The current plan is to have a 40-foot helix monument with a walkway displaying five obelisks commemorating various milestones in the history of the flag and the United States. It would also feature a large 50-foot flagpole displaying a 10-by-18-foot flag.

See also Flag Day

Further Reading

Fox Valley Patriotic Organization. 2017. "Monument Design Features." Flag Day Monument, Batavia, Illinois. Accessed March 2. http://flagdaymonument.com/monument-design-features/

Kanecountyconnects. 2016. "Celebrate 100th Anniversary of Flag Day on June 14 in Kane County, IL!" June 13. http://kanecountyconnects.com/2016/06/celebrate-100th-anniversary-of-flag-day-on-june-14-in-kane-county-il/

FLAG DESECRATION AMENDMENT

The American flag has held such a hallowed place throughout most of American history that individuals can sometimes bring tremendous attention to their cause by burning the flag or treating it in a controversial manner. In the late 19th century, after slavery had been abolished, flag displays and flag salutes became a common way to encourage patriotism in public schools, leading to the development of the pledge to the flag, which was subsequently revised. The flag, though, also became a frequent tool for advertisers. Such use of the flag for commercial gain led to a number of state laws designed to prevent such advertising. The court upheld one such law in *Halter v. Nebraska* (1907).

Protestors in opposition to the Vietnam War burned an American flag in Central Park in New York City in April 1967, after which Congress adopted a law to prevent those actions considered a form of flag desecration. Just two years later, in *Street v. New York* (1969), the U.S. Supreme Court overturned the conviction of an individual who burned a flag. In *Spence v. Washington* (1974), it overturned the conviction of an individual who taped a peace symbol to the flag, and that same year, in *Smith v. Goguen* (1974), it voided a Massachusetts law that had been used to convict an individual who wore a flag patch on the seat of his pants.

In *Texas v. Johnson* (1989), the Supreme Court voided the conviction, under a Texas state law, of an individual who burned an American flag outside the Republication National Convention in 1984. It did so on the basis that the act was symbolic speech and so protected by the First and Fourteenth Amendments. Although many members of Congress responded by proposing an amendment to prohibit such desecration (an amendment for which President George H. W. Bush announced his support at the Iwo Jima Memorial in Arlington, Virginia), Congress responded instead by drawing up legislation designed to provide additional legal protections to the flag. This legislation, however, was in turn invalidated in *United States v. Eichman* (1990), leading to new calls for an amendment to outlaw flag desecration.

Congress subsequently held votes in 1990, 1995, 1999, 2000, 2003, 2005, and 2006, but it continued to fall short of the necessary two-thirds of both houses of Congress that are required to propose such amendments. The only Senate vote in 2006 fell a single vote shy of this two-thirds majority. Proponents of the amendment, including justices on the Supreme Court who voted to upheld flag desecration laws, believed that the flag was a unique symbol that deserved governmental protection. Opponents believed that such an amendment would limit the guarantees of free speech that are enshrined in the First Amendment. Some critics further wondered whether individuals might evade the amendment by burning pictures or representations of flags rather than the flags themselves.

See also Exclusionary Flags; *Minersville School District v. Gobitis* (1940); *Smith v. Goguen* (1974); *Street v. New York* (1969); *Texas v. Johnson* (1989); *United States v. Eichman* (1990); *West Virginia State Board of Education v. Barnette* (1943)

Further Reading

Dorsen, Norman. 2000. "Flag Desecration in Courts, Congress, and Country." *Thomas M. Cooley Law Review* 17 (Michaelman Term): 417–442.

Goldstein, Robert J. 1995. *Saving "Old Glory": The History of the American Flag Desecration Controversy*. Boulder, CO: Westview Press.

Goldstein, Robert J. 2000. *Flag Burning and Free Speech.* Lawrence: University Press of Kansas.

Isaacson, Eric A. 1990. "The Flag Burning Issue: A Legal Analysis and Comment." *Loyola of Los Angeles Law Review* 23 (January): 535–600.

Pease, William H., and June H. Pease, eds. 1965. *The Antislavery Argument.* Indianapolis: Bobbs-Merrill.

Tushnet, Mark. 1990. "The Flag Burning Episode: An Essay on the Constitution." *University of Colorado Law Review* 61:39–53.

Vile, John R., 2015. *Encyclopedia of Constitutional Amendments, Proposed Amendments, and Amending Issues, 1789–2015.* 2 vols. 4th ed. Santa Barbara, CA: ABC-CLIO.

FLAG HOLIDAYS

Although Americans have the right to fly the flag on any day, there are some days that have been especially associated with the practice. The best known of these are Presidents' Day and/or Washington's and Lincoln's birthdays; Memorial or Decoration Day (May 30); Flag Day (June 14); Independence Day (July 4); and Labor Day (the first Monday in September).

A book published in Massachusetts in 1910 also suggests the following days are appropriate for flying the flag: New Year's Day (in honor of Lincoln's Emancipation Proclamation); Longfellow's birthday (February 24); the meeting of the first Congress (March 4); Inauguration Day (now January 20 each fourth year); the day the British evacuated Boston (St. Patrick's Day); Arbor Day (April); Patriot's Day (held on April 19 to commemorate the battles of Lexington and Concord, which started the Revolutionary War); the birthday of Horace Mann (May 4); Peace Day (May 18, which marked the first meeting of the Hague Arbitration Court); the Battle of Bunker Hill (June 17); Perry's victory on Lake Erie (September 10); the bombardment of Fort McHenry (September 13); Constitution Day (September 17); Columbus Day (October 12); the surrender of General Cornwallis (October 19); election day (the first Tuesday in November); Thanksgiving Day; the birthday of Whittier (December 17); and Forefathers' Day, marking the landing of the Pilgrims (December 21) (Whipple 1910, 140).

Omitting some of the more regional characteristics of the earlier list—and beginning with a mention of "All Patriotic Occasions" and "All State Holidays" and ending with "Such other days as may be proclaimed by the President of the United States"—Flags Unlimited, a contemporary website on flag etiquette, includes more-contemporary events. Its list includes Martin Luther King Day (January 20); Easter Sunday; Mother's Day (the second Sunday in May); Armed Forces Day (the third Saturday in May); Patriot Day (September 11); Navy Day (October 27); Veterans Day (November 11); Pearl Harbor Remembrance Day (December 7); and Christmas Day (December 25).

Both lists included approximately 25 holidays, or just over two a month.

See also Decoration Day (Memorial Day); Flag Day; Independence Day; Veterans Day

Further Reading

Flags Unlimited. 2017. "Flag Etiquette." Accessed February 5. http://www.usflags.com/flagetiquette.aspx

Whipple, Wayne. [1910] *The Story of the American Flag*. Bedford MA: Applewood Books [Philadelphia: Henry Altemus Company.

FLAG HOUSES

In addition to the Betsy Ross Flag House in Philadelphia, Pennsylvania, and the Star-Spangled Banner Flag House and Museum in Baltimore, Maryland, which honor Betsy Ross and Mary Pickersgill, respectively, some Americans have paid tribute to the flag by painting their houses to resemble it.

Elinor Horwitz describes one of the oddest and earliest such houses, a private home in Lebanon, Virginia, owned by a man named Charlie Fields:

> Painted the exterior and interior of his house with geometric designs, squiggles, and polka dots of red, white and blue. He painted the same decorations on the chairs, tables, clocks, stovepipes, and picture frames; on his many beehives; and on the suit he wore on Sundays when he opened his house to visitors. On the front door he painted a flag. Fields worked on the house for three decades until his death in 1926. (Horwitz 1976, 64–68)

Most modern flag houses, however, appear to have been inspired by the 1976 bicentennial celebrations marking the 200th anniversary of the Declaration of Independence. Others followed in the aftermath of terrorist attacks on New York City and Washington, D.C., on September 11, 2001.

Although most of these houses were designed to celebrate the owners' patriotism, a number appear to have been painted in reaction to what were considered to be restrictive zoning ordinances.

One house in Memphis, Tennessee, features a depiction of the battle flag of the confederacy on its second story. In Topeka, Kansas, a house located across from the notorious Westboro Baptist Church, whose members have received notoriety by protesting at the funerals of American servicemen and women, sports a rainbow flag and is known as the Equality House (Guenter 2015, 42, 46, 47).

See also Centennials, Bicentennials, and Other Commemorations; Landscape; Ross, Betsy

Further Reading

Faber, Judy. 2007. "Trump Fined in Florida Flag Flap." CBS News, January 19. http://www.cbsnews.com/news/trump-fined-in-florida-flag-flap/.

Guenter, Scot. 2015. "The Phenomenon of Flag Homes: Musings on Meaning." *Raven: A Journal of Vexillology* 22:27–53.

Hinrichs, Kit, Delphine Hirasuna, and Terry Heffernan. 2015. *100 American Flags: A Unique Collection of Old Glory Memorabilia*. Berkeley, CA: Ten Speed Press.

Horwitz, Elinor Lander, and J. Roderick Moore. 1976. *The Bird, the Banner, and Uncle Sam: Images of America in Folk and Popular Art*. Philadelphia: J. B. Lippincott Company.

FLAG MANUFACTURERS ASSOCIATION OF AMERICA

The Flag Manufacturers Association of America (FMAA) is an association of companies that manufacture flags in the United States. The association pushes for laws that require government agencies in particular to purchase American flags that have been manufactured in the United States. As of 2017, however, the FMAA has yet to persuade Congress to adopt a bill that would limit governmental purchases of flags to those manufactured on American soil.

The association's website lists several member companies, including the largest manufacturer of flags in the United States, Annin Flagmakers (or Annin & Co.), which began in New York in the 1820s and is now headquartered in New Jersey.

It also lists among its members Flag Zone; J.C. Schultz Enterprises, Inc.; the Flag Source; and Valley Forge Flag.

American flag makers generally face increased demand for their products during wars and other periods of national crisis (the terrorist attacks of 9/11, for example, spurred a massive surge in sales). Annin Flagmakers alone experienced a 40 percent increase in sales after 9/11 (Donovan 2002).

In 2015, a number of flag makers announced in the wake of attacks on African American worshipers in Charleston, South Carolina, that they would no longer manufacture Confederate flags, which have increasingly become a symbol of racial hatred (McAllister 2015).

See also All-American Flag Act; Confederate Flag; Mexican-American War; Terrorist Attacks of September 11, 2001

Further Reading

Donovan, Aaron. 2002. "Update/Annin & Company; 13 Stripes, 50 Stars, 800 Tired Workers." *New York Times*, March 10. https://www.nytimes.com/2002/03/10/business/update-annin-company-13-stripes-50-stars-800-tired-workers.html

Flag Manufacturers Association of America. 2017. Accessed February 21. http://www.fmaa-usa.com/about-profile_mission.php

McAllister, Edward. 2015. "Major U.S. Flag Makers to Stop Making Confederate Flags." Reuters, June 24. https://www.reuters.com/article/us-usa-shooting-south-carolina-flag/major-u-s-flag-makers-to-stop-making-confederate-flags-idUSKBN0P327E20150624

FLAG ON THE FLOOR ART EXHIBIT

One of the basic elements of flag etiquette is that the flag should not be allowed to touch the ground or floor. Another general rule stresses that nothing but a Bible or holy book should be placed on a flag. There are many accounts of flag bearers in battle who literally gave their lives so that the flag that they or their companions were carrying did not touch the ground.

This undoubtedly explains much of the reaction to an exhibit by Dread Scott at the School of the Art Institute in Chicago in 1989. Scott's piece was part of an exhibit designed to highlight the school's multiculturalism. He created a display entitled *What Is the Proper Way to Display a U.S. Flag?* It consisted of a 3-foot by 5-foot flag laid on the floor, with a shelf above it offering a notebook in which participants were asked to respond to the question posed by the display. Unless they removed the flag (which some did), participants would have to walk on the flag to reach the notebook and answer the question.

The display was widely criticized, with many people, especially veterans, demonstrating and picketing in protest. Although the school stood firm on its right to display the exhibit, even at the cost of some funding, Anthony Jones, the president of the school, refused a request to display the exhibit again at an exhibit of graduating students. He explained that he already had defended First Amendment rights during the first exhibit and did not want the subsequent show hijacked by attention to a single work of art.

In December 2016, Henry Sanchez Jr., a fine arts graduate student at the University of Cincinnati, caused considerable stir when, as part of an art class project, he displayed two American flags, one hanging upside down (a typical message of distress) and another hanging by a noose. He said that he did it as a response to the presidential election. The university said that the display was protected by the First Amendment (Harper 2016).

See also Flag Code; Flag Bearers, Standard-Bearers

Further Reading

Erickson, Jon. 1990. "Appropriation and Transgression in Contemporary American Performance: The Wooster Group, Holly Hughes, and Karen Finley." *Theatre Journal* 42 (May): 225–236.

Harper, Briana. 2016. "Student's American Flag Art Sparks Free Speech Debate at University of Cincinnati." WCPO, Last updated December 7, 2016. https://www.wcpo.com/news/education/higher-education/uc-news/students-american-flag-art-sparks-free-speech-debate-at-university-of-cincinnati

Jones, Anthony. 1990. "Stars and Bras: A Report from the Trenches." *Academe* 76 (July–August): 18–23.

FLAG PATCHES

The U.S. flag symbolizes diverse values—most typically independence, liberty, and democracy. Historian Rosalind Urbach Moss has argued that "because national flags are identified with official government policy and actions, they are most easily used by those who support such policies." She further notes that "by the mid-twentieth century, 'correct use' of national flags had been effectively limited to official (i.e., governmental) uses and private uses termed 'respectful' by regulations based on the privately published and promoted 1924 Flag Code" (Moss 1998, 18).

Civil rights demonstrators in the early 1960s often used flags to demonstrate how their goals aligned with American values. President Nixon and others had begun displaying flags and wearing flag lapel pins as a way of linking the Vietnam War to those same values. Moss writes:

> By 1969 police departments across the country had begun adding American flag patches and pins to their uniforms and stickers to their patrol cars. The New York *Times* reported that the mayor of Birmingham declared the flag to be "a symbol of law and order," a distinct change from its more traditional if vague associations with freedom, liberty, and the Constitution. (1998, 34)

Many police departments continue to incorporate a flag patch into their uniforms. Federal law specifies that "a flag patch may be affixed to the uniform of military personnel, firemen, policemen, and members of patriotic organizations" (Luckey 2008, 7).

See also Civil Rights Movement; Flag Code; Lapel Pins; Vietnam War

Further Reading

Luckey, John R. April 14, 2008. *The United States Flag: Federal Law Relating to Display and Associated Questions*. CRS Report for Congress. Washington, D.C.: Congressional Research Service.

Moss, Rosalind Urbach. 1998. "'Yes, There's a Reason I Salute the Flag': Flag Use and the Civil Rights Movement." *Raven: A Journal of Vexillology* 5:12–33.

FLYING THE FLAG

American flags, like those of other nationalities, are most commonly displayed on flag poles. Author Robert Phillips attributes this practice to the desire both to give the flag "greater visibility" and to highlight "the supremacy which it is intended to typify" (Phillips 1931, 74). Etiquette dictates that the American flag is always displayed higher than state flags and carried to the front right when on parade. When numerous national flags are flown together, it is acceptable for the U.S. flag to be at a similar height. For many years, however, the U.S. has not followed the custom of some other countries to dip its flag to Olympic hosts.

A flag flying from the top of a pole is said to be at full mast. Such flags are commonly raised at daybreak and fly until dusk. Etiquette calls for raising flags briskly and lowering them slowly.

Flags flown at half-mast, to denote the death of a ranking statesperson, are first raised to the top of the pole before being lowered. A flag flown upside down is a universally recognized signal of distress.

See also Flag Code; Half-Staff; Olympic Protocol

Further Reading

Phillips, Robert. 1931. *The American Flag: Its Uses and Abuses*. Boston: Stratford Company.

FOLDING THE FLAG

When the flag is lowered at the end of the day or at military funerals, it is customary to fold it lengthwise twice and then into triangles so that ultimately only the blue canton and its stars are showing.

This custom is believed to have originated during World War I. Some undocumented sources connect the triangle to the tricorner hat often worn by American soldiers during the Revolutionary War or to the division of powers among the legislative, executive, and judicial branches. Some military ceremonies use each of the folds symbolically, to represent such virtues as life, motherhood, citizenship, or the national motto "In God We Trust."

As with explanations for the colors of the flag, historian Marc Leepson believes it is likely that most such explanations are ex post facto justifications of a practice that largely developed for the sake of convenience. To support his claim, Leepson quotes Whitney Smith, a professional vexillologist and flag collector, who concluded: "There is no meaning to the triangle. It's simply a matter of convenience that [the] military came up with" (Leepson 2005, 264).

See also Colors of the Flag; World War I

Further Reading

"Folding the Flag." 2017. Accessed March 14. http://www.usflag.org/fold/flag.html
Leepson, Marc. 2005. *Flag: An American Biography*. New York: St. Martin's Press.

FORSTER FLAG

The Forster Flag is believed to be one of the oldest American flags that incorporates stripes in its canton. It appears to have been made originally as a regimental flag for the Manchester Company, 1st Regiment of Militia, of Essex County, Massachusetts, and is believed to have had the Union Jack in its canton, which was set within a wider field of red. Around the time of the Battles of Lexington and Concord, it appears as though the original canton was replaced by another patch of red silk, to which six short horizontal white stripes were added.

This flag was probably carried by Minutemen who heeded the alarm that was sounded when British troops began their march toward Lexington and Concord. The Manchester Company, headed by Lt. Samuel Forster, apparently did not take the flag into battle, however.

Remarkably, the flag was handed down continuously in the Forster family (hence the flag name) until being sold to the Flag Heritage Foundation in 1975. This foundation in turn sold this flag in 2014 in order to raise money for the Flag Heritage Fund at the University of Texas, which will be used to preserve the collection that vexillologist Whitney Smith left to that institution.

See also Revolutionary War; Revolutionary War Battle Flags; Smith, Whitney

Further Reading

Flag Heritage Foundation. 2017. "The Forster Flag." Accessed May 9. http://www.flagheritagefoundation.org/the-foundations-collections/the-forster/flag/
Owens, Barbara. 2014. "The Forster Flag, and the Conservation of a Revolutionary War Textile." *Inside the Conservator's Studio*. April 2. http://insidetheconservatorsstudio.blogspot.com/2014/04/the-forster-flag.html
Smith, Whitney. 2002. "The Forster Flag: The 'First American Flag Ever Made.'" *Flag Bulletin*, no. 205 (May–June): 82–118.

FORT MCHENRY FLAG

See Star-Spangled Banner (Flag)

FORT NIAGARA FLAG

In addition to the flag that flew over Fort McHenry and inspired Francis Scott Key to write "The Star-Spangled Banner," during the early part of the war, the British captured a flag that Americans had flown over Fort Niagara at the mouth of the river of the same name, when one of America's aims had been to capture Canada, then under British rule.

The Fort Niagara flag and other captured U.S. flags were given to Maj. Gen. Sir Gordon Drummond, who commanded British forces in upper Canada. They eventually ended up in Drummond's castle in Scotland. In 1969, the Fort Niagara flag was saved from a fire, and in 1993, the family sold it to the Old Fort Niagara Association in Youngstown, New York, where it remains as one of relatively few U.S. flags from this period. Like the flag that flew over Fort McHenry, it has 15 stars and 15 stripes.

See also Key, Francis Scott; Star-Spangled Banner (Flag)

Further Reading

Molotsky, Irvin. 2001. *The Flag, the Poet and the Song: The Story of the Star-Spangled Banner*. New York: Dutton.

FORT SUMTER FLAG

One of the nation's most historic flags is the storm flag that flew above Fort Sumter, just off the coast of Charleston, South Carolina, at the beginning of the Civil War. When President Lincoln attempted to supply U.S. troops, who had been moved from Fort Moultrie to Fort Sumter, Maj. Pierre G. T. Beauregard, who led rebel troops in Charleston, began firing at the fort. After seeing the

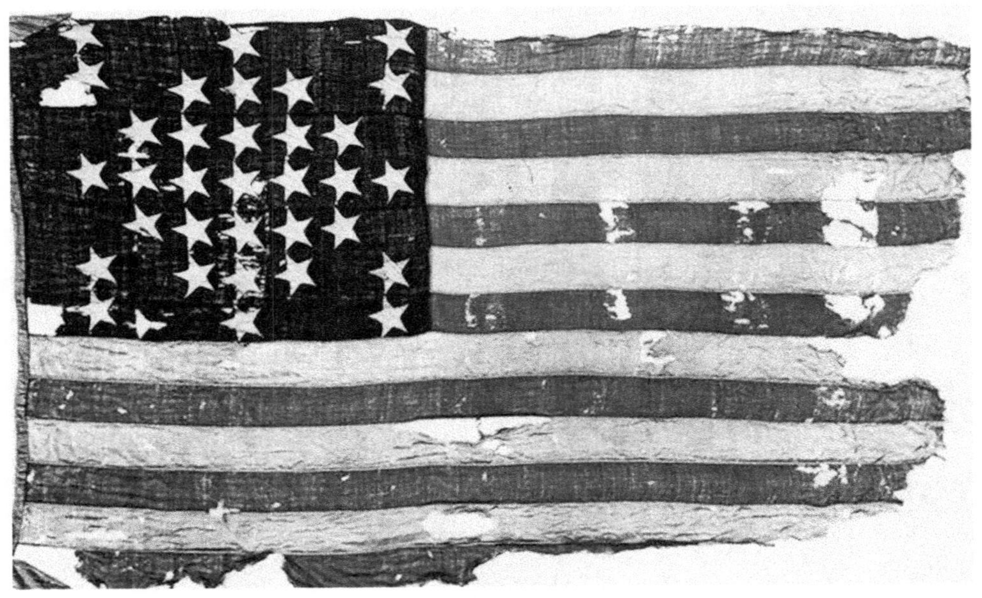

The storm flag present during the opening shots of the American Civil War at Fort Sumter in South Carolina. A storm flag is a small U.S. flag that is flown on military posts during storms. The storm flag was raised over Fort Sumter after the larger garrison flag had ripped. (National Park Service)

hopelessness of his situation, Maj. Robert Anderson raised both a flag of truce and an American flag, but was forced to lower the American flag before Confederate forces ceased firing.

Anderson was permitted to take the flag with him when he and his troops left the fort. As the federal soldiers departed, they "saluted their flag and sang 'Yankee Doodle'" at a time when the nation still had no official national anthem (Burke 1982, 42). On a sadder note, one Union soldier was killed and another mortally wounded during a planned 100-gun salute during the evacuation.

As Union forces withdrew, the South Carolina governor proudly noted that this was "the first time in the history of this country that the stars and stripes have been humbled" (Burke 1982, 42). Northerners also saw this turn of events as an insult to the flag but were determined to turn the tables. Anderson brought the flag to patriotic rallies in New York City, where, at a "monster rally," he placed it in the sculpted hands of a statue of George Washington in Union Square in Manhattan (Bonner 2003). That event also appears to have served as a catalyst for Frederic Edwin Church's oil sketch, quickly reproduced as a chromolithograph, of *Our Banner in the Sky*. The anonymous author of "The Battle-Cry of Freedom" observed that:

> Although causeless the blow
> That at Sumter laid low
> That flag, it was seed for the morrow;
> And a thousand flags flew,
> For the one that fell true,
> As traitors have found to their sorrow. (Schauffler 1917, 81)

On April 14, 1865, Major Anderson once again raised the flag over the fort after it was reclaimed by Union forces. That same day, William Lloyd Garrison, the fiery abolitionist who had published *The Liberator*, went to the grave of Sen. John C. Calhoun, one of the South's most ardent defenders of slavery, to announce, "Slavery is now buried deeper than you."

In 1905, Anderson's children presented the flag to William Howard Taft, who was then secretary of war. It was displayed in the War Department and the Pentagon before being transferred to Fort Sumter in 1954. The flag was further authenticated and preserved in the 1980s.

At the time the flag was made, the arrangement of stars in the canton had not been formalized. The flag featured 33 stars, with 2 stars in each of the four corners and a middle section consisting of a row of 7 horizontal stars flanked by rows of 5 stars, 3 stars, and 1 star, both above and below. Reproductions of the flag are available.

Henry Ward Beecher, who had delivered a speech extolling the flag at the beginning of the war, spoke at this ceremony as well. He intoned:

> Tell the air that not a spot now sullies thy whiteness. Thy red is not the blush of shame, but the flush of joy. Tell the dews that wash thee that thou are pure as they. Say to the night that thy stars lead toward the morning; and to the morning, that

> a brighter day rises with the healing in its wings. And then, oh glowing flag, bid the sun pour light on all thy folds with double brightness while thou art earing round and round the world the solemn joy—a race set free! A nation redeemed! (Burke 1982, 46)

Unfortunately, the day that the flag was raised and that Beecher spoke was also the day that President Lincoln was assassinated, a day when another flag became sacred as it cushioned the head of the president while he lay bleeding from a gunshot wound in the back of the head.

See also Beecher, Henry Ward; Civil War; Lincoln Flag; *Our Banner in the Sky*

Further Reading

Bonner, Robert E. 2003. "Star-Spangled Sentiment." *Common-Place* 3 (2). http://www.common-place-archives.org/vol-03/no-02/bonner/bonner-5.shtml

Burke, Doreen Bolger. 1982. "Frederick Edwin Church and 'the Banner of Dawn.'" *American Art Journal* 14 (Spring): 39–46.

Gutfeld, Arnon. 1968. "The Ves Hall Case, Judge Bourquin, and the Sedition Act of 1918." *Pacific Historical Review* 37 (May): 163–178.

Ness, William Boyd. 2008. *"Burning with Star-Fires": The National Flag in Civil War Poetry*. PhD thesis, University of Iowa.

"Preserving History: The Fort Sumter Flag." Westmont, IL: McCrone Associates, Inc. https://www.mccrone.com/filebin/PDFs/MA/case_studies/CaseStudy_SumterFlag.pdf

Schauffler, Robert Haven. 1917. *Our Flag in Verse and Prose*. New York: Moffat, Yard and Company.

FRANK, ROBERT

The Swiss-born American photographer Robert Frank (b. 1924) published a book in 1958 entitled *The Americans*. In contrast to many celebratory depictions of the U.S. flag, Frank juxtaposed photographs of flags with what Albert Bokme describes as "fragments of American life that bring out the dehumanization and anomie of Cold War society" (Boime 1998, 45).

Initially published in France, the book was republished by Grove Press in the United States in 1959. In one photograph taken in Hoboken, New Jersey, a flag blocks the vision of people peering out of an apartment building. A bar scene features a crumpled flag displayed between portraits of Washington and Lincoln.

Beat Generation novelist and poet Jack Kerouac wrote the introduction to the American edition of Frank's book, which appears to have inspired Jasper Johns and later artists who took liberties with flag depictions in order to highlight seamier sides of American life or opposition to governmental policies.

See also Johns, Jasper

Further Reading

Boime, Albert. 1998. *The Unveiling of National Icons: A Plea for Patriotic Iconoclasm in a Nationalist Era*. New York: Cambridge University Press.

Cotkin, George. 1985. "The Photographers in the Beat-Hipster Idiom: Robert Frank's *The Americans*." *American Studies* 26 (Spring): 19–33.

FREEDOM TO DISPLAY THE AMERICAN FLAG ACT (2005)

On July 24, 2006, President George W. Bush signed the Freedom to Display the American Flag Act of 2005, which both houses of Congress had adopted by unanimous consent. In a nation like the United States, which is so adorned with flags, it seems odd that Congress would need to adopt a law with this title, but this law was crafted in response to condominium and homeowners' association rules that had limited such displays.

Although no such case appears to have been decided by the U.S. Supreme Court, a number of state courts had upheld the constitutionality of rules when they had been part of restrictive covenants to which tenants had agreed. Although restrictive covenants per se do not constitute state action that the First and Fourteenth Amendments might prohibit, it is possible that court enforcement of such agreements might. Thus, in *Shelley v. Kraemer*, 334 U.S. 1 (1948), the U.S. Supreme Court held that it would be unconstitutional for courts to enforce racially restrictive covenants.

Although the law applied to the American flag, it did not provide a similar right to display state flags, military flags, or MIA/POW flags; similarly, the law does not apply to renters. Moreover, it allowed for appropriate "time, place, and manner" restrictions that might be applied to flags that were overly large or that blocked views of a neighboring house. A number of states had similar laws at the time.

Further Reading

Belmas, Genelle I. 2009. "Pushing Patriotism: Why Flag Encouragement Doesn't Fly." *Communication Law and Policy* 14 (Summer): 341–372.

Craig, Brian. 2007. "The Freedom to Display the American Flag Act: Construction and Constitutionality." *Raven: A Journal of Vexillology* 14:61–84.

Grussenmeyer, Elizabeth F. 2003. "Review of Selected 2002 California Legislation: Property: The Right to Display the American Flag in Common Interest Developments: Restrictions by Homeowners' Associations Not Tolerated." *McGeorge Law Review* 34 (Winter): 516–524.

FRITCHIE, BARBARA

Barbara Hauer Fritchie (1766–1862) was a resident of Frederick, Maryland, when the Civil War broke out in 1861, and her alleged gesture of flag-waving defiance against Confederate forces made her a legendary figure in 19th-century popular culture. Most notably, she became the heroine of an eponymous poem penned by John Greenleaf Whittier (1807–1892) and first published in the October 1863 issue of *The Atlantic Monthly*. Whittier apparently heard the story of Fritchie's defiance from Emma Dorothy Elizabeth Nevitt Southworth, a Georgetown novelist who was a fellow Quaker and abolitionist (Gardner 2012).

According to Whittier's beloved poem, Frietchie (his spelling) defied Confederate soldiers under the command of Stonewall Jackson as they rode past her house in Frederick, Maryland, by flying an American flag from her attic window. According to the poem, after Confederate troops shot the flag down, Fritchie leaned out of her windowsill to snatch "the silken scarf." Whittier continues:

> "Shoot, if you must, this old gray head,
> Just spare your country's flag," she said
> Jackson in turn blushed with shame:
> "Who touches a hair of yon gray head
> Dies like a Dog! March on!" he said.

Whittier continues by describing the flag as a "Flag of Freedom and Union" and as a "symbol of light and law."

Despite the stirring nature of the poem, the story it tells cannot be verified by contemporary testimony. Indeed, although there is evidence that Fritchie supported the northern cause and might even have waved a flag, there is no historical evidence that Jackson and Fritchie ever saw one another or that she waved a flag that in a manner that elicited any sort of Confederate response. There is evidence that a woman named Mary A. Quantrill from Frederick, Maryland, did display a small American flag, which, it seems, was cut down by a Confederate soldier (Leepson 2005, 115).

The myth of Fritchie was nonetheless memorialized by Clyde Fitch in a Broadway play named in her honor and performed in 1899 and 1900. The story is also recounted in the musical *My Maryland,* which was performed on Broadway in 1928 and 1929, and in silent movies in 1915 and 1924 (Leepson 2005, 114). A reconstruction of her house remains a tourist attraction at 154 West Patrick Street in Frederick, Maryland.

Whittier's description of Stonewall Jackson's reactions to the flag in "Barbara Frietchie" undoubtedly expressed the conflicts that must have been felt by some Confederate soldiers who had previously fought under the American flag. There is a story from East Tennessee about a Lieutenant White who was ordered to take a Confederate detachment and gather weapons from mountain folk who were largely Unionists. Warned by a judge that he must not molest an American flag that he would pass on his route, he and his men surrounded the flag as he was reputed to have given the following speech:

> Men, that was the flag under which we were born. It was under that flag our fathers fought and many of them died. While we are fighting under a new flag, still, that was the flag of our fathers. Let us honor it for its history and for the memory of the blood poured out so freely by our brave ancestors in its defense. Instead of doing it injury, I propose that we salute it.

The story further suggests that had the troops dishonored the flag, they would have been massacred by the mountaineers who silently surrounded them and whose weapons they never found (Ewing 1986, 51–53).

Whittier himself was sometimes conflicted about the flag. A strong abolitionist, he had sometimes regarded the flag as a symbol of slavery before the war. In a poem entitled "The New Year," which Whittier wrote in 1838, he pointed to "a stain on every fold" and concluded with the following stanza:

Shame! Shame! Its starry splendors glow
Above the slaver's loathsome jail;
Its folds are ruffling even now
His crimson flag of sale.

See also Civil War; Confederate Flags

Further Reading

Ewing, James. 1986. *It Happened in Tennessee*. Nashville: Rutledge Hill Press.
Gardner, Karen. 2012. "The Ballad of 'Barbara Frietchie:' Is Her Story Truth, Fiction or Somewhere in Between?" *Frederick News Post*, July 1.
Leepson, Marc. *Flag: An American Biography*. New York: St. Martin's Press.
McCartney, Robert. 2012. "Barbara Frietchie Didn't Wave that Flag." *Washington Post*, September 15.

G

GADSDEN FLAG

See Rattlesnake Flags

"GOD BLESS THE U.S.A."

One contemporary song with a particularly memorable line related to the U.S. Flag is Lee Greenwood's (b. 1942) "God Bless the U.S.A." Although it reflected other patriotic sentiments, Greenwood wrote the song in 1983 after the Soviet Union downed Korean Airlines Flight 007, killing 29 passengers, including 63 Americans. He released it the following year. The song went platinum in 2016 (Hawkins 2017).

Imagining that he woke up one day having lost everything but his wife and children, Greenwood proclaims that he would still be thankful because "the flag still stands for freedom," no matter what America's enemies do. The song, which praises those who have defended freedom, gets its title from the last line.

Greenwood has performed the song at the inaugurations of Ronald Reagan, George H. W. Bush, George W. Bush, and Donald Trump, but he does not consider the song to be political.

Further Reading

Hawkins, Derek. "'God Bless the U.S.A.': The (Apparently) Apolitical Origins of a GOP Inauguration Favorite." January 19, 2017. *Washington Post*. https://www.washingtonpost.com/news/morning-mix/wp/2017/01/19/god-bless-the-u-s-a-the-apparently-apolitical-origins-of-a-gop-inauguration-favorite/?utm_term=.a0207e99b13b

GRAND ARMY OF THE REPUBLIC (GAR)

The Grand Army of the Republic (GAR) was one of a number of veterans' and patriotic organizations that pushed for increased recognition of the flag, including the Pledge of Allegiance, the celebration of Decoration (later Memorial) Day, and the cultivation of flag etiquette. Members wore badges consisting of a metal eagle holding a small chiffon flag below which was a five-pointed metal star with a picture of a soldier and sailor shaking hands in front of a woman symbolizing liberty.

Formed by Union veterans in 1866 after the Civil War, the organization was divided into local posts and arranged hierarchically, like the military. Each year, it hosted national encampments. Initially somewhat political in its orientation, over time the organization narrowed its focus to lobbying for veterans' benefits

Membership certificate for the Grand Army of the Republic, from 1883. This organization of Union veterans consistently lobbied for increased recognition of the U.S. flag, and for increased attention to flag etiquette. (Library of Congress)

and issues related to the flag. Presidents Ulysses S. Grant, Rutherford B. Hayes, James Garfield, Benjamin Harrison, and William McKinley had all been members (Alford 2012, 319). In time, the organization was also accompanied by the Ladies of the Grand Army of the Republic, consisting of mothers, wives, sisters, and daughters of those who had served, and by the Woman's Relief Corps, which was especially influential in the establishment of Memorial Day.

Because they were limited to members associated with a single war, the GAR and its related organizations died out, but the Veterans of Foreign Wars (VFW), the Daughters of the American Revolution (DAR), and other organizations have furthered many of its concerns. The GAR held its last encampment in 1949, and Alfred Woolson, its last member, died in 1956 at the ripe age of 109.

See also Civil War; Decoration Day (Memorial Day); Pledge of Allegiance

Further Reading

Alford, Kenneth L. 2012. "Mormons and the Grand Army of the Republic." In *Civil War Saints* (pp. 316–339), edited by Kenneth L. Alford. Salt Lake City: Deseret Book.

O'Leary, Cecilia Elizabeth. 1999. *To Die For: The Paradox of American Patriotism*. Princeton, NJ: Princeton University Press.
Sons of Union Veterans of the Civil War. 2017. "Grand Army of the Republic History." Accessed April 2. http://www.suvcw.org/?page_id=167

GRAND UNION FLAG

See Union Flag

GREAT AMERICAN FLAG

Americans are known for believing that bigger is better. Sometimes size has a purpose. The flag that flew over Fort McHenry and inspired "The Star-Spangled Banner" was designed to be big enough that the British would have no trouble seeing it. Car dealerships often display giant flags to catch the attention of passersby and identify their products as "American." Creators of other large flags are simply inspired to do so by patriotism or the prospect of highlighting a significant flag-related holiday.

It's believed that for many years, the largest U.S. flag was the 230-by-90-foot flag that was displayed outside the J. L. Hudson Department Store on patriotic holidays, beginning with Armistice Day in 1923. Later purchased by the Great American Flag Association, it was damaged in 1991 when being lifted by a helicopter (Kincaid 2015, 29, 109).

As bicentennial celebrations of the Declaration of Independence approached in 1976, Len Silverfine, a marketing professor who was the grandchild of Russian immigrants, came up with the idea of constructing a bigger flag that could fly from the Verrazano-Narrows Bridge in New York City so that ships could see it as they came into the harbor. He subsequently constructed a 360-foot flag on June 28, 1976, only to discover that it acted as a giant sail and was significantly damaged the first time it was flown (Kincaid 2015, 38).

Silverfine went on to commission a larger flag (411 by 210 feet) that weighed seven tons. The flag was manufactured by Roger Milliken in Spartanburg, South Carolina, and sewn together at Anchor Industries in Evansville, Indiana. The flag has been unfurled on 12 occasions, including welcoming U.S. hostages back from Iran, in a remembrance for 9/11 victims in Pennsylvania, and on Flag Day events at the Washington Monument.

The sheer size and weight of the display made it difficult to display and to clean and dry. On one occasion, it was cleaned at the Wilson Sporting Goods plant in Humboldt, Tennessee, and on at least two occasions, helicopters have been used to help dry it out.

Faced with these difficulties, in 1983, Silverfine gave the flag to the U.S. government, which failed to display it regularly as promised. It was eventually sold to the Kansas Cosmosphere and Space Museum in Hutchinson, Kansas, which in turn found it difficult to display and sold it in an online bid to Ted Dorfman of Greensburg, Pennsylvania, in 2001. He unfurled it later that year to raise money for victims of the 9/11 terrorist attacks. It has been in storage since then.

Thomas “Ski’ Demski subsequently created a larger and lighter flag (the Superflag) that continues to be the nation’s largest.

See also Centennials, Bicentennials, and Other Commemorations; Star-Spangled Banner (Flag); Terrorist Attacks of September 11, 2001; Washington Monument Flag Display

Further Reading

Kincaid, Johnny. 2015. *The Great American Flag: The Story of the World’s Biggest Flag and the People Who Made It Possible*. Johnny Kincaid: Lexington, Kentucky.

GREAT SEAL OF THE UNITED STATES

See Hopkinson, Francis

GUILFORD FLAG

One of the most colorful early American flags, which is now owned by the North Carolina Historical Commission, is known as the Guilford (or Guilford Courthouse) Flag. Oral history links it to the Battle of Guilford Courthouse on March 15, 1781. The flag deviates from other designs from the time in that it has 13 eight-pointed (most others from the period have five or six points) blue stars against a white background in the canton as well as 12 blue and red stripes, although it is possible that one or more of the stripes has been removed. If the flag had 15 stripes, then it most likely dates to the 1790s, after the admission of Vermont and Kentucky.

See also Revolutionary War Battle Flags; Thirteen-Star Flags

Further Reading

Barrow, Healan. 2016. “The Guilford Flag.” DAR. Accessed February 20. http://www.ncdar.org/MicajahBullockChapter_files/html/guildfordflag.html

Cooper, Grace Rogers. 1973. *Thirteen-Star Flags: Keys to Identification*. Washington, D.C.: Smithsonian Institution Press.

Voigt, Robert C. 2006. “Guilford Courthouse Flag.” NCPedia. Last modified January 1. http://www.ncpedia.org/guilford-courthouse-flag

GUTHRIE, WILLIAM N.

As the nation became more diverse, individuals looked for ways to unify the people, and William Norman Guthrie (1868–1944) thought that the best way to do this was to promote reverence for the flag. Born in Scotland in 1868 and educated at the University of the South, he taught at a number of institutions before becoming rector of St. Mark’s Church-in-the-Bowery in New York City.

In *The Religion of Old Glory* (1919), which reflects the anti-German sentiment of the era, Guthrie made an exhaustive, if somewhat creative, examination of all aspects of the U.S. flag, including its colors, its stars, and its stripes. A believer in evolution, Guthrie asserted that the American flag, like poetry, music, and dance, had a way of tapping into man's primal nature. Although he recognized that African Americans and immigrants had brought about significant changes in America's makeup, he believed the color white on the flag stood for Caucasians. He explained that "'being white' does not however involve being literally a man of Caucasian blood; it only requires that, because of purity and price of blood, one affirms the Ideal of the Caucasian" (Guthrie 1919, 139). Moreover, he opined, regarding the people of the United States, that "the greatest loss to us was incurred by a too sudden, too extensive, and too simultaneously various immigration all but completely destroying our homogeneous flocking together, our instinctive integrity" (359).

Guthrie further sought a way of connecting people of different political persuasions and religions to unite under the flag, which he thought could be further enhanced through ceremony: "But if we are to make a Religion of it, a missionary religion, too, of Old Glory's Gospel—we must get us a rite of reverent worship" (308). He further explained:

> But as no other nation must ours look for the creation and stimulation and regular excitation of patriotic mass passion and self-devotion to its flag, which we found so marvelously capable of doing its unique and blessed work. (369)

Guthrie suggested that the individual might privately "place his own religion over the flag cult, if he like . . . but in the open and for all to behold let the shared 'by-worship' fly alone without rival" (381).

The bishop of the Protestant Episcopal Church of New York authorized Guthrie to perform a mystical ritual that he developed at his church on the Sunday afternoon after Thanksgiving of 1918 (Guenter 1990, 173). Following elaborate guidelines that Guthrie outlined in his book, the ceremony involved psalms to the flagpole and the eagle, "The Ceremony of Worship unto Old Glory," the incantation of Latin phrases, the singing of "The Star-Spangled Banner," and the introduction and explanation of numerous symbols.

After spreading the flag, the chief officiant would have reminded the people of "the nation chosen of God for a mighty purpose" (Guthrie 1919, 321). The ceremony would have continued thus:

> OFFICIANT:
> We are not worthy to behold thee
> FIRST ASSISTANT:
> We are not worthy to acclaim them,
> SECOND ASSISTANT:
> We are not worthy to serve thee,
> CHORUS:
> We are not worthy to die for thee,
> OFFICIANT:
> Yet shall we place at the foot of thy TREE OF LIFE,
> CHORUS:
> O Stars and Stripes—Old Glory (322)

Guthrie's controversial ceremony, which sought to combine Christianity and paganism, did not spread to other churches, but it remains a quintessential example of what many scholars call the cult of the flag and of the way that some individuals sought to use the flag to promote national unity.

One of Guthrie's more fascinating ideas was to create a flag temple for his pageants, but his description of such a place was notably vague:

> Not to be sure an armory. Not by any means a horseshow and circus space, a roofed and walled vacuum! Not an adopted and adapted Gothic structure, pathetically reminiscent of medieval paganism, wholly unfit for one single folk mass, with one single *kibleh*, or focus of raptured attention. What should it be? What style? Something true, so something new, making importations and adaptations seems cheap and nasty, and altogether out of the question! (401)

See also Baxter, Percival P.; Cult of the Flag; Folding the Flag; World War I

Further Reading

Boime, Albert. 1998. *The Unveiling of National Icons: A Plea for Patriotic Iconoclasm in a Nationalist Era*. New York: Cambridge University Press.

Guenter, Scot M. 1990. *The American Flag, 1777–1924: Cultural Shifts from Creation to Codification*. Cranbury, NJ: Associated University Presses.

Guthrie, William Norman. 1919. *The Religion of Old Glory*. New York: George H. Doran Company.

HALF-STAFF

One of the most detailed provisions (section 7, paragraph m) of the U.S. Flag Code, which National Flag Conferences proposed in 1923 and 1924 and which Congress approved by a Joint Resolution in 1942, relates to flying the flag at half-staff. Such a flag, which is raised to the top of the pole before being lowered half-way down, is used to commemorate the deaths of individuals who have served their country or to mark times of national mourning. The code specifies that the flag is only displayed at half-staff on Memorial Day until noon, after which it is to be raised to the top of the pole.

The president, as well as the mayor of the District of Columbia and state governors all have the power to order such displays. The flag code specifies that the flag will be lowered on the following occasions and for the following periods of time: 30 days on the death of a president or a former president; 10 days for a vice president, chief justice, or speaker of the U.S. House of Representatives; from death until the interment of an associate justice, a secretary of an executive or military department, a former vice president or governor; and on the day of death and the day following the death of a member of Congress. The Treue der Union Monument in Comfort, Texas, which honors Union supporters who were killed by Confederate forces during the Civil War, is the only such monument in the nation that daily displays its flag at half-staff (Kiel 2012).

One of the most bizarre uses of half-staff occurred in 1923 when Governor Percival Proctor of Maine ordered the flag over the state house to be lowered upon the death of his dog.

Flags often play an important role in the funerals of politicians. The first time that the flag was lowered at half-staff at the White House was on the death of newly inaugurated president William Henry Harrison in April 1841 (Marling 2004, 52). The U.S. Flag Code specifies that when a flag is used to cover a casket, the union should be placed at the head of the casket and over the left shoulder.

U.S. Flags are presented to surviving family members of veterans and are folded into triangles, which are often framed for display.

See also Baxter, Percival P.; Flag Code; Folding the Flag

Further Reading

Kiel, Frank Wilson. 2012. "Treue der Union: Myths, Misrepresentations, and Misinterpretations." *Southwestern Historical Quarterly* 115 (January): 282–292.

Luckey, John R. 2008. *The United States Flag: Federal Law Relating to Display and Associated Questions*. CRS Report for Congress. Washington, D.C.: Congressional Research Service.
Marling, Karal Ann. 2004. *Old Glory: Unfurling History*. Washington, D.C.: Library of Congress.

HALTER V. NEBRASKA (1907)

In *Halter v. Nebraska*, 205 U.S. 34 (1907), the U.S. Supreme Court upheld a conviction under a Nebraska anti–flag desecration statute against individuals accused of having sold a bottle of beer that included a picture of a U.S. flag on its label.

In a decision authored by John Marshall Harlan I, the court noted that more than half the states had similar statutes and that Congress had not chosen to preempt such legislation by adopting a law of its own. Harlan distinguished this case from an Illinois case, *Ruhstrat v. People*, 185 Ill. 133, which had overturned a law that it thought was discriminatory, and *People ex Rel. McPike v. Van De Carr*, 178 N.Y. 425, which had applied to items that had already been manufactured and was thus thought to deprive individuals of their property without due process of law.

In assessing the present case, Justice Harlan observed that "a state possesses all legislative power consistent with a republican form of government" and that states could use legislation to "provide not only for the health, morals, and safety of its people, but for the common good, as involved in the wellbeing, peace, happiness, and prosperity of the people." Harlan did not think that forbidding the use of the U.S. flag in advertising either infringed a right guaranteed by the U.S. Constitution or involved a matter exclusively delegated to the federal government. Harlan believed the legislation was designed to encourage a spirit of patriotism and that "when by its legislation the state encourages a feeling of patriotism towards the nation, it necessarily encourages a like feeling towards the state." He argued that the commercial use of the flag "tend[ed] to degrade and cheapen the flag in the estimation of the people, as well as to defeat the object of maintaining it as an emblem of national power and national honor." He further pointed to the role of the flag as "the symbol of the nation's power—the emblem of freedom in its truest, best sense."

The plaintiffs had argued that the law unfairly discriminated by permitting printing of the flag in newspapers, periodical, books, and pamphlets that was unconnected to advertising, but Harlan said that precedents had established that legislatures could make classifications based on reasonable grounds. He further noted that the law did not interfere with domestic trade but only with the right to use the U.S. flag for advertising purposes. This prohibition applied equally to all.

Justice Rufus Peckham dissented but did not provide a separate opinion.

The court rendered this decision before it began holding in *Gitlow v. New York* (1925) that some provisions of the Bill of Rights applied to the states via the due process clause of the Fourteenth Amendment. Moreover, when the court issued the opinion, it had not yet included commercial speech within the scope of the First Amendment.

Although it is unclear whether federal courts would enforce such laws, Congress did adopt a law that continues to prohibit the use of the flag for advertising purposes in Washington, D.C. (Luckey 2008, 14).

See also Advertising; *Ruhstrat v. Illinois* (1900)

Further Reading

Goldstein, Robert Justin. 1996. *Burning the Flag: The Great 1989–1990 American Flag Desecration Controversy*. Kent, OH: Kent State University Press.

Luckey, John R. 2008. *The United States Flag: Federal Law Relating to Display and Associated Questions*. CRS Report for Congress. Washington, D.C.: Congressional Research Service.

Scott, James Brown. 1917. "Respect for the American Flag." *American Journal of International Law* 11 (April): 410–413.

HARD HAT RIOT (1970)

Although the U.S. flag is often a unifying symbol, there are times when its use has become divisive. One such period was during the Vietnam War. As American military actions escalated in Vietnam and American and Vietnamese casualties mounted, Americans increasingly questioned whether the war was worth the cost. Many critics viewed the war as an example of American imperialism.

Members of the working class, whose children constituted the majority of the military recruits who bore the brunt of the conflict, tended to regard the flag as a symbol of their pride in serving and of their sacrifice (as evidenced by the flag-draped coffins of those who died in this conflict). By contrast, antiwar activists tended to see the war, and the flag under which the nation fought, as a betrayal of the national ideals that the flag represented. Protestors often lowered flags to half-mast to indicate disapproval of the war, painted peace signs or antiwar slogans on the flag, burned the flag, or waved flags of the North Vietnamese government.

On Friday, May 8, 1970—a day that came to be known as Bloody Friday—the mayor of New York City announced that the flag at city hall would be lowered to half-mast to honor four students who had been shot and killed by members of the national guard during an antiwar demonstration at Kent State University in Ohio. In reaction, about 200 construction workers in hard hats, encouraged by their unions and possibly by operatives working for President Richard M. Nixon, marched toward city hall and engaged in a huge brawl with antiwar demonstrators. The clash became particularly bitter after an unnamed man spat on the flag. The workers eventually succeeded in hoisting the flag to its full height while many sang the national anthem.

See also Flag Desecration Amendment; Vietnam War

Further Reading

Bryan-Wilson, Julia. 2007. "Hard Hats and Art Strikes: Robert Morris in 1970." *Art Bulletin* 89 (June): 333–359.

Teachout, Woden. 2009. *Capture the Flag: A Political History of American Patriotism*. New York: Basic Books.

HASSAM, (FREDERICK) CHILDE

American impressionist painter Childe Hassam (1859–1935) created some of the most iconic and recognizable depictions of American flags. Born in Boston, Massachusetts, he studied for a time in France but spent most of his life in New York City. In addition to being a Francophile, Hassam supported a movement to draft Theodore Roosevelt (who had run unsuccessfully as a Progressive, or Bull Moose, candidate in the previous presidential election) to run for president in 1916. Roosevelt had stressed the need for immigrants to cast off their associations with their nations of origin and embrace "Americanism" (Junker 2010, 27).

Hassam had been inspired by Claude Monet, who had composed some flag paintings in France, most notably for Bastille Day—for example, his *Rue Montorgueil Bedecked with Flags* (Gottlieb 1962, 179). In America, Hassam painted most of his flag paintings from 1916 to 1918, deriving much of his inspiration from Independence Day, Memorial Day, Liberty Bond, and Preparedness Day parades that he observed in New York City. The Preparedness Day Parade had involved more than 137,000 marchers and had lasted almost 13 hours (Junker 2010, 39). In most of about 30 paintings, the American flag predominated, but as the nation entered World War I, Hassam's paintings also featured flags of allies and the Red Cross. Some of his titles included *The Fourth of July* (1916); *Flags on the Waldorf* (1916); *Rainy Day Fifth Avenue* (1916); *The Avenue in the Rain* (1917), which has been displayed in the Oval Office; *Afternoon on the Avenue* (1917); *Allied Flags* (1917); *Allies Day* (1917); *Avenue of the Allies* (1917); *Flags on Fifty-Seventh Street* (1918); *Lincoln's Birthday* (1918); *The Union Jack, April Morning* (1918); and *Red Cross Drive* (1918).

Childe Hassam, who was born in Boston, was one of the most prolific artists whose primary focus was flags. As America entered World War I, Hassam, who was a Francophile, often mixed U.S. flags with those of America's allies, as in this depiction known as *Allies Day*, which he painted in 1917. (Universal History Archive/UIG via Getty Images)

In addition to his colorful outdoor scenes, Hassam painted at least two paintings—*The Flag Outside Her Window* (1918) and *The Fifty-Seventh Street Window* (1917)—of women watching soldiers marching by. In commenting on a self-portrait that does not feature a flag, Hassam observed, "It portrays me in a sport shirt. . . . My face is red my shirt is white and my hair is blue! My bandanna tie (a tie 'shows temperament' as the young lad art critic said) displays all the colors of the allied flags. As you know I am descended from that pure Arabian stock that landed in Dorchester in 1631. . . . So you see I have good reasons for being red white and blue" (Fort 1988, 108–109).

Hassam's paintings were generally well received. In 1920, the Pennsylvania Academy of the Fine Arts awarded Hassam a Gold Medal of Honor for his lifetime achievements. He spent the latter part of his life on Long Island and died in East Hampton in 1935.

That same year, William Doriani (1891–1958), who had returned to the United States after spending 13 years in Europe, composed an oil painting entitled *Flag Day*, which is owned by the Museum of Modern Art in New York. Mark Daly of Cincinnati, Ohio, has created a number of impressionist paintings similar to those of Hassam, most notably his *Flags, President Day*, which he composed in 2013.

See also World War I

Further Reading

Fort, Ilene Susan. 1988. *The Flag Paintings of Childe Hassam*. New York: Harry N. Abrams, Inc.

Gottlieb, Carla. 1962. "The Pregnant Woman, the Flag, the Eye: Three New Themes in Twentieth Century Art." *Journal of Aesthetics and Art Criticism* (Winter): 177–187.

Horwitz, Elinor Lander, and J. Roderick Moore. 1976. *The Bird, the Banner, and Uncle Sam: Images of America in Folk and Popular Art*. Philadelphia: J. B. Lippincott Company.

Junker, Patricia. 2010. "Childe Hassam, Marsden Hartley, and the Spirit of 1916." *American Art* 24 (Fall): 26–51.

Lubin, David M. 2015. *Flags and Faces: The Visual Culture of America's First War*. Oakland: University of California Press.

Rooney, E. Ashley, and Stephanie Standish. 2015. *Stars and Stripes: The American Flag in Contemporary Art*. Atglen, PA: Schiffer Publishing Ltd.

HEFT, ROBERT G.

One of the most endearing stories of flag design centers on Bob Heft (1942–2009). When Heft was a 17-year-old Boy Scout attending Lancaster High School near Columbus, Ohio, he designed and sewed a flag with nine alternating rows of 5 and 6 stars each in anticipation of Hawaii's entry into the Union (at the time the flag only had 49 stars). His history teacher gave him a B minus for the project, with the challenge that he would change the grade to an A if Heft's design were adopted (Wendell 2016).

Heft subsequently sent his flag to the Ohio governor, who displayed it in the Ohio State Capitol Building and the Governor's Mansion (Leepson 2005, 225). After the flag was returned to Heft, he gave it to his congressman, Walter Henry Moeller, who presented it to a design committee that Eisenhower had appointed. In time, Heft received a call from President Dwight D. Eisenhower, who told him that his design had been selected for the new flag and invited him to the White House. Heft's teacher then changed his grade to an A.

Heft served for 20 years as the mayor of Napoleon, Ohio, and gave many speeches describing his experience. Heft died in 2009, and his grave is marked by a red-white-and-blue tombstone that describes him as the "Designer of America's 50-Star Flag."

Charles A. Spain, the director of the Flag Research Center, threw a dash of cold water on the story in a blog post (response to the article by Wendall 2016). After likening the story to that of Betsy Ross, Spain stated, "There's no evidence for anything other than he was possibly one of many people who came up with the same design that was separately proposed by the military and adopted by President Eisenhower." Similarly, David B. Martucci observed: "The official designer is listed as the Army Institute of Heraldry. In fact, by the time Heft submitted his design, the final design probably had already been chosen" (2015, 73).

See also Ross, Betsy

Further Reading

Leepson, Marc. 2005. *Flag: An American Biography*. New York: St. Martin's Press.
Martucci, David B. 2015. "Wayne's World (of Flags)." *Raven: A Journal of Vexillology* 22:67–77.
"Robert G. Heft: 1942–2009—Creator of 50-Star Flag Was Teen in Lancaster." *The Columbus Dispatch*, December 14, 2009.
Wendall, Bryan. 2016. "A Boy Scout Designed the 50-Star American Flag." *Scouting Magazine*, June 14. http://blog.scoutingmagazine.org/2016/06/06/14/boy-scout-designed-50-star-american-flag/

HINRICHS, KIT

Kit Hinrichs (b. 1941) is a graphic designer and flag collector who is the principal and creative director of Studio Hinrichs in San Francisco, California, which he opened in 2009. Hinrichs earned his BFA degree at the Art Center School (now the ArtCenter College of Design) in Los Angeles and is a member of a member of the American Institute of Graphic Arts (AIGA), which awarded him its medal in 2014.

Hinrichs is one of the foremost collectors of American flags and associated memorabilia and has over 3,000 items in his collection. In 2014, he founded the Stars & Stripes Foundation, which is devoted to educating, conserving, and restoring U.S. flags. He has exhibited his memorabilia at several museums and libraries and has authored a number of related books.

See also Smith, Whitney; Zaricor Flag Collection

Further Reading

AIGA. 2017. "Kit Hinrichs." Accessed March 11. http://www.aiga.org/medalist-kithinrichs/
Hinrichs, Kit. 2016. *Long May She Wave: 100 Stars and Stripes Collectible Postcards*. Toronto, Canada: Potter Style.
Hinrichs, Kit, Delphine Hirasuna, and Terry Heffernan. 2015. *100 American Flags: A Unique Collection of Old Glory Memorabilia*. Berkeley, CA: Ten Speed Press.

HOAR, GEORGE F.

Sen. George Frisbie Hoar (1826–1904) was a grandson of Roger Sherman, who signed both the Declaration of Independence and the U.S. Constitution. George Hoar was born in Concord, Massachusetts, earned undergraduate and law degrees from Harvard University, and served both in the U.S. House of Representatives and the U.S. Senate. Hoar was a Republican who supported the rights of African Americans and women and who opposed American imperialism in the wake of the Spanish-American War.

Hoar made a statement about the U.S. flag in 1878, presumably from a longer speech, that is widely quoted:

> I have seen the glories of art and architecture and of river and mountain. I have seen the sun set on the Jungfrau [a summit in the alps] and the moon rise over Mont Blanc [another peak in the alps]. But the fairest vision on which these eyes ever rested was the flag of my country in a foreign port. Beautiful as a flower to those who love it, and terrible as a meteor to those who hate it, it is the symbol of the power and glory and of the honor of fifty millions of Americans. (Quoted in Brown 1919, 116–117)

In a speech that he gave in Congress in 1902, Hoar repeated the line "beautiful as a flower to those who love it, terrible as a meteor to those who hate it." He added that the flag "floats everywhere over peaceful seas and is welcomed everywhere in friendly ports as the emblem of peaceful supremacy and sovereignty in the commerce of the world." In the speech, Hoar opposed the American acquisition of the Philippines in the wake of the Spanish-American War (Torricelli and Carroll 2000, 7). At a time when many believed that the nation was at a crossroads, Hoar observed that American imperialists believed that the flag should "never be hauled down where it has once floated." By contrast, Hoar portrayed the flag as the symbol of the nation's highest ideals.

In the same year, Hoar contrasted U.S. policy toward Cuba and the Philippines. He observed, "You make the American flag in the eyes of a numerous people the emblem of sacrilege in Christian churches, and of the burning of human dwellings, and of the horror of the water torture." Hoar further accused his colleagues of repealing the Declaration of Independence, betraying the Monroe Doctrine, and of using the tactics of dictatorships. Responding to those who said the United States needed to adapt to the conduct of its enemies, Hoar observed, "I had supposed . . . that the question, whether a gentleman shall lie or murder or torture, depended on his sense of his own character, and not on his opinion of his victim."

See also Spanish-American War

Further Reading

Brown, Will H. 1919. *Patriotic Illustrations for Public Speakers*. Cincinnati: Standard Publishing Company.

Hoar, George Frisbie. "Subjugation of the Philippines Iniquitous." In *The World's Famous Orations*, edited by William Jennings Bryan. http://www.bartleby.com/268/10/25.html

Kinzer, Stephen. 2017. *The True Flag: Theodore Roosevelt, Mark Twain, and the Birth of American Empire*. New York: Henry Holt and Co.
Torricelli, Robert, and Andrew Carroll, eds. 2000. *In Our Own Words: Extraordinary Speeches of the American Century*. New York: Washington Square Press.

HOFFMAN V. UNITED STATES (1971)

In the case of *Abbie Hoffman v. United States*, 445 F.2d 226 (D.C. Cir. 1971), the court of appeals for the District of Columbia struck down a conviction against Abbie Hoffman (1936–1989), a political activist who had been convicted in a court of general sessions of desecrating the flag. Hoffman was the founder of the Youth International Party (the Yippies) and a member of the "Chicago Eight" who had led antiwar protests at the Democratic National Convention in Chicago in 1968.

Hoffman had worn a manufactured shirt that looked like an American flag. To this, he had pinned buttons reading "Wallace for President, Stand Up for America" and "Vote Pig Yippie in Sixty-Eight." When he was called before the Un-American Activities Committee of the U.S. House of Representatives, Hoffman explained, "I wore the shirt to show that we were in the tradition of the founding fathers of this country, and that that committee wasn't."

Although the senior judge (Charles Fahy) in the case cited previous cases like *Street v. New York* (1969), *Halter v. Nebraska* (1907), and *Stromberg v. California* (1931) to indicate that governments had an interest in protecting the flag against desecration, he also noted that the flag desecration statute had been specifically designed not to prohibit the mere expression of ideas. Although recognizing that Hoffman's behavior, which had included playing with a yo-yo, "had a distinct flavor of sarcasm or mockery," the judge did not believe that Hoffman had engaged in criminal conduct: "The wearing of the shirt was not a physical mutilation, defacement, or defilement of the flag as those words are used in the statute; nor were the two buttons pinned on the shirt."

Judge George MacKinnon wrote a concurring opinion in which he noted that there was no evidence "that appellant engaged in any physical act directed against the flag except wearing a shirt that had been made commercially from parts of an American flag to which were pinned two political-type buttons." Acknowledging that "a flag (or shirt) might be technically defaced by pinning such buttons thereon, such conduct alone does not 'cast contempt upon the flag.'" MacKinnon further distinguished between a flag and "a shirt made from parts of the flag." He observed, "If it is only a breach of custom to place a design upon a *flag* for which no penalty is imposed, it is certainly not to be inferred that Congress intended to make it a criminal offense to place a political-type button upon a *shirt resembling a flag*." MacKinnon believed that Hoffman had been prosecuted not for what he actually did but "because he was the person he was." As to any subjective intent, Hoffman appeared to be attempting to cast contempt on the committee before which he was appearing rather than on the flag itself.

Judge Roger Robb based his shorter opinion on the grounds that as a criminal statute, "the Flag Desecration Act must be strictly construed." He observed, "In my opinion he did not treat the flag with proper respect but I cannot say that his conduct was covered by the narrow terms of the statute."

On March 28, 1970, CBS electronically blocked out Hoffman's flag shirt when he appeared on *The Merv Griffin Show*, expressing concerns that some states might consider Hoffman's action to be a form of flag desecration.

Confirming the political nature of this prosecution, Laura Kidd observes that Gen. Richard Myers was photographed on a motorcycle wearing a similar flag and that many others have worn similar shirts without question (2007, 56).

In 1989, the U.S. Supreme Court struck down a Texas flag desecration law in *Texas v. Johnson*, and the following year, it struck down a similar federal statute in *United States v. Eichman*.

See also Flag Apparel; *Halter v. Nebraska* (1907); *Street v. New York* (1969); *Stromberg v. California* (1931); *Texas v. Johnson* (1989); *United States v. Eichman* (1990)

Further Reading

New York Times. 1970. "C.B.S. Blacks Out Chicago 7 Figure; 'Flag' Shirt Cited." March 28.
Kidd, Laura K. 2007. "Wave It or Wear It? The United States Flag as a Fashion Icon." *Raven: A Journal of Vexillology* 14:35–60.

HOLMAN, FRANCIS

The first known picture of the Stars and Stripes at sea was painted in 1779 by an English painter, Francis Holman (1729–1784), on behalf of Capt. William Parker. The painting depicted an engagement in which Parker's British ship, the *Bridgewater*, fended off an attack from the *Hampden*. The latter was an American privateering ship that had been commissioned by John Langdon of Portsmouth, New Hampshire, who would later serve as one of that state's two delegates to the Constitutional Convention of 1787 (Vile 2013, 156–160).

The *Hampden* had sailed to European waters in August 1778 and had several successes, including the recapture of a French ship, *Constance*, that had fallen prey to pirates. This capture had, however, resulted in some friction after the right of Lt. Samuel Pickering (the commander of the *Hampden*) to sell the cargo was subsequently questioned in French courts.

When Pickering's ship resumed its work, it encountered the *Bridgewater*, which ended up doing more damage to the *Hampden* than the *Hampden* did to it. The British ship was flying the British Union Flag and the American ship was flying the flag approved by Congress in 1777, consisting of 13 alternating red and white stripes and a blue canton with 13 stars.

Holman mostly painted nautical scenes, including *The Moonlight Battle Off Cape St. Vincent*, which depicted a battle between Britain and Spain that took place off the southern coast of Portugal.

See also Thirteen-Star Flags

Further Reading

More. Peter. 2016. "The Earliest Known Stars and Stripes." *Northern Mariner: Journal of the Canadian Nautical Research Society* 16 (October): 425–434.

Nye, James. 2012. "First Ever Recorded Image of Stars and Stripes Fetches over $100,000 at Auction in London." *Daily Mail*, November 22. http://www.dailymail.co.uk/news/article-2236880/First-recorded-image-Stars-Stripes-fetches-100-000-auction-London.html

Vile, John R. 2013. *The Men Who Made the Constitution: Lives of the Delegates to the Constitutional Convention*. Lanham, MD: Scarecrow Press, Inc.

HOPKINSON, FRANCIS

Contrary to a once-popular myth, Betsy Ross of Philadelphia did not design the first U.S. flag. To the degree that this honor can be attributed to any one person, that individual appears to have been Francis Hopkinson (1737–1791). Hopkinson was born in Philadelphia and graduated from the College of Philadelphia (today's University of Pennsylvania) before becoming a lawyer and government official. He was one of the signers of the Declaration of Independence and was serving as a U.S. district judge when he died.

Francis Hopkinson was one of the most talented and creative men in 18th-century America. As a writer, musician, and artist, he expressed his creative mind; as a lawyer and politician, Hopkinson served in numerous important roles. An individual of wide-ranging talents, Hopkinson designed an American flag, published the first book of American music, and signed the Declaration of Independence. (Library of Congress)

Hopkinson loved music, composed songs, and was interested in heraldry. He was a member of the Continental Navy Board, the treasurer of loans, and a judge of the Admiralty Court. He advised the second committee appointed by Congress to design the Great Seal of the United States, a seal that included a red-and-white-striped shield against a blue background. Similarly, Hopkinson's design for the seal of the Board of Admiralty included 13 alternative red and white bars (stripes) on a field of blue.

In 1780, Hopkinson presented a letter to the Continental Admiralty Board asking for "a Quarter Cask of the public Wine" in exchange for his work devising the following:

> The Flag of the United States of America
> 7 Devices for the Continental Currency
> A Seal for the Board of Treasury
> Ornaments, Devices & Checks for the new Bills of Exchange in Spain & Holland
> A Seal for the Board of Admiralty
> The Borders, Ornaments & Checks for the new Continental Currency now in the Press,—A Work of considerable Length
> A Great Seal for the United States of America, with a Reverse. (Williams, 44)

Congress did not reimburse Hopkinson, but it appears to have refused to do so largely on the basis that Hopkinson was a governmental employee at the time he made his designs and that he had therefore done his work as part of his regular job. Hopkinson's connection with the navy is probably important since flags largely originated as a way of identifying ships on the seas.

Francis's son, Joseph, composed the words to "Hail, Columbia," which was long considered as a possible national anthem before Congress finally settled on "The Star-Spangled Banner."

See also Ross, Betsy

Further Reading

Williams, Earl P., Jr. 1988. "The 'Fancy Work' of Francis Hopkinson: Did He Design the Stars and Stripes?" *Prologue: Quarterly of the National Archives* 20 (Spring): 42–52.

HOUSE OF FLAGS MUSEUM

The House of Flags Museum was founded on September 8, 2001, by George Scofield (1923–2008) and the Veterans of Foreign War Post 9116 in Columbus, North Carolina. It describes itself as "The ONLY House of Flags Museum in America," the purpose of which is to provide "a unique tourist destination in North Carolina dedicated to nurturing and promoting patriotism, flag etiquette, and historical understanding of the evolution of our Nation's flag."

The museum displays over 300 different flags, which its website describes as "full-size faithful reproductions accompanied with detailed descriptions of their story." Collections include *Defenders of Freedom*, *The Birth of a Nation*, *The Price of Liberty*, and *The United States of America*.

The museum is open from 10:00 a.m. to 1:00 p.m. on Tuesdays through Thursdays and from 10:00 a.m. to 4:00 p.m. on Saturdays. Its website claims that the House of Flags is the only museum that displays "all 27 official United States flags."

See also Veterans of Foreign Wars (VFW)

Further Reading

House of Flags Museum. 2017. "House of Flags Museum." Accessed March 28. http://www.houseofflags.org/

HUMAN FLAG

Just as some churches celebrate a "living Christmas tree," typically consisting of choir members arranged as a tree singing carols, so too individuals sometimes gather to display the Human Flag. The custom of creating "living flags," when students dressed in red, white, and blue or held flag-colored bunting, appears to have developed about the time of the Spanish-American War and was especially supported by the Daughters of the American Revolution and other patriotic groups. Ten thousand cadets participated in a living flag (which included the flag pole) on the parade ground of the U.S. Naval Training Station in Great Lakes, Illinois (Hinrichs and Hirasuna 2001, 22–23).

Such displays often involved children. In 1901, more than 1,000 African American children greeted President McKinley with such an exhibit when he visited New Orleans (Guenter 1990, 148). On May 14, 1903, another group of 2,000 students participated in a living flag at the encampment of the Indiana Department of the Grand Army of the Republic in Anderson, Indiana (Jackson 2015). Apparently, close to 6,500 students participated in such a display in Baltimore, Maryland, in 1914, marking the centennial of Francis Scott Key's composition of "The Star-Spangled Banner," which has since been designated as the national anthem. Their depiction of the flag was anachronistic, however, as theirs had 13 stripes rather than the original 15 of the 1812 flag (Phillips 1930, 78–79).

The American Flag Foundation, Inc., currently works with Fort McHenry to re-create this flag on patriotic holidays.

There is, of course, nothing limiting such affairs to depictions of the U.S. flag. In 1907, for example, schoolchildren formed a "Human Confederate Flag" in front of a monument to Robert E. Lee (O'Leary 1999, 126).

See also American Flag Foundation, Inc.; Cult of the Flag; Daughters of the American Revolution (DAR); Star-Spangled Banner (Flag)

Further Reading

Guenter, Scot M. 1990. *The American Flag, 1770–1924: Cultural Shifts from Creation to Codification*. Cranbury, NJ: Associated University Presses.

Hinrichs, Kit, Delphine Hirasuna, and Terry Heffernan. 2001. *Long May She Wave: A Graphic History of the American Flag*. Berkeley, CA: Ten Speed Press.

Jackson, Stephen T. 2015. "Stirring Living Flag Moves Civil War Veterans in 1903." *The Herald Bulletin*, November 1. http://www.heraldbulletin.com/community/stirring-living-flag-moves-civil-war-veterans-in/article_aa1c6704-ff6e-5e89-8b23-ef8a7f5031dd.html

O'Leary, Cecilia Elizabeth. 1999. *To Die For: The Paradox of American Patriotism*. Princeton, NJ: Princeton University Press.

Phillips, Robert. 1930. *The American Flag: Its Uses and Abuses*. Boston: Stratford Company.

I

IDENTIFYING THE AGE OF FLAGS

Flags, like historic documents, have often been reproduced, generally as items for tourists but especially during commemorative celebrations. Moreover, as flags are passed down from one generation to another, the stories surrounding them often become more and more elaborate. Some flags once believed to have flown during the American Revolution are now known to have been made later.

Undoubtedly, many individuals have come across flags, perhaps in a drawer or attic, with 13 stars and assumed that they were from the American founding period, but it turns out that there are quite a few such flags in existence. This is partly because they have been so often reproduced and partly because the navy permitted small boats to fly a 13-star flag at least as late as 2012 (Cooper 1973, vii).

Once a flag is designed, it can, of course, be copied, so it often takes an expert to decide whether a flag is an original or a reproduction. Grace Rogers Cooper has written an illuminating document that describes some clues as to a flag's provenance. She notes that any flag with six-ply cabled cotton thread must be dated after the 1860s, since it did not exist earlier than this time (Cooper 1973, 25). Similarly the earliest two-ply warp bunting dates to 1865 or thereafter (41). Cooper says that linen was most commonly used for stars on bunting flags in the first decade of the 19th century and that flags from 1813 and thereafter typically used cotton. No flags prior to the 1860s are known to have had grommets (43). Flags of the 18th century and early 19th century almost always used linen or wood thread, with cotton threads not being used until the 1820s (43). Any machine-stitched flag (other than for possible repairs) will date after 1850 (43).

See also Thirteen-Star Flags

Further Reading

Cooper, Grace Rogers. 1973. *Thirteen-Star Flags: Keys to Identification*. Washington, D.C.: Smithsonian Institution Press.

IMMIGRANTS AND FLAG-WAVING

One of the most contentious issues of recent years has centered on American immigration policies (Vile 2016). Many immigrants who have entered the nation, especially from Latin America, have done so illegally, often staying for decades and parenting children. Those children who have been born in the United States are citizens according to section 1 of the Fourteenth Amendment.

Although the Fourteenth Amendment was largely directed toward clarifying the status of African Americans, there have been a number of nativist movements, both before and after this amendment, that have used the U.S. flag as a symbol of exclusion. In turn, the movement in the 1880s to display flags in public schools and to include the pledge to the flag as part of a daily ritual was directed in part toward socializing immigrants to uphold American values.

Today, citizens and pundits alike have argued over whether "illegal" or "undocumented" aliens from Latin America contribute as much to society in work, taxes, and other areas as they take. The issue has been further enmeshed in fears that illegal immigrants, especially from predominantly Muslim nations in the Middle East and Africa, might also be connected to terrorism.

Congress has made several unsuccessful attempts to solve this problem, which became a major issue in the 2016 presidential campaign. Ten years earlier, there were a series of massive pro-immigration demonstrations and rallies throughout the United States. They included participation by many undocumented immigrants who often waved flags of their native countries, especially the flag of Mexico, which opponents widely criticized.

Richard D. Pineda and Stacey K. Sowards, from the University of Texas at El Paso, have analyzed these demonstrations and concluded that the protestors saw their flag-waving as a way of expressing their cultural pride and unity. They further saw it as a way of demonstrating that they had "attained cultural, if not legal, citizenship" (2007, 167). By contrast, those who were offended by the demonstrations typically viewed the waving of foreign flags as evidence of "immigrants' failure to assimilate, the deviance of non-American or noncitizen status, and the failure adequately to control immigration" (168).

As demonstrations continued, proponents of immigrant reform increasingly waved American flags in an effort to show that they were also proud of the United States. Such incidents demonstrate the continuing emotional symbolism connected not only to the U.S. flag but also to the flags of foreign countries.

U.S. citizenship ceremonies, which take place when new citizens are naturalized, include both an oath of citizenship and the Pledge of Allegiance to the U.S. flag.

See also Xenophobia, Nativism, and the U.S. Flag

Further Reading

Pineda, Richard D., and Stacey K. Sowards. 2007. "Flag Waving as Visual Argument: 2006 Immigration Demonstrations and Cultural Citizenship." *Argumentation and Advocacy* 43 (Winter and Spring): 164–174.

Vile, John R. 2016. *American Immigration and Citizenship: A Documentary History*. Lanham, MD: Rowman and Littlefield.

INDEPENDENCE DAY

Americans celebrate their independence from Great Britain every year on the fourth day of July. This marks the day that Congress officially adopted the Declaration of Independence. On June 7, 1776, Virginia's Richard Henry Lee had introduced a resolution in the Second Continental Congress. It proclaimed "that these United Colonies are and ought to be, free and independent states, that they are absolved from all allegiance to the British Crown; and that all political connection between them and the state of Great Britain is, and ought to be, totally dissolved." On June 11, Congress appointed five delegates to a committee to compose a justification for this action. Its members were Thomas Jefferson (Virginia), John Adams (Massachusetts), Benjamin Franklin (Pennsylvania), Robert Livingston (New York), and Roger Sherman (Connecticut).

Jefferson took the lead in drafting the document, which was subjected to minor edits by Adams and Franklin and much more extensive rewriting by Congress. Although the primary purpose of the declaration was to offer reasons for the decision for independence, the most-quoted part proclaimed, "We hold these Truths to be self-evident, that all Men are created equal, that they are endowed, by their CREATOR, with certain unalienable Rights, that among these are Life, Liberty, and the Pursuit of Happiness." The document had further proclaimed that the people had the right to overthrow governments that were not securing such rights and "to institute new Government, laying its Foundation on such Principles, and organizing its Power in such Form, as to them shall seem most likely to effect their Safety and Happiness." Jefferson's words reflected English social contract theory (Becker 1970) and may also have been influenced by Scottish common sense philosophy (Wills 1978).

Print titled "A flag that has waved one hundred years—A scene on the morning of the fourth day of July 1876." The illustration shows a group of people, including one African American man, raising the U.S. flag, with the Capitol Building in the background. The Centennial was used to emphasize American unity 11 years after the end of the bloody Civil War. (Library of Congress)

Because the colonists had previously directed most of their arguments against the authority of Parliament to tax them without their consent, this document now chiefly focused on King George III, who had rebuffed colonial petitions to side with them. The final paragraph of the declaration incorporated Richard Henry Lee's Resolution for Independence and ended with a mutual pledge of "our *Lives*, our *Fortunes*, and our *sacred Honour*."

Congress officially endorsed Lee's Resolution for Independence on July 2, which John Adams initially expected to be celebrated as Independence

Day. Congress adopted the Declaration of Independence, which explained the reasons for the resolution, on July 4. Contrary to popular mythology, most of the delegates signed the document over the next several months rather than on a single day.

Although John Adams incorrectly predicted that Americans would celebrate their independence on July 2, he was fairly accurate as to how the celebrations would proceed: "I am apt to believe that it will be celebrated, by succeeding Generations, as the great anniversary Festival. It ought to be solemnized with Pomp and Parade, with Shews, Games, Sports, Guns, Bells, Bonfires and Illuminations from one end of this Continent to the other from this Time forward forever more" (quoted in de Bolla 2007, 19).

Congress did not declare July 4 to be a national holiday until 1870, by which time many states had already declared it a holiday. Although the holiday sometimes became a partisan affair during the early republic (with Federalists stressing the role of George Washington in the revolution and Democratic-Republicans putting greater emphasis on Thomas Jefferson) and during the Civil War, in time the holiday was recognized as a day for national celebration. The holiday appeared to receive divine sanction on its 50th anniversary when both John Adams and Thomas Jefferson passed away (as would James Monroe five years later). By then, the celebrations had come to include ringing bells and firing cannons; military parades; services that typically included a prayer, songs, and an oration; the reading of the declaration; and exchanges of toasts (de Bolla 2007, 63–65). Even before the song was proclaimed as the national anthem, the holiday often included renditions of "The Star-Spangled Banner" (Svejda 1969, 132–146). The day was, and continues to be, marked by fireworks and ubiquitous displays of American flags. It and other patriotic holidays are also marked by picnics and sports events and sometimes by excessive consumption of alcohol, as is sometimes illustrated in paintings of the event (Schneider 2010).

In 1852, Frederick Douglass, who had fled from slavery and become a prominent abolitionist, gave a speech in which he asked, "What to the Slave Is the Fourth of July?" He pointed to the disparity between the aspirations of the Declaration of Independence celebrated on Independence Day and the institution of slavery (Vile 2017, 171–176). For a time, some African Americans celebrated July 5 as a form of protest (Kammen 2003, 190). African Americans have increasingly participated in traditional Independence Day celebrations since the adoption of the Thirteenth Amendment abolishing involuntary servitude—although many preferred to celebrate Emancipation Day instead (O'Leary 1999, 114). Initially tepid toward Independence Day celebrations, former southern states, who had fought under a rival banner during the war, also joined in the celebrations after the Civil War.

See also Civil War; Revolutionary War; Star-Spangled Banner (Flag)

Further Reading

Attebery, Jennifer Eastman. 2015. *Pole Raising and Speech Making: Modalities of Swedish American Summer Celebrations*. Logan: Utah State University Press.

Becker, Carl L. 1970. *The Declaration of Independence: A Study in the History of Political Ideas*. New York: Vintage Books.
De Bolla, Peter. 2007. *The Fourth of July and the Founding of America*. Woodstock, NY: Overlook Press.
Kammen, Michael. 2003. "Commemoration and Contestation in American Culture: Historical Perspectives." *Amerikastudien / American Studies* 48 (2): 185–205.
Maier, Pauline. 1997. *American Scripture: Making the Declaration of Independence*. New York: Alfred A. Knopf.
Neely, Mark E. 2011. *Lincoln and the Triumph of the Nation: Constitutional Conflict in the American Civil War*. Chapel Hill: University of North Carolina Press.
O'Leary, Cecilia Elizabeth. 1999. *To Die For: The Paradox of American Patriotism*. Princeton, NJ: Princeton University Press.
Schneider, Erika. 2010. "Temperance, Abolition, Oh My!: James Goodwyn Clonney's Problems with Painting the Fourth of July." *Pennsylvania History: A Journal of Mid-Atlantic Studies* 77 (Summer): 303–323.
Skeen, Edward. 2003. *America Rising*. Lexington: University Press of Kentucky.
Svejda, George J. 1969. *History of the Star-Spangled Banner from 1814 to the Present*. National Park Service, U.S. Department of the Interior.
Traves, Len. 1997. *Celebrating the Fourth: Independence Day and the Rites of Nationalism in the Early Republic*. Amherst: University of Massachusetts Press.
Vile, John R. 2015. *Founding Documents of America: Documents Decoded*. Santa Barbara, CA: ABC-CLIO.
Vile, John R. 2017. *The Jacksonian and Antebellum Eras: Documents Decoded*. Santa Barbara, CA: ABC-CLIO.
Warren, Charles. 1945. "Fourth of July Myths." *The William and Mary Quarterly* 2 (July): 237–272.
Wills, Garry. 1978. *Inventing America: Jefferson's Declaration of Independence*. New York: Doubleday.

INGERSOLL'S DECORATION DAY ORATION

One of the most lauded 19th-century orators was attorney Robert G. Ingersoll (1833–1899). Known as "the Great Agnostic" for his provocative advocacy of free thought, Ingersoll, who was also a Union veteran, was a strong proponent of American political ideals. He especially lauded the role of abolitionists in eliminating slavery. In 1882, Ingersoll delivered an address on Decoration Day (today largely supplanted by Memorial Day), which he ended with a tribute to the flag that has been frequently reprinted.

Decoration Day was designed to honor the war dead, and this speech was no exception. Beginning with the Revolutionary War, Ingersoll lauded the sacrifices that American soldiers had made. He especially emphasized those who had fought to uphold the Union and secure freedom for African Americans during the Civil War. He believed this war had abolished the inconsistency between the ringing ideals of the Declaration of Independence and the compromises that the U.S. Constitution had made with slavery. He observed that these soldiers had "neither paused nor swerved until a stainless flag, without a rival bloated over all our wide domain, and until every human being beneath its folds was absolutely free" (this and other quotations taken from the Secular Web, and verified through Smith 1908).

Ingersoll observed that "the Flag for which the heroes fought, for which they died, is the symbol of all we are, of all we hope to be." He further associated the flag with "equal rights," "freedom," "universal education," "the duty of every citizen to bear his share of the public burden," "the ballot-box," "the perpetual right of peaceful revolution," the elimination of "all distinctions based on birth or blood," and the idea that "there shall be a legal remedy for every wrong."

Almost as though he were thinking of the words that would one day be inscribed on the Statue of Liberty, Ingersoll further observed that the flag

> means national hospitality,—that we must welcome to our shores the exiles of the world, and that we may not drive them back. Some may be deformed by labor, dwarfed by hunger, broken in spirit, victims of tyranny and caste,—in whose sad faces may be read the touching record of a weary life, and yet their children, born of liberty and love, will be symmetrical and fair, intelligent and free.

He ended by observing that because of the sacrifices of Union soldiers, "for the first time since man has kept a record of events, the heavens bent above and domed a land without a serf, a servant or a slave."

See also Civil War; Decoration Day (Memorial Day)

Further Reading

Ingersoll, Robert Green. "Decoration Day 82." The Secular Web. Accessed March 15, 2017. https://infidels.org/library/historical/robert_ingersoll/decoration_day-82.html

Smith, Nicholas. 1908. *Our Nation's Flag in History and Incident*. 2nd ed. Milwaukee: Young Churchman Co.

Stob, Paul. 2016. "Sacred Symbols, Public Memory, and the Great Agnostic: Robert Ingersoll Remembers the Civil War." *Rhetoric and Public Affairs* 19 (Summer): 275–306.

IWO JIMA FLAG RAISING

A bronze statue of one of the most iconic photographs of an American flag has also become one of its most revered monuments. Both commemorate the raising of the American flag above Mount Suribachi at Iwo Jima by American soldiers in February 1945, during World War II. This was the first time that the U.S. flag had been raised in victory on Japanese soil since the 1941 attack on Pearl Harbor that had brought the U.S. into the war.

The soldiers had battled Japanese, who had tunneled into the landscape, for days before they were able to climb the mount, which is at the southern tip of the island, and raise the U.S. flag. This event was photographed by Louis Lowery, showing marines surrounding the flag after it had been raised.

After they raised the first such flag, military authorities decided that it was not large enough, and a second party of six men ascended the mountain to raise yet another. It was this flag raising that photographer Joe Rosenthal (1911–2006), of the Associated Press, ended up photographing. Standing atop rubble, six Marines—now believed to be Rene Gagnon, Harlon Block, Franklin Sousley, Ira

Hayes, Michael Strank, and Harold Schultz—are seen collectively putting the base of the flag into the ground and lifting the Stars and Stripes. The men form a triangular configuration typical of classical sculpture.

The press and the technology of the time did not allow Rosenthal to see the photograph before he sent it home. When *The New York Times* printed it on its front page, it quickly became one of the most requested photographs of its time, and it was awarded a Pulitzer Prize. The fact that this was the second flag-raising led some to charge that the event had been staged, but this was not the case.

One of a series of Marine photographer Lou Lowery's photos of the raising of the first flag on Iwo Jima, February 23, 1945. A short time later, the flag was replaced with a larger version, and the moment was captured by Associated Press photographer Joe Rosenthal in an even more iconic photograph now memorialized in a bronze memorial outside Arlington National Cemetery. (Library of Congress)

One endearing aspect of the photograph is that it captured six different soldiers from different walks of life. The group included a New Englander, a Texan, a Kentuckian, a Native American, and an immigrant from Czechoslovakia. It consisted of both Catholics and Protestants. Three soldiers who survived were ordered back to the United States, where they helped to sell bonds, but although they were lauded as heroes, they pointed out that the true heroes were those who had actually died in the conflict.

In 1945, a three-cent stamp was issued to commemorate the event, which Felix de Weldon (1907–2003), an Austrian immigrant who was serving in the U.S. Navy, subsequently incorporated into a model of clay and plaster and later of bronze. This memorial, which weighs more than 100 tons, is 80 feet from its base to the top of the flagpole (the marines are up to 32 feet tall) and is one of the world's largest bronze-cast statues. It is displayed at the Arlington National Cemetery outside Washington, D.C., where it was dedicated in 1954. After a Supreme Court decision in *Texas v. Johnson* (1989) protected flag burning as a form of symbolic speech, President George H. W. Bush used the monument as a backdrop to announce his support for a constitutional amendment banning flag desecration.

With the help of coauthor Ron Powers, James Bradley (the son of one of the six men believed to have raised the flag) wrote an inspiring book on the subject that became a *New York Times* best seller. Based on the research of Eric Krelle and Stephen Foley, however, experts now believe that while Bradley's father had participated in one of the flag-raisings, it was not the famous one that Rosenthal photographed.

The bloody fighting at Iwo Jima has been featured in the 1949 movie *Sands of Iwo Jima*, in a 2006 movie, based on and sharing the title of Bradley's book (*Flags of Our Fathers*), and in the 2006 movie *Letters from Iwo Jima*. Sgt. Bill Genaust, who was part of the photography unit of U.S. Marines but who did not survive the battle of Iwo Jima, also took some 16-millimeter color footage of the second flag-raising, which was featured in a documentary entitled *To the Shores of Iwo Jima* (Sorenssen 2013, 37).

Both Iwo Jima flags, at least one of which was damaged by the high winds on Mount Suribachi, are displayed at the National Museum of the Marine Corps, which is just outside the marine base in Quantico, Virginia. It was opened in 2006 and began expansion in 2013. The soaring design of the museum is designed to mimic that of the photograph and monument.

In 1968, Edward Kienholz composed *The Portable War Memorial* as a protest against the war in Vietnam. This mixed-media installation included an unflattering depiction of marines attempting to insert the staff of the flag into the umbrella hole in a patio table (Boime 1998, 52).

See also Flag Desecration Amendment; *Texas v. Johnson* (1989); World War II

Further Reading

Boime, Albert. 1998. *The Unveiling of National Icons: A Plea for Patriotic Iconoclasm in a Nationalist Era*. New York: Cambridge University Press.

Bradley, James, and Ron Powers. 2000. *Flags of Our Fathers*. New York: Bantam.

Burgan, Michael. 2011. *Raising the Flag: How a Photograph Gave a Nation Hope in Wartime*. North Mankato, MN: Compass Point Books.

Martin, Douglas. 2003. "Felix de Weldon Is Dead at 96; Sculptured Memorial to Marines." *The New York Times*, June 15. https://www.nytimes.com/2003/06/15/us/felix-de-weldon-is-dead-at-96-sculptured-memorial-to-marines.html

Michaels, Jim. 2016. "Marines Misidentified One Man in Iconic 1945 Iwo Jima Photo." *USA Today*, June 23. http://www.usatoday.com/story/news/world/2016/06/23/flag-riaser-marine-iwo-jima-photo/86254440/

Sorenssen, Bjorn. 2013. "The Forgotten Cinematographer of Mount Suribachi: Bill Genaust's Eight-Second Iwo Jima Footage and the Historical Facsimile." In *Eastwood's Iwo Jima: Critical Engagements with Flags of Our Fathers and Letters from Iwo Jima*, edited by Rikke Schubart and Anne Gjelsvik, 36–56. New York: Wallflower Press.

J

JEHOVAH'S WITNESSES

Few, if any, contemporary religious groups have had a greater influence on American law, and specifically on the practice of saluting the U.S. flag, than Jehovah's Witnesses.

Members of a denomination founded by Charles Taze Russell (1852–1916) in the late 1870s, Jehovah's Witnesses expect the imminent return of Christ to earth. They are often associated with the Watch Tower Society, which Russell founded in 1881. Although the denomination is non-Trinitarian, many of its views are based on very literalist readings of scripture. Jehovah's Witnesses have interpreted the Bible to forbid blood transfusions (they see this as "eating" blood and so contrary to Old Testament admonitions); to prohibit military service (they are conscientious objectors); and to refuse allegiance to the U.S. flag. They generally meet together in "Kingdom Halls" on Saturdays.

The Witnesses engage actively in door-to-door evangelism, selling literature, which has often brought them into conflict with more traditional believers. For many years, they were represented by a brilliant lawyer named Hayden Covington, who is credited with winning 85 percent of the 44 cases that he argued before the U.S. Supreme Court (Vile 2001, 1:134).

Jehovah's Witnesses refuse to salute the flag because they considered the practice to be a form of idolatry, in violation of the Ten Commandments. This has brought them into conflict with public school systems that require the practice. Prior to 1940, the Supreme Court had rejected appeals from Witnesses and other groups (like Mennonites) on at least four occasions—see *Leoles v. Landers*, 302 U.S. 656; *Hearing v. State Board of Education,* 303 U.S. 624; *Gabrielli v. Knickerbocker*, 306 U.S. 621; and *Johnson v. Deerfield*, 306 U.S. 621.

When the U.S. Supreme Court first accepted a case dealing with the subject in *Minersville School District v. Gobitis* (1940), Justice Felix Frankfurter wrote an opinion ruling against the Witnesses. In doing so, he deferred to legislative judgments that mandatory flag salutes promoted patriotism and national unity.

The decision was followed by a wave of violence against Jehovah's Witnesses throughout the United States. Three years later, the court reversed course in *West Virginia State Board of Education v. Barnette* (1943). Justice Robert Jackson wrote the opinion for the court majority, which ruled that compulsory flag salutes violated the guarantees of speech and religion as articulated in the First and Fourteenth Amendments to the U.S. Constitution.

The latter case noted that the Witnesses had offered to give the following pledge:

> I have pledged my unqualified allegiance and devotion to Jehovah, the Almighty God, and to his Kingdom, for which Jesus commands all Christians to pray.
>
> I respect the flag of the United States, and acknowledge it as a symbol of freedom and justice to all.
>
> I pledge allegiance and obedience to all the laws of the United States that are consistent with God's law, as set forth in the Bible.

Not surprisingly, Jehovah's Witnesses often faced even greater persecution abroad, especially in Nazi Germany. The fact that Hitler required personal salutes may have worked in favor of the Witnesses' stance against flag salutes.

See also *Minersville School District v. Gobitis* (1940); Tremain, Russell; *West Virginia State Board of Education v. Barnette* (1943)

Further Reading

Ellis, Richard J. 2005. *To the Flag: The Unlikely History of the Pledge of Allegiance*. Lawrence: University Press of Kansas.

Henderson, Jennifer Jacobs. 2005. "Conditional Liberty: The Flag Salute Before Gobitis and Barnette." *Journal of Church and State* 47 (Autumn): 747–767.

Manwaring, David. 1962. *Render unto Caesar*. Chicago: University of Chicago Press.

Newton, Merlin Owen. 1995. *Armed with the Constitution: Jehovah's Witnesses in Alabama and the U.S. Supreme Court, 1939–1946*. Tuscaloosa: University of Alabama Press.

Peters, Shawn Francis. 2000. *Judging Jehovah's Witnesses: Religious Persecution and the Dawn of the Rights Revolution*. Lawrence: University Press of Kansas.

Smith, Chuck. 2001. "The Persecution of West Virginia Jehovah's Witnesses and the Expansion of Legal Protection for Religious Liberty." *Journal of Church and State* 43 (Summer): 539–577.

Vile, John R. 2001. "Covington, Hayden C." In *Great American Lawyers: An Encyclopedia*, edited by John R. Vile, 134–140. 2 vols. Santa Barbara, CA: ABC-CLIO.

JOHNS, JASPER

Jasper Johns (b. 1930) is an American painter who has been a seminal figure in the development of abstraction expressionism and pop art. He is particularly known for a series of approximately 40 paintings of the American flag.

For many years, he was closely associated with Robert Rauschenberg, with whom he shared a studio. Rauschenberg's *Short Circuit* (1955) contained a door behind which one of Johns's first images of the flag, subsequently stolen, was hidden (Allen 2016).

Johns attributes one of his first paintings, composed between 1954 and 1956, simply identified as *Flag*, to a dream. He painted many others with titles such as *Two Flags*, *Three Flags*, and *The Large White Flag*. He composed most such paintings with encaustic, which uses wax rather than oil to bind pigments. The pigments in turn generally overlay a collage of newspaper print. The method allows for a greater focus on the way that brush strokes give the paintings a three-dimensional quality (Gottlieb 1962, 180). Noting that Johns's flags never flutter, one author observes, "It is a monument to a flag: the flag mummified" (Jones 2008).

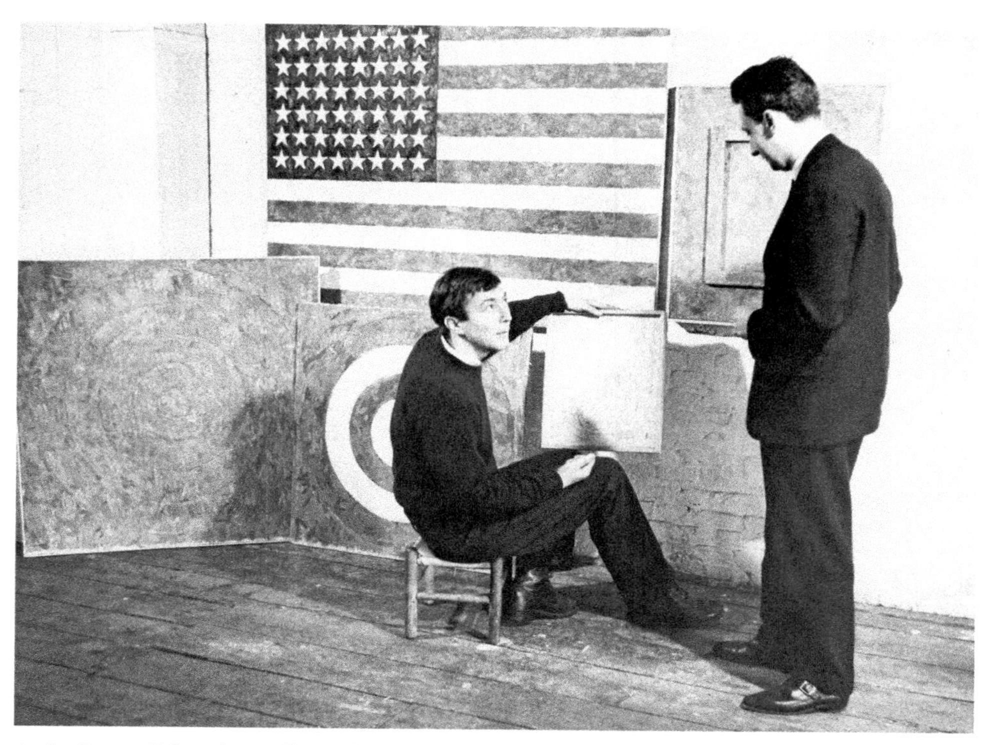

Artist Jasper Johns (seated) speaking with an unidentified man while setting up some of his work, including one of his signature depictions of U.S. flags, in his studio in 1958. (Peter Stackpole/The LIFE Picture Collection/Getty Images)

Although previous painters had often incorporated flags into landscapes, Johns found it liberating to use familiar objects such as flags and targets (another theme) in part because he thought the objects were so familiar that they were often overlooked. He explained: "Using the design of the American flag took care of a great deal for me because I didn't have to design it. . . . So I went on to similar things like the targets . . . things the mind already knows. That gave me room to work on other levels" (quoted in Carpenter 1977, 223).

Johns's parents named him after Sgt. William Jasper, who is immortalized in a monument in Madison Square, Savannah, Georgia, where he holds a flag aloft. During the Revolutionary War, Jasper had raised an American flag at Fort Sullivan (Moultrie) in Charleston harbor and had died during the siege of Savannah while attaching the regimental standards to the city walls (Boime 1998, 46).

Further Reading

Allen, Greg. 2016. "American Beauty: Jasper Johns, Robert Rauschenberg, and the Case of the Missing Flag." *Art News*, May 5. http://www.artnews.com/2016/05/10/american-beauty-jasper-johns-robert-rauschenberg-and-the-case-of-the-missing-flag/

Boime, Albert. 1990. "Waving the Red Flag and Reconstituting Old Glory." *Smithsonian Studies in American Art* 4 (Spring): 2–25.

Boime, Albert. 1998. *The Unveiling of National Icons: A Plea for Patriotic Iconoclasm in a Nationalist Era*. New York: Cambridge University Press.
Carpenter, Joan. 1977. "The Infra-Iconography of Jasper Johns." *Art Journal* 36 (Spring): 221–227.
Gottlieb, Carla. 1962. "The Pregnant Woman, the Flag, the Eye: Three New Themes in Twentieth Century Art." *The Journal of Aesthetics and Art Criticism* 21 (Winter): 177–187.
Jones, Jonathan. 2008. "The Truth beneath Jasper Johns' Stars and Stripes." *The Guardian*, October 24. https://www.theguardian.com/artanddesign/jonathanjonesblog/2008/oct/24/jasper-johns-jonathan-jones-flag

JULY 4 HOLIDAY

See Independence Day

K

KEIM, PETER

Dr. Peter Keim, of Austin, Texas, is among those flag collectors, including Whitney Smith and Ben Zaricor, who have not only amassed vast collections but have also contributed to public knowledge of the American flag and of U.S. history. Keim has observed both that people are quite "passionate . . . about our flag" but that "very few of them know the history of it at all" (quoted in Katsev 2016).

Keim served as a physician in the U.S. Army Medical Corp. He has specialized in collecting flags, some that never officially existed, with different numbers of stars. For example, Keim's collection includes a flag with 14 stars, despite the fact that because the United States went from a flag with 13 stars to one with 15, it never officially had a flag with 14 stars.

Keim coauthored a book with his son Peter, an architect, in which they traced the history of the United States through its respective flags. Although vividly illustrated with color photos, the book (titled *A Grand Old Flag* and published in 2007) contains considerable explanatory text.

See also Smith, Whitney; Zaricor Flag Collection

Further Reading

Katsev, Libbie. 2016. "U.S. flag Expert Peter Keim Collects History." *Pittsburg Post-Gazette*, June 14. http://www.post-gazette.com/life/holidays/2016/06/14/U-S-flag-expert-Peter-Keim-collects-history/stories/201606140002

Keim, Kevin, and Peter Keim. 2007. *A Grand Old Flag: A History of the United States through Its Flags*. New York: DK.

KEY, FRANCIS SCOTT

Francis Scott Key (1779–1843) of Frederick, Maryland, was a lawyer who authored "The Star-Spangled Banner," the song that has since been designated as American's national anthem.

Key was educated at St. John's College (which he would later loyally support) and became a prominent lawyer. After the British arrested Dr. William Beanes of Maryland during the War of 1812 and threatened to send him to Canada for a trial, Key arranged to meet several British military leaders aboard HMS *Tonnant* to negotiate his release. Fearing that Key may have gotten wind of British plans to attack Baltimore (the British had previously burned the nation's capital), Key was kept aboard a British ship for the attack on that city on September 13–14, 1814. After a night of heavy fire and great apprehension, Key was greatly relieved to spy the American flag still flying above the fort, which had repulsed the attack. Years after the event, Key described his sentiments on seeing the large flag, which Mary Pickersgill and her assistants had made, flying above the fort:

> I saw the flag of my country waving over a city, the strength and pride of my native state, a city devoted to plunder and desolation by its assailants. I witnessed the preparation for its assaults. I saw the array of its enemies as they advanced to the attack. I heard the sound of battle. The noise of the conflict fell upon my listening ear and told me that the brave and the free had met the invaders. (Quoted in Molotsky 2001, 97–98)

Key then wrote "The Star-Spangled Banner," drawing the tune from "Anacreon in Heaven," an English drinking song that appears to have been composed by John Stafford Smith (not Ralph Tomlinson, as was once believed). The song was almost immediately published, although Key did very little to tout his own role in its composition. The piece was initially published under the title "The Defense of Fort M'Henry."

This scene, of Francis Scott Key on a ship looking at the flag during the Battle of Baltimore, depicts Key's inspiration for writing the poem "The Star Spangled Banner." Asked to create an enormous flag to warn off the British after the War of 1812, Mary Young Pickersgill sewed a 30-foot by 42-foot red, white, and blue flag, with 15 stripes and 15 stars, that Key was proud to see flying the morning after the British bombardment. (Library of Congress)

Key was a religious man who had once considered becoming an Episcopalian priest and was affiliated with the American Bible Society. Although he owned slaves, he also helped found the American Colonization Society, which sought to solve the problem of slavery by transporting slaves back to Africa. As a lawyer, he defended both slaves and slave owners. Key is pictured in a painting by Edward Percy Moran entitled *By Dawn's Early Light*, which was painted about 1912 and portrays him as standing on a ship and looking toward the flag over the fort.

Key was a strong supporter of Andrew Jackson, and he went on to serve in his "kitchen cabinet."

Apparently, Key never visited Fort McHenry, nor was a flag displayed at his funeral (Molotsky 2001, 102). He has subsequently been honored, however, with the construction of monuments in San Francisco, California, and Frederick and Baltimore,

Maryland. A three-cent stamp was also issued in his honor (it features a 15-star flag on one side, a 48-star flag on the others, and has pictures of the Old Key Home and Fort McHenry) in 1948 and a four-cent stamp in 1960, which features the line "And this be our motto, in GOD is our TRUST." At least two bridges have been named after him. One is the Key Bridge, which spans the Potomac River. It was completed in 1923 and is now on the National Register of Historic Places. It has sometimes been humorously called the "The Car-Strangled Spanner" (Ferris 2014, 180). The other is the Francis Scott Key, or Outer Harbor, Bridge, which was completed in 1977 and spans the Patapsco River in Baltimore.

Key's sister married his law partner, Roger B. Taney, whom Andrew Jackson appointed as chief justice of the U.S. Supreme Court. Key's children ended up fighting for the Confederacy. Congress designated "The Star-Spangled Banner" as the national anthem on March 3, 1931.

See also Pickersgill, Mary Young; Postage Stamps; "Star-Spangled Banner" (Anthem); Star-Spangled Banner (Flag); War of 1812

Further Reading

Ferris, Marc. 2014. *The Star-Spangled Banner: The Unlikely Story of America's National Anthem*. Baltimore: Johns Hopkins University Press.

Leepson, Marc. 2014. *What So Proudly We Hailed: Francis Scott Key, A Life*. New York: Palgrave Macmillan.

Molotsky, Irvin. 2001. *The Flag, the Poet and the Song: The Story of the Star-Spangled Banner*. New York: Dutton.

Svejda, George J. 1969. *History of the Star-Spangled Banner from 1814 to the Present*. Washington, D.C.: National Park Service, U.S. Department of the Interior.

L

LAFAYETTE GRAVESITE

The grave of the Marquis de Lafayette (1757–1834) has, at least since the end of World War I, been marked by an American flag.

Lafayette was a French aristocrat who came to America at the age of 19 to participate in the American Revolution. He was wounded at the battle of Brandywine, fought at Yorktown, and was a close friend of George Washington, to whom, through Thomas Paine, he presented the key to the Bastille prison, which is on display at Washington's home at Mount Vernon. Lafayette also helped secure financial help for the American cause from King Louis XVI.

After returning to France, he sought to bring about peaceful political change, but he ultimately fled the nation during the French Revolution and was imprisoned for five years by the Prussians and Austrians before later becoming a member of the French Chamber of Deputies. In 1824, he participated in a much-heralded trip to the United States, where he visited all 24 states but expressed great concern about the continuation of slavery in a nation otherwise devoted to liberty.

The Picpus Cemetery, behind the chapel of Notre-Dame-de-la-Paix outside Paris, where Lafayette is buried, is located next to two mass graves of victims of the guillotine, including members of his wife's family. At his burial, soil from Bunker Hill was poured over his coffin. In a private ceremony held each July 4, the flag is replaced with a new one.

In 1824, Lafayette became the first foreign dignitary to address the U.S. Congress. In 2002, Congress conferred honorary U.S. citizenship upon him.

See also Independence Day; Revolutionary War

Further Reading

Kraut, Gary Lee. 2009. "Lafayette and the American Flag: The Fourth of July Ceremony." France Revisited. Last modified July 10. http://francerevisited.com/2009/07/lafayette-and-the-american-flag-the-fourth-of-july-ceremony/

Meier, Allison. 2013. "A Tale of Two Revolutions at the Grave of the Marquis de Lafayette." Atlas Obscura. Last modified July 4. http://www.atlasobscura.com/articles/a-tale-of-two-revolutions-in-paris

LAMBKIN, PRINCE

African Americans had little cause to celebrate the U.S. flag prior to their emancipation. The former slave Frederick Douglass was among those who contrasted the meaning of the Fourth of July and of American liberty for whites and for blacks.

Scottish poet Thomas Campbell connected the stripes on the American flag to the scars on the backs of American slaves.

However, after the Union finally conceded to requests by African Americans that they be allowed to participate in the Civil War to help secure their own freedoms, they became among the flag's most ardent defenders. One of the clearest indications of this shift is a speech recorded, in dialect, by Thomas Wentworth Higginson (1823–1911), a Unitarian minister from Massachusetts who was a captain in the 51st Massachusetts Infantry, after which he served as colonel of the 1st South Carolina Volunteers, which consisted of freedmen. In 1869, Higginson published a book entitled *Army Life in a Black Regiment*. In this book Higginson described how on the night of December 5, 1862, his troops engaged in singing and speechmaking.

He described a speech by Cpl. Prince Lambkin. After reviewing the contemporary political situation, which had included how African Americans had expected that they might receive their freedom on the July 4 that followed Abraham Lincoln's election, Higginson records how Lambkin "finally brought out one of the few really impressive appeals for the American flag that I have ever heard." The speech, as Higginson recorded it, is as follows:

> Our mas'rs dy hab lib under de flag, dey got dere wealth under it, and ebryting beautiful for
> Dere chilen. Under it dey hab grind us up, and put us in dere pocket for money. But de fus'
> Minute tey think dat ole flag mean freedom for we colored people, dey pull it right down,
> And run up de rag ob dere own. (Immense applause). But we'll neber desert de ole flag,
> Boys, neb er; we hab lib under it for eighteen hundred sixty-two years, and we'll die for it now.

Higginson observed, "I see already with relief that there will be small demand in this regiment for harangues from the officers; give the men an empty barrel for a stump, and they will do their own exhortation."

In addition to its heartfelt sentiments and its commitment to the American flag, Cpl. Lambkin's speech is notable for its observation that slave holders would rather give allegiance to a new flag than to interpret the U.S. flag to include freedom for African Americans.

See also Campbell, Thomas; Civil Rights Movement; Civil War; Confederate Flags

Further Reading

Higginson, Thomas Wentworth. 1900. *Army Life in a Black Regiment*. N.p.: Riverside Press. https://www.gutenberg.org/files/6764/6764-h/6764-h.htm#link2HCH0009

LANDSCAPE

Visitors to the United States are sometimes surprised by the number of U.S. flags and representations of flags that they encounter. Wilbur Zelinsky notes that the green, white, and red have increasingly been used to represent Italy, but he believes that Sweden may be the only other foreign country where flags are as conspicuous as they are in the United States (1984, 279).

Zelinsky observes that the flag was not as popular as the eagle, Miss Liberty, or pictures of Washington in the early republic. Moreover, portrayals of flags in early single-family dwellings were relatively sparse. In 1981 and 1982, Zelinsky took trips where he documented flags at private homes and found that approximately 4.7 percent displayed flags (with 4.2 displaying eagles). He noted that the red-white-and-blue shield was also relatively conspicuous, especially on national highway signs and corporate logos (1984, 278–279). He further found that the number of flag displays declined from Winchester, Virginia, southward (282). He observed that there was "an equally sharp disparity between North and South in the incidence of nationalistic place names, a development that long antedates the Civil War and has persisted ever since" (283). Zelinsky believes that the increased proliferation of flags in the American landscape is an indication that the American state, and its need for a unifying symbol, developed later than the American nation (285).

Flags are routinely displayed on certain holidays, including Independence Day and Flag Day. They are also more commonly displayed during times of war or crisis than at other times. Norman K. Denzin observed numerous flags being displayed in windows in the weeks immediately following the terrorist attacks of 9/11. Taking such flags as a way for Americans to feel "that Americans are patriotic, [and] that God is on Our Side," Denzin (2007, 21) observed that the flag is often mixed with other symbols:

> Now it is Christmas time 2002, and the flags are still here. Flags have taken over Christmas. Flags have taken over Santa Claus and his reindeer and sled. At Market Place Mall, Santa's suit is a flag, red, white and blue. His sled has flags on each side, and his Reindeer wear little hats made of flags. Flags are sprouting up everywhere. They are back in the windows of Central High [School]. People are putting up flag poles, and the couple in the house down the street make quite a ritual of taking down "Old Glory" just before night fall each day.

Jack Santino (1992) has observed that the flag is also increasingly displayed along with other symbols, such as yellow ribbons, which have become a symbol of welcoming back soldiers or prisoners, or holiday displays associated with Christmas, Easter, or Valentine's Day.

Scot Guenter (2015) has documented a number of homes that have been decorated as flags. Zoran Pavlovic has documented an even wider number of "flagscapes," which he defines as "unique landscapes depicting at least some elements of the national flag" (2008, 17). He finds such flagscapes to be particularly abundant in rural areas of the Interior Plains. In addition to finding flag depictions often used on commercial establishments, he has documented depictions of flags on garages, sheds, barns, fences, and mailboxes and on buildings and landmarks including water towers, painted rocks, and murals, as well as on other objects, almost all of which face the road.

See also Flag Homes; Terrorist Attacks of September 11, 2001

Further Reading

Denzin, Norman K. 2007. "Week 55: Flags in the Window (12-3-02)." *Counterpoints* 314:19–24.

Guenter, Scot. 2015. "The Phenomenon of Flag Homes: Musings on Meanings." *Raven: A Journal of Vexillology* 22:27–53.

Lowenthal, David. 1977. "The Bicentennial Landscape: A Mirror Held Up to the Past." *Geographical Review* 67 (July): 253–267.

Pavlovic, Zoran "Zok." 2008. "Flagscapes in the American Heartland." *FOCUS on Geography* 51 (Winter): 17–22.

Santino, Jack. 1992. "Yellow Ribbons and Seasonal Flags: The Folk Assemblage of War." *Journal of American Folklore* 105 (Winter):19–33.

Zelinsky, Wilbur. 1984. "O Say, Can You See?: Nationalistic Emblems in the Landscape." *Winterthur Portfolio* 19 (Winter): 277–286.

Zelinsky, Wilbur. 1988. *Nation into State: The Shifting Foundations of American Nationalism.* Chapel Hill: University of North Carolina Press.

LANE, FRANKLIN K.

Franklin Knight Lane (1864–1921) served as secretary of the interior from 1913 to 1920, having previously served as a commissioner of the Interstate Commerce Commission. During his tenure as leader of the Interior Department, Lane gave to employees what has become one of the most quoted speeches on the American flag. He delivered the speech, called either "Makers of the Flag" or "Flag Makers," on Flag Day, June 14, 1914.

Lane began his imaginative speech by recounting how every morning, when he passed by the flag on his way to his office, the flag addressed him with "Good Morning, Mr. Flag Maker." The speech continued as a conversation in which the flag does most of the talking. The flag exalts those who work hard, especially in government service. The flag thus referenced "the man who worked in the swelter of yesterday, straightening out the tangle of that farmer's homestead in Idaho," "the struggle which the boy in Georgia is making to win the Corn Club prize this summer," and the Michigan mother who worked "from sunrise until far into the night, to give her boy an education."

The flag identified itself not as "the flag" but "its shadow" and proclaimed (as it would do again in the penultimate paragraph), "I am whatever you make me, nothing more." Although at one point it says, "I am the Constitution and the courts, [and] statutes," it then proceeds to reference the "state-maker, soldier and dreadnaught, drayman and sweep, cook, counselor and clerk."

The end of the speech reinforces the idea that the flag reflects the collective work of citizens:

> I swing before your eyes as a bright gleam of color, a symbol of yourself, the pictured suggestion of that big thing which makes this nation. My stars and my stripes are your dreams and your labors. They are bright with cheer, brilliant with courage, firm

with faith, because you have made them so out of your hearts; for you are the makers of the Flag, and it is well that you glory in the making.

One of the fascinating aspects of Lane's speech is that unlike other speeches that focus chiefly on the inherent symbolism of the flag, the ideals of liberty and justice, or on the role of military personnel or first responders in protecting it, Lane's remarks focused both on commending the role of ordinary civil servants and ordinary citizens in advancing national ideals. H. Augustine Smith would later draw heavily on Lane's address in writing a patriotic service for children called *A Pageant of the Stars and Stripes* (Guenter 1990, 165). Part of the speech has also been used in the narrative of a work entitled *I Am the American Flag*, commissioned for the Air Force Band of Flight by Lt. Col. Alan Sierichs.

See also Flag Day

Further Reading

Jim Beckel Music. 2017. "About *I Am the American Flag*." Accessed May 22. http://jimbeckelmusic.com/Content/Pieces/AmFlag.htm

Guenter, Scot M. 1990. *The American Flag, 1777–1924: Cultural Shifts from Creation to Codification*. Cranbury, NJ: Associated University Presses.

Lane, Franklin K. 2017. "Flag Makers." Oocities.org. Accessed February 7. http://www.oocities.org/songkhla.geo/FlagMake.html?20177

LAPEL PINS

Although some laws have banned the use of flags in advertising (e.g., *Halter v. Nebraska*, 1907), it is increasingly common for police officers (who sometimes also have painted flags on their cars) and other public servants to wear flag patches and for politicians and ordinary citizens to wear lapel pins featuring depictions of the American flag. Such pins may symbolize either general patriotism or support for specific policies.

The appearance of flags on pins, patches, and other materials first attracted broad public attention in the late 1960s:

> Members of the establishment, the hawks, generally wore the flag in the form of a lapel pin or flag patches over their hearts or on their sleeves. Members of the anti-establishment, the doves, wore flag shirts and vests, used flags as shawls or blankets, and wore flag patches on their blue jeans, often over holes in the seat or knees of their jeans. (Kidd 2007, 54)

President Nixon wore a flag pin after construction workers gave him one in 1970, and his chief of staff, H. R. Haldeman, once urged cabinet members to wear such pins "to stick it to the liberals" (quoted in Teachout 2009, 212). Archie Bunker, television's quintessential redneck, wore a flag pin in the classic 1970s sitcom *All in the Family*. The movie *The Candidate* (1972), starring Robert Redford, satirized this practice, which it associated with symbolism rather than with substance, and flag pins generally went out of favor after the Watergate crisis and Nixon's resignation.

Such pins reappeared as prominent symbols after the terrorist attacks on the World Trade Center and other targets on September 11, 2001, when the president and members of his staff began wearing them (Teachout 2009, 208). Those who supported the subsequent invasion of Iraq tended to associate themselves more closely with flag displays than those who opposed this invasion. Fox News, which is generally associated with the right wing, directed all its staff to wear such pins in 2001, whereas other networks, fearful that displays of the flag would suggest support for war and detract from their perceived objectivity, banned them.

In early 2003, Bill Moyers, a journalist and former aide to President Lyndon B. Johnson, wore a flag pin on his lapel because, he wrote that year, he feared that "the flag's been hijacked and turned into a logo—the trade mark of a monopoly on patriotism"; he noted that prior to this time: "It no more occurred to me to flaunt the flag on my chest than it did to pin my mother's picture on my lapel to prove her son's love. Mother knew where I stood; so does my country."

U.S. law specifies that "the flag represents a living country and is itself considered a living thing" and "therefore, the lapel flag pin being a replica, should be worn on the left lapel near the heart" (Luckey 2008, 7).

A book originally published in 1910 includes a speech by Sen. John Mellen Thurston of Nebraska entitled "The Man Who Wears the Button," in which he extols veterans who wear a bronze button (Whipple 1910, 136). This would appear to have been the button issued by the Grand Army of the Republic to veterans of the Civil War; some of the buttons featured images of the U.S. flag.

See also Flag Apparel; Grand Army of the Republic (GAR); *Halter v. Nebraska* (1907); Iwo Jima Flag Raising; Terrorist Attacks of September 11, 2001

Further Reading

Borden, Sandra L. 2005. "Communitarian Journalism and Flag Displays after September 11: An Ethical Critique." *Journal of Communication Inquiry* 29 (January): 30–46.

Dionne, E. J., John McWethy, Alan Murray, and Alicia C. Shepard. 2003. "Running Toward Danger." In *The Media and the War on Terrorism*, edited by Stephen Hess and Marvin Kalb, 275–295. Washington, D.C.: Brookings Institution Press.

Gilman, John E. 1910. "The Grand Army of the Republic." Accessed 04/30/2018. http://civilwarhome.com/grandarmyofrepublic.htm

Kidd, Laura K. 2007. "Wave It or Wear It? The United States Flag as a Fashion Icon." *Raven: A Journal of Vexillology* 14:35–60.

Luckey, John R. 2008. *The United States Flag: Federal Law Relating to Display and Associated Questions*. CRS Report for Congress. Washington, D.C.: Congressional Research Service.

Marmo, Jennifer. 2010 "The American flag and the Body: How the Flag and the Body Create an American Meaning." *Kaleidoscope: A Graduate Journal of Qualitative Communication Research* 9:945–63.

Moyers, Bill. 2003. "Bill Moyers on Patriotism and the American Flag." *Now*, PBS, February 28. http://www.pbs.org/now/commentary/moyers19.html

Teachout, Woden. 2009. *Capture the Flag: A Political History of American Patriotism*. New York: Basic Books.

Whipple, Wayne. [1910]. *The Story of the American Flag*. Bedford, MA: Applewood Books [Philadelphia: Henry Altemus Company].

LIBBY, FREDERICK

Although he was born in Colorado, Frederick Libby (1891–1970) was working in Canada when World War I began. He joined the British Royal Flying Service, which deployed him to France, where he shot down 14 German airplanes.

At the suggestion of this squadron commander, he attached streamers made from stripes of the American flag to his plane. He carried these back to the United States as part of the Liberty Bonds drive to raise money for the war. The National Bank of Commerce subsequently bid $3.25 million for the streamers, which they returned to Libby.

Libby was subsequently transferred to the No. 22 Squadron of the U.S. Air Service at Hicks Field, Texas. He was able to regain the citizenship that he had forfeited for serving in a foreign force, but he became permanently disabled and was unable to serve. He went on to found Western Airlines and authored *Horses Don't Fly*.

See also World War I

Further Reading

Hudson, James J. *In the Clouds of Glory: American Airmen Who Flew with the British during the Great War*. Fayetteville: University of Arkansas Press.

Libby, Frederick. 2000. *Horses Don't Fly*. New York: Arcade Publishing.

LIBERTY TREES, LIBERTY POLES, AND LIBERTY CAPS

Although flags are often traced to battle ensigns and the identification of ships at sea, liberty trees and liberty poles probably also played a role in their development, especially in the United States. Significantly, the pledge to the American flag specifically identifies it as a symbol "with liberty and justice for all." Thomas Paine published a popular poem in the *Pennsylvania Magazine* of June 1775 in which he said that "the Goddess of Liberty" had transplanted "a fair budding branch from the gardens above" to "this peaceable shore," where "The fame of its fruit drew the nations around/ To seek out this peaceable shore." Thomas Jefferson would later proclaim, "The tree of liberty must be refreshed from time to time, with the blood of patriots and tyrants" (Schlesinger, 1952, 453).

The liberty tree appears to be an American innovation that grew out of the conflict with Great Britain over Parliament's adoption of colonial taxes including the Stamp Act, the Townsend Duties, and other such measures. A number of colonial trees had acquired significance even before the imposition of British taxes. Thus, Massachusetts long identified itself with a pine tree, Connecticut celebrated its Charter Oak, and Pennsylvania honored its Treaty Elm (Schlesinger 1952, 436–437).

The Stamp Act appears to have occasioned the first liberty trees, where individuals gathered to resist taxes and sometimes to post the names of or hang in effigy individuals whom they associated with such taxes. Such actions could serve to intimidate tax collectors or others whom patriots thought were not sufficiently committed to their cause. The Revolutionary Sons of Liberty were especially

British political cartoon published in 1774 entitled "The Bostonians paying the exciseman, or tarring and feathering." The issue of taxation was of tremendous importance in the decision made by the colonists to rebel against the British. Liberty trees and poles often served as gathering points for colonial resistance. (National Archives)

associated with gathering at such sites, where they sometimes displayed early flags with pine trees, rattlesnakes, or words like "Liberty" or "Don't Tread on Me."

Perhaps influenced by the British maypole, in time, liberty trees often gave way to liberty poles, which were stripped of branches and from which banners were often flown. Not surprisingly, British troops often tried to destroy these symbols, which multiplied as rebellion spread. As might be expected, rebel victories often led to the reconstruction of such monuments.

Liberty poles later became popular in France during the French Revolution, and the U.S. government minted a cent from 1793 to 1796 that was topped by a "liberty cap." It became even more prominent in France (Schlesinger 1952, 454), which did not have chattel slaves, whose owners might, like those in the United States, feel threatened by potential slave rebellions (Korshak 1987). This symbol had been borrowed from classical times, when it was used to symbolize freedom for a slave. The symbol was so powerful that Secretary of War Jefferson Davis (who would serve as president of the Confederate States of America) influenced a decision that resulted in the Statue of Freedom, which stands atop the Capitol Dome in Washington, D.C, wearing a helmet instead of this cap.

After the American Revolution, opponents of actions of the national government sometimes used the liberty pole, as during the Whiskey Rebellion and Fries Rebellion. Democratic-Republicans later used such poles to protest the Alien and Sedition Acts of 1798 (Smith 1955). Still later they were used in presidential elections, as when Andrew Jackson's supporters gathered round hickory poles and supporters of Henry Clay chose ash poles (Schlesinger 1952, 456). The practice of designating liberty trees or constructing liberty poles has largely died out, while flying the American flag has become increasingly ubiquitous.

The Museum of the American Revolution, which opened in Philadelphia on April 19, 2017, has an 18-foot-tall replica of America's first liberty tree in Boston.

See also Pine Tree Flag; Pledge of Allegiance; Revolutionary War Battle Flags

Further Reading

Harden, J. David. 1995. "Liberty Caps and Liberty Trees." *Past and Present*, no. 146, 66–102.

Korshak, Yvonne. 1987. "The Liberty Cap as a Revolutionary Symbol in America and France." *Smithsonian Studies in American Art* 1 (Autumn): 52–69.

Schlesinger, Arthur M. 1952. "Liberty Tree: A Genealogy." *New England Quarterly* 25 (December): 435–458.

Smith, James Morton. 1955. "The Federalist 'Saints' versus 'The Devil of Sedition': The Liberty Pole Cases of Dedham, Massachusetts, 1798–1799." *The New England Quarterly* 28 (June): 198–215.

LICENSE PLATES

States routinely issue license plates, primarily as proof that vehicles are registered and can be identified if they are involved in violating the law or in accidents. Such plates also become miniature traveling billboards that can be used to reinforce state and national identities.

States often issue standard or specialty license plates with representations or colors of the state and national flag. Sometimes these are disputed, as in the case of a Puerto Rican license that features both the U.S. and Puerto Rican flags (Lieb 2011, 32). License plates sometimes highlight historic celebrations and commemorations; thus, 18 states and the District of Columbia issued special plates for the bicentennial. Some states, most notably Indiana, have chosen license plates that combine both the motto "In God We Trust" and representations of the U.S. flag. Secular humanists in South Carolina received permission for a specialty license saying "In Reason We Trust" (32, 47).

In *Wooley v. Maynard*, 430 U.S. 705 (1977), the U.S. Supreme Court ruled that individuals could cover the words "Live Free or Die" on the New Hampshire license plate, and individuals could presumably also cover up other symbols other than the state name, which might be essential to vehicle identification. Despite the presence of such licenses in other states, the court ruled in *Walker v. Texas Division, Sons of Confederate Veterans*, 576 U.S. ____ (2015), that a state was not required to issue a specialty plate by the Sons of Confederate Veterans (SCV) featuring a Confederate flag. It did so on the basis that the license presented a type of governmental speech, which the state thus had the right to regulate as it chose.

See also Centennials, Bicentennials, and Other Commemorations; Confederate Flags

Further Reading

Billig, Michael. 1995. *Banal Nationalism*. London: Sage.

Lieb, Jonathan. 2011. "Identity, Banal Nationalism, Contestation, and North American License Plates." *The Geographical Review* 101 (January): 37–52.

LINCOLN, ABRAHAM

Although some presidents have done more to expand the number of stars on the flag, no president has done as much to preserve those that were there as Abraham Lincoln (1809–1865). He served as president from 1861 until his assassination in April 1865.

Lincoln was the 16th U.S. president and the first to be elected under the label of the Republican Party, which was formed out of the demise of the Whig Party and the division of the Democratic Party. Republicans took the position that slavery was a moral wrong that should not be permitted to spread in the territories. After his election, southern states began to assert their power to secede, and they fired on ships that sought to resupply Fort Sumter, off the coast of South Carolina, provoking a bloody Civil War.

In a speech that he gave at Lafayette, Indiana, on February 11, 1861, not long before his inauguration, Lincoln observed: "While some of us may differ in political opinions, still we are all united in one feeling for the Union. We all believe in the maintenance of the Union, [and] of every star and every stripe of the glorious flag" (Lincoln 1953, 4:192). On February 22, Lincoln appeared at Independence Hall in Philadelphia. There he announced in remarks to Theodore L. Cuyler, the president of the Select Council of Philadelphia, "I have never had a feeling politically that did not spring from the sentiments embodied in the Declaration of Independence" (4:240). Proceeding with more formal remarks to the audience in a flag-raising ceremony commemorating the addition of Kansas to the Union on January 29, 1861, Lincoln observed that "when that flag was originally raised here it had but thirteen stars." He continued:

Abraham Lincoln postcard commemorating the 100th anniversary of his birth. The Civil War did much to elevate the flag as a symbol of union. Confederate flags were less effective in rallying southerners to that cause. (John Vile)

> I wish to call your attention to the fact, that, under the blessing of God, each additional star added to that flag has given additional prosperity and happiness to this country until it has

> advanced to its present condition; and its welfare in the future, as well as in the past, is in your hands. Cultivating the spirit that animated our fathers, who gave renown and celebrity to this Hall, cherishing that fraternal feeling which has so long characterized us as a nation, excluding passion, ill-temper and precipitate action on all occasions, I think we may promise ourselves that not only the new star placed upon that flag shall be permitted to remain there to our permanent prosperity for years to come, but additional ones shall from time to time be placed there, until we shall number as was anticipated by the great historian, five hundred millions of happy and prosperous people. (4:141–242)

Fragments of this flag will be included (along with copies of the postbellum amendments) at a permanent exhibit and display funded by the Pew Charitable Trusts at the Constitution Center in Philadelphia.

Speaking later on January 29 to the Pennsylvania General Assembly in Harrisburg, Lincoln observed that in raising the flag, "I was a very humble instrument." He explained that:

> I had not provided the flag; I had not made the arrangement for elevating it to its place; I had applied but a very small portion of even my feeble strength in raising it. In the whole transaction, I was in the hands of the people who had arranged it, and if I can have the same generous co-operation of the people of this nation, I think the flag of our country may yet be kept flaunting gloriously. (4:245)

Lincoln expressed similar sentiments in raising a flag over a post office building on May 22, 1861 (4:383).

Thomas Nast visited Washington, D.C., at the time of Lincoln's inauguration and reported that there was a pall over the city with individuals snarling at one another. He further reports that it was broken the night of the inauguration when someone on the balcony of the Ebbitt House, directly opposite the Willard Hotel where he was staying, began to sing "The Star-Spangled Banner." According to Nast:

> The effect was magical, electrical. One window went up, and another, and heads popped out all over the neighborhood. People began to stir on the streets a Crowd soon gathered. The grand old song was taken up and sung by thousands.
>
> The spell was broken, and when the song was finished tongues were loosened, and cheers rent the air. (Fallows 1903, 63)

In an August 10, 1863, letter to a number of women in Philadelphia who had presented him with a flag, Lincoln observed the following:

> If anything could enhance to me the value of this representation of our national ensign, so elegantly executed and so gracefully bestowed, it would be the consideration that its price has been devoted to the comfort and restoration of those heroic men, who have suffered and bled in our flag's defense. We never should, and I am sure, never shall be niggard of gratitude and benefaction to the soldiers who have endured toil, privations and wounds, that the nation may live. (Lincoln 1953, 6:375–376)

Lincoln had opposed the exclusionary flag sentiments of the abolitionists, insisting that the conflict between North and South was a Civil War and not a War between the States (separate nation-states). So too was Lincoln adamant that because secession was illegal, the stars of the revolting states would not be removed. In words that may have proved prophetic, he observed, "I would rather be assassinated than remove stars from the flag" (quoted in Keim and Keim 2007, 114). Indeed, Lincoln was assassinated in Washington, D.C., on the same day that the American flag was being once again raised over Fort Sumter. As Lincoln lay dying on the floor, his head was cradled by an American flag.

The Lincoln Memorial in Washington, D.C., which features a giant sculpture by Daniel Chester French of Lincoln sitting in a chair, was the site of Marian Anderson's concert on Easter Sunday, 1939, and of Martin Luther King Jr.'s "I Have a Dream" speech on August 28, 1963. Congress added the words "under God," which Lincoln used in the concluding sentence of his Gettysburg Address, to the Pledge of Allegiance to the flag in 1954.

See also Beecher, Henry Ward; Civil War; Exclusionary Flags; Fort Sumter Flag; Lincoln Flag; Pledge of Allegiance

Further Reading

Fallows, Samuel, ed. 1903. *Story of the American Flag with Patriotic Selections and Incidents*. New York: Educational Publishing Company.

Keim, Kevin, and Peter Keim. 2007. *A Grand Old Flag: A History of the United States through Its Flags*. New York: DK.

Lincoln, Abraham. 1953. *The Collected Works of Abraham Lincoln*. Edited by Roy P. Basler. Vols. 4 and 6. New Brunswick, NJ: Rutgers University Press.

LINCOLN FLAG

Sometimes an ordinary flag can achieve an important place in the American mind because of its association with an extraordinary individual or event. This is certainly the case with respect to the 36-star flag now known as the Lincoln Flag.

According to the story that has most commonly surrounded the flag, it was initially used as bunting for the state box where Abraham Lincoln and his wife Mary sat as they watched *Our American Cousin* at Ford's Theatre on Good Friday, April 14, 1865, five days after Gen. Robert E. Lee had surrendered to Gen. Ulysses S. Grant at the Appomattox Court House.

Just after 10:00 p.m., as Lincoln watched the play, an actor named John Wilkes Booth entered the president's box and shot him in the back of the head. Charles Leale, a military physician, came to his aid and with the help with another doctor placed Lincoln on the floor, cushioning his head with Dr. Leale's handkerchief. After actress Laura Keene held Lincoln's head in her lap for some time, Thomas Gourlay, a stage manager and actor, folded the flag and placed it under Lincoln's head to cushion it. Ironically, Booth's escape was hindered when he caught his spur on a Treasury Guard Flag and broke his leg as he jumped from the President's box to the stage (this flag is currently exhibited in a museum in the basement of Ford's Theatre).

According to a long-accepted story, after Lincoln was transported across the street, Gourlay recovered the U.S. flag. He willed it to his daughter Jeannie Gourlay Struthers, who moved to Milford, Pennsylvania. She in turn willed it to her son, V. Paul Struthers, who donated the flag to the Milford Historical Society in 1954. This society now exhibits the flag at its Greek Revival home, known as "the Columns," which is located at 608 Broad Street.

The bloodstained flag was authenticated in a long report written by Joseph E. Garrera, then president of the Lincoln Group of New York, in 1996. The evidence that it was actually used to support Lincoln's head in his last moments, however, may not be as compelling as some claim. In 2015, Richard Smyth and Jim Garrett, who had previously researched Lincoln's assassination, noted that the Pike County Historical Society had fired its director Charles Clausen after he questioned the authenticity of the flag. They point out that the blood on the flag has not been specifically matched to Lincoln. They further say that reports that the flag had cushioned Lincoln's head did not emerge until many years later and is largely based on the family's oral history. They concluded that "in the end, the bloodied Lincoln Flag's history is either the genuine oral traditions held by a family for almost a century or a fabricated legend that later family members bought into" (2015, 65).

The Connecticut Historical Society houses another Treasury Guard Flag (it contains a flying eagle against a blue sky, surrounded by stars in the canton) that was in Ford's Theatre the night of Lincoln's assassination. In 1907, Henry A. Cobaugh, the head of Treasury Department security, passed the flag on to Edgar S. Yergason, a Civil War veteran and collector. His son, Dr. Robert M. Yergason, passed it to the Connecticut Historical Society in 1922. The flag was rediscovered in a box in 1998 and has now been restored. Ford's Theatre displays a similar Treasury Guard Flag.

The Chicago Historical Society stores yet another 34-star, 82-by-48-inch U.S. Army recruitment flag that is believed either to have been used to wrap Lincoln's body when it was transported from the Petersen House, where he died, to the White House or to have covered his coffin (Smyth and Garrett 2015, 82–83). Numerous flags were used on Lincoln's funeral train and in connection with commemorations surrounding his death.

Further Reading

Connecticut Historical Society. 2015. "A National Treasure Rediscovered." Last modified February 12. https://chs.org/2015/02/lincolnflag/

Coup, Jeannine. 2002. "The 'Lincoln Flag.'" The Political Bandwagon. Last modified May. http://thepoliticalbandwagon.com/articles/2002May.html

Ford's Theatre. 2017. "Treasury Guard Flag Decorating Lincoln's Box." Accessed February 17. https://www.fords.org/lincolns-assassination/treasury-guard-flag-decorating-lincolns-box/

Gallagher, Brian K. "The Lincoln Flag." April 10, 2012. http://ezinearticles.com/?The-Lincoln-Flag&id=6993406

Pike County Historical Society at the Columns. "The Lincoln Flag." Accessed 05/01/2018. http://pikehistorical.org/exhibits/the-lincoln-flag/

Smyth, Richard, and Jim Garrett. 2005. *The Lincoln Assassination: The Flags of Ford's Theatre*. U.S. Case Book Press.

LIVING FLAG

See Human Flag

LODGE, HENRY CABOT

Love for one's country does not necessarily equate to hatred for that of others, but to the degree that one elevates one's own nation and its ideals over others', it might become difficult to show similar respect for foreign countries, peoples, and ideals.

Sen. Henry Cabot Lodge (1859–1924) provides a sterling example of this potential. A Republican U.S. senator from Massachusetts and a friend of Theodore Roosevelt, Lodge was often quoted for his praise of the flag. He earned a PhD in history from Harvard University and served as Senate Majority leader and as chair of the Senate Foreign Relations Committee during his tenure in the Senate. A strong supporter of American imperial policies in the Spanish-American War and an advocate of restricting immigration, especially by southern Europeans and non-whites, Lodge criticized President Wilson for military weakness and then opposed both the Treaty of Versailles that Wilson helped negotiate to end the war and Wilson's plan for the United States to enter the League of Nations.

Influential Republican senator Henry Cabot Lodge from Massachusetts was a strong advocate of U.S. expansionism and urged U.S. intervention in Cuba. Referring with disgust to a "mongrel" flag at the end of World War I, Lodge disparaged the League of Nations that Woodrow Wilson had advocated as a means of avoiding future wars. (Library of Congress)

In a frequently quoted speech that he gave in Washington, D.C., on August 12, 1919, Lodge denied that there was any country in the world that could compare to the "ordered liberty" and "freedom" of the United States. He continued by observing, "I have always loved one flag and I cannot share that devotion [with] a mongrel banner created for a League." Recognizing that some might call him "selfish," "conservative," or "reactionary," Lodge said, "I must think of the United States first," in part because it carried "the best hopes of mankind" with it.

Reflecting great fear of internationalism in foreign affairs, Lodge observed:

> I have never had but one allegiance—I cannot divide it now. I have loved but one

> flag and I cannot share that devotion and give affection to the mongrel banner invented for a league. Internationalism, illustrated by the Bolshevik and by the men to whom all countries are alike provided they can make money out of them, is to me repulsive.

Lodge further contrasted his own realistic policy with what he considered the "visionary" dreams of Wilson and others.

Much like President Washington had done in his *Farewell Address*, Lodge warned about entangling alliances. Lodge argued that if the United States joined the League, its politics would be "distracted and embittered by the dissentions of other lands." He also feared that the American people would be unwilling to send troops to support League of Nations commitments, thus eroding American credibility (Hewes 1970, 245).

Ironically, the League of Nations never adopted an official flag. Its successor, the United Nations, which has its headquarters in New York City, adopted a blue flag, which highlights a world map with white continents surrounded by two white olive branches. The flag is displayed slightly apart from those of the other 193 nation-states in front of the U.N. Headquarters in New York City.

See also Spanish-American War; World War I

Further Reading

Endrst, Elsa B. 1992. "So Proudly They Wave . . . Flags of the United Nations." *UN Chronicle*, December, 74–75. https://www.questia.com/magazine/1G1-13344189/so-proudly-they-wave-flags-of-the-united-nations

Hewes, James E., Jr. 1970. "Henry Cabot Lodge and the League of Nations." *Proceedings of the American Philosophical Society* 114 (August 20): 245–255.

Lodge, Henry Cabot. 2017. "Henry Cabot Lodge on the League of Nations, 12 August 1919." FirstWorldWar.com. Accessed April 4. http://www.firstworldwar.com/source/lodge_leagueofnations.htm

"LONG MAY IT (SHE) WAVE"

The second stanza of "The Star-Spangled Banner," which was authored by Francis Scott Key and which has been designated as the national anthem, ends with the following lines:

> 'Tis the Star-Spangled Banner, O Long may it wave
> O'er the land of the free and the home of the brave.

"Long may it wave" has since become a common phrase associated with the American flag.

A waving flag almost always evokes more emotion than one that is not, perhaps in part because such movement gives the impression that the flag is alive. Consistent with early representations of America as a woman (Columbia, Pocahontas, and Lady Liberty), today it appears more common to say "long may she wave"—as in Ray Stevens's song "Stand Up," when he asks:

Do you stand for Old Glory?
Long may she wave.

This feminine usage thus further identifies the flag as a living thing.

It is not uncommon, however, to question whether those individuals waving the flag (like those who figuratively are said to wrap themselves in the flag) are more patriotic than those going about the business of the nation.

A 1914 silent film comedy entitled *Long May It Wave* featured Oliver Hardy as a drunken man who has taken his wife to a play—possibly George M. Cohan's *George Washington, Jr*, which featured the song "You're A Grand Old Flag." Although the play resolves most issues by waving the flag, the husband finds that he is not as successful at placating his wife at home by employing the same tactic.

See also National Anthem; "Star-Spangled Banner" (Anthem); "You're a Grand Old Flag"

Further Reading

Ferris, Marc. 2017. "'Long May It Wave.'" The American Legion. Accessed April 24. https://www.legion.org/magazine/224572/long-may-it-wave

"MAN WITHOUT A COUNTRY"

One of the most emotional stories that has stoked love of the flag is Edward Everett Hale's "The Man without a Country." Hale was a Unitarian minister who lived from 1822 to 1909. His fictional story, written in 1863 when many people were weary of the Civil War, was printed in many school texts and was long thought by many people to be true. It tells the tale of Philip Nolan, an American naval officer who after being caught up in Aaron Burr's scheme to create a new America in the South and Southwest proclaimed at his trial, "Damn the United States! I wish I may never hear of the United States again!"

A judge gave him his wish, and Nolan was transported from port to port but was forced to remain aboard ship with a crew that was ordered never to mention America to him again. It was not until his deathbed that a friend finally told him how the nation had progressed from the days of the Jefferson administration to that of Andrew Jackson. When the friend entered Nolan's stateroom, he found that Nolan had created "a little shrine" in his room. Hale explained: "The stars and stripes were traced up above and around a picture of Washington, and he had painted a majestic eagle, with lightning blazing from his beak and his foot just clasping the whole globe, which his wings overshadowed."

Nolan was thrilled to learn that the flag now had 34 stars and wanted to know the name of each new state and when it had been admitted. He had guessed that Kentucky, Michigan, Indiana, Mississippi, and Ohio had been admitted, but he did not know the names of the other "fourteen" (Hale may have been a bit confused since Kentucky and Vermont had been the 14th and 15th states, which were commemorated on the flag from 1795–1818), the time during which the judge would have imposed Nolan's penalty.

In the story, Nolan left instructions that he be buried at sea but that a plaque be set up "at Fort Adams or at Orleans" with his name and rank and the words "He loved his country as no other man has loved her; but no man deserved less at her hands."

See also Civil War

Further Reading

Hale, Edward Everett. 1863. "The Man without a Country." *The Atlantic*, December. http://www.theatlantic.com/magazine/archive/1863/12/the-man-without-a country/308751/

Quaife, Milo M., Melvin J. Weig, and Roy E. Appleman. 1961. *The History of the United States Flag from the Revolution to the Present, Including a Guide to Its Use and Display*. New York: Harper and Brothers.

MASTAI, BOLESLAW, AND MARIE-LOUISE D'OTRANGE

Boleslaw Mastai (1904–2002) and Marie-Louise D'Otrange Mastai (1920–2001) were a married couple who amassed an impressive collection of American flags over the course of their lives together. Their flags are now part of the Zaricor Flag Collection, the largest collection of U.S. and foreign flags in the world. Boleslaw was born in Cracow, Poland, and immigrated to the United States, where he founded and edited *Mastai's National Directory of the U.S. Art and Antique Trade*. His wife, a native of Louisiana, was a writer and painter and one-time curator of the Parrish Art Museum in Southampton, New York.

The Mastais published a volume in 1973 that not only highlighted color photographs of their extensive flag collection but also provided considerable text giving the historical background of individual flags. The Mastais had one of the world's largest collections of Revolutionary War flags.

See also Keim, Peter; Zaricor Flag Collection

Further Reading

Martucci, David. 2000. "The 13 Stars and Stripes: A Survey of 18th Century Images." *NAVA News*, April–June. Addenda published in *NAVA News* in July–September 2000, April–June 2003, and October–December 2005.

Mastai, Boleslaw, and Marie-Louise D'Otrange. 1973. *The Stars and the Stripes: The American Flag as Art and as History from the Birth of the Republic to the Present*. New York: Alfred A. Knopf.

MEMORIAL DAY

See Decoration Day (Memorial Day)

MENNONITES AND AMISH

Heirs of the Anabaptist tradition, Mennonites and Amish often came to the United States to escape religious persecution in Europe. Different groups accept varying degrees of technology and adaptation to modern dress. They often wear black, and women in their communities typically keep their heads covered in accord with what they believe to be Biblical commands. Mennonites and Amish typically are not actively involved in American politics.

Although they are otherwise more theologically orthodox, Mennonites, like Jehovah's Witnesses (who would later adjudicate numerous cases related to religious freedom before the U.S. Supreme Court), are overwhelmingly pacifist. In part because they sometimes associate the American flag with militarism, they typically refuse to salute the flag, although it is displayed in some Mennonite churches and on some Mennonite campuses (Ottoson 2010, 690, 692). When the draft was in effect for military service, Mennonites worked out an alternate service plan with the government so they would not be called upon to fight.

Many Mennonites, like Quakers, were active in the antiwar movement during the Vietnam War era. In *Wisconsin v. Yoder*, 406 U.S. 205 (1972), Amish parents won the right to stop the formal education of their children in school after the eighth grade, but in *United States v. Lee*, 455 U.S. 252 (1982), they were denied an exemption from contributing to Social Security on behalf of their employees.

See also Jehovah's Witnesses; Vietnam War

Further Reading

Ottoson, Robin Deich. 2010. "The Battle Over the Flag: Protest, Community Opposition, and Silence in the Mennonite Colleges in Kansas during the Vietnam War." *Journal of Church and State* 52 (Autumn): 686–711.

MEXICAN-AMERICAN WAR

The Mexican-American War (1846–1848) followed America's 1845 annexation of Texas, which had previously been an independent republic, and President James K. Polk's subsequent decision to place American troops in disputed territory claimed by both Mexico and the United States. In addition to securing disputed territory in Texas, the war also resulted in the Treaty of Guadalupe Hidalgo, which ceded 525,000 square miles of territory, including all or part of New Mexico, Arizona, Colorado, Nevada, Utah, and California to the United States. The treaty thus became an important landmark in furthering American dreams of its "manifest destiny"—the expansion of its territorial reach to the Pacific.

Abraham Lincoln was among those who opposed the war, in part because he believed Polk was the provocateur (Vile 2017, 131–133). He probably also feared—like other congressional proponents of the Wilmot Proviso (1846), which would have prohibited the expansion of slavery into any territories acquired as a result of the war—that its acquisitions would further expand the reach of slavery. Similarly, Henry David Thoreau refused to pay a poll tax that was being used to support the war. Nonetheless, the war appears to have been fairly popular with the American public, which was generally supportive of measures to increase the nation's landholdings for economic development.

The Mexican-American War marked the first time that U.S. troops regularly marched into battle under the American flag rather than regimental colors, which they had used in previous military conflicts. In fact, by the time the Mexican-American War erupted, as O'Leary notes, "the association of patriotism with military expansion, masculinity, and the flag resonated broadly." Discussing the effect of the war, O'Leary further observes, "Consecrated in the blood of battle, soldiers and citizens alike began to look at the Stars and Stripes as the symbolic repository of their patriotic sentiments" (O'Leary 1999, 21–22). Demand for American flags became so intense that in 1847, the Annin Company of New York became the first ever company to mass produce flags.

American military victories from this war continue to be celebrated in the "Marines' Hymn." Its reference to the Halls of Montezuma is a reference to the Battle of Chapultepec, where U.S. Marines stormed a Mexican castle. The second stanza to the hymn observes, "Our flag's unfurled to every breeze/ From dawn to setting sun."

U.S. Army troops under General Winfield Scott land at Vera Cruz, Mexico, in March 1847, during the Mexican-American War. This was the first conflict in which American troops regularly marched into battle under the U.S. flag rather than under regimental colors. (Library of Congress)

A hand-colored lithograph from the war by Louis Nagel entitled *Death of Major Ringgold, of the Flying Artillery, at the Battle of Palo Alto, May 8, 1846*, is notable for depicting a flag that contains 23 six-pointed stars arranged in two concentric ovals (Furlong and McCandless 1981, 196–197). As noted above, as a result of the war, the U.S. would eventually add the southwestern states of Arizona, California, Colorado, Nevada, New Mexico, and Utah. Walt Whitman thus correctly predicted that the war would "furnish a cluster of new stars for the spangled banner" (quoted in Boime 1998, 20).

Some of the military leaders who served during the Mexican-American War would later fight under separate flags during the Civil War. Jefferson Davis had been among the war's heroes. O'Leary notes that when they met at Appomattox to end the Civil War, Gen. Ulysses S. Grant helped break the silence with Gen. Robert E. Lee by reminding him that they had first served together in Mexico. Officers from the two sides who had served in this war subsequently sought out one another (O'Leary 1999, 118).

See also Civil War; Flag Manufacturers Association of America; Lincoln, Abraham

Further Reading

Boime, Albert. 1998. *The Unveiling of National Icons: A Plea for Patriotic Iconoclasm in a Nationalist Era*. New York: Cambridge University Press.

Furlong, William Rea, and Byron McCandless. 1981. *So Proudly We Hail: The History of the United States Flag*. Washington, D.C.: Smithsonian Institution Press.
O'Leary, Cecilia Elizabeth. 1999. *To Die For: The Paradox of American Patriotism*. Princeton, NJ: Princeton University Press.
Vile, John R. 2017. *The Jacksonian and Antebellum Eras, Documents Decoded*. Santa Barbara, CA: ABC-CLIO.

MINERSVILLE SCHOOL DISTRICT V. GOBITIS (1940)

The U.S. Supreme Court decision in *Minersville v. Gobitis*, 310 U.S. 586 (1940), continues to be one of the most controversial in its history. The case orbited around William and Lillian Gobitis, who were 10 and 12 years old, respectively, when they were expelled from school for refusing to salute the U.S. flag as part of a daily school exercise. At the time, this would have involved repeating the words of the pledge (which then referred to "my flag" and did not include the words "under God") with students extending their right hand toward the flag. The children did not participate because they were Jehovah's Witnesses, whose religious beliefs include the conviction that saluting the flag is equivalent to bowing down to a graven image. The U.S. District Court and the Third Circuit Court of Appeals had both upheld the children's right to refuse to participate on the basis of the due process clause of the Fourteenth Amendment, which had been held to incorporate the protections for freedom of speech and religion against state laws. As in other states, Pennsylvania state law mandated that children their age be in school.

Justice Felix Frankfurter, who was a great advocate of judicial restraint, authored the Supreme Court's eight-to-one decision upholding the school system's mandatory flag salute. Acknowledging broad constitutional protection for religious belief, Frankfurter observed that "the religious liberty which the Constitution protects has never excluded legislation of general scope not directed against doctrinal loyalties of particular sects." Moreover, he noted other cases, including *Hamilton v. Regents* (1934), in which the court had failed to exempt students (in that case, college students) from mandatory military training.

Pennsylvania obviously thought that the Pledge of Allegiance promoted "national cohesion," which Frankfurter identified as "an interest inferior to none in the hierarchy of legal values." He further observed that "national unity is the basis of national security" and cited a dilemma of Lincoln's: "Must a government of necessity be too strong for the liberties of its people, or too weak to maintain its own existence?"

Frankfurter observed that governments "presuppose the existence of an organized political society" and that the "binding tie of cohesive sentiment . . . is fostered by all those agencies of the mind and spirit which may serve to gather up the traditions of a people, transmit them from generation to generation, and thereby create that continuity of a treasured common life which constitutes a civilization." He continued: "'We live by symbols.' The flag is the symbol of our national unity, transcending all internal differences, however large, within the framework of the Constitution."

Frankfurter did not think that "the wisdom of training children in patriotic impulses" was an appropriate matter for judicial review and observed that parents opposed to compulsory flag salutes had the option of sending their children to private schools.

Justice (later Chief) Harlan Fiske Stone authored the solitary dissent. He noted that the children who refused to salute the flag were doing so out of genuine religious convictions. Classifying the Pennsylvania law as "unique in the history of Anglo-American legislation," he noted that it not only prohibited the free exercise of religion but sought "to coerce these children to express a sentiment which, as they interpret it, they do not entertain, and which violates their deepest religious convictions." He lauded the "guaranties of civil liberty" as "guaranties of freedom of the human mind and spirit and of reasonable freedom and opportunity to express them." Such liberties included "the freedom of the individual from compulsion as to what he shall think and what he shall say." He further questioned whether compelled speech would engender the same feelings of patriotism as speech voluntarily offered.

Stone's decision in *U.S. v. Carolene Products* (1938) had contained his famous "Footnote Four," which showed particular concern for the protection of fundamental rights and the rights of "discrete and insular minorities." Stone thought that both were at issue in this case. He observed that the Constitution is "an expression of faith and a command that freedom of mind and spirit must be preserved, which government must obey, if it is to adhere to that justice and moderation without which no free government can exist."

The decision in this case unleashed nationwide violence against the Jehovah's Witnesses (Peters 2000, 72–152). In 1943, the court overturned the decision in *West Virginia State Board of Education v. Barnette* (1943).

See also Jehovah's Witnesses; Pledge of Allegiance; *West Virginia State Board of Education v. Barnette* (1943)

Further Reading

DiAgostino, Grace. 2016. "Pledging Allegiance: Negotiating National Responsibility, Religious Liberty, and the First Amendment." *Social Education* 80 (September): 219–223.

Ellis, Richard J. 2005. *To the Flag: The Unlikely History of the Pledge of Allegiance*. Lawrence: University Press of Kansas.

"The Flag Salute." (Editorial) 1943. *Journal of the National Educational Association* 32 (December): 265–266.

Peters, Shawn Francis. 2000. *Judging Jehovah's Witnesses: Religious Persecution and the Dawn of the Rights Revolution*. Lawrence: University Press of Kansas.

N

NATIONAL ANTHEM

It took more than 100 years between the time that Francis Scott Key wrote "The Star-Spangled Banner" in 1814 and the time that President Herbert Hoover signed a law designated this song as the national anthem in 1931. (President Wilson had previously designated it as the anthem for the armed forces.) Much of the effort to so designate the song was spearheaded by veterans' organizations like the Grand Army of the Republic (GAR) and the Veterans of Foreign Wars (VFW) as well as by hereditary associations such as the Daughters of the American Revolution (DAR) and the Sons of the American Revolution (SAR).

There were numerous other songs that had been suggested for the national anthem and that were sometimes used for ceremonial events prior to the designation of "The Star-Spangled Banner." The central contenders were "Hail, Columbia," "Columbia, the Gem of the Ocean," "Yankee Doodle," "My Country, 'Tis of Thee," "America the Beautiful," "God Bless America," "The Battle Hymn of the Republic," and "Dixie."

"Hail, Columbia," which was used as the presidential anthem before being replaced by "Hail to the Chief," now serves as the anthem for the vice president. Written by Philip Phile for George Washington's first inauguration in 1789, the song describes America (personified by Columbia) as a "happy land" and lauds "Washington's great name," without mentioning the U.S. flag. It was particularly popular in the 19th century.

"Columbia, the Gem of the Ocean," was authored by Thomas A. Becket Sr. in 1843 and probably comes as close as any other contender in its focus on the flag. Its second line borrows from "The Star-Spangled Banner" by specifically referencing "The home of the brave and the free." Other lines speak of the nation's "banners" and of "the red, white, and blue." It also references the nation's "Army and Navy," which might have enhanced its popularity among members of the armed forces.

"Yankee Doodle" has an older vintage, dating back to the Revolutionary War. The tune is catchy, but the lyrics do more to laud homespun American ingenuity than national symbols.

"My Country, 'Tis of Thee" was written by Samuel Francis Smith in 1831 and is much easier for most people to sing than "The Star-Spangled Banner." One liability of this song is that it is to the tune of "God Save the Queen," which the British use as their national anthem.

Katharine Lee Bates, an English professor at Wellesley, wrote "America the Beautiful" in 1893 after visiting the World's Columbian Exposition ("thine alabaster cities") and Pikes Peak ("purple mountain majesties"). Samuel A. Ward supplied a tune based on "O Mother Dear Jerusalem."

"God Bless America," a favorite authored by Irving Berlin in 1918 and popularized by Kate Smith after it was revised in 1938, achieved admiration too late to be considered as the national anthem (Hutchinson 2014). Far less militaristic than "The Star-Spangled Banner," it takes the form of a prayer that God will bless the nation and does not mention its flag. It may be the most religiously oriented of the songs that have been in contention for the national anthem.

In 1940, Woody Guthrie composed "This Land Is Your Land" as an alternative—but after the national anthem had already been designated. His most controversial verse, which is usually omitted, denigrated private property by noting that the back of a "No Trespassing" sign, which said nothing, "was made for you and me." It also made a fairly awkward reference to hungry people waiting at a relief office.

Julia Ward Howe (who also wrote a popular poem entitled "The Flag") wrote "The Battle Hymn of the Republic" in 1861 to the tune of "John Brown's Body." Both songs were popular among Union soldiers but not those in the South.

"Dixie" originated from blackface minstrel shows in the 1850s, and while popular in both the North and South, it was more successful in unifying southerners than northerners. Unlike "The Star-Spangled Banner," it did not specifically mention the flag. "Dixie" eventually became the unofficial anthem of the South, although it received some competition from "The Bonnie Blue Flag," which Harry Macarthy wrote after the president of the Mississippi Secession Convention was handed a blue flag with a white star (but which did not otherwise resemble any of the Confederate flags that were actually adopted). "Maryland, My Maryland," which was written by James Ryder Randall after reports that the 6th Massachusetts had killed Confederate sympathizers in a Maryland mob, was also fairly popular as a southern anthem, although insufficient to entice that state to join the Confederacy (McWhirter 2012, 79–82).

George M. Cohan's "You're a Grand Old Flag," which was written for his musical *George Washington, Jr.* in 1906, combines references to "Yankee Doodle," "Dixie," and "Auld Lang Syne," as well as to Uncle Sam. Like John Philip Sousa's "Stars and Stripes Forever," Cohan's tune explicitly references the U.S. flag.

Of all of these songs, "The Star-Spangled Banner" was most closely tied to a specific historical event. Its eyewitness testimony to an American flag waving after a dramatic battle may have contributed to its popularity with the public.

See also Grand Army of the Republic (GAR); Key, Francis Scott; "Star-Spangled Banner" (Anthem); "Stars and Stripes Forever"; Veterans of Foreign Wars (VFW); "You're a Grand Old Flag"

Further Reading

Cerulo, Karen A. 1989. "Sociopolitical Control and the Structure of National Symbols: An Empirical Analysis of National Anthems." *Social Forces* 68 (September): 76–99.

Cerulo, Karen A. 1993. "Symbols and the World System: National Anthems and Flags." *Sociological Forum* 8:243–271.

Ferris, Marc. 2014. *Star-Spangled Banner: The Unlikely Story of America's National Anthem*. Baltimore: Johns Hopkins University Press.
Hutchinson, Lydia. 2014. "Irving Berlin's 'God Bless America.'" Performing Songwriter. Last modified May 11. http://performingsongwriter.com/god-bless-america/
McWhirter, Christian. 2012. *Battle Hymns: The Power and Popularity of Music in the Civil War*. Chapel Hill: University of North Carolina Press.
Molotsky, Irvin. 2001. *The Flag, the Poet and the Song: The Story of the Star-Spangled Banner*. New York: Dutton.
Svejda, George J. 1969. *History of the Star-Spangled Banner from 1814 to the Present*. Washington, D.C.: National Park Service, U.S. Department of the Interior.
Taylor, Lonn, Kathleen M. Kendrick, and Jeffrey L. Brodie. 2008. *The Star-Spangled Banner: The Making of an American Icon*. Washington, D.C.: Smithsonian Books.

NATIONAL FLAG FOUNDATION (NFF)

The National Flag Foundation (NFF), which is located in Pittsburgh, Pennsylvania, is a nonprofit organization that was founded in 1968 by George F. Cahill, a World War II veteran previously associated with the Boy Scouts. Its mission is to promote "a deeper appreciation of our Nation's founding principles and its first and principal emblem, the Flag of the United States of America, by serving as a primary resource for patriotic and Flag Education" (Great Nonprofits 2017). Its national headquarters in Pittsburgh's Flag Plaza is the home of a *Flags of America* art collection.

The National Flag Foundation website (2017) describes its goals as follows:

> Encourage understanding and respect for the Flag
> Highlight the historic and factual as well as the symbolic and emotional aspects of our Flag
> Make the Flag a more significant part of contemporary culture conversation and media.

The organization targets schoolchildren with Young Patriots multimedia programs and organizes Flags across America sites. The organization has been described by one historian as "the twenty-first-century equivalent of [James A.] Moss's United States Flag Association" (Leepson 2005, 203).

See also United States Flag Association

Further Reading

Great Nonprofits. 2017. "National Flag Foundation." Accessed January 28. http://greatnonprofits.org/org/national-flag-foundation
Leepson, Marc. 2005. *Flag: An American Biography*. New York: St. Martin's Press.
National Flag Foundation. 2017. "Raising the Standard." Accessed January 28. http://www.nationalflagfoundation.org/about/

NATIVE AMERICAN ART

Native American carvings, pottery, and other objects are prized by collectors. Beadwork is particularly prominent in some tribes, including those of the Plains Indians. Although as many as 40 tribes have included flag imagery in their arts, and particularly in their beadwork, the large majority of such items are attributed to the Lakota.

Schmittou and Logan have divided Native American perspectives on the symbolism of the U.S. flag into four time periods, which they identify as "contact–1849, 1850–90, 1890–1916, and 1917 to the present" (2002, 562). During the first period, when American officials presented flags as gifts or when flags may have been captured in battle, they appear to have been highly valued and even considered to be magic. During the second period, which involved diplomacy and conflict, the flag was often the symbol of Native American enemies who would have carried such flags into battle. The third period was marked by the advent of Wild West shows and Independence Day celebrations, which would have increased Native American exposure to the flag. The fourth period, beginning with World War I, marked increased Native American participation in the U.S. military and pride in their battlefield achievements.

Much of the trade in Native American art would have been determined by market demand, and Americans increasingly came to cherish the American flag in the period from the Civil War forward. As a result, some Native Americans incorporated the flag into their art during this period. Schmittou and Logan believe that as former enemies who had defeated the U.S. at the Battle of Little Big Horn, Lakota may also have regarded it as a way to curry favor with whites or to demonstrate their own devotion to the nation, even prior to the time that many made a name for themselves by participating in the U.S. Armed Forces. They point out that Chief Red Cloud sometimes used the flag as a shawl and that his house contained flags as well as images of Jesus and the Virgin Mary.

One fascinating aspect of Lakota beadwork involving flags is that a fair number of works display American flags upside down, at half-staff, or with different colors. Given the usual Lakota attention to detail, Logan and Schmittou (2007) hypothesize that these images may have been an internal code language to express their feelings of mourning, distress, or mistreatment.

See also Flag Apparel; Half-Staff

Further Reading

Herbst, Tony, and Joel Kopp. 1993. *The Flag in American Indian Art*. Cooperstown, NY: New York State Historical Association and University of Washington Press.

Logan, Michael H., and Douglas A. Schmittou. 2007. *Plains Anthropologist* 52 (May): 209–227.

Powell, Timothy B. 1999. "Narratives Woven in Beads: Reading the Material Culture of the Sioux at the Height of the Ghost Dance." *Multiculturalism and Narrative* 7 (May): 131–146.

Schmittou, Douglas A., and Michael H. Logan. 2002. "Fluidity of Meaning: Flag Imagery in Plains Indian Art." *American Indian Quarterly* 26 (Autumn): 559–604.

NEW YORK CITY FIREMEN PHOTOGRAPH

One of the most traumatic events in recent U.S. history was the terrorist attack on the New York World Trade Center on September 11, 2001, that resulted in about 3,000 deaths.

One of the iconic images that emerged from this disaster was a photo taken by Thomas Franklin that showed three New York City firemen raising the colorful American flag against a mound of gray rubble in the background. The firemen appear to have taken the flag from a yacht that was moored at a small marina just west of Lower Manhattan when the World Trade Center attacks took place (Guerre 2016).

The firemen—George Johnson, Dan McWilliams, and Billy Eisengrein—were all white. As in Joe Rosenthal's famous photograph of soldiers raising the flag at Iwo Jima, in Franklin's image the three firemen, together with the pipe that forms the pole, provide a triangular focus to the picture. Scholar Woden Teachout has observed that in contrast to the sense of victory evoked by the Iwo Jima photograph, the 9/11 photo focuses on "civil servants" rather than "soldiers" and "is an image of a country united not in war but in rebuilding" (2009, 219–220). Historian Louis Masur further observes that "there is a religious sensibility to the image, the twisted steel seeming to form a cathedral and suggesting the shape of a cross (2008, 177).

The development firm Forest City Ratner subsequently commissioned a statue of the photograph, which it planned to display at the headquarters of the New York City Fire Department. The artist who was commissioned decided to portray one of the men as Hispanic and another as African American in an attempt to stress the contributions that all Americans had made to the tragedy. This led to criticism that the sculptor was sacrificing authenticity for political correctness, and the project was canceled.

In response to the terrorist attacks and the later invasion of Iraq, many Americans began flying flags. The Sunday after 9/11, a group climbed a 13,000-foot Colorado mountain to mount a 10-by-16-foot flag on its peak (Johnson et al. 2011). Others followed. In time, one of the flags was burned, and a note was left behind expressing opposition to the invasion of Iraq.

These incidents reveal the way that art involving the American flag can bring solace but also provoke conflict during times of national crisis.

A flag that was believed to be the one that the fireman raised flew over a 9/11 prayer service at Yankee Stadium and over the aircraft carrier USS *Roosevelt*, but that turns out to have been a somewhat larger flag (Feyerick 2016). After CNN aired a film entitled *The Missing Flag* in 2013, an individual who said that he was a retired Marine named Brian came to a fire station in Everett, Washington, with a flag that he claimed had been given to him by the widow of a New York firefighter. Forensic tests and photographic comparison later confirmed this to be the original flag in the photograph. It is now displayed at the National September 11 Memorial and Museum. The flag's recovery was documented on a History Channel special on the 15th anniversary of the 9/11 attacks.

Six months after the 9/11 attacks, President George W. Bush hosted the firemen at the Oval Office, where he unveiled a 45-cent stamp of them raising the flag (Mortensen 2013, 26). Apparently, fearing that the photo overly simplified the event, the creative director of the National September 11 Memorial and Museum initially decided not to include the photo in its exhibits, but later relented (Chumley 2013).

In 2017, during an outbreak of wildfires in California, Josh Edelson took a picture of two firemen lifting a third to remove a flag flying from a luxury home in the town of Oroville. They appear to be either trying to save it or to prevent it from serving as a source of ignition for blowing embers (Coleman 2017). The entire picture is tinted with orange smoke, which obscures all the colors except for the red and white stripes of the flag.

See also Iwo Jima Flag Raising; Terrorist Attacks of September 11, 2001

Further Reading

Chumley, Cheryl K. 2013. "U.S. Flag Photo Nearly Cut from 9/11 Museum, Deemed Too Patriotic, Books Says." *Washington Times,* July 29. http://www.washingtontimes.com/news/2013/jul/29/us-flag-photo-nearly-cut-911-museum

Coleman, Nancy. 2017. "Surrounded by Flames, California Firefighters Rescue US Flag from Wildfire." CNN.com, July 10. http://www.cnn.com/2017/07/10/us/california-wildfires-firefighter-photo-trnd/index.html

Feyerick, Deborah. 2016. "Iconic 9/11 Flag, Missing for Years, Returns to New York City." CNN.com, September 9. http://www.cnn.com/2016/09/09/us/ground-zero-flag-returns/

Guerre, Kristine. 2016. "The Iconic 9/11 Flag That Disappeared 15 Years Ago Has Been Found—Nearly 3,000 Miles Away." *Washington Post*, September 8.

Johnson, Kirk, et al. 2011. "Across the Nation, Tragedy Spawned Inspiration." *New York Times*, September 11. http://www.nytimes.com/2011/09/12/us/12vignettes.html

Marling, Karal Ann. 2001. "ART/ARCHITECTURE; Salve for a Wounded People." *New York Times,* October 14.

Masur, Louis P. 2008. *The Soiling of Old Glory: The Story of a Photograph That Shocked America*. New York: Bloomsbury Press.

McPhee, Michele. 2002. "FDNY Cancels 9/11 Statue Commish to Rethink Memorial after Flap over Race." *The New York Times*, January 18.

Mortensen, Mette. 2013. "The Making and Remakings of an American Icon: 'Raising the Flag on Iwo Jima' from Photojournalism to Global, Digital Media." In *Eastwood's Iwo Jima: Critical Engagements with Flags of Our Fathers and Letters from Iwo Jima*, edited by Rikke Schubart and Anne Gjelsik, 15–35. New York: Columbia University Press.

Teachout, Woden. 2009. *Capture the Flag: A Political History of American Patriotism*. New York: Basic Books.

Willis, Susan. 2002. "Old Glory." *The South Atlantic Quarterly* 101:375–383.

NICKNAMES FOR THE U.S. FLAG

Although the Pledge of Allegiance refers to "the flag of the United States of America" (the original version directed itself to "my flag"), throughout its life, the American flag has acquired a number of nicknames. Each reflects a different aspect of its history.

As with other flags, people sometimes refer to the U.S. flag as an ensign or standard; the first is a reference to a flag on a ship and the second to a flag indicating the presence of a leader. The flag may also be referred to, somewhat generically, as a banner, as in Frederick Edwin Church's oil *Our Banner in the Sky*.

Although the American flag's combination of colors are not unique, individuals sometimes use "the Red, White, and Blue" as an identifying phrase for the flag. It is thus common to have flag bearers make a "presentation of colors" at formal ceremonies such as convocations or graduations or even at sports events.

"The Star-Spangled Banner," also the name of the national anthem written by Francis Scott Key during the War of 1812, is another popular designation for the flag. Although the term "spangled" is used relatively rarely outside such a context, this appellation directs attention to the flag's derivation from the idea that America was a new political constellation (Shalev 2011).

The term "Stars and Stripes" is one that calls attention to the most prominent visual elements in the flag. John Philip Sousa incorporated this designation in "The Stars and Stripes Forever," which has since been designated as the national march.

"Old Glory" is another nickname. This term derives from the name that retired ship captain William Driver gave to an American flag that he flew around the world and later protected during the Civil War. Stanley Forman entitled an iconic photograph of a Boston racist using a flag staff to attack an African American attorney as *The Soiling of Old Glory*.

In 1885, Lt. James S. Ostrander gave a speech in which he simply referred to "the Old Flag." Henry Cuyler Bunner wrote a poem with the same name (Harrison 1914, 279). George M. Cohan referred in his play *George Washington, Jr.* to "a Grand Old Flag."

See also Colors of the Flag; Confederate Flags; National Anthem; Old Glory Flag; Ostrander, James S.; *Our Banner in the Sky*; Pledge of Allegiance; *Soiling of Old Glory, The* (Photograph); "Stars and Stripes Forever"; "There's a Star-Spangled Banner Waving Somewhere"; "You're a Grand Old Flag"

Further Reading

Harrison, Peleg D. 1914. *The Stars and Stripes and Other American Flags*. 5th ed. Boston: Little, Brown, and Company.

Shalev, Eran. 2011. "'A Republic Amidst the Stars' Political Astronomy and the Intellectual Origins of the Stars and Stripes." *Journal of the Early Republic* 31 (Spring): 39–73.

O

OLD GLORY FLAG

References to the American flag as "Old Glory" appear to have originated in the 19th century with William Driver (1803–1866), a sea captain from Salem, Massachusetts. When he was a young man (historians differ on the exact year), his mother and "the girls of Salem" gave him a 12-by-24-foot flag (Pomeroy 2013, 165). Consistent with the number of states in the Union at the time, it contained 24 stars. Driver subsequently took the flag on long voyages, leaving his wife, Martha Silsbee Babbidge, to care for their three children. On one of his trips, Driver returned descendants of *Bounty* mutineers from Tahiti to Pitcairn Island in the South Pacific.

Driver was quite proud of his flag, which he called: "my staunch companion and protection. Savages and heathens, lowly and oppressed, hailed and welcomed it at the far end of the wide world. Then, why should it not be called Old Glory?" (quoted by Jenkins 2013).

Shortly after he returned home from his trip to Pitcairn Island, Driver's wife died. In 1837, he moved with his children to Nashville. There he married Sarah Jane Park, with whom he would have nine additional children.

As a Nashville resident, Driver displayed Old Glory on important holidays like Washington's birthday and Independence Day as well as on presidential election day. In a parade in 1856, he was presented with a merino (wool) flag made by the ladies of Nashville, which he also regularly displayed.

Shortly after Lincoln's election, Driver removed Old Glory from public display and sought to restore it. At this time, he added an anchor to the canton.

Grave of William Driver, Nashville City Cemetery in Tennessee. (J.S.A. Brown)

After restoring the flag, he had it quilted into a bed cover and hid it, not even telling his family where he had kept it. On at least two occasions, he had to resist attempts by pro-Confederate neighbors to seize it. Residents of Salem knew of his efforts through letters that he wrote during the war.

When Union forces captured Nashville in 1862, Driver offered his flag to Gen. William "Bull" Nelson, who commanded the 6th Ohio. Nelson's men hoisted the flag above the capitol, and the regiment adopted "Old Glory" as its motto (Jenkins 2013). Driver later took it down to save it from wind damage and replaced it with his merino flag. Driver was appointed to the Nashville city council, volunteered to serve against Confederate forces who threatened Nashville, and later served on a relief commission, where he expressed special sympathy for former slaves.

On July 10, 1873, Driver gave Old Glory as a gift to a daughter, Mary Jane Roland, who had married a Union soldier. He told her:

> This is my old ship flag Old Glory. I love it as a mother loves her child; take it and cherish it as I have always cherished it; for it has been my steadfast friend and protector in all parts of the world—savage, heathen and civilized. (Quoted in Jenkins 2013)

Roland took the flag West. Sarah Park died in 1878 and William in 1886. He was buried with a flag in Nashville City Cemetery, and his monument was inscribed "His Ship, His Country, and his flag, Old Glory" (Pomeroy 2013, 175).

In 1896, James Whitcomb Riley published the poem "The Name of Old Glory." The third verse include the following words:

> And seeing you fly, and the boys marching by,
> There's a shout in the throat and a blur in the eye,
> And an aching to live for you always—or die,
> If, dying, we still keep you waving on high. (Keim and Keim 2007, 113)

In time, a dispute developed when a niece, Harriet Ruth Waters Cooke, donated a 12-by-6-foot flag that she claimed to be Old Glory to the Essex Institute (now the Peabody Essex Museum) in Salem, Massachusetts, which later loaned it to the Smithsonian Institution. Mary Jane wrote a book entitled *Old Glory: The True Story* (1908) and eventually gave her flag to President Warren G. Harding, who gave it to the Smithsonian Institution, which still regards her flag as the original. In recent years, however, the Smithsonian has begun renewed investigations of the so-called Peabody Flag. Initial results indicate that it does not have wear consistent with having flown at sea, but it still could have also belonged to Driver. The Peabody Museum had some souvenir patches, purportedly from Old Glory, that may have been cut from the flag that flew over the Tennessee State Capitol building.

Driver's devotion to the flag is a reminder that not all individuals in the seceding states supported rending the Union. A drawing of Gay Street in Knoxville, Tennessee, by an imprisoned Confederate soldier shows recruitment on that street by both Union and Confederate forces, each under their respective flags. Parson Brownlow, an East Tennessean who opposed secession, was reputedly the last person in East Tennessee to take his flag down. His daughter reputedly pulled a gun on soldiers who came to the house. A similar story tells how, on May 22, 1861, a Mrs. McEwin of Nashville displayed a flag at her house and threatened to shoot anyone who sought to take it down (Preble 1872, 374).

Although the name Old Glory has stuck, it has not been without its critics. Writing in 1906, educator Edward S. Holden felt that while "there is no question that those who use this name intend to express their affection for the national symbol," nonetheless "the excessive familiarity and lack of respect in the phrase offends, to some degree, against good taste" (49–50). He observed, "There is certainly a shade of boastfulness in the 'Glory'; and there is too much triviality and familiarity in the 'Old'" (50). He further added that "our flag, which is, we hope, not for a day but for all time must not be spoken of as if it were a boon companion, but rather a sacred symbol of great ideals" (51).

Similarly, in "The Name of Old Glory," Riley observed:

> *We*—Tom, Dick and Harry—each swinging his hat
> And hurrahing "Old Glory!" like you were our kin.
> When—*Lord!*—we all know we're as common as sin! (Fallows 1903, 101)

See also Civil War

Further Reading

Fallows, Samuel, ed. 1903. *Story of the American Flag with Patriotic Selections and Incidents*. New York: Educational Publishing Company.

Holden, Edward S. 1906. *Our Country's Flag and the Flags of Foreign Countries*. New York: D. Appleton and Company.

Jenkins, Sally. 2013. "How the Flag Came to be Called Old Glory." *Smithsonian Magazine*. http://www.smithsonianmag.com/history/how-the-flag-came-to-be-called-old-glory-18396/?utm_campaign=201310-hist&utm_medium=email&page=4&utm_so

Keim, Kevin, and Peter Keim. 2007. *A Grand Old Flag: A History of the United States through Its Flags*. New York: DK.

Pomeroy, Dan E. 2013. "'His Ship, His Country and his Flag,' William Driver and Old Glory." *Tennessee Historical Quarterly* 72 (Fall): 1650–1682.

Preble, Henry. 1872. *Our Flag. Origin and Progress of the Flag of the United States of America, with an Introductory Account of the Symbols, Standards, Banners and Flags of Ancient and Modern Nations*. Albany, NY: Joel Munsell.

Scott, Emma Look. 1915. *How the Flag Became Old Glory*. New York: Macmillan Company.

Shades of Gray and Blue. 2017. "Gay Street, Knoxville, Tenn. 1861." Accessed April 14. http://www.civilwarshades.org/gay-street-knoxville/

"OLD IRONSIDES"

Flags were once far more prominent at sea, where they served as means of identification, than they were on land. It is thus fitting that one of the best-known poems about the American flag was written in an attempt to save the ship USS *Constitution*, also sometimes known as Old Ironsides, from destruction. This 18th-century frigate had defeated HMS *Guerriere* during the War of 1812. The poem was written by Oliver Wendell Holmes Sr., a Harvard-educated physician who taught at both Dartmouth and Harvard before transitioning to a literary career. Holmes also was the father of Supreme Court justice Oliver Wendell Holmes Jr. Holmes was highly patriotic and a strong supporter of the Union cause during the Civil War. He wrote "Old Ironsides" in 1830. The most notable aspect of the poem is the manner in which it connects the ship, whose alternate name also ties it to the U.S. Constitution, to the U.S. flag.

The first stanza is probably the best known. Although it does not specifically reference the blue canton and its stars, it uses a number of terms ("on high," "banner in the sky," and "clouds") to direct attention heavenward:

Ay, tear her tattered ensign down!
    Long has it waved on high,
And many an eye has danced to see
    That banner in the sky;
Beneath it rung the battle shout,
    And burst the cannon's roar,—
The meteor of the ocean air
    Shall sweep the clouds no more.

Holmes thus equated the scuttling of Old Ironsides to tearing down the flag under which she sailed. The power of this stanza may also stem in part from the frequently used metaphor of "the ship of state."

The second verse, while not specifically mentioning the flag, ties to two of its three colors:

Her deck, once red with heroes' blood,
    Where knelt the vanquished foe,
When winds were hurrying o'er the flood,
    And waves were white below,
Nor more shall feel the victor's tread,
    Or know the conquered knee;—
The harpies of the shore shall pluck
    The eagle of the sea!

Notably, the last line of this stanza further connects the flag to the eagle, which is another popular national symbol.

The third stanza suggests that it would be better for the ship to sink than for it to be dismantled:

Oh, better that her shattered hulk
    Should sink beneath the wave;
Her thunders shook the might deep,
    And there should be her grave;
Nail to the mast her holy flag,
    Set every threadbare sail,
And give her to the god of storms,
    The lightning and the gale!

Much like Julia Ward Howe's "The Battle Hymn of the Republic," this stanza identifies the flag with holiness.

William Boyd Ness observed that of Holmes's 11 best-known poems, all but two of them have flag references, and two of them, "God Save the Flag!" and "The Flowers of Liberty," are entirely built around a flag theme (Ness 2008, 117–118).

Partly as a result of Holmes's poem, the navy decided not to scrap the ship, which remains a prominent national symbol. It continues to float in Boston Harbor, where it has become a popular tourist destination.

See also Eagle

Further Reading

Holmes, Oliver Wendell. 1830. "Old Ironsides." *Boston Daily Advertiser*, September 16.

Ness, William Boyd. 2008. *"Burning with Star-Fires": The National Flag in Civil War Poetry*. PhD thesis, University of Iowa.

Novick, Sheldon M. 1989. *Honorable Justice: The Life of Oliver Wendell Holmes*. Boston: Little, Brown and Company.

OLYMPIC PROTOCOL

Many people think of the 1936 Summer Olympic Games as the event where Jesse Owens and other African American athletes contested the superiority of Adolf Hitler's so-called Aryan master race. These games were also notable for the American delegation's refusal to dip the American flag to Hitler during the opening ceremonies. Although this quickly developed into the legend, largely fueled *New York Times* Olympic correspondent Arthur Daley, that the United States had never dipped its colors to a foreign potentate, the story was more mixed. In point of fact, the U.S. Olympic team had dipped the flag in 1912, 1924, and 1932, but not in 1908—although new photographic evidence suggests that it did so during a parade but not a march past the monarch (Wilcock 2011, 44)—1920, or 1928 (Dyreson 2008a, 148).

Drawing from the American Legion's early flag code, in 1942, Congress passed a law regarding "respect for the flag" that stipulated that "the flag should not be dipped to any person or thing." By contrast, the International Olympic Committee (IOC) adopted a resolution indicating that national delegations should dip their flags to honor the host (Dyreson 2008b, 164).

A recent study of pictures from the 1936 Olympics shows that three American men—Cornelius Johnson (gold), David Abritton (silver), and Delos Thurber (bronze), the first two of whom were African American—who swept the men's long-jump competition used the so-called Bellamy salute when they received their recognition on the last day of the competition. It consisted of pointing their right arms toward the flag and turning it with palm upward. They did this rather than use the Nazi salute with their arms pointed forward, or the Olympic salute, which consisted of the right arm at 90 degrees to the right (Stefani 2015). Hitler had exited his box at the Olympics prior to their recognition.

When the Olympics resumed in 1948, the U.S. adhered to its 1942 law. Over the next several Olympics, the American delegation was often the only nation that refused to dip its flag to the leader of the host country. This decision elicited negative reactions from other nations, which regarded it as a display of arrogance. During the Cold War, the Soviet Union and other Soviet bloc nations sometimes imitated the U.S. practice. By 1992, the U.S. practice had become standard.

It was apparently not until 1932 that the Olympic Games formalized the practice of playing the national anthem and raising the flag of the gold medalist after each sporting victory. In earlier days, all the awards were given out on the same day rather than after each event (Molotsky 2001, 149–150). In the 1968 Olympic Games in Mexico City, African Americans Tommie Smith and John Carlos (who had respectively won gold and bronze medals in the 200-meter race) raised gloved, fisted hands in support of black power while the American flag was raised and the national anthem was played.

American Olympic competitors are almost always dressed in uniforms that include the red, white, and blue colors of the U.S. flag. It is common for winning U.S. track stars to take victory laps carrying an American flag in their hands.

See also Flag Apparel; Flag Etiquette; Sports

Further Reading

Bass, Amy. 2002. *Not the Triumph but the Struggle: The 1968 Olympics and the Making of the Black Athlete*. Minneapolis: University of Minnesota Press.

Dyreson, M. 2008a. "'This Flag Dips for No Earthly King': The Mysterious Origins of an American Myth." *The International Journal of the History of Sport* 25 (February 15): 142–162.

Dyreson, M. 2008b. "'To Dip or Not to Dip': The American Flag at the Olympic Games since 1936." *The International Journal of the History of Sports* 25 (February 15): 163–184.

Luckey, John R. 2008. *The United States Flag: Federal Law Relating to Display and Associated Questions*. CRS Report for Congress. Washington, D.C.: Congressional Research Service.

Mallon, Bill, and Ian Buchanan. 1999. "To No Earthly King." *Journal of Olympic History* 7 (September): 21–28.

Molotsky, Irvin. 2001. *The Flag, the Poet and the Song: The Story of the Star-Spangled Banner*. New York: Dutton.

Stefani, Raymond T. 2015. "Johnson, Albritton, and Thurber's Patriotic and Defiant Bellamy Salute in Response to Hitler's Snub at Berlin in 1936." *Sport Journal* (September): 1.

Wilcock, Bob. 2011. "This Flag Dips to No Earthly King." *Journal of Olympic History* 19 (March): 39–45.

ORDER OF THE STAR SPANGLED BANNER

See Xenophobia, Nativism, and the U.S. Flag

OSTRANDER, JAMES S.

Of all periods in American history, few generated as many speeches about the American flag as the Civil War. James S. Ostrander (1822–1895) gave one of the most emotional talks on this subject at the annual meeting of the Ohio Commandery of the Military Order of the Loyal Legion in 1885. He was simply identified as a first lieutenant from Richmond, Indiana. The speech was entitled "The Old Flag."

After reviewing the use of flags and standards throughout history, Ostrander used religious terminology to explain how the flag was a symbol of something much larger than itself:

> Men seal their devotion to an idea, a principle, with their lives; but the mind is so constituted that the abstract thought must have material existence, and this the flag supplies, for by some occult process of transubstantiation it becomes in the eyes of the patriot the visible State, the embodiment of all that is grand and good and true in the structure of the nation; its defense the one lesson of patriotism, treason to its cause the unpardonable sin.

Although he acknowledged that the U.S. flag was not the world's oldest, Ostrander observed that in its "century of life is compassed more of human progress, more of grandeur and glory, than the world has witnessed since the morning stars sang together." Ostrander proceeded to trace the history of the flag from battlefields of the Revolutionary War to the War of 1812, the War with Mexico, and the Civil War, the last of which was of particular interest to the audience he was addressing:

> We saw its stars go down in darkness at Sumter. We watched its varying fortunes through the night of war. Four ponderous years its colors hung like an avenging Nemesis bathed in the lurid clouds of battle. We saw it in the hour of victory, when the last field was won. Scarred, with the wounds of deadly strife; tattered, in the tempest of conflict; stained, with the red record of battle. A flag of shreds and patches. Royalty in rags! But "every inch a king!" And when the light of that April morning irradiates its folds the last shackle of bondage is melted in the fervent heat of patriotism, the one blot of shame gone from our escutcheon.

Although Ostrander identified the southern cause with treason, he nonetheless sought reconciliation:

> The Nation lives! Advance your Standard! Peerless Republic, "Not a stripe erased, not a scar obscured." O, banner of beauty and glory! Glinted by the first rays of the morning, as you crown the blue waters of the Atlantic, a beacon of liberty to all the lands; kissed by the light of noonday as you wave over the great Mississippi Valley and spread your protecting shadow in majestic sweep from the unsalted seas to the land of the Montezumas; gorgeous in the golden sunset of that far occident, whose rivers tumble to the tide and hear no sound, save their own dashing; gathering a continent in your embrace, sheltering one great country under the benison of one mighty flag. Your flag! Misguided Southrons. Your flag! Men of the Northland. Doubly your flag! Companions of the Legion; tenderly protecting, staunchly supporting, mother at once and wife. Who shall declare divorce?

A later version of the speech ends with a quotation from "The Star-Spangled Banner" and an unattributed poem:

We know to-day no North nor South, erased all boundary bars,
For o'er us float from palm to pine, unmarred, the stripes and stars.
The pangs of war have rent the vail, and low! God's high decree,
One heart, one hope, one destiny, one flag from sea to sea. (Fallows 1903, 86)

See also Civil War; Fort Sumter Flag

Further Reading

Fallows, Samuel, ed. 1903. *Story of the American Flag with Patriotic Selections and Incidents*. New York: Educational Publishing Company.
Ostrander, James S. 1887. "The Old Flag." *Circular Papers and Annual Meeting of the Ohio Commandery of the Military Order of the Loyal Legion during the Year 1885*. N.p.: H. C. Sherick.

OUR BANNER IN THE SKY

One of the most unusual images of the U.S. flag emerged in the spring of 1861, shortly after American troops were forced to lower their flag and withdraw from Fort Sumter, off the coast of Charleston, South Carolina. This event, which was considered to be a national humiliation, led to huge rallies in the North in which American flags became a rallying point.

About this time, Frederic Edwin Church (1826–1900), an artist who was then chiefly known for his landscapes, painted an oil sketch entitled *Our Banner in the Sky*. It was subsequently made into a popular chromolithograph, which was published by Goupil and Co. (Burke 1982, 39).

Church's painting portrays an image of a morning sky in which white clouds form the shape of stripes against a black sky through which a canton of stars reveal themselves. On the left-hand side of the flag is a bare tree, which, much like earlier liberty poles, looks like a bent flagpole, over which an eagle flies. The author of this encyclopedia owns a similar picture in which a sentry with a gun fulfils a similar function to the tree.

Church's image was especially evocative not only of the Civil War but also of the origin of the flags on the flag canton from the night sky.

See also Civil War; Constellation; Fort Sumter Flag; Liberty Trees, Liberty Poles, and Liberty Caps

Further Reading

Burke, Doreen Bolger. 1982. "Frederic Edwin Church and 'The Banner of Dawn.'" *American Art Journal* 14 (Spring): 39–46.

P

PARKS, GORDON

See American Gothic, Washington, D.C. (Photograph)

PEACE FLAG

See Whipple Flag

PEOPLE'S FLAG SHOW

The American flag is a powerfully evocative symbol, both for those who celebrate its meaning and for those who question the values for which they think it stands. Laws against flag desecration reflect concern over depictions that focus on the latter. At times, however, such laws have conflicted with artistic expression.

The *People's Flag Show* was exhibited at the Judson Memorial Church in Washington Square Park in New York in November 1970 to protest flag desecration laws. African American artist Faith Ringgold designed a poster for the flag show that has subsequently been recognized as an iconic image. The exhibit itself featured over 150 works that incorporated the American flag in one fashion or another, including a flag cake, a flag made of soda cans, a flag draped over a toilet bowl, and a sculpture of a flag shaped like a penis by Alex Gross (Glueck 1970). Celebrated dancer-choreographer Yvonne Rainer also reported that she performed *Trio A*, one of her best known pieces, with several other dancers at the opening of the exhibit "in the nude . . . with five-foot American flags tied around our necks" (Rainer 2009, 13).

At the exhibit's opening, sculptor Paul von Ringelheim said, "We're not trying to test the laws but to discuss them" (quoted in Glueck 1970). Abbie Hoffman showed up with a shirt made from a flag, for which he had been arrested at a hearing of the House Un-American Activities Committee.

Police subsequently closed the show for flag desecration. In time, three artists, who became known as the Judson Three, were fined, although their convictions were later invalidated.

See also Flag Desecration Amendment

Further Reading

Glueck, Grace. 1970. "A Strange Assortment of Flags Is Displayed at 'People's Show.'" *The New York Times*, November 10.

New York Times. 1971. "Flag Show Artists Fined $100 Apiece." May 25.

Rainer, Yvonne. 2009. "Trio A: Genealogy, Documentation, Notation." *Dance Research Journal* 41 (Winter): 12–18.
Wallace, Michele. 2010. "The People's Flag Show by Faith Ringgold." *Ringgold in the 1960s*. May 26. http://ringgoldinthe1960s.blogspot.com/2010/05/peoples-flag-show-1970.html

PICKERSGILL, MARY YOUNG

Although historians doubt that Betsy Ross stitched the first American flag, there is general agreement that Philadelphia-born Mary Young Pickersgill (1776–1857) stitched the flag that flew over Fort McHenry during the British bombardment of Baltimore in 1814. That was the flag that inspired Francis Scott Key to write "The Star-Spangled Banner," which has become the national anthem. Mary's mother, Rebecca Young, was a flag maker as well.

After Mary's husband, John Pickersgill, died in in Philadelphia in 1805, she moved to Baltimore in 1807, where she set up a business making flags. In 1813, Maj. George Armistead, who was responsible for guarding the Baltimore Harbor from Fort McHenry, commissioned Pickersgill to make a large flag. She is believed to have been helped by her daughter, Caroline; some nieces; and possibly a free black woman who lived with them. Her mother, though not in good health, may also have helped with the design.

The massive flag of wool bunting that they produced was 30 by 42 feet and weighed about 80 pounds. It was waved from a 90-foot pole. Consistent with the designs of the day, it contained both 15 stars and 15 stripes. The stars, made of cotton, were approximately two feet from point to point and were made using a reverse applique method so the stars would be visible from both sides (Molotsky 2001, 76). The stripes were each two feet wide. The flag had approximately 350,000 stitches. The flag was so large that the material had to be laid out on the floor of the Claggertt's Brewery's malthouse.

This is the flag that Francis Scott Key saw the morning after Fort McHenry repulsed an attempted invasion by the British Navy. A smaller storm flag (still a formidable 15 by 25 feet) would have actually flown on the night of the battle. Pickersgill's flag was recently restored by the Smithsonian Institution, although its length is now shorter than the original in part because many individuals had over the years clipped off pieces as souvenirs.

Pickersgill's work continues to be celebrated at the Star-Spangled Banner Flag House (her home) in Baltimore. In addition to her work on the flag, Pickersgill is also known for her support (including a stint as president) of the Impartial Female Humane Society, which assisted destitute women.

See also Key, Francis Scott; National Anthem; Star-Spangled Banner (Flag); War of 1812

Further Reading

Molotsky, Irvin. 2001. *The Flag, the Poet and the Song: The Story of the Star-Spangled Banner*. New York: Dutton.

Poole, Robert M. 2008. "Star-Spangled Banner Back on Display." *Smithsonian Magazine*, November. http://www.smithsonianmag.com/history/star-spangled-banner-back-on-display-83229098/

PINE TREE FLAG

One of the regional flags that was used to muster troops before Congress adopted the Stars and Stripes was known as the Pine Tree Flag. It was particularly popular in New England, and especially in Massachusetts. It featured a profile of a green pine tree on a white background, typically with the words "An Appeal to Heaven." That expression was used by John Locke and other English philosophers to refer euphemistically to an appeal to arms to resolve otherwise intractable conflicts. This philosophy, in turn, was behind the reasoning of the Declaration of Independence.

The term "pine tree" apparently covered not only today's pines but also "oaks, willows, and possibly others" (Martucci 2006, 26). The Iroquois League may have used the pine tree symbol prior to the Pilgrims' arrival (26–27). Apparently, the symbol of the pine tree had also been displayed at the corner of the "first flag of New England." The Pine Tree Flag itself was used as the first naval flag of Massachusetts (Cox 1908, 438).

As scholar John Monsky observed, "the pine tree had a special meaning for Americans, as it was the focus of an important industry and a sign of wealth, commerce and power" (2002, 245). The industry in question was shipbuilding, for "the tall white pines of New England were key elements of the King's Navy as a unique source of tall, durable masts" (245).

Although simple in design and sentiment, the flag generally retained its regional association and was more suitable for rallying troops in Massachusetts and the rest of New England against perceived oppression than continuing to unite the colonies in common union. The Pine Tree Flag may have served as partial inspiration for liberty trees and liberty poles, which were often rallying points for resistance to what colonials considered to be British violations of their rights (Schlesinger 1952).

John Trumbull's 1786 painting *The Death of General Warren at the Battle of Bunker's Hill, June 17, 1774* which he largely drew from memory, portrays a pine tree flag in its upper-left-hand corner (Corcoran 2002, 23–24).

See also Liberty Trees, Liberty Poles, and Liberty Caps; Revolutionary War Battle Flags

Further Reading

Corcoran, Michael. 2001. *For Which It Stands: An Anecdotal Biography of the American Flag.* New York: Simon and Schuster.

Cox, E. J. 1908. "The Development of 'Old Glory.'" *The Journal of Education* 67 (16): 535, 539.

Martucci, David B. 2006. "Flag and Symbol Usage in Early New England." *Raven: A Journal of Vexillology* 13:1–40.

Monsky, John R. 2002. "From the Collection: Finding America in Its First Political Textiles." *Winterthur Portfolio* 37 (Winter): 239–264.

Schlesinger, Arthur M. 1952. "Liberty Tree: A Genealogy." *The New England Quarterly* 25 (December): 435–458.

PLEDGE OF ALLEGIANCE

The Pledge of Allegiance to the United States was not developed until the 1890s, when it was formulated in preparation for the celebration of the 400th anniversary of Columbus's discovery of America. This event was largely coordinated by James B. Upham and Francis Bellamy, both of whom were then working for *The Youth's Companion*, a popular magazine that sought to coordinate plans for a nationwide celebration of the flag in U.S. schools.

Perhaps in part as a way of assimilating immigrants, many of whom were no longer northern European Protestants, *The Youth's Companion* joined with a variety of veterans' groups in pushing for a ceremony that would be suitable for children in public schools. George Thacher Balch, a retired military officer who became an auditor for the New York City Board of Education, wrote the first pledge. It was as follows: "We give our Head!—and our Hearts!—to God! And our Country! One Country! One Language! One Flag."

Francis Bellamy, a former Baptist preacher who favored socialism, subsequently wrote the predecessor to the modern pledge, which Upham quickly approved. It was as follows: "I pledge allegiance to my flag, and to the republic for which it stands, one nation with liberty and justice for all." In 1923, the words "my flag" (which might have been confusing to immigrant students who had lived under

Pledge of Allegiance
I pledge allegiance to the flag of the United States of America and to the Republic for which it stands, one Nation indivisible, with liberty and justice for all.
THE GUARDIANS OF OUR NATION
© MWM

The flag continues to be especially identified with those who fight in defense of the nation. This card was printed prior to 1954, when, facing the threat of international communism, Congress added the words "under God" to the Pledge of Allegiance. (John Vile)

a different flag) were changed to "the flag of the United States," and in 1924, the words "of America" were added. In 1954, during an escalation in Cold War tensions, Congress voted to add the words "under God" (similar to the words "In God We Trust" on American currency) as a way of further distinguishing the United States from the Soviet Union and its godless communism. This change moved the Bellamy pledge closer to its Balch predecessor.

Like confessions of faith, the pledge, although almost always repeated within a group, begins with the individual person, "I." The term "pledge" denotes a promise, and "allegiance" denotes loyalty, and thus the Pledge of Allegiance resembles an oath (the only such oath in the U.S. Constitution is the one wherein the president promises to "preserve, protect and defend the Constitution of the United States"). The term "pledge" is less likely to offend members of some religious groups who do not believe it is appropriate to "swear." The wording "of the United States" that was initially added and the "of America," which was later added, refers to a federal system in which individual states retain some elements of sovereignty.

The term "republic" is typically used to distinguish representative, or republican, government from a pure democracy. In *Federalist* no. 10, James Madison argued that the two fundamental differences were that a republic was an indirect, rather than a direct, form of democracy and that as a result it could cover a much larger land area since individuals did not have to make all their decisions in a common assembly.

The "God" of the pledge appears to be generic enough to cover almost all belief systems, although it would appear more attuned to theistic than to nontheistic ones. It allows participants to fill in the god under which they think the nation rests, leading many to conclude that it is a term appropriate for "civil religion," rather than confessional faiths. Although it was especially developed for schools, where it is not always clear that students understand its meaning (Moser and David, 1936), it is common to engage in the pledge in meetings of civic groups and at public events.

The idea of nationhood is generally associated with a people united by ethnicity, culture, ideology, religion, language, and shared history. As a "melting pot," it is not clear that the United States actually constitutes a single nation rather than an amalgam of nations. The very practice of saluting the flag undoubtedly fosters a feeling of nationhood that transcends ethnicity and national origin. Balch emphasized this when he included the words "One Language!" in his original salute.

The term "indivisible" reinforces the idea, articulated after the Civil War in *Texas v. White*, 74 U.S. 700 (1869), that the Constitution "looks to an indestructible Union, composed of indestructible states." In many situations, individuals reciting the pledge may also see a state flag in the background.

Perhaps surprisingly, the pledge does not specifically reference either the Declaration of Independence, which referred to the equal rights of all men to pursue "life, liberty, and the pursuit of happiness," or the U.S. Constitution and the rule of law that the latter symbolizes. Were the pledge to have begun with a collective "we" rather than the singular "I," the opening words of the Constitution—"We the People"—might have been appropriate. The terms "liberty" and "justice" arguably intend to convey the central values of these and other American documents. "Liberty" is sometimes used to denote orderliness (as opposed to unlimited "freedom," or license), and "justice" is typically associated with law.

Bellamy's papers indicate that he had considered borrowing the slogan "Liberty, Equality, [and] Fraternity" from the French Revolution but realized that it might be too controversial. He decided that the phrase "with liberty and justice for all" was preferable "because it would be 'applicable to either an individualistic or a socialistic state, and could not be gainsaid by any party" (quoted in Ellis 2005, 29).

William Tyler Page, who authored the American's Creed, wrote: "We have pledged allegiance to the Flag of our County and to the Republic for which is stands. But without the Constitution there could be no Republic, there could be no Flag." He therefore proposed that we should say, "*I pledge allegiance to the Constitution of the United States of America, protector of the liberties of a free people, and to the Republic which it created*" (Page 1937, 40).

In *Minersville School District v. Gobitis* (1940), the U.S. Supreme Court ruled that public schools could expel students who refused to salute the flag. In *West Virginia State Board of Education v. Barnette* (1943), the court reversed course and decided that under the First and Fourteenth Amendments, states could not compel individuals to affirm that which they did not believe. In both cases, children of Jehovah's Witnesses had refused to salute the U.S. flag because they considered it to be a form of idolatry. The latter ruling does not necessarily prevent social pressures for children to conform to the pledge. In *Elk Grove Unified School District v. Newdow* (2004), a Supreme Court majority denied that a noncustodial parent had the right to challenge school flag salutes, but four justices indicated that they did not think that the practice violated the Establishment Clause of the First Amendment.

In *Texas v. Johnson* (1989) and *United States v. Eichman* (1990), the Supreme Court later upheld the right of individuals to burn the flag in protest of U.S. policies. Such actions may garner public attention precisely because they appear to be contravening fundamental values of patriotism that many children have learned at school.

Participants in the flag salute initially stood and extended their right hands toward the flag. Although participants still commonly face the flag, because the initial posture resembled the Nazi salute, this was changed so that most participants place their right hands over their heart. Men typically remove their hats, while those in uniform may instead stand at attention in a military salute. The event is often associated with playing or singing "The Star-Spangled Banner," which focuses on the flag and which Congress has designated as the national anthem.

See also American's Creed; Balch, George Thacher; Bellamy, Francis J.; *Elk Grove Unified School District v. Newdow* (2004); *Minersville School District v. Gobitis* (1940); *Texas v. Johnson* (1989); Under God; *United States v. Eichman* (1990); *West Virginia State Board of Education v. Barnette* (1943); *Youth's Companion*

Further Reading

Baer, John W. 1992. *The Pledge of Allegiance: A Centennial History, 1892–1992*. Annapolis, MD: Free State Press, Inc.

Ellis, Richard J. 2005. *To the Flag: The Unlikely History of the Pledge of Allegiance*. Lawrence: University Press of Kansas.

Hamilton, Alexander, James Madison, and John Jay. (1787–1788) 1961. *The Federalist Papers*. New York: New American Library.

Harris, Louise. 1971. *The Flag Over the Schoolhouse*. Providence, RI: C. A. Stephens Collection, Brown University.

Moser, A. C., and Bert B. David. 1936. "I Pledge A Legion." *The Journal of Educational Sociology* 9 (March): 436–440.

Olander, Herbert T. 1941. "Children's Knowledge of the Flag Salute." *The Journal of Educational Research* 35 (December): 300–305.

Page, William Tyler. 1937. "The Romance of the Constitution." *Records of the Columbia Historical Society, Washington, D.C.* 37/38:31–40.

Teachout, Woden. 2009. *Capture the Flag: A Political History of American Patriotism*. New York: Basic Books

POSTAGE STAMPS

The U.S. flag is a popular subject for U.S. postage stamps, but it was not always so. Indeed, the U.S. did not issue the first stamp showing an image of an American flag until 1869. Prior to this time, the eagle and the shield (which included stars at the top and stripes at the bottom) were much more common. Reverence for the flag increased significantly during the Civil War, however, and in the late 1880s, the post office began using a cancellation mark that depicted a waving flag. In the late 1920s, the post office removed the canton from the mark, leaving only the waving stripes still used today (Hinrichs, Hirasuna, and Heffernan 2015, 14).

When stamps first began to portray the flag, it was often in the background, and the monochromatic designs make it difficult to discern the stars and stripes. By contrast, many postcards that were privately produced in the late 19th and early 20th centuries featured brightly colored flags, especially in conjunction with celebrations of the birthdays of George Washington and Abraham Lincoln and for holidays such as Independence Day. Especially during times of war, envelopes were sometimes also decorated with flags, eagles, and other patriotic representations.

On January 2, 1952, the post office released a stamp commemorating the birth of Betsy Ross; it featured a picture of Charles H. Weisgerber's 1893 painting entitled *The Birth of Our Nation's Flag*, which perpetuated the popular myth that Ross created the first U.S. flag (Lidman, 1971). In 1948, the post office issued another three-cent stamp honoring Francis Scott Key, the author of "The Star-Spangled Banner."

In 2013, scholar Jeremy Lifsey observed: "About three-quarters of the stamps which show the complete flag prominently in the foreground have been issued in the past 35 years. This means that three times as many flag stamps have been issued in the past 25 years as were issued in the first 134 years of stamp production."

For the most part, the inclusion of flag imagery on postage stamps has been welcomed by members of the American public as well as collectors. But even this practice has not been without detractors. It is common, for example, for the post office to "cancel" stamps by printing a date on them so that they cannot be reused. During debates over flag desecration, some individuals have questioned whether this action could be considered to be a form of flag desecration.

Flag imagery has also seeped into other areas of postal operations. Public mailboxes, for example, which used to be painted green, are now typically painted red, white, and blue (Zelinsky 1988, 177).

See also *Birth of Our Nation's Flag*; Civil War; Eagle; Key, Francis Scott; Postcards; Ross, Betsy

Further Reading

Hinrichs, Kit, Delphine Hirasuna, and Terry Heffernan. 2015. *Long May She Wave: 100 American Flags: A Unique Collection of Old Glory Memorabilia*. Berkeley, CA: Ten Speed Press.

Lidman, Davis. 1971. "Betsy Ross Stamp Perpetuates a Myth." *New York Times*, April 25.

Lifsey, Jeremy. 2013. "United States Flags on United States Stamps." Philatelic Database. Last modified March 9. http://www.philatelicdatabase.com/united-states/united-states-flags-on-united-states-stamps/

Zelinsky, Wilbur. 1988. *Nation into State: The Shifting Symbolic Foundations of American Nationalism*. Chapel Hill: University of North Carolina Press.

POSTCARDS

In a world dominated by the Internet and e-mail, postcards—like letters of personal correspondence and greeting cards—have declined in popularity. During the late 19th and early 20th centuries, however, postcards were very popular modes of communication for Americans. Then, as now, postcards featured a picture on the front side and, on the back, a space to write message and attach a stamp. Many were simply photographs of famous places, but others were humorous cartoons or depictions of holiday symbols.

Many postcards from the period featured American flags. Washington's and Lincoln's birthdays appear to have been particularly observed with flag depictions, as was the centennial of Lincoln's birth in 1909. Independence Day postcards almost always featured flags (and fireworks), as did Memorial Day and Veterans Day cards and cards commemorating famous battles or places (e.g., Independence Hall).

Occasionally, Valentine's Day or even Thanksgiving or Christmas cards would also feature flags. The red in the flag was especially appropriate for Valentine's greetings. For a time, many businesses printed cards with flags on them, but there was eventually a backlash about such advertising, which some considered to be a form of flag desecration (Guenter 1990, 137–144).

During the Civil War, envelopes and stationery often contained images of American flags, sometimes in conjunction with pictures of President Lincoln, a cannon, an eagle, an elephant, or a man on horseback (Mastai and D'Otrange 1973, 150–151).

Today, postcards do not occupy as prominent a place in personal communications between Americans. But postcards are still frequently utilized as tourist souvenirs or to commemorate special occasions, and just as they did more than a century ago, postcards focused on historic places and events often incorporate flag imagery into their artwork.

As this Valentine's Day postcard shows, although flag depictions are routinely associated with patriotic holidays, they sometimes also find their way into other holiday commemorations. (John Vile)

See also Advertising; Independence Day; Postage Stamps

Further Reading

Guenter, Scot. 1990. *The American Flag, 1777–1924: Cultural Shifts from Creation to Codification*. Cranbury, NJ: Associated University Presses.

Hinrichs, Kit. 2016. *Long May She Wave: 100 Stars and Stripes Collectible Postcards*. New York: Potter Style.

Mastai, Boleslaw, and Marie-Louise D'Otrange. *The Stars and the Stripes: The American Flag as Art and as History from the Birth of the Republic to the Present*. New York: Alfred A. Knopf.

Wood, Jane. 1991. *The Collector's Guide to Post Cards*. Gas City, IN: L.-W. Promotions.

POSTERS IN WARTIME

The American flag was one of the most popular motifs for recruiting posters and liberty bond drives during World Wars I and II. Flags were often combined with images of idealized women (or images of German Huns attacking such women), iconic landmarks like the Statue of Liberty, and patriotic appeals.

President Woodrow Wilson organized the Committee on Public Information in order to generate support for U.S. intervention in World War I. It was headed by George Creel, a journalist who had campaigned for Wilson. He had the help of Charles Dana Gibson, the nation's highest-paid illustrator and creator of the "Gibson Girl," who largely donated his services and headed the Division of Pictorial Publicity (DPP) (Vogt 2000–2001, 39).

There may have been as many as 2,000 different designs for World War I posters alone (Lubin 2015, 32). Leading illustrators included Howard Chandler Christy (who is also known for his depictions of the Constitutional Convention of 1787), Harrison Fisher, and James Montgomery Flagg. Flagg was responsible for the "I Want You for the U.S. Army" poster, which one scholar described as "perhaps the single best-known, most universally recognized artifact of the First World War" (Lubin 2015, 17). The latter image features a picture of Uncle Sam, clad in red, white, and blue and pointing his forefinger directly at the viewer and asking them to report to the nearest recruiting station.

Although there were some dissenting voices, especially prior to America's entry into the war, most artists used their craft to support the war effort. Childe Hassam was especially known for his colorful flag paintings during this period.

See also Hassam, Childe; Uncle Sam; World War I; World War II

Further Reading

Lubin, David M. 2015. *Flags and Faces: The Visual Culture of America's First World War.* Oakland: University of California Press.

Vogt, George L. 2000–2001. "When Posters Went to War: How America's Best Commercial Artists Helped Win World War I." *Wisconsin Magazine of History* 84 (Winter): 38–47.

PREBLE, GEORGE HENRY

George Henry Preble (1816–1885) was a U.S. naval officer who served from 1835 to 1878. He participated in both the Mexican-American War and Civil War and ultimately achieved the rank of rear admiral. In addition to his distinguished military career, Preble is also remembered as the author of one of the most impressive 19th-century books on the history of the U.S. flag. This work, *Our Flag: Origin and Progress of the Flag of the United States of America, with an Introductory Account of the Symbols, Standards, Banners and Flags of Ancient and Modern Nations*, was originally published in 1872 and remains in print today.

In the process of researching flags, Preble incorrectly stated that the flag that had flown over Fort McHenry and that had inspired Francis Scott Key to write "The Star-Spangled Banner" was rolled up and covered in dust. Georgiana Armistead Appleton, who was the guardian of the flag, corrected him, and Preble asked to photograph it. To this end, she shipped it to him, where he secured the flag to a backing and took the first such photograph of the flag on June 21, 1873, at the Boston Navy Yard (Taylor, Kendrick, and Brodie 2008, 93). He published stories on the Fort McHenry flag that eventually helped transform it into a national icon.

See also Civil War; Mexican-American War; Star-Spangled Banner (Flag)

Further Reading

Preble, Henry. 1872. *Our Flag. Origin and Progress of the Flag of the United States of America, with an Introductory Account of the Symbols, Standards, Banners and Flags of Ancient and Modern Nations*. Albany, NY: Joel Munsell.

Taylor, Lonn, Kathleen M. Kendrick, and Jeffrey L. Brodie. *The Star-Spangled Banner: The Making of an American Icon*. Washington, D.C.: Smithsonian Books.

PRISONERS OF WAR

Members of the military typically have a special relationship to the American flag. This is especially true of those who are captured in wartime and held as prisoners of war. This affection for the flag dates back to the earliest days of the country's existence. For example, during the Revolutionary War, American prisoners who were held in the Mill Prison in England (a place that housed two future husbands of Betsy Ross) celebrated the Fourth of July with the flag, according to one such prisoner's account:

> This morning when we were let out, we all hoisted the American flag upon our hats, except about five or six who did not choose to wear them. The agent, seeing us all with those papers on our hats, asked for one to look at, which was sent to him, and it happened to be one with "independence" written on the top, and at the bottom "Liberty or Death." He, not knowing the meaning of it, and thinking we were going to force the guard, directly ordered a double sentry at the gate. Nothing happened till one o'clock; we then drew up thirteen divisions, and each division gave three cheers, till at last we all cheered together, all of which was conducted with the greatest regularity. We kept our colors hoisted till sunset, and then took them down. (Quoted in Cogliano 1998, 27)

Writing about the Civil War, William Boyd Ness observed that "prisoners were known to make their own flags out of articles of clothing or whatever fabric could be found" (2008, 38). On the same page, he cited a letter that was printed in *Harper's Weekly* on February 11, 1865, in which a former prisoner of Andersonville Prison reacted to seeing the flag for the first time:

> I shall never forget the feeling that overwhelmed me when, for the first time in months, I saw the old flag again—the dear old flag under which I had so often fought—for which I was ready to die in honorable battle. How we cried when we found ourselves under its folds on the deck of a loyal ship!

Historian Edward S. Holden reports that before 500 members of the 16th Regiment of Connecticut surrendered during the Civil War, they cut their regimental flag into small fragments that they carried with them to a prison camp. They reputedly kept these pieces until the end of the war, after which they reconstructed the flag and sent it to the state house in Hartford (Schauffler 1917, 28).

More recently, when North Vietnam held American prisoners in a wretched POW camp nicknamed the Hanoi Hilton, a prisoner of war named Mike Christian made a bamboo needle and sewed an American flag. After his guards discovered this and beat him severely, he began making another (Citizens Flag Alliance 2017).

It is common to see the POW/MIA flag flown in conjunction with the American flag. Indeed, Congress adopted a law in 1997 requiring post offices and other federal buildings to fly that flag several times during the year (Martini 2007, 241). The flag is black with a silhouetted solder in the center, against a white background featuring a guard tower and a barbed-wire fence, with the letters "POW" and "MIA" separated by a star at the top and the words "YOU ARE NOT FORGOTTEN" at the bottom below what appears to be a stylized wreath.

See also Civil War; Revolutionary War; Vietnam War

Further Reading

Citizens Flag Alliance. 2017. "The Story of Mike Christian, Vietnam POW." Accessed February 17. http://www.citizensflagalliance.org/stories/story-mike-christianvietnam-pow

Cogliano, Francis D. "'We All Hoisted the American Flag:' National Identity among American Prisoners in Britain during the American Revolution." *Journal of American Studies* 32 (April): 19–37.

Martini, Edwin A. 2007. *The American War on Vietnam, 1976–2000*. Amherst: University of Massachusetts Press.

Ness, William Boyd. 2008. *"Burning with Star-Fires": The National Flag in Civil War Poetry*. PhD thesis, University of Iowa.

Schauffler, Robert Haven, ed. 1917. *Our Flag in Verse and Prose*. New York: Moffat, Yard and Company.

PROPORTIONS OF THE AMERICAN FLAG

It was not until President William Howard Taft issued an executive order on October 29, 1912, that federal law specifically delineated the proportions of the U.S. flag and the specific arrangement of stars. Taft's executive order arose from the fact that 66 different sizes of national flags were being used at the time.

According to Executive Order No. 1637, the fly (length) of the flag should be 1.9 times its width. The union, or canton, should in turn be seven-thirteenths of the hoist (length) of the flag and the length should be 0.76 of the length. Each stripe should be one-thirteenth of the width of the hoist.

Taft further established that the 48-star flag would consist of six rows of 8 stars each. The order did permit small boats to bear 13-star flags, and it specified that the field of the president's flag should be blue.

See also Executive Order No. 1556 of 1912 and Its Successors

Further Reading

Wikipedia. "Executive Order 1637." https://en.wikisource.org/wiki/Executive_Order_1637

Q

QUILTS

American historic quilts are prized, especially those that deal with patriotic themes. Quilts might be made by an individual seamstress or by groups of quilters, especially for civic-related displays.

A colorful collection of historic quilts shows both that certain patterns are commonly reproduced in certain eras and that certain historic events and commemorations are especially likely to generate quilt making (Bishop and Houck 1986, 7–9). Such occasions have included wars, presidential campaigns (especially those centering on Whig candidates), centennials and bicentennials, and world fairs and expositions. Quilts sometimes incorporate handkerchiefs that were manufactured for these occasions. Some were also made from premium flag patches issued by cigarette companies.

Historically, the bald eagle and images of George Washington began as more prominent symbols in quilts, carvings, and other textiles (coverlets, kerchiefs, and patriotic ribbons, for example) than the American flag (Hornung 1973, 2:788–828). The flag appears to have risen in prominence after federal troops were driven from Fort Sumter at the beginning of the Civil War.

One quilt from this time period that features an American flag in the middle was made for a Union soldier. It included such admonitions as "Ye are Martyrs in a good cause," "Be true to humanity and to freedom," "Touch not intoxicating drinks," "Quiet Conscience gives quiet sleep," "Touch not Tobacco—a curse on it," "REBELS: They mock our peaceful labor/ They scorn our useful toil/ But on their vain pretensions/ The Blow will sure fall" (Bishop and Houck 1986, 28; see illustration 22). The Spanish-American War was the occasion for some of the most colorful quilts utilizing the flag motif.

Interestingly, although the U.S. Flag Code is not legally enforceable, it contains a provision that "the flag should not be used "as wearing apparel, bedding, or drapery" (Luckey 2008, 6).

The Statue of Liberty was an especially popular symbol among quilt makers at the time of its centennial, in 1986.

See also Centennials, Bicentennials, and Other Commemorations; Civil War; Eagle; Flag Code; Washington Kerchief Flags

Further Reading

Bishop, Robert, and Carter Houck. 1986. *All Flags Flying: American Patriotic Quilts as Expressions of Liberty*. New York: E. P. Dutton.

Hornung, Clarence P. 1973. *Treasury of American Design*. 2 vols. New York: Harry N. Abrams, Inc.

Luckey, John R. 2008. *The United States Flag: Federal Law Relating to Display and Associated Questions*. CRS Report for Congress. Washington, D.C.: Congressional Research Service.

R

"RAGGED OLD FLAG"

Country legend Johnny Cash, who was known throughout his long and prolific career in popular music for his identification with the downtrodden, released "Ragged Old Flag," one of his best-known songs, in 1974. This song about the American flag is divided into five stanzas. The first tells about coming to a courthouse square and observing there to an old man that the courthouse is run down and that the pole is displaying a "ragged old flag." The old man responds that they are "kinda proud" of the flag.

The old man proceeds in the next two stanzas to describe how the flag had weathered battles dating back to Washington's crossing of the Delaware, through the War of 1812, the Civil War, two world wars, Korea, Vietnam, and desecration on the home front. He concludes that "she's in good shape" despite her tumultuous history.

The last stanza describes how the town raises and lowers the flag each day and ends with the man changing his mind about not liking to brag, bragging about the pride he has for the flag.

Later in life, Cash told a crowd that he was proud of the flag and American freedoms—"even the right to burn the flag." After getting some undoubtedly anticipated boos, he added, "We've also got a right to bear arms and if you burn my flag, I'll shoot ya" (Betts 2016).

Further Reading

Betts, Stephen L. 2016. "Flashback: Johnny Cash Raises Political Voice with 'Ragged Old Flag.'" *Rolling Stone,* July 4. https://www.rollingstone.com/music/videos/flashback-johnny-cash-raises-political-voice-with-ragged-old-flag-20160704

RALLY 'ROUND THE FLAG EFFECT

The alleged phenomenon identified by political scientists as the "rally 'round the flag effect" is not really about the U.S. flag, which often serves as a rallying point for soldiers in battle, but about increased support for U.S. presidents in time of crisis. The expression is important in that the president, a unitary figure who is elected on a nationwide basis, is often taken, like the flag, to represent national ideals.

A notable study of the subject by John R. Oneal and Anna Lillian Bryan (1995) finds that the average increase of support for presidents in times of international crises is relatively mild but that it increases when the United States becomes involved in a war and when this war is reported extensively. Another study by

Lambert, Schott, and Scherer (2011) suggests that such support increases with anger, especially in the case of surprise attacks against the United States such as Pearl Harbor in 1941 or the terrorist attacks on the World Trade Center in New York City in 2001. Presidents can increase the rally 'round the flag effect by enacting policies and making speeches that emphasize America's capacity to withstand such blows (Baker and Oneal 2001).

See also Flag Desecration Laws; Flag Lapel Pins; Vietnam War

Further Reading

Baker, William D., and John R. Oneal. 2001. "Patriotism or Opinion Leadership?: The Nature and Origins of the 'Rally 'Round the Flag' Effect." *The Journal of Conflict Resolution* 45 (October): 661–687.

Lambert, Alan J., J. P. Schott, and Laura Scherer. 2011. "Threat, Politics, and Attitudes: Toward a Greater Understanding of Rally-'Round-the-Flag Effects." *Current Directions in Psychological Science* 20 (December): 343–348.

Oneal, John R., and Anna Lillian Bryan. 1995. "The Rally 'Round the Flag Effect in U.S. Foreign Policy Crises, 1950–1985." *Political Behavior* 17 (December): 379–401.

RANTOUL, ROBERT S.

Robert S. Rantoul (1832–1922), a member of a prominent Massachusetts reform family, earned his undergraduate and law degrees from Harvard University. He served in a number of political posts including collector of the Port of Salem, state representative, and mayor of Salem before service as vice president and president of the Essex Institute (now the Essex Museum), which described itself as "a literary, historical and scientific society."

On February 28, 1900, not long after the Spanish-American War, Rantoul penned a letter in his capacity as president of the Essex Society. In the letter, later reprinted in Peleg D. Harrison's *The Stars and Stripes and Other American Flags* (1918), he observed, "The flag of a free country does not take care of itself." Explaining that "whether it shall command respect or not is to be determined by the quality of the Nation's life," Rantoul opined that "it is for us and those who shall come after us, to say whether its ancient glory shall play about it still."

Referring to the "mighty deeds" that the flag had already inspired, Rantoul continued his discourse on the flag:

> It speaks at once of aspirations and of achievement,—it stands at once for memory and for hope. It is a pledge, it is the Solemn Covenant of our common liberties. It is a badge of brotherhood and of common destiny. It links together, by an indissoluble tie, with the Nation's past and future, the whole mighty family of her living sons.

In order to maintain popular respect, the flag needed to continue standing "for majesty and might," as well as "for purity and justice and honor." Respect for the flag would erode if national standards lowered:

> A little lowering of the patriotic standards,—a little blunting of the national conscience,—a little falling off in the collective honor of the people,—and that

generous pride with which we hail its lustrous folds lapses into the blink idolatry of emblem-worship,—a heartless and a hollow sham.

Rantoul concluded, "If we would respect the majesty of the flag, we must keep it the badge of worth as well as the badge of power, that all men, unchallenged, shall make haste to pay obeisance to it" (quoted in Harrison 1914, 276).

See also Spanish-American War

Further Reading

Curti, Merle E. 1932. "Robert Rantoul, Jr., 'The Reformer in Politics.'" *New England Quarterly* 5 (April): 264–280.

Harrison, Peleg D. 1918. *The Stars and Stripes and Other American Flags*. 5th ed. Boston: Little, Brown, and Company.

Philllips Library Digital Collections. 2017. "Biographical Sketch." Accessed April 11. http://phillipslibrarycollections.pem.org/cdm/ref/collection/0p15928coll1/id/1100

RATTLESNAKE FLAGS

One of the most distinctive flags that arose at the beginning of the Revolutionary War was the Rattlesnake Flag, often called the Gadsden Flag after its designer Christopher Gadsden, a Georgia-born brigadier general in the Revolutionary War. The flag was especially popular in Pennsylvania and South Carolina and apparently came in a number of forms.

Although the image of a snake might at first seem somewhat repulsive (the serpent was used in Genesis, chapter 3, as a symbol for the devil), the biblical book of Numbers describes Moses lifting a bronze snake on a pole that brought healing to those who looked upon it (Numbers 21:9). An article in *The Scots Magazine* of July 1776 further notes, "It is a rule in heraldry that the worthy properties of the animal in the crest borne shall be considered, and the base ones cannot be intended" (quoted in Desbler 1892, 182). Moreover, the very first political cartoon in the United States was a woodcut of a snake cut in parts and labeled "Join, or Die," drawn by Benjamin Franklin (Vile 2015, 65). Franklin observed that because the rattlesnake had no eyelids, it was "an emblem of vigilance," that "she never begins an attack, nor, when once engaged, ever surrenders," and that the rattles, though "distinct and independent of each other," were yet "united together, so as never to be separated but by breaking them in pieces" (quoted in Hamilton 1852, 76–77). Moreover, the rattlesnake is indigenous to the Americas and so would be a particularly potent symbol of rebellion against the British. It also was generally regarded in colonial times as "a symbol of vigilance and deadly striking power" (Eggenberger 1959, 14). Historian William Guthrie further elaborates that "it was natural for the rattler to be viewed by our forefathers as the type of a defensive fighter, brave, formidable, desperate, but chivalrous, not smiting the enemy ere giving due warning, but when he delivers the blow, deadly indeed" (1919, 48).

Scholars have identified the rattlesnake with a banner used by minutemen in Culpepper County, Virginia. That flag featured a coiled rattler against a white field and the words "Liberty or Death" (attributed to Patrick Henry) or "Don't Tread

Benjamin Franklin's *Join, or Die*, believed to be the first political cartoon, was published in the *Pennsylvania Gazette* on May 9, 1754. The cartoon warns the Albany Congress that the American colonies need to "join, or die," and to unite in the face of French and Native American interests. Franklin's drawing shows the American colonies as a segmented snake, with the segments representing the colonies: "S.C." (South Carolina), "N.C." (North Carolina), "V." (Virginia), "M." (Maryland), "P." (Pennsylvania), "N.J." (New Jersey), "N.Y." (New York), and "N.E." (New England, representing the colonies of Massachusetts, Rhode Island, Connecticut, and New Hampshire). (Library of Congress)

on Me" (Eggenberger 1919, 14). It is also associated with the Gadsden Flag, an emblem of Col. Christopher Gadsden, who was a delegate to the Continental Congress from South Carolina. That flag, which also featured the words "Don't Tread on Me," featured a black-and-white outline of a rattler against yellow background. John Proctor's Westmoreland County Battalion in Pennsylvania also used a coiled rattlesnake and the words "Don't Tread on Me" ("Mystery of Reversed Lettering Is Resolved" 1975, 229). A variant of these flags apparently was also flown by U.S. naval ships at sea (Hoff 1929, 562), at least two examples of which apparently showed "the snake undulating against a background of white and red stripes" (Monsky 2002, 246).

Although a potent symbol of rebellion and resistance to tyranny at the start of the Revolutionary War, the Rattlesnake Flag was arguably not as good a symbol of national aspiration and unity as the flags with stars and stripes that followed. Indeed, a parlor song entitled "Down with the Traitor's Serpent Flag," published in Chicago in 1861, portrays a union soldier standing on a Palmetto Flag, which was sometimes used by Confederate forces, and puncturing it with his sword (Hartvigsen 2011).

In the early 21st century, the conservative Tea Party Movement, which opposes increased federal power, embraced both the rattlesnake image and the words "Don't Tread on Me" on flags and other promotional materials to rally supporters.

Further Reading

Desbler, Charles D. 1892. "How the Declaration Was Received in the Old Thirteen." *Harper's New Monthly Magazine* 85 (July): 165–187.

Eggenberger, David. 1959. *Flags of the U.S.A.* New York: Thomas Y. Crowell Company.

Guthrie, William Norman. 1919. *The Religion of Old Glory*. New York: George H. Doran Company.

Hamilton, Schuyler. 1852. *History of the National Flag of the United States*. Philadelphia: Lippincott, Grambo, and Co.

Hartvigsen, Kenneth. 2011. "Picturing Flag Violence in Civil War Sheet Music: The Case of 'Down with the Traitors' Serpent Flag.'" In *Proceedings of the 24th International Congress of Vexillology*, 407–424. Washington, D.C.

Hoff, Daniel. 1929. "Flags Important in American History." *The Journal of Education* 109 (May 20): 559–563.

Monsky, John R. 2002. "From the Collection Finding America in Its First Political Textile." *Winterthur Portfolio* 37 (Winter): 239–264.

"Mystery of Reversed Lettering Is Resolved." 1975. *History News* 30 (October): 229.

Rankin, Hugh F. 1954. "The Naval Flag of the American Revolution." *William and Mary Quarterly* 22 (July): 339–353.

Vile, John R. 2015. *Founding Documents of America, Documents Decoded*. Santa Barbara, CA: ABC-CLIO.

Walker, Rob. 2017. "The Shifting Symbolism of the Gadsden Flag." *New Yorker*, October 2. http://www.newyorker.com/news/news-desk/the-shifting-symbolism-of-the-gadsden-flag

RESPECT FOR AMERICA'S FALLEN HEROES ACT

Congress adopted the Respect for America's Fallen Heroes Act in 2006 in reaction to demonstrations carried out at military funerals. Although the Supreme Court later ruled in *Snyder v. Phelps* (2011) that the First Amendment barred the imposition of civil penalties against Fred Phelps (who, along with other members of his church, thought that U.S. casualties were a result of U.S. support for homosexuals) and such other protestors, the law at issue applies to government-owned cemeteries that are not, like sidewalks and parks, typically areas for protest.

The law specifically prohibits "the display of any placard, banner, flag, or similar device, unless such a display is part of a funeral, memorial service, or ceremony" (Government Printing Office). An article in *The Washington Post* claims that the law bans individuals from carrying any flag into the Arlington National Cemetery (Shapiro 2017).

See also Flag Desecration Laws

Further Reading

Government Printing Office. "109th Congress Public Law 109-228." https://www.gpo.gov/fdsys/pkg/PLAW-109publ228/html/PLAW-109publ228.htm

Hudson, David L., Jr. 2009. "Funeral Protests." In *Encyclopedia of the First Amendment*, edited by John R. Vile, David L. Hudson Jr., and David Schultz, 496–497. Washington, D.C.: CQ Press.

Shapiro, T. Rees. 2017. "What Can't You Take to Arlington National Cemetery on July 4? An American Flag." *Washington Post*, July 4. https://www.washingtonpost.com/local/virginia-politics/what-cant-you-take-to-arlington-national-cemetery-on-july-4-an-american-flag/2017/07/03/b3a1241c-5fae-11e7-a4f7-af34fc1d9d39_story.html?noredirect=on&utm_term=.d1a5a8e9ad67

REVOLUTIONARY WAR

The U.S. flag was born during the Revolutionary War, largely as a way of distinguishing American soldiers and sailors from their British counterparts. Initially, American soldiers fought under a variety of flags. Some, like the Pine Tree Flag, were more indicative of their state or region than of the nation as a whole. In battle, regimental flags were typically used up to the Mexican-American War of 1848. Many of the flags shown on subsequent paintings from the earlier era, like *The Spirit of '76* or *The Birth of Our Nation's Flag*, are thus anachronistic.

On June 14, 1777, the Continental Congress adopted a Resolution that specified "that the flag of the thirteen United States be thirteen stripes, alternate red and white; [and] that the union be thirteen stars, white in a blue field, representing a new constellation." This resolution did not, however, specify how the stars were to be arranged, and there are reports of flags with 9 (rather than 13) stripes and with alternating red, white, and blue stripes.

Francis Hopkinson, and not Betsy Ross, is now believed to have designed the first U.S. flag, but the flag was not initially the unifying symbol that it has since become, and it would have been more commonly used at sea than on land. Francis D. Cogliano has documented that American privateers who were held in British prisons were among the first to attach special significance to flag designs. They made flags with slogans like "Independence" and "Liberty or Death" in celebrations on July 4, 1778, and crafted an American flag after hearing news of the British surrender at Yorktown (1998, 26–27).

See also *Birth of Our Nation's Flag*; Hopkinson, Francis; Ross, Betsy; *Spirit of '76*; Stripes on the Flag

Further Reading

Architect of the Capitol. 2017. "Surrender of Lord Cornwallis." Accessed February 3. https://www.aoc.gov/art/historic-rotunda-paintings/surrender-lord-cornwallis

Cogliano, Francis D. 1998. "'We All Hoisted the American Flag:' National Identity among American Prisoners in Britain during the American Revolution." *Journal of American Studies* 32 (April): 19–37.

REVOLUTIONARY WAR BATTLE FLAGS

At the beginning of the Revolutionary War, American soldiers marched under a variety of banners, including the Pine Tree Flag, the Rattlesnake Flag, and other state emblems. It was not until June 14, 1777, that Congress specified that the official American flag would have 13 stars in a blue canton and 13 red and white stripes. The resolution, however, did not specify how the stars would be arranged. Moreover, there are subsequent records of flags being made with red, white, and blue stripes, and it was far more common to carry regimental banners on the battlefield than it was the U.S. flag.

In 2006, four such flags were auctioned at Sotheby's for $17.4 million. All were made of silk. The flag receiving the highest bid was the flag of Col. Elisha Sheldon's Continental Light Dragoons, which was captured by British officer Banastre Tarleton on July 2, 1779, at Pound Ridge, New York. The flag consists of 13 alternating red and white stripes with an inset middle panel with "a winged thundercloud, ten golden thunderbolts shooting in every direction" and a banner with a Latin phrase that means "When their Country calls, her sons answer in tones of thunder" (Miller 2010, 2). Measuring 30 by 36 inches, the flag has a silver fringe.

Tarleton captured the three other flags that belonged to Lt. Col. Abraham Buford's Virginia regiment at Waxhaws, on the border of Virginia and North Carolina, on May 29, 1780. One is on gold silk and portrays a beaver gnawing at a palmetto tree, Carolina's state symbol. The flag also features a banner with the motto "Perseverando" imprinted on it. The other two flags, one of which is blue and the other of which is gold, simply have the word "Regiment" emblazoned across their surfaces.

All four flags were exhibited at Colonial Williamsburg's DeWitt Wallace Decorative Arts Museum from December 22, 2007, through mid-July of 2009.

Other examples of Revolutionary War–era flags include the Bennington Flag and the Forster Flag.

See also Bennington Flag; Forster Flag; Pine Tree Flag; Rattlesnake Flags

Further Reading

Bahls, Roy A. 2007. "Revolutionary War Battle Flags Head Home." *Virginia Pilot*, October 17. https://pilotonline.com/news/military/revolutionary-war-battle-flags-head-home/article_a95e202f-d9f8-59df-9235-bb6c89f9a80e.html

Bahls, Roy A. 2009. "Revolutionary War Battle Flags Soon to Wave Goodbye." *Virginia Pilot*, July 3. https://pilotonline.com/news/local/article_fe785d47-eddb-5e86-88b9-b575ac3b35e1.html

Goodman, Brian. 2006. "Revolutionary War Flags Go for $17.4 M." CBS News, June 13. https://www.cbsnews.com/news/revolutionary-war-flags-go-for-174m/

Miller, Marla R. 2010. *Betsy Ross and the Making of America*. New York: Henry Holt and Company.

RINGGOLD, FAITH

See People's Flag Show

"RIP VAN WINKLE"

One of the most fascinating early 19th-century references to the American flag is found in the story of Rip Van Winkle, which author Washington Irving

(1783–1859) published in 1819. The tale, which is set in the Catskill Mountains, chronicles how a henpecked husband, largely known for his ability to evade work, meets a group of strange men who are playing nine-pins and then wakes up some 20 years later, in the mid-1790s, to find that the world very much changed.

As Rip Van Winkle wanders down the mountains to his village inn after awakening, he finds that it has been replaced with "The Union Hotel, by Jonathan Doolittle." He further finds that the iconography with which he was familiar has changed:

> Instead of the great tree that used to shelter the quiet little Dutch inn of yore, there now was reared a tall naked pole, with something on the top that looked like a red nightcap, and from it was fluttering a flag, on which was a singular assemblage of stars and stripes—all this was strange and incomprehensible. He recognized on the sign, however, the ruby face of King George under which he had smoked so many a peaceful pipe, but even this was singularly metamorphosed. The red coat was changed for one of blue and buff, a sword was held in the hand instead of a scepter, the head was decorated with a cocked hat, and underneath was painted in large characters, "GENERAL WASHINGTON."

In analyzing this scene, scholar Benjamin Irvin observes that "we see a triptych of early U.S. national identity: the liberty cap, a token of radical resistance, the memento of the people out of doors; the flag of the United States, the fancy work of Francis Hopkinson, adopted by Congress to signify a rising constellation; and George Washington, the hero of the war, now a president in the place of a king" (2011, 281).

Van Winkle finds this quite confusing, and he is similarly bewildered when he faces questions about "whether he was Federal or Democrat." Indeed, the villagers accuse him of being a Tory after he confesses that he was "a loyal subject of the King, God bless him!" before discovering "that the country had thrown off the yoke of old England—and that, instead of being a subject to his Majesty George the Third, he was now a free citizen of the United States."

See also Stars and Stripes

Further Reading

Irvin, Benjamin H. 2011. *Clothed in Robes of Sovereignty: The Continental Congress and the People Out of Doors*. New York: Oxford University Press.

Irving, Washington. "Rip Van Winkle." http://etc.usf.edu/lit2go/171/american-short-fiction/3461/rip-van-winkle/

ROSENTHAL, JOE

See Iwo Jima Flag Raising

ROSS, BETSY

Of all the stories surrounding the American flag, none is more endearing or mythical than the one that attributes creation of the first U.S. flag to Betsy Ross (1752–1836). Ross was a Philadelphia seamstress, and she did make flags. However, the story that Gen. George Washington and a committee from Congress met with her to design the flag originated long after her death. It came about when her grandson

William J. Canby read a paper entitled "The Origin of the American Flag" to the American Historical Society in 1870. According to Ross's story, his grandmother was chosen to make the first flag after she demonstrated how a seamstress could make five-cornered flags. This allegedly gave her an edge over other seamstresses who had proposed the more complex six-cornered flags.

Despite the presence of affidavits that Canby secured from relatives (Harker 2005), his story gradually fell apart, in part because he had alleged that Betsy had sewn the flag prior to the time that Congress had approved its design and in part because there is no historical evidence that Ross met with George Washington. This did not prevent a famous depiction of a meeting between Ross and Washington in Charles H. Weisgerber's *The Birth of the American Flag*, which depicts Ross as an American Founding Mother. This picture was highlighted on a three-cent stamp on the 200th anniversary of Ross's birth. The canton of the flag in this painting arranged the stars in a circle. Although most scholars now discount the story, it continues to be a favorite among the authors of children's books, and a house on the street where Ross lived in Philadelphia is still a favorite tourist spot. Descendants of Betsy Ross subsequently sold small replicas of the flag attributed to her (Spicer 2013). Another depiction of Ross presenting the flag to Washington and two other men is found in a drawing by Joseph Boggs Beale (1841–1926), which he finished about 1899.

Ross was raised a Quaker but was expelled from her congregation after she married John Ross, who was of a different denomination. John died during the Revolutionary War, and Betsy married Joseph Ashburn in 1780. He died in a British jail after being captured for privateering. In 1783, Betsy married John Claypoole, who had met Ashburn in prison.

The design of the U.S. flag is generally attributed to Francis Hopkinson, who played a part in the design of the American shield. Mary Young Pickersgill, the daughter of Rebecca Young, another Philadelphia flag maker, made the flags that flew over Fort McHenry during the battle for Baltimore during the War of 1812 that Francis Scott Key commemorated by writing "The Star-Spangled Banner."

See also *Birth of the American Flag, The*; Hopkinson, Francis; Pickersgill, Mary Young; Star-Spangled Banner (Flag)

Further Reading

Crews, Ed. 2008. "The Truth about Betsy Ross." *Colonial Williamsburg Journal* (Summer). https://www.history.org/foundation/journal/summer08/betsy.cfm

Harker, John B. 2005. "Betsy Ross: An American Legend and Patriot Revisited." *Raven: A Journal of Vexillology* 12:87–99.

Menezes, Joann. 1997. "The Birthing of the American Flag and the Invention of an American Founding Mother in the Image of Betsy Ross." In *Narratives of Nostalgia, Gender, and Nationalism*, edited by Jean Pickering and Suzanne Kehde, 74–87. Washington Square: New York University Press.

Miller, Marla R. 2011. *Betsy Ross and the Making of America*. New York: Henry Holt and Company.

Spicer, Gwen. 2013. "The Conservation of a Betsy Ross Flag." *Inside the Conservator's Studio*, June 14. http://insidetheconservatorsstudio.blogspot.com/2013/06/betsy-ross.html

RUHSTRAT V. ILLINOIS (1900)

In *Ruhstrat v. Illinois*, 185 Ill. 133; 57 N.E. 41 (1900), Chief Justice Benjamin D. Magruder of the Illinois Supreme Court wrote a decision ruling that a state law restricting the use of flag and depictions of flags in advertising (in this case on cigar boxes) violated both the state constitution and the Fourteenth Amendment to the U.S. Constitution.

The court ruled that the state constitution's guarantee of happiness and due process as well as the privileges and immunities clause of the Fourteenth Amendment were designed to allow individuals to pursue common occupations without undue state interferences. National law allowed for trademarks that incorporate the colors of the American flag, and such advertising is legitimate.

States do have police powers to regular public health and comfort, but legislative judgements on such matters are subject to judicial review, especially where private conduct does not directly impinge on the rights of others. Judging by such criteria, Magruder thus argued:

> It is difficult to see how the Flag law of April 22, 1899, tends in any way to promote the safety, welfare or comfort of society. The use of a likeness of the flag upon a label or as part of the trade-mark of a business man in the lawful prosecution of his business, cannot be regarded otherwise than as an act which is harmless in itself. It may violate the ideas, which some people have of sentiment and taste, but the propriety of an act, considered merely from the standpoint of sentiment and taste, is a matter, about which men of equal honesty and patriotism may differ.

Tracing the use of flags, to identification of flags at least, the court observed that "a flag is emblematic of the sovereignty of the power which adopts it." The right to display such a flag is a privilege and immunity of U.S., rather than of state, citizenship. Moreover, Congress has not adopted any legislation on the subject.

The court further argued that the law was discriminatory in character because it contained an exemption for those who incorporated the flag in art exhibitions. Three justices dissented from the decision.

Moreover, in *Halter v. Nebraska* (1907), the U.S. Supreme Court upheld a similar state law against advertising, distinguishing it in part on the basis that it was not discriminatory. This decision should, in turn, be interpreted in the light of increasingly extensive protections for commercial speech under the First Amendment and in light of decisions in *Texas v. Johnson* (1989) and *U.S. v. Eichman* (1990) invalidating state and federal flag desecration laws.

See also Advertising; *Halter v. Nebraska* (1907); *Texas v. Johnson* (1989); *United States v. Eichman* (1990)

Further Reading

Corcoran, Michael. 2002. *For Which It Stands: An Anecdotal Biography of the American Flag*. New York: Simon and Schuster.

S

SCHULLER, ROBERT H.

Over the course of American history, many speeches variously titled "I Am the Flag," or "I Am the American Flag," often unattributed and sometimes combining passages from several historic speeches together, have been delivered and publicized. One well-known speech with the latter title was delivered by Robert H. Schuller (1926–2015) at his Crystal Cathedral on July 1, 2007. Schuller was a minister of the Reformed Church of America; he emphasized the power of positive thinking and was best known as the founding pastor of the Crystal Cathedral in Orange County, California, from which he broadcast the nationally syndicated *Hour of Power* television program.

Writing from the perspective of the flag in the first person, Schuller professed to speak "from the wisdom of a long life" and stressed, "I have earned the right to be heard." Citing numerous military engagements throughout the nation's history, his flag offers three primary messages.

The first is to "be proud of your country." This pride stems from all that is "beautiful, compassionate, tender, powerful, yet gentle" about the nation. Acknowledging that the nation is "imperfect," the flag points to the millions of people whom American soldiers have liberated. It also highlighted the goodwill that American doctors, missionaries, and others have spread abroad. Schuller asserts that "no country knows greater freedom, under law, than my country," and cites freedom to travel, "to try anything," "to speak, write, praise, question or criticize anyone," "to save and build a fortune," "to worship or not to worship," "to start your own business," and so on. This pride blends into the assurance that Americans can "do anything you want to," to "climb any mountain," and to "dream a beautiful dream."

The second appeal that the flag makes is to "BE HUMBLE." This part of the speech stressed that "FREEDOM DEPENDS ON MORALITY." It ties America's foundations to "the Ten Commandments, the Sermon on the Mount and the Word of God." It further evokes the words of Emma Lazarus on the Statue of Liberty about welcoming immigrants.

The flag's third message is to "BE RENEWED!" This calls for renewed "faith in God" and in "His Holy Word." The flag attributes America's long survival, including through the Civil War and the Great Depression, to its faith and urges America to dream new and greater dreams. It closes by envisioning "little children, teenagers, young people who haven't been in religion coming back to the root."

Continuing in the first person, the sermon ends with: "I see adults who have been drifting into heathenistic secularism and agnosticism coming back. You heard me speak. Now take a good look at my face."

Further Reading

Schuller, Robert H. 2017. "I Am the American Flag." Accessed May 22. http://libertyworks.com/i-am-the-american-flag/

SCHUYLER FLAG

One of the most beautiful of America's earliest flags is the Schuyler Flag, which appears to date to 1784. Originally described as a regimental flag, it seems more likely that it was a national symbol. The flag contains an eagle in the blue canton with an olive branch in one claw, arrows in the other, and a shield on its chest. A banner streams from its beak, and a circle of 13 stars is over its head. The rest of the flag consists of 13 alternating red and white stripes. The flag is from the family of Philip Schuyler (1733–1804), who fought at the battle of Saratoga and is probably best known as the father-in-law of Alexander Hamilton.

Although there are some differences in detail, as the date suggests, the pattern on the canton appears closely tied to the Great Seal of the United States, which was adopted in 1782 (Vile 2015, 125–126). In the seal, the banner contains the words "E Pluribus Unum" (From many, one).

According to one historian, the eagle-and-star design "may well have been one of the more common early designs for national flags. It continued in use in the nineteenth century as late as the 1840s" and appeared in Charles Willson Peale's 1782 portrait *Washington at Yorktown* (Cooper 1973, 6). The United States Indian Department appears to have ordered such flags to give to Native American tribes (Miller 2010).

The eagle appears to have initially been a more popular symbol in early American than the flag itself, so the idea of combining the images was a wise one. The flag of the U.S. president is probably the most commonly recognized current U.S. flag that uses the eagle as an emblem.

See also Eagle; Quilts

Further Reading

Cooper, Grace Rogers. 1973. *Thirteen-Star Flags: Keys to Identification.* Washington, D.C.: Smithsonian Institution Press.

Miller, Marla R. 2010. *Betsy Ross and the Making of America.* New York: Henry Holt and Company.

Vile, John R. 2015. *Founding Documents of America: Documents Decoded.* Santa Barbara, CA: ABC-CLIO.

SEDITION ACT OF 1918

After first adopting an Espionage Act in 1917, Congress also adopted a Sedition Act the following year. Clearly designed to quell dissent during World War I, the second act is notable for including a provision that specifically related to the American flag, giving it the same level of legal protection as the government, the Constitution, and the U.S. military. The law thus made it a crime to willfully

> utter, print, write, or publish any disloyal, profane, scurrilous, or abusive language about the form of government of the United States, or the Constitution of the United States, or the military or naval forces of the United States, or the flag of the United States, or the uniform of the Army or Navy of the United States, or any language intended to bring the form of government of the United States, or the Constitution of the United States, or the military or naval forces of the United States, or the flag of the United States, or the uniform of the Army or Navy of the United States into contempt, scorn, contumely, or disrepute.

The law also make it a crime to "willfully display the flag of any foreign enemy."

A number of state laws had similar provisions. Thus, an individual who refused a mob's request to kiss a U.S. flag was sentenced to 10–20 years of hard labor by a Montana court relying on such a state law. The federal judge who heard a habeas corpus appeal in *Ex Parte Starr* (1920) upheld the verdict even though he thought it would have been more appropriate to punish members of the mob.

Both the Espionage and Sedition Acts resulted in numerous Supreme Court decisions, almost all of which upheld the laws, despite modern judgments that they were violations of the First Amendment. Both acts have been subsequently repealed.

Despite national Flag Protection Acts of 1968 and 1989, the Supreme Court ruled in *Texas v. Johnson* (1989) and *United States v. Eichman* (1990) that such laws were unconstitutional.

See also *Ex Parte Starr* (1920); Flag Protection Acts of 1968 and 1989; *Texas v. Johnson* (1989); *United States v. Eichman* (1990); World War I

Further Reading

Gutfeld, Arnon. 1968. "The Ves Hall Case, Judge Bourquin, and the Sedition Act of 1918." *Pacific Historical Review* 37 (May): 163–178.

SEE YOU AT THE POLE (SYATP) EVENTS

Most schools in the United States fly flags. The flag pole thus arguably marks a hallowed, and easily identifiable, space for individuals to gather. Since 1990, some Christian students have gathered at school flag poles in See You at the Pole (SYATP) events prior to school openings to pray for their schools and fellow students. These gatherings, which occur on the fourth Wednesday in September, have typically garnered the most support from conservative Protestant denominations. Such gatherings in part may be a reaction to a series of Supreme Court decisions that have restricted collective religious activities, such as Bible reading and prayer, in public schools during regular school hours as violations of the Establishment Clause of the First Amendment but that have allowed student-led religious activities on an equal basis with other extracurricular activities.

Activities at a flag pole are, as with other speech allowed by the First Amendment, subject to reasonable time, place, and manner restrictions and cannot be officially "sponsored" by public schools, which remain subject to First Amendment Establishment Clause prohibitions.

See also Flying the Flag

Further Reading

Gwyn, Brian S. 2015. "Adopting a Respectful Posture toward Teacher Religious Expression: An Establishment Clause Analysis of North Carolina's Respect for Student Prayer and Religious Activity Law." *First Amendment Law Review* 13 (Spring): 426–470.

RelgiousTolerance.org. 2017. "'See You at the Pole' Public School Prayer Event." Accessed January 27. http://www.religioustolerance.org/chr_syatp.htm

Shanafelt, Robert. 2008. "The Nature of Flag Power: How Flags Entail Dominance, Subordination, and Social Solidarity." *Politics and the Life Sciences* 27 (September): 13–27.

SHIFFLER, GEORGE

See Xenophobia, Nativism, and the U.S. Flag

SMITH, WHITNEY

Of all the scholars of flags, probably none has had more influence than Whitney Smith (1940–2016). A Massachusetts native, he was born in Arlington and grew up in Lexington and Winchester. He acquired a love of flags at an early age. At the age of 18, he combined the Latin word for "flag," *vexillum*, with the Greek suffix *logia*, meaning "study," to coin the word "vexillology" for the study of flags.

After earning an undergraduate degree in political science from Harvard and his PhD in the same subject from Boston University, where he taught for a time, he left in 1970 to devote himself to vexillology. He amassed a collection of more than 4,000 flags and 10,000 books on the subject, most of which are now housed in the Dr. Whitney Smith Flag Research Center Collection at the Briscoe Center for American History at the University of Texas at Austin, which acquired it in 2013.

When he was only 20, Smith helped design Guyana's national flag and subsequently consulted on a number of others. Although he opposed flag burning, he believed that the right was protected by the First Amendment of the U.S. Constitution.

Smith wrote 27 books on flags, the most notable of which is *Flags Through the Ages and Across the World*, which he first published in 1975. He also organized the First International Congress of Vexillology, which took place in the Netherlands; founded the North American Vexillological Association; and helped found *The Flag Bulletin* and the Flag Research Center.

Smith died in Peabody, Massachusetts, in 2016, at the age of 76.

Further Reading

Marquard, Bryan. 2016. "Whitney Smith, 76; Coined Term for Scholarly Study of Flags." *Boston Globe*, November 29.

New York Times. 2016. "Flag Fanatic Invented His Own Scholarly Discipline." December 4.

Smith, Whitney. 1975. *Flags Through the Ages and Across the World*. New York: McGraw-Hill.

SMITH V. GOGUEN (1974)

In *Smith v. Goguen*, 415 U.S. 566 (1974), the U.S. Supreme Court affirmed lower court decisions in determining that a Massachusetts statute that provided punishment to an individual who "treats contemptuously" the U.S. flag was unconstitutionally vague and overbroad. The case arose when police arrested Valerie Goguen for displaying a four-by-six-inch flag on the left rear of his blue jeans. Goguen was convicted under a state law that applied to anyone who "publicly mutilates, tramples upon, defaces or treats contemptuously the flag of the United States." Notably, Goguen was not charged with physical flag desecration but with contemptuous treatment.

Justice Lewis Powell wrote the opinion on behalf of five justices. Powell observed that the doctrine of vagueness was designed to incorporate notions of fair notice or warning. He further noted that standards of contemptuous behavior varied widely, particularly when it came to youthful fashion. Given the unlikelihood that the Massachusetts law was designed to criminalize every informal use of the flag, the law needed to set forth a standard that individuals of common intelligence could understand in advance: "Where inherently vague statutory language permits such selective law enforcement, there is a denial of due process."

Justice Byron White authored a concurring decision disagreeing with Powell's rationale. White did not think the law was vague with regard to Goguen's conduct: "It should not be beyond the reasonable comprehension of anyone who would conform his conduct to the law to realize that sewing a flag on the seat of his pants is contemptuous of the flag." White further believed that Congress and the states had the right to preserve the physical integrity of the flag as well as "its use, display, and disposition." For him, this would include limiting advertising involving the flag. Although White would therefore "affirm Goguen's conviction . . . had he been convicted for mutilating, trampling upon, or defacing the flag, or for using the flag as a billboard for commercial advertisements or other displays," he thought that the "treats contemptuously" provision involved "communicating ideas about the flag." He believed that decisions in *West Virginia State Board of Education v. Barnette* (1943), involving flag saluting; *Street v. New York* (1969), in which flag desecration was linked to speech against the flag; or *Stromberg v. California* (1931), which involved anti-governmental communication, all suggested that laws directed to speech about the flag violated the First and Fourteenth Amendments. If, by contrast, the state believed that Goguen's conduct did not communicate anything, then there would be no reason for finding that he had acted "contemptuously."

Justice Harry Blackmun wrote a dissenting opinion joined by Chief Justice Warren Burger. Blackmun did not believe the law was unconstitutionally vague. He thought that it was proper for the state to preserve its physical integrity by preventing it from being worn on the seat on an individual's pants.

Justice William Rehnquist authored a dissent also joined by C. J. Burger. Rehnquist did not believe the statute was unconstitutionally vague. Acknowledging that the case contained elements of symbolic speech, Rehnquist did not think that Goguen was exempt from prosecution simply because he owned the flag.

He believed that the term "contemptuously" should be understood within the context of the wider law, which he believed punished individuals for contemptuous use regardless of its purpose. He observed that: "Massachusetts has not merely prohibited impairing of the physical integrity of the flag by those who would cast contempt upon it, but equally by those who would seek to take advantage of its favorable image in order to facilitate any commercial purpose, or those who would seek to convey any message at all by means of imprinting words or designs on the flag." Rehnquist believed that Goguen's conviction was consistent with the tests established in *United States v. O'Brien* (1968), involving the burning of draft cards, which permitted regulations of conduct involving incidental restrictions on speech when such restrictions are within governmental powers, when they further an important governmental interest unrelated to the suppression of free expression, and when they are not greater than necessary to secure this interest.

Much as he would later do in flag-burning cases, Rehnquist cited numerous historical references on the importance of the U.S. flag. Rehnquist would thereby distinguish Goguen's acknowledged right "to express verbally whatever views it was he was seeking to express by wearing a flag sewn to his pants," but he believed the action was itself contemptuous and therefore subject to punishment.

See also Flag Desecration; *Street v. New York* (1969); *Stromberg v. California* (1931); *West Virginia State Board of Education v. Barnette* (1943)

Further Reading

Goldstein, Robert. 1995. *Saving "Old Glory": The History of the American Flag Desecration Controversy*. Boulder, CO: Westview Press.

Pollitt, Daniel H. 1992. "Reflections on the Bicentennial of the Bill of Rights: The Flag Burning Controversy: A Chronology." *North Carolina Law Review* 70 (January): 553–614.

SOILING OF OLD GLORY, THE (PHOTOGRAPH)

On April 5, 1976, Stanley Forman (b. 1945) took a Pulitzer Prize–winning photograph of a white teenager, Joseph Rakes, appearing to use the staff of an American flag as a spear to attack a Yale-educated African American attorney named Ted Landsmark in Boston's City Hall Plaza. Landsmark's nose was broken in the incident, which occurred during a protest by white demonstrators against court-ordered busing to desegregate the city's schools. Landsmark was an innocent bystander who happened to be in the square for other business when he was attacked.

The photo, which was first published in *The Boston Herald America*, won Forman his second Pulitzer Prize. It became known as *The Soiling of Old Glory*. The event captured in the photograph was later depicted in Dana Chandler's colorful painting, entitled the *Ted Landsmark Incident* (Boime 1990, 19–21).

Louis P. Masur further describes the background of this incident in a book published in 2008. Masur notes that the photograph evoked earlier images by Paul Revere of the Boston Massacre, brought to mind the role of Crispus Attucks in that event, and may even have evoked images of the sword being thrust in the side of Jesus at his crucifixion (2008, 68–69, 75). The photograph was in sharp contrast to heroic photos of the flag raising on Iwo Jima.

The photograph was cropped for effect, and contrary to appearances, a white person (Jim Kelly) who appeared to be holding Landsmark so that Rakes could strike him was actually trying to raise him from the ground and protect him. Moreover, rather than using the flag as a spear, Rakes was actually waving it from side to side, and evidence suggests that it did not actually strike Landsmark (Masur 2008, 87–88).

Forman eventually switched from still photography to video. Landsmark went on to hold a variety of public service positions in Boston, eventually earning a PhD in history. Rakes, who received a two-year suspended sentence and a two-year probation for assaulting Landsmark, eventually apologized to Landsmark.

See also Civil Rights; Iwo Jima Flag Raising; Old Glory Flag

Further Reading

Boime, Albert. 1990. "Waving the Red Flag and Reconstituting Old Glory." *Smithsonian Studies in American Art* 4 (Spring): 2–25.

Encarnacao, Jack. 2016. "Boston Icon Ted Landsmark Reflects on Busing Attack." *Boston Herald* March 21.

Masur, Louis P. 2008. *The Soiling of Old Glory: The Story of a Photograph That Shocked America*. New York: Bloomsbury Press.

SOUSA, JOHN PHILIP

See "Stars and Stripes Forever"

SPACE PROGRAM, AMERICAN FLAG AND THE

On July 20, 1969, astronauts Neil Armstrong and Edwin "Buzz" Aldrin, who were part of the crew of the Apollo 11 mission, planted an American flag on the surface of the moon. In announcing the space program in September 1962, President John F. Kennedy had said, "We mean to lead, for the eyes of the world now look into space, to the moon and to the planets beyond, and we have vowed that we shall not see it governed by a hostile flag of conquest, but by a banner of freedom and peace" (quoted in Platoff 1993).

European explorers had planted their nations' flags in the New World to denote territorial claims. However, the United Nations Treaty on Principles Governing the Activities of States in the Exploration and Use of Outer space, Including the Moon and Other Celestial Bodies had already specified that "outer space, including the moon and other celestial bodies, is not subject to national appropriation by claim of sovereignty, by means of occupation, or by any other means." Planting a U.S. flag on the moon was thus framed as a symbolic gesture meant to highlight the achievements of the American astronauts and of the country that had paid for their endeavor, rather than an attempt to stake a formal claim to new territory.

Astronaut Buzz Aldrin stands beside a U.S. flag on the moon on July 20, 1969, during the Apollo 11 mission into space. Nationalism and competition with the Soviet Union were key factors in motivating America's race to the moon. (National Aeronautics and Space Administration)

The National Aeronautics and Space Administration (NASA) "has used three images—nationalism, romanticism, and pragmatism—to build political support over its history" (Byrnes 1994, 3). The flag certainly appealed to the first two of these. Significantly, the lunar module was named the *Eagle*, which is the national bird, and after touching down, Armstrong radioed, "Houston, Tranquility base here. The *Eagle* has landed" (86). When he touched the moon's surface, Armstrong stated, "That's one small step for a man, one giant leap for mankind." The event was an occasion of great national pride, topping what President Nixon described as "the greatest week in the history of the world since the Creation."

The nation had previously decorated its space capsules and space suits with flags, and Congress had expressed opposition to Americans planting foreign or international flags on the moon. The flag was a three-by-five-foot nylon flag, which was carried on the Lunar Module ladder, where it had to be shielded in a protective shroud to keep it from being destroyed by heat during lunar entry. Because there was no wind on the moon, the flag had to be mounted with a cross bar to give it the effect of waving; this effect was enhanced with ripples when the astronauts could not pull the horizontal telescoping rod all the way out. Subsequent moon landings have also included flag deployments.

Ever since the bicentennial of the Declaration of Independence in 1976, the Vehicle Assembly building (VAB) at the Kennedy Space Center in Florida has also sported a massive (209 feet by 110 feet) painting of a flag on the outside (Platoff 2007, 164).

After the terrorist attacks on the United States on September 11, 2001, the space shuttle *Endeavor* took more than 6,000 flags to and from the International Space Station to distribute to families of those who had been killed in that catastrophe (Philonoe 2002, 7).

See also Eagle; Terrorist Attacks of September 11, 2001

Further Reading

Byrnes, Mark E. 1994. *Politics and Space: Image Making by NASA*. Westport, CT: Praeger.

Philonoe. 2002. "At Large and at Small: A Piece of Cotton." *The American Scholar* 71 (Winter): 5–9.

Platoff, Anne M. 2007. "Flags in Space: NASA Symbols and Flags in the U.S. Manned Space Program." *Flag Bulletin: The International Journal of Vexillology* 46 (September–December): 143–221.

Platoff, Anne M. 1993. "Where No Flag Has Gone Before: Political and Technical Aspects of Placing a Flag on the Moon." Paper presented to the 26th Meeting of the North American Vexillological Association, San Antonio, Texas, October 11. http://www.hq.nasa/gov/alsj/alsj-usflag.html

SPANISH-AMERICAN WAR

In 1898, the United States went to war with Spain after reports of Spanish atrocities in Cuba, a longtime territory of Spain, and the sinking of the American warship *Maine*, which was docked in the harbor at Havana, Cuba's capital. Although Americans were convinced that the sinking of the *Maine* was the result of a Spanish attack, historians believe that the ship's boiler exploded. Another factor in America's decision to use its military to pry Cuba loose from Spain was that many Americans had come to see their nation as one prepared to seize the mantle of global leadership from Spain and other old European powers of yesteryear. Cuba was seen by many Americans as a stepping stone in that march toward empire.

The Spanish-American War occurred near the end of a decade in which there had been major national efforts to encourage military drills and the salute to the flag in American schools, in part as a way of combatting fears that immigrants would not otherwise become familiar with American ideals. It also came at a time when Americans like Theodore Roosevelt (who would later lead a regiment of Rough Riders in the Battle of San Juan Hill in Cuba) were stressing the need for American manhood and social Darwinists touted imperialism as a way for superior (white) races to spread civilization to those who were less civilized.

The Spanish-American War was the first time that the U.S. Army appointed ex-Confederate officers to serve in the officer corps. Enthusiastic crowds of southerners waved American flags as Roosevelt's troops passed from New Orleans on their way to Tampa, where U.S. forces were being transported over to Cuba. Hearst newspapers, which had pushed vigorously for the war, printed full-page images of the flag for people to post in their homes (O'Leary 1999, 121, 138, 139).

A relatively quick American victory resulted in the U.S. acquisition of Guam, Cuba, and the Philippines. In the last, it quickly encountered a popular insurgency,

Theodore Roosevelt and his Rough Riders on San Juan Hill in 1898. The Spanish-American War raised the question of what rights "followed the flag" into America's newly acquired foreign territories. (Library of Congress)

which would take more than 125,000 U.S. soldiers to end. American commanders often treated native Filipinos much as they had treated Native Americans during the winning of the West. The war stirred debate between war hawks such as Theodore Roosevelt and individuals such as the writer Mark Twain, who bemoaned what he considered to be American imperialism.

Even though the Philippines was largely Roman Catholic, President William McKinley subsequently defended the U.S. decision to keep it as a colony by saying that after praying to God, he had concluded that "there was nothing left for us to do but to take them all, and to educate the Filipinos, and uplift and civilize and Christianize them, and by God's grace do the very best we could by them, as our fellow-men from whom Christ also died." The Spanish-American War was thus "reshaped into a religious mission" (O'Leary 1999). Meanwhile, many Americans expressed pride in the idea that the American flag was flying in far-flung corners of the globe. As one veteran of the Grand Army of the Republic stated: "Old Glory is God's chosen banner. When one flag was raised on these islands and proclaimed freedom and independence to the inhabitants, it was like a voice from heaven" (142).

The United States raised a 120-by-43-foot flag over its arsenal in Havana on New Year's Day of 1899. Adm. George Dewey's flagship flew a red-white-and-blue pennant over 500 feet long when it returned to the United States (Guenter 1990,

147–148). The war was the first to be filmed, with cameramen generating footage showing servicemen returning with war dead, reenactments of battles, and narratives of the war. One of the reenactments, called *Raising Old Glory Over Morro Castle,* is believed to be the first instance when the raising of a U.S. flag was captured on film (Eberwein 2013, 83–84).

See also Bruner, Frank C.; Civil War; Cult of the Flag; Hoar, George F.; Grand Army of the Republic (GAR)

Further Reading

Eberwein, Robert. 2013. "Following the Flag in American Film." In *Eastwood's Iwo Jima: Critical Engagements with Flags of Our Fathers and Letters from Iwo Jima*, edited by Rikke Schubart and Anne Gjelsviki. New York: Columbia University Press.

Guenter, Scot M. 1990. *The American Flag, 1777–1924: Cultural Shifts from Creation to Codification*. Cranbury, NJ: Associated University Presses.

Kinzer, Stephen. 2017. *The True Flag: Theodore Roosevelt, Mark Twain, and the Birth of American Empire*. New York: Henry Holt and Company.

McConnell, Stuart. 1996. "Reading the Flag: A Reconsideration of the Patriotic Cults of the 1890s." In *Bonds of Affection: Americans Define Their Patriotism*, edited by John Bodnar, 102–119. Princeton, NJ: Princeton University Press.

Neuman, Gerald L., and Tomilo Brown-Nagin, eds. 2015. *Reconsidering the Insular Cases: The Past and Future of the American Empire*. Cambridge, MA: Human Rights Program at Harvard Law School.

O'Leary, Cecilia Elizabeth. 1999. *To Die For: The Paradox of American Patriotism*. Princeton, NJ: Princeton University Press.

Sparrow, Bartholomew H. 2006. *The Insular Cases and the Emergence of American Empire*. Lawrence: University Press of Kansas.

SPENCE V. WASHINGTON (1974)

In *Spence v. Washington*, 418 U.S. 405 (1974), the U.S. Supreme Court overturned the conviction of a college student who had hung a U.S. flag from his apartment in Seattle, Washington. Harold Omand Spence, a student at the University of Washington in Seattle, hung a three-by-five-foot flag upside down (a recognized symbol of distress); he had taped a peace symbol to both sides with black removable tape. Seattle police arrested him and charged him with violating Washington state's "improper use" statute.

The statute provided that:

> No person shall, in any manner, for exhibition or display:
>
> (1) Place or cause to be placed any word, figure, mark, picture, design, drawing or advertisement of any nature upon any flag, standard, color, ensign or shield of the United States or of this state . . . or
>
> (2) Expose to public view any such flag, standard, color, ensign or shield upon which shall have been printed, painted or otherwise produced, or to which shall have been attached, appended, affixed or annexed any such word, figure, mark, picture, design, drawing or advertisement.

Spence was tried before a local justice court and found guilty. He then received a new jury trial before the King County Superior Court, during which time he explained that he had hung the flag to protest the U.S. invasion of Cambodia and the killings at Kent State University and that he desired to associate the flag with peace. The jury also convicted him. Although the Washington Court of Appeals reversed his conviction, the Washington Supreme Court reversed the Appeals Court decision and affirmed Spence's conviction.

The U.S. Supreme Court's per curiam opinion overturning Spence's conviction rested on several observations. The majority noted that Spence owned the flag in question and he displayed it on private property and thus committed "no trespass or disorderly conduct." It further observed that there was no evidence of "any risk of breach of the peace." Moreover, Spence was "engaged in a form of communication." The court noted that cases such as *Stromberg v. California* (1931) and *West Virginia State Board of Education v. Barnette* (1943) had "recognized the communicative connotations of the use of flags." Context often gives "meaning to the symbol."

The court noted that while the Washington Supreme Court had rejected the breach-of-the-peace argument, the state counsel had relied on that rationale in oral arguments. The court found that it was "totally without support in the record." As to the argument for protecting the sensibilities of individuals who passed by, *Street v. New York* (1969) and other cases had established that "the public expression of ideas may not be prohibited merely because the ideas are themselves offensive to some of their hearers." People who passed by were not captive and could avert their eyes. The majority did not think Spence could "be punished for failing to show proper respect for our national emblem."

The state court had argued that Washington had "an interest in preserving the national flag as an unalloyed symbol of our country." The Supreme Court acknowledged, "For the great majority of us, the flag is a symbol of patriotism, of pride in the history of our country, and of the service, sacrifice, and valor of the millions of Americans who in peace and war have joined together to build and to defend a Nation in which self-government and personal liberty endure." Further acknowledging that interest in preserving the flag as a symbol was legitimate, the court did not think that there was any risk "that appellant's acts would mislead viewers into assuming that the Government endorsed his viewpoint. To the contrary, he was plainly and peacefully protesting the fact that it did not." Moreover, the state did not charge him with flag desecration, and he did not "permanently disfigure the flag or destroy it."

In a brief concurring opinion, Justice William O. Douglas relied on a ruling by the Iowa Supreme Court in *State v. Kool*, 212 N.W.2d 518. The court had decided that an individual's actions in hanging a peace symbol wrapped in tinfoil against a flag constituted a form of constitutionally protected symbolic speech.

In a brief dissenting opinion, Chief Justice Warren Burger suggested that however unwise the law might be, "it should be left to each State and ultimately the common sense of its people to decide how the flag, as a symbol of national unity, should be protected."

Justice William Rehnquist wrote a dissent joined by Burger and Byron White. Although Rehnquist agreed that Spence had engaged in a form of communication, he did not think that this insulated his action from further scrutiny. He believed the precedent in *Halter v. Nebraska* (1907) had established the government's right to protect usages of the flag that might cheapen or degrade it. Rehnquist emphasized that the intent of the law was not to protect the cloth or the resale value of the flag but its importance as a symbol of nationhood and unity. The purpose of this law, which Rehnquist approved, was simply to withdraw "a unique national symbol from the roster of materials that may be used as a background for communications."

This decision would ultimately be one of the cases that laid the groundwork for U.S. Supreme Court decisions in *Texas v. Johnson* (1989) and *United States v. Eichman* (1990) protecting the right of individuals to burn the flag as an act of symbolic protest.

See also *Halter v. Nebraska* (1907); *Stromberg v. California* (1931); *Texas v. Johnson* (1989); *United States v. Eichman* (1990); *West Virginia State Board of Education v. Barnette* (1943)

Further Reading

Goldstein, Robert Justin. 1995. *Saving "Old Glory": The History of the American Flag*. Boulder, CO: Westview.

Post, Robert. 1995. "Recuperating First Amendment Doctrine." *Stanford Law Review* 47 (July): 1249–1281.

SPIRIT OF '76

One of the most famous paintings that depicts an American flag, albeit anachronistically, is *The Spirit of '76*. It was painted by Archibald Willard (1836–1918) of Ohio and largely marketed by James F. Ryder, who owned a photography shop and pioneered chromolithography.

Originally displayed under the title *Yankee Doodle*, the massive 8-by-10-foot painting was exhibited at the Centennial Exposition in Philadelphia in 1876, sent on a tour of several U.S. cities, and exhibited at the Corcoran Gallery in Washington, D.C. Gen. John H. Devereux eventually purchased it and donated it to Marblehead, Massachusetts, where it remains on display. The painting, reproductions of which are sometimes cropped to eliminate a dead soldier in the foreground, contains three central figures, two of whom are playing drums and one a fife. Willard patterned the middle figure, an aged drummer, after his father, Samuel Willard, an itinerant Baptist preacher who had recently died. The fifer to his right was modeled by Hugh Moser, a Civil War veteran and friend of Willard, while the young drummer on the left resembled Henry K. Devereux, the son of General Devereux, who eventually bought the painting. There are soldiers behind them following a flag with stars and stripes. This flag most closely resembles the so-called Cowpens Flag, with 12 stars in a canton surrounding one in the middle.

The painting is anachronistic because Congress had not yet established the U.S. flag in 1776, and most soldiers would have marched under regimental, rather than U.S., colors. In addition to numerous lithographs, which spread the fame of the painting, Willard made several copies. Willard returned to patriotic themes and

Archibald Willard's famous painting entitled *Yankee Doodle*, became better known as *The Spirit of '76*. The image, a tribute to the patriots of the American Revolution, was painted for the Centennial Exposition in Philadelphia, Pennsylvania, in 1876. Depictions of this scene often crop out the picture of the dead soldier in the foreground. (Library of Congress)

imagery on several other occasions in his career as an illustrator as well. For example, one of his later works was a picture known variously as *The Divine Origin of the Flag*, the *Stars and Stripes and the Magi*, or *Allegory of the Flag*. He also utilized flag imagery in a number of murals (Pauly 1976, 447).

Although Willard's painting is most frequently associated with centennial celebrations, the image of his painting was revived during the Spanish-American War and World War I as well as during the bicentennial of American independence.

See also Betsy Ross Flag; Cowpens Flag; Centennials, Bicentennials, and Other Commemorations; Spanish-American War; World War I.

Further Reading

Pauly, Thomas H. 1976. "In Search of 'The Spirit of '76." *American Quarterly* 28 (Autumn): 445–464.

Zaretsky, Natasha. 2007. *No Direction Home: The American Family and the Fear of National Decline, 1968–1980*. Chapel Hill: University of North Carolina Press.

SPORTS

Sports play an important role in American life and are often identified with the flag and with the national anthem that celebrates it.

In 1936, Americans refused to dip the U.S. flag toward Adolf Hitler during the Olympic Games, and it subsequently was one of the few nations who refused to dip the flag to any leader, including American presidents, when the games were held in American cities.

One of the high points of Olympic competitions occurs when winners of the gold, silver, and bronze medals stand on a platform as their national anthem is played and their flag is raised. In the Mexico City Olympics in 1968, during that ceremony, Tommie Smith (gold winner) and John Carlos (bronze winner) raised a hand with a black gloved fist in a black power salute. After African American sprinters Wayne Collett and Vince Matthews turned their backs as "The Star-Spangled

Banner" was being played, the International Olympic Committee barred them from future competition.

The practice of singing "The Star-Spangled Banner" before sports events, which is now standard practice, began in World War I, before it was officially designated as the national anthem. The first performance of "The Star-Spangled Banner" by a band at a sports event, however, took place in 1898 at New York City's Polo Grounds (Guenter 1990, 167). The practice of singing the national anthem before baseball games was continued during World War II and thereafter. Over time, the practice spread to other athletic events. In 1931, for example, writer Robert Phillips observed that "a characteristic feature of the [college] football games of recent years . . . has been the raising of the national standard to the accompanying tune of the Star Spangled Banner" (Phillips 1931, 137).

The musical range of the anthem is out of reach for many individuals without musical training, so being asking to sing or play the national anthem is a high honor. Renditions of the anthem can also subject performers to considerable scrutiny. In 1965, Robert Goulet, who had been raised in Canada, flubbed the lines in a performance for the heavyweight boxing title in Lewiston, Maine (Ferris 2014, 211). In 1969, Jose Feliciano's folk rendition of the tune offended many listeners, but not nearly so much as Roseanne Barr's tasteless parody in 1990, which included grabbing her crotch and spitting, in what some called the "Barr-Mangled Banner" (242). Also notable for departing from the traditional tune was Marvin Gaye's rendition of the anthem at the 1983 NBA All-Star Game.

In 2011, NBC Sports stirred controversy when it omitted the words "under God" from a video of the Pledge of Allegiance that it showed before the U.S. Open Golf Tournament. It subsequently apologized for the omission (Matheson 2011).

In 1996, Mahmoud Abdul-Rauf of the Denver Nuggets basketball team refused for a time to stand for the national anthem, claiming that this conflicted with his Islamic beliefs (Ferris 2014, 245). During the 2016 football season, Colin Kaepernick, the quarterback for the San Francisco 49ers, refused to stand for the playing of the national anthem, saying "I am not going to stand up to show pride in a flag for a country that oppresses black people and people of color." Many observers have speculated that as a direct result of Kaepernick's controversial decision, no NFL team was willing to sign him to a contract for the 2017 season. Consistent with the Supreme Court's decision forbidding compulsory flag salutes in *West Virginia State Board of Education v. Barnette* (1943), Kaepernick certainly had a constitutional right to express his views, but this did not shield him from considerable displeasure among fans. For much of the 2017 NFL season, however, players on multiple teams knelt during the national anthem in peaceful protest against alleged police brutality and social injustice.

In Baltimore, where "The Star-Spangled Banner" was composed and whose team, the Orioles, are sometimes known simply as the O's, the audience remains quietly standing during the anthem until fans shout out the "O" when the verse "O Say, does that star-spangled banner yet wave. " Similarly, fans of the Atlanta Braves often substitute the term "Braves" for "brave" in the last line of the song (Molotsky 2001, 2). The game of baseball is so closely tied to the Star-Spangled Banner that

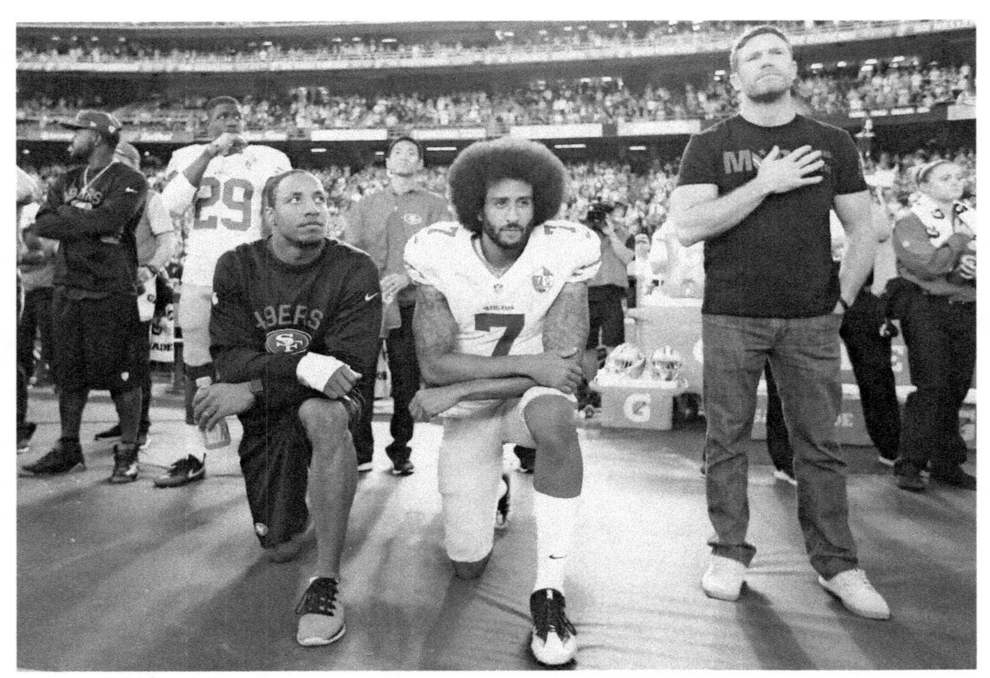

San Francisco 49er Colin Kaepernick (center) kneels during the national anthem before a game against the San Diego Chargers in San Diego, California, September 1, 2016. According to Kaepernick, his protest of "The Star Spangled Banner" was due to his unwillingness to show pride in the American flag because he believes the United States oppresses people of color. (Michael Zagaris/San Francisco 49ers/Getty Images)

Ferris observes that some children are said to believe the last words of the anthem are "play ball" (2014, 1).

It is increasingly common to unfurl flags that cover an entire playing field at sports events. Teams may play a few thousand dollars to rent such a flag for a special game. Sometimes the volunteers recruited to hold the flag above the ground (touching the ground is considered to be disrespectful) will shake their arms to create ripples so the flag appears to be flapping in the wind.

See also Civil Rights Movement; National Anthem; Olympic Protocol; *West Virginia State Board of Education v. Barnette* (1943); World War I; World War II

Further Reading

Branch, John. 2008. "American Flags as Big as Fields." *New York Times,* July 4. http://www.nytimes.com/2008/07/04/sports/04flags.html

Butterworth, Michael L. 2005. "Ritual in the 'Church of Baseball': Suppressing the Discourse of Democracy after 9/11." *Communication and Critical/Cultural Studies* 2 (June): 107–129.

Chiari, Mike. 2017. "Colin Kaepernick Reportedly Will Stand for National Anthem Next Season." Bleacher Report, Inc. Last modified March 2.http://bleacherreport.com/articles/2695776-colin-kaepernick-reportedly-will-stand-for-national-anthem-next-season

Ferris, Marc. 2014. *Star-Spangled Banner: The Unlikely Story of America's National Anthem*. Baltimore: Johns Hopkins University Press.

Guenter, Scot M. 1990. *The American Flag, 1777–1924: Cultural Shifts from Creation to Codification*. Cranbury, NJ: Associated University Presses.

Laband, David N., Ram Pandit, John P. Sophocleus, and Anne M. Laband. 2009. "Patriotism, Pigskins, and Politics: An Empirical Examination of Expressive Behavior and Voting." *Public Choice* 138:97–108.

Matheson, Alison. 2011. "NBC Apologizes for Cutting 'Under God' from Pledge at U.S. Open." *Christian Post*, June 20. https://www.christianpost.comnews/nbc-apolotizes-after-cutting-under-god-from-pledge-at-us-open-51341

Molotsky, Irvin. 2001. *The Flag, the Poet and the Song: The Story of the Star-Spangled Banner*. New York: Dutton.

Phillips, Robert. 1931. *The American Flag: Its Uses and Abuses*. Boston: Stratford Company.

Polacek, Scott. 2017. "Multiple Browns Players Kneel during National Anthem vs. Giants." Bleacher Report, Inc. Last modified August 21. http://bleacherreport.com/articles/2728743-multiple-browns-players-kneel-during-national-anthem-vs-giants

Voigt, David Q. 1974. "Reflections on Diamonds: American Baseball and American Culture." *Journal of Sport History* 1 (Spring): 3–25.

Wyche, Steve. 2016. "Colin Kaepernick Explains Why He Sat during the National Anthem." NFL. Last modified August 27. http://www.nfl.com/news/story/0ap3000000691077/article/colin-kaepernick-explains-why-he-sat-during-national-anthem

STAFFORD FLAG

As the popularity of the U.S. flag has increased, so have the myths surrounding its history, which are fueled by the public's desire to view relics. One such myth was long associated with a flag that was flown over the American warship *Bonhomme Richard*, which John Paul Jones commanded during the Revolutionary War. The legend began in 1861, when Sarah Smith Stafford claimed on the death of her father, James Bayard Stafford, that he had rescued the flag after an encounter with the British warship *Serapis* in September 1779. She further claimed that the flag subsequently had been awarded to her father in recognition of his valor.

Despite evidence that the American flag had gone down with the ship, the flag that Sarah Strafford produced was displayed at events in the North at the beginning of the Civil War (she also sent a small piece to President Abraham Lincoln) and later displayed at centennial celebrations in Philadelphia in 1876. In 1887, the Grand Army of the Republic, a Civil War veterans' organization that did much to encourage the display of, and reverence for, the U.S. flag, displayed it at its national encampments, where it was honored as "the first Stars and Stripes ever made" (quoted in Guenter 1990, 99).

After the family donated the flag to President William McKinley, it was displayed at the Smithsonian Institution until the 1930s. At that time, though, historians called its provenance into question, and the Smithsonian withdrew it from public viewing.

See also Centennials, Bicentennials, and Other Commemorations; Civil War; Grand Army of the Republic (GAR); Ross, Betsy

Further Reading

Guenter, Scot M. 1990. *The American Flag, 1777–1924: Cultural Shifts from Creation to Codification*. Cranbury, NJ: Associated University Presses.

Smith, Nicholas. 1908. *Our Nation's Flag in History and Incident*. 2nd ed. Milwaukee: Young Churchman Co.

STANDARD-BEARERS

See Flag Bearers, Standard-Bearers

STARS, ARRANGEMENT OF ON U.S. FLAGS

Since 1777, the U.S. flag mostly has had one star for each state. At one time, the flag also had one stripe for each state, but this number has subsequently been reduced to 13, to stand for each of the original states.

Although stars have long been arranged in rows, the specific patterns were not determined until the 20th century. It is therefore common to see early flags where 13 stars are displayed in a circle (often called the Betsy Ross flag), where 12 stars arranged in a circle (the Cowpens Flag) or square (the Trumbull Flag) surround a 13th, or where stars are arranged in a medallion, an hourglass, a bomb, a cross, a wreath or double wreath, a flower, a diamond, a medallion, a large star, or other patterns (Mastai 1973).

See also: Constellation; Stripes on the Flag

Further Reading

Mastai, Boleslaw, and Marie-Louise D'Otrange. 1973. *The Stars and the Stripes: The American Flag as Art and as History from the Birth of the Republic to the Present*. New York: Alfred A. Knopf.

Selkirk, Keith. 1992. "Old Glory: A Practical Investigation into Pattern." *Mathematics in School* 21 (March): 42–45.

Wilson, Chris. 2010. "13 Stripes and 51 Stars." *Slate*, June 9. http://www.slate.com/articles/life/do_the_math/2010/06/13_stripes_and_51_stars.html

STARS AND STRIPES

One of the most common names for the United States flag is the Stars and Stripes. As with the nicknames the Red, White, and Blue and the Star-Spangled Banner, this term (early versions sometimes reversed the current order and referred, as in "The Star-Spangled Banner," to "broad stripes and bright stars") is based directly on the flag's design. Its field features 13 red and white stripes representing the original 13 states and a canton with a star for each state. John Philip Sousa's "The Stars and Stripes Forever" has been designated as the nation's official march.

Today the term is also used for a military newspaper that is distributed to members of the armed forces. A newspaper by the same name was printed during the Civil War, near Bloomfield, Missouri, beginning in 1861. The current paper operates from the Department of Defense but is editorially independent of it.

During the Civil War, the U.S. Navy acquired a steamer that it operated from 1861 to 1865 and named USS *Stars and Stripes*. The navy used it as both a gunboat and a tugboat.

Bloomfield, Missouri, is the site of the Stars and Stripes Museum and Library, which contains the largest collection of past issues of the newspaper as well as other books and artifacts related to U.S. military history.

See also Nicknames for the U.S. Flag; Stars, Arrangement of on U.S. Flags; "Stars and Stripes Forever"; Stripes on the Flag

Further Reading

Cornebise, Alfred E. 1984. *The Stars and Stripes: Doughboy Journalism in World War I.* Westport, CT: Greenwood Press.

The Stars and Stripes Museum/Library. http://www.starsandstripesmuseumlibrary.org/who-we-are/home

"STARS AND STRIPES FOREVER"

Declared the national march in 1987, John Philip Sousa's "The Stars and Stripes Forever" remains an American classic. It is better known for its martial tune than for the words, which Sousa also composed.

Born in Washington, D.C., in 1854, Sousa was enlisted as an apprentice in the United States Marine Band in 1868. After spending some time in a theatrical orchestra, he became head of the Marine Band in 1880 and had a hand in the design of the sousaphone. Sousa would later form his own band, for which he composed "The Stars and Stripes Forever." The formal debut of the piece occurred in Philadelphia on May 14, 1897, though it had probably been played as an encore in Augusta, Maine, two weeks earlier, on May 1 (Warfield 2013, 264).

Sousa claimed that "my idea was to climax the march with three themes—one representing the North, a broad sweeping theme; the South with its languorous beauty and romance, and the West, a strong, pushing melody carrying all before it" (quoted in Warfield 2013, 265). The march was well-received from the beginning and undoubtedly gained part of its appeal by the patriotism being generated by the prospect (soon realized) of a war with Spain. One reviewer observed that the work was "stirring enough to rouse the American eagle from his crag and set him to shriek exultantly while he hurls his arrows at the aurora borealis" (267). Sousa authored another march, "El Capitan," about this same time, which portrayed the Spanish administration of colonial Peru as incompetent (Hess 1998).

Sousa died of a heart attack in 1932 after a concert that concluded with "The Stars and Stripes Forever."

Because the piece is a march, it is rarely sung, unlike "America" or "The Star-Spangled Banner." The chorus of the march notes that:

> Other nations may deem their flags the best
> And cheer them with fervid elation
> But the flag of the North and South and West
> Is the flag of flags, the flag of Freedom's nation.

The first verse of the march proclaims, "The red and white and starry blue/ Is freedom's shield and hope." Another verse refers to "the banner of the right" and later combines this "right" with "might." Similarly, the march ends with the words "That by their might and by their right/ It waves forever."

Sousa once said, "I would rather be the composer of an inspirational march than a manufactured symphony" (Van Outryve 2006, 15). He seems to have gotten his wish with his most famous march. A 1952 film about Sousa is also entitled *The Stars and Stripes Forever*. In 1987, his march by that name was designated as the official National March of the United States.

See also Spanish-American War; "Star-Spangled Banner" (Anthem)

Further Reading

Hess, Carol A. 1998. "John Philip Sousa's El Capitan: Political Appropriation and the Spanish-American War." *American Music* 16 (Spring): 1–24.

Van Outryve, Karen. 2006. "Idea Bank: Appreciating an Old Favorite: Sousa's All-Time Hit." *Music Educator's Journal* 92 (January): 15.

Warfield, Patrick. 2013. *Making the March King: John Philip Sousa's Washington Years, 1854–1893*. Urbana-Champaign: University of Illinois Press.

"STAR-SPANGLED BANNER" (ANTHEM)

"The Star-Spangled Banner," which Congress designated as the national anthem in 1931, was written by Francis Scott Key, an American lawyer who was kept aboard a British ship during the British bombardment of Fort McHenry outside Baltimore, Maryland, on the night of September 13–14, 1814, during the War of 1812. Key had been meeting with the British in an attempt to free a doctor, William Beanes, whom the British had captured.

The words of the song reflect Key's relief on seeing the massive American flag flying over the fort at daybreak as the British forces retreated. Scott describes the flag as waving not only as a reference to the stormy weather of the night but arguably to the wider tempests to which the war had subjected the nation. The flag Key observed, which had been stitched by Mary Pickersgill and her assistants of Baltimore, had 15 stars and stripes, denoting the 15 states then in the Union.

Key wrote his song to the tune of a British drinking song named "Anacreon in Heaven," which had been composed by John Stafford Smith. Anacreon was a Greek poet who celebrated parties and was associated in the song with Venus (the goddess of love) and Bacchus (the god of wine).

Key's lyrics fairly quickly became popular. The song consists of four stanzas, each of which ends with the same phrase: "O'er the land of the free and the home of the brave."

The first stanza, which is typically the only one that is sung at public events, is as follows:

O say! Can you see, by the dawn's early light,
What so proudly we hail'd at the twilight's last gleaming?
Whose broad stripes and bright stars, thro' the perilous fight,
O'er the ramparts we watched were so gallantly streaming?

And the rockets' red glare, the bombs bursting in air
Gave proof thro' the night that our flag was still there.
O say! Does that star-spangled banner yet wave
O'er the land of the free and the home of the brave?

Sheet music, printed in 1861, of "The Star Spangled Banner" with a cover illustration of a Union soldier holding the Stars and Stripes at an encampment. The lyric of the song was written during the War of 1812 and the song gained popularity through the 19th century, until it was finally officially adopted as the anthem of the United States in 1931. (Library of Congress)

The reference to stars highlights not only the design of the flag's canton but also the fact that Key had endured a night of anxiousness as he awaited the outcome of the conflict. The sounds he referenced were from bombs that the British had fired at the fort. The last two lines point both to the American view of the fight (an attempt to preserve "liberty") and to the bravery of American soldiers in beating back the British attack. A spangle is a bright shiny object. The term "star-spangled" had earlier twice appeared in Shakespearean plays.

The use of the second person in the opening line seems to invite those who are singing the song to join the author as he looks toward the flag (the language quickly turns to the first person plural, "we"). Both Key's opening and closing lines end in questions, as if to further engage those who read or sing the song. The most vivid imagery in the first stanza stems from the contrast between Key's fear at twilight, which could have marked the end of the republic, and his joy at daybreak when he observed that the flag was still waving. Benjamin Franklin had utilized a similar metaphor on the last day of the Constitutional Convention of 1787. After observing a painted sun at the top slat of the Chippendale chair on which George Washington had been seated as he presided over the convention, Franklin observed that while painters had found it difficult to distinguish a rising from a setting sun, he was confident that the sun was rising rather than setting over America (Vile 2016, 2:755–757).

The second stanza of "The Star-Spangled Banner" continues as follows:

On the shore, dimly seen thro' the mist of the deep,
Where the foe's haughty host in dread silence reposes.

What is that which the breeze, o'er the towering steep,
As it fitfully blows, half conceals, half discloses?
Now it catches the gleam of the morning's first beam,
In full glory reflected now shines in the stream.
'Tis the star-spangled banner, O long may it wave
O'er the land of the free and the home of the brave.

Key associated the British, who had just sacked Washington, D.C., with arrogance (a "haughty host"). The British navy was the world's most powerful, so a victory over its navy was particularly impressive.

The third stanza of the song has received the most criticism. Originally, this criticism focused on anti-British sentiments that became especially inconvenient when America allied with her in both world wars. More recent critics have noted that Key's reference to "the hireling and slave" is a reference to slaves to whom the British had promised freedom in exchange for their military services in fighting against Americans. This somewhat undermines Key's tribute to "the land of the free."

And where is that band who so vauntingly swore,
That the havoc of war and the battle's confusion
A home and a country should leave us no more?
Their blood has wash'd out their foul footstep's pollution.
No refuge could save the hireling and slave
From the terror of flight or the gloom of the grave,
And the star-spangled banner in triumph doth wave
O'er the land of the free and the home of the brave.

The fourth stanza, which is the first to evoke God (and the origin of the term "In God We Trust," which is now displayed on American currency), is as follows:

O thus be it ever when freemen shall stand
Between their lov'd home and war's desolation,
Blest with vict'ry and peace, may the Heav'n-rescued land
Praise the pow'r that hath made and preserv'd us a nation.
Then conquer we must, when our cause it is just,
And this be our motto, "In God is Our Trust."
And the star-spangled banner in triumph shall wave
O'er the land of the free and the home of the brave.

This verse associates the American victory with God's providence, but it also gains much of its power both from Key's hope that this victory will result in "peace" and from the fact that Americans are fighting to defend their homes. The song does not reference the fact that early in the war, many Americans had also hoped to conquer British Canada but stresses that Americans had little choice—"Then conquer we must"—but to seek to repel the British attack.

During the Civil War, "The Star-Spangled Banner" was largely claimed by the northern states (the South often used "Dixie"), which is somewhat ironic since the War of 1812 had been widely opposed in the North, where it had wrecked New England commerce. In 1861, Oliver Wendell Holmes Sr. (the father of a supreme court justice with his name) wrote a fifth verse to "The Star-Spangled Banner" that was included in a number of collected songs of the day and appeared to contemplate slave emancipation. This additional stanza was worded as follows:

> When our land is illum'd with Liberty's smile,
> If a foe from within strike a blow at her glory,
> Down, down, with the traitor that dares to defile
> The flag of her stars and the page of her story!
> By the millions unchain'd who our birthright have gained
> We will keep her bright blazon forever unstained!
> And the Star-Spangled Banner in triumph shall wave
> While the land of the free is the home of the brave.

After the war, all sections of the nation embraced "The Star-Spangled Banner."

The tune, which has a high range, has often been criticized for being more difficult to sing than some other patriotic songs. As is typical of the period, it also contains a number of contractions designed to match the words with the meter. Still, popular fondness for the song appears to have risen with respect for the flag.

Although some Americans have expressed a preference for a less martial song, the battle Key described was a defensive one, involving the protection of home and hearth, rather than a battle for foreign conquest. It seems a bit unusual that while mentioning the "star-spangled banner" and "broad stripes and bright stars," the only reference to colors is the "red glare" of the rockets rather than the red, white, and blue colors of the flag itself.

The original draft of "The Star-Spangled Banner" passed from Key to Judge Joseph H. Nicholson. He passed it on to his granddaughter, Mrs. Edward Shippen. Henry Walters, a Baltimore collector, subsequently purchased it and donated it to the Walters Art Gallery in Baltimore. The gallery later sold it to Catherine Key Jenkins, a Key descendant, who donated it to the Maryland Historical Society, where it is carefully preserved (Ferris 2014, 185).

See also Civil War; Key, Francis Scott; National Anthem

Further Reading

Ferris, Marc. 2014. *The Star-Spangled Banner: The Unlikely Story of America's National Anthem*. Baltimore: Johns Hopkins University Press.

Leepson, Marc. 2014. *What So Proudly We Hailed: Francis Scott Key, A Life*. New York: St. Martin's Press.

Lichtenwanger, William. 1977. "The Music of 'the Star-Spangled Banner': From Ludgate Hill to Capitol Hill." *Quarterly Journal of the Library of Congress* 34 (July): 136–170.

Molotsky, Irvin. 2001. *The Flag, the Poet and the Song: The Story of the Star-Spangled Banner*. New York: Dutton.

Montgomery, Henry C. 1948. "Anacreon and the National Anthem." *The Classical Outlook* 26 (December): 30–31.

Shafer, Leah. 2013. "Francis Scott Key and the Complex Legacy of Slavery." *U.S. Capitol Historical Society—A Blog of History*, June 14. https://uschs.wordpress.com/tag/oliver-wendell-holmes/

Siegel, Eli, and Edward Green. 2014. "'The Star-Spangled Banner' as a Poem." *Choral Journal* 55 (November): 28–35.

Svejda, George J. 1969. *History of the Star-Spangled Banner from 1814 to the Present*. Division of History: Office of Archeology and Historical Preservation: National Park Service, U.S. Department of the Interior.

Taylor, Lonn, Kathleen M. Kendrick, and Jeffrey L. Brodie. 2008. *The Star-Spangled Banner: The Making of an American Icon*. Washington, D.C.: Smithsonian Books.

Vile, John R. 2016. *The Constitutional Convention of 1787: A Comprehensive Encyclopedia of America's Founding*. Rev. 2nd ed. Clark, NJ: Talbot Publishing.

STAR-SPANGLED BANNER (FLAG)

No physical flag in the United States is more iconic than the flag that flew over Fort McHenry during the battle for Baltimore in the War of 1812. It inspired Francis Scott Key to write "The Star-Spangled Banner," which is now the national anthem. Although the term "Star-Spangled Banner" has become a favorite nickname for the U.S. flag, it remains especially associated with the flag that flew over Fort McHeny, which is now on permanent display at the Smithsonian Institution in Washington, D.C.

The flag was commissioned by Maj. George Armistead, who was responsible for defending Fort McHenry. It was created by a local flag maker, Mary Young Pickersgill, and her assistants. Made of wool bunting, it was originally 30 by 42 feet. Consistent with legislation adopted in 1795, the flag had 15 stars (Kentucky and Vermont had entered as states, joining the original 13 states) and stripes. Congress subsequently reduced the number of stars back to the original 13.

The original "Star Spangled Banner" that inspired Francis Scott Key's song is shown displayed at the Boston Naval Yard in 1873. It was moved to the Smithsonian Institution in 1907, removed for safekeeping during World War II, returned, and painstakingly restored. (Bettmann/Getty Images)

The British had approached Baltimore, then the nation's third largest city, after winning the battle of Bladensburg just outside of Washington, D.C. That victory enabled British forces to invade the capital of Washington, D.C., and burn the White House, the Capitol Building, and other structures. Key observed the bombardment of Fort McHenry from a British ship where he was being held after trying to negotiate the release of a local doctor whom the British had imprisoned. Key was joyful upon rising the morning after that fierce bombardment to see the U.S. flag still flying over the fort. His song, as did Andrew

Jackson's military victory in New Orleans, did much to increase national pride and highlighted the role of the flag as a national symbol.

Armistead acquired the flag before he died in 1818 and then passed it down to his widow, Louisa, who willed it to her daughter Georgiana Armistead Appleton. It was displayed during the Marquis de Lafayette's visit to Baltimore in 1824, was exhibited at Peale's Museum and Gallery of the Fine Arts in 1830, was draped above the platform when president-elect William Henry Harrison visited in 1841, was displayed at the Young Men's Whig National Convention in Baltimore in May 1844, and was apparently regularly brought out at Baltimore's annual Defenders' Day Celebrations (Taylor, Kendrick, and Brodie, 2001, 83–85).

Consistent with practice of the day, pieces of the flag, including one of the massive stars, were sometimes cut out and given as mementos. This practice ended, however, when it was given to the Smithsonian in 1907. Louisa Armistead had also sewn a red chevron in the shape of the letter *A* on one of the white stripes near the bottom of the flag (Taylor, Kendrick, and Brodie 2001, 92).

Georgiana Armistead Appleton sent the flag to George Henry Preble, the author of a classic work on the flag. Preble had a canvas backing stitched to it and had the first photograph of it taken as it hung from the side of a building in the Boston Naval Yard in 1873. Although the flag was sent to the Centennial Exposition in Philadelphia, it was not displayed there but was returned to Georgiana, whose son, Eben Appleton, inherited it in 1878. He kept it locked in a safe for most of the time that he owned it, though he did consent to have it carried in a military parade in Baltimore in 1880.

He loaned the flag to the Smithsonian Institution in 1907 and converted the loan to a gift in 1912, stipulating that it would never leave that institution. In 1914, the Smithsonian commissioned Amelia Fowler of Boston, an embroidery teacher who had previously help preserve flags for the U.S. Naval Academy in Annapolis, to help preserve the flag. She and her assistants did so by removing the backing that Preble had added and sewing on a new linen backing that required 1.7 million stitches. Because they used the same side as the previous backing, the flag had to be displayed, contrary to the suggested flag code of 1923, with the canton facing the right of the viewer rather than on the left (Taylor, Kendrick, and Brodie 2001, 110–111). The top part of the flag was displayed in a case in the Arts and Industries Building, with the lower half folded at the bottom of the case.

In 1942, the Smithsonian transported the Star-Spangled Banner and numerous other artifacts to warehouses outside Luray, Virginia, for safekeeping in the event of possible Axis attacks. These artifacts remained there until late 1944, when they returned to Washington, D.C.

In 1964, the flag was moved to the Museum of History and Technology (now called the National Museum of American History), where it was suspended vertically from the Museum's Flag Hall until 1998. Two years before, the Smithsonian held a conference to discuss the preservation and future exhibition of the flag. The flag then underwent years of painstaking restoration (much of which was financed by designer Ralph Lauren), which included cleaning and removing the flag backing that Amelia Fowler had added and replacing it with Stabiltex, a lighter polyester material.

Since 2008, the Star-Spangled Banner has been displayed in a largely horizontal position in a carefully regulated chamber in dim light in the Smithsonian's National Museum of American History.

See also Key, Francis Scott; National Anthem; Nicknames for the U.S. Flag; Pickersgill, Mary Young; "Star-Spangled Banner" (Anthem)

Further Reading

Ferris, Marc. 2014. *Star-Spangled Banner: The Unlikely Story of America's National Anthem.* Baltimore: Johns Hopkins University Press.

Molotsky, Irvin. 2001. *The Flag, the Poet and the Song: The Story of the Star-Spangled Banner.* New York: Dutton.

Poole, Robert M. 2008. "Star-Spangled Banner Back on Display." *Smithsonian Magazine*, November. http://www.smithsonianmag.com/history/star-spangled-banner-back-on-display-83229098/

Svejda, George J. 1969. *History of the Star-Spangled Banner from 1814 to the Present.* Division of History: Office of Archeology and Historical Preservation: National Park Service, U.S. Department of the Interior.

Taylor, Lonn, Kathleen M. Kendrick, and Jeffrey L. Brodie. 2008. *The Star-Spangled Banner: The Making of an American Icon.* Washington, D.C.: Smithsonian Books.

STAR-SPANGLED BANNER FLAG HOUSE

The Star-Spangled Banner Flag House is located at 844 East Pratt Street in Baltimore, Maryland. It was built in 1793 and once served as the home and business of Mary Pickersgill, who moved there in 1806 after the death of her husband in Philadelphia. Pickersgill directed the sewing of the large flag that flew above Fort McHenry during the attempted invasion of Baltimore in the War of 1812. It was this flag that served as an inspiration to Francis Scott Key in the writing of "The Star-Spangled Banner," which later became the country's official national anthem.

The city of Baltimore purchased the house in 1927, and the Star-Spangled Banner House Association established the museum that remains there today. The house contains exhibits that describe both the defense of Baltimore and Mary Pickersgill and her family.

See also Key, Francis Scott; Pickersgill, Mary Young; War of 1812

Further Reading

Visit Baltimore. 2017. "The Star-Spangled Banner Flag House." Accessed January 20. http://baltimore.org/info/star-spangled-banner-flag-house

STREET V. NEW YORK (1969)

The case of *Street v. New York*, 394 U.S. 576 (1969), deferred answering the question, later addressed in *Texas v. Johnson* (1989) and *United States v. Eichman* (1990), as to whether laws prohibiting the burning of the U.S. flag were constitutional.

The case arose after a Brooklyn, New York, resident named Sidney Street, after hearing of the assassination of civil rights leader James Meredith, went to a street corner and burned an American flag. A police officer who came to the scene found Street talking with a group of about 30 people saying, "We don't need no damn flag." When the officer questioned him about the flag, Street responded, "Yes; that is my flag; I burned it. If they let that happen to Meredith, we don't need an American flag." Street was subsequently convicted under a New York law that made it a crime to "publicly mutilate, deface, defile, or defy, trample upon, or cast contempt upon either by words or act" any flag of the United States. A criminal court judge convicted Street of malicious mischief, and the New York Court of Appeals affirmed the judgment. Street appealed his conviction on grounds that the law was overbroad, vague, and imprecise and that the act of flag burning was an act of expression protected by the Fourteenth Amendment.

Justice John Marshall Harlan II's opinion avoided answering the last two questions by focusing instead on his concern that Street's conviction might have been based on the words he said rather than the action that he took in burning the flag. Harlan found that Street's attorneys had appropriately raised the issue of whether he had been convicted on the basis of what he said. He further ruled that on the basis of *Stromberg v. California* (1931), which had involved the display of a red flag, and other cases, that it was the court's duty to reverse a conviction if it might have been based on his words alone or on his words in combination with his action. In this specific case, he observed that the trial court had taken both words and actions into account. If, therefore, the section prohibiting individuals from speaking against the flag were unconstitutional, the law could not stand.

Harlan examined each of four interests that the state might have asserted in punishing words directed against the flag. The first involved deterring words that might incite others to commit unlawful acts. Prior cases, however, "prohibit the States from imposing criminal punishment for public advocacy of peaceful change in our institutions." The second involved the state's interest "in preventing appellant from uttering words so inflammatory that they would provoke others to retaliate physically against him, thereby causing a breach of the peace." Harlan did not think that Street's words rose to the level of "fighting words" that the state could prohibit. The third involved the state's interests in "protecting the sensibilities of passers-by who might be shocked by appellant's words about the American flag." Harlan determined that any shock would have derived from the "content of the ideas expressed" and that prior cases had prohibited convictions based on such content. The fourth involved the state's interests in seeing that Street "showed proper respect for our national emblem." Harlan cited the court's decision in *West Virginia State Board of Education v. Barnette* (1943), the second flag-salute case, to show that the state had no right to require such respect from those who did not want to give it.

Chief Justice Earl Warren authored a dissent in this case because he thought the court should have directly answered the issue of whether the First and Fourteenth Amendments allowed legislation prohibiting flag desecration. Warren thought that the record clearly established that Street had been convicted for burning the flag rather than for what he said and that the statements elicited had only been used to show his illegal intent. Warren said that he believed that "Both those who seek constitutional shelter for acts of flag desecration perpetrated in the course of a political protest and those who must enforce the law are entitled to know the scope of constitutional protection." For his part, he believed that both "the states and the Federal Government do have the power to protect the flag from acts of desecration and disgrace," but he did not delineate his reasons for this belief.

In a separate dissent, Justice Hugo Black also thought that Street had been convicted for burning the flag rather than for his accompanying words. Although he was an absolutist when it came to free speech, he did not believe it covered actions like flag burning.

Justice Byron White also thought the conviction had been based on flag burning. He too would sustain a conviction based on flag burning, absent a compelling argument that such actions were protected under the Constitution.

Justice Abe Fortas authored yet a fourth dissent indicating that he did not regard laws against flag burning any differently than he would laws that prohibited the burning of one's clothing in public intersections. Citing the conviction in *Halter v. Nebraska* (1907) for improperly using the flag for advertising purposes, Fortas further noted: "The flag is a special kind of personality. Its use is traditionally and universally subject to special rules and regulation." He ended by observing: "Protest does not exonerate lawlessness. And the prohibition against flag burning on the public thoroughfare being valid, the misdemeanor is not excused merely because it is an act of flamboyant protest."

See also *Halter v. Nebraska* (1907); *Stromberg v. California* (1931); *Texas v. Johnson* (1989); *United States v. Eichman* (1990); *West Virginia State Board of Education v. Barnette* (1943)

Further Reading

Goldstein, Robert Justin. 1996. *Desecrating the American Flag: Key Documents of the Controversy from the Civil War to 1995*. Syracuse, NY: Syracuse University Press.

STRIPES ON THE FLAG

The 13 alternating red and white stripes on the U.S. flag represent the original 13 colonies that declared their independence from Great Britain in 1776 and subsequently joined together as a single nation, first under the Articles of Confederation and then under the Constitution that was written in 1787. Many of America's early flags also had 13 stars, 1 for each colony or state. In some early flags, as in the flag sometimes included in the depiction of the battle between John Paul Jones's ship the *Bonhomme Richard* and the English *Serapis*, the stripes were red, white, and blue.

Stripes were not unique to the U.S. flag. Ships of the English East India Company had 13 red and white stripes (sometimes the number varied) and a canton with the cross of St. George (Horner 1915, 112). During this same period, there were 11 cities and nations with striped ensigns, at least 6 of which used red and white stripes (Rankin 1954, 341). Stripes were especially effective for signaling (Moeller 1995).

The Sons of Liberty, who may have exhibited striped flags as early as the 1760s, may well have likened perceived British abuses to the stripes that were used as punishment for slaves and criminals (Keim and Keim 2007, 36). Stripes had previously also been associated with prisoners, who wore striped clothing; with prostitutes, who in Europe were sometime forced to wear striped stockings; and with other oddities and misfits. A leading scholar of the subject observed: "Everything changes after 1775. In one decade, the decade of the American Revolution, the stripe, still rare and exotic a generation earlier, begins to invade the world of clothing, textiles, emblems, and décor. This is the beginning of the romantic and revolutionary stripe born in the New World, but which is going to find the soil of old Europe particularly fertile ground" (Pastoureau 2001, 45).

Although most early U.S. flags have 13 stripes, a competing early tradition resulted in flags of 9 stripes. This symbolism was tied to John Wilkes (1725–1797), an Englishman who edited *The North Briton* and was elected to parliament for voicing his opposition to the policies of King George III. Like the colonists, Wilkes had opposed general warrants, which had authorized the ransacking of his house, and he won a substantial judgment against the government. However, as one scholar observed: "Nine was a volatile number in the colonies. . . . As the sum of four and five, it referred to the forty-fifth edition of the North Briton newspaper in which publishers John Wilkes had lambasted King George" and which had led to his arrest (Teachout 2009, 30).

Given the existence of early flags that sported 9 and 12 stripes, it has been suggested that the British cut away stripes from the colonies that they captured during the Revolutionary War (O'Dell, n.d., 11). Historians have also taken note of a 21-star flag with only 12 stripes; this flag's appearance may have arisen from a shortage of the materials needed to make a flag with a full complement of stripes (Keim and Keim 2007, 66).

Congressional legislation of 1777 specified that states would continue to be individually represented by both stars and stripes. When Vermont and Kentucky entered the Union, the number of stripes was accordingly increased to 15. Indeed, the flag flying over Fort McHenry in 1814 that Francis Scott Key memorialized in "The Star-Spangled Banner," which later became the nation's national anthem, has 15 stars and 15 stripes.

In 1818, Congress reduced the number of stripes on the flag from 15 to 13 but specified that the number of stars would continue to increase as new states were added. Capt. Samuel Reid is believed to have advised New York representative Peter Wendover that the 13 stripes could represent the original 13 states and the stars all of those in the Union (Guenter 1990, 46).

Francis Scott Key highlighted the "broad stripes and bright stars" in "The Star-Spangled Banner." It is possible that the Marquis de Lafayette may have been the first to describe the flag as "the stars and the stripes" (Mastai and D'Otrange 1973, 29). In his poem "To the United States of North America," Thomas Campbell likened the stripes on the American flag to the stripes that slaves received when they were disciplined, and some abolitionists picked up on this theme. *Emancipator and Free American* thus published lyrics emulating those of "The Star-Spangled Banner" that read: "O say, does that blood-striped banner still wave / O'er the land of the fetter and the hut of the slave?" (Taylor, Kendrick, and Brodie 2001, 51). This may be one reason that southerners preferred to describe the design on their flag as bars rather than stripes. The *Charleston Mercury* of March 23, 1861, thus observed: "We protest against the word 'stripes' as applied to the broad *bars* of the flag of our Confederacy. The word is quite appropriate as applied to the Yankee ensign or a barber's pole; but it does not correctly describe the red and white divisions of the flag of the Confederate states. The word is *bars*—we have removed from under the stripes" (quoted in Ness 2008, 38).

One variant of the stripes on the U.S. flag is found on the U.S. Customs Ensign, which has long flown over the U.S. Customs and Border Protection headquarters and over ports of entry. It contains 16 vertical stripes (there were 16 states when the flag was designed) in the field and an eagle in the white canton and would have identified ships at sea with authority to stop ships to collect customs. Nathaniel Hawthorne makes a reference to this flag in *The Scarlet Letter* (1850).

See also Campbell, Thomas; Confederate Flag; East India Company Flag; Key, Francis Scott; Stars and Stripes; Star-Spangled Banner (Flag); Union Flag: Washington's Coat of Arms

Further Reading

Cash, Arthur H. 2006. *John Wilkes: The Scandalous Father of Civil Liberty*. New Haven: Yale University Press.

Guenter, Scot M. 1990. *The American Flag, 1777–1924: Cultural Shifts from Creation to Codification*. Cranbury, NJ: Associated University Presses.

Hinrichs, Kit. 2016. *Long May She Wave: 100 Stars and Stripes Collectible Postcards*. New York: Potter Style.

Horner, Harlan H. 1915. "The American Flag." *Proceedings of the New York State Historical Association* 14:108–121.

Keim, Kevin, and Peter Keim. 2007. *A Grand Old Flag: A History of the United States through Its Flags*. New York: DK.

Mastai, Boleslaw, and Marie-Louise D'Otrange. 1973. *The Stars and the Stripes: The American Flag as Art and as History from the Birth of the Republic to the Present*. New York: Alfred A. Knopf.

Moeller, Henry W. 1995. *Shattering an American Myth: Unfurling the History of the Stars and Stripes*. Mattituck, NY: Amereon House.

Ness, William Boyd. 2008. *"Burning with Star-Fires": The National Flag in Civil War Poetry*. PhD thesis, University of Iowa.

O'Dell, Heather. N.d. *History of Our Flag*. Gettysburg, PA: Americana Souvenirs and Gifts.

Pastoureau, Michel. 2001. *The Devil's Cloth: A History of Stripes*. Translated by Jody Gladding. New York: Washington Square Press.

Rankin, Hugh F. 1954. "The Naval Flag of the American Revolution." *William and Mary Quarterly* 11 (July): 339–353.

Taylor, Lonn, Kathleen M. Kendrick, and Jeffrey L. Brodie. 2008. *The Star-Spangled Banner: The Making of an American Icon*. Washington, D.C.: Smithsonian Books.

Teachout, Woden. 2009. *Capture the Flag: A Political History of American Patriotism*. New York: Basic Books.

U.S. Customs and Border Protection. 2017. "Flag Day: CBP's Ensign Was America's First for Government Agency." Accessed May 25. https://www.cbp.gov/newsroom/spotlights/flag-day-cbps-ensign-was-americas-first-government-agency

STROMBERG V. CALIFORNIA (1931)

In *Stromberg v. California*, 283 U.S. 359 (1931), the U.S. Supreme Court overturned a California conviction of a 19-year-old woman who, as a member of the Young Communist League, was running a youth camp for 10- to 15-year-olds. Yetta Stromberg had been convicted in the Superior Court of San Bernardino County of violating provisions of the state law that provided for the following:

> Any person who displays a red flag, banner or badge or any flag, badge, banner, or device of any color or form whatever in any public place or in any meeting place or public assembly, or from or on any house, building or window as a sign, symbol or emblem of opposition to organized government or an invitation or stimulus to anarchistic action or as an aid to propaganda that is of a seditious character is guilty of a felony.

Stromberg's conviction was upheld by the District Court of Appeal and denied a hearing by the Supreme Court of California.

Stromberg had participated in a daily ceremony in which the red flag, which symbolized both Soviet Russia and the Communist Party of the United States, had been raised. As this occurred, children stood at salute and recited a pledge "to the worker's red flag, and to the cause for which it stands; one aim throughout our lives, freedom for the working class." Although Stromberg also kept a library that contained communist propaganda, there was no evidence that children had consulted it.

The trial court observed that the jury could have convicted Stromberg for violating any of the three concerns expressed by the law and that violation of any one would be sufficient to convict her. In writing his opinion for seven justices, however, Chief Justice Charles Evans Hughes expressed concern that Stromberg may have been convicted for her opposition to organized government apart from whether she sought to replace it through peaceful means. Noting that U.S. Supreme Court decisions in *Gitlow v. New York*, 268 U.S. 652 (1925); *Whitney v. California*, 272 U.S. 357 (1927); and *Fiske v. Kansas*, 274 U.S. 380 (1927) had all established that the Fourteenth Amendment applied the guarantees of freedom of speech in the First Amendment to the states, Hughes acknowledged that the right to free speech was not absolute: "A statute which upon its face, and as authoritatively construed, is so vague and indefinite as to permit the punishment of the fair use of this opportunity [that of seeking to change the government through peaceful means] is repugnant to the guaranty of liberty contained in the Fourteenth Amendment."

Justices James McReynolds and Pierce Butler both wrote dissents. McReynolds did not think the lower court permitted a review of the issue that Hughes had raised. After examining the instructions to the jury, which had distinguished between advocacy of peaceful and violent means of change, Justice Butler was convinced that Stromberg was not convicted for the former and would therefore have also upheld her conviction.

Although this case concerned a red flag rather than a U.S. flag, it demonstrates that the court has recognized for some time that individuals can convey speech through symbolic means like flags. In part because of this symbolic connection, the court would in *West Virginia State Board of Education v. Barnette* (1943) invalidate compulsory flag salutes in public schools as well as the conviction of a protestor who burned an American flag in *Street v. New York* (1969) and in *Texas v. Johnson* (1989) and *United States v. Eichman* (1990).

See also *Street v. New York* (1969); *Texas v. Johnson* (1989); *United States v. Eichman* (1990)

Further Reading

Goldstein, Robert Justin. 2000. *Flag Burning and Free Speech: The Case of* Texas v. Johnson. Lawrence: University Press of Kansas.

Sullenger, D. Wes. 2005. "Burning the Flag: A Conservative Defense of Radical Speech and Why It Matters Now." *Brandeis Law Journal* 43 (Summer): 796–666.

SUFFRAGISTS AND THE U.S. FLAG

Long before women in the United States secured the right to vote, they were engaged in political activities, including opposition to slavery, prohibition, and other issues. In 1848, a group of women gathered in New York for the Seneca Falls Convention, which issued a Declaration of Sentiments, patterned after the Declaration of Independence, affirming that "all men and women are created equal" and that women were entitled to the right to vote.

It was not until 1920, however, that women secured the right to vote. This right, secured through passage of the Nineteenth Amendment to the constitution, only came to be after years of political protest. These protests took many forms, including parades in which members of the National Woman's Suffrage Congressional Union, a major force in the suffrage movement, often marched under a flag with three vertical stripes of purple, white, and gold. Explanations for this color selection varied. *The Suffragist* published a story that said: "Purple is the color of loyalty, constancy to purpose, unswerving steadfastness to a cause. White, the emblem of purity, symbolizes the quality of our purpose; and gold, the color of light and life, is as the torch that guides our purpose, pure and unswerving" (quoted in LaCroix). Grace Hoffman White later said that the purple represented the "royal glory of womanhood"; white, "purity in home and politics"; and gold, the "crown of victory" (quoted in LaCroix).

Scholars have observed how suffragists drew attention to their cause through pageants, where women were often portrayed through an icon of justice (Collins 2012) and through public parades, where symbols were often used in support of their message of political equality (Tickner 1988). Such parades garnered publicity in part because of their effective use of "spectacle" and "iconography" (Borda 2002). A review of images of such parades in the archives of the Library of Congress and at other sites reveals that they also prominently featured U.S. flags, sometimes fairly large ones.

Suffragists carrying U.S. flags march in New York City for the right to vote, May 6, 1912. After more than 70 years of effort, women finally won the right to vote when the Nineteenth Amendment became law in August 1920. (Library of Congress)

Dr. Anna Shaw (1847–1919), who was active both in the Women's Christian Temperance Union (WCTU) and the movement for woman's suffrage, gave a well-known tribute to the flag:

> This is the American flag. It is a piece of bunting and why is it that, when it is surrounded by the flags of all other nations, your eyes and mine turn first toward it and there is a warmth at our hearts such as we do not feel when we gaze on any other flag? It is not because of the beauty of its colors, for the flags of England and France which hang beside it have the same colors. It is not because of its artistic beauty, for other flags are as artistic. It is because you and I see in that piece of bunting what we see in no other. It is not visible to the human eye but it is to the human soul.

She continued:

> We see in every stripe of red the blood which has been shed through the centuries by men and women who have sacrificed their lives for the idea of democracy; we see in every stripe of white the purity of the democratic ideal toward which all the world is tending, and in every star in its field of blue we see the hope of mankind that some day the democracy which that bit of bunting symbolizes shall permeate the lives of men and nations, and we love it because it enfolds our ideals of human freedom and justice. (1922, 758)

Similar to the strategy employed by the Seneca Falls Convention attendees of patterning their pleas after the Declaration of Independence, suffragists carried the flag as a way to indicate that they were appealing to American ideals. Civil rights protestors in the late 1950s and early 1960s, as well as modern immigrants, employed a similar strategy.

Marilyn Artus, who is preparing a project to commemorate the centennial of women's suffrage in 2020, is among modern women activists who use flag-related pieces of art to advocate for women's rights (Baker 2017).

See also Civil Rights Movement; Colors of the Flag; Immigrants and Flag-Waving

Further Reading

Baker, Melinda. 2017. "'Her Flags' Exhibit at the Arts Company Explores the American Female Experience." *Tennessean*, July 2.

Borda, Jennifer L. 2002. "The Woman Suffrage Parades of 1910–1913: Possibilities and Limitations of an Early Feminist Rhetorical Strategy." *Western Journal of Communication* 66 (Winter): 25–52.

Collins, Kristin A. 2012. "Representing Injustice: Justice as an Icon of Woman Suffrage." *Yale Journal of Law and the Humanities* 24:191–220. http://www.bu/edu/law/faculty/scholarship/workingpapers/2012.html

LaCroix. Allison. "The National Woman's Party and the Meaning Behind Their Purple, White, and Gold Textiles." National Woman's Party at Belmont-Paul Women's Equality National Monument. http://nationalwomansparty.org/the-national-womans-party-and-the-meaning-behind-their-purple-white-and-gold-textiles/.

Shaw, Anna. 1922. "Dr. Shaw's Tribute to the American Flag, Given Many Times." In *The History of Woman Suffrage*, edited by Susan B. Anthony and Ida Husted Harper. Vol. 5. Rochester, NY: Susan B. Anthony.

Tickner, Lisa. 1988. *The Spectacle of Women: Imagery of the Suffrage Campaign 1907–14*. Chicago: University of Chicago Press.

T

TAYLOR V. MISSISSIPPI (1943)

This companion case to *West Virginia State Board of Education v. Barnette* (1943) involved an appeal from three Jehovah's Witnesses who had been prosecuted under a Mississippi law that made it a felony for individuals who spoke or distributed a publication that "reasonably tends to create an attitude of stubborn refusal to salute, honor or respect the flag or government of the United States, or of the state of Mississippi." Their convictions had been upheld by the Mississippi Supreme Court.

The lead defendant, Carlos Taylor, had told women who had lost sons in World War II that the sacrifice of their sons had been useless and that saluting the flag was a form of idolatry. The other defendants had distributed literature containing similar messages.

Citing the companion case, Justice Owen J. Roberts noted on behalf of the court that if individuals had the right under the First and Fourteenth Amendments to refrain from saluting the flag, then they also had the right to express opposition to such salutes.

See also Jehovah's Witnesses; *Virginia State Board of Education v. Barnette* (1943); World War II

Further Reading

McAninch, William Shepard. "A Catalyst for the Evolution of Constitutional Law: Jehovah's Witnesses in the Supreme Court." *University of Cincinnati Law Review* 55 (1987): 997–1077.

TERRORIST ATTACKS OF SEPTEMBER 11, 2001

The surprise terrorist attacks on the World Trade Center and the Pentagon during the presidency of George W. Bush on September 11, 2001, brought about a surge in American patriotism and devotion to the American flag. It also was cited as a key factor in broad public support for subsequent American military actions in Iraq, Afghanistan, and elsewhere. The 2001 attacks resulted in almost 3,000 deaths and many more injuries in New York City alone.

Police officers and fire fighters who served as first responders after the attacks were among those who lost their lives when the towers collapsed. Both those who lived and those who died were hailed as heroes in the aftermath (Peabody and Jenkins 2017, 213–214). Indeed, one of the most iconic photographs to arise after the attack was one taken by Tom Franklin that showed three firemen raising a U.S. flag against the backdrop of debris covered in gray ash. The attack also served as the inspiration for Charlie Daniels's song "This Ain't No Rag, It's a Flag," which was released in 2001, and Toby Keith's song "Courtesy of the Red, White and Blue," which was released the next year and lauded subsequent U.S. efforts to hit the terrorists back.

Congress called on the American people to honor and remember those who lost their lives in the attacks by flying their flags at half-mast for 30 days after the attacks. A huge flag also was displayed from one side of the Pentagon, which had also been attacked (Goddard 2008). There was a surge in demand for flags in the immediate aftermath of the attacks (Donovan 2002), and a five-story flag was hung from a building that overlooked Ground Zero. In time, however, the flag began to symbolize those who sought foreign military action in response to the attacks. "Within weeks . . . the post-9/11 flag of unity began to harden again into the flag of war" (Teachout 2009, 208). Supporters of the later war against Iraq were thus more likely to wear flag lapel pins than those who opposed such military actions.

Newspapers also continued to used flag images to commemorate subsequent anniversaries of 9/11. In this context, "The flag served as collective comfort, much like a religious icon, soothing when people felt vulnerable" (Winfield, Li, and Page 2014, 145).

See also "Courtesy of the Red, White and Blue"; Lapel Pins; New York City Firemen Photograph; "This Ain't No Rag, It's a Flag"

Further Reading

Donovan, Aaron. 2002. "Update/Annin & Company; 13 Stripes, 50 Stars, 800 Tired Workers." *New York Times*, March 10. http://www.nytimes.com/2002/03/10/business/update-annin-company-13-stripes-50-stars-800-tired-workers.html

Gitlin, Todd. 2006. *The Intellectuals and the Flag*. New York: Columbia University Press.

Goddard, Kristian. 2008. "The Resilience of the Stars and Stripes." December 4. http://www.kristiangoddard.net/Blog/americanflag.htm

Lyubansky, Mikhail. 2010. "On 9-11, Patriotism, and the U.S. flag." *Psychology Today*, September 10. https://www.psychologytoday.com/us/blog/between-the-lines/201009/9-11-patriotism-and-the-us-flag

Peabody, Bruce, and Krista Jenkins. 2017. *Where Have All The Heroes Gone?* New York: Oxford University Press.

Teachout, Woden. 2009. *Capture the Flag: A Political History of American Patriotism*. New York: Basic Books.

Winfield, Betty Houchin, You Li, and Janis Teruggi Page. 2014. "'And Our Flag Was Still There': The American Flag News Images following 9-11." *Americanist* 27 (1): 131–47.

TEXAS V. JOHNSON (1989)

Texas v. Johnson, 491 U.S. 397 (1989), is one of the Supreme Court's most controversial decisions. The case arose when Gregory Lee Johnson, who was protesting at the Republican National Convention in Dallas in 1984, unfurled an American flag and burned it as a crowd of supporters chanted "America, the red, white, and blue, we spit on you." Texas charged Johnson with violating a Texas law prohibiting destruction of a venerated object, and he was convicted. The Court of Appeals for the Fifth District of Texas affirmed the conviction, only to have the Texas Court of Criminal Appeals overturn it. The U.S. Supreme Court subsequently agreed to consider the case.

Justice William J. Brennan wrote the opinion for the U.S. Supreme Court's five-to-four majority. Brennan observed that the trial court had convicted Johnson for desecration of the flag rather than for the words that he and the protestors uttered. Prior cases had established that the First and Fourteenth Amendments protected symbolic speech. These cases included *Spence v. Washington* (1974) (attaching a peace sign to a flag), *West Virginia State Board of Education v. Barnette* (1943) (compulsory flag salute), *Stromberg v. California* (1931) (displaying a red flag), and *Smith v. Goguen* (1974) (wearing a flag on the seat of one's pants). Brennan observed, "Pregnant with expressive content, the flag as readily signifies this Nation as does the combination of letters found in 'America.'" Prior cases had sought to understand flag displays in context, recognizing that "the government generally has a freer hand in restricting expressing conduct than it has in restricting the written or spoken word."

Gregory Lee Johnson, whose conviction for burning an American flag was overturned by the Supreme Court in *Texas v. Johnson* (1989), poses on June 28, 1989. In its controversial decision, the court ruled that flag burning was a form of symbolic speech that was protected by the First and Fourteenth Amendments. (Bettmann/Getty Images)

In upholding a law that forbade the burning of draft cards in *United States v. O'Brien* (1968), the court sought to establish whether governmental interests in regulating the nonspeech element of an act could justify incidental limitations on free expression. In this case, Texas justified its actions as a way of avoiding breaches of the peace and preserving the flag as a symbol of national unity. Brennan did not believe the evidence in this case was not implicated in this case since it did not result in such a breach or provoke a riot. He further observed that burning the flag was not a form of "fighting words" subject to regulation, as in *Chaplinsky v. New Hampshire* (1942), because Johnson's actions were not directed to a specific person, nor did the words rise to creating an imminent lawless action, such as

Brandenburg v. Ohio (1969), involving a speech at a Ku Klux Klan rally, presented. Notably, Texas did not see fit to use its breach of the peace statutes in this case.

Although previous cases had recognized the role of the flag as a symbol of nationhood and national unity, this interest is directly tied to Johnson's own right to free expression and is content-based in that it would permit speech favoring the flag but not criticizing it. Brennan observed, "If there is a bedrock principle underlying the First Amendment, it is that the government may not prohibit the expression of an idea simply because society finds the idea itself offensive or disagreeable." Moreover, "to conclude that the government may permit designated symbols to be used to communicate only a limited set of messages would be to enter territory having no discernible or defensible boundaries." Brennan observed that there was no constitutional text that would enable the court to treat the flag differently than other symbols and that American Framers had themselves expressed contempt for the English Union Jack.

Brennan did think that government had the right to enact "precatory [recommendatory] regulations describing the proper treatment of the flag," but he expressed hope that "the flag's deservedly cherished place in our community will be strengthened, not weakened, by our holding today." He explained, "Our decision is a reaffirmation of the principles of freedom and inclusiveness that the flag best reflects, and of the conviction that our toleration of criticism such as Johnson's is a sign and source or our strength." He further observed, "We can imagine no more appropriate response to burning a flag than waving one's own, [and] no better way to counter a flag burner's message than by saluting the flag that burns."

Justice Anthony Kennedy wrote a brief concurring opinion indicating that the judiciary sometimes had to issue decisions that it did not like.

Chief Justice William Rehnquist wrote a ringing dissent, joined by Justices Byron White and Sandra Day O'Connor, in which he cited numerous poems and historical events to indicate that "the American flag has occupied a unique position as the symbol of our Nation, a uniqueness that justifies a governmental prohibition against flag burning in the way respondent Johnson did here." Rehnquist cited national laws and symbols involving the U.S. flag, and the fact that 48 of 50 states, as well as Congress, had adopted legislation seeking to protect it. He stated:

> The American flag . . . throughout more than 200 years of our history, has come to be the visible symbol embodying our Nation. It does not represent the views of any particular party, and it does not represent any particular political philosophy. The flag is not simply another "idea" or "point of view" competing for recognition in the marketplace of ideas.

To Rehnquist, burning the flag was "the equivalent of an inarticulate grunt or roar . . . most likely to be indulged in not to express any particular idea, but to antagonize others." He observed that the majority decision went beyond previous flag cases, and he considered Brennan's decision to be "patronizing." Rehnquist believed that the case constituted an example of trying to set up the justices as a set of Platonic guardians.

Justice John Paul Stevens authored a separate dissent, based on the intangible meaning of the flag and on the fact that Johnson was prosecuted not for what he said but for what he did. Stevens did not think Johnson's actions were much different than if he had chosen to spray-paint or project his sentiments onto a national monument.

In reaction to this decision, numerous members of Congress advocated a constitutional amendment to prohibit flag desecration. Instead, Congress adopted national legislation that the court invalidated in *United States v. Eichman* (1990).

See also Flag Desecration Amendment; *Smith v. Goguen* (1974); *Spence v. Washington* (1974); *Stromberg v. California* (1931); *United States v. Eichman* (1990); *West Virginia State Board of Education v. Barnette* (1943)

Further Reading

Goldstein, Robert Justin. 1995. *Saving "Old Glory:" The History of the American Flag Desecration Controversy*. Boulder, CO: Westview Press.

Goldstein, Robert Justin. 2000. *Flag Burning and Free Speech: The Case of* Texas v. Johnson. Lawrence: University Press of Kansas.

"THERE'S A STAR-SPANGLED BANNER WAVING SOMEWHERE"

One of the classic tunes that emerged from World War II was entitled "There's a Star-Spangled Banner Waving Somewhere." It was first recorded by Elton Britt on March 19, 1942. Britt was born in Arkansas and was barred from service because of a congenital heart defect. His recording became the first time a country singer won a gold record, and it topped the sales of both sheet music and records in 1943 (Hatchett and McNeil 2005, 34–35). The lyrics appear to have been written by Paul Roberts, which was the stage name of Paul Roberts Metivier, who served in the army during World War II. Much of the marketing was done by Shelby Darnell, a pseudonym for Bob Miller.

The song was written from the perspective of a "crippled" "mountain boy," who is trying to enlist in the armed service despite his disability. It evokes patriotic heroes from Washington and Lincoln to Colin Kelly (a U.S. pilot who was shot down while attacking Japanese ships during World War II).

The song demonstrates how the flag often serves as a rallying point, especially during times of crisis and war. It further associates the flag with the willingness of Americans to die for their country.

See also World War II

Further Reading

Hatchett, Louis, and W. K. McNeil. 2005. "There's a Star-Spangled Banner Waving Somewhere." In *Country Music Goes to War*, edited by Charles K. Wolfe and James E. Akenson, 33–42. Lexington: University Press of Kentucky.

THIRTEEN-STAR FLAGS

Few flag patterns stir the American imagination like the original flags with 13 stars, representing (like the stripes) the 13 original states. Such flags were the official flags from 1777 until 1795, after which a flag with 15 stars and 15 stripes (like that which flew over Fort McHenry and inspired "The Star-Spangled Banner") was adopted.

Part of the beauty of the 13-star flags is that they were produced before there were any regulations as to how the stars would be placed. As a consequence, numerous patterns of stars were utilized in these early flags, including three horizontal rows of 4-5-4, five horizontal rows of 3-2-3-2-3, three vertical rows of 4-5-4, two vertical rows of 7-6, and even diagonal rows of 4-5-4 (Cooper 1973; Martucci 2000). Among the most popular patterns was one in which the 13 stars were arranged in a circle (the so-called Betsy Ross flag). Another common pattern featured 12 stars in a circle surrounding a 13th star in the circle's center. Such patterns reinforced the idea that the United States represented a new constellation. Because these patterns are both aesthetically pleasing and historically significant, they are among the most reproduced of all the flag patterns in U.S. history. These patterns were especially prominent during celebrations of the centennial and bicentennial of the Declaration of Independence. The pattern is also used as the U.S. Navy "Boat" Flag.

It is important for collectors to realize that such banners could have been made anytime from 1776 forward.

See also Bennington Flag; Betsy Ross Flag; Constellation; Cowpens Flag; Easton Flag; Revolutionary War Battle Flags; Schuyler Flag; Union Flag

Further Reading

Cooper, Grace Rogers. 1973. *Thirteen-Star Flags: Keys to Identification*. Washington, D.C.: Smithsonian Institution Press.

Martucci, David. 2000. "The 13 Stars and Stripes: A Survey of 18th Century Images." *NAVA News*, April–June. Addenda published in *NAVA News* in July–September 2000, April–June 2003, and October–December 2005.

"THIS AIN'T NO RAG, IT'S A FLAG"

The lyrics of country music star Charles Daniels's (b. 1936) "This Ain't No Rag, It's a Flag" attempted to use the imagery of the U.S. flag, which Daniels has incorporated into the design of his guitar, to generate support for the U.S. war against terrorism. The contrast of a flag to a rag is striking (the lyrics to "You're a Grand Old Flag" were changed after objections to the original lines "You're a Grand Old Rag").

The song, first performed in 2001, begins by saying "It's a flag and we don't wear it on our heads" (a reference to Muslims, sometimes derogatorily referred to as "rag heads," because they wear head scarves). It is filled with invective—the terrorist attacker is "a coward and a fool" who has "shot us in the back" and has been "pulling our chain." Daniels proclaims that "these colors don't run," and promises that

America will hunt down terrorists. He also likens the enemy to a mole crawling into his hole (probably a reference to Saddam Hussein). The flag, which is variously described as "flying high," as "old glory red white and blue," and as "the stars and stripes," is also associated with the flying eagle. The final lines repeat the song's title and associate the flag with "the USA."

Initially scheduled to perform at a Salvation Army benefit for the victims of 9/11, Daniels decided not to perform after sponsors thought the song was more provocative than healing. Daniels complained, "I don't feel that this is the time for healing. I feel that this is the time to rub salt in the wounds and keep America focused on the job at hand" (TruthorFiction.com 2017). Daniels ultimately released a recording of the song that enjoyed modest success on the country music charts in late 2001.

Daniels was even more confrontational in "An Open Letter to the Hollywood Bunch," which he posted on his website. There he specifically identified liberal actor and director and Bush administration critic Sean Penn as "a traitor to the United States of America" and ridiculed those who "scoff at our military whose boots you're not even worthy to shine" (Rudder 2005, 221).

See also "Courtesy of the Red, White and Blue"; Terrorist Attacks of September 11, 2001

Further Reading

Rudder, Randy. 2005. "In Whose Name? Country Artists Speak Out on Gulf War II." In *Country Music Goes to War*, edited by Charles K. Wolfe and James E. Akenson. Lexington: University Press of Kentucky.

TruthorFiction.com. 2017. "Charlie Daniels' Letter about the Country Freedom Concert and His Song, 'This Ain't No Rag, It's a Flag.'" Accessed February 28. https://www.truthorfiction.com/charliedaniels/

TOP OF THE FLAGPOLE

Flagpoles are typically topped by a ball or spear. Poles designed for the American flag are typically topped by a figure of the bald eagle. These tops are called finials, although common usage in the military refers to the top as a "truck."

The top is both decorative and functional. Early battle flags were topped with a pike or spear that could be used as a last resort by a soldier in combat (Riley 2014). Other tops might have identified a regiment (though many early flags served the same purpose). Any metal top would protect the pole itself from seeping water. In 1976, Stanley Forman took an iconic photograph, called *The Soiling of Old Glory*, of a white teenager using the tip of a flag to attack an African American attorney in Boston.

A popular urban legend, which apparently dates back to the Cold War, suggested that ball tops contained a razor blade, a match, and a bullet to be used to prevent the flag from falling into enemy hands.

Flags of organizations might be topped with a symbol of that organization (thus a cross might adorn the top of a pole displaying the Christian flag), although this is generally considered to be inappropriate for an American flag, which governs Christians and non-Christians.

See also Eagle; *The Soiling of Old Glory* (Photograph)

Further Reading

Hornung, Clarence P. 1973. *Treasury of American Design*. 2 vols. New York: Harry N. Abrams, Inc.

Riley, John. 2014. "Myths and Legends of the Flag Pole." Last modified January 16. http://www.myguidon.com/index.php?option=com_content&task=view&id=16788

TREMAIN, RUSSELL

Scholars typically begin their discussions of compulsory flag-salute cases with the U.S. Supreme Court decision in *Minersville School District v. Gobitis* (1940), to uphold the requirement, and with the court's decision three years later, in *West Virginia State Board of Education v. Barnette* (1943), to overturn it. Controversies over compulsory acknowledgments of the flag, however, predate these cases. In 1918, for example, Ora Troyer, a Mennonite in West Liberty, Ohio, was successfully prosecuted because his daughter refused to salute the flag. That same year, school officials in Sarpy County, Nebraska, fired a teacher who was a member of the Church of God for failing to salute the flag (Bergman 1997, 217).

Another notable case concerned that of nine-year-old Russell Tremain of Whatcom County in the state of Washington in 1925. Russell was the son of John and Ethel Tremain, who belonged to the Elijah Voice Society (EVS), "a splinter group of the Russellites, the original Jehovah's Witnesses" (Henderson 2005, 750). The EVS expected Christ to return to earth soon, opposed war, and regarded the flag salute as a symbol of militarism. The Washington State School Law of the era, though, required that all children must participate in such a salute at least once a week. When authorities refused to exempt Russell from this requirement, his parents took him out of school. Judge W. P. Brown of the Superior Court in Whatcom County fined John Tremain $25 and placed him in the county jail for failing to send his child to school and for contributing to the delinquency of a minor. At another juvenile court hearing, the judge subsequently placed Russell in a county detention center. He was later sent to the Washington Children's Home in Seattle, where authorities sought to place Russell for adoption by another family.

Although the American Civil Liberties Union (ACLU) sought to intervene, their efforts were stymied both by the Tremain family and the Elijah Voice Society, neither of which recognized the authority of U.S. courts or were willing to authorize the ACLU to proceed on their behalf. The ACLU further found that public opinion was heavily against the family. At one point, Rev. Dr. Sydney Strong successfully brokered a compromise whereby Russell would return to a public school, but none would accept him if he refused to salute the flag, and the parents refused to allow him to attend a private YMCA school. After 26 months, authorities eventually returned Russell to his parents, with the stipulation that he attend school.

See also Jehovah's Witnesses; *Minersville School District v. Gobitis* (1940); *West Virginia State Board of Education v. Barnette* (1943)

Further Reading

Bergman, Jerry. 1997. "The Modern Religious Objection to Mandatory Flag Salute in America: A History and Evaluation." *Journal of Church and State* 39 (Spring): 215–236.

Henderson, Jennifer Jacobs. "Conditional Liberty: The Flag Salute Before Gobitis and Barnette." *Journal of Church and State* 47 (Autumn 2005): 747–767.

Hodgdon, Daniel R. 1947. "School Law Review: No More Compulsory Flag Salutes Allowed." *Clearing House* 21 (April): 499–500.

TWENTY-FOUR-HOUR FLAG DISPLAYS

Most U.S. flags are flown during the day, although there is no law that prohibits flying them at night. The U.S. Flag Code, which is not legally enforceable, does recommend that they be illuminated after dark.

Federal laws have specifically designated eight sites where the flag may be flown during both day and night. Each has a connection to the U.S. flag or to military memorials. The designated sites are as follows:

Fort McHenry National Monument, Baltimore, Maryland
Flag House Square, Baltimore, Maryland
The U.S. Marine Corps War Memorial, Arlington, Virginia
Lexington, Massachusetts (first battle of the Revolutionary War)
The White House, Washington, D.C.
Washington Monument, Washington, D.C.
United States Customs ports of entry
Valley Forge State Park, Pennsylvania (Luckey 2008, 9–0).

See also Iwo Jima Flag Raising; Star-Spangled Banner (Flag); Washington Monument Flag Display

Further Reading

Luckey, John R. 2008. *The United States Flag: Federal Law Relating to Display and Associated Questions*. CRS Report for Congress. Washington, D.C.: Congressional Research Service.

U

UNCLE SAM

Of all American images, few are as iconic as that of Uncle Sam. Most studies of the term have attributed its origin to the War of 1812 and specifically to Samuel Wilson, who set up a meatpacking business in Troy, New York. He shipped his product in casks marked "U.S.," which a soldier jokingly said referred not to the United States but to "Uncle Sam" (Ketchum 1990).

Another scholarly study of this subject by Professor Donald R. Hickey, however, suggests a number of problems with this story as well as a number of others that have been circulated with respect to the origins of Uncle Sam. Hickey found some references from earlier in the War of 1812, including a diary entry from Isaac Mayo, who served as a midshipman on USS *Wasp* and used Uncle Sam as a nickname for the U.S. government in 1810 (Hickey 2015, 688). Hickey does believe that the expression gained fairly wide circulation during the War of 1812, typically in articles appearing in New England Federalist publications criticizing the war. An editor writing shortly after the war, for example, described Uncle Sam as "a cant [popular or fashionable] term in the army for the United States" (691). By the next decade, however, "Uncle Sam finally cast off his negative associations and became acceptable for broader consumption" (691).

This World War I recruiting poster is the most famous of 46 posters designed for the U.S. government by James Montgomery Flagg, one of America's leading early 20th-century illustrators. An adapted version of this poster was also used during World War II. Uncle Sam is almost always depicted in red, white, and blue colors and/or with one or more stars. (Library of Congress)

As a symbol of the United States, it is fitting that Uncle Sam is typically dressed in the colors and the motif of the flag: "The look of his costume takes its inspiration from the U.S. flag, adding to the patriotic effect. He wears red and white striped slacks, a blue jacket, and a top hat, often adorned with a band of stars" (Watts 2007). Over time, Uncle Sam largely supplanted earlier patriotic portrayals of Yankee Doodle and Brother Jonathan, the latter of whom was almost always clean shaven (Kidd 2007, 38).

Modern images that typically portray Uncle Sam as a tall thin figure with a goatee largely date to Thomas Nast's cartoons from the 1870s in *Harper's Weekly* and from James Montgomery Flagg's iconic "I WANT YOU" World War I recruiting posters. Uncle Sam items have become highly collectible (Vogt 2000–2001, 41; Czulewicz 1995).

Female figures, including Pocahontas (or other Native American figures—see Fleming 1965), Lady Liberty, and Columbia, have also been used as symbols for the United States. They are often depicted wearing clothing or holding shields with the colors of the U.S. flag (Miller 2010; Guenter 2010).

See also Posters in Wartime; War of 1812

Further Reading

Czulewicz, Gerald E., Sr. 1995. *The Foremost Guide to Uncle Sam Collectibles*. Paducah, KY: Collector Books.

Fleming, E. McClung. 1965. "The American Image as Indian Princess 1765–1783." *Winterthur Portfolio* 2:65–81.

Guenter, Scot. 2010. "Juxtaposing Symbols in Civil Religion: The Lady and the Flag." *Raven: A Journal of Vexillology* 17:1–22.

Hickey, Donald R. 2015. "A Note on the Origins of 'Uncle Sam,' 1810–1820." *New England Quarterly* 88 (December): 681–692.

Ketchum, Alton. 1990. "The Search for Uncle Sam." *History Today* 40 (April): 20–26.

Kidd, Laura K. 2007. "Wave It or Wear It? The United States Flag as a Fashion Icon." *Raven: A Journal of Vexillology* 14:35–60.

Miller, Ruth. 2010. "Stuck or Star-Struck with Uncle Sam? Reevaluating Relations between the U.S. and Its National Personification." *Americana* 8:16–33.

Roberts, Sam. 2016. "Alternate Uncle Sam Spotted in the Mists of New York History." *New York Times*, April 19. https://www.nytimes.com/2016/04/20/nyreg8ion/alternate-uncle-sam-spotted-in-the-mists-of-new-york-history.html

Vogt, George L. 2000–2001. "When Posters Went to War: How America's Best Commercial Artists Helped Win World War I." *Wisconsin Magazine of History* 84 (Winter): 38–47

Watts, Linda S. 2007. *Encyclopedia of American Folklore*. New York: Facts on File, Inc.

UNDER GOD

The Pledge of Allegiance to the American flag, originally composed by Francis Bellamy for the celebration of the 400th anniversary of Columbus's discovery of America, has undergone a number of changes over the years. Among the most profound was the addition of the words "under God," which Congress added in 1954.

The impetus for this move originated in 1951 at meetings of the Knights of Columbus (an organization with the Roman Catholic Church), which forwarded the suggestion to Republican Congressman Edmund Radwan from New York. He entered the idea into the *Congressional Record* on March 25, 1953. Democrat congressman Louis Rabaut of Michigan subsequently introduced a House Joint Resolution on April 21, 1953, proposing that this change to the pledge be made.

In a Lincoln Day sermon delivered on February 7, 1954, to an audience that included President Dwight D. Eisenhower, George M. Docherty, a minister of the New York Avenue Presbyterian Church in Washington, D.C. advocated this addition. Docherty observed that Abraham Lincoln had used this term in the Gettysburg Address (Canipe 2003, 315–316). Three days later, Senator Homer Ferguson, a Wisconsin Republican, introduced a joint resolution of his own.

Much of the impetus for this addition centered on America's situation with respect to the Cold War, which many viewed as pitting Christian civilization against godless communism. Rabaut thus observed, "From the root of atheism stems the evil weed of communism" (quoted in Canipe 2003, 317). Other members of Congress were quick to point out that the words "under God" did not constitute an establishment of religion in violation of the First Amendment because they were nonsectarian. President Eisenhower, who with his preacher had helped create the Foundation for Religious Action in the Social and Civil Order, announced at its first conference that it would show how to "take the Bible in one hand and the Flag in the other, and march ahead" (quoted in Fitzgerald 2017, 185).

In May, the House and Senate Judiciary Committees recommended the measure. Congress passed the measure on June 1954, and President Eisenhower signed it into law on June 14, 1954 (Flag Day). Later that day, a military band played "Onward Christian Soldiers," as a new flag was raised above the Capitol Dome (Canipe 2003, 319).

In 1956, Congress established "In God We Trust" as the national motto. The term, which first appeared on national coins in 1864, began to be used on paper currency the following year.

In 2000, Michael Newdow successfully challenged the revised pledge before the U.S. Ninth Circuit Court of Appeals, which found that the words violated the Establishment Clause of the First Amendment. In *Elk Grove Unified School District v. Newdow* (2004), however, the U.S. Supreme Court invalidated this ruling on the basis that, as a noncustodial father, Newdow did not have proper standing to bring the suit. Since *Minersville School District v. Gobitis* (1940), which was decided even prior to the addition of "under God," courts have ruled that flag salutes in public schools are not compulsory.

The words "under God" are sometimes interpreted as a manifestation of civil religion, which seeks to appeal across faiths. This does not mean that individuals who say the words necessarily make a distinction between the characteristics of the God they worship and the God of the United States. Numerous individuals have sought to read religious meanings into the design of the U.S. flag (Smith 2009).

See also Bellamy, Francis J.; *Elk Grove Unified School District v. Newdow* (2004); *Minersville School District v. Gobitis* (1940); Pledge of Allegiance

Further Reading

Canipe, Lee. 2003. "Under God and Anti-Communist: How the Pledge of Allegiance Got Religion in Cold War America." *Journal of Church and State* 45 (Spring 2003): 305–323.

Cloud, Matthew W. 2004. "'One Nation, Under God': Tolerable Acknowledgement of Religion or Unconstitutional Cold War Propaganda Cloaked in American Civil Religion?" *Journal of Church and State* 46 (Spring): 311–340.

FitzGerald, Frances. 2017. *The Evangelicals: The Struggle to Shape America.* New York: Simon and Schuster.

Goldstein, Jared A. 2017. "How the Constitution Became Christian." *Hastings Law Journal* 68 (February): 259–308.

Kao, Grace Y. 2007. "'One Nation Under God' or Taking the Lord's Name in Vain?: Christian Reflections on the Pledge of Allegiance." *Journal of the Society of Christian Ethics* 27 (Spring/Summer): 183–204.

McCarthy, Martha M. 2005. "Parental Choice and Excellence: Just How 'Distinctive' Should Public Schools Be?" *Educational Horizons* 83 (Winter): 92–97.

Smith, Whitney. 2009. " 'One Nation Under God' The Crusade to Capture the American Flag." In *Proceedings: The XIX International Congress of Vexillology York 23–27 July 2001*, 67–74. U.K.: Flag Institute.

U.S. Department of the Treasury. 2017. "History of 'In God We Trust.'" Accessed January 20. https://www.treasury.gov/about/education/pages/in-god-we-trust.aspx

UNION FLAG

One of the earliest American flags has been variously called the Union Flag, the Cambridge Flag, the Somerville Flag, the Grand Union Flag, the Continental Flag, and even the Congress Flag. Apparently, it was first flown from the *Black Prince,* later renamed USS *Alfred*, beginning in December 1775, and in early January 1776, it was flown from George Washington's camp on Prospect Hill outside Boston (Balderston 1969). Ansoff (2006) believes that the flag was actually the British Union Flag, but DeLear (2014) identifies it with the American Union Flag.

The flag carried a mixed message since the colonies had not yet declared their independence from Britain. It thus consisted of the design of the British Union Jack (which contained the intersecting British crosses of St. Andrew and St. George against a field of blue) in the upper-left canton, with a field of 13 alternating red and white stripes. These were apparently created by sewing white stripes across the British red ensign (Balderston 1969, 78). The stripes would have been a symbol of the unity of the 13 colonies against British taxation and other oppressive measures.

The two known depictions of the Union Flag, one recreated from North Carolina currency, differ as to whether the canton rested on the third red stripe or on the fourth white stripe (Mastai and D'Otrange 1973, 18). When the flag was first raised on Prospect Hill, the similarity between the canton on the U.S. flag and the British flag apparently led some Loyalists to believe that Washington was surrendering. It is uncertain who designed this flag. One theory is that it was the work of Benjamin

Franklin, Benjamin Harrison, and Thomas Lynch, whom the Continental Congress had appointed to advise Washington on his army (Leepson 2005, 16).

Each year the town of Somerville holds a ceremony on New Year's Day commemorating what is believed to be Washington's first use of the flag on Prospect Hill (Orchard 2013).

See also Union Jack; Stripes on the Flag

Further Reading

Ansoff, Peter. 2006. "The Flag on Prospect Hill." *Raven: A Journal of Vexillology* 13:77–100.

Balderston, Marion. 1969. "The Flag John Paul Jones Really Fought Under." *Huntington Library Quarterly* 33 (November): 77–83.

DeLear, Byron. 2014. "Revisiting the Flag at Prospect Hill: Grand Union or Just British?" *Raven: A Journal of Vexillology* 21:19–70.

Leepson, Marc. 2005. *Flag: An American Biography*. New York: St. Martin's Press.

Mastai, Boleslaw, and Marie-Louise D'Otrange. 1973. *The Stars and the Stripes: The American Flag as Art and as History from the Birth of the Republic to the Present*. New York: Alfred A. Knopf.

Orchard, Chris. 2013. "Research Upholds Traditional Prospect Hill Flag Story." *Somerville Patch*, December 30. https://patch.com/massachusetts/somerville/research-upholds-traditional-prospect-hill-flag-story

UNION JACK

The foreign flag from which the United States flag is most closely derived is the Union Jack, the name given to the flag of Great Britain. It consists of three colors—red, white, and blue—all of which have significant symbolism. According to historian Florence Withrow, "in heraldry red indicates courage, white purity and blue, integrity" (1917, 27). The Union Jack known to the American colonists, however, was somewhat different from the current emblem of Great Britain.

The flag of England consisted of a red cross against a white background and is associated with King Richard I (the Lionheart). He fought crusades under the banner of St. George, who is considered the patron saint of England. The term "Jack" originated from displaying the flag on the coat, or *jacques* (French term), that knights would have worn over a coat of mail (Withrow 1917, 23). In time, the term was used for any small flag hung on a ship's bow to indicate its nationality.

In 1603, James I, who had been King of Scotland, also became King of England. The Scottish flag consisted of a white St. Andrew's Cross, which is diagonal (like an X) against a blue background. James thus combined the two crosses on the new flag, with additional white lines to keep colors from touching one another. Although discontinued for a time under the rule of Oliver Cromwell, and somewhat modified under Queen Anne, this would have been the British flag in use at the time of the American Revolution. The Union (or Grand Union) Flag that George Washington is believed to have flown from Prospect Hill outside Boston would have used this design for its canton and 13 red and white stripes, representing each of the colonies, for its field.

When Northern Ireland joined the United Kingdom in 1801, the diagonal red cross of St. Patrick was added to the British Flag, creating the current design of the Union Jack.

See also Colors of the Flag; Union Flag

Further Reading

Marshall, Tim. 2017. *Worth Dying For: The Power and Politics of Flags*. London: Elliott and Thompson.

Patriot Wood. 2017. "The Flags That Make Up the Union Jack." Accessed May 11. https://www.patriotwood.com/blogs/news/37922689-the-flags-that-make-up-the-union-jack

Withrow, Florence. 1917. "The Story of the Union Jack." *Public Health Journal* 8 (January): 23–27.

UNITED STATES FLAG ASSOCIATION

The United States Flag Association was founded in Washington, D.C., on April 24, 1924, the year after the Flag Conference of 1923. It was the brainchild of Col. James A. Moss (1871–1941), a retired army officer. Moss may be best known for having formed the 25th Infantry Bicycle Corps in 1896 from African American volunteers, known as Buffalo Soldiers. Prior to this time, forces had to travel either by foot or by horse.

Moss, who was born in Lafayette, Louisiana, was a graduate of the U.S. Military Academy. He won a Silver Star in Cuba during the Spanish-American War, and he later served both in the Philippines and in France. He is buried in Arlington National Cemetery.

On its founding, Moss became director general of the United States Flag Association, which had 13 founding members "drawn from the various religious, racial, and political element composing our population, and representing the thirteen stripes of the flag" (Phillips 1831, 97). Moss said that the purpose of the organization was "to foster reverence for the flag of the United States and combat any and all influences hostile to the ideals, traditions, principles and institutions for which the flag stands" (98).

Moss authored a short book, with an introduction by Woodrow Wilson, entitled *Our Flag and Its Message* (1917). An article in the May 19, 1930, issue of *The Journal of Education* observed that the association had "organized a Supply Service whose function is to supply Flags, National Bunting, Flag Books, Flag Charts, and other patriotic products," the profit of which would support "the patriotic education of the youth of America." An article later published in *The Journal of Criminal Law and Criminology* in 1934 indicated that the organization was sponsoring a National Anti-Crime Conference seeking to deter criminals "from declarations in favor of flogging for the more serious offenses to universal finger-printing." The conference also focused on "educating youth to prevent the development of criminal tendencies" and on asking "that Congress prohibit the sale, manufacture or possession of pistols, machine guns or other firearms, except for police purposes," which was arguably in violation of the Second Amendment to the U.S. Constitution.

In 1941, Moss was credited with the idea of spotlighting the U.S. flag for an entire week. Presidents Calvin Coolidge, Herbert Hoover, and Franklin D. Roosevelt all served as honorary presidents of the organization.

The organization, which perpetuated the myth that Betsy Ross designed the first flag and lobbied against the purchase of Japanese-made U.S. flags, faltered after Moss's death in a car accident in 1941.

See also Ross, Betsy

Further Reading

"Interesting Announcement." 1930. *The Journal of Education* 111:574.

"It's Flag Day All Year in Quartermaster's Depot." 1941. *The Science News-Letter* 29 (June): 359.

Leepson, Marc. 2005. *Flag: An American Biography*. New York: St. Martin's Press.

Leon, Philip W. 1994. "'Here They Came!' The Bicycle Rescue in 'A Connecticut Yankee.'" *Mark Twain Journal* 32 (Spring): 27–32.

Moss, James A., and M. B. Stewart. 1917. *Our Flag and Its Message*. Philadelphia: J. P. Lippincott Company.

"National Anti-Crime Conference." 1934. *Journal of Criminal Law and Criminology* 24 (January–February): 973.

Phillips, Robert. 1931. *The American Flag: Its Uses and Abuses*. Boston: Stratford Company.

UNITED STATES V. EICHMAN (1990)

Soon after the Supreme Court issued its decision in *Texas v. Johnson* (1989) that the First and Fourteenth Amendments protected the symbolic speech of individuals who burned American flags in protest, Congress adopted the Flag Protection Act of 1989. It provided that "whoever knowingly mutilates, defaces, physically defiles, burns, maintains on the floor or ground, or tramples upon any flag of the United States shall be fined under this title or imprisoned for not more than one year." The law made an exception for individuals who burn a flag "when it has become worn or soiled."

After several individuals were prosecuted under this law for flag burning in protest of American domestic and foreign policy, lower courts ruled their convictions unconstitutional. The issue was appealed to the U.S. Supreme Court in the case of *United States v. Eichman*, 496 U.S. 310 (1990). As in *Texas v. Johnson* (1989), the court issued a five-to-four ruling that the new law, like the Texas laws that it had invalidated in *Texas v. Johnson*, was unconstitutional.

As in the previous case, Justice William J. Brennan authored the majority opinion. It began with a review of the previous year's decision, which had determined that Johnson's action was "conduct 'sufficiently imbued with elements of communication' to implicate the First Amendment" and that "the State's asserted interest 'in preserving the flag as a symbol of nationhood and national unity,' was an interest" related to suppressing free expression. As in the previous case, the conduct at issue in this case "constituted expressive conduct," and as in that case, the court did not think such conduct was entitled to less protection than other First Amendment rights.

Per Brennan's opinion, the only relevant question was thus whether the Flag Protection Act was "sufficiently distinct from the Texas statute that it may constitutionally be applied to proscribe appellees' expressive conduct." Whereas the Texas law focused on acts that might offend onlookers, the current law "proscribes conduct (other than disposal) that damages or mistreats a flag, without regard to the actor's motive, his intended message, or the likely effects of his conduct on onlookers." However, "although the Flag Protection Act contains no explicit content-based limitation on the scope of prohibited conduct, it is nevertheless clear that the Government's asserted interest is 'related to the suppression of free expression . . . and concerned with the content of such expression." Although the government seeks to preserve "the flag's status as a symbol of our Nation and certain national ideals . . . the mere destruction of disfigurement of a particular physical manifestation of the symbol, without more, does not diminish or otherwise affect the symbol; itself in any way." Thus, the law would not prohibit individuals from burning a flag in their basement. The language of the law further "confirms Congress' interest in the communicative impact of flag destruction." As with the Texas law, the act thus "suppresses expression out of concern for its likely communicative impact." Such a law requires "the most exacting scrutiny," which this law does not meet. Officials may seek to foster national unity by "persuasion and example," but "the Flag Protection Act goes well beyond this by criminally proscribing expressive conduct because of its likely communicative impact." The act of flag burning is offensive to many people, but so are other forms of speech that the court has permitted.

Justice John Paul Stevens wrote the dissenting opinion. Stevens believed that expressive actions may be prohibited in the three following cases:

> a) the prohibition is supported by a legitimate societal interest that is unrelated to suppression of the ideas the speaker desires to express; (b) the prohibition does not entail any interference with the speaker's freedom to express those ideas by other means; and (c) the interest in allowing the speaker complete freedom of choice among alternative methods of expression is less important than the societal interest supporting the prohibition.

Stevens continued to believe that the government had an interest in preserving the symbolic importance of the flag: "In times of national crisis, it inspires and motivates the average citizen to make personal sacrifices in order to achieve societal goals of overriding important; at all times, it serves as a reminder of the paramount importance of pursuing the ideals that characterize our society." He believed that "the Government's legitimate interest in preserving the symbolic value of the flag is . . . essentially the same regardless of which of many different ideas may have motivated a particular act of flag burning." Regulating flag burning would be little different than regulating "a gigantic fireworks display or a parade of nude models in a public park." In weighting individual interests against national interests, Stevens said that the court needed to make judgments on: "(1) The importance of the individual interest in selecting the preferred means of communication; (2) the importance of the national symbol; and (3) the question whether tolerance of flag burning will enhance or tarnish that value." He stated that although the individual interest is of "great importance," it is not "absolute." Burning a flag is not the same as burning a public building; it still detracts from its meaning. Indeed, Stevens believed that the previous case had already eroded national understanding of the meaning of the flag, which had been further eroded by "leaders who seem to advocate compulsory worship of the flag . . . who seem to manipulate the symbol of national purpose into a pretext for partisan disputes about meaner ends."

See also *Texas v. Johnson* (1989)

Further Reading

Gey, Steven G. 1990. "This Is Not a Flag: The Aesthetics of Desecration." *Wisconsin Law Review* 1990 (December): 1549–1595.

Goldstein, Robert Justin. 1996. *Burning the Flag: The Great 1989–1990 American Flag Desecration Controversy*. Kent, OH: Kent State University Press.

V

VETERANS DAY

One of the holidays that is most closely associated with the display of flags is Veterans Day. President Woodrow Wilson originally proclaimed November 11 as Armistice Day because it was the day that leaders signed the truce ending World War I (then known as the Great War), which, to that date, had been the most destructive war in world history.

Whereas Decoration Day (later called Memorial Day) was designed to honor those who had died in the service of their country, Armistice Day was designed to honor all who had served in military conflicts. Celebrations of the two holidays, however, were often a similar mix of commemorative activities (including parades often featuring veterans) and leisure activities such as ball games and picnics.

Congress subsequently adopted a concurrent resolution on June 4, 1926, recognizing that 27 states had already proclaimed November 11 to be a holiday. Congress accordingly called upon the president

> to issue a proclamation calling upon the officials to display the flag of the United States on all Government buildings on November 11 and inviting the people of the United States to observe the day in schools and churches, or other suitable places, with appropriate ceremonies of friendly relations with all other peoples. (Office of Public and Governmental Affairs 2017)

Congress subsequently made the day a legal holiday in 1938.

In 1954, Congress replaced the word "Armistice" with "Veterans," thus using the holiday to acknowledge not only those who had served in World War I but also those who had served in other wars, including World War II, Korea, and those conflicts that followed. In 1968, the Uniform Holiday Bill further provided that Washington's Birthday, Memorial Day, Veterans Day, and Columbus Day all be celebrated on Mondays, to provide three-day weekends for federal employees. After some criticism and confusion, in 1975, President Gerald R. Ford signed a law returning Veterans Day to November 11 beginning in 1978.

See also Decoration Day (Memorial Day)

Further Reading

Drake, Sarah E. 2002. "The Postwar Home Front: Memorializing Veterans." *OAH Magazine of History* 17 (October): 60–64.

Office of Public and Governmental Affairs. 2017. "History of Veterans Day." Accessed April 9. https://www.va.gov/opa/vetsday/vetdayhistory.asp

VETERANS OF FOREIGN WARS (VFW)

Like the Grand Army of the Republic (GAR) that preceded it, the Veterans of Foreign Wars (VFW) organization has had a major role in promoting respect for the flag and rules of flag etiquette, in establishing a flag code and urging its adoption by Congress, and in advocating for governmental support for veterans and their families.

Founded after the Spanish-American War, the VFW is organized, like the GAR before it, into local posts. In 1913, the organization adopted as its motto the words "One country, one language, one flag," which it had taken from the original pledge to the flag composed by George Thacher Balch (Ellis 2005, 56). The VFW, which as of 2017 reported 1.7 million members in its main organization and auxiliary (family members of VFW veterans), remains active in promoting exercises in schools to recognize and promote respect for the flag.

See also Balch, George Thacher; Flag Code; Pledge of Allegiance

Further Reading

Ellis, Richard J. 2005. *To the Flag: The Unlikely History of the Pledge of Allegiance*. Lawrence: University Press of Kansas.

Veterans of Foreign Wars. 2017. "The Veterans of Foreign Wars of the U.S.—VFW." Accessed December 20. https://www.vfw.org/

VIETNAM MEMORIAL

The Vietnam War was one of the most divisive wars in American history, and the memorial designed to commemorate the American soldiers who lost their lives in the conflict touched a deep nerve. Located in Constitutional Gardens next to the National Mall and maintained by the National Park Service, the center of the memorial consists of two tapering walls of black reflective stone, on which the names of more than 58,000 U.S. casualties from the war are engraved. Funded by the Vietnam Veterans Memorial Fund (VVMF), the winning design was submitted by Maya Lin (b. 1959), who was, at the time, an undergraduate at Yale University. When the winning design was announced, it was harshly criticized by veterans who thought that it was too bleak and unheroic. Many others defended the design, however, and "the Wall," as it came to be known, was completed in 1982.

Partly as a result of the criticism of Lin's design, the Government's Fine Art Commission subsequently agreed to add an eight-foot statue of three solders, designed by Frederick Hart and entitled *Three Infantrymen*. It was set against the background of a flag flying from a 55-foot flag pole, which was installed on July 1, 1983. Even this move proved to be somewhat controversial, as both the statue and pole formed part of the entrance to the memorial rather than being placed in the middle, at the conjunction of the two walls, as many had hoped. Others thought that Hart's piece shouldn't have been added at all because it compromised Lin's design.

The wall and accompanying statue draw many visitors, many of whom make rubbings of the names of lost love ones. Many visitors report that the wall has helped them heal from their losses, and in the more than 30 years since the memorial was completed and opened to the public, most of the controversy around it has faded. Today "the Wall" is generally regarded as a moving, powerful tribute to Americans killed in the Vietnam War.

See also Vietnam War

Further Reading

Hogopian, Patrick. 2009. *The Vietnam War in American Memory*. Amherst: University of Massachusetts Press.

New York Times. 1983. "Statue and Flag Voted for Vietnam Memorial." February 9. http://www.nytimes.com/1983/02/09/us/statue-and-flag-voted-for-vietnam-memorial.html

VIETNAM WAR

In contrast with most previous wars, during American participation in the Vietnam War (1955–1975), the American flag often became a symbol of national division rather than of unity.

In 1954, the Geneva Convention had divided Vietnam, which had previously been colonized by France, into two distinct nations, one in the north and one in the south. North Vietnam was controlled by communists aligned with the Soviet Union and communist China and led by Ho Chi Minh, who was determined to unify the nation under communist control. South Vietnam, which had a succession of regimes, aligned itself with the United States and her allies, who viewed saving the south from such a fate as part of its worldwide containment policy against communism.

The role of Americans moved from advising the South Vietnamese to direct combat against both the North Vietnamese army and the Viet Cong—communist guerrillas operating in the south. America steadily committed greater forces to the conflict. A pivotal moment in this regard came in August 1964, when U.S. officials came to believe (probably in error) that an American ship had been attacked by communist forces in the Gulf of Tonkin. President Lyndon Johnson sought broad authorization for U.S. military action, which he received in the Gulf of Tonkin Resolution (Congress later adopted the War Powers Resolution of 1973, in which it attempted to set limits to presidentially authorized foreign interventions). Johnson subsequently increased American participation in Vietnam until the U.S. presence reached more than half a million troops, many of whom were drafted. Johnson also ramped up bombing of strategic targets in the north, but that seemed to have little effect.

American disillusionment with the Vietnam War intensified in early 1968 when enemy forces launched the so-called Tet Offensive against towns and cities across South Vietnam. The scale of the offensive made American claims of imminent victory appear hollow. Further doubts were raised by reports of the participation of U.S. soldiers in the My Lai Massacre of civilians that same year. Civil rights leader Martin Luther King Jr. was among those who questioned the wisdom and morality of the war.

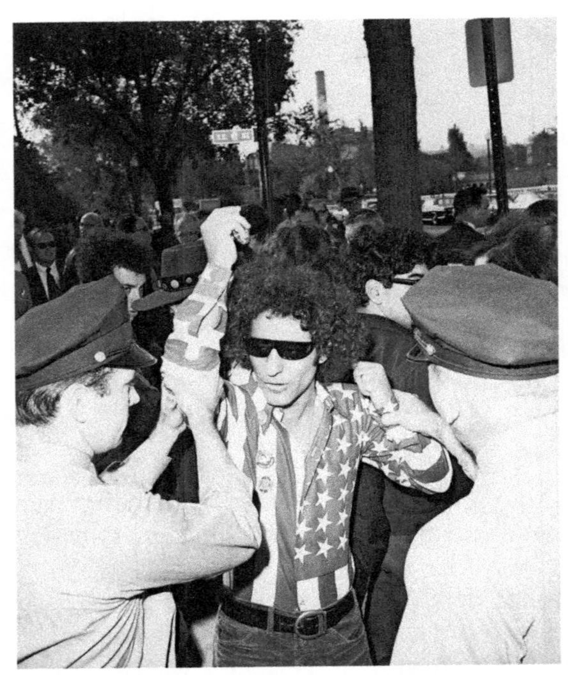

Abbie Hoffman is arrested while trying to interrupt a meeting of a subcommittee of the House Committee on Un-American Activities (HUAC), October 1, 1968. HUAC was investigating the riots at the 1968 Democratic National Convention the previous August. A federal appellate court struck down Hoffman's conviction for desecrating the flag by wearing a shirt made from a flag. *The Merv Griffin Show* electronically blocked out the shirt when he appeared on that program. (Bettmann/Getty Images)

President Johnson chose not to seek reelection in 1968, and the election went to Richard Nixon, who proposed Vietnamization (turning over the war to locals) of the war; he also called for an all-volunteer military force. Shortly after Gerald Ford replaced Nixon, however, Saigon, the capital of South Vietnam, was overrun, and the remaining Americans were forced to leave.

The surge in U.S. domestic opposition to the war occurred as American troop levels increased. In 1970, four students were killed by national guard troops during antiwar protests at Kent State University in Ohio. As the antiwar movement grew, it embraced a wide variety of slogans and symbols. The peace symbol, consisting of a circle dissected by a vertical line intersected by two diagonal lines near the bottom, which had originally been designed for the British Campaign for Nuclear Disarmament in the 1950s, often superimposed on flags, became one popular way of expressing opposition to continuing American participation in the conflict. Some college protestors carried North Vietnamese flags while others carried American flags upside down (a signal of distress) or publicly burned them. Others publicly burned their draft cards, although the Supreme Court upheld a law against this action in *United States v. O'Brien* (1968).

Congress adopted a flag desecration law in 1968, but in *Street v. New York* (1969), the Supreme Court overturned the conviction of someone who burned a flag in protest of the death of civil rights leader Medgar Evers, and in *Spence v. Washington* (1974), it overturned the conviction of a student for hanging a flag from his apartment with a peace symbol taped over it. According to the court, the student's alteration of the flag was a form of symbolic speech protected by the First Amendment. The U.S. Supreme Court would later rule in *Texas v. Johnson* (1989) and *United States v. Eichman* (1990) that burning the flag also was a form of symbolic speech.

President Nixon had come into office with appeals to what he called the "silent majority." Significantly, both he and Archie Bunker in television's *All in the Family* sported flag pins, while an increasing number of police officers, who identified the flag with "law and order" and protestors with bums and countercultural hippies and flower children, wore flag patches. In 1968, Abbie Hoffman was arrested after wearing a flag shirt to a meeting of the House Committee on Un-American Activities. In *Smith v. Goguen* (1974), the Supreme Court overturned a decision that had imprisoned an individual for wearing a flag on the seat of his jeans.

In contrast, New York City construction workers who supported President Nixon's Vietnam policies engaged in a publicized fight with student protestors after the mayor sought to lower the U.S. flag to half-staff to honor the students who were killed at Kent State. A popular slogan directed against flag protestors proclaimed, "America, love it or leave it."

Numerous artists protested the Vietnam War. John Prine wrote lyrics to "Your Flag Decal Won't Get You into Heaven Anymore," in which he proclaimed "that heaven is "overcrowded/ From your dirty little war" and that "Jesus don't like killin'/ No matter what the reason's for." Artist Seymour Chwast produced a 1967 poster entitled *End Bad Breadth*, in which a green-faced red-white-and-blue Uncle Sam opens his mouth to reveal planes dropping bombs (Goddard 2008). William Copley's (1919–1996) painting *Model for American Flag* (1961), which replaces the stars in the canton of the flag with the word THINK, has also been associated with opposition to the war (Tommaney 2016).

Long after the Vietnam War has ended, people continue to wave MIA/POW flags to memorialize those who died missing in action or who served as prisoners of war. Although protestors sometimes blamed Americans who served in the conflict, attitudes appear to have shifted to the recognition that many were doing what they considered to be their duty. The completion in 1983 of the Vietnam Memorial in Washington, D.C., which contains the engraved names of each of the American soldiers who died during the conflict, appears to have had a healing effect. An American flag was added to the entrance of the memorial in 1983.

See also Federal Flag Protection Acts of 1968 and 1989; Flag Patches; Hard Hat Riot (1970); Prisoners of War; *Smith v. Goguen* (1974); *Spence v. Washington* (1974); *Street v. New York* (1969); *Texas v. Johnson* (1989); *United States v. Eichman* (1990)

Further Reading

Fanning, Charles. 1987. "John Prine's Lyrics." *American Music* 5 (Spring): 48–73.

Goddard, Kristian. 2008. "The Resilience of the Stars and Stripes." December 4. http://www.kristiangoddard.net/Blog/americanflag.htm

Huebner, Andrew J. 2008. *The Warrior Image*. Chapel Hill: University of North Carolina Press.

Teachout, Woden. 2009. *Capture the Flag: A Political History of American Patriotism*. New York: Basic Books.

Tommaney, Susie. 2016. "X-Rated, Pop Art and Political Themes by William N. Copley on View at the Menil." *Houston Press*, February 15. http://www.houstonpress.com/arts/x-rated-pop-art-and-political-themes-by-william-n-copley-on-view-at-the-menil-8152013

WAR OF 1812

The War of 1812's closest connection to the U.S. flag is that an incident in this war between the United States and Great Britain inspired Francis Scott Key to write "The Star-Spangled Banner," which has since been designated as the national anthem.

The U.S. was drawn into the war, much as in its earlier undeclared naval war against France, as both powers sought to restrict American shipping to the other side. Great Britain, which did not recognize the right of its subjects to accept foreign citizenship, also sought to impress U.S. seamen whom they believed had fled from royal service. Younger war hawks in Congress further hoped that the war might be an occasion for the U.S. acquisition of British-held Canadian territory to the north.

Although this hope was not achieved, the U.S. gained international prestige as it fought the British to a standstill that was finally ended with the Treaty of Ghent in 1814. Because it took time for news of the treaty to arrive, one of America's greatest victories at the Battle of New Orleans actually took place after the treaty was signed.

Although there were 18 states in the Union during the war, the flag still featured 15 stars and stripes, which had been formalized in 1795 after Vermont (1791) and Kentucky (1792) had joined the Union.

See also Key, Francis Scott; "Star-Spangled Banner" (Anthem); Star-Spangled Banner (Flag)

Further Reading

Borneman, Walter R. 2005. *1812: The War That Forged a Nation*. New York: Harper Perennial.

Furlong, William Rea, and Byron McCandless. 1981. *So Proudly We Hail: The History of the United States Flag*. Washington, D.C.: Smithsonian Institution Press.

Randall, Willard Stern. 2017. *Unshackling America: How the War of 1812 Truly Ended the American Revolution*. New York: St. Martin's Press.

WASHINGTON CROSSING THE DELAWARE

One of the most iconic works of art in American history is Emanuel Leutze's 12-by-20-foot painting entitled *Washington Crossing the Delaware*. The painting features 13 diversely dressed men (one of whom is African American) squeezed into a small boat. They include George Washington and James Monroe, who are both standing, with the latter clutching an American flag. Numerous commentators

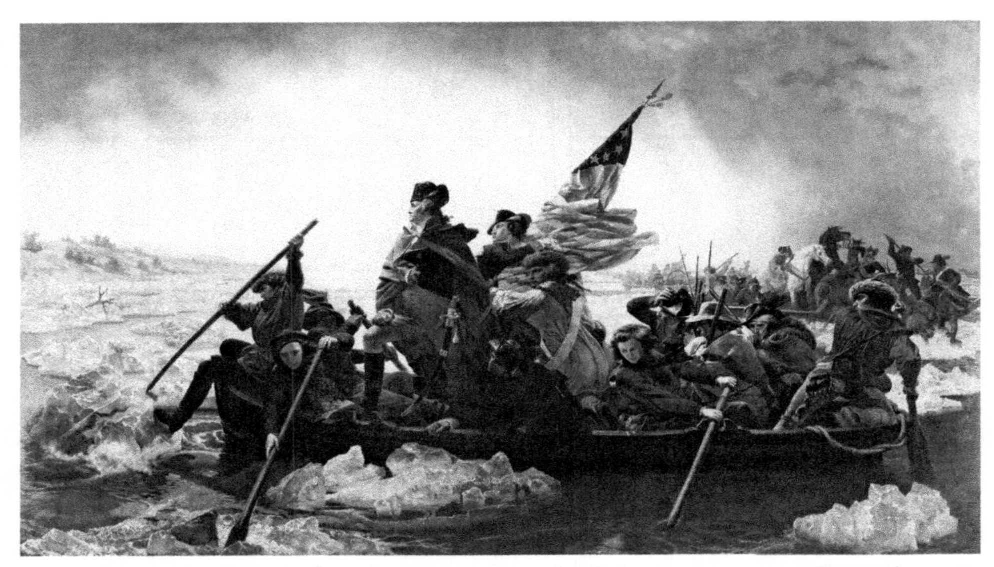

Emanuel Leutze's painting of Washington crossing the Delaware to surprise British forces in 1776 is anachronistic, but continues to evoke strong patriotic emotions among many American citizens. (The Metropolitan Museum of Art/Gift of John Stewart Kennedy, 1897)

have observed that the flag is historically inaccurate since Washington usually fought under a regimental flag and the flag design featured in the picture was not approved by Congress until 1777, while the event being recorded took place on Christmas Day of 1776.

Leutze was a German-American immigrant who was attracted to democratic principles and who returned to Europe, where he hoped to spread American revolutionary ideals. He finished the painting in 1850. Partially damaged by a fire in his studio, the painting was exhibited in the Bremen Art Museum until it was destroyed in a raid by the British Royal Air Force on September 5, 1942.

Leutze subsequently painted another copy, which came to America in 1851 with great fanfare and was exhibited in the rotunda of the Capitol Building. John S. Kennedy bought the painting in 1897 and donated it to the Metropolitan Museum of Art, although it spent some time in the Dallas Art Museum and in the Washington Crossing State Park in Pennsylvania.

Although Leutze did not paint the correct flag, he understood that Washington's crossing of the Delaware to defeat Hessian soldiers was a major turning point in the Revolutionary War and in world history (Fischer 2004, 5). Leutze's painting has been mimicked in numerous subsequent works. These included a version by George Caleb Bingham painted sometime between 1856 and 1871, by Larry Rivers in 1953, by Peter Saul in 1975, by Robert Colescott in 1975 (his is entitled *George Washington Carver Crossing the Delaware*), and Sandow Birk's undated *(North Swell) Washington Crossing the Delaware*. Around 1900, meanwhile, a postcard by Raphael Tuck purporting to reproduce Leutze's famous portrait banished the African American from the boat (Fischer 2004, 44). It has also been noted that Grant Wood's deeply ironic painting *Daughters of the Revolution* (1932) includes the Leutze painting in the background behind three aged women, one of whom has an English teacup in her hand (Fischer 2004, 425–457).

See also Daughters of the American Revolution (DAR); Postcards; Revolutionary War

Further Reading

Fischer, David Hackett. 2004. *Washington's Crossing*. New York: Oxford University Press.

WASHINGTON KERCHIEF FLAGS

One of the most iconic American textiles (chosen as the first to be discussed in a book on the Smithsonian's collection) is a calico-printed linen kerchief featuring a portrait of Gen. George Washington on a horse and surrounded by the words "George Washington, Esq. Foundator and Protector of America's Liberty and Jndependency." Notably, both the terms "Foundator" and "Jndependency" vary somewhat from more common English usages of the day. The kerchief, which may have been intended as the centerpiece for a quilt, is printed in two shades of red against a white background (Collins 1979, 48). This image was in turn copied from an English print from September 1775, which had been published by "C. Shepherd" (Monsky 2002, 240). The kerchief has reliably been attributed to John Hewson, who had immigrated to Philadelphia from London and who is known to have made kerchiefs for Martha Washington.

The circular motto is, in turn, surrounded by cannons and four distinct flags. One resembles the Union (or Grand Union) Flag, which portrayed the British Union Jack in the upper-right canton, against a field of white with red stripes. However, instead of picturing the British Union Jack in the canton, the flag portrays a radiating group of 13 alternating red and white stripes.

This early kerchief, attributed to John Hewson, and probably printed in 1776 prior to the adoption of a more standardized flag, displays a number of early flags including the Grand Union Flag, the Pine Tree Flag, the Rattlesnake Flag, and a flag with alternating red and white stripes. (Collection of the New York Historical Society, USA/Bridgeman Images)

Another is the Pine Tree Flag, often associated with Massachusetts and other New England colonies, portraying a pine tree against a white background, but without the words "An Appeal to Heaven," which this flag often bore. By contrast, the Rattlesnake Flag depicted on the kerchief does contain the motto "Don't Tread upon Me," a slight variation on the more familiar "Don't Tread on Me." The snake appears to have rattles, possibly 13, which would be another sign of colonial unity (Monsky 2002, 247). The kerchief also contains a flag with alternating stipes (13 appear to be red and 12 white) and no distinct canton, which one scholar has interpreted as "a symbol of Revolutionary unity" similar to those used in cartoons prior to the time that Congress adopted the 13 stripes, in 1777 (Monsky 2002, 245). Monsky calls this the "Rebel Stripes" flag.

The kerchief is believed to have been printed in Philadelphia in 1776, prior to the congressional resolution on the flag of the following year. The flag indicates that Washington was visualized as the "father" of the nation early in the Revolution and that his image initially may have been a more unifying symbol than the flags, some of which had distinct regional associations.

See also Pine Tree Flag; Rattlesnake Flags; Union Flag

Further Reading

Collins, Herbert Ridgeway. 1979. *Threads of History Americana Recorded on Cloth 1775 to the Present*. Washington, D.C.: Smithsonian Institution Press.

Monsky, John R. 2002. "From the Collection Finding America in Its First Political Textile." *Winterthur Portfolio* 37 (Winter): 239–264.

WASHINGTON MONUMENT FLAG DISPLAY

In early American history, pictures of George Washington were much more ubiquitous than displays of the U.S. flag. The capital city, as well as many other towns and cities, were named after him, and beginning in 1885, an official holiday (since changed to President's Day) was dedicated to his memory. Early postcards often features pictures of George Washington and/or Abraham Lincoln in connection with flags and national holidays, especially the Fourth of July. In addition, a number of well-known paintings, with more appeal to sentiment than historical accuracy, portray Washington consulting with Betsy Ross about the design of the first American flag.

The Washington Monument, which was commissioned in 1799 but not completed until 1884, is one of the most visible structures in the nation's capital. It consists of a freestanding obelisk, which, at over 555 feet, is the world's tallest such structure. In 1868, Sgt. Gilbert Bates lifted the American flag that he had carried 1,300 miles throughout the South above the unfinished monument. America's largest flag, the so-called Superflag, has also been flown from the structure.

On February 23, 1920, a flag display, then consisting of 48 flags on wooden poles, was arranged around the monument for Washington's birthday. Similar displays continued on national holidays. Beginning in 1958, these flags have been flown continuously from aluminum poles, with the number being increased from 48 to 50 with the admission of Alaska and Hawaii to the United States.

Initially, the United States Park Police conducted a flag raising and retiring ceremony at the beginning and end of each day. Beginning on July 4, 1971, however, President Richard M. Nixon ordered that the flags be flown constantly. The Park Service has favored keeping all the flags identical rather than flying state flags (as is done at the entrance to the Mount Rushmore Memorial) or historic flags. On Flag Day in 1991, and again in 1992, the memorial was the site at which the Great American Flag (210 by 399 feet) was displayed (Kincaid 2015, 101–105, 110).

Fifty American flags encircle the Washington Monument on the Mall in Washington, D.C. (Splosh/Dreamstime.com)

Unlike some heroes, especially those from the later Civil War, who are revered in one section of the country and not in others, Washington is claimed in the north and south, the east and west. After noting that American flags surround the monument, constitutional scholar Sanford Levinson observed:

> It is, altogether clearly, Washington the national liberator, the founding father of a New Union, who is being honored, not Washington the Virginian, as is less unambiguously the case in Richmond, which might well want us to believe that Washington, like Robert E. Lee, would have given priority to his Virginia identity over his national one had the two ever emerged sharply in conflict. (Levinson 1994–1995, 1085)

See also Bates, Gilbert; Great American Flag; Ross, Betsy

Further Reading

Hoover, Michael D. 1992. *The Origins and History of the Washington Monument Flag Display*. National Park Service National Capital Parks—Central Cultural Resources Management.

Horwitz, Elinor Lander, and J. Roderick Moore. 1976. *The Bird, the Banner, and Uncle Sam: Images of America in Folk and Popular Art*. Philadelphia: J. B. Lippincott Company.

Kincaid, Johnny. 2015. *The Great American Flag: The Story of the World's Biggest Flag and the People Who Made It Possible*. Lexington, KY: Johnny Kincaid.

Levinson, Sanford. 1994–1995. "They Whisper: Reflections of Flags, Monuments, and State Holidays, and the Construction of Social Meaning in a Multicultural Society." *Chicago-Kent Law Review* 70:1079–1119.

WASHINGTON'S COAT OF ARMS

Although few people in the United States had coats of arms during the era of the Revolution, the Washington family had a coat of arms that included three red stars and two red stripes (Smith 1999, 43). It is commonly believed that these may have provided the inspiration for the stars and stripes on the U.S. Grand Union or Continental Flag, but apart from visual similarity, there is little evidence to support this assertion. Moreover, there were at least 11 nations whose ships sailed under striped flags, including at least 6 that used red and white ones (Rankin 1954, 341).

The idea that Washington's coat of arms may have influenced the flag design appears to have derived from a play entitled *Washington: A Drama, in Five Acts*, written by Martin F. Tupper and published for the American centennial. In scene 3 of act 2, a Quaker named Nathan engages in a conversation with Benjamin Franklin after asking "Why choose stripes and stars?" Franklin responds:

> Yes, Nathan, I proposed it to the Congress
> It was their leader's old crusading blazon,
> Washington's coat, his own heraldic shield. (Tupper 1876, 25)

Nathan wonders whether Washington, like Oliver Cromwell, was too ambitious, and Franklin responds:

> It is not known, and it was not ambition.
> He never heard of it till fixed and done.
> For on the spur, when we must choose a flag,
> Symbolling [sic] independent unity,
> We, and not he—all was unknown to him—
> Took up his coat of arms, and multiplied
> And magnified it every way to this
> Our glorious national banner. (25)

Franklin further claimed to have "searched it out and known it for myself":

> When late in England there, at Herald's College,
> And found the Washington of Wessyugton
> In County Durham and of Sulgrave Manor
> County Northampton, bore upon their shield
> Three stars atop, two stripes across the field.
> Gules—that is red—on white, and for the crest
> An eagle's head upspringing to the light,
> Its motto, Latin, "Issue proveth acts."
> The architraves at Sulgrave testify,
> As sundry painted windows in the hall
> At Wessynton, this was their family coat.
> They took it to their new Virginian home:
> And at Mount Vernon I myself have noted
> An old cast iron scutcheoned chimney-back
> Charged with that heraldry. (26)

Washington did take an interest in heraldry, and had it applied to numerous personal objects as well as his fireplace mantel (Capps 2012).

See also Stripes on the Flag; Union Flag

Further Reading

Capps, Alan. 2012. "Coat of Arms." MountVernon.org. Edited by Joseph F. Stoltz III, Mount Vernon Estate. http://www.mountvernon.org/digital-encyclopedia/article/coat-of-arms/
Rankin, Hugh F. 1954. "The Naval Flags of the American Revolution." *The William and Mary Quarterly* 11 (July): 339–353.
Smith, Whitney. 1999. "American Perspectives on Heraldry and Vexillology." *Raven: A Journal of Vexillology* 6:41–53.
Tupper, Martin F. 1876. *Washington: A Drama, in Five Acts*. New York: J. Miller.

WEBSTER, DANIEL

Daniel Webster (1782–1852), who was born in New Hampshire but who served in Congress for Massachusetts and as the nation's secretary of state, was a lawyer (he graduated from Dartmouth College and got his legal training as a lawyer's apprentice) who was recognized as one of the most powerful orators of the 19th century. He was a strong nationalist who replied in January 1830 to a speech in the U.S. Senate by South Carolina Senator Robert Hayne, who advanced the doctrine of nullification, which Vice President John C. Calhoun, also a South Carolinian, had advocated. Southerners, who were chaffing under high tariffs that were designed to increase domestic manufacturing that was primarily located in the North and that raised the prices of imported goods, had advanced the notion that individual states could nullify such laws. This doctrine would eventually end in the doctrine of secession, which would justify state exiting the Union, as 11 southern states would later do over the issue of slavery.

In the penultimate paragraph of his speech, Webster said that he had never looked "beyond the Union, to see what might be hidden in the dark recess behind." He further likened disunion to an abyss whose consequences were happily hidden behind a veil. In his closing paragraph, Webster sought to invoke the flag as a guard against such disunion:

> God grant that in my day, at least, that curtain may not rise! God grant that on my vision never may be opened what lies behind! When my eyes shall be turned to behold for the last time the sun in heaven, may I not see him shining on the broken and dishonored fragments of a once glorious Union; on states dissevered, discordant, belligerent; on a land rent with civil feuds, or drenched, it may be, in fraternal blood! Let their last feeble and lingering glace rather behold the gorgeous ensign of the republic, now known and honored throughout the earth, still full high advanced, its arms and trophies streaming in their original luster, not a stripe erased or polluted, nor a single star obscured, bearing for its motto no such miserable interrogatory as "What is all this worth?" nor those other words of delusion and folly, "Liberty first and Union afterwards"; but everywhere, spread all over in characters of living light, blazing on its ample folds, as they float over the sea and over the land, and in every wind under the whole heavens, that other sentiment, dear to every true American heart—Liberty and Union, now and forever, one and inseparable! (Webster 1853, 111–112)

The most notable aspect of this paragraph may be the way that Webster ties the image of the shining sun to what he calls "the living light" of the stars, which are themselves suns, to the stars and stripes of the floating flag.

Notably, Webster's approach differed from that of some early abolitionists and from later seceding states, who preferred to divide the Union (and reduce the number of stars or stripes on the flag) rather than to seek unity. President Abraham Lincoln was among those who insisted that the flag under which Union forces fought during the Civil War contained stars representing both northern and southern states. Some northern battle flags contained the words "Liberty," "Union," or both.

See also Civil War; Confederate Flag; Exclusionary Flags

Further Reading

Vile, John R. 2017. *The Jacksonian and Antebellum Eras: Documents Decoded*. Santa Barbara, CA: ABC-CLIO.

Webster, Daniel. 1853. *The Great Orations and Senatorial Speeches of Daniel Webster*. Rochester, NY: Wilbur M. Hayward.

WEST VIRGINIA STATE BOARD OF EDUCATION V. BARNETTE (1943)

In *West Virginia State Board of Education v. Barnette*, 319 U.S. 624, which was issued on Flag Day of 1943, the U.S. Supreme Court overturned its decision of three years before in *Minersville School District v. Gobitis* (1940) by invalidating a compulsory flag salute in the public schools. The decision, authored by Justice Robert Jackson, is among the most elegant that the Supreme Court has ever issued, lauding the principles of the First Amendment.

As in the earlier case, this one involved children of Jehovah's Witnesses who refused to salute the U.S. flag in class because they believed that doing so violated the Biblical prohibition against worshiping graven images. Relying on *Minersville*, the school expelled the children and prosecuted the parents for contributing to their delinquency. A three-judge district court had enjoined enforcement of the penalties, and the school board had appealed directly to the Supreme Court.

Jackson observed that failure to salute the flag did not bring students "into collision with rights asserted by any other individual." He further cited Justice Harlan Fiske's dissent in the earlier case to stress that this case involves "a compulsion of students to declare a belief." In speaking of the flag, Jackson observed:

> The flag salute is a form of utterance. Symbolism is a primate but effective way of communicating ideas. The use of an emblem or flag to symbolize some system, idea, institution, or personality is a short-cut from mind to mind. Causes and nations, political parties, lodges, and ecclesiastical groups seek to knit the loyalty of their followings to a flag or banner, a color or design.

The flag salute and accompanying pledge "requires affirmation of a belief and an attitude of mind." Prior cases had not permitted "censorship" other than in cases that presented a "clear and present danger," which was not at stake in this case.

Jackson reviewed the central arguments that *Minersville* had raised. In responding to Lincoln's question as to whether a government must "be too strong for the liberties of its people, or too weak to maintain its own existence," Jackson said, "It may be doubted whether Mr. Lincoln would have thought that the strength of government to maintain itself would be impressively vindicated by our confirming power of the State to expel a handful of children from school." Jackson further emphasized that "free public education . . . will not be partisan or enemy of any class, creed, party, or faction."

As to Frankfurter's fears that intervening would transform the court into a national school board, Jackson said that the First and Fourteenth Amendments protected citizens and observed that in adopting a flag code in 1942, Congress had not required that it be compulsory. On the related issue as to whether the court had competence to rule in this area, he observed:

> The very purpose of a Bill of Rights was to withdraw certain subjects from the vicissitudes of political controversy, to place them beyond the reach of majorities and officials, and to establish them as legal principles to be applied by the courts. One's right to life, liberty, and property, to free speech, a free press, freedom of worship and assembly, and other fundamental rights may not be submitted to vote; they depend on the outcome of no elections.

Jackson further opined that when the Court is interpreting the Fourteenth Amendment application of First Amendment guarantees, much of the vagueness behind the term "due process of law" disappears. He contrasted this to the Court's general review of most economic legislation in which the state merely needed to demonstrate a "rational basis" for its decisions.

As to arguments that the flag salute promoted national unity, Jackson said that it could best be promoted "by persuasion and example" rather than by "compulsion." He compared attempts to stamp out dissent to those of the Roman Empire attempting to stamp out Christianity and to modern totalitarianism: "Those who begin coercive elimination of dissent soon find themselves exterminating dissenters. Compulsory unification of opinion achieves only the unanimity of the graveyard." Arguing that "freedom to differ is not limited to things that do not matter much," Jackson delivered what has become the most quoted part of his decision: "If there is any fixed star in our constitutional constellation, it is that no official, high or petty, can prescribe what shall be orthodox in politics, nationalism, religion, or other matters of opinion, or force citizens to confess by word or act their faith therein." Consciously or not, Jackson therefore tapped into the idea, dating back to the birth of the U.S. flag, that the stars on its canton represented a "new constellation" (Shalev 2011).

Justices Owen Roberts and Stanley Reed would have reaffirmed the *Minersville* precedent. Justices Hugo Black and William O. Douglas, who had joined the earlier decision, authored a concurrence. Observing that their vote in the earlier case had been based on their "reluctance to make the Federal Constitution a rigid bar against state regulation of conduct thought inimical to the public welfare," they now stressed religious freedom and the manner in which the compulsory flag salute was akin to the test oaths that the Constitution had outlawed. Justice Frank Murphy also authored a concurring opinion in which he stressed: "The right of freedom of thought and religion, as guaranteed by the Constitution against

State action, includes both the right to speak freely and the right to refrain from speaking at all, except insofar as essential operations of government may require it for the preservation of an orderly society."

Justice Felix Frankfurter, who had authored the *Minersville* opinion, wrote the most passionate dissent. Highlighting his own status as a Jewish immigrant, he stressed that "as judges, we are neither Jew nor Gentile, neither Catholic nor agnostic." As in the earlier decision, he stressed the court's lack of competence in the area of education and the need for judicial restraint. He did not agree with the idea that the court should treat certain rights as more important than others. Jackson made a fairly strong distinction between freedom of belief and the state's right to make laws of general applicability that might fall harder on some groups than on others. Using a flag analogy, he noted, "Nor does waving the banner of religious freedom relieve us from examining into the power we are asked to deny the states." Frankfurter noted the wide variety of religious denominations in the United States and the difficulty of designing legislation that affected them all equally.

For Frankfurter:

> Symbolism is inescapable. Even the most sophisticated live by symbols. But it is not for this Court to make psychological judgments as to the effectiveness of a particular symbol in inculcating concededly indispensable feelings, particularly if the state happens to see fit to utilize the symbol that represents our heritage and our hopes.

Perhaps with a view toward the example of American refusal to dip the U.S. flag toward Adolf Hitler at the Olympics, Frankfurter further distinguished saluting the flag from saluting a dictator. He observed that "to reject the swastika does not imply rejection of the Cross."

Frankfurter noted that prior to *Minersville*, the court had dismissed four similar compulsory flag salute convictions for lack of a substantial federal question, and he reiterated the need for judicial restraint. Acknowledging that "patriotism cannot be enforced by the flag salute," he observed that "neither can the liberal spirit be enforced by judicial invalidation of illiberal legislation."

See also Flag Day; Jehovah's Witnesses; *Minersville School District v. Gobitis* (1940)

Further Reading

Ellis, Richard J. 2005. *To the Flag: The Unlikely History of the Pledge of Allegiance*. Lawrence: University Press of Kansas.

Peters, Shawn Francis. 2000. *Judging Jehovah's Witnesses. Religious Persecution and the Dawn of the Rights Revolution*. Lawrence: University Press of Kansas.

Shalev, Eran. 2011. "'A Republic Amidst the Stars' Political Astronomy and the Intellectual Origins of the Stars and Stripes." *Journal of the Early Republic* 31 (Spring): 39–73.

WHIPPLE FLAG

Wayne Whipple (1856–1942) was a newspaper editor and prolific author whose books included *The Story of the American Flag*, *The Story of the White House*, and *The Story of the Liberty Bell*. He proposed a colorful design for a flag, sometimes called the New Flag or Peace Flag, which left the arrangement of red and white stripes in the field unchanged but proposed a unique arrangement of white stars in the blue canton. Because many individuals had proposed designs prior to standardization, it is sometimes incorrectly reported that Whipple's flag was chosen from some 500 designs submitted (Martucci 2015, 71).

A middle grouping of stars to create a star consisted of 13 identically shaped five-pointed stars in the shape of a six-star flag arranged in rows of one, four, three, four, and one and all pointing upward. It was in turn surrounded by a circle of 25 stars, which represented additional states that had entered the Union in the nation's first 100 years, and another group of 10 stars (initially 8), distributed evenly around the circle and representing those that had entered subsequently (Leepson 2005, 179).

Although Whipple included pictures of his flag in subsequent editions of his book on the flag, his proposed flag design was never adopted as the national emblem. Instead, President William Howard Taft issued an executive order on June 24, 1912, accepting the recommendation of a panel headed by Adm. George Dewey for a design that provided for a canton of six horizontal even rows, each containing eight stars each pointing upward.

Addie G. Weaver, the author of *The Story of Our Flag*, proposed a design similar to Whipple's. John F. Earhart had proposed an even more radical design which would have called for a nine-pointed star in the middle of the field of stripes, by which he hoped to celebrate "the birth of imperialism" (Martucci 2015, 74). John C. Lettra of Oaks, Pennsylvania, also proposed a 48-star pennant that came close to Whipple's design (75).

See also Executive Order No. 1556 of 1912 and Its Successors; Stars, Arrangement of on U.S. Flags

Further Reading

Leepson, Marc. 2005. *Flag: An American Biography*. New York: St. Martin's Press.

Martucci, David B. 2015. "Wayne's World (of Flags)." *Raven: A Journal of Vexillology* 22:67–77.

Whipple, Wayne. 1910. *The Story of the American Flag*. Philadelphia: Henry Altemus.

WHITTIER, JOHN GREENLEAF

See Fritchie, Barbara

WILSON, WOODROW

See Flag Day; Veterans Day

WINTHROP, ROBERT C.

Robert C. Winthrop delivered one of the most quoted speeches on the U.S. flag on the occasion of the presentation of a flag to the 22nd Regiment Massachusetts Volunteer Infantry on the Boston Common on October 8, 1861. Winthrop, a descendant of John Winthrop (1587–1649), one of the Puritan Founding Fathers of the Massachusetts Bay Colony, was a Harvard graduate who had studied law under Daniel Webster and had served in 1847–1849 as speaker of the U.S. House of Representatives. He spent the latter part of his life as the chairman of the Peabody Education Fund Trustees.

In the early part of the speech, Winthrop outlined the situation that the Union faced in light of the attempted secession of the southern states. He cited the motto "E Pluribus Unum" as an indication of the need for "duty to our whole country; of devotion to its Union; of allegiance to its rules; of loyalty to its Constitution; and of undying love to that old Flag of our Fathers, which was associated with the earliest achievement of our liberty, and which we are resolved shall be associated with its latest defence." Winthrop continued, "It is nothing more, and nothing less, than a determination that neither fraud nor force, neither secret conspiracy nor open rebellion, shall supplant that flag on the come of out Capitol, or permanently humble it anywhere beneath the sun." Winthrop said that, eschewing any thought of "revenge or hatred," the nation and its defenders should be motivated "only to enforce the laws; only to sustain the government; only to uphold the Stars and Stripes; only to aid in restoring to the whole people of the land that quiet enjoyment of liberty, which nothing but the faithful observance of the Constitution of our Fathers can secure to us and our posterity."

Winthrop invoked the names of contemporary American heroes, including Colonel Anderson, who had defended Fort Sumter. Winthrop observed how "lifting his banner upon the wings of prayer, and looking to the guidance and guardianship of the God in whom he trusted, went through that fiery furnace unharmed." Noting that some men "measured the value of our country to the world by a nobler standard than the cotton crop," Winthrop observed with a reference to Daniel Webster's speech that "all are seen rallying beneath a common flag, and exclaiming with one heart and voice, 'The American Union,—it must be, and shall be, preserved.'"

The end of Winthrop's speech is the most frequently quoted and falls into four paragraphs. The first focuses on the spirit of the flag:

> It is the National ensign, pure and simple; dearer to all our hearts at this moment, as we lift it to the gale, and see no other sign of hope upon the storm-cloud which rolls and rattles above it, save that which is reflected from its own radiant hues; dearer, a thousand-fold dearer to us all, than ever it was before, while gilded by the sunshine of prosperity and playing with the zephyrs of peace. It will speak for itself, far more eloquently than I can speak for it.

Each of the next three paragraphs begins with an admonition to look at the flag and listen to it. The first of these remaining three paragraphs thus says:

> Behold it! Listen to it! Every star has a tongue; every stripe is articulate. There is no language or speech where their voices are not heard. There's magic in the web of it. It has the answer for every question of duty. It has a solution for every doubt and every perplexity. It has a word of good cheer for every hours of gloom or of despondency.

Winthrop's next paragraph recounted the history that the flag represents:

> Behold it! Listen to it! It speaks of earlier and of later struggles. It speaks of victories, and sometimes of reverses, on the sea and on the land. It speaks of patriots and heroes among the living and among the dead; and of him, the first and greatest of them all, around whose consecrated ashes this unnatural and abhorrent strife has so long been raging,—'the abomination of desolation standing where it ought not.' But before all and above all other associations and memories,—whether of glorious men, or glorious deeds, or glorious places,—its voice is ever of Union and liberty, of the Constitution and the laws.

The final paragraph on the flag, and the penultimate of the speech, is similar:

> Behold it! Listen to it! Let it tell the story of its birth to those gallant volunteers as they march beneath its folds by day, or repose beneath its sentinel stars by night. Let it recall to them the strange, eventful history of its rise and progress; let it rehearse to them the wondrous tale of its trials and its triumphs, in peace as well as in war; and, whatever else may happen to it or to them, it will never be surrendered to rebels; never be ignominiously struck to treason; nor ever be prostituted to any unworthy and unchristian purpose of revenge, depredation, or rapine.

Winthrop's speech came at a time just after the beginning of the Civil War when there was renewed national attention to the flag, which became a symbol of both liberty and union. He gave another speech on August 27, 1862, at a mass-recruiting meeting on the Boston Common, in which his penultimate paragraph again focused on the flag, which seems to be displayed even more ubiquitously than in the previous speech:

> Let us keep our eyes and our hearts steadily fixed upon the old flag of our fathers,—the same today as when it was first lifted in triumph at Saratoga, or first struck down in madness at Sumter. That flag tells our whole story. We must do whatever we do, and whatever is necessary to be done, with the paramount purpose of preserving it, untorn and untarnished, in all its radiance and in all its just significance. We must be true to every tint of its red, white, and blue. Beyond it at this moment streaming from every window and watch-tower and cupola of our fair city. It has a star for every State. Let us resolve that there shall still be a State for every star. Let this be our watchword, in speech and in song, and still more in the whole civil and military policy of the war,—A STAR FOR EVERY STATE, AND A STATE FOR EVERY STAR,—And, by the blessing of God, and our own strong arms, we may once more see that flag waving in triumph from the Atlantic to the Pacific.

Winthrop's speech serves as a reminder that President Lincoln had insisted that the American flag continue to represent each of the states, including those that were in rebellion.

See also Civil War; Fort Sumter Flag; Lincoln, Abraham; Webster, Daniel

Further Reading

Winthrop, Robert C. 1895. *Addresses and Speeches on Various Occasions from 1852 to 1867*. Vol. 2. Boston: Little, Brown, and Company.

WORLD WAR I

World War I (1914–1918) was one of the most devastating wars of the 20th century. It pitted the Allied Powers, including Great Britain, France, Russia, and their colonies, against the Central Powers, chiefly Germany, the Austro-Hungarian Empire, and the Ottoman Empire. When war was triggered by the assassination of Archduke Franz Ferdinand of Austria by a Yugoslavian nationalist in Serbia, each side brought in their allies.

The United States managed to avoid participation in the conflict (President Woodrow Wilson ran for a second term on the theme "He Kept Us Out of War") until April 17, 1917. It eventually entered it in part because of the sinking of passenger ships including the *Lusitania* by German U-boats (submarines) and because of a growing belief that it was necessary to join the Allies in order to "make the world safe for democracy." Wilson, who was generally regarded as a Progressive, further advertised this war as "a war to end all wars," but his so-called "Fourteen Points," his principles for bringing about world peace, ended up being as honored in their breach as their execution, with the Allied Powers not about to give up their colonies for a broad principle like national self-determination. Moreover, the punitive sanctions assessed on Germany paved the way for discontent and resentment that would lead to another world war in just over 20 years.

America sent 2 million troops, many of whom participated in the deadly trench warfare that had marked so much of the war, and many songs of the period celebrated their sacrifices and lauded the flag's symbolism. The war led to such an increased demand for American flags, in fact, that the Federal Trade Commission launched an investigation into possible price fixing (Guenter 1990, 163). Aside from American action to quash insurgency in the Philippines after the Spanish-American War, this was the first time a massive number of troops had fought on noncontiguous foreign soil. The U.S. flag was increasingly used as a symbol of American resolve. The year before American entry, Wilson had established June 14 as Flag Day. That same year, President Wilson signed an order making "The Star-Spangled Banner" the official anthem of America's armed services.

A U.S. Army recruitment poster, ca. 1917. (Library of Congress)

After the war began, the nation adopted the Espionage Act of 1917 and the Sedition Act of 1918, the latter of which made it a crime to disparage the flag of the United States or to display the flag of a foreign enemy. These and other state laws led to some of the Supreme Court's most notable early decisions on First Amendment rights.

Wilson organized a Committee on Public Information to generate support for the war, and illustrators like Howard Chandler Christy, Harrison Fisher, and James Montgomery Flagg helped design recruiting posters utilizing stark images and lots of red, white, and blue. Childe Hassam painted numerous pictures of U.S. and Allied flags waving in the streets of New York City. Frederick Libby, who had begun flying for France prior to the U.S. entry into the war, helped raise money for war bonds by offering the stripes of the American flag that he had flown from his airplane at a public auction.

In a stirring speech that he gave on Flag Day of 1918, Rep. Frederick C. Hicks of New York used Wilsonian language to laud the American flag and the flag of the Allies as flying over armies "consecrated in a holy cause—the salvation of civilization and the protection of humanity." He further said, "It will fly until military autocracy has been annihilated and until arrogant Prussia shall be driven suppliant to her knees before the enlightened democracy of triumphant America" (Hicks 1918, Appendix, 2).

The war introduced the practice, apparently conceived by Capt. Robert L. Queisser of the 5th Ohio Infantry, of handing a small flag with a red border, a white center, and a blue star to be displayed in a house window for every family member serving in the service. Those who lost a loved one would replace the blue star with a gold one, and those who have lost children in the armed services in war are still known as gold star parents (Blue Star Mothers 2017). A poem of the period entitled "The Service Flag" associated the flag with mothers, wives, and sweethearts left behind (Herschell 1918, 487).

On the darker side, mobs sometimes harassed individuals, especially those of German heritage, who they thought were disrespecting the flag, and courts jailed them. Some states outlawed the teaching of German. The Sedition Act of 1918 made it a crime to publish words that were disloyal to the flag or to fly the flag of an enemy nation. The years between 1917 and 1920 further marked the so-called Red Scare, a time of high-handed government raids against subversive groups, especially against communists, who had taken control in Russia in the Revolution of 1917 and advocated a worldwide revolution of the proletariat (working class) against capitalism (Hagedorn 2008).

After the war, Wilson designated the day that the truce was signed as Armistice Day, the precursor to today's Veterans Day. By contrast, New York ceased celebrating Evacuation Day (when the British had left the state after the Revolutionary War), largely because Americans now regarded the British as allies rather than enemies. When the Tomb of the Unknown Soldier was opened in Arlington National Cemetery on March 4, 1921, it contained an unidentified soldier from World War I who had been exhumed from a cemetery in France.

It's probable that no one pushed adulation of the U.S. flag further than William Guthrie, who published *The Religion of Old Glory* (1919), a book in which he prescribed elaborate ceremonies to honor the flag.

There was considerable disillusionment during the years between World War I and II, with many people believing that arms dealers had been behind the conflict. Nonetheless, in the years immediately after the war, flag conferences held in 1923 and 1924 further solidified the flag code. It received strong support from the American Legion and other veterans' groups.

The National World War I Museum and Memorial in Kansas City, Missouri, has a Centennial Flag Program in which it provides three-by-five-foot flags that have been flown over the museum to individuals who give gifts to support it.

See also American Legion; Evacuation Day; Flag Day; Guthrie, William N.; Hassam, (Frederick) Childe; Libby, Frederick; Posters in Wartime; Sedition Act of 1918; Veterans Day; Wilson, Woodrow

Further Reading

Blue Star Mothers. 2017. "About the Service Flag." Accessed May 2. https://www.bluestarmothers.org/service-flag

Dewitt, Petra. 2012. *Degrees of Allegiance: Harassment and Loyalty in Missouri's German-American Community during World War I*. Athens: Ohio University Press.

Guenter, Scot M. 1990. *The American Flag, 1777–1924: Cultural Shifts from Creation to Codification*. Cranbury, NJ: Associated University Presses.

Guthrie, William Norman. 1919. *The Religion of Old Glory*. New York: George H. Doran Company.

Hagedorn, Ann. 2008. *Savage Peace: Hope and Fear in America, 1919*. New York: Simon and Schuster.

Herschell, William. 1918. "The Service Flag." *The Journal of Education* 87 (May 2): 487.

Hicks, Frederick C. 1918. *The Flag of the United States: Address Delivered by Hon. Frederick C. Hicks of Long Island in the House of Representatives, June 14, 1917*. Washington, D.C.: Government Printing Office.

Lubin, David M. 2015. *Flags and Faces: The Visual Culture of America's First World War*. Oakland: University of California Press.

O'Leary, Cecilia Elizabeth. 1999. *To Die For: The Paradox of American Patriotism*. Princeton, NJ: Princeton University Press.

WORLD WAR II

World War II (1939–1945) was largely a consequence of the rise of German expansionism in Europe and Japanese expansionism in the Pacific. Although America did not officially enter the war until the surprise Japanese attack on U.S. ships in Pearl Harbor, Hawaii, on December 7, 1941, the U.S. had aided Britain through a massive lend-lease program prior to this time. Moreover, the opening words of Irving Berlin's "God Bless America" (written much earlier but released in 1939)—"While the storm clouds gather far across the sea"—indicated that many Americans already recognized the rising threat.

The United States joined the Allied Powers of Great Britain, Russia (which had little ideological affinity with them but was opposed to Nazism, after Adolf Hitler broke an agreement with Joseph Stalin and invaded Russia), and Chinese nationalist forces in opposition to the Axis powers of Germany, Italy, and Japan.

The Axis powers were committed to authoritarian government and ideas of racial supremacy. The war did not end until the Allies launched a massive invasion of Europe that ended in the defeat of Germany in Berlin, and until the United States dropped two atomic bombs on Japan. Soon after the war ended, the United States and Western European powers became aligned against the Soviet Union and its Eastern European puppets and the communists who had gained control of China.

The ideological differences between democracy and Nazism (like that between democracy and communism) were stark, and the stakes were high, and these were often reflected in issues related to the flag. Thus in 1940, the U.S. Supreme Court ruled in *Minersville School District v. Gobitis* that children of Jehovah's Witnesses (who thought that the ceremony was a form of idolatry) could be forced either to salute the American flag or be dismissed from school. On July 4 of the next year, Chief Justice Harlan Fiske Stone led the American people by radio in a pledge to the flag. As Americans witnessed Nazi youth saluting the Nazi flag, opinions eventually changed, and in *West Virginia State Board of Education v. Barnette* (1943), the Supreme Court used Flag Day to announce that it had changed its mind. That same year, Congress officially recognized the pledge, formally adopted the flag code, and advised students to place their right hand over their heart—rather than extending the hand toward the flag with palms up, which had resembled the Nazi salute.

As World War II continued, "the American flag was an important symbol of the war effort for American troops on the fields of battle in Europe, Africa, Asia, and the Pacific, as well as on the home front" (Leepson 2005, 205). Dry cleaners were deluged after they offered to dry clean flags for free and "citizens everywhere flew flags as a sign of support for the war effort" (206). About 16 million Americans, more than 400,000 of whom died, served in the conflict, and as in World War II, many families hung service flags in their windows indicating that they had one or more family members who were participating in the conflict. The identification of the flag with the war effort was probably never more pronounced than in July 1942, when more than 400 magazines incorporated pictures of U.S. flags on their covers. That same year, the Smithsonian Institution temporarily moved the flag that had inspired "The Star-Spangled Banner" (and other historic artifacts) to a storage facility in the Shenandoah National Park, near Luray, Virginia, for safekeeping.

Apart from the initial attack at Pearl Harbor, World War II was fought abroad. This was emphasized in the song "There's a Star-Spangled Banner Waving Somewhere," which was released in 1942. That same year, a movie musical entitled *Yankee Doodle Dandy* recounted the life of George M. Cohan and included patriotic songs like "You're a Grand Old Flag."

The most flag-worthy moment of the war undoubtedly occurred when a picture of American marines raising a U.S. flag on Mount Suribachi on Iwo Jima was printed on the first page of *The New York Times* and subsequently became one of the most requested photographs in U.S. history. The surviving participants were subsequently brought to the United States to raise money for war bonds, and the moment was embodied in a bronze memorial in Arlington, Virginia.

When the Japanese finally surrendered on the *Missouri*, Americans displayed the flag that U.S. commodore Matthew Perry had flown on his first visit to Japan in 1853. The White House also flew a flag that had survived the Pearl Harbor attack; it was also flown at the United Nations Charter meeting in San Francisco, California, and at the Conference of the Big Three Powers in Potsdam, Germany, in 1945 (*Our Flag* 2003, 5). Following the attack on Pearl Harbor, President Roosevelt continued to fly the same flag that had flown over the Capitol during that attack (it was typically replaced from day to day) until Congress passed its declaration of war (Schneider 2003, 127–128).

As Soviet troops moved into Eastern Europe and set up puppet regimes (creating what Winston Churchill called the Iron Curtain) and communists gained control of China with the nationalists retreating to Taiwan, the postwar world ushered in a Cold War. It aligned America with Western Europe against Russia and China and was played out throughout much of the world. African American veterans who returned from the war fighting racism abroad often encountered similar racism at home, and many formed the backbone of civil rights protests in the United States.

The flag of the United States during World War II, like that during World War I, contained 48 stars since Alaska and Hawaii had not yet been admitted. After the war, the Philippines, which America had acquired as a colony during the Spanish-American War and which had been the scene of intense fighting, became independent.

Especially in the aftermath of protracted conflicts in Vietnam, Iraq, and Afghanistan, Americans sometimes look back at World War II as "the Good War" (Lukacs 2010) and to those who fought it in as "the Greatest Generation." A massive World War II Memorial was dedicated in Washington, D.C., on May 29, 2004, and includes 4,000 sculpted gold stars, to remind visitors of the sacrifices involved in this conflict.

The National WWII Museum (formerly the D-Day Museum) in New Orleans was founded in 2000 and highlights the amphibious assault on Normandy Beach that was facilitated by so-called Higgins boats that were manufactured in that city. The museum contains a number of U.S. flags from the war. Its site also has lesson plans for schoolchildren entitled *The Stories That Flags Can Tell Us*. There is another National D-Day Memorial in Bedford, Virginia, whose soldiers suffered particularly heavy casualties during the invasion of Normandy, which President George W. Bush dedicated on D-Day in 2001.

See also Civil Rights; Flag Code; Iwo Jima Flag Raising; *Minersville School District v. Gobitis* (1940); *West Virginia State Board of Education v. Barnette* (1943); World War I

Further Reading

Bradley, James, and Ron Powers. 2000. *Flags of Our Fathers*. New York: Bantam.

Leepson, Marc. 2005. *Flag: An American Biography*. New York: St. Martin's Press.

Lukacs, John. 2010. *The Legacy of the Second World War*. New Haven: Yale University Press.

Marvin, Carolyn, and David W. Ingle. 1999. *Blood Sacrifice and the Nation: Totem Rituals and the American Flag*. New York: Cambridge University Press.

National WWII Museum. *The Stories that Flags Can Tell Us: Primary Sources from WWII.* New Orleans: National WWII Museum.

Our Flag. 2003. Washington, D.C.: U.S. Government Printing Office.

Schneider, Richard H. 2003. *Stars and Stripes Forever: The History, Stories, and Memories of Our American Flag.* New York: William Morrow.

XENOPHOBIA, NATIVISM, AND THE U.S. FLAG

In some periods of American history, the U.S. flag has assumed heightened importance as a symbol of the nation. Especially since the Civil War, citizens have generally revered the flag as a symbol of national unity, but it is not uncommon for special interests and causes to seek to appropriate the flag for their own uses. In the period from the end of the War of 1812 until the Civil War, American nativists (favoring those who had been born on American soil rather than naturalized) sought to appropriate the flag as a symbol of white Protestant America and as a sign of xenophobic opposition to immigrants.

This usage was especially prominent in the events that led to riots in the city of Philadelphia, Pennsylvania, in 1844. Historian Woden Teachout traces the origins of the riots to Lewis Levin, a gifted orator who railed against alcohol, Catholicism, and Irish immigrants and helped found what was known as the American Republican Party (not to be confused with the party of Abraham Lincoln that would follow). Levin was also editor of a nativist newspaper, *The Daily Sun*, which, like others, included an American flag on its masthead. Levin was among those who helped drive a wedge between Irish working men and native-born workers who were often at the margins of Philadelphia society. One flash point was the Bible, with Catholics seeking to allow their Douay version to be read in public schools (or eliminate the practice altogether) rather than the King James Version, which was the staple of American Protestantism (Dorsey 2008).

Riots broke out after Levin gave a provocative speech in the Irish part of town against the backdrop of an American flag. In the ensuing melee, which would leave much of the Irish quarter in Kensington (especially Catholic churches) burned, nativist supporter George Shiffler grasped the flag and raised it above his head before taking six bullets to his chest, from which he died. Nativists used his death as a further rallying point, adding a new verse to "Auld Lang Syne":

> Our Flag's insulted, friends are slain,
> And must we quiet be?
> No! No! we'll Rally round the Flag.
> Which leads to Victory. (Teachout 2009, 67)

Some Irish families were able to save their homes by stitching U.S. flags and displaying them, almost like talismans, on their doors during the riots.

Nativists subsequently held a gigantic Independence Day parade, which featured numerous flags, including one held by Shiffler himself. They also carried Liberty figures, liberty caps, images of bald eagles, and portraits of George Washington.

"Beware Foreign Influence" was the most frequently displayed slogan, along with banners proclaiming allegiance to 'Our Native Land' and "virtue, Liberty, and Independence.'" (Miers 2000, 493). John L. Magee subsequently composed a lithograph, published by Wm. Smith of Philadelphia, entitled the *Death of George Shifler, in Kensington*, showing three men coming to the aid of Shiffler, who clutches the flag in one hand and his heart with the other.

This symbolism has been described by Teachout as "nationalist patriotism"—loyalty to a group rather than to the people as a whole or its government (2009, 69). She contrasts this with what she describes as "humanitarian patriotism," which she associates with the ideals or liberty and equality articulated in the Declaration of Independence and other documents.

At the national level, a secret organization known as the Order of the Star-Spangled Banner, founded in 1849, gained popularity and developed into the American, or Know-Nothing, Party, which opposed Roman Catholics and immigrants. it largely faded with the rise of the Republican Party, which resulted in the election of Abraham Lincoln in 1860. Lincoln strongly repudiated nativist sentiments and sought a union of all the people. In a letter to Joshua F. Speed, Lincoln explained his sentiments:

> I am not a Know-Nothing. That is certain. How could I be? How can any one who abhors the oppression of negroes, be in favor of degrading classes of white people? Our progress in degeneracy appears to me to be pretty rapid. As a nation, we begin by declaring that "all men are created equal." We now practically read it "all men are created equal, except negroes." When the Know-Nothings get control, it will read "all men are created equal, except negroes, and foreigners, and catholics." When it comes to this I should prefer emigrating to some country where they make no pretence of loving liberty—to Russia, for instance, where despotism can be taken pure, and without the base allow of hypocracy. (Lincoln 1902, 216–217)

Groups like the Ku Klux Klan and the Knights of the White Camelia would later revive nativist, racist, and xenophobic sentiments with symbols of their own, most notably white hoods and robes and burning crosses. Often, however, they would combine these symbols with national symbols like the American flag. In 1925, for example, 40,000 robed members of the Ku Klux Klan marched down Pennsylvania Avenue in Washington, D.C., carrying U.S. flags.

See also Independence Day; Lincoln, Abraham

Further Reading

Dorsey, Bruce. 2008. "Freedom of Religion: Bibles, Public Schools, and Philadelphia's Bloody Riots of 1844." *Pennsylvania Legacies* 8 (May): 12–17.

Lincoln, Abraham. 1902. *Abraham Lincoln: Complete Works*. Edited by John G. Nicholay and John Jay. Vol. 1. New York: Century Company.

Miers, Charlene. 2000. "Slavery, Nativism, and the Forgotten History of Independence Hall." *Pennsylvania History: A Journal of Mid-Atlantic Studies* 67 (Autumn) 481–501.

Teachout, Woden. 2009. *Capture the Flag: A Political History of American Patriotism*. New York: Basic Books.

Y

"YOU'RE A GRAND OLD FLAG"

One of America's most beloved songs to the flag originated from a Broadway musical penned by George M. Cohan (1878–1942). Cohan—as his lyrics in "I'm a Yankee Doodle Dandy" suggest—claimed to have been born on July 4, although historians believe that he was actually born the day before (Marling 2004, 16). He composed more than three dozen musicals during his career. These musicals include numerous famous songs including "Over There," "Give My Regards to Broadway," and "The Yankee Doodle Boy," many of which contained highly patriotic themes.

"You're a Grand Old Flag" was one such song. It was composed for the play *George Washington, Jr.*, first performed in 1906, which includes Mount Vernon and Washington, D.C., among its settings. In the original play, the musical referred to the American flag as "a grand old rag," but this, as well as a scene in which Cohan wrapped himself in the flag, were considered to be in bad taste, and the lyrics were changed.

The lyrics to the two main stanzas are arguably a bit corny, with the first stanza attempting, much like "The Stars and Stripes Forever," to unite North and South around the Red, White, and Blue:

> There's a feeling comes a-stealing
> And it sets my brain a-reeling
> When I'm list'ning to the music of a military band
> Any tune like "Yankee Doodle"
> Simply sets me off my noodle
> It's the patriotic something
> That no one can understand
> "Way down South in the land of cotton"
> Melody untiring
> Ain't that inspiring!
> Hurrah! Hurrah! We'll join the jubilee
> And that's going some
> For the Yankees, by gum!
> Red, white and blue
> I am for you
> Honest, you're a grand old flag.

The most recognized and most powerful part of the song is found in the chorus, which, unlike the earlier reference to "a military band," expresses the wish that "forever in peace may you wave":

You're a grand old flag,
You're a high flying flag
And forever in peace may you wave.
You're the emblem of
The land I love.
The home of the free and the brave.
Ev'ry heart beats true
'neath the Red, White and Blue,
Where there's never a boast or brag.
Should auld acquaintance be forgot,
Keep your eye on the grand old flag.

The line "There's never a boast or a brag" seems a bit more modest than that of a "grand" or "high flying" flag.

The second stanza continues with popular vernacular but proceeds in a more militaristic direction than the first. It also invokes Uncle Sam and the colors of the flag:

I'm a cranky hanky panky
I'm a dead square honest Yankee
And I'm might proud of that old flag
That flies for Uncle Sam
Though I don't believe in raving
Ev'ry time I see it waving
There's a chill runs up my back
That makes me glad I'm what I am
Here's a land with a million soldiers
That's if we should need 'em
We'll right for freedom!
Hurrah! Hurrah! For ev'ry Yankee tar
And old G.A.R.
Ev'ry stripe, ev'ry star
Red, white and blue
Hats off to you
Honest, you're a grand old flag.

The song then ends with a repetition of the chorus, which is the last song in the musical. In analyzing the song, scholar Scot M. Guenter observed that a musical tradition has developed that a "patriotic pitch can often win an audience" and that such a pitch almost always requires the use of the flag (Guenter 1990, 157).

See also "Star-Spangled Banner" (Anthem); "Stars and Stripes Forever"; "This Ain't No Rag, It's a Flag"; Uncle Sam

Further Reading

Guenter, Scot M. 1990. *The American Flag, 1777–1924: Cultural Shifts from Creation to Codification*. Cranbury, NJ: Associated University Presses.

Marling, Karal Ann. 2004. *Old Glory: Unfurling History*. Washington D.C.: Library of Congress.
McCabe, John. 1973. *George M. Cohan: The Man Who Owned Broadway*. Garden City, NY: Doubleday.
Whitmer, Mariana. 2005. "Songs with Social Significance: An Introduction." *OAH Magazine of History* 19 (July): 9–16, 22.

YOUTH'S COMPANION

The Youth's Companion was a magazine, based in Boston, owned by Daniel Sharp Ford (1822–1899) for much of its existence. He purchased it in the late 1850s and converted it into "a publishing powerhouse" (Ellis 2005, 5). One of the magazine's innovations was to give discounts on a variety of goods for subscribers who sold subscriptions. In 1888, the magazine began including American flags among such goods, and it subsequently joined a movement to place a flag in each school and to have a nationwide school celebration to commemorate the 400th anniversary of Christopher Columbus's discovery of America. The magazine sent certificates that students could sell at 10 cents apiece in order to raise the $10 needed to purchase a flag (Guenter 1990, 125).

The two individuals who took the lead in this effort were James B. Upham, a nephew of Ford who headed the magazine's Premium Department, and Francis Bellamy, a former Baptist preacher who believed in socialism. The latter of these individuals subsequently wrote a pledge to the flag, which declared, "I pledge allegiance to my Flag and to the Republic for which it stands—one Nation indivisible—with Liberty and Justice for all." That pledge replaced a former pledge that George Balch had written. With some modifications, it remains the basis for the current Pledge of Allegiance.

The proposed Columbus Day program touted by the magazine included raising the flag, saluting it with right arms and upraised palms extended toward it, an "Acknowledgement of God," a prayer and Bible reading, a rendition of the "Song of Columbus Day," and the reading of an address, "The Meaning of the Four Centuries," and an ode entitled "Columbia's Banner" (Ellis 2005, 20). The *Companion* further suggested that this should be followed by an afternoon parade that would include Civil War veterans.

Commemorations were carried out in schools across the country. In a fascinating twist, Francis Bellamy gave a speech in which he emphasized the importance of America's Anglo-Saxon rather than its Spanish roots. This did not keep many—especially Roman Catholics, who were uncomfortable with daily school exercises that typically included readings from Protestant versions of the Bible—from focusing on the role of Columbus and from criticizing compulsory public education (Ellis 2005, 22–23).

See also Balch, George Thacher; Bellamy, Francis J.; Pledge of Allegiance

Further Reading

Ellis, Richard J. 2005. *To the Flag: The Unlikely History of the Pledge of Allegiance*. Lawrence: University Press of Kansas.

Guenter, Scot M. 1990. *The American Flag, 1777–1924: Cultural Shifts from Creation to Codification*. Cranbury, NJ: Associated University Presses.
Harris, Louise. 1971. *The Flag over the Schoolhouse*. Providence, RI: C. A. Stephens Collection, Brown University.

Z

ZARICOR FLAG COLLECTION

The Zaricor Flag Collection is one of the world's most important collections of U.S. flags. It was created by Ben Zaricor, the former chief executive of Good Earth Tea, who began collecting when he was in college. The collection now includes over 3,500 artifacts, including 900 U.S. flags, many associated with historic events. Zaricor is particularly proud of his collection of eight 13-star flags that date from early American history. Although usually kept in storage, the flags have been exhibited on a number of occasions.

A graduate of Overton High School in Memphis, Tennessee, Zaricor subsequently earned a graduate degree in sociology from Washington University in St. Louis. He became fascinated with flags when he saw a man beaten up and arrested for wearing a vest with stars and stripes (Steinberg 2011).

As devoted as he is to the flag, Zaricor opposes flag desecration laws: "I don't think we have to protect the flag from its people. We have a bottom-up, people's flag. It wasn't created by the government and handed down" (Tucker 2011).

Further information about the Zaricor Flag Collection is available at its website, at www.flagcollection.com. The website indicates that the collections include 11 personal collections previously belonging to Boleslaw and Marie-Louise D'Otrange Mastai, William Guthman, Norm Flayderman, Howard Madaus, Calvin Bullock, Howard Hughes, Judge John Ball, Matthew Ridgway, Robert Eichelberger, Jim Mountain, and Louise Veninga.

See also Mastai, Boleslaw and Marie-Louise D'Otrange; Thirteen-Star Flags

Further Reading

Schrambling, Regina. 2014. "A Lifelong Pledge." *Robb Report*, June 17. http://robbreport.com/art-collectibles/lifelong-pledge/

Steinberg, Becki. 2011. "Q&A with Ben Zaricor: American Flag Collector." *The Hill*, August 5. http://thehill.com/capital-living/cover-stories/175651-qaa-with-ben-zaricor-american-flag-collector

Tucker, Neely. 2011. "Ben Zaricor Is a Flag Waver." *Washington Post*, August 3. https://www.washingtonpost.com/lifestyle/style/ben-zaricor-is-a-flag-waver/2011/11/21/gIQAqddqsI_story.html?utm_term=.e7b47e6dedb3

Womack, Tiffany. 2003. "American Flag: A Living Symbol." CBS News, July 3. http://www.cbsnews.com/news/american-flag-a-living-symbol/

Glossary

Allegiance

Loyalty.

All-Weather Flag

A flag made of synthetic materials that can withstand inclement weather.

Band

Narrow strip of canvas, sometimes called a "heading," that is next to the staff.

Bible Flags

Flags that were small enough to fit inside the covers of Bibles that soldiers carried into battle.

Bunting

Red, white, and blue cloth (typically wool in the 19th century) used as patriotic decoration. Flag etiquette requires that the blue be on the top, the white in the middle, and the red on the bottom.

Canton

The upper-left-hand portion of a flag. In the U.S. flag, it consists of a blue background representing a constellation, with one star for each of the 50 states.

Cavalry Flag

Typically swallowtail in shape, it is often used in battle.

Civil Religion

Generic religious sentiments that bind a nation together and that are generally strong on emotional and sentimental ideals and relatively weak in terms of traditional religious doctrines.

Colors

A term sometimes used to describe either national or regimental flags, especially of the infantry.

Continental Flag

Early U.S. flag used on ships, with British crosses in the canton and 13 alternating red and white stripes.

Cult of the Flag

A term used to describe the increasing focus on the U.S. flag that developed during the 1880s, 1890s, and thereafter.

Desecrate

To violate or treat a sacred object, like a flag, with disrespect.

Dip

To lower a flag, as in a salute.

Does the Constitution Follow the Flag?

A question used to ascertain the degree to which American constitutional law is applied to U.S. possessions. In the Insular Cases, the Supreme Court decided that the law did follow the flag but only with regard to those rights that were considered to be most fundamental.

Ensign

The designation of the national flag by the U.S. Navy. An ensign was initially an officer charged with carrying a flag into battle.

Escutcheon

A shield with a coat of arms.

Estoiles

Six-pointed stars, typically wavy, that were sometimes used on early U.S. flags.

Federalism

A system that divides governmental authority between a central authority (sometimes called the federal government) and constituent subcomponents, which in the U.S. are called states.

Fimbriations

Thin lines or stripes, generally white or silver, that separate colors in heraldic symbols and those flags that are derived from them, such as in the Union Jack of Great Britain.

Finial

An object, like a ball or an eagle, on top of a flag pole.

Fly

A name for the horizontal dimensions of a flag. Flags flown by federal executive agencies must be 1.9 times their width.

Fringe

Trim that is sometimes used for indoor flags.

Garrison Flag

A flag that is used for special occasions.

Gonfanon

A heraldic flag used as a rallying point for soldiers, often with a swallowtail or streamers and suspended from a crossbar.

Grommets

The rings through which the halyards pass to attach the flag to a pole.

Guidon

A flag held aloft on a staff as with a battle, or cavalry, flag.

Half-Staff (or Half-Mast) Flags

Used to mourn the death of important governmental officials.

Halyard

The rope or tackle used to raise a flag or sails on a ship.

Hoist

The vertical dimension (width) of a flag. Also a verb used for the process of raising a flag.

Iconography

A set of symbols, often including a flag, that help provide emotional ties that bind individuals together.

Indivisible

Not capable of being divided. This term, which is part of the Pledge of Allegiance to the U.S. flag, was probably written with a view toward rejecting the attempt by the Confederate states to secede from the Union.

Jack

A naval flag, typically flown at the ship's bow.

Mullet

A five-pointed star like that currently used on U.S. flags.

Nation

A group of people bound together by common ties of language, belief, and ethnicity, whose identity is sometimes symbolized by flags. A nation-state may consist of one or more nations.

Nationalism

Sentiments that bind individuals into nation states. The iniquitousness of flags and of flag colors and images, which Michael Billig identifies with "banal nationalism," may often go largely unnoticed. Militant nationalism is sometimes associated with expansionism.

Nativist

An individual who seeks to give special status to individuals born in the United States. American nativists have typically been hostile to immigrants, especially Catholics or people of color.

Obverse

The front of a flag when an observer sees the hoist on the left.

OG Red and OG Blue

Official colors of the U.S. flag, with "OG" standing for "Old Glory." These colors apparently come close to 281C Blue and 193C Red on the standardized color matching system (Pantone).

Old Glory

A name that Capt. William Driver gave to his U.S. flag, which he had to hide during the Civil War. It has become a popular nickname for the U.S. flag.

Patriotism

Love for and devotion to one's country. One reason the U.S. flag is such a potent patriotic symbol is that many people identify it with the nation as a whole.

Polysemous

A word or object (such as a flag) with multiple meanings.

Post Flag

A flag that flies over a government installation. Sometimes also called a Camp Flag.

Quincuncial Pattern

A pattern, used in early American flags, where stars were arranged in groups of five, with alternating rows of three stars and two stars.

Rally 'Round the Flag Effect

Increased support for the U.S. President during times of national crisis.

Raven: A Journal of Vexillology

The most prominent scholarly journal devoted to the study of flags.

Republic

A government, sometimes distinguished from a pure democracy, in which people are indirectly represented through their elected representatives. Republics can cover much larger areas than pure democracies, where people have to physically gather to make decisions. Also a term used in the salute to the U.S. flag to designate representative, or republican, government.

Reverse

The side of the flag opposite the obverse.

Shield

A shield with alternating vertical red and white stripes is one of the most ubiquitous symbols of the United States other than the U.S. flag. Francis Hopkinson appears to have had his hand in the design of both. The shield is especially prominent in corporate logos.

Spangled

Covered with bright shiny objects (spangles), for example, the stars in the canton of the U.S. flag.

Staff

Another name for the pole on which a flag is displayed.

Standard

A name for the flag of the cavalry.

Standard-Bearer

The person, also known as a flag-bearer, who carries a flag into battle.

Stars and Stripes

Another name for the U.S. flag, focusing on its two central features.

Star-Spangled Banner

The name of the banner that flew over Fort McHenry and of the national anthem, composed by Francis Scott Key. This term is also used as a name for the U.S. flag.

State

Either a national entity (a nation-state) with control over the use of legitimate force within its borders or one of the constituent parts of the U.S. government or of other federal systems.

Storm Flag

A flag used during inclement weather.

Strike a Flag

To lower a flag in surrender or submission.

Symbol

A drawing or object that stands for something else.

Under God

Words added to the Pledge of Allegiance during the Cold War when the nation was battling (atheistic) communism, serving as a sign that the flag salute is part of America's civil religion.

Union

Another designation of the starred blue canton on the U.S. flag.

Union Jack

A name either for the blue star-spangled canton on the U.S. flag that the U.S. Navy used from 1777 to 2002, to identify ships' nationality, or for the Union Flag of the United Kingdom.

Vexillology

The scientific study of flags. The term was coined by flag collector Whitney Smith from the Latin *vexillum* for "flag" and the Greek *logia* for "study."

Vexillum

A flag or standard used in ancient Roman armies.

Waving the Flag

A term used for moving the flag about to catch the air in a patriotic gesture.

Wrapping One's Self in a Flag

Describes an individual who attempts to exonerate him or herself or divert criticism by associating his or her cause with the flag.

Bibliography

Articles, Essays, Reports, Websites, and Book Chapters

Adriansen, Inge. 2014. "The Danish National Flag as a Gift from God: A National-Religious Myth," *Kirchliche Zeitgenschichte* 27: 277–298.

Aikman, Lonnelle. 1959. "New Stars for Old Glory." *National Geographic Magazine* 116 (July): 87–171.

Anthony, Susan B., and Ida Husted Harper, eds. "Dr. Shaw's Tribute to the American Flag, Given Many Times." In *The History of Woman Suffrage*. Vol. 5. Rochester, NY: Susan B. Anthony.

Baker, Russell. 1976. "The Flag." In *Mom, the Flag, and Apple Pie*, compiled by editors of *Esquire*, 15–20. Garden City, NY: Doubleday and Company, Inc.

Baker, William D., and John R. Oneal. 2001. "Patriotism or Opinion Leadership? The Nature and Origins of the 'Rally 'Round the Flag' Effect." *The Journal of Conflict Resolution* 45 (October): 661–687.

Belmas, Genelle I. 2009. "Pushing Patriotism: Why Flag Encouragement Doesn't Fly." *Communication Law and Policy* 14 (Summer): 341–372.

Bergman, Jerry. 1997. "The Modern Religious Objection to Mandatory Flag Salute in America: A History and Evaluation." *Journal of Church and State* 39 (Spring): 215–236.

Billig, Michael. 2005. *Banal Nationalism*. Los Angeles, CA: Sage.

Boime, Albert. 1990. "Waving the Red Flag and Reconstituting Old Glory." *Smithsonian Studies in American Art* 4 (Spring): 2–25.

Bonner, Robert E. 2002. "Flag Culture and the Consolidation of Confederate Nationalism." *The Journal of Southern History* 68 (May): 293–332.

Bonner, Robert E. 2003. "Star-Spangled Sentiment." *Common-Place* 3 (2). http://www.common-place-archives.org/vol-03/no-02/bonner/bonner-5.shtml.

Borda, Jennifer L. 2002. "The Woman Suffrage Parades of 1910–1913: Possibilities and Limitations of an Early Feminist Rhetorical Strategy." *Western Journal of Communication* 66 (Winter): 25–52.

Borden, Sandra L. 2005. "Communitarian Journalism and Flag Displays after September 11: An Ethical Critique." *Journal of Communication Inquiry* 29 (January): 30–46.

Bruff, Harold H. 2015. *Untrodden Ground: How Presidents Interpret the Constitution*. Chicago: University of Chicago Press.

Burke, Doreen Bolger. 1982. "Frederic Edwin Church and 'The Banner of Dawn.'" *American Art Journal* 15 (Spring): 39–46.

Canipe, Lee. 2003. "Under God and Anti-Communist: How the Pledge of Allegiance Got Religion in Cold War America." *Journal of Church and State* 45 (Spring): 305–323.

Cerulo, Karen A. 1989. "Sociopolitical Control and the Structure of National Symbols: An Empirical Analysis of National Anthems." *Social Forces* 68 (September): 76–99.

Cerulo, Karen A. 1993. "Symbols and the World System: National Anthems and Flags." *Sociological Forum* 8 (June): 243–271.

Cloud, Matthew W. 2004. "'One Nation, Under God': Tolerable Acknowledgement of Religion or Unconstitutional Cold War Propaganda Cloaked in American Civil Religion?" *Journal of Church and State* 46 (Spring): 311–340.

Coffman, Elesha. 2008. "Do You Know the History of the Christian Flag?" *Christianity Today*, August 8. https://www.christianitytoday.com/history/2008/august/do-you-know-history-of-christian-flag.html.

Cogliano, Francis D. 1998. "'We All Hoisted the American Flag:' National Identity among American Prisoners in Britain during the American Revolution." *Journal of American Studies* 32 (April): 19–37.

Collins, Kristin A. 2012. "Representing Injustice: Justice as an Icon of Woman Suffrage." *Yale Journal of Law and the Humanities* 24:191–220.

Coulter, E. Merton. 1953. "The Flags of the Confederacy." *Georgia Historical Quarterly* 37 (September): 188–199.

Cox, E. J. 1908. "The Development of 'Old Glory.'" *The Journal of Education* 67 (April 16): 435, 439.

Craig, Brian. 2007. "The Freedom to Display the American Flag Act: Construction and Constitutionality." *Raven: A Journal of Vexillology* 13:61–84.

Crews, Ed. Summer 2008. "The Truth About Betsy Ross." *Colonial Williamsburg Journal*, Summer. https://www.history.org/foundation/journal/summer08/betsy.cfm.

Davis, Derek H. 2003. "The Pledge of Allegiance and American Values." *Journal of Church and State* 45 (Autumn): 657–668.

Desbler, Charles D. 1892. "How the Declaration Was Received in the Old Thirteen." *Harper's New Monthly Magazine* 85 (July): 165–187.

DiAgostino, Grace. 2016. "Pledging Allegiance: Negotiating National Responsibility, Religious Liberty, and the First Amendment." *Social Education* 80 (September): 219–223.

Dionne, E. J., John McWethy, Alan Murray, and Alicia C. Shepard. 2003. "Running Toward Danger." In *The Media and the War on Terrorism*, edited by Stephen Hess and Marvin Kalb, 275–295. Washington, D.C.: Brookings Institution Press.

Dorsen, Norman. 2000. "Flag Desecration in Courts, Congress, and Country." *Thomas M. Cooley Law Review* 17 (Michaelmas): 417–442.

Dorsey, Bruce. 2008. "Freedom of Religion: Bibles, Public Schools, and Philadelphia's Bloody Riots of 1844." *Pennsylvania Legacies* 8 (May): 12–17.

Drake, Sarah E. 2002. "The Postwar Home Front: Memorializing Veterans." *OAH Magazine of History* 17 (October): 60–64.

Durrill, Wayne K. 2006. "Ritual, Community and War: Local Flag Presentation Ceremonies and Disunity in the Early Confederacy." *Journal of Social History* 39 (Summer): 1105-1122.

Dyreson, M. 2008a. "'This Flag Dips for No Earthly King': The Mysterious Origins of an American Myth." *The International Journal of the History of Sport* 25 (February 15): 142–162.

Dyreson, M. 2008b. "'To Dip or Not to Dip': The American Flag at the Olympic Games since 1936." *The International Journal of the History of Sports* 25 (February 15): 163–184.

Eberwein, Robert. 2013. "Following the Flag in American Film." In *Eastwood's Iwo Jima: Critical Engagements with Flags of Our Fathers and Letters from Iwo Jima*, edited by Rikke Schubart and Anne Gjelsviki, 81–99. New York: Columbia University Press.

Ferris, Marc. 2014. "'Long May It Wave.'" *The American Legion Magazine*, September 11. https://www.legion.org/magazine/224572/long-may-it-wave.

Flag Manufacturers Association of America. 2017. Accessed February 2017. http://www.fmaa-usa.com/about-profile_mission.php.

Fox Valley Patriotic Organization. 2017. "Monument Design Features." Flag Day Monument, Batavia, Illinois. Accessed March 2. http://flagdaymonument.com/monument-design-features/.

Gey, Steven G. 1990. "This Is not a Flag: The Aesthetics of Desecration." *Wisconsin Law Review* 1990 (December): 1549–1595.

Goddard, Kristian. 2008. "The Resilience of the Stars and Stripes." December 4. http://www.kristiangoddard.net/Blog/americanflag.htm.

Goldstein, Jared A. 2017. "How the Constitution Became Christian." *Hastings Law Journal* 68 (February): 259–308.

Goldstein, Robert Justin. 1990. "The Great 1989–1990 Flag Flap: An Historical, Political, and Legal Analysis." *University of Miami Law Review* 45 (September): 19–106.

Greenstein, Nicole. 2013. "Why the U.S. Flag is Red, White and Blue." *Time*, July 4. http://swampland.time.com/2013/07/04/why-the-u-s-flag-is-red-white-and-blue/.

Guenter, Scot M. 2009. "Flag Tattoos: Markers of Class and Sexuality." In *Proceedings: The XIX International Congress of Vexillology, York, 23–27 York July 2001*. U.K.: Flag Institute.

Guenter, Scot M. 2015. "The Phenomenon of Flag Homes: Musings on Meaning. *Raven: A Journal of Vexillology* 22:27–53.

Hamilton, Alexander, James Madison, and John Jay. 1961. *The Federalist Papers*. New York: New American Library.

Harden, J. David. 1995. "Liberty Caps and Liberty Trees." *Past and Present*, no. 146, 66–102.

Hartvigsen, Kenneth. 2011. "Picturing Flag Violence in Civil War Sheet Music: The Case of 'Down with the Traitors' Serpent Flag.'" In *Proceedings of the 24th International Congress of Vexillology*, 407–424. Washington, D.C.

Hatchett, Louis, and W. K. McNeil. 2005. "There's a Star-Spangled Banner Waving Somewhere." In *Country Music Goes to War*, edited by Charles K. Wolfe and James E. Akenson, 33–42. Lexington: University Press of Kentucky.

Henderson, Jennifer Jacobs. 2005. "Conditional Liberty: The Flag Salute Before Gobitis and Barnette." *Journal of Church and State* 47 (Autumn): 747–767.

Hickey, Donald R. 2015. "A Note on the Origins of 'Uncle Sam,' 1810–1820." *New England Quarterly* 88 (December): 681–692.

Homer, Harlan H. 1915. "The American Flag." *Proceedings of the New York State Historical Association* 14:108–121.

Isaacson, Eric A. 1990. "The Flag Burning Issue: A Legal Analysis and Comment." *Loyola of Los Angeles Law Review* 23 (January): 535–600.

Johnson, Jason. 2016. "Star-Spangled Bigotry: The Hidden Racist History of the National Anthem." *The Root*, August 4. https://www.theroot.com/star-spangled-bigotry-the-hidden-racist-history-of-the-1790855893

Johnson, Kirk, et al. 2011. "Across the Nation, Tragedy Spawned Inspiration." *New York Times*, September 12. http://www.nytimes.com/2011/09/12/us/12vignettes.html.

Jones, Anthony. 1990. "Stars and Bras: A Report from the Trenches." *Academe* 76 (July–August): 18–23.

Joselit, Jenna Weissman. 2017. *Set in Stone: America's Embrace of the Ten Commandments*. New York: Oxford University Press.

Joyner, Russell. 1989. "Flags, Symbols and Controversy." *ETC: A Review of General Semantics* 46 (Fall): 217–220.

Kao, Grace Y. 2007. " 'One Nation Under God' or Taking the Lord's Name in Vain? Christian Reflections on the Pledge of Allegiance." *Journal of the Society of Christian Ethics* 27 (Spring/Summer): 183–204.

Ketchum, Alton. 1990. "The Search for Uncle Sam." *History Today* 40 (April): 20–26.

Kidd, Laura K. 2007. "Wave It or Wear It? The United States Flag as a Fashion Icon." *Raven: A Journal of Vexillology* 14:35–60.

Koukoulopoulos, Dimitris, and Johann Thiel. 2012. "Arrangements of Stars on the American Flag." *The American Mathematical Monthly* 119 (June–July): 443–450.

Lambert, Alan J., J. P. Schott, and Laura Scherer. 2011. "Threat, Politics, and Attitudes: Toward a Greater Understanding of Rally-'Round-the-Flag Effects." *Current Directions in Psychological Science* 20 (December): 343–348.

Lane, Megan. 2011. "Five Hidden Messages in the American Flag." *BBC News Magazine*, November 14. http://www.bbc.com/news/magazine-15634606.

Lee, Lois. 2015. *Recognizing the Non-Religious: Reimagining the Secular*. New York: Oxford University Press.

Levinson, Sanford. 1994–1995. "They Whisper: Reflections of Flags, Monuments, and State Holidays, and the Construction of Social Meaning in a Multicultural Society." *Chicago-Kent Law Review* 70:1079–111

Lidman, Davis. 1971. "Betsy Ross Stamp Perpetuates a Myth." *New York Times*, April 25.

Lifsey, Jeremy. 2013. "United States Flags on United States Stamps." Philatelic Database. Last modified March 9. http://www.philatelicdatabase.com/united-states/united-states-flags-on-united-states-stamps/.

Lowe, John. 2001. "From 'Flags in the Dust' to Banners of Defiance: Tales of a Symbol's Transformations." *Callaloo* 24 (Winter): 117–122.

Lowenthal, David. 1977. "The Bicentennial Landscape: A Mirror Held Up to the Past." *Geographical Review* 67 (July): 253–267.

Lyubansky, Mikhail. 2010. "On 9-11, Patriotism, and the U.S. flag." *Psychology Today*, September 10. https://www.psychologytoday.com/blog/between-the-lines/201009/9-11-patriotism-and-the-us-flag.

Madriaga, Manuel. 2007. "The Star-Spangled Banner and 'Whiteness' in American National Identity." In *Flag, Nation and Symbolism in Europe and America*, edited by Thomas Hylland Eriksen and Richard Jenkins, 53–67. New York: Routledge.

Martucci, David. 2000. "The 13 Stars and Stripes: A Survey of 18th Century Images." *NAVA News*, April–June. Addenda published in *NAVA News* in July–September 2000, April–June 2003, and October–December 2005.

Martucci, David. 2006. "Flag and Symbol Usage in Early New England." *Raven: A Journal of Vexillology* 13:1–40.

Menezes, Joann. 1997. "The Birthing of the American Flag and the Invention of an American Founding Mother in the Image of Betsy Ross." In *Narratives of Nostalgia, Gender, and Nationalism*, edited by Jean Pickering and Suzanne Kehde, 74–87. Washington Square, New York: New York University Press.

Mortensen, Mette. 2013. "The Making and Remakings of an American Icon: 'Raising the Flag on Iwo Jima' from Photojournalism to Global, Digital Media." In *Eastwood's Iwo Jima: Critical Engagements with Flags of Our Fathers and Letters from Iwo Jima*, edited by Rikke Schubart and Anne Gjelsik, 15–35. New York: Columbia University Press.

Moss, Rosalind Urbach. 1998. "'Yes, There's a Reason I Salute the flag': Flag Use and the Civil Rights Movement." *Raven: A Journal of Vexillology* 5:12–33.

Moyers, Bill. 2003. "Bill Moyers on Patriotism and the American Flag." *Now*, PBS, February 28. http://www.pbs.org/now/commentary/moyers19.html.

O'Leary, Cecilia Elizabeth. 1999. *To Die For: The Paradox of American Patriotism*. Princeton, NJ: Princeton University Press.

Oneal, John R., and Anna Lillian Bryan. 1995. "The Rally 'Round the Flag Effect in U.S. Foreign Policy Crises, 1950–1985." *Political Behavior* 17 (December): 379–401.

Ostrander, James S. "The Old Flag," 1887. *Circular Papers and Annual Meeting of the Ohio Commandery of the Military Order of the Loyal Legion During the Year 1885*. N.p.: H.C. Sherick.

Ottoson, Robin Deich. 2010. "The Battle Over the Flag: Protest, Community Opposition, and Silence in the Mennonite Colleges in Kansas during the Vietnam War." *Journal of Church and State* 52 (Autumn): 686–711.

"Our Federal Sun: Planetary Politics before the Civil War." 2018. *American Political Thought: A Journal of Ideas, Institutions, and Culture* 7 (Spring): 189–215.

Parry-Jones, Cai. 2014. "Flying the Flag for Freedom: The Star-Spangled Banner and the American Abolitionist Movement." October 16. Adam Matthew: A Sage Company. http://qa.amdigital.co.uk/m-editorial-blog/flying-the-flag-for-freedom/

Pauly, Thomas H. 1976. "In Search of 'The Spirit of '76.'" *American Quarterly* 28 (Autumn): 445–464.

Pavlovic, Zoran "Zok." 2008. "Flagscapes in the American Heartland." *FOCUS on Geography* 51 (Winter): 17–22.

Perry, Lewis. 2008. "Harriet Jacobs and the 'Dear Old Flag.'" *African American Review* 42 (Fall/Winter): 595–605.

Pickerell, Ryan. March 1, 2017. "Why is the American Flag Flying at Rallies for South Korea's Impeached President?" http://dailycaller.com/author/ryan-pickerell/. Accessed 6/238/17.

Platoff, Anne M. 2007. "Flags in Space: NASA Symbols and Flags in the U.S. Manned Space Program." *Flag Bulletin: The International Journal of Vexillology* 46 (September–December): 143–221.

Saas, William O., and Rachel Hall. 2016. "Restive Peace: Body Bags, Casket Flags, and the Pathologization of Dissent." *Rhetoric and Public Affairs* 19 (Summer): 177–208.

Schmittou, Douglas A., and Michael H. Hogan. 2002. "Fluidity of Meaning: Flag Imagery in Plains Indian Art." *American Indian Quarterly* 26 (Autumn): 559–604.

Scott, Cord. 2007. "Written in Red, White, and Blue: A Comparison of Comic Book Propaganda from World War II and September 11." *Journal of Popular Culture* 40:325–343.

Scott, James Brown. 1917. "Respect for the American Flag." *American Journal of International Law* 11 (April): 410–413.

Shanafelt, Robert. 2008. "The Nature of Flag Power: How Flags Entail Dominance, Subordination, and Social Solidarity." *Politics and the Life Sciences* 29 (September): 13–27.

Shalev, Eran. 2011. "'A Republic Amidst the Stars' Political Astronomy and the Intellectual Origin of the Stars and Stripes," *Journal of the Early Republic* 31 (Spring) 39–73.

Sica, Morris G. 1990. "The School Flag Movement: Origin and Influence." *Social Education* 54 (October): 380–384.

Smith, Chuck. 2001. "The Persecution of West Virginia Jehovah's Witnesses and the Expansion of Legal Protection for Religious Liberty." *Journal of Church and State* 43 (Summer): 539–577.

Smith, Whitney. 1999. "American Perspectives on Heraldry and Vexillology." *Raven: A Journal of Vexillology* 6:41–53.

Smith, Whitney. 2009. "'One Nation Under God' The Crusade to Capture the American Flag." In *Proceedings: The XIX International Congress of Vexillology York 23–27 July 2001*, 67–74. U.K.: Flag Institute.

Steinberg, Becki. 2011. "Q&A with Ben Zaricor: American Flag Collector." *The Hill*, August 5. http://thehill.com/capital-living/cover-stories/175651-qaa-with-ben-zaricor-american-flag-collector.

Sullenger, D. Wes. 2005. "Burning the Flag: A Conservative Defense of Radical Speech and Why It Matters Now." *Brandeis Law Journal* 43 (Summer): 796–666.

Tushnet, Mark. 1990. "The Flag Burning Episode: An Essay on the Constitution." *University of Colorado Law Review* 61:39–53.

Uhrbrock, Richard Stephen. 1930. "We'll Rally 'Round the Flag, Boys." *Social Science* 5 (May, June, July): 328–33.

U.S. Department of the Treasury. 2017. "History of 'In God We Trust.'" https://www.treasury.gov/about/education/pages/in-god-we-trust.aspx.

Walker, Rob. 2017. "The Shifting Symbolism of the Gadsden Flag." *New Yorker*, October 2. http://www.newyorker.com/news/news-desk/the-shifting-symbolism-of-the-gadsden-flag.

Wallace, Michele. 2010. "The People's Flag Show by Faith Ringgold." *Ringgold in the 1960s*. May 26. http://ringgoldinthe1960s.blogspot.com/2010/05/peoples-flag-show-1970.html.

Waltzer, Michael. 1967. "On the Role of Symbolism in Political thought." *Political Science Quarterly* 82 (June): 191–204.

Warren, Charles. 1945. "Fourth of July Myths." *William and Mary Quarterly* 2 (July): 237–272.

Webster, Gerald R. 2011. "American Nationalism, the Flag, and the Invasion of Iraq." *Geographical Review* 101 (January): 1–18.

Wheeler, Brian. 2008. "The Pledge of Allegiance in the Classroom and the Court: An Epic Struggle over the Meaning of the Establishment Clause of the First Amendment." *Brigham Young University Education and Law Journal* 2008:281–324.

Williams, Earl P., Jr. 1988. "The 'Fancy Work' of Francis Hopkinson: Did He Design the Stars and Stripes?" *Prologue: Quarterly of the National Archives* 20 (Spring): 42–52.

Willis, Susan. 2002. "Old Glory." *South Atlantic Quarterly* 101:375–383.

Wilson, Chris. 2010. "13 Stripes and 51 Stars." *Slate*, June 9. http://www.slate.com/articles/life/do_the_math/2010/06/13_stripes_and_51_stars.html.

Young, Rowland L. 1977. "'Liberty and Justice for All.'" *American Bar Association Journal* 63 (June): 828–831.

Zelinsky, Wilbur. 1984. "O Say, Can You See? Nationalistic Emblems in the Landscape." *Winterthur Portfolio* 19 (Winter): 277–286.

Zelinksy, Wilbur. 1988. *Nation Into State: The Shifting Symbolic Foundations of American Nationalism*. Chapel Hill: University of North Carolina Press.

Books, Pamphlets, and Government Documents

Abbott, Samuel. 1919. *The Dramatic Story of Old Glory*. New York: Boni and Liveright.

All-American Flag Act: Report of the Committee on Homeland Security and Governmental Affairs United States Senate to Accompany S. 1214. to Require the Purchase of Domestically Made Flags of the United States of America for Use by the Federal Government. 2014. Washington, D.C.: U.S. Government Printing Office.

Allentown Art Museum. 1976. *The American Flag in the Art of Our Country*. Allentown, PA: Allentown Art Museum.

Anderson, Peggy. 1974. *The Daughters: An Unconventional Look at America's Fan Club—The DAR*. New York: St. Martin's Press.

Applegate, Debby. 2007. *The Most Famous Man in America: The Biography of Henry Ward Beecher*. New York: Three Leaves.

Attebery, Jennifer Eastman. 2015. *Pole Raising and Speech Making: Modalities of Swedish American Summer Celebrations*. Logan: Utah State University Press.

Baer, John W. 1992. *The Pledge of Allegiance: A Centennial History, 1892–1992*. Annapolis, MD: Free State Press, Inc.

Balch, George T. 1890. *Methods of Teaching Patriotism in the Public Schools*. New York: D. Van Nostrand.

Bass, Amy. 2002. *Not the Triumph but the Struggle: The 1968 Olympics and the Making of the Black Athlete*. Minneapolis: University of Minnesota Press.

Bates, Gilbert H. 1868. *Sergeant Bates' March Carrying the Stars and Stripes Unfurled from Vicksburg to Washington: Being a Truthful Narrative of the Incidents Which Transpired during His Journey on Foot, Without a Cent, through the Late Rebellious States, and Showing How the Good Old Flag Was Received as the Harbinger of Peace and New Hope to the Distressed People of the South*. New York: B. W. Hitchcock.

Becker, Carl L. 1970. *The Declaration of Independence: A Study in the History of Political Ideas*. New York: Vintage Books.

Billig, Michael. 1995. *Banal Nationalism*. London: Sage.

Bishop, Robert, and Carter Houck. 1986. *All Flags Flying: American Patriotic Quilts as Expressions of Liberty*. New York: E. P. Dutton.

Blair, William A. 2004. *Cities of the Dead: Contesting the Memory of the Civil War in the South, 1865–1914*. Chapel Hill: University of North Carolina Press.

Boime, Albert. 1998. *The Unveiling of National Icons: A Plea for Patriotic Iconoclasm in a Nationalist Era*. New York: Cambridge University Press.

Bonner, Robert E. 2002. *Colors and Blood: Flag Passions of the Confederate South*. Princeton, NJ: Princeton University Press.

Boulton, Mark. 2014 *Failing Our Veterans: The G.I. Bill and the Vietnam Generation*. New York: NYU Press.

Bradley, James, and Ron Powers. 2000. *Flags of Our Fathers*. New York: Bantam.

Brown, Will H. 1919. *Patriotic Illustrations for Public Speakers*. Cincinnati: Standard Publishing Company.

Bruff, Harold H. 2015. *Untrodden Ground: How Presidents Interpret the Constitution*. Chicago: University of Chicago Press.

Buenter, Scot M. 1990. *The American Flag, 1777–1924. Cultural Shifts from Creation to Codification*. Cranbury, NJ: Associated University Presses.

Burgan, Michael. 2011. *Raising the Flag: How a Photograph Gave a Nation Hope in Wartime*. North Mankato, MN: Compass Point Books.

Burstein, Andrew. 2001. *America's Jubilee: How in 1826 a Generation Remembered Fifty Years of Independence*. New York: Knopf.

Byrnes, Mark E. 1994. *Politics and Space: Image Making by NASA*. Westport, CT: Praeger.

Carson, Hampton L., ed. 1889. *History of the Celebration of the One Hundredth Anniversary of the Promulgation of the Constitution of the United States*. 2 vols. Philadelphia; J. J. Lippincott.

Cash, Arthur H. 2006. *John Wilkes: The Scandalous Father of Civil Liberty*. New Haven: Yale University Press.

Chang, Ina. 1994. *A Separate Battle: Women and the Civil War*. New York: Scholastic, Inc.

Child, Lydia Maria. 1997. *The Stars and Stripes. A Melo-Drama.* Edited by Glynis Carr. The Online Archive of Nineteenth-Century U.S. Women's Writings. http://www.facstaff.bucknell.edu/gcarr/19cUSWW/LB/S&S.html.

Collins, Herbert Ridgeway. 1979. *Threads of History: Americana Recorded on Cloth 1775 to the Present.* Washington, D.C.: Smithsonian Institution Press.

Cooper, Grace Rogers. 1973. *Thirteen-Star Flags: Keys to Identification.* Washington, D.C.: Smithsonian Institution Press.

Corcoran, Michael. 2002. *For Which It Stands: An Anecdotal Biography of the American Flag.* New York: Simon and Schuster.

Cornebise, Alfred E. 1984. *The Stars and Stripes: Doughboy Journalism in World War I.* Westport, CT: Greenwood Press.

Crane, Stephen. 1957. *The Red Badge of Courage and Other Stories.* New York: Dodd, Mead and Company.

Crothers, David D. 1962. *Flags of American History.* Maplewood, NJ: C. S. Hammond and Company.

Czulewicz, Gerald E., Sr. 1995. *The Foremost Guide to Uncle Sam Collectibles.* Paducah, KY: Collector Books.

Davies, Wallace Evan. 1955. *Patriotism on Parade: The Story of Veterans' and Hereditary Organizations in America 1783–1900.* Cambridge, MA: Harvard University Press.

De Bolla, Peter. 2007. *The Fourth of July and the Founding of America.* Woodstock, NY: Overlook Press.

Dewitt, Petra. 2012. *Degrees of Allegiance: Harassment and Loyalty in Missouri's German-American Community during World War I.* Athens: Ohio University Press.

D'Imperio, Chuck. 2013. *Unknown Museums of Upstate New York.* Syracuse, NY: Syracuse University Press.

Dittmer, Jason. 2013. *Captain America and the Nationalist Superhero.* Philadelphia: Temple University Press.

Ebel, Jonathan H. 2010. *Faith in the Fight: Religion and the American Soldier in the Great War.* Princeton: Princeton University Press.

Eggenberger, David. 1959. *Flags of the U.S.A.* New York: Thomas Y. Crowell Company.

Ellis, Richard J. 2005. *To the Flag: The Unlikely History of the Pledge of Allegiance.* Lawrence: University of Kansas Press.

Ewing, James. 1986. *It Happened in Tennessee.* Nashville: Rutledge Hill Press.

Fallows, Samuel, ed. 1903. *Story of the American Flag with Patriotic Selections and Incidents.* New York: Educational Publishing Company.

Ferris, Marc. 2014. *Star-Spangled Banner: The Unlikely Story of America's National Anthem.* Baltimore: Johns Hopkins University Press.

Fischer, David Hackett. 2004. *Washington's Crossing.* New York: Oxford University Press.

FitzGerald, Frances. 2017. *The Evangelicals: The Struggle to Shape America.* New York: Simon and Schuster.

Fort, Ilene Susan. 1988. *The Flag Paintings of Childe Hassam.* Los Angeles: Los Angeles County Museum of Art and New York: Harry N. Abrams, Inc.

Furlong, William Rea, and Byron McCandless. 1981. *So Proudly We Hail: The History of the United States Flag.* Washington, D.C.: Smithsonian Institution Press.

Ganz, Cheryl R. 2008. *The 1933 Chicago World's Fair: A Century of Progress.* Urbana-Champaign: University of Illinois Press.

Gitlin, Todd. 2006. *The Intellectual and the Flag.* New York: Columbia University Press.

Glassberg, David. *American Historical Pageantry: The Uses of Tradition in the Early Twentieth Century*. Chapel Hill: University of North Carolina Press.

Goldstein, Robert Justin. 1995. *Saving "Old Glory": The History of the American Flag Desecration Controversy*. Boulder, CO: Westview Press.

Goldstein, Robert Justin. 1996. *Burning the Flag: The Great 1989–1990 American Flag Desecration Controversy*. Kent, Ohio: Kent State University Press.

Goldstein, Robert Justin, ed. 1996. *Desecrating the American Flag: Key Documents of the Controversy from the Civil War to 1995*. Syracuse, NY: Syracuse University Press.

Gores, Stan. 1974. *1876 Centennial Collectibles and Price Guide*. Fond Du Lac, WI: Haber Printing Co.

Griswold, F. Gray. 1926. *The House Flags of the Merchants of New York, 1800–1860*. N.p.: F. Gray Griswold.

Guenter, Scot M. 1990. *The American Flag, 1777–1924: Cultural Shifts from Creation to Codification*. Cranbury, NJ: Associated University Presses.

Guthrie, William Norman. 1919. *The Religion of Old Glory*. New York: George H. Doran Company.

Hagedorn, Ann. 2008. *Savage Peace: Hope and Fear in America, 1919*. New York: Simon and Schuster.

Hamilton, Alexander, James Madison, and John Jay. (1787–1788) 1961. *The Federalist Papers*. New York: New American Library.

Hamilton, Schuyler. 1852. *History of the National Flag of the United States*. Philadelphia: Lippincott, Grambo, and Co.

Harris, Louise. 1971. *The Flag Over the Schoolhouse*. Providence, RI: C. A. Stephens Collection, Brown University.

Harrison, Peleg D. 1914. *The Stars and Stripes and Other American Flags*. 5th ed. Boston: Little, Brown, and Company.

Herbst, Tony, and Joel Kopp. 1993. *The Flag in American Indian Art*. Cooperstown: New York State Historical Association and University of Washington Press.

Hicks, Frederick C. 1918. *The Flag of the United States: Address Delivered by Hon. Frederick C. Hicks of Long Island in the House of Representatives, June 14, 1917*. Washington, D.C.: Government Printing Office.

Hinrichs, Kit. 2016. *Long May She Wave: 100 Stars and Stripes Collectible Postcards*. Potter Style.

Hinrichs, Kit, Delphine Hirasuna, and Terry Heffernan. 2001. *Long May She Wave: A Graphic History of the American Flag*. Berkeley, CA: Ten Speed Press.

Hinrichs, Kit, Delphine Hirasuna, and Terry Heffernan. 2015. *100 American Flags: A Unique Collection of Old Glory Memorabilia*. Berkeley, CA: Ten Speed Press.

Hogopian, Patrick. 2009. *The Vietnam War in American Memory*. Amherst: University of Massachusetts Press.

Holden, Edward S. 1906. *Our Country's Flag and the Flags of Foreign Countries*. New York: D. Appleton and Company.

Hoover, Michael D. 1992. *The Origins and History of the Washington Monument Flag Display*. National Park Service National Capital Parks—Central Cultural Resources Management.

Hornung, Clarence P. 1973. *Treasury of American Design*. 2 vols. New York: Harry N. Abrams, Inc.

Horwitz, Elinor Lander, and J. Roderick Moore. 1976. *The Bird, the Banner, and Uncle Sam: Images of America in Folk and Popular Art*. Philadelphia: J. B. Lippincott Company.

Irvin, Benjamin H. 2011. *Clothed in Robes of Sovereignty: The Continental Congress and the People Out of Doors*. New York: Oxford University Press.

Johnson, Willis Fletcher. 1930. *The National Flag: A History*. Boston: Houghton Mifflin Company.

Joselit, Jenna Weissman. 2017. *Set in Stone: America's Embrace of the Ten Commandments*. New York: Oxford University Press.

Kass, Amy A., and Leon R. Kass. 2013. *Flag Day: The American Calendar*. Washington, D.C: What So Proudly We Hail.

Keim, Kevin, and Peter Keim. 2007. *A Grand Old Flag: A History of the United States through Its Flags*. New York: DK.

Kinzer, Stephen. 2017. *The True Flag: Theodore Roosevelt, Mark Twain, and the Birth of American Empire*. New York: Henry Holt and Co.

Kosek, Joseph Kip, ed. 2017. *American Religion American Politics: An Anthology*. New Haven, CT: Yale University press.

Lee, Lois. 2015. *Recognizing the Non-Religious: Reimagining the Secular*. New York: Oxford University Press.

Leepson, Marc. 2005. *Flag: An American Biography*. New York: St. Martin's Press.

Leepson, Marc. 2014. *What So Proudly We Hailed: Francis Scott Key, A Life*. New York: Palgrave Macmillan.

Libby, Frederick. 2000. *Horses Don't Fly*. New York: Arcade Publishing.

Lincoln, Abraham. 1902. *Abraham Lincoln: Complete Works*. Edited by John G. Nicholay and John Jay. Vol. 1. New York: Century Company.

Lincoln, Abraham. 1953. *The Collected Works of Abraham Lincoln*. Edited by Roy P. Basler. Vols. 4 and 6. New Brunswick, NJ: Rutgers University Press.

Little, David B. 1974. *America's First Centennial Celebration: The Nineteenth of April 1875 at Lexington and Concord, Massachusetts*. 2nd ed. Boston: Houghton Mifflin.

Lubin, David M. 2015. *Flags and Faces: The Visual Culture of America's First War*. Oakland: University of California Press.

Lukacs, John. 2010. *The Legacy of the Second World War*. New Haven: Yale University Press.

Maier, Pauline. 1997. *American Scripture: Making the Declaration of Independence*. New York: Alfred A. Knopf.

Manwaring, David. 1962. *Render unto Caesar*. Chicago: University of Chicago Press.

Marling, Karal Ann. 2004. *Old Glory: Unfurling History*. Washington, D.C.: Library of Congress.

Marshall, Tim. 2017. *Worth Dying For: The Power and Politics of Flags*. London: Elliott and Thompson.

Martini, Edwin A. 2007. *The American War on Vietnam, 1976–2000*. Amherst: University of Massachusetts Press.

Marvin, Carolyn, and David W. Ingle. 1999. *Blood Sacrifice and the Nation: Totem Rituals and the American Flag*. New York: Cambridge University Press.

Mastai, Boleslaw, and Marie-Louise D'Otrange. 1973. *The Stars and the Stripes: The American Flag as Art and as History from the Birth of the Republic to the Present*. New York: Alfred A. Knopf.

Masur, Louis P. 2008. *The Soiling of Old Glory: The Story of a Photograph That Shocked America*. New York: Bloomsbury Press.

McCabe, John. 1973. *George M. Cohan: The Man Who Owned Broadway*. Garden City, NY: Doubleday.

McWhirter, Christian. 2012. *Battle Hymns: The Power and Popularity of Music in the Civil War*. Chapel Hill: University of North Carolina Press.

Miller, Marla R. 2011. *Betsy Ross and the Making of America*. New York: Henry Holt and Company.

Moeller, Henry W. 1995. *Shattering an American Myth: Unfurling the History of the Stars and Stripes*. 2nd ed. Mattituck, NY: Amereon House.

Molotsky, Irvin. 2001. *The Flag, the Poet and the Song: The Story of the Star-Spangled Banner*. New York: Dutton.

Neely, Mark E. 2011. *Lincoln and the Triumph of the Nation: Constitutional Conflict in the American Civil War*. Chapel Hill: University of North Carolina Press.

Ness, William Boyd. 2008. *"Burning with Star-Fires": The National Flag in Civil War Poetry*. PhD thesis, University of Iowa.

Neuman, Gerald L., and Tomilo Brown-Nagin, eds. 2015. *Reconsidering the Insular Cases: The Past and Future of the American Empire*. Cambridge, MA: Human Rights Program at Harvard Law School.

Newson, Merlin Owen. 1995. *Armed with the Constitution: Jehovah's Witnesses in Alabama and the U.S. Supreme Court, 1939–1945*. Tuscaloosa: University of Alabama Press.

O'Dell Heather. N.d. *History of our Flag*. Gettysburg, PA: Americana Souvenirs and Gifts.

O'Leary, Cecilia Elizabeth. 1999. *To Die For: The Paradox of American Patriotism*. Princeton, NJ: Princeton University Press.

Our Flag. 2003. Washington, D.C.: U.S. Government Printing Office.

Pastoureau, Michel. 2001. *The Devil's Cloth: A History of Stripes*. Translated by Jody Gladding. New York: Washington Square Press.

Peabody, Bruce, and Krista Jenkins. 2017. *Where Have All The Heroes Gone?* New York: Oxford University Press.

Pease, William H., and June H. Pease, eds. 1965. *The Antislavery Argument*. Indianapolis: Bobbs-Merrill.

Pencak, William. 1989. *For God and Country: The American Legion, 1919–1941*. Boston: Northeastern University Press.

Peters, Shawn Francis. 2000. *Judging Jehovah's Witnesses: Religious Persecution and the Dawn of the Rights Revolution*. Lawrence: University Press of Kansas.

Phillips, Robert. 1931. *The American Flag: Its Uses and Abuses*. Boston: Stratford Company.

Preble, Henry. 1872. *Our Flag. Origin and Progress of the Flag of the United States of America, with an Introductory Account of the Symbols, Standards, Banners and Flags of Ancient and Modern Nations*. Albany, NY: Joel Munsell.

Quaife, Milo M., Milvin J. Weig, and Roy E. Appleman. 1961. *The History of the United States Flag from the Revolution to the Present, Including a Guide to Its Use and Display*. New York: Harper and Brothers.

Rooney, E. Ashley, and Stephanie Standish. 2015. *Stars and Stripes: The American Flag in Contemporary Art*. Atglen, PA: Schiffer Publishing, Ltd.

Schauffler, Robert Haven, ed. 1912. *Flag Day: Its History, Origin, and Celebration as Related in Song and Story*. New York: Moffat, Yard and Company.

Schauffler, Robert Haven, ed. 1917. *Our Flag in Verse and Prose*. New York: Moffat, Yard and Company.

Schneider, Richard H. 2003. *Stars and Stripes Forever: The History, Stories, and Memories of Our American Flag*. New York: William Morrow.

Scott, Emma Look. 1915. *How the Flag Became Old Glory*. New York: Macmillan.

Skeen, Edward. 2003. *America Rising*. Lexington: University Press of Kentucky.

Smith, Nicholas. 1908. *Our Nation's Flag in History and Incident*. 2nd ed. Milwaukee: Young Churchman Co.

Smith, Whitney. 1975. *Flags Through the Ages and Across the World*. New York: McGraw Hill.

Smith, Whitney. 2001. *The American Flag*. 2nd ed. New York: Friedman/Fairfax.

Smyth, Richard, and Jim Garrett. 2005. *The Lincoln Assassination: The Flags of Ford Theatre*. U.S.: Case Book Press.

Sparrow, Bartholomew H. 2006. *The Insular Cases and the Emergence of American Empire*. Lawrence: University Press of Kansas.

Stewart, Charles W. 1914. *The Stars and Stripes from Washington to Wilson, 1777–1914*. Washington, D.C.: Navy Publishing Co.

Svejda, George J. 1969. *History of the Star-Spangled Banner from 1814 to the Present*. Washington, D.C.: National Park Service, U.S. Department of the Interior.

Tappan, Eva March. [1917]. *The Little Book of the Flag*. Boston: Houghton Mifflin. Reprinted by CreateSpace in 2016.

Taylor, Lonn, Kathleen M. Kendrick, and Jeffrey L. Brodie. 2008. *The Star-Spangled Banner: The Making of an American Icon*. Washington, D.C.: Smithsonian Books.

Teachout, Woden. 2009. *Capture the Flag: A Political History of American Patriotism*. New York: Basic Books.

Teachout, Woden Sorrow. 2003. *Forging Memory: Hereditary Societies, Patriotism and the American Past, 1876–1898*. PhD thesis, Harvard University.

Thomas, William Widgery, Jr. 1893. *Sweden and the Swedes*. Chicago: Rand, McNally, and Company.

Tickner, Lisa. 1988. *The Spectacle of Women: Imagery of the Suffrage Campaign 1907–14*. Chicago: University of Chicago Press.

Torricelli, Robert, and Andrew Carroll, eds. *In Our Own Words: Extraordinary Speeches of the American Century*. New York: Washington Square Press.

Travers, Len. 1997. *Celebrating the Fourth: Independence Day and the Rites of Nationalism in the Early Republic*. Amherst: University of Massachusetts Press.

Tupper, Martin F. 1876. *Washington: A Drama, in Five Acts*. America: W. F. Millard.

Vile, John R. 2013. *The Men Who Made the Constitution: Lives of the Delegates to the Constitutional Convention*. Lanham, MD: Scarecrow Press, Inc.

Vile, John R. 2014. *Re-Framers: 170 Eccentric, Visionary, and Patriotic Proposals to Rewrite the U.S. Constitution*. Santa Barbara, CA: ABC-CLIO.

Vile, John R. 2015a. *Encyclopedia of Constitutional Amendments, Proposed Amendments, and Amending Issues, 1789–2015*. 4th ed. 2 vols. Santa Barbara, CA: ABC-CLIO.

Vile, John R. 2015b. *Founding Documents of America, Documents Decoded*. Santa Barbara, CA: ABC-CLIO.

Vile, John R. 2016a. *American Immigration and Citizenship: A Documentary History*. Lanham, MD: Rowman and Littlefield.

Vile, John R. 2016b. *The Constitutional Convention of 1787: A Comprehensive Encyclopedia of America's Founding*. 2nd ed. 2 vols. Clark, NJ: Talbot Publishing.

Vile, John R. 2017. *The Jacksonian and Antebellum Eras: Documents Decoded*. Santa Barbara, CA: ABC-CLIO.

Vile, John R., ed. 2001. *Great American Lawyers: An Encyclopedia*. 2 vols. Santa Barbara, CA: ABC-CLIO.

Vile, John R., David L. Hudson Jr., and David Schultz. 2009. *Encyclopedia of the First Amendment*. 2 vols. Washington, D.C.: CQ Press.

Warfield, Patrick. 2013. *Making the March King: John Philip Sousa's Washington Years, 1854–1893*. Urbana-Champaign: University of Illinois Press.

Webster, Daniel. 1853. *The Great Orations and Senatorial Speeches of Daniel Webster*. Rochester: Wilbur M. Hayward.

Wescher, H. 1977. *Flags*. Winchester, MA: North American Vexillological Association.

Whipple, Wayne. [1910] *The Story of the American Flag*. Bedford, MA: Applewood Books. Originally published Philadelphia: Henry Altemus Company, 1910.

Williams, Earl P., Jr. 1987. *What You Should Know About the American Flag*. Gettysburg, PA: Thomas Publications.

Wills, Garry. 1978. *Inventing America: Jefferson's Declaration of Independence*. New York: Doubleday.

Winthrop, Robert C. 1895. *Addresses and Speeches on Various Occasions from 1852 to 1867*. Vol. 2. Boston: Little, Brown, and Company.

Woefly, S. J. 1914. *Under the Flag: History of the Stars and Stripes*. Revised by M. H. Stine. Harrisburg, PA: United Evangelical Press.

Wood, Jane. 1991. *The Collector's Guide to Post Cards*. Gas City, IN: L.-W. Promotions.

Zelinsky, Wilbur. 1988. *Nation into State: The Shifting Symbolic Foundations of American Nationalism*. Chapel Hill: University of North Carolina Press.

Zaretsky, Natasha. 2007. *No Direction Home: The American Family and the Fear of National Decline, 1968–1980*. Chapel Hill: University of North Carolina Press.

About the Author and Contributors

The Author

Dr. John R. Vile is a professor of political science and dean of the University Honors College at Middle Tennessee State University. He has written and edited numerous previous works, including *The Encyclopedia of Constitutional Amendments, Proposed Amendments, and Amending Issues, 1789–2015*; *The Constitutional Convention of 1787: An Encyclopedia of America's Founding*; *Re-Framers: 170 Eccentric, Visionary, and Patriotic Proposals to Rewrite the U.S. Constitution*; and four volumes for ABC-CLIO's Documents Decoded series.

The Contributors

Dr. Larry L. Burriss is a professor in the School of Journalism at Middle Tennessee State University, where he teaches media law and mass media and national security.

Derek W. Frisby is a lecturer and faculty coordinator at Middle Tennessee State University. A USMC veteran, he is a historical consultant to military units and organizations concerning warfare and culture. He has written for other ABC-CLIO publications, including the *Encyclopedia of the American Civil War* (2000).

Kenneth Hartvigsen holds a PhD in art history from Boston University. He has published multiple articles on flags in art and culture and was awarded the William Driver Award by the North American Vexillilogical Association in 2011 for his work on violent flag imagery in sheet music illustrations during the Civil War. He is the curator of American art at the BYU Museum of Art in Provo, Utah.

Marc Leepson is a journalist and historian and the author of nine books, including *Flag: An American Biography* (2005), a history of the Stars and Stripes from its beginnings to the early 21st century.

Marla R. Miller teaches and directs the public history program at the University of Massachusetts Amherst and is the author of *Betsy Ross and the Making of America* (2010).

Gregory N. Reish is the director of the Center for Popular Music and a professor of music history at Middle Tennessee State University. A musicologist with a broad range of interests, he is also a performing musician and record producer specializing in traditional musics of the South.

Eran Shalev is the chair of the History Department at Haifa University, Israel, and the author of *American Zion: The Bible as a Political Text from the Revolution to the Civil War* (2013) and *Rome Reborn on Western Shores: Historical Imagination and the Creation of the American Republic* (2009). He is currently writing a book on popular understandings of astronomy and American politics.

Woden Teachout is a professor of graduate studies in the master of arts program at Union Institute and University in Middlesex, Vermont, and the author of *Capture the Flag: A Political History of American Patriotism*.

Index

Boldface page numbers indicate main entries in the encyclopedia.
Italicized page numbers indicate photographs or illustrations.